# HUNTER-GATHERER ECONOMY IN PREHISTORY

# HUNTER-GATHERER ECONOMY IN PREHISTORY

A EUROPEAN PERSPECTIVE

EDITED BY GEOFF BAILEY

CAMBRIDGE UNIVERSITY PRESS

CAMBRIDGE

LONDON    NEW YORK    NEW ROCHELLE

MELBOURNE    SYDNEY

CAMBRIDGE UNIVERSITY PRESS
Cambridge, New York, Melbourne, Madrid, Cape Town, Singapore, São Paulo, Delhi

Cambridge University Press
The Edinburgh Building, Cambridge CB2 8RU, UK

Published in the United States of America by Cambridge University Press, New York

www.cambridge.org
Information on this title: www.cambridge.org/9780521106207

First published 1983
This digitally printed version 2009

*A catalogue record for this publication is available from the British Library*

*Library of Congress Catalogue Card Number: 82-9505*

ISBN 978-0-521-23742-0 hardback
ISBN 978-0-521-10620-7 paperback

# CONTENTS

# CONTRIBUTORS

Kathryn Allwarden, Department of Anthropology, University of
   Chicago, Illinois, U.S.A.
Paul G. Bahn, Department of Prehistoric Archaeology, University
   of Liverpool.
Geoffrey N. Bailey, Department of Archaeology, University of
   Cambridge.
Patrick L. Carter, Museum of Archaeology and Anthropology,
   Cambridge.
Geoffrey A. Clark, Department of Anthropology, Arizona State
   University, U.S.A.
Iain Davidson, Department of Prehistory and Archaeology,
   University of New England, Armidale, Australia.
Clive S. Gamble, Department of Archaeology, University of
   Southampton.
Helen P. Higgs, Department of Organic and Inorganic Chemistry,
   University of Cambridge.
Michael A. Jochim, Department of Anthropology, University
   of California, Santa Barbara, U.S.A.
Richard G. Klein, Department of Anthropology, University of
   Chicago, Illinois, U.S.A.
Marsha A. Levine, Department of Archaeology, University
   of Cambridge.
Marcie M. Madden, Department of Anthropology, Grenfell
   College, Memorial University of Newfoundland,
   Cornerbrook, Newfoundland.
Peter A. Rowley-Conwy. Department of Archaeology,
   University of Cambridge.
Lawrence G. Straus, Department of Anthropology, University
   of New Mexico, Albuquerque, New Mexico, U.S.A.
Robin Torrence, Department of Prehistory and Archaeology,
   University of Sheffield.

H. Martin Wobst, Department of Anthropology, University of
Massachusetts, Amherst, Mass., U.S.A.
Cornelia Wolf, Department of Anthropology, University
of Chicago, Illinois, U.S.A.

# PREFACE

Studies of hunters and gatherers have gained a wide
popularity in recent years. Within archaeology they have
created an international focus for people working in many
different areas of the world. At a broader level they have
provided a meeting ground for a range of disciplines concerned
in one way or another with various features of human behaviour. The exotic remoteness of hunters and gatherers
from our more immediate experience of human life has
added to the sense of intellectual challenge. In the resulting
interplay of new ideas and theoretical perspectives, analysis
of the prehistoric record has inevitably lagged behind,
preoccupied with fundamental technical problems of dating,
stratigraphic correlation, data-interpretation, and field survey
of the many remaining geographical blanks in our knowledge
of the Palaeolithic era. Interest in the traditional Palaeolithic
sequences of Europe has been further overshadowed by the
excitement of new discoveries, new dates and new culture
sequences in Africa, Australasia and the Far East. The
intellectual attractions and imperative urgency, as well as
the humanitarian claims of ethnographic and ethnoarchaeological work in the few remaining areas where this is
still possible, have offered further diversions. The result has
been, if anything, a widening of the gap between theories
and ideas on the one side, and their practical realization
through analysis of archaeological data on the other. This
book is intended to stimulate a more effective interaction

between theory and data — between knowledge of the present
and knowledge of the past — by bringing together a series
of case studies which combine an awareness of recent
developments in hunter-gatherer theory with a commitment
to the analysis and interpretation of prehistoric material.
Students of developments in archaeological thought during
the past decade will recognize the influence of a number of
theoretical 'schools' in the chapters that follow (functionalist,
ecological, palaeoeconomic and social, to name only the
most obvious). Such plurality, and the divergence of thinking
that accompanies it, is perhaps the best indication of future
potential in the subject — of problems remaining to be solved
(and hence of new directions to be explored). It is also
hopefully the best antidote to the imperialistic ambitions
of new and intolerant orthodoxies. I am grateful to the
contributors for providing a range of chapters which has
forced me to reconsider the problem of integration in
archaeology (without arriving at any satisfactory solution
to it), and for their various comments and occasional disagreements. I am further indebted to Tim Murray for cheer-
fully challenging all my assumptions about knowledge of the
prehistoric past; to Suzanne Bailey for tolerating my frequent
neglect of matters in the present; to Sue Rowley for preparing
the index; and to Robin Derricourt and Kate Owen at
Cambridge University Press for their helpful advice and
encouragement.

Geoff Bailey

Chapter 1

**Hunter-gatherer behaviour in prehistory:
problems and perspectives**
Geoff Bailey

**Introduction**

In the fourteen years since the publication of the *Man
the Hunter* symposium (Lee and DeVore 1968a), there has
been a considerable growth of research interest in hunter-
gatherer behaviour. The proposition that human societies
have spent over 99% of their cultural history as hunters and
gatherers has become almost a truism, and little justification
is required for a field of research which is seen as providing
both a cultural baseline for the emergence of agricultural
and urban societies and a behavioural and evolutionary link
between our remote biological origins and our present-day
condition. Yet, despite the fact that over 99% of the world's
hunters and gatherers lived in the prehistoric past and are
amenable to study only through archaeological methods,
most theorizing about hunters and gatherers has been
supported largely by ethnographic and ecological data, and
empirical research in prehistoric archaeology has been
relatively slow to respond to the development of new
theoretical perspectives. The interaction between theory and
archaeological data has tended to be at best a one-way process
in which ideas established in other disciplines are brought in to
help explain or interpret existing features of the archaeological
record or to predict what ought to be there. There has been
little exploration of the ways in which data about the
prehistoric past can make their own distinctive contribution
to the creation of new theoretical concepts, and the influence
of prehistory on the development of theory, apart from

demonstrating the long time-spans over which hunter-gatherer
behaviour patterns have persisted, has remained negligible.

Broadly two major trends can be discerned in the
development of hunter-gatherer studies during the past decade.
The first is the development of general models and theoretical
concepts about the fundamental principles of hunter-gatherer
adaptation. The concept of adaptation focuses on patterns of
reproductive success and subsistence. Hence interest has
mainly centred on subsistence ecology and demography as
the primary clues to a unifying perspective (Wobst 1974a,
1976; Durham 1976; Jochim 1976; Keene 1979; Bettinger
1980; L.R. Binford 1980; Earle and Christenson 1980;
Winterhalder 1980, 1981), but has also included studies of
the influence of social organization and ideology (Sahlins
1974; Wobst 1976, 1977; Ingold 1980, 1981). The
archaeological input to this literature – with rare exceptions –
has been relatively minor. Where archaeological data have
been referred to at all, they have usually been used as
illustrations of established principles rather than as raw
material for the building of new theoretical structures.
Inspiration has rather been sought in the theoretical models
of other disciplines such as ecology, social anthropology and
ethology (including sociobiology), in the mathematical
simulation techniques derived from game theory and decision
theory, and in the examination of ethnographically observed
case studies as test data.

A second trend, characteristic of specifically archaeological research, has been the development of operational concepts by which to transform the inert data of the material record into behavioural patterns — middle-range theory in Binford's (1977a) terminology — and in the analysis and interpretation of particular historical patterns. Major growing points have been the archaeology of early hominids and the very earliest steps towards a recognizably distinctive human pattern of hunting and gathering (Isaac and McCown 1976; Leakey and Lewin 1977; Isaac 1978; Binford 1981) where the biological and palaeontological features of human evolution viewed within the established framework of natural selection theory continue to provide a dominant focus of interpretation; the very latest stages of hunting and gathering where they merge into early agriculture (Higgs 1972, 1975; Megaw 1977; Reed 1977; Jarman *et al.* in press); and the ethnoarchaeological study of surviving or recently observed hunters and gatherers (Yellen 1977; Binford 1978a; R.A. Gould 1980; Smiley *et al.* 1980).

It is not without interest or significance that these growing points all lie on the peripheries of the archaeological record, at the very beginning or the very end of the hunter-gatherer chronological span. At first sight these developments would appear to represent a diversion from the primary goal of analysing prehistoric hunter-gatherer behaviour, a retreat from the central core of the prehistoric archaeological record, albeit a retreat that might ultimately facilitate a more effective attack. In part this reflects the current perception that the earliest and latest periods of the hunter-gatherer span are where the dramatic changes in sociocultural evolution occur, the intervening millennia offering less interesting or less easily studied material either from the biological or the cultural point of view. But it is also symptomatic of the immense difficulties that impede theoretical interpretation of archaeological data in their own terms, and a measure of the centrifugal force exerted by the ambiguities of the archaeological record in pushing the centre of theoretical interest out towards the lesser uncertainties of the biological past or the agricultural and ethnographic present.

A number of factors have contributed to the pattern of these recent developments, including theoretical preconceptions as well as practical limitations of the data. One factor is the normative concept of hunting and gathering as a single 'way of life' which, despite its long duration, can be summed up in a few simple generalizations, a notion that is not discouraged by the relative rarity of surviving hunter-gatherer societies available as test data. It is here, perhaps, that recent archaeological research, by concentrating on the boundaries of the hunter-gatherer world, has had its greatest impact. This is apparent in the challenge to the classificatory division between hunter-gatherers and farmers (Higgs 1972, 1975; Jarman *et al.* in press), in the detection of different principles of organizing subsistence strategies amongst ethnographically observed hunter-gatherers (Binford 1980), and in the examination of the relationship between hunting,

scavenging and other forms of non-human or pre-human predation in the earliest stages of human development (Isaac 1978; Binford 1981). The latter theme also recurs at the other end of the chronological scale in discussions of early agriculture and animal domestication (Jarman and Wilkinson 1972; Rindos 1980). The erosion and replacement of the monolithic conception implied by 'hunting and gathering' has been one of the more original consequences — and to some extent a justification — of recent tendencies in archaeological thinking, and this is an interest which has now begun to be tackled from an anthropological point of view as well (Ingold 1980; Woodburn 1980).

A second restraint on the archaeological study of hunters and gatherers is the very real difficulty of reconstructing patterns of behaviour from the material record. The formidable technical problems posed by data recovery, excavation, sampling, dating and palaeoenvironmental control hardly need emphasizing, while the investment of time, effort and money that is required to bring to final publication the excavation of even a single site should not be underestimated. Regional studies multiply the practical problems. Satisfactory results may be achieved only after decades of work, and it is not unknown for the completion of large-scale field projects to represent a posthumous tribute to the vision of their originators.

Added to this is the problem that by far the most prolific type of data surviving in palaeolithic deposits, namely lithic artefacts, is also one of the most ambiguous indicators of behavioural patterning. The difficulties of analysing and interpreting variability in lithic material have given rise to a virtually autonomous field of inquiry with its own literature and methodology. Although this has its own growing points in the development of mathematical techniques, use-wear analyses and raw-material studies, many of its major preoccupations are necessarily far removed from the ultimate objective of recovering behavioural activities and adaptations. The archaeological prominence of lithic debris and the ambiguities of its interpretation are also primary motivations for the diversion of effort away from prehistoric research into ethnoarchaeological analysis, in the search for general principles by which to transform material data into patterns of behaviour.

Finally, the difficulties of working with material data have given rise to a special use of theoretical procedures, in which theoretical models are used not so much to explain patterns of past behaviour but to aid in recreating those patterns by filling gaps in the prehistoric record for which material data are lacking. Hence the theories tell the archaeologist what past behavioural patterns ought to look like rather than explain directly observable or independently verifiable patterns visible in the record. Clearly theories of this sort are immune to archaeological testing, except by circular argument, since they are the source of the patterns derived from the archaeological record. This further weakens the case for prehistoric research.

However, the most influential restraint on prehistoric research, and one which in some measure contributes to the other factors already discussed, is the paralysing ambiguity of uniformitarian orthodoxy. Uniformitarianism can mean different things: that there are constants or universals underlying visible patterns of diversity and variation; that events in the past should be explained by processes observable in the present; or that change is slow and gradual rather than sudden and disruptive. Belief in any one of these does not necessarily entail acceptance of the others. The first meaning corresponds to S.J. Gould's (1965) definition of methodological uniformitarianism – a belief in universal principles. The other two meanings broadly correspond to his definition of substantive uniformitarianism – a belief that processes and rates of change were similar in the past to those visible in the present. These two definitions are not necessarily incompatible, although they may be, depending on the nature of the subject matter. Substantive uniformitarianism has long been rejected in geological theory. In biological theory it is an integral part of the neo-Darwinian synthesis of evolution by natural selection, although increasingly under attack (Gould and Eldredge 1977). In archaeology and the human sciences generally there has been relatively little explicit discussion of this point, although a belief in substantive uniformitarianism is the implication of most studies (Bailey 1981a; Dalton 1981). In archaeological research uniformitarian principles usually rest on the belief that people in the past behaved much as they do in the present, with similar social structures, economic strategies and cognitive abilities. Essentially the belief is that there are certain continuities of human thought and behaviour which provide a link through time, enabling our ignorance of what happened in the past to be enlightened by our knowledge of the present.

In one respect uniformitarian assumptions can have a liberating influence on archaeological research, especially at the operational level, where they are used as a means to an end rather than as the ultimate object of inquiry, offering a key with which to unlock information from the archaeological record that would otherwise remain hidden, rather than providing the final answer. Thus Binford (1978a, 1981) has emphasized the advantage in faunal studies that animal anatomy provides a known framework which can serve as a reference point for measuring variation in the pattern of prehistoric faunal exploitation (see Part 1 below).

Site territorial analysis and the associated concept of the site exploitation territory (see Parts 2 and 3) exemplify both the potentials and the pitfalls of this sort of approach, employing the uniformitarian principle of least effort and the 2-hour walk in order to define potential areas of habitual exploitation around archaeological sites. However, the notion that the aim of site territorial analysis in archaeology is to illustrate or test the principle of least effort, or to define the boundary of site exploitation territories as an end in itself, would strike most field practitioners as absurd. Although there are certain restrictive conditions under which such a test

might be possible without recourse to circular reasoning, it would be irrelevant to many archaeological research designs. Rather the aim is to provide a framework within which to obtain a sharper focus on the relationship between subsistence data, site location and the natural environment. As many practitioners have pointed out, the precise accuracy of a postulated universal such as the 2-hour territorial boundary is not really at issue when the objectives of analysis are to detect broad relative variations between sites or regions. The important point in these sorts of analyses is that the relationship under scrutiny is between two (or three) sets of data, *all of which are archaeologically visible* (or potentially so). In effect one set of relationships (the relationship between human energy expenditure and food returns) is being held constant in order to provide some control on another set of relationships, that between environment, site location and subsistence. Thus the aim is to play off against each other two or three sets of independently verifiable data, rather than to explain one set of data in terms of another set which is archaeologically invisible and can only be derived by extrapolation from a non-archaeological context. This is a major principle underlying much ethnoarchaeological research, where the expressed intention is usually to establish some uniformities in the relationship between the material record and the behaviour patterns that produce it. However, the literature on site catchment analysis is ample testament to the confusions that can arise over misuse of this principle, and to the narrow line that separates the self-fulfilling prophecy from the signpost to an empirically knowable but as yet unknown reality.

The ambiguity of uniformitarian assumptions, as well as the latent paradox they embody, becomes even more marked when one moves from the level of operational procedures to general theory. For if the aim of archaeological inquiry is to identify unifying principles of general applicability, and if it is assumed that these principles can be derived in their entirety from the study of contemporary or near-contemporary societies, then prehistory becomes irrelevant except as an end in itself, capable of being enlightened by theoretical knowledge, but contributing nothing to it. Taken to its logical extreme substantive uniformitarianism condemns archaeological research to 'ethnography with a shovel' (Wobst 1978: 303), or an idiographic discipline concerned with individualities rather than generalization, and thus an exercise appealing to diggers and antiquarians but to few others. Moreover the insistence that past patterns of behaviour should look like present ones imposes a commitment on the archaeologist to reconstruct the past in the same sort of detail and with the same sort of expectations as would be attempted in ethnographic or ecological or ethological studies. Categories and concepts derived from other disciplines thus propel archaeological research forward in a frantic and never-ending search for the elusive goal of better data – for more carefully controlled samples, more detailed stratigraphies and more accurate dating methods — discarding along the way as inadequate a vast quantity of already accumulated data. Substantive uniformitarianism can thus have a doubly paralysing effect on archaeological research, demanding a resolution and a detail from the archaeological record which current techniques are scarcely able to fulfil, yet denying the theoretical relevance of any patterns they might yield.

This consequence is further sanctioned by the theoretical premises of two of archaeology's most powerful disciplinary neighbours, ethology and social anthropology. Both have made a virtue of necessity, developing comparative methods for deriving general principles from a diversity of contemporary instances, and favouring theories which do not depend on historical knowledge. Ethology, despite its interest in the evolutionary history of behaviour patterns, is forced back on indirect methods, since there is no behavioural equivalent of palaeontology (Hinde and Tinbergen 1958). Moreover the emphasis on the biological basis of behaviour has usually carried with it an acceptance of neo-Darwinian evolutionary theory with its strong implication that large-scale evolutionary patterns can be explained in terms of the small-scale selection processes that lie within the range of focus of the contemporary observer—in effect that the evolution of horses can be understood by looking at fruitflies. Whatever the power and success of this approach in animal behaviour studies, or the validity of natural selection as a working hypothesis in human behaviour, attempts to derive theories of human social evolution via the hybrid terminology of 'biogrammars' and 'culturgens' has done little to assuage the well-deserved scepticism of anthropological commentators (Gluckman 1972; Leach 1981), or to bring into focus the behavioural potential of the archaeological record which forms the historical bridge between our animal ancestry and our present-day behaviour.

Social anthropologists have generally been more cautious about deriving theories of historical change from contemporary observations, and indeed have tended to favour theories with an emphasis on the synchronic, in which history is deemed largely irrelevant. Although the value of historical knowledge is periodically re-emphasized in anthropoligical study of contemporary societies (Evans-Pritchard 1961; Goody 1976, 1977), there nevertheless remains a lingering sense in the discipline at large that theories of long-term change can be derived by extrapolation from contemporary observations or by logical elaboration of a few axiomatic principles, and that any novel behavioural patterns thrown up by prehistory would be little more than exotic variations on themes whose main outlines were already clearly defined.

One of the attractions of concentrating archaeological research on the early hominid or the ethnographic and agricultural ends of the hunter-gatherer spectrum lies in the fact that these are all areas of research which lie very close to the data and theories of well-established disciplines. Evolutionary biology, social anthropology and agricultural economics provide secure and sensible launching points from which to explore the unknowns of the prehistoric past, but at the same time immediate surroundings of diverse interest, easy accessibility and frequent controversy which provide ample excuses for resisting departure. If there is to be a sense of future direction in hunter-gatherer studies, it will require a strong commitment to the exploration and comparison of prehistoric case studies, awareness of the reference points provided by other disciplines without subservience to them, and ultimately a belief that history and anthropology (in the broadest sense of those terms) can be reunited in a dialogue fruitful to both, in which an understanding of historical patterns not only benefits from existing theoretical knowledge but contributes to it.

One does not have to search far for clues as to what sort of historical knowledge might be theoretically valuable. The conception of behaviour as an integration of processes operating at different time-scales and with different periodicities has long been familiar in biology (Haldane 1956; Gould 1965) (although overshadowed to a large extent by the highly successful reductionism of neo-Darwinian theory). Braudel (1972) has made famous a similar conception of human history as being separable into different layers, ranging from the deep and slowly-moving currents of 'geographical history' to the more fast-moving and ephemeral surface changes of social and individual history, each layer being in contact with the others but not reducible to them. Such a notion of history provides a far more enlightening perspective than other examples of the historian's approach more usually held up as models for archaeological imitation. Bonner (1980) has recently suggested a similar resolution of the current impasse between biological and sociological theories of human behaviour, emphasizing the concern of the former with the limits to variation and the ways in which those limits change over the long term, and the concern of the latter with the short-term, small-scale variations that occur within those limits. Such a perspective does not of course exclude the possibility that variations in behaviour at a small scale might overcome pre-existing limits and generate long-term changes. Changes of social organization, for example, especially in so far as they affect patterns of reproduction and demography, can have far-reaching biological and social consequences (see Part 4). Thus interactions of many different kinds can occur between different scales of behaviour (Holly 1978).

Turning to more specific issues, the current uncertainty about the reliability of the ethnographic record as a mirror of 'typical' hunters and gatherers (Wobst 1977; Schrire 1980) helps to emphasize the point that ethnographically observed societies are the outcome of a long historical process which it is the purpose of archaeological study to trace and explain. Wobst (1977) has pointed out that patterns of behaviour among ethnographically observed hunter-gatherers may have been influenced by contact with colonizing cultures. Schrire (1980) has suggested that the !Kung Bushmen, widely quoted as a typical example of the hunter-gatherer way of life, may formerly have been farmers who have only recently resorted to hunting and gathering as a preferable livelihood in a marginal environment. These cautions do not undermine the potential value of comparative ethnographic studies as clues to general organizational principles. But they do highlight the problems of distinguishing what is truly universal in human behaviour from what is peculiar to the circumstances of particular geographical and historical contexts, and hence the need for time depth in comparative studies as well as geographical 'width'.

Sahlin's famous ethnographic characterization of stable affluence as the typical hunter-gatherer mode has already begun to give way to a more dynamic view under the impetus of an archaeological perspective (Cohen 1977; Bender 1978). There is also growing evidence to suggest that some of the unifying features of modern hunters and gatherers, such as the integration of local bands into larger social and biological units through reciprocal social ties and affiliations, may be a relatively recent development, and one closely related to the cultural and economic innovations and demographic changes which characterize the emergence of the European Upper Palaeolithic (see Part 4). In a broader evolutionary perspective, it is apparent that the decisive shift from a predominantly biological to a predominantly cultural mode of evolution took place in the prehistoric past, and that archaeological data should throw important light on the nature and causes of this transformation.

These are all pointers as to where new directions may be sought, and they are directions which the archaeologist is uniquely qualified to pursue. These are the goals which we can aim for, however intractable the data base may seem to be, and it is in this spirit that the present volume has been conceived.

Studies of subsistence economy form an obvious starting point for understanding hunter-gatherer behaviour, especially in its prehistoric dimension, since data on subsistence are more easily accessible to the archaeologist and more amenable to interpretation than the less tangible patterns of social organization and ideology. However, this is not to say that studies of subsistence will provide a sufficient understanding of hunter-gatherer behaviour, and a more general label is required to define the focus of study. For this purpose I have preferred the use of the general term *economy*.

Although there is room for considerable disagreement about the definition and purposes of economic prehistory and economic archaeology, the term economy may be used in its broadest sense as a descriptive term to refer to the exploitation and organization of resources used in the maintenance of human populations and societies, without commitment to one or other of the theoretical viewpoints currently in competition (Sheridan and Bailey 1981). The resources in question obviously include food as a primary target of study. But resources of time required in the manufacture and deployment of material technology (Part 1), and social resources embodied in patterns of social organization, and the ways in which these influence or are influenced by patterns of food exploitation (Part 4), are here treated as appropriate

fields for research under the heading of economy. A general definition of this sort is preferred here because it helps to focus on the nexus of interrelations between environmental and ecological factors on the one side, and social factors on the other, without giving undue emphasis to either side of the relationship. Such a definition is also intended to avoid prejudgement about what if any are the primary driving forces of social and cultural evolution, while encouraging exploration of the widest range of data sources. Food remains, site locations and palaeoenvironmental data figure prominently in many of the chapters in this volume, but there are also major discussions of stone artefacts (Parts 1 and 3) and artistic data (Part 4). The term adaptation provides an alternative characterization of the general field of study. But I have preferred to avoid its use for this purpose and to leave its discussion to individual authors, both because of the teleological implications imputed to it by its critics, and because it is open to varying definitions each with quite specific theoretical connotations.

The emphasis on Europe is a matter of practical convenience rather than a statement of belief about the primacy of this part of the world in human evolution, and reflects the growth of interest in reinterpretation of the European Palaeolithic rather than the absence of comparable work elsewhere. Even in Europe it is scarcely possible to do justice in a single volume to the new work in progress, and many areas are necessarily not represented. Europe has been rightly described as a peninsula on the edge of a continent, and the majority of the data presented here is further confined to western Europe, a truly parochial entity in relation to global geography. At the same time charges of Eurocentrism still lurk uneasily between the lines of the hunter-gatherer archaeological literature, in understandable reaction to the historical dominance of Franco-Cantabria in Palaeolithic studies. It may therefore be useful to emphasize some of the advantages of a European focus for present purposes in order to counteract any charges of extreme parochialism on the one hand or residual hints of cultural imperialism on the other.

In the first place, unlike the Americas, Africa, Australia, or parts of Asia, there is no historical continuity between the Palaeolithic record and an ethnographically observed hunter-gatherer present. While this obviously precludes the sort of ethnoarchaeological work that has been such a stimulus elsewhere, it also reduces the temptation to fill in the blank spaces of one's archaeological knowledge with plausible ethnographic colour. Any ethnographically supported principles applied to the European Palaeolithic must be of a high order of generality if they are to be of any serious use. This is reinforced by the fact that the European environment during the last glacial period had a number of ecological characteristics for which there is no modern parallel. Low temperatures combined with the insolation of middle latitudes produced an unusually rich periglacial flora and fauna. Europe is thus potentially the source of distinctive variations in behavioural patterns as well as a useful challenge to the validity of postulated general principles. Admittedly the latter point can probably be claimed for most areas of the world inhabited during the last glacial period, and is thus as much an argument for prehistoric study in general as for a European focus in particular.

A second important point is that long sequences and large samples of data are typical of the European Palaeolithic, both at the level of individual sites and at the regional scale. While much of the data was collected by former generations of archaeologists and can be questioned on the grounds that it may lack the quality and resolution that one would expect from application of modern techniques, it nevertheless represents the sort of large-scale sample that provides a useful starting point for the detection of major variations in the overall limits to behavioural patterning. In particular it provides a context within which to examine the long-term processes that are within the range of focus of the prehistorian. One such issue is the way in which subsistence exploitation and social organization responded to large-scale environmental changes induced by the onset of glacial maxima and subsequent deglaciation (Parts 3 and 4). Long-term variations in the geographical extent or localization of artistic expression and stylistic patterning in artefacts offer other rich possibilities for the examination of large-scale trends (Part 4).

Europe is also well placed geographically for the study of major changes in the limits to behavioural variation. For, although it was geographically peripheral to the main centres of Old World habitation throughout most of the Pleistocene, at the same time it represents a frontier region on the very margins of effective human occupation, and therefore a region sensitive to the development of new behavioural strategies. This is reflected in the evidence that the ecological and geographical limits to the human habitat were considerably expanded during the later Pleistocene, with effective colonization of the periglacial steppe and tundra, and territorial expansion into the northerly latitudes of Siberia and ultimately the New World (Part 4).

Finally, as regards the specific problems associated with the reconstruction of subsistence economies, it is probable that plant foods were relatively unimportant resources, especially during glacial periods or in higher latitudes. This is not to say that they can be completely ignored or that their importance did not vary. However, in as much as plant foods are notoriously invisible in the archaeological record, their likely scarcity in European palaeoenvironments provides a convenient simplification of the methodological problems posed by studies of prehistoric subsistence. Thus emphasis on faunal remains is likely to produce a less distorted view of subsistence and land-use patterns than might be the case in warmer climates or at lower latitudes.

The temporal focus of this volume is primarily the last glacial period as conventionally defined (*c.* 70 000 b.p. to 10 000 b.p.), and the early postglacial, and thus covers developments in the latter part of the Upper Pleistocene and the early Holocene. This is likewise a product of convenience and practical necessities, intended to convey some sense of the possibilities offered by archaeological study of long time-spans, while necessarily ignoring the potential of earlier periods. Although many of the issues discussed in this volume have relevance to earlier periods, limitations of dating and data control in the Lower and Middle Pleistocene, and the nature of the behavioural and evolutionary issues that can be resolved within those limitations, pose formidable problems requiring separate study in their own right.

The chapters are organized in terms of four major themes forming a rough hierarchy of scale in order to highlight underlying problems of theory and method. The first focuses on the primary data — animal bones and stone artefacts recovered from excavation, which represent the most tangible and immediate sources of information. Successive themes broaden the range of focus, moving through discussions of spatial variation and temporal trends at the regional level, to the large-scale interactions that highlight major social and cultural changes. Interpretation of large-scale trends poses the greatest degree of uncertainty because it focuses on a wide range of factors, including the archaeologically elusive variable of social organization, and its success depends on controlling the smaller-scale spatial and regional components of variability, and on understanding the limitations inherent in the use of primary sources of excavated material as test data. At the same time large-scale patterns bring into focus problems that can suggest new ways of analysing or interpreting smaller-scale regional or site-specific data. At the other extreme the focus on faunal and lithic data strikes at the very heart of what is involved in trying to reconstruct behaviour patterns from material data — of what the limitations are and how they can be overcome, of the questions that can be answered and those that may lie beyond the resolution of current techniques. It should be emphasized that the primary data sources raise their own issues of theory and of large-scale change no less than of method, while spatial and temporal trends pose their own problems of method as well as of theory. Thus the four major themes are strongly interdependent, and in the interest of flexible research design a number of chapters span two or more themes. The thematic boundaries defined here are not to be applied too rigidly. Indeed their replacement by others, as new problems and issues emerge, will be a measure of the extent to which archaeological study of prehistoric hunters and gatherers can promote self-sustaining growth as a vigorous and healthy empirical discipline worthy of the name.

# PART ONE

## Primary data sources: problems of theory and method

Chapter 2

## Editorial

Animal bones accumulated as food refuse and artefacts of stone (and less often of bone) together represent the primary materials recovered in excavation of prehistoric hunter-gatherer sites. They are the primary data sources which support interpretation in relation to the issues examined in Parts 2, 3 and 4 of this book. They can also be analysed in their own right to provide information on a range of behavioural and cultural issues. As such they offer a useful initial focus on some of the basic problems posed in the analysis and interpretation of prehistoric behaviour.

Traditionally both types of materials have been exploited for their chronological implications. Archaeological analysis of artefacts has been used to build up a relative time—space framework of cultural variation. Zoological analysis of the faunal remains and their evolutionary status and palaeoenvironmental implications has been used to provide a framework for inter-regional and inter-continental correlation. The development of radiometric dating, aided by more sensitive palaeoenvironmental techniques based on such indicators as pollen, beetles or the oxygen-isotope content of marine foraminifera (Butzer 1971a; Evans 1978), has progressively eliminated the need for such chronological studies (as well as exposing the inadequate assumptions on which many were founded). This in its turn has helped to break down the barrier between stone artefacts as reflections of human culture and animal bones as reflections of the natural environment, and to encourage new theoretical perspectives and new methods relating both types of material more directly to cultural and behavioural issues.

In the case of faunal studies this has increasingly involved the active participation of the archaeologist both as interpreter and analyst, and has thus placed increasing demands on the training of individuals within an archaeozoological rather than a narrowly zoological frame of reference (Brothwell and Higgs 1969). Artefact studies, meanwhile, have moved towards increased emphasis on the value of specialist studies of other disciplines, such as geological sourcing or the study of fracture mechanics (Hayden 1979).

Apart from the relatively obvious relationship between fauna and cultural behaviour via the subsistence economy, there have been a number of suggestions about the ways in which faunal data might be harnessed to cultural problems or artefactual data to biological and ecological concerns. These ideas range across a wide spectrum from 'functionalist' exhortations about the role of artefacts as extra-somatic aids to adaptation (L.R. Binford 1962) to 'structuralist' assertions about the culture-symbolic patterning preserved in spatial distributions of animal-bone refuse (Tilley 1981). Studies of stylistic variation in material culture represent one promising focus for the integration of functionalist and culture-symbolic interests (Wobst 1977). They involve special considerations which are treated more fully in Part 4 in the context of large-scale social change. Despite these developments it is still relatively rare for the bone and stone material from an excavation to be treated together in integrated fashion, or with equal emphasis, or to be seen as equally important contributors to a common objective. In part this reflects on-going traditions of training and disciplinary demarcation, in which expertise in the analysis of one set of material is held to exclude expertise in the other. In part it reflects a lack of any coherent or methodologically well-founded theoretical framework in which both sets of data can participate on equal terms. Theoretical concepts which define relevant variables and supply a framework for interpreting observations of the basic data are as yet little developed in relation to either set of materials in isolation, let alone in combination. A continuing problem is the lack of clear or widely agreed guide-lines about so-called 'middle-range theory' — about how patterns of material data are to be transformed into patterns of past behaviour (Schiffer 1976; Binford 1977a). These problems affect faunal and lithic studies alike, although in differing degree.

The interpretation of artefact data in terms of behaviour is much less advanced in comparison with faunal studies, partly because general concepts about the causes of artefact variability have been little developed, and partly because the middle-range theory that would allow the transformation of artefact variability into patterns of behaviour is still very poorly understood. The function of most categories of prehistoric stone tools is still mainly a matter of speculation. Even the very definition of what constitutes a specific tool type is a subject of considerable debate. Attempts to interpret assemblage variability in functional terms through comparison with site locations and environmental patterning may entail a number of quite complex issues which are extremely difficult to control for archaeologically, even in apparently favourable circumstances (see, for example, Parkington 1980 and comments). Statistical correlation techniques are unlikely to have much additional impact without some initial decisions as to what constitute relevant variables and what might constitute significant correlations. Use-wear analysis is still beset by an array of technical issues and is in an early stage of development in which its ultimate potential remains difficult to assess. It is perhaps scarcely surprising that stone-artefact analysis has tended to gain a certain notoriety in the wider archaeological community as a rather sterile end in itself, rather than a means to a further end. However, as Torrence emphasizes in chapter 3 of this volume, stone artefacts are usually far more abundant than faunal remains, and on many sites are the only surviving evidence of human activity.

One approach suggested by Binford (1973) on the basis of his analysis of Mousterian variability and subsequent ethnographic work is to concentrate on the general structure of an assemblage in terms of patterns of tool manufacture and discard, in addition to measurement of morphological differences and typological categories. Binford's conceptual distinction between *curated tools* (made in anticipation of future needs) and *expedient tools* (made for the needs of the moment) has suggested new ways of thinking about artefact analysis which clearly have potential for detailed application and further development in archaeological contexts (e.g. Marks and Friedel 1977). Torrence develops this approach by focusing on the use of time as a crucial variable affecting hunter-gatherer decisions, and the ways in which time is budgeted or scheduled between different activities. This emphasis on time budgeting is of particular theoretical interest because it draws attention to a fundamental variable in human behaviour which is not only of relevance to artefact studies but which has a wider application to a whole range of behavioural issues including subsistence.

Her argument in broad outline is that certain types of environment will be 'time-stressed', notably ecologically specialized environments with a limited range of relatively mobile and unpredictable resources. Survival in these conditions is likely to be especially dependent on the efficient use of time, for example by scheduling activities into different time slots to avoid distracting conflicts, and by increasing the speed and efficiency with which critical activities such as the capture and retrieval of elusive prey can be effected. In these conditions material equipment is likely to take the form of a relatively wide range of highly specialized and complex tools, each designed to achieve efficiently a limited range of tasks. The investment in advance production of complex equipment will be facilitated by scheduling, and rewarded by the more efficient completion of the designated task. Conversely in more generalized environments with a wider range of resource options, including relatively predictable and easily collected resources such as plant foods, constraints on efficient time budgeting will be relaxed, with concomitant changes towards more 'generalized' tool-kits characterized by multi-purpose tools, and simpler designs and manufacturing processes. A number of important qualifications on this general theme, and the problems of its practical application, are elaborated.

Torrence's approach is interesting in two ways. In the first place at least two of the three proposed measures of assemblage structure, namely composition (functional categories of tools), diversity (number of tool types) and complexity (number of parts per tool-kit), would seem to lend themselves to measurements of relative differences between assemblages, independently of any knowledge about the specific function of particular artefacts. At least this is the case for the latter two measures.

Secondly the theory emphasizes time budgeting as an underlying variable in all human decision-making and hence as a potentially unifying focus for the study both of material culture and of subsistence data. The distinction between time-stressed and 'time-relaxed' environments recalls Binford's (1980) distinction between logistical and foraging exploitation strategies (see Part 2). Thus we might expect to find correlations between variations in assemblage structure and variations in the structure of the natural environment and the subsistence strategies used in its exploitation. There is clearly some measure of support for this expectation in Torrence's analysis of ethnographic data. These considerations further suggest a realistic prospect for undertaking archaeological tests in which analyses of prehistoric assemblage structure are compared with independently derived palaeoeconomic and palaeoenvironmental data. The regional sequences discussed in Part 3 provide abundant evidence of substantial changes in assemblage structure against a background of changing environments and exploitation strategies. In particular Clark and Straus (chapter 12 of this volume) give some detailed analyses of variations in assemblage structure which indicate possibilities of development along these lines.

At the present, faunal analysis is in some ways in a more privileged position than lithic analysis, to the extent that theories of animal behaviour and ecology and the knowledge of animal anatomy provide a well-established framework within which to examine variability in food-refuse patterns. Various features of faunal assemblages of relevance to the human use of animal populations can be analysed within this framework, such as the proportional representation of species, patterns of bone breakage, or the analysis of mortality patterns. The last is the theme of the other two chapters in this section and has a direct bearing on one of the more contentious issues in human social evolution, namely the origins of animal domestication.

Analysis of mortality patterns was originally developed as an alternative to the reliance on morphological indicators in studies of early domestication. An initial assumption was that hunting strategies would produce a random cull in which the age at death of the exploited animals reflects the natural age structure of the living population, whereas domestication would produce a selective cull in which certain age classes, notably the immature, are disproportionately represented (Perkins 1964; Ducos 1978). Higgs and Jarman (1969) observed that a high percentage of immature animals are found in assemblages of supposedly wild animals in early contexts (for example rhinoceros in the Middle Palaeolithic), an observation intended less to assert the existence of early domestication than to challenge the conventional division of animals into Pleistocene 'wild' and Holocene 'domesticated', and to encourage critical appraisal of the criteria by which such a division had been maintained. In the aftermath of the debate that ensued (see, for example, Jarman and Wilkinson 1972; Jarman 1976 and discussion), it became apparent that reliable interpretation of mortality patterns would require a detailed understanding of the ecological factors that influence variability in the natural population structure of the prey species, as well as the development of appropriate techniques for distinguishing age classes in prehistoric faunal material.

Hunting strategies, as both Levine and Klein *et al.* emphasize (chapters 4 and 5), may give rise to two quite different mortality patterns, depending on the hunting techniques employed and the behaviour of the prey species: (1) *catastrophic mortality patterns*; and (2) *attritional mortality patterns*.

Catastrophic mortality patterns can be produced by a variety of strategies. These include mass slaughter of whole social groups, for example by driving techniques, but would by no means be limited to that technique. They could also include random hunting by stalking or trapping individual animals, as discussed by Levine. Attritional mortality patterns are characteristic of stalking individual animals and typically result in an age profile weighted towards the weaker and more vulnerable individuals, such as the young and the old. With some species it would appear that a high percentage of immature animals, once thought to be a sign of domestication, may in fact be what would be predicted in some types of hunting strategies, both random and attritional.

Levine elaborates a number of variations on the two basic patterns of mortality in the context of horse exploitation, with particular reference to Middle and Upper Palaeolithic assemblages in France and Germany. She emphasizes the effect that horse social behaviour can have on population structure, leading to the segregation of particular age (and/or sex) classes in different geographical ranges at certain seasons or during certain stages of the life cycle. Fluctuating environmental conditions can also affect herd structure by leading to disproportionate representation of particular year classes, depending on the varying balance of natural mortality and natality factors from year to year. Klein *et al.* similarly employ catastrophic and attritional mortality patterns in their discussion of red deer exploitation in Upper Palaeolithic Cantabria and Mesolithic Britain. It is interesting to note that both chapters propose slaughter of whole social groups as the most likely hunting strategy in the majority of cases (see also Clark and Straus, chapter 12 below).

On the methodological side, simple classification into immature and adult categories has long been superseded by more detailed ageing criteria. Here both authors use crown height measurements as a means of placing individual teeth within more or less narrow time-spans. These may not be assignable to specific age classes with any accuracy, but are nevertheless useful in discriminating different mortality patterns. This technique provides a useful complement to the better known tooth eruption and wear sequences worked out for the common farmyard animals (Higham 1967; Payne 1973) and for red deer (Lowe 1967). It also has the additional advantage that it is not limited to mandibles but can be applied to finds of isolated teeth, an advantage which greatly increases the sample size in most assemblages.

Several remaining problems may be noted. One is the possibility that juvenile teeth may be systematically under-represented because of differential representation, an objection that can be mitigated if not wholly overcome by applying a systematic adjustment factor (Levine), or by considering the state of preservation of other material (Levine and Klein *et al.*). Another potential difficulty is small sample size. A further uncertainty lies in the possibility that quite different exploitation strategies might give rise to similar mortality patterns. For example, the culling policy recommended in some patterns of animal husbandry would produce an attritional mortality pattern not unlike that created by some hunting strategies. The difficulty of reliably sexing adequate samples of horse or deer material is a major handicap here. Differential culling of young males is a feature of livestock management, and differentiation of males and females in prehistoric mortality profiles would provide useful additional information in discriminating between alternative strategies. Detailed antler studies can sometimes throw light on this problem in deer species (e.g. Sturdy 1975). But interpretation is usually hampered by small samples and by the likelihood that the representation of antlers will be distorted by their use as raw material for making artefacts. Other more indirect information can sometimes clarify the nature of the exploitation strategy, for example the evidence of site locations (see chapters 7, 8, 13 and 15). Nevertheless the value of establishing differences and similarities between assemblages is clearly apparent in Levine's comparison of natural and archaeological assemblages. Similarly Klein *et al.* show the usefulness of comparing assemblages from sites which, on independent evidence, appear to have served different economic functions.

Chapter 3

Time budgeting and hunter-gatherer technology
Robin Torrence

This chapter addresses the need for theoretical approaches to the study of prehistoric stone tools. It is argued that time stress is a major factor determining variations in technological behaviour among hunter-gatherers. Two effects of time budgeting are discussed: scheduling of procurement, manufacture and maintenance activities; and determination of assemblage structure. In particular predictions for the composition, diversity and complexity of tool-kits are illustrated by way of an analysis of tools used in the procurement of food. Although further work is needed before the ideas presented here can be implemented in the study of archaeological material, this preliminary attempt at theory building demonstrates that future research must account for the role of time in shaping prehistoric hunter-gatherer assemblages.

### The importance of time

Recent years have witnessed some important theoretical developments in the study of hunter-gatherer subsistence and settlement (e.g. Jochim 1976; Winterhalder 1977; L.R. Binford 1978a, 1978b, 1980; Keene 1979; Bettinger 1980; Perlman 1980). Consequently, analytical techniques applied to several categories of archaeological data, particularly faunal and floral remains, have become highly developed and are now central to hunter-gatherer research. In contrast, research focused on lithic artefacts has not contributed significantly to these newer trends. With the notable exception of micro-wear analysis, a set of techniques still in its infancy (e.g. Hayden 1979; Keeley 1979; Odell and Odell-Vereecken 1980), methodology for the analysis of chipped stone artefacts has altered only slightly in

recent years, merely broadening in scope to include waste by-products of manufacture as well as completed tools (e.g. Swanson 1975).

A more serious problem, however, is the poverty of the theory which is directed to the explanation of variability in hunter-gatherer technology. Due to the overwhelming dominance of lithic remains in the archaeological record of the Pleistocene, this deficiency cannot be taken lightly. Since organic remains decay rapidly in comparison with their stone counterparts, a great majority of hunter-gatherer sites are composed largely, if not entirely, of lithic artefacts. Unless a means is devised for using chipped stone materials to answer questions about human behaviour, archaeologists may never be able to explain adequately many features of prehistoric hunter-gatherer adaptation.

Although there are undoubtedly several factors which have contributed to the particular make-up of the technology employed by a hunter-gatherer group, only one of these, the effects of time, will be explored in depth here. Certainly material culture responds to a series of different kinds of stresses which impinge on the larger system. The role of technology in the efficient use of energy has been stressed by many authors, but as Wobst (1977) has pointed out, tools can also be used to convey information. In this chapter I have chosen to concentrate on the way technology responds to a need for effective use of time because the importance of this variable has not been given the theoretical consideration which I believe its marked effects merit. In fact, I think it can be demonstrated that limitations in the time available to complete a task are a key variable in explaining differences in the structure of hunter-gatherer tool-kits as well as in the patterns of procurement, manufacture and discard of artefacts.

In discussing human adaptations, anthropologists and archaeologists have long stressed the role of energetic efficiency (cf. E. Smith 1979: 55). On the whole the emphasis has been placed on the overall *quantity* rather than the *rate* of energy capture. In contrast, Smith has convincingly argued for the importance of 'time budgeting as a primary adaptive constraint' (1979: 53). According to his argument, an increase in the rate of energy capture is important in all cases whether the amount of energy available is scarce or not. Although I do not agree with Smith that groups will necessarily attempt to maximize the rate of energy capture (1979: 70), I do think that in many cases time is likely to be a more critical limiting factor for human survival than is simply the quantity of energy available. If optimum use of time can be assumed to lead ultimately to increased reproductive fitness, that is, be 'adaptive' in terms of neo-Darwinian theory, then it seems reasonable to assume that technology will reflect one of the areas where time budgeting will take place.

### The role of scheduling

Given the basic assumption that time budgeting is crucial to hunter-gatherer behaviour, the technology used by these groups can be expected to vary according to both the severity and the character of time stress. The degree of stress will mainly condition the quantity of the response, whereas the type of stress will determine the quality of adaptive technological behaviour. The nature of the quality of behaviour can be grouped into two types of response. First, if the total amount of time available is limited, tools which increase the speed at which the activity is carried out will be employed; I will return to this possibility later. In other cases the overall quantity of time may be sufficient, but it may be necessary to *schedule* certain types of behaviour in order to avoid competition among various activities for particular periods of time. This second response is likely to involve the division of time into small parcels which are then juggled according to some set of priorities in order to fit in all the competing demands.

The concept of scheduling activities to maximize the use of resources which are available for limited periods of time is one of the most important guides to the understanding of hunter-gatherer subsistence behaviour (e.g. Jochim 1976; Binford 1978b). It should not be surprising, therefore, that the same type of behaviour should also have adaptive value in other spheres of hunter-gatherer life. Unlike subsistence, however, technology is not a sub-system in and of itself but is used as an aid in a range of activities. For this reason scheduling constraints are usually imposed on technology by

the nature of the time stress operating in other realms; in order to understand how technology responds to these demands, one must, therefore, go beyond the tools themselves. In other words, the relationship between scheduling behaviour in the procurement, manufacture, use and discard of tools needs to be examined within the context of a wider range of activities.

At this point, a few examples which demonstrate the role of scheduling behaviour in determining the configuration of hunter-gatherer technology might be instructive. Binford (1973, 1977b, 1979a, 1979b) has previously described several cases among the Nunamiut Eskimo in which the production and maintenance of stone tools are scheduled in order to avoid interference with subsistence activities. Procurement of lithic raw materials, for example, is tied into and 'embedded' in subsistence strategies so that valuable time which could be spent in food getting is not wasted by making special purpose trips to quarry locations. The collection of stone takes place, instead, at times when it can be conveniently slotted into the more important subsistence system (Binford 1979a, 1979b). Manufacture and repair of tools among the Nunamiut is another task which is often embedded within the more time-stressed occupation of caribou hunting. For instance, Binford (1978b; pers. comm.) notes that these activities commonly take place at hunting stands while the Eskimo wait for the game.

In another case study Binford (1977b) has shown that when tools which are used in the procurement of food are manufactured, the character of the work is affected by the nature of the time stress operating on the subsistence pattern. The production of tools in anticipation of use, a strategy which Binford (1973, 1977b) has defined as 'curation', is an additional response to the need to schedule time effectively. In the case of hunting caribou, the major source of food for the Nunamiut, the time available for capture of the resource is limited due to the high mobility of the animal and to its seasonal occurrence in the area. Production of tools used to kill caribou must therefore be planned so as not to detract from the small amount of 'pursuit time' (Schoener 1971; cf. below). Consequently, tools are manufactured well in advance of sighting the game. Furthermore, in situations when amounts of time are restricted, there is no room for repair of tools until after the caribou has been safely secured. The result is that large amounts of time and energy are invested in the production and maintenance of hunting equipment, long before their use is required, to ensure that the tools will survive without breakage until the task is completed. Binford (1977b) has already discussed at length some consequences of the need for the large inputs into tool production for the formation processes of the archaeological record. In brief, he argues that tools will not be thrown away after one use but are carried around to be used repeatedly in order to reap the returns of the initial investments. If broken, tools are frequently repaired or recycled; discard will therefore not necessarily take place at the location of tool use since even worn out equipment can be stockpiled at base camps for later conversion into another tool.

Since the occurrence of intensive manufacturing activities will be carefully segregated from the time devoted to subsistence when the latter is limited, certain long periods of time may therefore be scheduled exclusively for the necessarily elaborate preparation of hunting gear. For example, during the month or so after the autumn caribou migration, some Eskimo groups live off stored food in order to manufacture and repair tools and other equipment such as tents and clothing (e.g. Damas 1972).

These examples from Binford's ethnographic work among the Nunamiut serve to illustrate just two important ways that technological behaviour can be scheduled in order to make optimum use of limited time. In the first place, procurement, manufacture and maintenance tasks can be fitted into small time slots which occur within the contexts of other activities. Secondly, large investments of time in technology which is used in tasks requiring an uninterrupted duration will be beneficial. Although the high inputs of time may be parcelled out over a very long period, it may also be necessary in some instances to schedule large blocks of time solely for this purpose. There are likely to be additional types of scheduling behaviour; archaeologists need to identify as many as possible and to recognize the resulting implications for patterning in the archaeological record as Binford has done so elegantly for curation (1977b). My purpose here is simply to argue that where maximization in the efficient use of time is to be expected because of its adaptive consequences, then one outcome that could be predicted is the scheduling of the procurement, production and discard of tools. Once the importance of time budgeting is recognized, its effects on a whole host of related activities, for example the selection of raw material types, the character of the reduction strategy utilized to fabricate artefacts, the role of craft specialist production, the timing and location of production, repair and discard, can also begin to be incorporated into a general theory of hunter-gatherer technology.

### Assemblage structure

The recognition of scheduling in response to time stress is certainly an important insight into hunter-gatherer technology. As suggested previously, there is, however, another category of behaviour which has not received adequate attention by archaeologists: the use of particular tools to increase the speed at which activities are carried out. Whereas, in a very general sense, scheduling primarily affects the *organization* of technological behaviour, the need for speed is mainly reflected in the *structure* of the tool assemblage. Three dimensions of hunter-gatherer assemblage structure can be related to time stress. The first property is the *composition* of the assemblage in terms of the functional categories of tools present. Secondly, the *diversity* of tools within a functional class can be measured by simply counting the numbers of tool

types present. Finally, the *complexity* of the tools in terms of either the average number of parts per tool or simply the total number of components in the tool-kit will be affected by the need to minimize the expenditure of time.

Assemblage composition can be studied in terms of the degree to which tools are effective at reducing the time spent in a task. Given a knowledge of the nature of time stress and an independent measure of the efficiency of tools, one could then predict which tools should be present in a given hunter-gatherer tool-kit. Since tool typologies have not previously been established with time minimization in mind, it is difficult to give a specific example of how composition could be studied in this way; the detailed discussion of subsistence given below, however, may help clarify the suggested procedure.

The diversity of tool-kits should be negatively correlated with the amount of time available to complete a job; with small quantities of time, the diversity of tool use will be large. This prediction is based on the assumption that highly specialized tools, that is, artefacts designed to be used in a small number of functions, are more efficient than general-purpose equipment. The use of special-purpose gear means that a range of different tools will all participate in the same activity. A specialized tool-kit, then, creates a very diverse assemblage. The logical conclusion is that diversity is caused, at least in part, by attempts to use time efficiently.

In addition to the postulated relationship with time, specialized and therefore diverse tool-kits may be found when the range of activities requiring technology is small. In contrast, general-purpose assemblages exhibiting a low level of diversity will occur when the tools must be used in many different tasks. Due to the relatively high mobility of most hunter-gatherer groups, the gross number of artefacts which can be carried between residences is ultimately limited. Given this constraint, the degree to which specialization of tools can take place is restricted. Generalized assemblages will be expected in cases where tools are needed for a wide range of jobs.

Like functional specialization, the third dimension of assemblage structure, complexity of tools, can be predicted to be inversely related to the availability of time. In this case I assume that the greatest pay-off to the investment of additional time required in the manufacture of a complex tool is time saved as a result of using that tool rather than a simpler but functionally equivalent artefact. Additional factors contributing to the need for complex tools appear to me also to be ultimately linked to the optimal use of time. For example, it could be argued that some complex tools, such as hafted stone implements or tools in which stone points are inset into a shaft, are beneficial because individual parts can be replaced easily if worn out or broken, thereby avoiding the need to manufacture an entirely new tool from scratch. Nevertheless, the time gained by the ease in substituting new parts has only been won as a result of a high initial investment in the manufacture of all the separate parts. In other words, this strategy may be based on the ability to schedule manufacturing time so that the long time used for manufacture is followed by a long period of use with only small interruptions to replace separate parts. Complexity, therefore, can assist time budgeting by increasing the speed of a task or through aiding the scheduling of manufacture and repair of equipment.

The power of the general hypotheses concerning assemblage structure can perhaps be best demonstrated by reference to a specific case. In the remainder of the chapter the composition, diversity and complexity of one functional class of implements, tools used by hunter-gatherers to procure food, will be examined in order to determine the extent to which these traits are sensitive to differences in the amount of time available to secure adequate food resources. Fortunately the job of testing hypotheses concerning hunter-gatherer subsistence technology has been aided considerably by the large catalogue of ethnographic data compiled by Wendall Oswalt (1973, 1976; cf. Lustig-Arecco 1975). For the purpose of his study Oswalt has proposed the useful term *subsistant* to refer to hunter-gatherer food-getting technology. He defines a subsistant as 'an extrasomatic form that is removed from a natural context or manufactured and is applied directly to obtain food' (1976: 46). On the basis of charts summarizing the data, Oswalt makes some very interesting observations about technology, but his empirical generalizations lack explanatory power because they are divorced from theories of hunter-gatherer behaviour (cf. Binford 1977a: 5–6; 1978b: 358–60). Regardless of the shortcomings of Oswalt's inductive approach to the evolution of technology, the data can still be used to verify a different set of propositions about the structure of hunter-gatherer assemblages.

**Measuring time stress**
In order to predict the effects of time budgeting on the structure of hunter-gatherer subsistants, one must first devise a way to measure the degree of time stress experienced by various subsistence practices. One important variable is obviously the length of time during the year in which resources can be exploited. Edible plant foods, for example, can be obtained in equatorial rain forests at any period of the year, but in other environments the availability of vegetable resources is restricted by rainfall, sunlight and temperature to a growing season of limited duration. Similarly, for most environments animal foods are not constant in their occurrence throughout the year; many species migrate seasonally whereas others hibernate during the periods when their food is scarce. The amount of periodicity or seasonality in annual terms, then, will determine the need for subsistence strategies to be efficient in their use of time.

An additional factor which contributes to the potential amount of time for subsistence activities is the nature of the resources being exploited. The key factors in this regard have been described by ecologists as the time involved in locating a resource, called the *search time*, and the time which elapses

from detection until capture, the *pursuit time* (e.g. MacArthur and Pianka 1966; Schoener 1971). As Jochim has emphasized in relation to human subsistence (1976: 27–8; cf. Keene 1979: 376–7), the mobility of the resource affects the length of both components of time; search time is also dependent on the density of the potential food, whereas pursuit time relates to the aggregated or dispersed nature of the resources.

In ideal circumstances the prediction of subsistant composition, diversity and complexity would be based on measurements of the mobility, density and aggregation of the resources exploited as well as the length of time during the year in which they were available. From this data it should then be possible to devise an 'optimal tool-kit' in much the same way that previous scholars have modelled subsistence using principles from optimal foraging theory in ecology (e.g. Winterhalder 1977; Keene 1979; Reidhead 1979: 555–62). At this preliminary stage in the development of theory for technology, however, such detailed analyses are not really necessary or appropriate, although the formation of more specific models should be the ultimate goal. In the meantime, I have opted for approximate measures and have concentrated on the effects of resource availability and mobility.

Although there are several possible measures of the time in which edible resources are present, I propose to use latitude in the preliminary analyses of subsistants which follow. Ecologists have demonstrated that all other things being equal (e.g. altitude, rainfall) the length of the growing season for plants decreases on a global scale with increasing latitude. Further tests of the hypotheses will need to devise more sophisticated measures of resource availability, but for the purpose of evaluating the general validity of the argument, latitude should be sufficiently accurate. The approach adopted here for estimating the mobility of resources is fairly crude, but it does serve to emphasize the relationship between mobility and time and to highlight some important differences in the role of time among various hunter-gatherer economies. Since plants are immobile, both search and pursuit times required in their exploitation will be generally lower than for animal resources. Reductions in the amount of time in plant collection are difficult to achieve. Because outputs are directly related to the size of energy inputs, plant gathering is an energy maximizing strategy, in ecological terms (Schoener 1971: 376). In contrast, the exploitation of mobile animal resources is almost entirely dependent on the effective use of time both in terms of search and pursuit. Unlike plant-gathering strategies, an increase in the amount of energy invested in hunting does not necessarily lead to greater quantities of animals taken. The success of a subsistence strategy based on animals is the speedy and effective capture of a resource when it is encountered; failure can lead to the additional inputs of considerable amounts of time and effort in the continued pursuit of a mobile prey species. Since the dichotomy between hunting animals and collecting plants also represents a marked difference in the degree to which the efficient use of time is necessary, the percentage of plants in

Table 3.1. *Hunter-gatherer subsistants: numbers of tools and technounits*

| Group | Latitude | Instruments | | | Weapons | | Tended facilities | | Untended facilities | | Total | |
|---|---|---|---|---|---|---|---|---|---|---|---|---|
| Tiwi | 12 | 3 | (2) | 6 | 6 | 6 | 2 | 2 | 0 | 0 | 11 | 14 |
| Andamanese | 12 | 4 | (2) | 8 | 4 | 31 | 3 | 12 | 0 | 0 | 11 | 51 |
| Ingura | 14 | 3 | (3) | 3 | 6 | 19 | 3 | 8 | 1 | 2 | 13 | 32 |
| Chenchu | 16 | 7 | (7) | 13 | 7 | 26 | 6 | 16 | 0 | 0 | 20 | 55 |
| Naron Bushman | 19 | 2 | (1) | 5 | 5 | 19 | 3 | 5 | 2 | 11 | 12 | 40 |
| Aranda | 24 | 4 | (2) | 7 | 4 | 21 | 7 | 10 | 1 | 4 | 16 | 42 |
| Owens Valley Paiute | 37 | 4 | (4) | 9 | 9 | 44 | 10 | 30 | 5 | 24 | 28 | 107 |
| Surprise Valley Paiute | 42 | 7 | (3) | 15 | 9 | 27 | 19 | 41 | 4 | 14 | 39 | 97 |
| Tasmanian | 42 | 3 | (2) | 3 | 3 | 3 | 4 | 8 | 1 | 1 | 11 | 15 |
| Klamath | 43 | 9 | (5) | 18 | 7 | 35 | 22 | 70 | 5 | 28 | 43 | 151 |
| Twana | 48 | 4 | (1) | 7 | 12 | 70 | 19 | 96 | 13 | 64 | 48 | 237 |
| Tlingit | 58 | 4 | (0) | 7 | 8 | 25 | 8 | 34 | 8 | 55 | 28 | 121 |
| Tanaina | 60 | 7 | (0) | 13 | 16 | 83 | 3 | 17 | 14 | 111 | 40 | 224 |
| Ingalik | 62 | 6 | (1) | 14 | 13 | 64 | 15 | 61 | 21 | 157 | 55 | 296 |
| Nabesna | 63 | 1 | (1) | 1 | 8 | 36 | 8 | 23 | 8 | 45 | 25 | 105 |
| Caribou | 63 | 3 | (0) | 12 | 10 | 39 | 13 | 37 | 8 | 30 | 34 | 118 |
| Angmaksalik | 66 | 4 | (0) | 18 | 18 | 151 | 9 | 20 | 2 | 13 | 33 | 202 |
| Iglulik | 69 | 3 | (0) | 8 | 20 | 142 | 8 | 27 | 11 | 48 | 42 | 225 |
| Copper | 70 | 4 | (0) | 16 | 8 | 53 | 11 | 36 | 4 | 17 | 27 | 122 |
| Taremiut | 71 | 1 | (0) | 3 | 18 | 133 | 10 | 41 | 6 | 28 | 35 | 205 |

*Note*: the first number given in each case is the number of *tools* in each class. The second number is the total number of *techno-units*. In the case of instruments, the figure in parenthesis is the number of instruments used only in conjunction with plants. Based on Oswalt 1976: 157, 173, tables 8.1, 9.1.

the diet can be used as a rough measure of the severity of time stress experienced by a group.

With the proposed measures for each of the two variables which condition the relative amount of time that hunter-gatherers can use to procure food – availability throughout the year and mobility of resources – the effects of time on the assemblage structure of subsistants can be investigated. Once again I must stress that the following is not meant to be a definitive analysis of hunter-gatherer technology; the purpose of the investigation is merely to examine the role of time.

### Assemblage composition of subsistants

As a preliminary step towards studying variability in the composition of hunter-gatherer subsistants, it might be profitable to adopt the basic structure of Oswalt's typology of tools, which was based on the ideas first proposed by Wagner (1960). Oswalt has defined three major types of artefact: instruments, weapons and facilities. Instruments 'are used to impinge on masses incapable of significant motion and relatively harmless to people' (1976: 64); a digging stick is a good example of an instrument. On the other hand, both weapons and facilities are applied to mobile resources, although the former type kill the resources whereas the latter 'controls the movement of a species or protects it to man's advantage' (1976: 105). In these terms spears, bows and arrows, and

throwing sticks are weapons; traps, weirs, hunting blinds are classified as facilities. Another distinction can be made among these types. Implements and weapons use human energy directly whereas 'facilities are designed to apply human energy indirectly, through attracting, containing, holding, restraining, or redirecting a living mass' (1973: 26). Facilities are subdivided further into tended and untended varieties which are differentiated by whether they operate in the presence or absence of man. For my purposes Oswalt's distinctions between artefact and 'naturefact' and between simple and complex forms are not helpful (1976: 17–27, 50).

Given the definition of instruments as tools used to procure immobile resources, it is not surprising that in Oswalt's data (1976: 157, 173), presented here in tables 3.1 and 3.2, there is a strong positive relationship between the percentage of the diet comprised of immobile resources (largely plants) and the incidence of instruments. Similarly, among the hunter-gatherers which Oswalt studied, weapons and facilities are associated with the importance of animal resources in the subsistence pattern (table 3.2). These results simply follow logically from the typology of subsistants.

What is more interesting from a theoretical point of view is the differences between weapons and facilities. One way to investigate this distinction is to evaluate the potential of each class of artefact for maximizing either search or pursuit time.

Table 3.2. *Hunter-gatherer subsistants: percentage composition of tools, technounits and diet*

| Group | Diet | | Artefacts | | | | | | | |
|---|---|---|---|---|---|---|---|---|---|---|
| | % immobile resources | % mobile resources | Instruments | | Weapons | | Tended facilities | | Untended facilities | |
| Tiwi | 50 | 50 | 27 | 43 | 55 | 43 | 18 | 14 | 0 | 0 |
| Andamanese | 40 | 60 | 36 | 16 | 36 | 61 | 27 | 24 | 0 | 0 |
| Ingura | 70 | 30 | 23 | 9 | 46 | 59 | 23 | 25 | 8 | 6 |
| Chenchu | 70 | 30 | 35 | 24 | 35 | 47 | 30 | 29 | 0 | 0 |
| Naron Bushman | 60 | 40 | 17 | 13 | 42 | 48 | 25 | 13 | 17 | 28 |
| Aranda | 60 | 40 | 25 | 17 | 25 | 50 | 44 | 24 | 6 | 10 |
| Owens Valley Paiute | 70 | 30 | 14 | 8 | 32 | 41 | 36 | 28 | 18 | 22 |
| Surprise Valley Paiute | 65 | 35 | 18 | 15 | 23 | 28 | 49 | 42 | 10 | 14 |
| Tasmanian | 40 | 60 | 27 | 20 | 27 | 20 | 36 | 53 | 9 | 7 |
| Klamath | 40 | 60 | 21 | 12 | 16 | 23 | 51 | 46 | 12 | 19 |
| Twana | 5 | 95 | 8 | 3 | 25 | 30 | 40 | 41 | 27 | 27 |
| Tlingit | 10 | 90 | 14 | 6 | 29 | 21 | 29 | 28 | 29 | 45 |
| Tanaina | 5 | 95 | 18 | 6 | 40 | 37 | 8 | 8 | 35 | 50 |
| Ingalik | 5 | 95 | 11 | 5 | 24 | 22 | 27 | 21 | 38 | 53 |
| Nabesna | 5 | 95 | 4 | 1 | 32 | 34 | 32 | 22 | 32 | 43 |
| Caribou | 3 | 97 | 9 | 10 | 29 | 33 | 38 | 31 | 24 | 25 |
| Angmaksalik | 7 | 93 | 12 | 9 | 55 | 75 | 27 | 10 | 6 | 6 |
| Iglulik | 3 | 97 | 7 | 4 | 48 | 63 | 19 | 12 | 26 | 21 |
| Copper | 6 | 94 | 15 | 13 | 30 | 43 | 41 | 30 | 15 | 14 |
| Taremiut | 3 | 97 | 3 | 1 | 51 | 65 | 29 | 20 | 17 | 14 |

*Note*: the first figure is the percentage of tools; the second figure is the percentage of technounits. Based on Oswalt 1976: 157, 173, 193, tables 8.1, 9.1, 9.4.

In the first instance, search time can be most effectively reduced by using untended facilities, such as traps, because they operate independently of the hunter; in this way several different searches can be carried out concurrently, thus allowing the hunter to maximize his options. None of the other subsistants which Oswalt has described are very effective during the search stage of procurement, but there are other artefacts in hunter-gatherer assemblages which help to reduce search costs. For example, tools which convey information about the state of the environment (e.g. stone cairns marking places where streams can be crossed easily) or games and toys which ultimately teach children how to find resources efficiently must serve to minimize search costs. Many of these tools would normally be classified in Binford's typology of material culture as ideotechnic or sociotechnic although they are important for subsistence (Binford 1972a: 24–5). There is much to be learned about how tools themselves, rather than merely their artistic or stylistic features (cf. Wobst 1977), function to communicate information which helps diminish search time.

On the whole subsistant technology is not well suited for minimizing search time. Since this parameter is determined by the density as well as the mobility of the resource, search time can be effectively reduced by manipulation of plants and animals through controlling their occurrence in the environment (e.g. by simple techniques of herd movement, use of fire or selective weeding) or, at the extreme end of the continuum of possible options, by means of full domestication.

Weapons and facilities are primarily directed towards the pursuit of resources. Although ecologists calculate pursuit time in terms of predator and prey speeds and fields of vision, Keene rightly points out that 'human predators generally rely on technology rather than speed to capture prey' (1979: 376–7). For this reason he suggests that pursuit time is determined by 'critical distance' which he defines as 'the distance at which predation is perceived minus the distance from which the hunter can successfully strike' (1979: 377). Technology could be used to reduce the critical distance in two ways. To begin with, the effective range of the tools which kill the animal could be increased by using weapons. Further reductions of critical distance could be made by enhancing the power of a weapon by adding parts to it; for example, by using an atlatl rather than just a spear. The benefits of this latter strategy are further discussed in conjunction with tool complexity. Another similar strategy would be to restrict the mobility of the prey so that the hunter can get close enough to kill it with a simple weapon. This second goal could be accomplished with the aid of tended facilities such as fish dams, cairns placed along caribou drives, or hunting blinds. As Oswalt's data show (1976: 235–94),

Table 3.3. *Relationship between technology and resource type*

| | Artefact type | | | | | | | | | | | |
| | Instruments | | | Weapons | | | Tended facilities | | | Untended facilities | | |
| Resource type | 1 | 2 | 3 | 1 | 2 | 3 | 1 | 2 | 3 | 1 | 2 | 3 |
|---|---|---|---|---|---|---|---|---|---|---|---|---|
| Plants | 37 | 71 | 1.9 | – | – | – | – | – | – | – | – | – |
| Birds | – | – | – | 27 | 95 | 3.5 | 7 | 24 | 3.4 | – | – | – |
| Waterfowl | – | – | – | 10 | 48 | 4.8 | 13 | 37 | 2.8 | 9 | 41 | 4.6 |
| Small mammals (terrestrial) | 9 | 24 | 2.7 | 7 | 29 | 4.1 | 15 | 30 | 2.0 | 33 | 185 | 5.6 |
| Large mammals (terrestrial) | 6 | 14 | 2.3 | 22 | 117 | 5.3 | 52 | 118 | 2.3 | 27 | 158 | 5.9 |
| Mammals (size unknown) (terrestrial) | 2 | 5 | 2.5 | 55 | 231 | 4.2 | 4 | 9 | 2.3 | 5 | 32 | 6.4 |
| Marine mammals | 7 | 10 | 1.4 | 32 | 357 | 11.1 | 6 | 28 | 4.7 | 1 | 7 | 7.0 |
| Fish | 21 | 62 | 3.0 | 39 | 180 | 4.6 | 69 | 324 | 4.7 | 30 | 212 | 7.1 |

*Column numbers*: 1 Total number of tools; 2 Total number of technounits; 3 Average number of technounits per tool.

*Note*: based on Appendix, 'Subsistants and their technounits', in Oswalt 1976: 235–94.

tended facilities are especially important in the exploitation of resources which are aggregated, such as large terrestrial mammals or fish (table 3.3). In these cases, then, tended facilities are highly beneficial because they control animal movement so that the hunter can achieve multiple kills in a short amount of time (cf. Oswalt 1976: 103). On the contrary, when resources are not aggregated, one would expect weapons to dominate assemblages. Since tended facilities are always used in association with weapons, all subsistant tool-kits will contain a reasonable proportion of weapons.

One can conclude that in general untended facilities will be found where search time is high due to the low density and high mobility of resources; that weapons will become important where pursuit time is large; and tended facilities will also be used when the pursuit time is high but will mainly come into use with the exploitation of aggregated resources. If these principles are to be used to predict assemblage composition, the nature of the resource as well as the overall time stress of the environment must be considered. It must be recalled that all subsistence time, including both search and pursuit times, will be more limited in high-latitude environments with short growing seasons than nearer the equator. The effects of this variable on assemblage composition can be seen, for example, in the proportion of untended facilities in subsistant tool-kits as one moves away from the equator (tables 3.1 and 3.2). The decline witnessed in arctic settings, contrary to expectation, can be explained by the nature of sea-mammal hunting which dominates the most northerly procurement systems; despite the need to minimize search time, it would be extremely difficult to design an untended facility for sea-mammal hunting that could function adequately in the open sea.

The case of small-mammal procurement also illustrates how assemblage composition responds to scarcity of time measured on a yearly basis. Although small mammals form part of the diet of all hunter-gatherer groups, the type of tool used in their capture varies latitudinally. Near the equator where time is not limiting, small mammals are hunted largely with weapons and instruments, whereas in the far north, untended facilities, such as traps and snares, dominate the relevant tool-kits (table 3.4). A similar pattern also applies to large terrestrial mammals; as seasonality increases, tended facilities are brought more and more into play in the subsistence strategy (Oswalt 1976: 233–94).

The principles discussed here could be used to predict composition of hunter-gatherer subsistant tool-kits given data on resource use and seasonality. Conversely, archaeologists could infer subsistence practices on the basis of artefactual data. Nevertheless, at present the function of prehistoric artefacts can rarely be inferred accurately and so there is unlikely to be any immediate benefit from using assemblage composition to analyse subsistence. My point here is simply a general one: it is possible to understand certain aspects of assemblage composition in terms of the quantity of time.

### Diversity of tool-kits

Diversity, or the number of different kinds of tools, is not totally independent of assemblage composition. For example, if search costs are high, then the number of untended facilities present is partly a result of the degree to which that tool type is beneficial to the procurement strategy and partly due to the variety of functional equivalents used, as predicted previously. The latter property, the variability of subsistants within a tool class, that is, the diversity, is determined by the

Table 3.4. *Artefact types used to procure small mammals*

| Group | Latitude | Instruments | | Weapons | | Tended facilities | | Untended facilities | |
|---|---|---|---|---|---|---|---|---|---|
| Tiwi | 12 | 1 | 4 | | | | | | |
| Andamanese | 12 | | | | | | | | |
| Ingura | 14 | | | | | | | | |
| Chenchu | 16 | | | | | | | | |
| Naron Bushman | 19 | 1 | 4 | | | | | | |
| Aranda | 24 | 1 | 4 | | | | | 1 | 7 |
| Owens Valley Paiute | 37 | | | 2 | 7 | 2 | 5 | 2 | 11 |
| Surprise Valley Paiute | 42 | 2 | 2 | | | 4 | 6 | 2 | 8 |
| Tasmanian | 42 | | | | | 1 | 1 | | |
| Klamath | 43 | | | 1 | 4 | | | 2 | 11 |
| Twana | 48 | | | 1 | 7 | | | | |
| Tlingit | 58 | | | | | | | 2 | 19 |
| Tanaina | 60 | 3 | 9 | 1 | 4 | | | 3 | 30 |
| Ingalik | 62 | 1 | 1 | 1 | 6 | 3 | 16 | 6 | 54 |
| Nabesna | 63 | | | | | 3 | 10 | | |
| Caribou | 63 | | | | | | | 3 | 12 |
| Angmaksalik | 66 | | | | | | | 1 | 6 |
| Iglulik | 69 | | | 1 | 1 | | | 3 | 11 |
| Copper | 70 | | | | | 1 | 1 | 2 | 8 |
| Taremiut | 71 | | | | | | | 1 | 7 |

*Note*: in each case the first number given is the total number of tools and the second is the number of technounits. Based on Oswalt 1976: 235–94.

number of tasks undertaken or, in this case, the number of resource types which normally comprise the diet of the hunter-gatherer group in question.

Specialized hunter-gatherers such as the Eskimo who exploit only a few prey species will develop a very diverse subsistant assemblage composed of tools which have a very limited range of functions (cf. Oswalt 1976: 102). Due to the small number of resources available, hunter-gatherers in these situations have few alternatives if they fail to procure one species effectively. Therefore, when the number of options is low such that the dependence on any one resource is high, the optimal solution is to minimize risk by reducing the time spent on procuring the resource. This can be achieved by increasing the technological component of subsistence practices (cf. Oswalt 1976: 183). As well as utilizing a larger number of tools, it will be beneficial to devise highly efficient, special-purpose tools for each of the small number of tasks involved. In contrast, for generalized procurement patterns the need for diverse subsistants is not only small, because the number of resource options is high, but investment in tools which are specialized for particular tasks would be maladaptive. If the range of prey types which may be encountered in a given period is likely to be large, then it would be difficult to transport a tool-kit specialized for the pursuit of each species. A better solution would be to employ a few general-purpose tools capable of capturing a wide range of resource types.

As Harris (1969) and Gamble (1978a) have argued, the

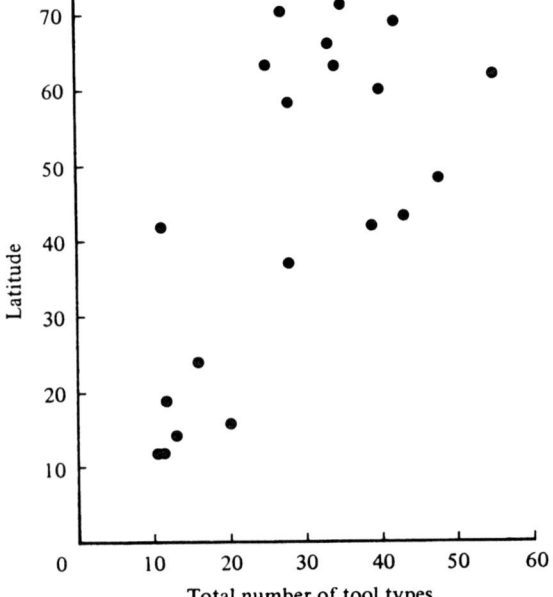

Fig. 3.1. Scatterplot of assemblage diversity and latitude (based on data in table 3.1).

degree of specialization of hunter-gatherer subsistence patterns can be directly related to the ecological maturity of the environment, which in turn is roughly correlated with latitude. Since this is the case, then the hypothesis for subsistant diversity can be tested by comparing diversity with latitude. Oswalt's data (1976: 157, 173) confirm that there is a significant linear relationship between the diversity of tools, as reflected in the number of different subsistant types, and resource specialization, as monitored by latitude ($r = 0.6903$; $p < 0.01$; fig. 3.1).

### Subsistant complexity

Oswalt's most recent book on technology, *An Anthropological Analysis of Food-Getting Technology* (1976), concentrates on the analysis of subsistant complexity. When introducing the notion of complexity, Oswalt discusses two possible ways of measuring variability along this dimension: 'To count all the forms in an inventory yields a gross assessment of total complexity. To total all technounits of an inventory provides a more precise statement of complexity' (p. 43).

The first solution refers to the property which I have previously described as diversity. Like Oswalt I would prefer to restrict the definition of complexity to mean only the number of separate parts which make up tools, as opposed to the quantity of separate tool types. As a means of measuring complexity, Oswalt has devised the concept of technounit, which is defined as 'an integrated physically distinct, and unique structural configuration that contributes to the form of a finished artefact' (p. 38). Following on from this, 'the number of technounits that create a finished artefact is offered as a measure of an artefact's complexity' (p. 34) but for assemblages, 'the average number of technounits per form is considered the most satisfactory measure of technological complexity' (p. 44). Nevertheless, when comparing assemblages Oswalt finds it more convenient to use the total number of technounits per group rather than the averages because the latter have a wider range of variability (p. 191). For archaeologists the technounit total is a more realistic measure because it can be monitored easily, whereas in many cases it is not yet possible to assign every unique technounit to one specific tool type.

If complex tools are utilized to reduce the expenditure of time, then one would expect that in general, because of the distribution of stress, the tool-kits of high-latitude hunter-gatherers would be more complex than those from lower latitudes. This hypothesis is supported by the scatterplot of the numbers of technounits found in hunter-gatherer tool-kits against latitude (fig. 3.2; cf. Oswalt 1976: 194, fig. 9.4); the linear relationship between the two variables is significant ($r = 0.7470$; $p < 0.01$). The alternative measure of complexity, which is calculated by the average number of technounits per artefact, is also significantly correlated with latitude ($r = 0.6841$; $p < 0.01$). Oswalt (1976: 154) predicted that 'the biomes occupied by foragers' will correlate with the complexity of the subsistants, but he does not explain why this should be the case except 'that peoples who occupied broadly similar habitats exploited edibles in similar ways'. When the connections among seasonality of an environment,

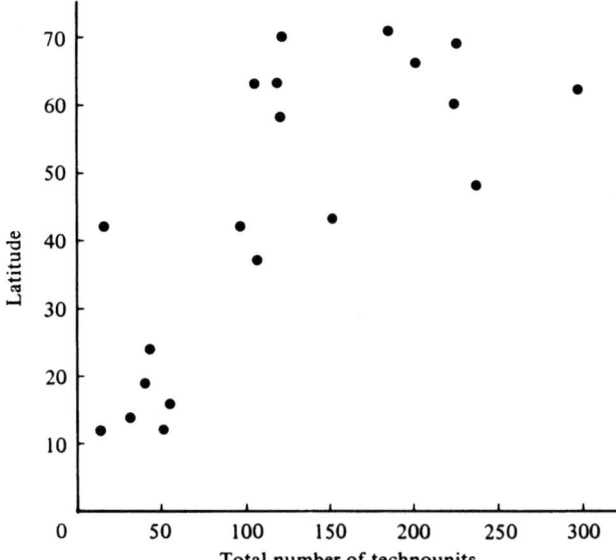

Fig. 3.2. Scatterplot of assemblage complexity and latitude (based on data in table 3.1).

time stress and complexity can be recognized, the posited relationships can be understood more clearly.

In addition to the assemblage as a whole, the degree of complexity will vary among various artefact classes according to the relative potential of each for maximizing time. Untended facilities are the most efficient time-saving devices because they operate in the absence of humans and therefore consume very little of a person's limited time. Since weapons are normally designed to operate with or without the assistance of tended facilities, one might expect that they would be more complex than the latter type. Instruments are applied to immobile resources which by definition will involve the least amount of time stress and therefore they should always be the least complex tool type in any environment; instruments used on plants should also be more simple than those used for animals. These hypotheses can be evaluated by examining the data in table 3.3, which was compiled from Oswalt's (1976) catalogue. The predicted ranking of tools according to complexity is generally correct, although it is notable that because sea-mammal procurement has to depend on weapons rather than either of the facilities (cf. above), in these economies the former type is much more complex than either of the latter.

The finding that individual tool types can be ranked according to their average complexity leads to the conclusion that the two dimensions composition and complexity are very much interdependent. Complexity increases with latitude partly because each tool type has more technounits, but in addition, the composition of the assemblages alters to include new tool types, such as facilities, that are more complex. For instance, bows and arrows as well as leisters from assemblages at different latitudes all have about the same number of parts. Similarly, wherever they are found, traps, snares and deadfalls

Table 3.5. *Average number of technounits for particular artefact types*

| Group | Weapons used on terrestrial mammals | Traps, snares, deadfalls | Fish traps, weirs |
|---|---|---|---|
| Tiwi | 2.5 | | |
| Andamanese | 9.5 | | |
| Ingura | 3.0 | | 2.0 |
| Chenchu | 6.8 | | |
| Naron Bushman | 4.8 | 5.5 | |
| Aranda | 5.3 | 4.0 | |
| Owens Valley Paiute | 4.6 | 4.0 | 8.0 |
| Surprise Valley Paiute | 4.7 | 5.5 | 3.0 |
| Tasmanian | 3.0 | | |
| Klamath | 4.2 | 3.0 | 6.0 |
| Twana | 5.5 | 7.0 | 10.3 |
| Tlingit | 3.5 | 8.2 | 9.0 |
| Tanaina | 4.0 | 8.7 | 11.5 |
| Ingalik | 5.0 | 9.1 | 9.6 |
| Nabesna | 13.5 | 6.8 | 4.5 |
| Caribou | 6.0 | 4.0 | |
| Angmaksalik | 6.0 | 7.0 | |
| Iglulik | 3.3 | 4.3 | |
| Copper | 10.0 | 6.0 | |
| Taremiut | 5.2 | 5.0 | 6.0 |

*Note*: based on Oswalt 1976: 235–94.

for mammals as well as fish traps and weirs tend to be fairly complex artefacts (table 3.5). Archaeologists should be pleased at this finding because it means that complexity, a trait easily monitored, can be used as a guide to the function of tools represented in an assemblage.

Not surprisingly, given the definitions of search and pursuit time (cf. above), Oswalt notes that for the technologies which he studied the complexity of weapons and the mobility of the resources are correlated (1976: 101–2). Throughout his analysis of subsistants, he also finds that tool types which are employed in the exploitation of aquatic species are more complex than their counterparts which are utilized on land (1976: 101, 128–9, 147, 183). For example, weapons used to capture wild species on land average 4.0 technounits per tool whereas for wild aquatic species the technounit average per tool is 6.3 and the pattern is repeated for all tool classes: instruments used on land, 1.8; on water, 2.4; tended facilities on land, 2.3; on water, 4.0; untended facilities used on land, 5.0; on water, 5.3 (Oswalt 1976: 76, 101, 128, 148). In addition, the numbers of parts which comprise artefacts used to procure the same resource type vary according to the setting in which the exploitation takes place. Therefore, when Eskimos hunt sea mammals on the ice, the harpoons used range from 7 to 17 parts, but harpoons used in open water have between 17 and 26 components (p. 183).

The explanation given by Oswalt for this interesting difference between terrestrial and aquatic tool-kits is that the potential mobility of animals in water is greater than for those

on land (p. 183). While part of the contrast between tools employed on land and those in water must be due to variations in mobility, I doubt that this one variable provides a totally adequate explanation. Variations in the density and aggregation of the prey might be important because these properties affect search and pursuit time. Since both these variables are low in the case of sea mammals, the occurrence of a complex technology is not surprising. Fishing technology, however, poses a problem because it is more complex than hunting gear used for terrestrial mammals, which are often more sparsely distributed in the environment than are fish. Obviously there is yet another facet of complexity which must be considered.

Besides the search and pursuit components of food procurement, ecologists consider a phase called *handling* (Schoener 1971: 378–9). Some tools perform the function of handling as well as pursuit and/or search and as a result are very complex. Handling, in terms of human subsistence practices, can be divided into two stages each of which is dealt with by a separate functional class of tools. First the resource must be *retrieved*; subsistants can be utilized in this phase. Secondly, the food may need to be *processed* so that it can be consumed. Tools used in the processing of food are not subsumed in Oswalt's definition of subsistants and so will not be considered further here, although the role of time stress in the assemblage structure of processing tools should be broadly similar to that for subsistants.

Not all hunting strategies will involve a stage of retrieval. For example, if a deer is successfully shot and killed, no retrieval will be necessary and the processing, in this case butchery, can begin with no further work. In contrast, resources captured in the water necessitate complicated retrieval strategies. For instance, marine mammals once hit by a harpoon must still be recovered from the water and brought to shore. Similarly, a fish once speared must also be brought successfully out of the water. Furthermore, the time available for retrieval of aquatic species before they sink is limited. Since the time for retrieval will always be least for animals captured in water, the complexity of the subsistants which serve this function will be high. On the whole, hunter-gatherers do not employ special-purpose tools whose only function is to retrieve resources. This additional task is usually shouldered by hunting implements and facilities. For example, harpoons are commonly attached by a line to a float made out of sealskin or a bladder (Oswalt 1976: 96–7); fish spears or leisters usually have a series of barbed points which not only strike the fish but also hang on to it so that it can be removed from the water. The result is that subsistants which both pursue and retrieve will be extremely complex.

### Archaeological applications

Since one of the major problems in archaeology is the interpretation of variability among different assemblages of artefacts, it would be extremely helpful if the hypotheses for assemblage structure, that I have tested using Oswalt's collection of ethnographic data on hunter-gatherer subsistants, could also be applied to the archaeological record. Although I believe that this will eventually be possible, further research is required before specific applications can be made. In the first place, one will need to create a series of bridging arguments, or middle-range theory (Binford 1977a: 7), to link the predictions to the types of data which are recoverable from archaeological sites. This is not an easy task, but it is essential if the theory is to be of use in interpreting the past. A whole range of methodologies will be required in order to implement the general theory proposed here, but this difficulty is not peculiar to technology; all archaeological facts are static and must be subject to a series of transformations before they can be utilized (Binford 1977a: 7). The challenge is for archaeologists to develop the appropriate methodology that allows them to answer relevant questions about the past. The first problem to tackle will be to devise a means to correlate the types and numbers of non-perishable, e.g. lithic, artefacts to the original tool-kit. This will require a middle-range theory which predicts what kinds of raw material will be used for particular tool types under given conditions. A second area where improved methodology will be needed is in the measurement of tool function. Recent advances in the development of appropriate techniques are encouraging (e.g. Hayden 1979; Keeley 1979; Odell and Odell-Vereecken 1980).

Regardless of deficiencies in present analytical techniques, one can, nevertheless, suggest areas of research in Europe which could profit from considering the hypotheses about hunter-gatherer subsistant technology given support by Oswalt's data. Changes in the diversity and complexity of subsistants throughout the Pleistocene, for example, are likely to be due to shifts in subsistence strategies. If the fluctuations between specialized and generalized hunting strategies as documented by Gamble (1978a, 1979), Straus (1977a) and Freeman (1973a) for instance, are correct, then the technology should have responded to differences in time stress related to these subsistence practices (see also Part 3 below).

Taking another approach, technology could be used to inform about subsistence. For instance, it would be extremely interesting to evaluate the role of plants in hunter-gatherer economies from the end of the Pleistocene (cf. D.L. Clarke 1976) until the adoption of agriculture. As demonstrated previously, instruments are less complex than weapons; therefore in plant-based economies, the subsistants are less complex. The pursuit of immobile resources means that constraints placed on technology as a result of demands for scheduling activities are reduced. The shift which can be noted in many parts of Europe, from distinct, recognizable and reasonably standardized tool types in the Mesolithic to the highly irregular flake and blade industries of the Neolithic can perhaps be understood partly in these terms. Not only do the Neolithic tools tend to be less complex, but also it seems clear that Mesolithic subsistants were more highly curated than their later counterparts. Clearly, these are only very tentative suggestions, but they do serve to illustrate the potential benefits to be gained from studying the effects of time stress on the assemblage structure of subsistants. There is no reason to doubt that other types of tools could be analysed in similar terms.

### Further areas for theory building

At the beginning of this chapter I outlined two major responses of hunter-gatherer technology to limitations in time. Although the importance of scheduling activities was discussed, I have emphasized several basic ways in which assemblage structure is affected by time stress. Since both these responses are interrelated, many of the arguments leading to predictions for the composition, diversity and complexity of subsistants can be extended to encompass scheduling behaviour. For example, it has been argued above that time is most limited in highly seasonal environments in which mobile resources are exploited. As a result a high proportion of facilities in the hunter-gatherer tool-kit was expected and assemblages were predicted to be very diverse and complex. Scheduling in the procurement, manufacture and maintenance of tools should also be highly developed in these same circumstances. It is therefore not surprising that curation and embedded procurement were first noted by Binford (1977b, 1979a, 1979b) since he worked among a hunter-gatherer group, the Nunamiut Eskimo, who occupy a highly time-stressed environment. Future attempts at theory building should further develop the relationships between degrees of scheduling and differences between assemblage structures with regard to time stress.

Once time has been recognized as a key variable, its role in shaping a wide range of technological behaviour can begin to be explored in greater depth. To take just one area of research which has become extremely important due, at least in part, to the 'Mousterian controversy' over the meaning of assemblage variability (e.g. Binford 1973; Bordes 1973): the investigation of stylistic attributes (e.g. Sackett 1973; 1977; Wobst 1977; Close 1978; Part 4 below). Although the characteristics discussed here could all be classified as functional, one could still argue that the same principles hold for stylistic traits. That is, that time is an important variable conditioning differences between assemblages. Wobst (1977) has suggested that some attributes convey information which facilitates interaction among hunter-gatherer groups. Since it could be argued that the need for conveyance of information is partly dependent on the distribution and amount of time available for tasks, then the degree to which these attributes are expressed in an assemblage should be dependent on the nature of the time stress. For example, I would expect that the need for communication among small bands of people is partly a function of the distribution of resources in the environment through time. As a consequence, when resources are only available for a short period of time throughout the year or are highly mobile, there would be an adaptive pay-off to employing methods to increase interaction and exchange of information among scattered groups of hunter-gatherers. Restrictions in time, then, should contribute to the use of stylistic traits in hunter-gatherer assemblages.

This brief example is only meant to emphasize how the adoption of a different perspective on technology can lead to new and profitable areas of research. Certainly, time is not the only variable which affects the differences in hunter-gatherer technology observed in the archaeological record. Nevertheless, I hope that I have demonstrated that it is a very important factor which has numerous ramifications for the study of material culture. For this reason the extent to which hunter-gatherer tool-kits respond to limitations in the amount of time available is a subject worthy of further study; I have only been able to sketch out some proposals for future research. Although the ideas presented here need to be developed much further and tested against archaeological data, the value to archaeology of devising a body of general theory appropriate to technology cannot be disputed.

*Acknowledgements*

The ideas expressed in this paper have been developing over a long period of time and therefore owe their growth to a large number of scholars, not all of whom can be mentioned here. L. Binford guided my initial efforts and R. Hunter-Anderson made some key suggestions when the approach was first presented. The chapter was mainly written while I was a visiting lecturer at Northwestern University; the enthusiasm and scepticism of the students in my seminar on technology were extremely valuable. Further discussion with L. Binford, R. Boydston, J. Brown, R. Joslin-Jeske, L. Keeley and R. Vierra have been particularly helpful. I hope these colleagues will not be too disappointed with the outcome.

Chapter 4

**Mortality models and the interpretation of horse population structure**
Marsha A. Levine

Assemblages of prehistoric horse teeth are aged to reveal the structure of the animal populations from which they were derived. The material is from French and German Pleistocene deposits, some natural and some archaeological in origin. Two systems of relative ageing are employed here: eruption–wear sequences and crown–height curves. The age patterns derived from the various assemblages are compared with one anoth.... and with various mortality models. The results of this study suggest that the horses from the archaeological deposits examined here were probably not domesticated.

**Introduction**
Assemblages of prehistoric horse teeth have been aged in order to reveal the structures of the carcase populations from which they have been derived. An assemblage might never have been representative of any living animal population, but it should be representative of the individuals whose carcases comprised it. If that is true, it should be possible to suggest from its age structure how the assemblage might have been formed. In the case of material from an archaeological deposit it should be possible to learn something about the subsistence patterns of the people who created it. The material used in this study is from 13 Pleistocene deposits; 9 are archaeological in origin and 4 are natural (table 4.1). All but one (a German site) are French.

Two interlocking and internally coherent tooth ageing systems have been employed in the analyses carried out here: eruption–wear sequences and crown–height wear curves

(Levine 1979). They are relative ageing techniques, but used together they constitute an ageing system of considerable precision and one which is easily applicable to a wide range of material. The age patterns thus derived are compared with one another and with various mortality models. Cluster analysis techniques are used in an attempt to discover patterns not otherwise apparent.

Although sophisticated methods of demographic analysis have been developed for studies of both men and animals, they are not strictly applicable here because of the inadequacy of the fossil data. However, generalizations based upon analyses of modern comparative data can help to explain some of the fossil patterns observed below.

**Mortality patterns**
Palaeontologists frequently classify fossil assemblages according to two basic mortality types: catastrophic and attritional (Craig and Oertel 1966; Hallam 1972). Voorhies writes: 'it may be said that catastrophic mortality furnishes a sample of the standing crop of the vertebrate community while attritional mortality mainly reflects the rate of turnover of biomass within the community' (1969: 23).

*Natural catastrophes* include floods, droughts and volcanic eruptions. An equivalent *archaeological catastrophe* is the herd drive in the course of which a large number of animals are frightened over a precipice or into an enclosure

Table 4.1. Assemblage unit list and tooth: bone ratios

*Combe Grenal*

| Site and assemblage unit | Level or square | Geological period | Industry and C14 date (if any) | Teeth | Bones | Bone fragments no. | Bone fragments % | Bones, excluding fragments | Teeth:bone-fragments |
|---|---|---|---|---|---|---|---|---|---|
| CG10 | 10 | Würm II | Typical Mousterian | 7 | 2 | 1 | 50.0 | 1 | 7.0:1.0 |
| CG11 | 11 | Würm II | Denticulate Mousterian | 135 | 3 | 1 | 33.3 | 2 | 67.5:1.0 |
| CG12 | 12 | Würm II | Denticulate Mousterian (39 000 ± 1500 b.p., GRN-4304 or 30 300 ± 350 b.p., GRN-4311) | 20 | 2 | 1 | 50.0 | 1 | 20.0:1.0 |
| CG14 | 14 | Würm II | Denticulate Mousterian | 435 | 14 | 11 | 78.6 | 3 | 145.0:1.0 |
| CG15 | 15 | Würm II | Denticulate Mousterian | 56 | 2 | 0 | 0.0 | 2 | 28.0:1.0 |
| CG20 | 20 | Würm II | Denticulate Mousterian (non-Levallois) | 25 | 5 | 3 | 60.0 | 2 | 12.5:1.0 |
| CG21 | 21 | Würm II | Quina Mousterian | 55 | 2 | 0 | 0.0 | 2 | 27.5:1.0 |
| CG22 | 22 | Würm II | Quina Mousterian | 200 | 49 | 15 | 30.6 | 34 | 5.9:1.0 |
| CG23 | 23 | Würm II | Quina Mousterian | 173 | 30 | 13 | 43.3 | 17 | 10.2:1.0 |
| CG24 | 24 | Würm II | Quina Mousterian | 40 | 5 | 0 | 0.0 | 5 | 8.0:1.0 |
| CG25 | 25 | Würm II | Qunia Mousterian | 42 | 4 | 1 | 25.0 | 3 | 14.0:1.0 |
| CG27 | 27 | Würm II | Ferrassie-type Mousterian | 34 | 0 | 0 | 0.0 | 0 | — |
| CG28 | 28 | Würm II | Typical Mousterian | 6 | 0 | 0 | 0.0 | 0 | — |
| CG29 | 29 | Würm II | Typical Mousterian | 10 | 0 | 0 | 0.0 | 0 | — |
| CG31 | 31 | Würm II | Typical Mousterian | 10 | 0 | 0 | 0.0 | 0 | — |
| CG70 | I | Würm II | Quina Mousterian? | 65 | 14 | 3 | 21.4 | 11 | 5.9:1.0 |
| CG33 | 33 | Würm II | Ferrassie-type Mousterian | 6 | 0 | 0 | 0.0 | 0 | — |
| CG34 | 34 | Würm II | Ferrassie-type Mousterian | 4 | 0 | 0 | 0.0 | 0 | — |
| CG35 | 35 | Würm II | Ferrassie-type Mousterian | 36 | 9 | 1 | 11.1 | 8 | 4.5:1.0 |
| CG36 | 36 | Würm II | Typical Mousterian | 5 | 2 | 1 | 50.0 | 1 | 5.0:1.0 |
| CG37 | 37 | Würm II | Typical Mousterian | 22 | 1 | 0 | 0.0 | 1 | 22.0:1.0 |
| CG38 | 38 | Würm I | Denticulate Mousterian | 12 | 0 | 0 | 0.0 | 0 | — |
| CG40 | 40 | Würm I | Typical Mousterian | 16 | 2 | 1 | 50.0 | 1 | 16.0:1.0 |
| CG47 | 47 | Würm I | Mousterian (type uncertain) | 13 | 1 | 0 | 0.0 | 1 | 13.0:1.0 |
| CG49 | 49 | Würm I | Mousterian (type uncertain) | 7 | 0 | 0 | 0.0 | 0 | — |
| CG50 | 50 | Würm I | Typical Mousterian | 94 | 3 | 1 | 33.3 | 2 | 47.0:1.0 |
| CG98 | 50A | Würm I | Typical Mousterian | 31 | 2 | 0 | 0.0 | 2 | 15.5:1.0 |
| CG51 | 51 | Würm I | Typical Mousterian | 13 | 1 | 1 | 100.0 | 0 | — |
| CG52 | 52 | Würm I | Typical Mousterian | 54 | 2 | 1 | 50.0 | 1 | 54.0:1.0 |
| CG55 | 55 | Würm I | Typical Mousterian | 4 | 0 | 0 | 0.0 | 0 | — |
| CG56 | 56 | Riss III | Upper Acheulian | 6 | 0 | 0 | 0.0 | 0 | — |
| CG57 | 57 | Riss III | Upper Acheulian | 6 | 0 | 0 | 0.0 | 0 | — |

| | | | | | | | | | |
|---|---|---|---|---|---|---|---|---|---|
| *Le Morin* | | | | | | | | | |
| MO01 | AI | Late Würm | Magdalenian VI | 57 | 20 | 2 | 10.0 | 18 | 3.2:1.0 |
| MO03 | AIII | Late Würm | Magdalenian VI | 106 | 26 | 1 | 3.8 | 25 | 4.2:1.0 |
| MO04 | AIV | Late Würm | Magdalenian VI | 98 | 37 | 2 | 5.4 | 35 | 2.8:1.0 |
| MO05 | BI | Late Würm | Magdalenian V | 39 | 20 | 4 | 20.0 | 16 | 2.4:1.0 |
| MO12 | AI/AII | Late Würm | Magdalenian VI | 72 | 24 | 3 | 12.5 | 21 | 3.4:1.0 |
| *Pech de l'Aze* | | | | | | | | | |
| PA01 | 1 | surface | Ferrassie-type Mousterian | 11 | 0 | 0 | 0.0 | 0 | — |
| PA21 | 2G or 2G1 | Würm I | Typical Mousterian | 4 | 0 | 0 | 0.0 | 0 | — |
| PA03 | 3 | Würm I | Typical Mousterian | 4 | 0 | 0 | 0.0 | 0 | — |
| PA04 | 4 | Würm I | probably Typical Mousterian | 8 | 1 | 0 | 0.0 | 1 | 8.0:1.0 |
| PA41 | 4A2 | Würm I | Typical Mousterian | 4 | 0 | 0 | 0.0 | 0 | — |
| PA42 | 4B | Würm I | Denticulate Mousterian | 36 | 0 | 0 | 0.0 | 0 | — |
| PA43 | 4C2 | Würm I | Typical Mousterian | 26 | 1 | 0 | 0.0 | 1 | 26.0:1.0 |
| PA05 | 5 | Würm I | almost sterile | 15 | 1 | 0 | 0.0 | 1 | 15.0:1.0 |
| PA51 | 5R | Würm I ? | almost sterile | 7 | 1 | 1 | 100.0 | 0 | — |
| PA06 | 6 | Riss II | Acheulian | 85 | 21 | 1 | 4.8 | 20 | 4.3:1.0 |
| PA67 | 6/7 | Riss II | Acheulian | 5 | 2 | 0 | 0.0 | 2 | 2.5:1.0 |
| PA69 | 6/7B | Riss II | Acheulian | 5 | 5 | 0 | 0.0 | 5 | 1.0:1.0 |
| PA07 | 7 | Riss II | Acheulian | 55 | 20 | 1 | 5.0 | 19 | 2.9:1.0 |
| PA08 | 8 | Riss I | Acheulian | 73 | 22 | 7 | 31.8 | 15 | 4.9:1.0 |
| PA09 | 9 | Riss I | Acheulian | 91 | 32 | 7 | 21.9 | 25 | 3.6:1.0 |
| *Chatillon-St-Jean* | | | | | | | | | |
| CSJ0 | | probably Riss | natural | 15 | 115 | 4 | 3.5 | 111 | 0.14:1.0 |
| *La Fage-Aven I* | | | | | | | | | |
| F123 | 2/3 | Riss | natural | 18 | 13 | 2 | 15.4 | 11 | 1.6:1.0 |
| *La Fage-Aven II* | | | | | | | | | |
| F201 | 1 | probably Upper Pleistocene | natural | 18 | 56 | 29 | 51.8 | 27 | 0.7:1.0 |
| F202 | 2 | probably Upper Pleistocene | natural | 78 | 343 | 182 | 53.1 | 161 | 0.5:1.0 |
| F203 | 3 | probably Upper Pleistocene | natural | 8 | 85 | 26 | 30.6 | 59 | 0.1:1.0 |
| *Jaurens* | | | | | | | | | |
| JA01 | | Würm II, III or II/III | natural (29 300 ± 1400 b.p., Ly-359) | 593 | 970 | 47 | 4.8 | 923 | 0.6:1.0 |

Table 4.1. continued.

| Site and assemblage unit | Level or square | Geological period | Industry and C14 date (if any) | Teeth | Bones | Bone fragments no. | Bone fragments % | Bones, excluding fragments | Teeth:bone-fragments |
|---|---|---|---|---|---|---|---|---|---|
| *Roc de Marsal* | | | | | | | | | |
| RM02 | II | Early to Middle Würm | Denticulate Mousterian | 4 | 0 | 0 | 0.0 | 0 | – |
| RM03 | III | Early to Middle Würm | Denticulate Mousterian | 11 | 0 | 0 | 0.0 | 0 | – |
| RM04 | IV | Early to Middle Würm | Typical Mousterian | 26 | 2 | 0 | 0.0 | 2 | 13.0:1.0 |
| RM05 | V | Early to Middle Würm | Typical Mousterian | 46 | 0 | 0 | 0.0 | 0 | – |
| RM06 | VI | Early to Middle Würm | Typical Mousterian | 65 | 1 | 1 | 100.0 | 0 | – |
| RM07 | VII | Early to Middle Würm | Typical Mousterian | 54 | 0 | 0 | 0.0 | 0 | – |
| RM09 | IX | Early to Middle Würm | Quina Mousterian | 69 | 0 | 0 | 0.0 | 0 | – |
| RM19 | IXA | Early to Middle Würm | Quina Mousterian | 20 | 0 | 0 | 0.0 | 0 | – |
| RM29 | IXB | Early to Middle Würm | Quina Mousterian | 54 | 0 | 0 | 0.0 | 0 | – |
| RM10 | X | Early to Middle Würm | Quina Mousterian | 42 | 0 | 0 | 0.0 | 0 | – |
| RM11 | XI | Early to Middle Würm | Quina Mousterian | 68 | 1 | 1 | 100.0 | 0 | – |
| RM21 | XIA | Early to Middle Würm | Quina Mousterian | 18 | 0 | 0 | 0.0 | 0 | – |
| RM12 | XII | Early to Middle Würm | Quina Mousterian | 21 | 0 | 0 | 0.0 | 0 | – |
| *Gönnersdorf* | | | | | | | | | |
| FG15 | | pre-Allerod, Late Glacial | Late Magdalenian (10 500 b.c., Ly-768) | 220 | 440 | 165 | 37.5 | 275 | 0.8:1.0 |
| *Blot* | | | | | | | | | |
| BL22 | 22 | Late Würm | Proto-Magdalenian | 13 | 0 | 0 | 0.0 | 0 | – |
| BL23 | 23 | Late Würm | Proto-Magdalenian | 137 | 43 | 24 | 55.8 | 19 | 7.2:1.0 |
| BL26 | 26 | Late Würm | Proto-Magdalenian | 7 | 0 | 0 | 0.0 | 0 | – |
| BL27 | 27 | Late Würm | Proto-Magdalenian | 62 | 8 | 7 | 87.5 | 1 | 62.0:1.0 |
| BL28 | 28 | Late Würm | Proto-Magdalenian | 4 | 0 | 0 | 0.0 | 0 | – |

| Unit | Code | Period | Culture | | | | | | |
|---|---|---|---|---|---|---|---|---|---|
| BL30 | 30 | Late Würm | Proto-Magdalenian? | 15 | 0 | 0 | 0.0 | 0 | — |
| BL34 | 34 | Late Würm | Proto-Magdalenian | 4 | 0 | 0 | 0.0 | 0 | — |
| BL99 | HA | Late Würm | | 4 | 0 | 0 | 0.0 | 0 | — |
| *Arlay* | | | | | | | | | |
| AR01 | 1 | Late Würm | Magdalenian | 150 | 54 | 2 | 3.7 | 52 | 2.9:1.0 |
| *Gigny* | | | | | | | | | |
| GI15 | XV | Würm II | Ferrassie-type Mousterian | 12 | 0 | 0 | 0.0 | 0 | — |
| GI18 | XVIII | Würm I | Typical Mousterian? | 8 | 0 | 0 | 0.0 | 0 | — |
| GI19 | XIX | Würm I | Typical Mousterian | 10 | 11 | 1 | 9.1 | 10 | 1.0:1.0 |
| GI29 | XIXA | Würm I | Typical Mousterian | 9 | 0 | 0 | 0.0 | 0 | — |
| GI39 | XIXB | Würm I | Typical Mousterian | 14 | 0 | 0 | 0.0 | 0 | — |
| GI49 | XIXC | Würm I | Typical Mousterian | 54 | 0 | 0 | 0.0 | 0 | — |
| GI20 | XX | Würm I | Typical Mousterian (about 31 500 b.p., Ly-804) | 21 | 2 | 0 | 0.0 | 2 | 10.5:1.0 |
| GI21 | XXIA | Würm I or II | possibly Acheulian | 8 | 0 | 0 | 0.0 | 0 | — |
| *Solutré* | | | | | | | | | |
| SO1M | Sq. M12 | Würm III | Lower Aurignacian | 65 | 270 | 82 | 30.4 | 188 | 0.3:1.0 |
| SO2L | Sq. L13 | Würm III | Upper Perigordian | 275 | 548 | 74 | 13.5 | 474 | 0.6:1.0 |
| SO3P | Sq. P16 | Würm IV | Final Magdalenian (12 580 ± 250, Ly-393) | 422 | 898 | 249 | 27.7 | 649 | 0.7:1.0 |
| SO3N | Sq. N16 | Würm IV | Final Magdalenian | 53 | 55 | 15 | 27.3 | 40 | 1.3:1.0 |
| Total | | | | 5238 | 4303 | 996 | 23.1 | 3308 | 1.6:1.0 |
| Total in archaeological units | | | | 4508 | 2717 | 703 | 25.9 | 2015 | 2.2:1.0 |

*Note*: this table includes all the teeth from all the assemblage units studied here, even those not appropriate for ageing. A horse skeleton includes 205 bones and 36 permanent teeth (but a total of 60 teeth if deciduous ones are included). Therefore the ratio of teeth to bones is from 36:205 (0.18:1.00) to 60:205 (0.29:1.00).

and slaughtered *en masse*. Examples of *natural attritional mortality* are disease, malnutrition, senescence, predation and the accidents that affect individuals rather than populations. Those most affected are usually the very young and the very old (Kurtén 1964; Caughley 1966; Voorhies 1969; Mech 1970). A pattern of *archaeological attritional mortality* develops out of those kinds of man–animal interactions in which animals are withdrawn from the living population more or less individually. Either hunting or pastoralism may generate attritional patterns. The shape of the archaeological attritional distribution is not as uniform as that of the natural one. It will depend upon the particular hunting or slaughtering techniques employed and, in the case of some species, the season of the kill.

*Coursing* (chasing on foot) and *scavenging* dead or unfit individuals should produce the same pattern as natural attrition. A *trapping* pattern will depend upon the kind of traps used, but in most cases it should look random: age classes will probably be taken from the living population in the proportions in which they were represented in that population. However in the archaeological situation most samples of trapped ungulates will probably be too small to show any systematic structure. *Stalking* is an attritional hunting technique, which may produce a non-random, non-representative distribution. A good hunter can often choose his prey. Amongst the Bisa and the Hadza of eastern Africa the preferred prey is a large, fat, healthy male (Woodburn, pers. comm.; Marks 1976). However, when hungry, people will eat whatever they can get. Caughley attests to the utility of such an opportunistic strategy in his discussion of ungulate management: 'there is usually little or nothing to be gained from harvesting age classes at different rates. The optimum strategy turns out to be the unselective harvest' (Caughley 1977: 189). In contrast to natural attrition, scavenging and coursing, this strategy takes a low proportion of juveniles and a high proportion of prime adults. Moreover, 'Should mortality be excessively high at the adult stage but juvenile mortality is at a normal level for the species this is *prima facie* evidence that the decline is caused by excessive hunting. Most other agents of mortality act more heavily on juveniles' (Caughley 1977: 171).

When, as with a species like the horse, a number of social units occupy overlapping home ranges, slaughter of whole social units is probably the most efficient hunting strategy: 'Disturbance is minimized thereby and food and other resources made available by the removal of a group are open to utilization by other groups' (Caughley 1977: 187). Driving individual family groups or bachelor groups into enclosures, water or deep snow could achieve this end. It is, in effect, a small-scale catastrophe, affecting all age classes in proportion to their representation in the relevant type of social group.

The only quantitative structural model of *pastoral nomadism* available to me was that devised by Dahl and Hjort with reference to East African cattle husbandry. A short discussion of this model brings up several points probably

Table 4.2. *A life table based upon Dahl and Hjort's 'base-line herd model' for cattle*

| Age (in years) | Mortality rate (%) | Survival Frequency | % | Mortality Frequency | % |
|---|---|---|---|---|---|
| 0–1 | 20.0 | 1000.0 | 13.7 | 200.0 | 20.0 |
| 1–2 | 7.0 | 800.0 | 11.0 | 56.0 | 5.6 |
| 2–3 | 7.0 | 744.0 | 10.2 | 52.2 | 5.2 |
| 3–4 | 7.0 | 691.0 | 9.5 | 48.4 | 4.8 |
| 4–5 | 5.0 | 643.5 | 8.8 | 32.2 | 3.2 |
| 5–6 | 5.0 | 611.3 | 8.4 | 30.6 | 3.1 |
| 6–7 | 5.0 | 580.7 | 8.0 | 29.0 | 2.9 |
| 7–8 | 10.0 | 551.7 | 7.6 | 55.2 | 5.5 |
| 8–9 | 10.0 | 496.5 | 6.8 | 49.7 | 5.0 |
| 9–10 | 20.0 | 446.9 | 6.1 | 89.4 | 8.9 |
| 10–11 | 33.0 | 357.5 | 4.9 | 118.0 | 11.8 |
| 11–12 | 49.0 | 239.5 | 3.3 | 117.4 | 11.7 |
| 12–13 | 90.0 | 122.2 | 1.7 | 109.9 | 11.0 |
| 13–14 | 100.0 | 12.2 | 0.2 | 12.2 | 1.2 |

*Note*: this model presumes a life expectancy of 9–14 years.

The first column of the table shows the age span during which the deaths are occurring. The second column shows the mortality rate for each age span. The third and fourth columns show respectively the number and proportion of individuals alive at the beginning of each age span. The fifth and sixth columns show respectively the number and proportion of individuals dead by the end of each age span.

*Source*: Dahl and Hjort 1976: 45–6.

relevant to all kinds of large ungulate husbandry. Dahl and Hjort's 'base-line herd model' has been constructed from a number of sources and represents a stable population with a static age structure. According to the model, cows first produce young at 2 to 4 years of age and continue breeding until approximately their twelfth year. They have a life expectancy of 9 to 14 years (Dahl and Hjort 1976). If we follow a cohort (in demographic terms, a group of animals born simultaneously) of cattle from birth, when they numbered 1000, to the death of the last individual, employing the suggested mortality rates, the age structure of the 'population' can be presented in the form of a simplified life table (see table 4.2 and figs. 4.1 and 4.2). When the mortality frequency is plotted, the age distribution resembles that predicted for natural attrition (see table 4.2 and fig. 4.3).

It cannot be assumed that prehistoric horse husbandry would necessarily have produced the same kind of age distribution as East African cattle husbandry. The physiological differences between the two species more or less ensure that they will play somewhat different roles in human subsistence. The little information available concerning horse nomadism (for example, among the Kazaks of Central Asia) indicates that milk production of horses is markedly inferior to that of cattle. Kazak horses can produce about two quarts of milk a day

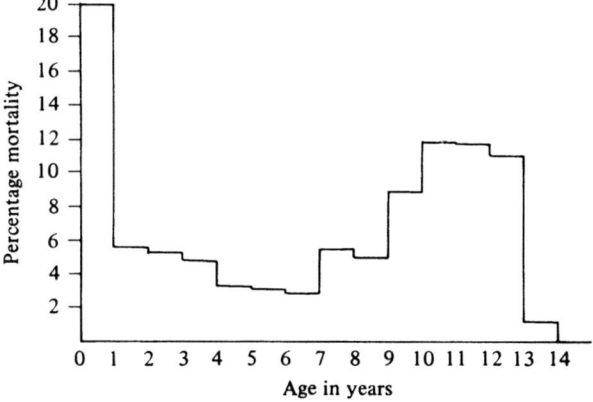

Fig. 4.1. Cattle mortality based on Dahl and Hjort's 'base-line herd model' (see table 4.2).

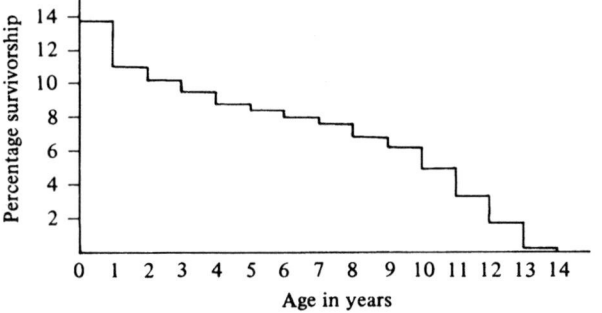

Fig. 4.2. Cattle survival based on Dahl and Hjort's 'base-line herd model'.

during 4 months of the year for human consumption (Forde 1934). East African cattle produce, on average, 1.5 kg or 1.7 quarts a day during 7 to 9 months of the year for human consumption in marginal dry lands (Dahl and Hjort 1976). Cow's milk is a staple, while mare's milk is a luxury. The sheep herds of the Kazak are larger than their horse herds and represent their major food resource. The greatest importance of the horse lies in the mobility it provides. Poor Kazak families with few horses do not milk their mares at all, 'but reserve their strength for use as riding and baggage animals' (Forde 1934: 339).

East African cattle are primarily milk producers. Meat is of secondary importance, consumed or traded for other products in times of need or when the animals are old or even dying. Dahl and Hjort (1976) have estimated that in the case of a cattle herd with a normal growth rate, 8% of the animals could be slaughtered each year without prejudicing the growth of the herd (that is, roughly between 4 and 12 animals per family per year). Usually most of the animals killed are young bullocks (4 to 5 years old and fully grown), while the rest are usually old and unproductive cows and bulls. Apparently horse meat is sometimes consumed by the Kazak, but information concerning the quantity and age distribution of those animals is unavailable (Forde 1934). However, since horses reach sexual maturity relatively late and since a mare produces on average only one offspring every two years, it may be suggested

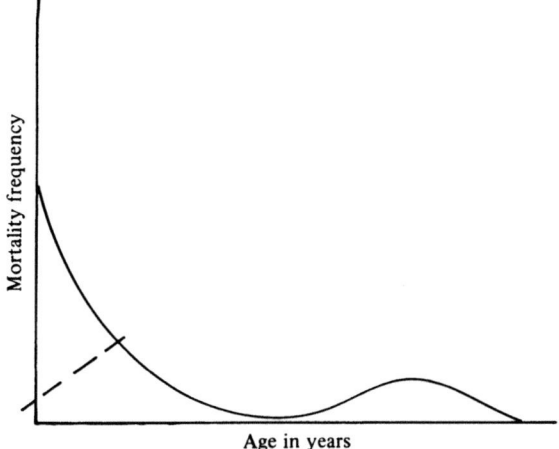

Fig. 4.3. The attritional death model.

that the horse would be an inefficient meat producer by comparison with sheep, goats and possibly even cattle (Dahl and Hjort 1976).

Although the data are inadequate and the role of the horse is likely to differ somewhat from that of cattle, it is not unreasonable to suggest that horse herding would produce an age structure similar to that of cattle herding. Infant mortality in both cases should be high; mortality during the productive years, relatively low. Mares bear their first offspring at about 3 years, approximately one year later than cows, and may continue breeding past their twentieth year (Tyler 1969; Mohr 1971). Horses on average appear to have a longer life span than cattle. This should be reflected in the mortality curve by an extended period of low mortality.

**Mortality models**

The behavioural patterns discussed above can be used to define a series of formal models representing various patterns of mortality.

*The attritional assemblage model*

The mortality distributions for natural attrition, scavenging, coursing and pastoral nomadism are all similar to figure 4.3. This curve is sometimes described as 'U-shaped' or 'fish-hook shaped'. Mortality is low for adults during their reproductive years, and high for juveniles and senescent adults (Caughley 1966).

*The carnivorous husbandry model*

As explained above, neither horses nor cattle are productive enough to be raised primarily for meat in a non-industrial society. However a mortality curve somewhat like that in figure 4.4 might be generated if a pattern of slaughter at maturity of all surplus males were superimposed upon the usual pastoral pattern of attritional mortality. Only isolated segments of the model might be archaeologically visible if the killing (or scavenging) of the various age and sex classes were separated by time or space.

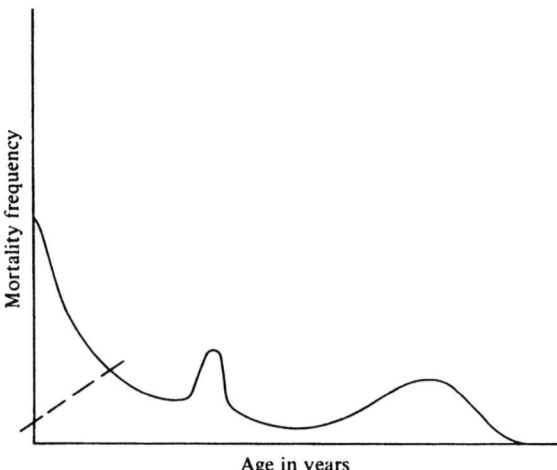

Fig. 4.4. The carnivorous husbandry model.

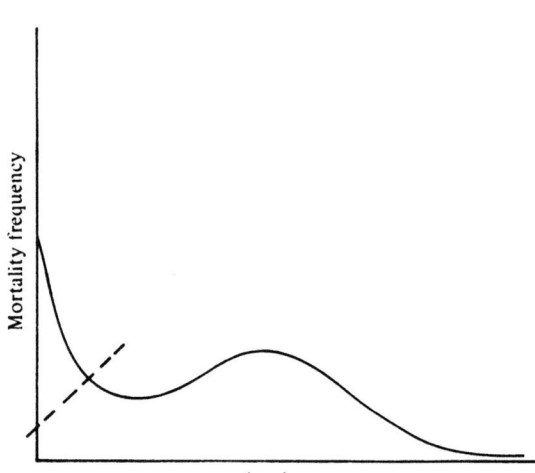

Fig. 4.6. The family group model.

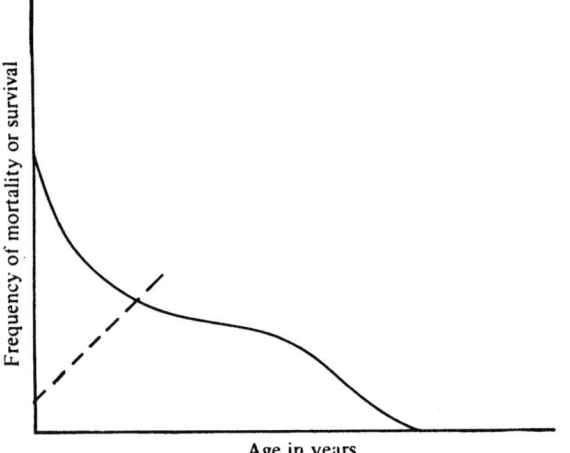

Fig. 4.5. The life assemblage or catastrophe model.

### The life assemblage or catastrophe model

The obverse of the U-shaped curve is the 'sigmoidal' or 'S-shaped curve', characteristically 'concave in early life, reflecting high but gradually diminishing juvenile mortality; approaching the straight diagonal in middle life, and convex when senescence sets in and mortality rates again build up' (Kurtén 1964; 101—3) (fig. 4.5). This curve is representative either of a living population (when it is referred to as a survivorship curve), a catastrophe assemblage, or an assemblage in which all age classes are represented as they would be in the living population because of completely random (and therefore representative) sampling.

### Social group models (variants of the life assemblage model)

The hunting of whole social groups might produce a variety of patterns. The structure of an assemblage, composed of one or several social units, may be dependent upon the degree of heterogeneity manifested by the various types of social groups characterized by a particular species. For

example, the horse has two types of social unit: the family group and the bachelor group. The family group is composed of one mature male over 5 or 6 years old, a number of adult mares (on average, two to three) and their young (on average, two to three). From the ages of 2 years to $4\frac{1}{2}$ years the male young leave the family group to join bachelor groups (Levine 1979). A number of different group types in one deposit may result in a pattern indistinguishable from that of the life assemblage model, especially if the stratigraphy of that deposit is not well understood.

### The family group model

The family group assemblage should, when enough data are considered, have an age distribution very similar to that of the total species population. The main difference should be the relatively low proportion of adolescents marking the absence of bachelor males. The actual effect of bachelor mobility on the age structure has not been established for a living population. It may, however, be suggested that the proportion of individuals 3 to 6 years old will be relatively low (fig. 4.6).

### The bachelor group model

There is little quantitative data about horse social structure and almost none concerning the age structure of bachelor groups. However it has been observed among both zebra and horse that bachelor groups are often segregated from family groups. This segregation is probably at least partly ecological in nature (Klingel 1965; Rubenstein 1978). The most obvious difference in the age structures of the two types of social groups is the absence of individuals less than about 2 years old from bachelor groups. From the age of 5 or 6 years some males leave the bachelor groups to build up their own family groups. However it is likely that some males remain in bachelor groups or solitary throughout their lives (Rubenstein, pers. comm.). A hypothetical bachelor-group age distribution is suggested in figure 4.7.

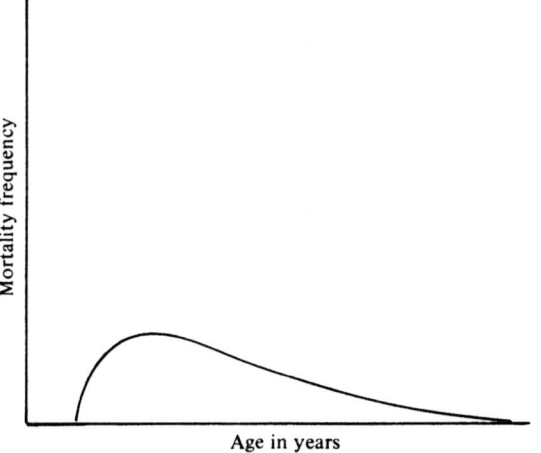

Fig. 4.7. The bachelor group model.

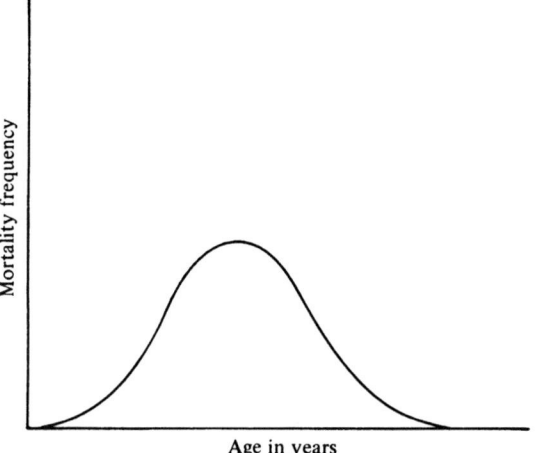

Fig. 4.8. The stalking model.

### The stalking model

Hunting mainly prime adults should produce a distribution approximating a bell-shaped curve (fig. 4.8). Identification of the stalking assemblage will probably be handicapped by the intrinsically small sample produced by such a hunting strategy. Stalking may produce a pattern archaeologically indistinguishable from bachelor-group hunting.

### Problems related to mortality-type interpretation

There are three kinds of problems involved in mortality-type interpretation: (1) problems of data interpretation (fitting the ageing data to a population structure); (2) problems of pattern interpretation (fitting the population structure to a mortality model); (3) problems of statistical analysis.

### Problems of data interpretation

Immature teeth are probably not as poorly preserved in a fossil deposit as immature bone. However, it is likely that the incomplete mineralization of jaw bones and teeth will result in the under-representation of juvenile teeth. This may distort assemblage age distributions as indicated by the broken lines

in figures 4.3 to 4.6. That is, the area above the line may not be represented in the fossil assemblage. This is a critical problem, because it means that material representing a random sample of the living population, or resulting from a catastrophe or family-group hunting, could produce a pattern resembling a stalking or bachelor-group distribution. Special consideration is therefore given here to estimating a hypothetical adjustment factor to compensate for the probable under-representation of immature teeth.

Despite the absence of quantitative measurements of differential preservation of teeth at various ages, it is obvious that immature teeth are much less sturdy than mature teeth. Moreover, each tooth type (e.g. Upper $P_3$, Upper $P_4$, Lower $M_1$ and so on) develops – mineralizes, erupts and wears – according to its own schedule. A model has been constructed, setting an average (hypothetical but not unreasonable) value for the development of all tooth types for each of the years from 0 to 5. Such a model can be useful without any pretensions to accuracy.

The little information available concerning unmanaged, feral horses suggests that 13% to 19% of a living population may be 0 to 1 year old (Rubenstein 1978). Estimates for other age classes cannot be used, as the criteria for membership within them are not compatible with the needs of the model proposed here; that is, they are behavioural rather than chronological criteria. However if 13% to 19% is accepted as the approximate membership for the first year, the adjustment model can be devised so that on average it recreates a population structure which is not too different from that of living horse populations.

For the purposes of this model it is assumed that throughout the first five years of life tooth preservation increases linearly (see fig. 4.9, curve A). The actual shape of the curve is probably convex, with an initial high rate of increase in preservation that tapers off as maturity is reached at about 4 or 5 years, after which it remains constant (see fig. 4.9, curve B). The real situation is complicated by the fact that the total number of teeth per individual varies throughout the first five years of the horse's life, as demonstrated in table 4.3. In the case of a fossil assemblage, the number in the third column is probably more meaningful than that in the second column. Each tooth in each row is at a different point in its development. Since the relative durability of each individual tooth type at each point cannot (at this time) be measured, the actual probability that any tooth at any point will be represented in a fossil assemblage cannot be determined. From 2 to 3 or 4 years of age the over-representation of tooth types probably compensates somewhat for poor tooth preservation (fig. 4.9, curve C). Therefore a convex adjustment model would probably over-adjust for those teeth aged 2 to 4 years. A linear model decreases the preservation rate where adjustment could be most distorted by the large number of teeth in each jaw. Therefore it is the linear model that will probably best illustrate how differential preservation can affect the shape of a fossil age distribution.

Table 4.3. *Change in the number of teeth in a horse throughout its first 5 years of life (approximate values)*

| Age | Total number of teeth | Number of well-developed teeth |
|---|---|---|
| Birth | 16 | 16 |
| 2 months | 28 | 20 |
| 9 months | 32 | 26 |
| 10 months | 32 | 28 |
| 1¼ years | 36 | 32 |
| 1½ years | 48 | 32 |
| 1¾ years | 56 | 46 |
| 2½ years | 60 | 54 |
| 3 years | 50 | 44 |
| 4–4½ years | 36 | 36 |

*Source*: Küpfer 1937: 149, 160–73.

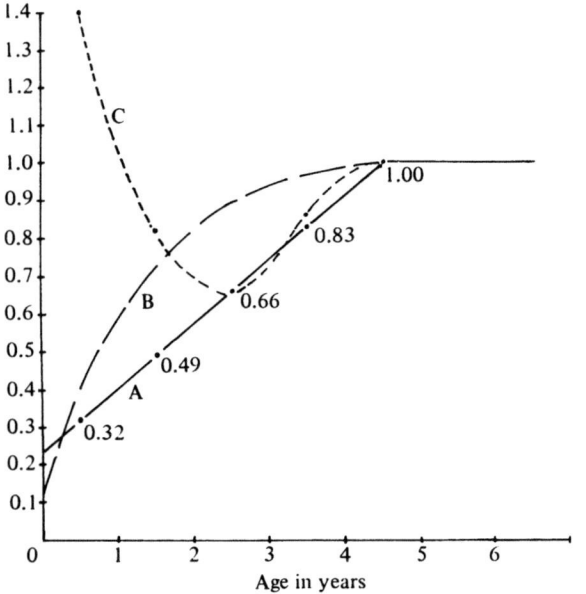

Fig. 4.9. The adjustment factor used in tooth age distribution histograms (fig. 4.10 to 4.23, and 4.25 to 4.30), to account for differential preservation of immature teeth. Curve A is used to adjust the age distribution histograms to account for the differential preservation of immature teeth. The values given are the average values for each whole year (e.g. 0–1, 1–2, 2–3 etc.). The formula for the line is $y = 0.23 + 0.17 \times age$. At 5 years old the teeth are completely mineralized. Curve B shows the probable shape of the actual preservation curve.

$$\text{Curve C} = \frac{\text{The number of teeth in an adult}}{\text{The number of teeth at a given age}}$$

Curve A is approximately equal to Curve B × Curve C.

It is assumed that all teeth are completely mineralized and have ceased growing by the age of 5 years and that thereafter teeth from all age classes have an approximately equal chance of being preserved. In the case of extremely old animals that may not be true. However, such individuals are rare in any population and doubtless of negligible importance here.

The formula for the preservation curve is: $y = 0.23 + 0.17$ (age). When this equation is plotted on a graph, 0.23 equals the $y$ intercept; 0.17 is the slope of the line; and 'age', the average age for each age class (e.g. the 0 to 1 age range is equal to 0.5) (fig. 4.9). What this means is that approximately 32% of the teeth from a horse up to one year old would be preserved; at 1 to 2 years 49% would be preserved and so on. Multiplying the frequency of teeth in each age class from 0 to 5 years by $1/[0.23 + 0.17 \text{ (age)}]$ gives the average adjusted frequency for each age class. The adjusted frequencies can then be converted into percentages and plotted as histograms.

The adjustment formula used here raises the proportion of teeth up to one year old in the pooled assemblages from approximately 4% to 12%, which is close to the lower limit for living equid populations (fig. 4.10). It is also comparable with Dahl and Hjort's mortality estimate for the 'base-line herd model' (figs. 4.1 and 4.2). If anything, in most cases it probably underestimates the bias against immature teeth.

For deposits where preservation is bad, the value of the slope could probably be set lower than where it is good — except that the method of adjustment employed here is probably too crude for such manipulations to be worthwhile. A further guide is the comparative preservation of bones and teeth. To my knowledge there have been no quantitative studies but it is not improbable that the relationship between the two is roughly linear. If that is true, the bone preservation state should provide some idea of how well immature teeth will be preserved in a particular assemblage (Levine 1979). Moreover if a linear model is at all suitable, the tooth:bone ratio will provide a further indication of differential preservation. That is, there are approximately four times more bones than teeth in a horse skeleton. Therefore the deviation of the actual ratio in each assemblage from the ideal ratio

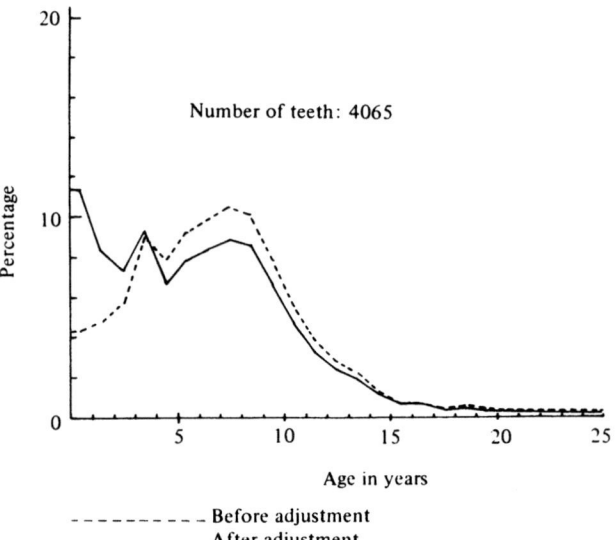

Fig. 4.10. Tooth age distribution – all assemblage units pooled.

could provide a rough assessment of the preservation conditions in that deposit (table 4.1). If two deposits are compared – for example, Gönnersdorf with a tooth:bone ratio of 0.8:1.0 and Jaurens with a ratio of 0.6:1.0 – it may be suggested that preservation is better at Jaurens than at Gönnersdorf. These results are comparable with those from bone preservation studies carried out on the same sites (Levine 1979).

Another type of interpretation problem is the possible absence of skulls from a site. The structure of an archaeological deposit is more complicated than that of a natural deposit. Taphonomic processes may affect both similarly, but human decisions will have an important impact on archaeological fossil distributions (Levine 1979). If the carcase of a large animal must be carried far, the skull may be left at the kill site. However if the skull has some special importance aside from its food value, its size may not bias its representation. Because bone preservation is generally much poorer than tooth preservation in archaeological deposits, the only reliable evidence for skull abandonment would be the virtual absence of teeth from a large bone assemblage. No such pattern has been observed in this study.

Poplin has observed that the skull bones and teeth of horse are under-represented at Gönnersdorf (evidently an open-air habitation site) by comparison with those of smaller animals such as fox, hare and reindeer. His tentative interpretation of this pattern is that small game would have been brought back whole to the habitation site; while large game, such as the horse, would have been butchered at the kill site and only the meat-bearing bones brought back (Poplin 1976). However, small teeth are probably more likely to be preserved than large ones in an environment in which trampling is an important agent of destruction – as it should be at a habitation site. Also, an experimental study in the South Dakota Badlands has indicated, with regard to teeth, that 'body size is an important criterion in understanding differential damage to species, particularly the relative tooth volume to enamel thickness. In most small mammals there seems to be no dehydration cracking of the teeth. . . Large teeth splinter very quickly' (Hill 1975: 158). Poplin's estimate for the bone MNI is 13; mine is 12 (Poplin 1976). My estimate for the tooth MNI is 10. The MNI estimates for teeth and bones are not significantly different (using Poplin's estimate $z = 0.63$, $p > 0.05$). Neither the bone preservation state, nor the tooth:bone ratio, nor the tooth age distribution suggest that the skulls were abandoned. However if skull abandonment were a pattern characteristic of small deposits, the samples might be too small for analysis. No evidence has been uncovered for special cultural functions of horse teeth or skulls. This may be because of poor preservation or it may be that the relevant information has not been available to me. In any case it seems likely that the deposits studied here were, like those at Gönnersdorf, at or near kill sites (Levine 1979).

For several reasons the proportion of male horses in a fossil assemblage cannot be determined directly from the teeth in a deposit. The cheek teeth and incisors do not show sexual dimorphism. And although only males have well-developed permanent canines, these teeth do not even begin to grow until the animal is about $2\frac{1}{2}$ years old. They erupt between the ages of 4 and $5\frac{1}{2}$ years. Nothing further can be said with any precision about the age of loose canines, once in wear. Moreover, because of their odd shape and relative fragility, canines will probably be under-represented in fossil deposits (Levine 1979). Therefore inferences about the sex structure of a fossil population must be made through an interpretation of its age structure or through some other kind of analysis of sexual dimorphism.

*Problems of pattern interpretation*

A series of patterns has been distinguished thus far according to the various agents of mortality. However, the archaeologist can never be certain that he has not uncovered a palimpsest of patterns rather than a single event. What is taken to be a homogeneous assemblage may have been deposited in a series of hunting episodes, for example, each employing a different hunting strategy and each recovering a different segment of the prey population structure. Moreover in the archaeological situation an attritional pattern may look like a catastrophe pattern if populations are sampled in a random fashion. If it is certain that only a small number of animals had been killed, there is no problem; since a small accumulation by definition cannot constitute the type of catastrophe discussed above. If the deposit is large but carefully excavated, it should be possible to disentangle the various patterns according to the context of the assemblage and the depositional sequence. However, collection of the necessary data is often neglected. Small assemblages cannot usually be assigned confidently to any of the models. If more than one agent of accumulation is responsible for the deposit, interpretation of the distribution may be impossible. Moreover, if the proportion of males in a population is very much lower than the proportion of females, a representative sample may produce a pattern resembling the family group model rather than the life assemblage model.

Poor preservation is not the only bias against the representation of immature animals in the tooth/bone assemblage. They will also be under-represented when agents of mortality other than those which have caused the death assemblage have already removed them from the living population. Such agents include predation, malnutrition, disease, floods and drought – all of which hit juveniles more heavily than healthy adults. When that happens a catastrophe, family-group or random distribution may resemble a stalking or bachelor-group distribution.

*Problems of statistical analysis*

The fossil data studied here have two important drawbacks ruling out statistical analysis based upon significance testing: non-independence of observations and overlapping age spans.

The fatal deficiency of the data is the non-independence of observations. Obviously there was a time when each tooth was embedded in a jaw. In the fossil situation and particularly in the archaeological situation most jaws are broken up, and in most cases only a small number of them can be reconstructed. All or some of the teeth from a particular jaw may remain in a deposit and be recovered in excavation. It may reasonably be assumed that once a tooth is fully developed, the probability that it will be preserved remains equal to that of any other fully developed tooth of that type in that deposit and is not dependent upon its exact age. Therefore ageing individual teeth rather than individual animals should not distort the general shape of an age distribution. However this does mean that the true sample size, the number of carcases, is smaller than the apparent sample size, the number of teeth. As the true sample size cannot be determined, no level of statistical significance can be established. Therefore significance tests comparing the age distributions of the various assemblages cannot be carried out.

The second serious fault in the data is overlapping age classes. Some teeth can be assigned an age span of one year (e.g. 1 to 2, 2 to 3, 3 to 4 years old). In other cases the age determinations are broader and often overlapping (e.g. 2 to 4, 3 to 6 years old). That occurs when teeth are aged by eruption and wear sequences, when they are broken, or when the exact tooth type cannot be determined (e.g. $P_3$ or $P_4$, $M_1$ or $M_2$) (Levine 1979). Teeth with age spans of ten years or more are excluded from the age distribution histograms.

There are two reasons for the inclusion of teeth with age spans greater than one year in the age distribution histograms. One is that exclusion of those cases would reduce the size of the already barely adequate samples available for study. The second and more important reason is that omission of this data would bias the distributions by under-representing adult cheek teeth when they are at their maximum length. That is, teeth at their maximum length are, by reason of their long, thin shape, more likely to be broken than older stubbier teeth. The broken cheek teeth can be assigned a minimum age by virtue of their wear state and a maximum age by virtue of their length. Because age determination becomes increasingly inaccurate beyond 15 years, very old teeth must be assigned relatively broad age spans.

Incisors are not as well represented in the age distributions as cheek teeth because they cannot be as closely aged and because their representation in fossil deposits is relatively poor; that is, they are small, fragile and loosely held in the jaw. Canines are completely excluded from the age distribution study, as they are rare, difficult to age and sex-linked.

When a tooth is assigned an age span greater than one year, it is divided between as many columns of the histogram as necessary. In this way a tooth aged 2 to 4 years will add 0.5 to the column for 2 to 3 years, and 0.5 to the column for 3 to 4 years. Thus the values for each column are not true frequencies, but the area covered by the histogram is correct.

Despite the limitations of the data discussed above, it is believed that the age distributions as presented by the histograms are representative of the age distributions of the fossil assemblages under consideration.

**Analyses of age distribution histograms**

This study includes 95 assemblage units, each containing at least 10 teeth. Of these, 72 units have enough data to be used in a cluster analysis. Eight are of sufficient interest to be discussed individually and in some detail. Pooling assemblage units is useful here for two reasons. One, it increases the functional sample size by allowing inclusion of data from units otherwise too small for consideration. Two, classes of data (for example, natural deposits and archaeological deposits) can be compared with one another and with individual assemblage units in order better to understand the nature of the variability.

*Natural assemblages*

It is useful to look at natural assemblage units first, in order to have examples of age distributions presumably unaffected by man, to which archaeological assemblage units can be compared.

The pooled natural assemblage unit includes one very rich unit, Jaurens, and five small units from La Fage and Chatillon-Saint-Jean. Out of 610 ageable teeth 498 are from Jaurens. This unit obviously dominates the age distribution of the pooled natural data (figs. 4.11–4.13). However when the natural assemblage units are pooled excluding Jaurens, the age distribution remains similar, although it no longer resembles a smooth curve (fig. 4.13). It is not possible to make useful generalizations about the small samples from Chantillon-Saint-Jean and La Fage.

An extensive bone deposit, dated by C14 to 29 300 ±

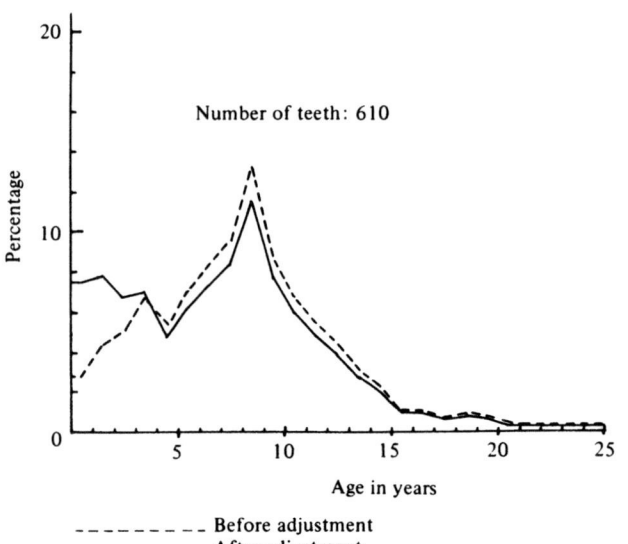

Fig. 4.11. Tooth age distribution – all natural assemblage units pooled.

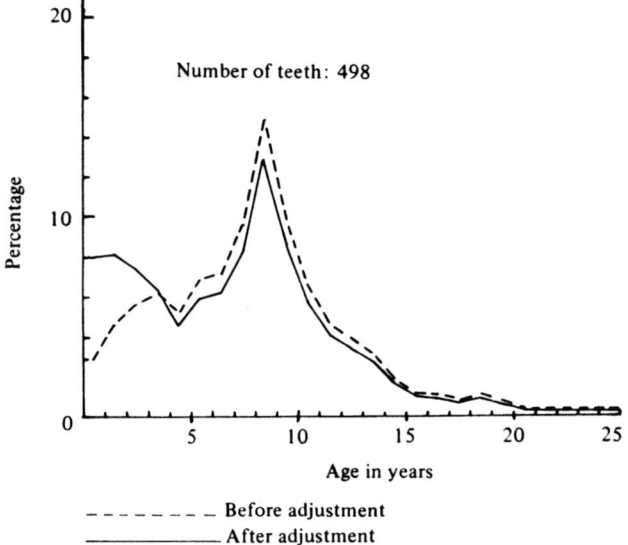

Fig. 4.12. Tooth age distribution – Jaurens.

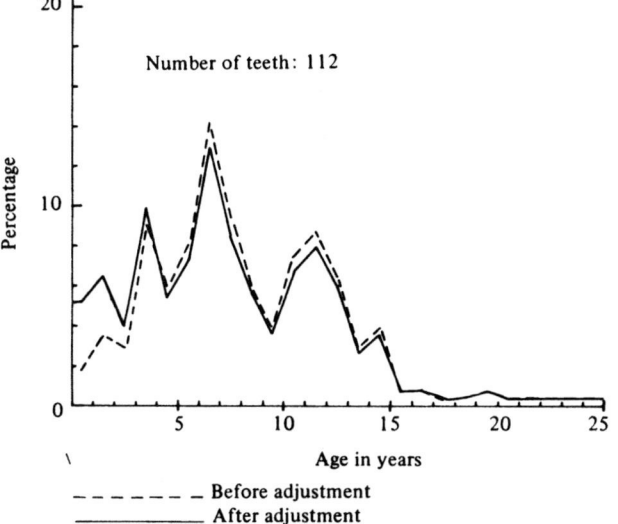

Fig. 4.13. Tooth age distribution – natural assemblage units pooled excluding Jaurens.

1400 years b.p. (Ly-359), was found in Jaurens, a cave site (fig. 4.12). The deposit was probably formed when a flood swept the carcases of a large number of animals of various species into the cave (Guerin 1969, 1970; Levine 1979). The preservation state of the skeleton material from this site is excellent (table 4.1; Levine 1979).

The adjusted age distribution histogram for Jaurens most closely fits the family group assemblage model except that, even when adjusted, the percentage of teeth up to one year old is low. A bone cluster analysis (employing the Ward's Method dendrogram and a principal components analysis from the *Clustan* computer package) carried out on the astragali, metacarpal II, metatarsal III and anterior phalange II suggests that Jaurens represents a number of family groups with an average stallion:mare:juvenile ratio of 1.0:2.2:3.0 (Levine 1979). This interpretation is strongly dependent upon the assumption that the separation of the clusters associated with mares and juveniles has been created by the absence of bachelor males. An examination of the age distribution of the teeth from Jaurens confirms this hypothesis. If it is assumed that the horse carcases from Jaurens had been derived from a stable living population, the low representation of teeth 4 to 7 years old may be explained as follows. If males leave their family groups when they are 2 to 4 years old, during the year 4–5 there may be no adolescent males at all in those groups. Males leave the bachelor groups to acquire their own families from 5 years old at the earliest. But for most this will probably happen several years later or not at all. If most stallions are 7 to 9 years old when they begin collecting mares, that would perhaps explain the high proportion of teeth 8 to 9 years old at Jaurens.

The adult:juvenile ratio (stallions + mares:juveniles) suggested by the bone cluster analysis is 1.0:0.7. If the tooth frequency trough at 4 to 7 years is identified with the break between the bone clusters representing adults and juveniles, the focal point of the break is probably located at the centre of the trough at about 5 to 6 years. If juveniles, then, are roughly equated with individuals 6 years or younger, the adult:juvenile tooth ratio is 1.0:0.5, unadjusted, or 1.0:0.7, adjusted. Comparable data for the plains zebra yields an adult:juvenile ratio of 1.0:0.8 (Klingel 1969). The close agreement of these results lends support to the hypothesis that this assemblage unit comprises a number of family groups.

The family-group structure does not explain the low proportion of teeth 0 to 1 year old. Both the bone-preservation state and the tooth:bone ratio, 0.6:1.0, indicate that preservation conditions at Jaurens were excellent (table 4.1). This suggests that, although the adjusted proportion of teeth in the first year is only 8%, it is more likely to overestimate than to underestimate the true percentage for that year. Therefore the low proportion of teeth 0 to 1 year old is likely to reflect the under-representation of this age class in the population of carcases swept into the cave. There are at least three plausible explanations for this pattern. One, the catastrophe, which was probably a flood, occurred, as floods often do, in the early spring before the horses' main breeding season. Two, infant mortality for that year was unusually high before the catastrophe (or the birth rate unusually low). Three, since the hydraulic behaviour of foal carcases is probably different from that of adults, they may have been deposited elsewhere.

The results of the Jaurens tooth analysis support the hypothesis which holds that this assemblage unit was composed of a number of family groups killed in a flood from which most or all bachelors were excluded, possibly because of the ecological separation of the two types of social groups.

### Archaeological assemblages

The shape of the age distribution for the pooled archaeological assemblage unit, when adjusted, resembles the sigmoidal curve of the life assemblage model (figs. 4.5 and

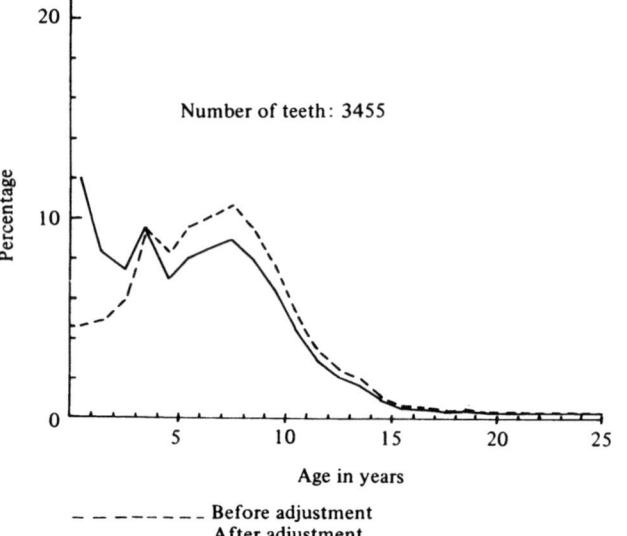

Fig. 4.14. Tooth age distribution – all archaeological assemblage units pooled.

4.14). The adjusted percentage of teeth 0 to 1 year old, 12%, is close to the lower limit suggested by the comparative data for feral horses. Although this age distribution is broadly representative of a living, stable population of horses, it also has its anomalies. The somewhat low proportion of teeth 4 to 7 years old is reminiscent of (though not as extreme as) the pattern at Jaurens, associated there with the absence of bachelor males. However, the data from the pooled archaeological assemblage unit are an amalgam of many different units. There is therefore a strong possibility that they reflect an amalgam of strategies. An emphasis on family-group hunting, possibly with some preference for prime individuals might account for the apparent bias.

The second anomaly in the age distribution of the pooled archaeological data is the high proportion of teeth 3 to 4 years old. One possible explanation is selective mortality. By the age of 3 to 4 years most juveniles have left their natal family groups. This may be the period when they are most mobile and therefore least protected. Moreover it is the year when females first bear young, which makes them all the more vulnerable (Tyler 1969; Mohr 1971; Bureau of Land Management 1973). An alternative explanation is differential preservation. That is, at this stage in the horse's tooth growth a relatively large number of teeth are well developed and may therefore be preserved (table 4.3). If the adjustment factor used is not quite right, the shape of the age distribution might be somewhat biased. If this hypothesis were correct a similar anomaly might be expected in the Jaurens age distribution. In fact there is a slight mortality peak at 3 to 4 years in that assemblage, but it disappears when the data are adjusted (figs. 4.11 and 4.12). The absence of the anomaly in Jaurens is not conclusive, however, since it might be caused by two factors peculiar to natural assemblages. For one thing, if, as the evidence suggests, Jaurens really is a catastrophe site, the relative vulnerability of horses 3 to 4 years old should be low

or even manifested as a deficiency rather than as an excess of individuals. That is, a proportion of individuals from this age class should already have succumbed to other, more selective, agents of mortality than the catastrophe. Moreover, the preservation state of material from natural deposits is usually better than that from archaeological deposits (table 4.1). It may be that the superior conditions of preservation at Jaurens have resulted in a superior representation of teeth 1 to 3 years old, contrasting with the archaeological over-representation of teeth 3 to 4 years old.

The anomalies of the pooled archaeological assemblage unit do not prejudice its identification with the life assemblage model. Such an age distribution is best accounted for by a generally opportunistic adaptation. That is, the problem of the prehistoric people concerned was not so much to select a particular age class or sex from the animal population as it was to select a strategy or series of strategies – for example, stalking, trapping, scavenging and herd driving – that would provide most efficiently for their immediate needs. This is the tactic of the hunter, not the pastoralist.

*Large archaeological assemblage units*

Each assemblage unit containing a total of 150 or more teeth is discussed individually. This is, of course, an arbitrary limit; it means in effect that a relatively large sample has been excavated. The larger the sample the more likely that it will be representative of the age distribution of the animals interred in the deposit.

*Combe Grenal–level 14 (CG14)* (fig. 4.15). This site has the greatest total number of teeth of any archaeological assemblage unit studied here. Yet it contains only 14 pieces of bone, of which 11 are fragments of shaft or articulation; two are metapodials and one is a second phalange. Bone preservation here is very poor indeed. The tooth:bone ratio at CG14 is perhaps rather extreme, 145:1, which may mean that the adjustment factor under-compensates here for

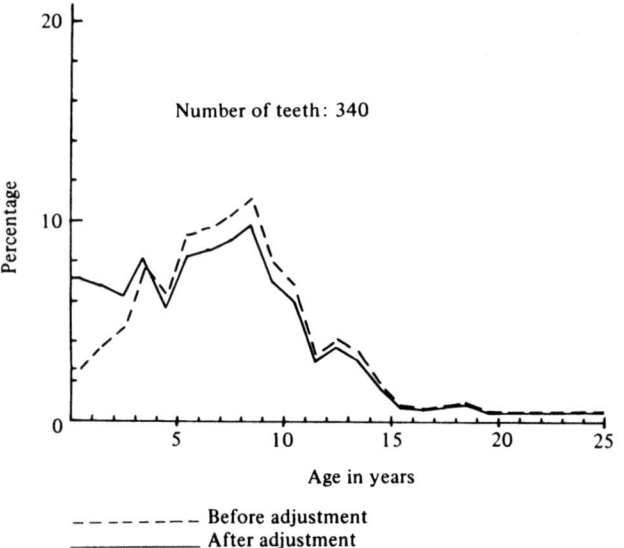

Fig. 4.15. Tooth age distribution – Combe Grenal, level 14.

differential representation of immature teeth. If that is so, the relatively low proportion of teeth 0 to 1 year old in the adjusted distribution, 7.1%, may not adequately reflect their original representation in this assemblage unit. The proportion of teeth 3 to 4 years old is somewhat high, indicating either adolescent vulnerability or, particularly in this unit, the inadequacy of the adjustment factor. The percentage of teeth 4 to 5 years old is somewhat low, perhaps indicating a low proportion of bachelor males. From 5 to 9 years the mortality rate is at its highest and it remains relatively high until 11 years.

Combe Grenal—level 14, like Jaurens, most closely fits the family group model. That the absence of teeth 4 to 6 years old is not as marked here as it is at Jaurens might suggest that the exclusion of bachelor males is not as systematic. There is practically no information available about the context and disposition of the bones and teeth within CG14. The MNI is 18, but the true number of horses is almost certainly much greater. The population structure and the quantity and density of material within the deposit suggest that the hunting technique most often employed here might have been herd driving.

*Combe Grenal—level 22 (CG22)* (fig. 4.16). There are 200 teeth in Combe Grenal—level 22, 152 of which are ageable. The tooth:bone ratio is 5.9:1.0, significantly lower than that of Combe Grenal—level 14 ($\chi^2 = 51.5$, $p < 0.001$). The difference between the two ratios suggests that preservation is better at CG22 than at CG14. The mean age of the teeth in CG22 is lower than that in CG14. The adjusted percentage of teeth 0 to 1 year old, 16.7%, fits well within the limits suggested by the comparative data for feral horses. However the proportion of teeth 2 to 4 years old is rather higher than expected and the drop in mortality at 4 years rather abrupt. From 4 to 10 years the percentage of teeth in each age class remains more or less constant.

This assemblage unit is not a very large one. Therefore although the data are undoubtedly useful, it is not certain that they are completely representative of the animals originally deposited in level 22. For example, the high proportion of teeth 2 to 4 years old might be interpreted most plausibly in three ways. One, it might be a chance distortion, arising from the inadequate sample size. Two, it might be truly representative of the age distribution and accounted for by the killing of inexperienced adolescents. Three, it could be the result of an unstable age structure; for example, caused by increased resources (e.g. grazing) or decreased predation from the years 0 to 4. In the absence of contextual information (as in the case of CG14), it is not possible to give any of these alternatives precedence over the others. Even so, the shape of the adjusted age distribution is, on the whole, most similar to that of the sigmoidal life assemblage model. With an MNI of 10, the horses of CG22 could have been killed in a herd drive, in several group drives, in random stalks and scavenging, or any combination of these.

*Combe Grenal—level 23 (CG23)* (fig. 4.17). Combe Grenal—level 23 is similar to the pooled archaeological assemblage unit in its size, general shape and preservation state. It contains however a higher proportion of teeth 0 to 1 year old than either the pooled archaeological assemblage unit or any of the other large archaeological or natural units. When adjusted, the proportion, 22.4%, for that year surpasses the limits suggested by the comparative feral horse data. Yet, since preservation in this unit is relatively poor and the tooth: bone ratio rather high, it is unlikely that the adjustment factor over-compensates for juvenile under-representation. As in the case of the pooled archaeological assemblage unit, the proportion of teeth 4 to 6 years old is relatively low.

The shape of the CG23 age distribution resembles that

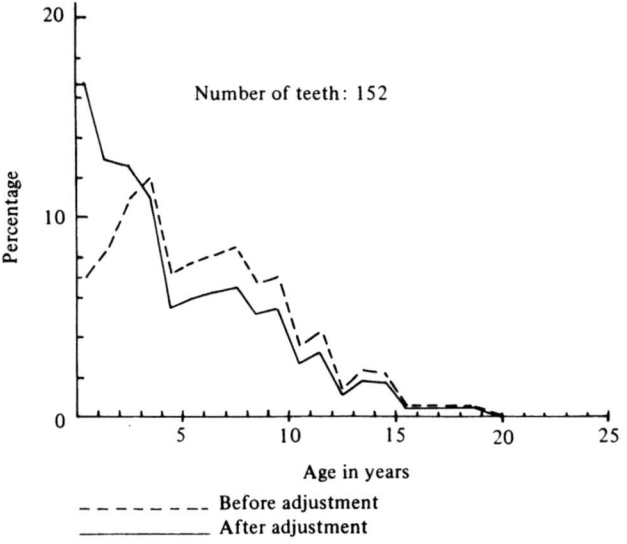

Number of teeth: 152

- - - - - - - Before adjustment
_____ After adjustment

Fig. 4.16. Tooth age distribution – Combe Grenal, level 22.

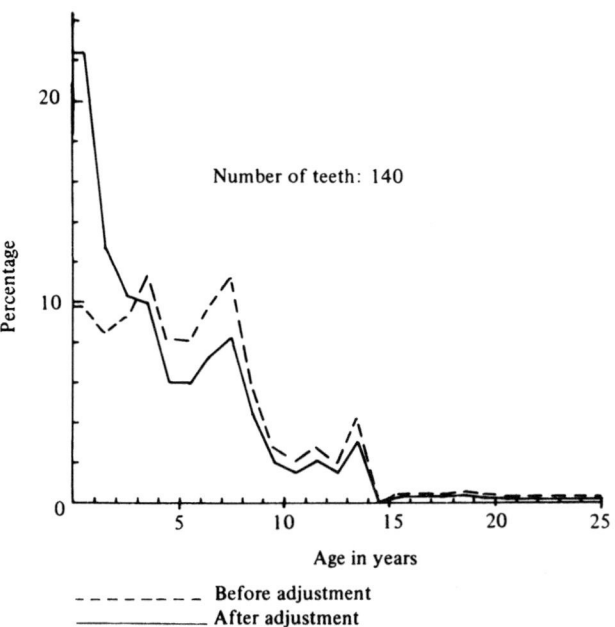

Number of teeth: 140

- - - - - - - Before adjustment
_____ After adjustment

Fig. 4.17. Tooth age distribution – Combe Grenal, level 23.

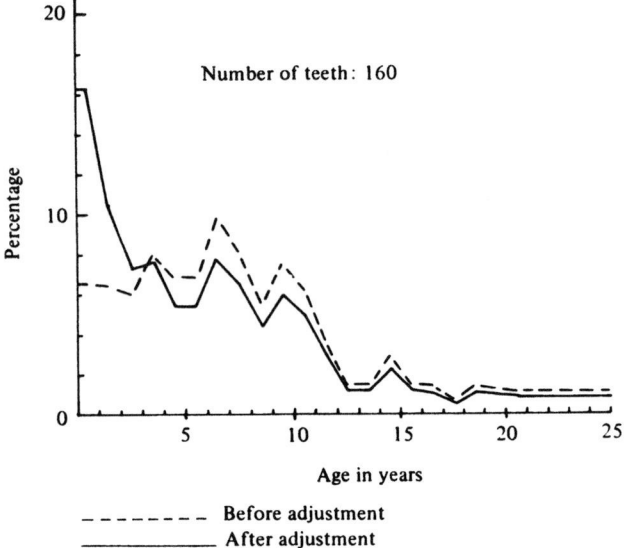

Fig. 4.18. Tooth age distribution – Gönnersdorf.

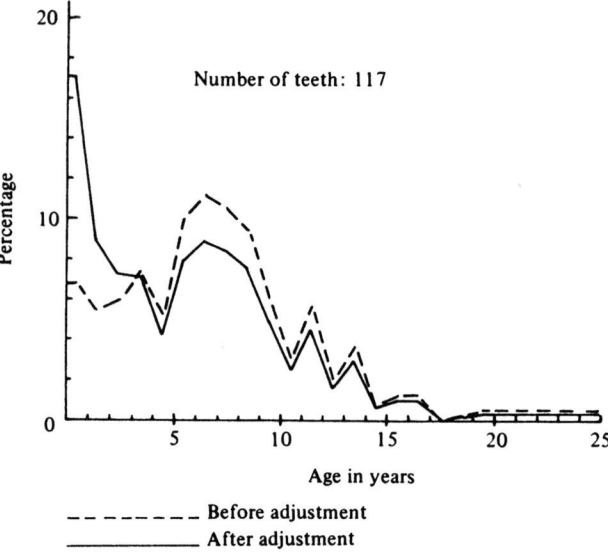

Fig. 4.19. Tooth age distribution – Arlay, level 1.

of the life assemblage model, but the sample is too small to distinguish between two similar patterns: the one including, the other excluding, bachelor males. The high proportion of teeth 0 to 1 year old suggests that the animals had been killed in an unusually productive year, perhaps during the main breeding season. However the sample is also small enough that chance might explain both that and the low proportion of teeth over 8 or 9 years old. Stalking, trapping and scavenging or driving could explain the age distribution manifested here.

*Gönnersdorf (FG15)* (fig. 4.18). The age distribution at Gönnersdorf is similar to those of the archaeological units already discussed. The proportion of teeth 0 to 1 year old, 16.3%, fits within the limits suggested by the comparative data. But since the tooth:bone ratio, 0.8:1.0, is significantly lower in FG15 than in the pooled archaeological assemblage unit ($\chi^2 = 125.06$, p $<$ 0.001), it is quite possible that the adjustment factor over-compensates here for the hypothetical under-representation of immature teeth.

As with several of the other assemblage units already discussed, the sample at FG15 is not large enough to define unambiguously the shape of the distribution. However the general pattern is that of the life assemblage model – possibly somewhat deficient in bachelor males. Considering the context and environment of this assemblage unit, it is likely that the horses were killed over a relatively short period of time (Poplin 1976). I would also suggest that whole social groups were hunted and that, most probably, driving techniques were employed.

*Arlay–level 1 (AR01)* (fig. 4.19). Arlay–level 1 is the smallest of the large assemblage units. The relative inadequacy of the sample is reflected by the irregularity of the distribution. However the overall pattern is not very different from those of the archaeological units discussed. The adjusted proportion of teeth 0 to 1 year old, 17.1%, fits within the limits of the comparative data. There is a low percentage of teeth 4 to 5

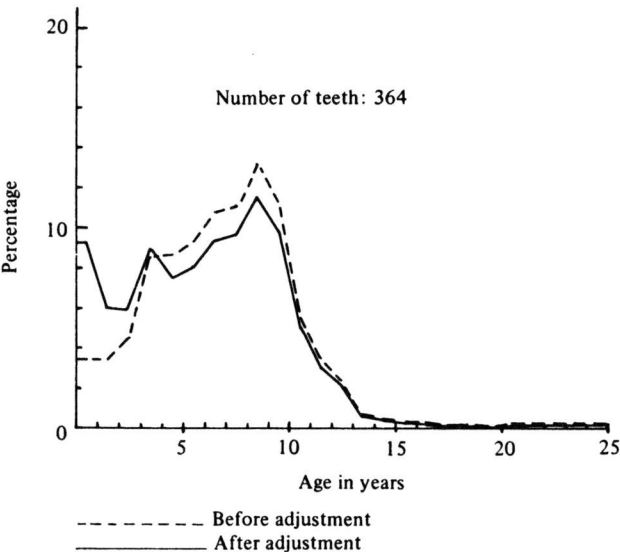

Fig. 4.20. Tooth age distribution – Solutré, square P 16.

years old. The tooth:bone ratio, 2.9:1.00, is close to the average ratio for all assemblages combined (see table 4.1, last line). This suggests that the degree of preservation at Arlay is similar to that at the other deposits studied here and hence that the adjustment factor used to compensate for the under-representation of immature teeth is applicable here.

The pattern is apparently again that of the life assemblage model, possibly deficient in bachelor males. The distribution is best explained by a hunting strategy of group or herd driving. However information concerning the formation of this deposit is so sparse that random (and ultimately, representative) stalking, trapping and scavenging cannot be ruled out.

*Solutré–square P16 (SO3P)* (fig. 4.20). As regards teeth, SO3P is the second largest archaeological assemblage unit examined here. Both the tooth:bone ratio, 0.7:1.0, and a

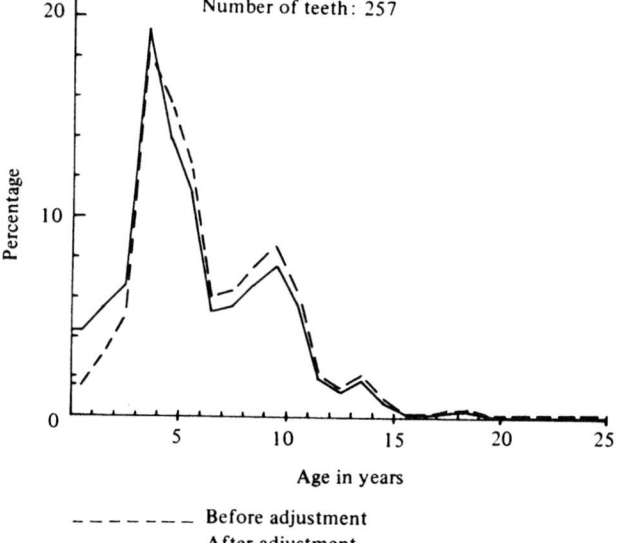

Fig. 4.21. Tooth age distribution – Solutré, square L 13.

differential bone representation study indicate that preservation in this assemblage unit is excellent, though perhaps inferior to that at Jaurens and Solutré–square L13 (Levine 1979). Aside from the rather low proportion of teeth 0 to 3 years old, SO3P looks very much like the pooled archaeological assemblage unit. The low proportion of juveniles might reflect a chance sampling bias, the inadequacy of the adjustment factor, a relatively high proportion of bachelor males, an unstable age distribution – for example, reflecting a gradually deteriorating environment – or any combination of these factors. The rather high, but relatively unimportant, representation of teeth 3 to 4 years old might be explained by a high proportion of young dams and bachelor males, a sampling bias, or an ageing bias. That the proportion of teeth in each age class increases from 4 to 9 years might indicate an unstable age distribution, the return of bachelor males as stallions to family groups or again merely a sampling bias. The SO3P age distribution most closely resembles the life assemblage model. It was probably composed of the butchering refuse from a hunters' herd drive (Levine 1979).

*Solutré–square L13* (SO2L) (fig. 4.21). Solutré–square L13, from the Upper Perigordian breccia level, is an important assemblage unit from an important site. With 275 teeth, of which 257 are ageable, it is the third largest archaeological assemblage unit studied here. Like Jaurens it has a very low tooth:bone ratio, 0.6:1.0. The SO2L bone preservation state is not as good as that of Jaurens, but better than that of any other archaeological assemblage unit (Levine 1979).

Site SO2L has an age distribution rather different from that of any other unit or model described in this study. The percentage of teeth 0 to 3 years old is unusually low even when adjusted. The preservation state, if anything, indicates that adjustment probably over-compensates for differential preservation of immature teeth. The percentage of teeth 3 to 6

years old is extremely high. The decrease at 6 years is very steep and the proportion of teeth 6 to 9 years old somewhat low. Three hypotheses will be discussed to account for these anomalies: (1) pastoralism; (2) an emphasis on hunting bachelor males; (3) hunting an unstable population.

Because archaeologists habitually use domestication to explain unusual age distributions, that possibility will be discussed first. If this were a pastoralists' slaughter site, it would appear that few horses 0 to 3 years old were killed, but many 3 to 6 years old. From 6 to 11 years slaughter would be moderate, and thereafter, extremely rare. This pattern is very different from the model based upon the Dahl and Hjort data (table 4.2, figs. 4.1 and 4.2). The low representation of teeth 0 to 3 years old and especially 0 to 1 year old might be accounted for if natural mortality took those individuals while at pasture, and if they were rarely killed at the slaughter site. Despite the almost complete absence of comparative data, this hypothesis seems plausible. The slaughter rate at SO2L then would be highest during the horses' early reproductive years. That would make sense only if young males, almost exclusively, were killed.

As noted earlier, there are no data available concerning the age structure of horse herds belonging to pastoral nomads. However the shape of the age distribution for the living domesticated cattle population synthesized by Dahl and Hjort is a sigmoidal curve. If that general structure were also characteristic of domesticated horse herds (as is not unlikely), then according to Dahl and Hjort's data, 26.7% of the living population would be 3 to 6 years old (or taking into account the fact that cattle may begin breeding one year earlier than horses, 28.5%) (Dahl and Hjort 1976). Probably only half of those individuals, 13–14%, would be males. If an age and sex class containing only 13–14% of the postulated living population had contributed 46.5% (the percentage of teeth 3 to 6 years old recovered from SO2L) to the archaeological assemblage, then it is clear that individuals could not have been butchered in proportion to their representation in the living population. No accurate size estimate can be provided for the 'magma' or breccia level, but it certainly comprised hundreds and probably thousands of horses (Levine 1979). Moreover the disposition of the bones and associated artefacts (as yet unpublished) suggests to me that the material had probably been deposited within a relatively short period of time. If half of those hundreds or thousands of horses consisted of 3 to 6 year old males, as hypothesized above, then the living herds from which the slaughtered animals were drawn must have been at least three times greater than the total number of slaughtered animals. If this were so, the living herds must have been vast; much larger than the herds of most pastoral nomads and particularly most domesticated horse herds (Levine 1979).

Approximately 81.6% of the teeth at SO2L were from horses slaughtered between the ages of 3 and 10 years. That is the most important reproductive period of the horse. Such a slaughter pattern would be most unusual for pastoral nomads (unfortunately data have not been available for comparison with meat producers like the Chukchi). That such a large quantity of animals should have been killed in one place, within a relatively short period of time, is itself uncharacteristic of pastoralist behaviour. Also, the large quantity of whole bones and bones in connection suggests butchering techniques too wasteful to be attributed to pastoralists.

That adults in their prime reproductive years were the main victims of the kill suggests some kind of hunting strategy for SO2L. The high proportion of teeth 3 to 4 years old could be the result of an emphasis on bachelor-group hunting. But a rather different kind of explanation is also possible. That is, until now it has been assumed that survivorship and the rate of increase in the population from which SO2L was derived remained constant over a relatively long period of time. However, that is not necessarily the case. Changes in either of those two variables could have induced the pattern observed at SO2L. Caughley states that: 'A positive rate of increase is. . . generated by lowering density, thereby increasing the resources available to the survivors' (Caughley 1977: 175). For example, if survivorship had been low in the first years of life for the cohorts now 6 to 8 years old, then when conditions had improved, the rate of increase would rise because of the increased resources per head. That increase might perhaps be reflected in the high proportion of teeth 3 to 6 years old. The low proportion of teeth 0 to 3 years old could result from low fertility in age classes older than 6 years or from the return of unfavourable living conditions. Natural conditions, such as disease or drought, could generate such oscillations in the age structure. Alternatively, man could also effect such changes. Heavy predation of the cohorts over 6 years old during some stage in their development may have reduced population density to a level at which hunting was no longer practical. The ensuing low predation of the cohorts in the age classes 3 to 6 years and the increased resources available to them could have brought about the exceptionally high growth rate for those years.

It is not possible to prove that horses were not domesticated at SO2L (or any other prehistoric site for that matter); however, the data fit a hunting strategy far more satisfactorily. The general context of the deposit suggests that the main technique employed was herd driving – possibly into an enclosure against the cliff face (Levine 1979).

*Comparing large and small assemblage units*
Small assemblage units do not have the same value as large ones because the role of chance is so much greater where small samples are concerned. However it has been demonstrated that pooling assemblage units, including small ones, will often provide useful insights into the general structure of the data. Figures 4.22 and 4.23 show the unadjusted and adjusted age distributions for all large assemblage units pooled (those with 150 or more teeth), and for all small assemblage units pooled (those with fewer than 150 teeth).

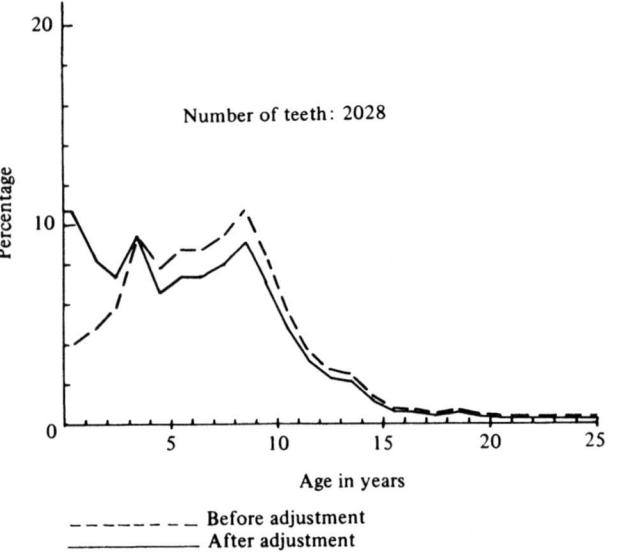

Fig. 4.22. Tooth age distribution – large assemblage units pooled (those with 150 or more teeth).

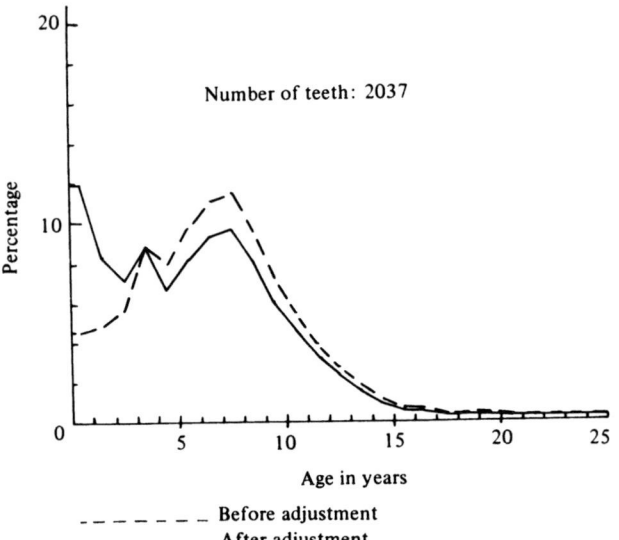

Fig. 4.23. Tooth age distribution – small assemblage units pooled (those with fewer than 150 teeth).

The distributions for the large pooled assemblage unit and the small pooled assemblage unit are remarkably similar to one another and to the life assemblage model. That is, on average, both large and small units seem to withdraw a representative sample from the living population.

*The clustering of assemblage units*
A cluster analysis is used here to show variability among units of all sizes. The variables employed are the descriptive statistics: the mean, standard deviation, skewness and kurtosis. These four statistics taken together define most of the shape of the age distribution. They are the most convenient variables because they can be used to describe any assemblage unit containing ageable teeth, even when the sample is very small. The cluster analysis techniques used here are the Ward's

Table 4.4. *Cluster unit size and chronology*

| Cluster unit | | Assemblage unit | Geological period | Industry | Number of ageable teeth | Mean number of ageable teeth |
|---|---|---|---|---|---|---|
| IA | 1 | CG11 | Würm II | Denticulate Mousterian | 91 | |
| | 13 | CG29 | Würm II | Typical Mousterian | 9 | |
| | 5 | CG20 | Würm II | Denticulate Mousterian | 19 | |
| | 31 | PA01 | surface | | 8 | |
| | | | | Total | 127 | 31.8 |
| IB | 27 | MO03 | Late Würm | Magdalenian VI | 84 | |
| | 28 | MO04 | Late Würm | Magdalenian VI | 73 | |
| | 58 | FG15 | Late Glacial | Late Magdalenian | 160 | |
| | 62 | AR01 | Late Würm | Magdalenian | 117 | |
| | 44 | JA01 | Würm II, III or II/III | | 498 | |
| | 67 | GI39 | Middle Würm | Typical Mousterian | 10 | |
| | 68 | GI49 | Middle Würm | Typical Mousterian | 43 | |
| | 3 | CG14 | Würm II | Denticulate Mousterian | 340 | |
| | 24 | CG70 | Würm II | Quina Mousterian | 40 | |
| | 15 | CG37 | Würm II | Typical Mousterian | 8 | |
| | 18 | CG50 | Würm I | Typical Mousterian | 65 | |
| | 37 | PA42 | Würm I | Denticulate Mousterian | 24 | |
| | 42 | F202 | Upper Pleistocene | | 52 | |
| | 40 | CSJ0 | Riss | | 14 | |
| | | | | Total | 1528 | 109.1 |
| IC | 72 | SO3P | Würm IV | Final Magdalenian | 364 | |
| | 30 | MO12 | Late Würm | Magdalenian VI | 66 | |
| | 70 | SO2L | Würm III | Upper Perigordian | 257 | |
| | 4 | CG15 | Würm II | Denticulate Mousterian | 45 | |
| | 6 | CG21 | Würm II | Quina Mousterian | 39 | |
| | 8 | CG23 | Würm II | Quina Mousterian | 140 | |
| | 49 | RM06 | Early to Middle Würm | Typical Mousterian | 47 | |
| | 20 | CG52 | Würm I | Typical Mousterian | 38 | |
| | 34 | PA07 | Riss | Acheulian | 41 | |
| | | | | Total | 1037 | 115.2 |
| IIA | 29 | MO05 | Late Würm | Magdalenian V | 35 | |
| | 59 | BL23 | Late Würm | Proto-Magdalenian | 84 | |
| | 2 | CG12 | Würm II | Denticulate Mousterian | 11 | |
| | 7 | CG22 | Würm II | Quina Mousterian | 152 | |
| | 11 | CG27 | Würm II | Ferrassie-type Mousterian | 26 | |
| | 56 | RM21 | Early to Middle Würm | Quina Mousterian | 16 | |
| | 53 | RM11 | Early to Middle Würm | Quina Mousterian | 52 | |
| | 50 | RM07 | Early to Middle Würm | Typical Mousterian | 48 | |
| | 48 | RM05 | Early to Middle Würm | Typical Mousterian | 40 | |
| | 45 | RM02 | Early to Middle Würm | Denticulate Mousterian | 3 | |
| | 16 | CG40 | Würm I | Typical Mousterian | 9 | |
| | 35 | PA08 | Riss I | Acheulian | 51 | |
| | 36 | PA09 | Riss I | Acheulian | 46 | |
| | | | | Total | 573 | 44.1 |

Table 4.4. continued.

| Cluster unit | | Assemblage unit | Geological period | Industry | Number of ageable teeth | Mean number of ageable teeth |
|---|---|---|---|---|---|---|
| IIB | 71 | SO3N | Würm IV | Final Magdalenian | 43 | |
| | 60 | BL27 | Late Würm | Proto-Magdalenian | 35 | |
| | 61 | BL30 | Late Würm | Proto-Magdalenian | 7 | |
| | 69 | SO1M | Würm III | Lower Aurignacian | 57 | |
| | 9 | CG24 | Würm II | Quina Mousterian | 30 | |
| | 12 | CG28 | Würm II | Typical Mousterian | 6 | |
| | 14 | CG35 | Würm II | Ferrassie-type Mousterian | 32 | |
| | 65 | GI20 | Middle Würm | Typical Mousterian | 16 | |
| | 55 | RM19 | Early to Middle Würm | Quina Mousterian | 15 | |
| | 57 | RM29 | Early to Middle Würm | Quina Mousterian | 47 | |
| | 54 | RM12 | Early to Middle Würm | Quina Mousterian | 14 | |
| | 51 | RM09 | Early to Middle Würm | Quina Mousterian | 59 | |
| | 47 | RM04 | Early to Middle Würm | Typical Mousterian | 25 | |
| | 32 | PA04 | Würm I | Typical Mousterian | 4 | |
| | | | | Total | 390 | 27.9 |
| IIC | 26 | MO01 | Late Würm | Magdalenian VI | 54 | |
| | 10 | CG25 | Würm II | Quina Mousterian | 33 | |
| | 52 | RM10 | Early to Middle Würm | Quina Mousterian | 30 | |
| | 46 | RM03 | Early to Middle Würm | Denticulate Mousterian | 10 | |
| | 17 | CG47 | Würm I | Mousterian | 9 | |
| | 25 | CG98 | Würm I | Typical Mousterian | 20 | |
| | 19 | CG51 | Würm I | Typical Mousterian | 7 | |
| | 22 | CG56 | Riss III | Upper Acheulian | 6 | |
| | 66 | GI29 | Würm I | Typical Mousterian | 8 | |
| | 63 | GI18 | Würm I | Typical Mousterian | 8 | |
| | 64 | GI19 | Würm I | Typical Mousterian | 9 | |
| | 38 | PA43 | Würm I | Typical Mousterian | 13 | |
| | 39 | PA51 | Würm I ? | almost sterile | 2 | |
| | 33 | PA06 | Riss II | Acheulian | 51 | |
| | 41 | F123 | Riss | | 18 | |
| | 43 | F203 | probably Upper Pleistocene | | 7 | |
| | | | | Total | 285 | 17.0 |

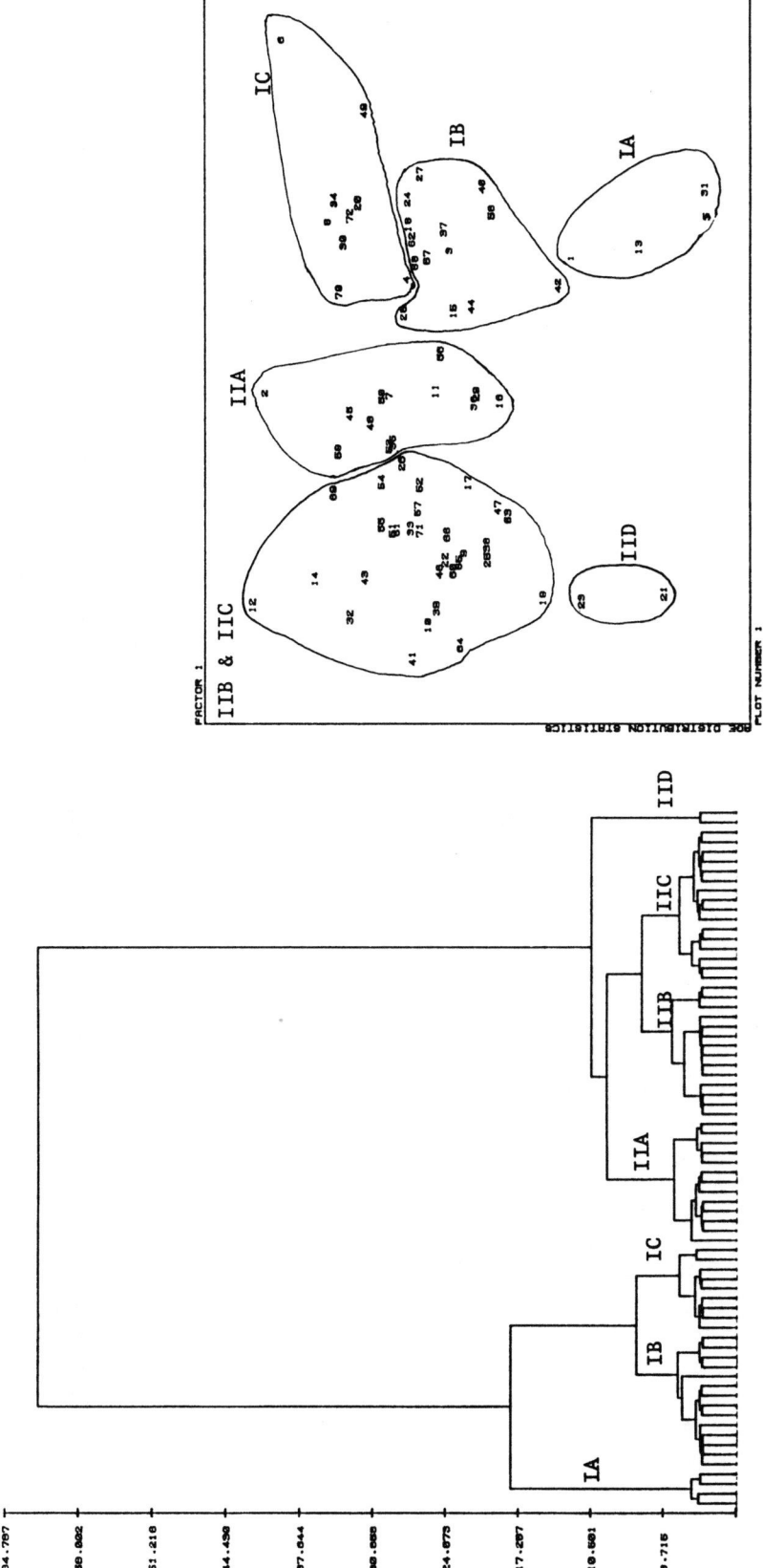

Fig. 4.24. Cluster analysis of tooth age distribution statistics (data in table 4.4).

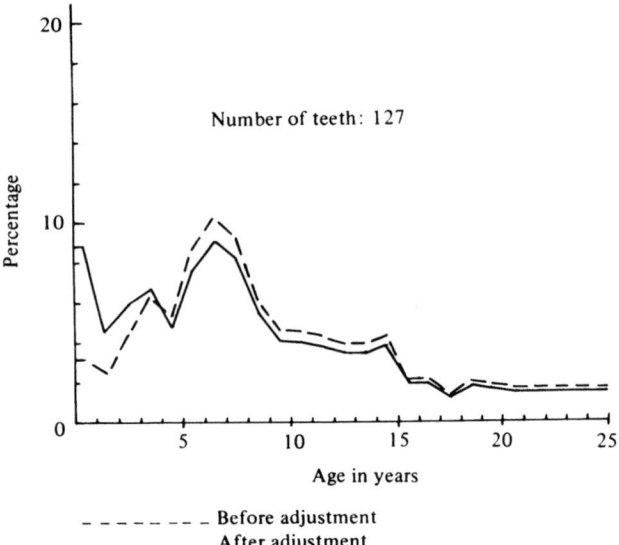

Fig. 4.25. Tooth age distribution – cluster unit IA.

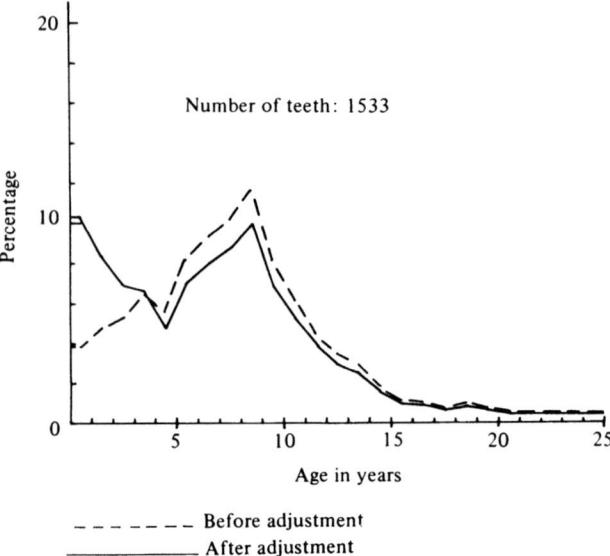

Fig. 4.26. Tooth age distribution – cluster unit IB.

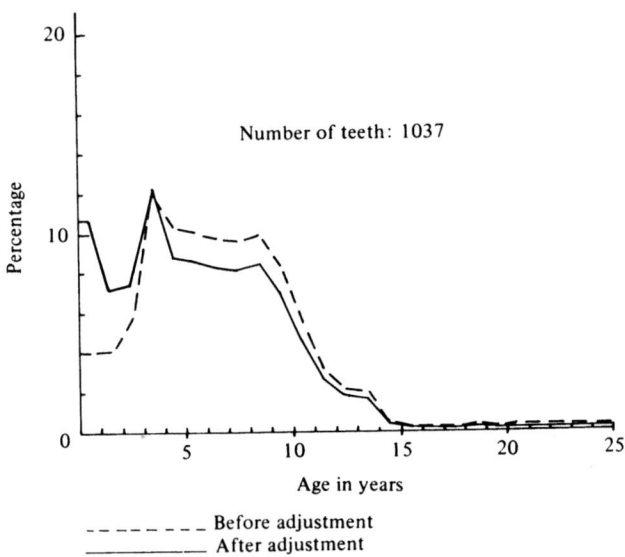

Fig. 4.27. Tooth age distribution – cluster unit IC.

Method dendrogram and a scatter diagram based upon a principal components analysis (Ward 1963; Wishart 1975; Levine 1979; fig. 4.24).

Assemblage units with data occupying fewer than ten columns (ten is an arbitrary, but plausible number) of the histogram are excluded from the cluster analysis. In that case the probability would have been high that all the teeth in that unit would have come from only a very few animals. If that were so, the statistics would be measuring the accuracy of the ageing technique rather than the shape of the age distribution. Of the 23 assemblage units thus excluded from the cluster analysis, 17 have an MNI of 1 and the rest of 2 or 3. Seventy-two assemblage units are suitable for inclusion in the cluster analysis in table 4.4.

According to the scatter diagram, not even the two main clusters identified by Ward's Method are discretely separate from one another. This suggests that the units do not easily fall into types. However, when the data from the 'clustered' units are pooled and histograms from that data plotted, some interesting distributions are generated.

*Cluster IA* (fig. 4.25). Cluster IA, with 127 ageable teeth, is the smallest of the clusters discussed here. It comprises only four assemblage units (IID contains only 8 ageable teeth and is therefore not discussed at all). Only one unit has more than 100 teeth; it accounts for 91 (or 72%) of the ageable teeth. The age distribution for IA is relatively flat – especially when the data are adjusted. The proportion of senescent teeth is unusually high. The percentage of teeth 0 to 3 years old is low by comparison with the pooled archaeological assemblage unit. However the preservation state of all these deposits is relatively poor. Such a small sample allows only for provisional interpretation. However it can be said that this age distribution resembles a somewhat flattened life assemblage model. It might reflect the hunting of rather aged family groups, random

stalking with an emphasis upon adults, trapping (some traps only capture adults), or stalking and scavenging.

*Cluster IB* (fig. 4.26). With 1533 ageable teeth, cluster IB is much larger than IA. The relevant units are relatively large. Four have over 100 ageable teeth; six have 40 to 100; and only four have less than 40. The overall pattern for this cluster is that of an almost ideal aggregate of family groups.

*Cluster IC* (fig. 4.27). Cluster IC is composed of 1037 ageable teeth. None of the assemblage units included here is very small. Three have over 100 ageable teeth, and the rest contain 38 or more each. Aside from the low proportion of teeth 0 to 3 years old and the rather high proportion 3 to 4

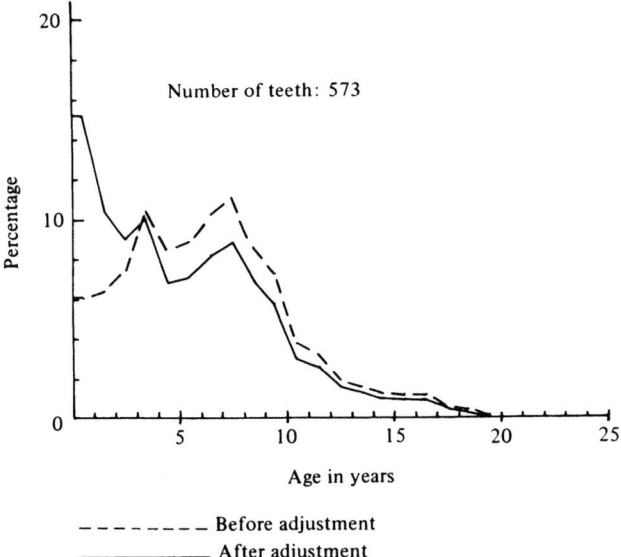

Fig. 4.28. Tooth age distribution – cluster unit IIA.

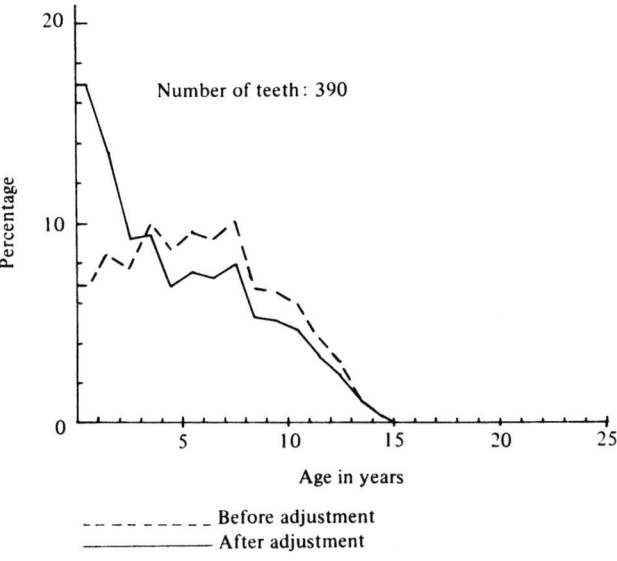

Fig. 4.29. Tooth age distribution – cluster unit IIB.

years old, the adjusted age distribution for this cluster is consistent with the life assemblage model.

*Cluster IIA* (fig. 4.28). The constituent assemblage units of clusters IIA–C are, on average, smaller than those of IA–C. Moreover the average size of the units comprising each cluster decreases from IIA to IIC.

Cluster IIA is composed of a relatively large number of medium to small assemblage units. Only one of these units contains more than 100 ageable teeth. Six contain 40 to 100, and six contain less than 40 each. IIA is then a cluster of medium-size assemblage units. The histogram for this cluster closely resembles the life assemblage model, although teeth 3 to 4 years old are somewhat over-represented and teeth 4 to 6 years old somewhat under-represented as in the pooled archaeological assemblage unit.

*Cluster IIB* (fig. 4.29). Cluster IIB comprises more assemblage units, but fewer teeth than IIA and it resembles the life assemblage model perhaps even more closely than does IIA. Apparently all age classes are sampled according to their representation in the whole population (rather than just the family group). The individuals comprising these assemblage units may have accumulated through any agency operating randomly or representatively on the whole population. Opportunistic stalking, trapping or driving could have produced the manifested pattern.

*Cluster IIC* (fig. 4.30). Cluster IIC is composed of a relatively large number of small and very small assemblage units. The age distribution as regards the archaeological units in this cluster is particularly interesting, because it so markedly fits the stalking model (fig. 4.8). That is, it contains a low proportion of teeth less than 3 years old and greater than 10 years old, but a high proportion between 3 and 10 years old. It looks very much as if the hunters responsible for these tooth deposits were choosing large, prime adults.

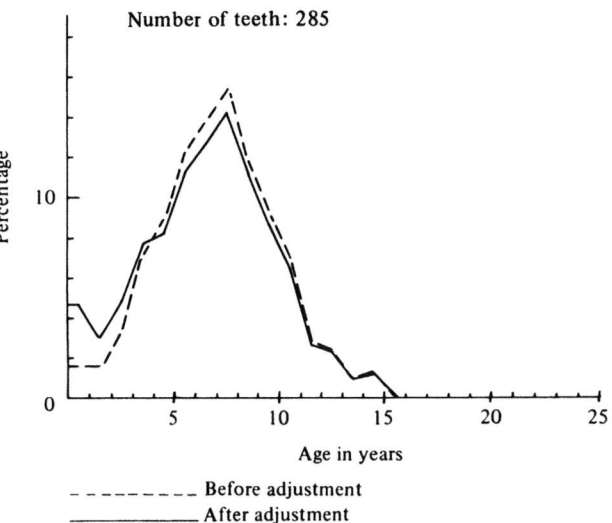

Fig. 4.30. Tooth age distribution – cluster unit IIC.

### Age distribution and chronology

On the whole it appears that the type of age distribution manifested by a particular assemblage unit is not linked to its chronology (table 4.4). This is not surprising, since all the hunting techniques needed should have been well within human capabilities throughout all the time periods relevant here. That various strata within one site seem to have similar age distributions – for example, belong to the same cluster – could probably be explained by the site's ecology and the traditions of the human groups reoccupying it repeatedly over time. There may be some significance in the fact that cluster IIC includes a rather large proportion of Würm I assemblage units. However, such a temporal clustering may be chance (the site sample in reality being very small); or it may

be that the units cluster together because the tooth samples
for those units are small, rather than because of the particular
type of hunting strategy employed.

### Conclusion

The results of this age-distribution study are of particular
interest because they deal with one of the major problems of
Pleistocene archaeology — the question of the subsistence
level of Palaeolithic man. Throughout the development of the
discipline workers have taken various and often conflicting
points of view in their interpretations of Pleistocene man—
animal relationships (Perkins 1964, 1969; Higgs 1972; Sturdy
1972; Bahn 1978a; Levine 1979).

Comparison of fossil material with data from living
populations shows that the age classes best represented in the
archaeological assemblages studied here have been those of
mature animals. This pattern is most similar to that of the life
assemblage model in which each age class is represented as it
would be in a living population or as it would be if an
opportunistic hunting strategy were employed. This pattern is
in marked contrast to the attritional type of mortality pattern
predicted for a population of large domesticated ungulates.
These results have been repeated for individual assemblage
units whenever the samples have been large enough to be
compared with the models. Thus it may be concluded that the
age distribution patterns for the sites studied here are
characteristic of hunting, not pastoralism. This makes sense,
especially as the horse is not particularly suitable as a milk or
meat domesticate. It matures slowly and produces on average
only one offspring every two years. Historically its most
important function has been to provide transport; that is a
role in which individuals are almost never intentionally killed
during their prime reproductive years.

We must, then, ask why in some situations animals are
domesticated, while in others they are not. It cannot be
assumed that there was any more reason for Palaeolithic man
to have domesticated the horse than there has been for the
Hadza to domesticate the zebra. Since there can be no first-
hand knowledge of the earliest domestication of animals, we
cannot judge how, in the absence of prior knowledge about

domestication, such a concept would have evolved amongst
more or less isolated human groups. However, information
about contemporary and historical pastoralist groups indicates
that pastoralism is largely restricted to regions too marginal
for either cultivation or hunting. That is, animal domestication
would apparently have been necessary for those regions
to have been inhabited (Beardsley 1953). However, the
Pleistocene low latitude tundra and steppe, with its allegedly
tremendous carrying capacity, would not have been a marginal
environment for Palaeolithic hunters (Butzer 1971a). Hunting
would probably have been the most efficient strategy (in terms
of energy expenditure) by which to exploit such an
environment. There is little information available about the
relative energy inputs into the various subsistence strategies,
however. Paine states that 'what should be stressed is the
multiplicity of husbandry tasks, whereby the herd is handled
as a complex aggregation of assets. . . the principle of least
effort has no place in the pastoral adaptation. . . this is an
underlying difference between the herder and hunter' (Paine
1971: 161). This, of course, does not rule out the possibility
that Palaeolithic pastoralist adaptations were of a completely
different form from contemporary and historical ones.
However there is no evidence to support such a hypothesis.

*Acknowledgements*

I would like in particular to thank Geoff Bailey and Dan
Rubenstein, who read and criticized this study. For my fossil data I
was dependent upon the cooperation and hospitality of French
palaeontologists and archaeologists including: F. Prat, R. Delpech,
F. Bordes and M. Lenoir (Université de Bordeaux); J. Bouchud
(Institute de Paléontologie Humaine, Paris); F. Poplin (Muséum
National d'Histoire Naturelle, Paris); H. Delporte (Musée des Antiquités
Nationales); M. Vuillemey (Lons-le-Saunier); C. Mourer-Chauviré,
C. Guerin and M. Sirven (Université de Lyon); M. Philippe (Muséum
d'Histoire Naturelle de la Ville de Lyon); J. Combier (Directeur des
Antiquités Préhistoriques de la Circonscription Rhône-Alpes) and
P. Ayroles (assistant director at Solutre). I am also grateful to D.E.
Walters (A.R.C. Unit of Applied Biology, Cambridge) who advised me
about statistics; M.Z. Oakley and R. Stibbs (Cambridge University
Computing Service); and G.P. Smith. I would also like to thank Wolfson
College for financial assistance in the form of travelling grants.

Chapter 5

**The calculation and interpretation of ungulate age profiles from dental crown heights**
Richard G. Klein, Kathryn Allwarden and Cornelia Wolf

Analysis of a sample of known-age wapiti (North American red deer) indicates that the relationship between age and dental crown height is both close enough and systematic enough to estimate age from crown height, when the goal is simply to determine the broad age structure of a group of individuals. The wapiti data further indicate that the basic shape of an age profile can be readily approximated by estimating age using a set of theoretical assumptions about the relationship between age and crown height, when this cannot be established empirically. These assumptions will probably provide useful age profiles for most high-crowned ungulates, particularly for various cervids and bovids, all of which have teeth that are very similar to those of wapiti in shape and structure. The age profiles that result from age estimates based on crown heights allow inferences about how ancient people exploited a species, whether, for example, they stalked individuals or commonly trapped entire groups.

**Problems in sex and age determination**

High-crowned ungulates are the most common species in many, if not most, archaeological faunas, reflecting their persistent and widespread importance to human populations. In recent years, archaeologists have increasingly come to realize that the presence or abundance of an ungulate species by itself says little about how the species was exploited by the ancient inhabitants of a site. Much more pertinent are data on the age and sex composition of the species, from which it may be possible to deduce whether people hunted or herded it, and in either case the methods they used.

Although most ungulate species exhibit sexual dimorphism in bone morphology, size, or both, there are serious practical obstacles to estimating the sex ratio in most fossil ungulate samples. This is even true for the bovids and cervids, which are strikingly dimorphic in their horncores and antlers respectively. In all bovid and cervid species, females either lack these structures or have ones that are quite different from those of males in size or shape. The major problem is that many samples which are rich in other bony elements are poor in horncores or antlers, sometimes because they were not brought to a site (or were taken from it), but very often because they are particularly susceptible to destruction during post-depositional leaching, profile compaction, and so on. Female structures (or the portion of the skull that would bear them) are especially fragile, so that the sex ratio may become distorted in favour of males, even in large samples. The relative rarity of horncores or antlers at many sites, coupled with the possibility of selective addition or removal, leaves few samples in which they may be used to infer a reliable sex ratio.

An alternative method of determining the sex ratio derives from the fact that, in many species, bones of males are larger on average than their homologues in females (Boessneck and von den Driesch 1978, with references). The bones involved are often relatively durable, with little or no difference in durability between the sexes. The most useful bones are ones that bear weight (e.g. the metapodials), since they are the ones that will most clearly reflect larger male size. There is the difficulty, however, that even where a difference in mean size is evident, it is usually relatively small, and the sexes often overlap substantially in bone size. Except in very large samples, it is therefore difficult to demonstrate the presence of size bimodality due to sex, and it is even more difficult to argue that the proportional relationship of the modes reliably reflects the proportional representation of the sexes at the site. As a result, there have been few successful attempts to estimate the sex ratio from bone size bimodality in archaeological samples. Perhaps a more promising method when bones are relatively complete is the simultaneous use of multiple measurements to maximize the extent of separation between males and females. Bedord (1978) has illustrated this method with respect to metapodials of archaeological bison (*Bison bison*) from the western United States.

The determination of age is much less problematic than the determination of sex in fossil ungulates because the most appropriate parts — the teeth — are usually abundant in fossil samples, primarily due to their durability. Furthermore, with the exception of teeth from very young animals, teeth from individuals of different ages are about equally durable, so that post-depositional destructive processes are less likely to distort an age profile than a sex ratio. In any case, it is usually possible to evaluate the likelihood of significant distortion from the state of bone preservation and fragmentation, or more generally from the depositional context of a fossil sample.

There are three basic methods of estimating age from ungulate teeth (Morris 1972; Spinage 1973). The first is subjective comparison of the state of eruption and wear versus eruption and wear in a series of known-age specimens. The second involves counting the number of growth increments or 'annuli' present in dental cementum (or less commonly dentine). The third is the measurement of a dimension that clearly varies with age, particularly crown height.

Subjective comparison is problematic, partly because it depends on the ability of different investigators to reach the same subjective conclusion, and partly because it requires complete or nearly complete demi-mandibles or maxillae. In many archaeological samples, demi-mandibles or maxillae are rare, while isolated teeth are abundant. The principal difficulty with age determination via annuli counts is that it is destructive and time-consuming. Additionally, in many, perhaps most, fossil samples, only a small proportion of teeth will probably exhibit readily identifiable annuli (Spiess 1979; K.A., personal experience). Under the circumstances, we believe that the least problematic method of age determination in fossil ungulates is the measurement of a dental dimension, particularly crown height.

In a previous paper (Klein *et al.* 1981), we analysed a sample of known-age American red deer (*Cervus elaphus canadensis*) to show that ages estimated from crown heights closely approximate true ages, when both estimated and true ages are grouped into broad but still useful age classes. In this chapter we recapitulate and extend the earlier analysis to argue the point even more strongly and to show that certain 'theoretical' assumptions about dental attrition can be used to estimate age from crown height, even where an empirical relationship has not been established. Following common North American usage, we have referred to the American red deer as 'wapiti' to distinguish it clearly from the conspecific European form, *Cervus elaphus elaphus*.

### The relationship between age and crown height

As far as we know, the empirical relationship between age and crown height has not been thoroughly established for any high-crowned ungulate species. The principal reason is the rarity of large samples of known-age dentitions, particularly ones from a wide variety of age classes. In the absence of a sound body of empirical observations, the estimation of age from crown height requires some 'theoretical' assumptions on the nature and rate of crown attrition. In our work to this point, we have made the following assumptions:

(1) that reduction in crown height is roughly constant through the life of a tooth, that is, that the relationship between decreasing crown height and advancing age is approximately linear.

(2) that for a deciduous tooth, the chronological age of complete crown reduction — when the crown is all but worn away — is the age when the tooth is replaced by its permanent counterpart. For a permanent tooth, the chronological age of complete crown reduction is the age past which no individuals survive in the wild, sometimes known as 'potential ecological longevity'. The dental eruption/replacement schedule and 'potential ecological longevity' for most species may be obtained directly from wildlife biology publications or indirectly by inference from publications on closely related species of similar size.

(3) that the amount of crown height lost per unit time on a deciduous tooth equals the initial unworn crown height divided by the time interval between age of eruption (usually birth) and age of replacement by a permanent tooth. The amount of crown height lost per unit time on a permanent tooth equals the initial unworn crown height divided by the time interval between age of eruption and age at potential ecological longevity. Initial unworn crown height may usually be estimated from unworn or lightly worn teeth occurring in any sample that is large enough to warrant mortality profile construction. In our experience, individual variability in unworn crown heights within a local population of a species tends to be very limited, so that the mean in a fossil sample is an adequate estimate, even if it is based on very few specimens.

In our previous paper (Klein *et al.* 1981) we showed that these assumptions lead to the following age-prediction formulae:

For a deciduous tooth:    $AGE = AGEs - (AGEs/CHo) \times$ (crown height)

For a permanent tooth:    $AGE = AGEpel - [(AGEpel - AGEe)/CHo] \times$ (crown height) where AGEs is the age at which a deciduous tooth is shed, AGEe is the age at which a permanent tooth erupts, AGEpel is the age past which no individuals appear to survive in the wild ('potential ecological longevity'), and CHo is initial (unworn) crown height.

Among our various assumptions, perhaps the most questionable one is that the rate of crown attrition is constant throughout the life of a tooth. Spinage (1971, 1972, 1973) in particular has suggested that very early on, when the occlusal surface of a tooth is roughest, crown reduction will be relatively rapid, while much later, when the occlusal surface has become quite smooth, wear will proceed very slowly. Only in mid-life will wear occur at a more or less constant rate. In order to accommodate a rate of wear which varies in this way, Spinage has proposed age-estimation formulae that have the following form, when they are expressed using the terms we have used above:

For a deciduous tooth: $\text{AGE} = \text{AGEs}[(\text{crown height} - \text{CHo})/\text{CHo}]^2$

For a permanent tooth: $\text{AGE} = (\text{AGEpel} - \text{AGEe})[(\text{crown height} - \text{CHo})/\text{CHo}]^2 + \text{AGEe}$

The two sets of theoretical formulae may be algebraically rewritten to take the following generalized form:

For a constant rate of wear: $\text{AGE} = a - b(\text{CH})$

For a variable rate of wear of the kind suggested by Spinage: $\text{AGE} = a - c(\text{CH}) + d(\text{CH})^2$

where 'a' is the age at which crown height reaches '0' (age shed for a deciduous tooth, 'potential ecological longevity' for a permanent one), and 'b', 'c', and 'd' are constants that reflect the rate of crown reduction. They are derived from appropriate algebraic combinations of initial (unworn) crown height (CHo) and age shed, age erupted, and/or age at potential ecological longevity, depending upon the tooth.

The age-estimation formulae incorporating a, b, c and d are identical in algebraic form to linear and quadratic regressions of age on crown height that can be calculated from a sample of known-age animals. It follows that the regressions may be used to evaluate the theoretical formulae, assuming that the regressions themselves provide a reasonable means of estimating age from crown height. The next section is devoted to an analysis of the relevant regressions in a sample of known-age wapiti, and the regressions are compared to the corresponding 'theoretical' formulae in the following section. We should emphasize that the choice of wapiti as a test species was determined entirely by the availability of the known-age sample, and there is no a priori reason to suppose that wapiti ages should be better estimated from the theoretical formulae than those of any other hypsodont ungulate. The wapiti case thus represents a reasonable test of the general utility of the theoretical estimation formulae, at least as applied to bovids and cervids, all of which have teeth that are very similar in shape and structure to those of wapiti.

### Age and crown height in a known-age sample of wapiti

Our known-age wapiti sample is essentially the same one that was used by Quimby and Gaab (1957) to demonstrate the utility of subjective eruption and wear as age criteria in wapiti. The sample, to which a few individuals have been added since Quimby's and Gaab's study, is currently housed in the Department of Wildlife Biology at Montana State University, where one of us (C.W.) made the measurements analysed below.

The sample comprises 170 measurable individuals, ranging in age from approximately half a year (5 months) to approximately $21\frac{1}{2}$ years (260 months). Ages were known from tagging shortly after birth by the Montana Fish and Game Department, the U.S. Park Service, or the U.S. Forest Service. All the wapiti came from the general vicinity of Yellowstone National Park, though mainly from outside it. Most were hunters' kills, but some were found dead of natural causes. In a few instances, sex had not been recorded and could not be judged directly, because the part of the skull that bears the antlers (present only in males) had been removed. We suspect these were mainly trophy males, but we have treated them as 'sex unknown'. Up to the age of about $5\frac{1}{2}$ years there was about an equal number of males and females, but older animals of known sex were almost exclusively females (table 5.1). The reason may be that hunters often failed to turn in the skulls of older males.

The sample was collected over several years, but always between October and January (the hunting season). Since Yellowstone wapiti are almost all born between mid-May and mid-June, this means that individual ages form a series of discrete age clusters, each spanning 3–4 months, and separated by gaps of 8–9 months from adjacent clusters (table 5.1 and figs. 5.2 and 5.3). The youngest age cluster has an approximate mean age of $\frac{1}{2}$ year, the next oldest of $1\frac{1}{2}$ years, and so forth. This means the sample can be used to evaluate the extent to which the crown heights of archaeological wapiti might be used to determine seasonality in site occupation (see below).

The crown height measurement we use is illustrated in figure 5.1. It is the minimum distance between the occlusal surface and the line separating the enamel of the crown from the dentine of the roots, measured on the buccal surface of mandibular teeth and on the lingual surface of maxillary ones. On multilobed teeth, we make the measurement on the anteriormost lobe. The measurement is readily made on isolated teeth, but can be problematic on ones that are still set in jaws, because the line separating the enamel of the crown from the dentine of the roots may be masked by jaw bone. In wapiti, for example, this is generally true of first molars ($M_1$) in individuals under $2\frac{1}{2}$ years, and of second molars ($M_2$) and third molars ($M_3$) in individuals under $5\frac{1}{2}$ years of age. This is the reason that the number of 'measurable' wapiti $M_1$, $M_2$ and $M_3$ teeth in table 5.1 is smaller than the number of individuals in the youngest age categories. Although in this instance we simply had to ignore crowns partially masked by jaw bone, in others we have found that the crown base may be readily revealed either by X-ray photography or

Table 5.1. *The numbers of males, females, and individuals of both sexes in each cohort represented in the sample of known-age wapiti, compared to the numbers of individuals on which the crown heights of* $dP_4$, $M_1$, $M_2$ *and* $M_3$ *could be measured*

| Age cohorts (in years) | Males | Females | Males, females and unknowns | Measurable | | | |
|---|---|---|---|---|---|---|---|
| | | | | $dP_4$ | $M_1$ | $M_2$ | $M_3$ |
| $\frac{1}{2}$ (5–10 mths) | 26 | 15 | 41 | 41 | – | – | – |
| $1\frac{1}{2}$ (17–20 mths) | 19 | 18 | 39 | 39 | 20 | – | – |
| $2\frac{1}{2}$ (27–32 mths) | 9 | 10 | 25 | 3 | 25 | – | – |
| $3\frac{1}{2}$ (40–44 mths) | 4 | 17 | 24 | – | 24 | 6 | 2 |
| $4\frac{1}{2}$ (53–56 mths) | 6 | 6 | 14 | – | 14 | 7 | 2 |
| $5\frac{1}{2}$ (65–68 mths) | 3 | 5 | 10 | – | 9 | 10 | 3 |
| $6\frac{1}{2}$ | – | – | – | – | – | – | – |
| $7\frac{1}{2}$ (92 mths) | – | 1 | 1 | – | 1 | 1 | 1 |
| $8\frac{1}{2}$ (101–104 mths) | – | 7 | 9 | – | 9 | 9 | 9 |
| $9\frac{1}{2}$ (113–114 mths) | – | 3 | 3 | – | 2 | 3 | 3 |
| $10\frac{1}{2}$ | – | – | – | – | – | – | – |
| $11\frac{1}{2}$ (138 mths) | – | 1 | 1 | – | 1 | 1 | 1 |
| $12\frac{1}{2}$ | – | – | – | – | – | – | – |
| $13\frac{1}{2}$ | – | – | – | – | – | – | – |
| $14\frac{1}{2}$ | – | – | – | – | – | – | – |
| $15\frac{1}{2}$ (185 mths) | 1 | 1 | 2 | – | – | 2 | 2 |
| $16\frac{1}{2}$ | – | – | – | – | – | – | – |
| $17\frac{1}{2}$ | – | – | – | – | – | – | – |
| $18\frac{1}{2}$ | – | – | – | – | – | – | – |
| $19\frac{1}{2}$ | – | – | – | – | – | – | – |
| $20\frac{1}{2}$ | – | – | – | – | – | – | – |
| $21\frac{1}{2}$ | – | 1 | 1 | – | – | – | – |
| Totals | 68 | 85 | 170 | 83 | 105 | 39 | 23 |

by careful incision to remove masking jaw bone. Both methods work best with mandibular dentitions. For this reason, and also because mandibular teeth are usually more common than maxillary ones in fossil samples, we generally rely on mandibular teeth to calculate age profiles.

In order to construct a complete age profile, it is necessary to have crown height measurements on a deciduous tooth and on a permanent tooth that erupts before the deciduous tooth is shed. In our experience with cervids and bovids, the most suitable teeth are generally the fourth deciduous premolar ($dP_4$) and one of the three permanent molars ($M_1$, $M_2$ or $M_3$). We completely ignore the incisors because they are usually much less abundant than cheek teeth in fossil samples, reflecting their relative fragility. They can also be difficult to assign to species, when two or more cervids or bovids of similar size are present in a sample. Finally, incisors appear to be much more variable in the rate of wear than cheek teeth, probably for reasons suggested by Spinage (1973). We also usually ignore the anteriormost premolars, whether deciduous ($dP_2$ and $dP_3$) or permanent ($P_2$ and $P_3$), both because they are generally less numerous than other cheek teeth in fossil samples and because they are more variable in their rate of wear.

The linear and quadratic regressions of wapiti age on crown height in our known-age samples of $dP_4$, $M_1$, $M_2$ and $M_3$ teeth are presented in figures 5.2 and 5.3 and on the left-hand side of table 5.3. These results are based on all measurable specimens, regardless of sex. We initially calculated the regressions separately for males and females, but found that the results were essentially the same when the male and female samples comprised approximately equal numbers of individuals in various age categories. This suggests that there are no essential differences between the sexes in the nature or rate of crown attrition. Mitchell *et al.* (1977) also found no difference in rate of wear between the sexes in Scottish red deer.

However, in a study of wapiti populations in four Canadian National Parks, Flook (1970) found that males in three of the parks appeared to wear their teeth more rapidly than females, while in the fourth park there was no obvious difference. Taken together, our findings, those of Mitchell *et al.*, and those of Flook, suggest that both the presence and extent of a difference may vary from place to place. We note, however, that Flook's samples did not involve known-age animals. Instead, he analysed the relationship between age estimated from subjective wear and eruption and age estimated from cementum annuli counts (the latter taken as 'true' age).

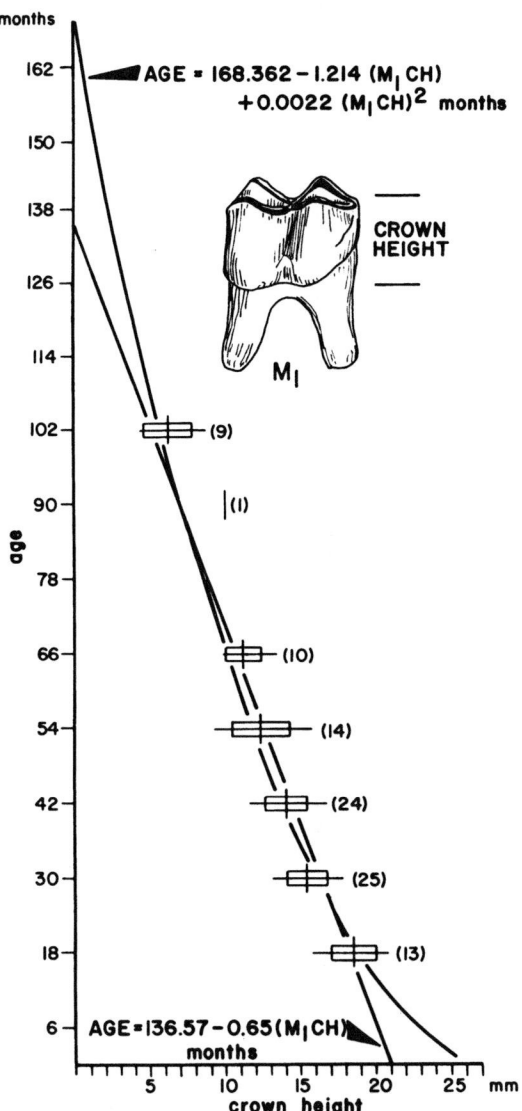

months

$$AGE = 168.362 - 1.214\,(M_1\,CH)$$
$$+\,0.0022\,(M_1\,CH)^2 \text{ months}$$

CROWN
HEIGHT

$M_1$

$$AGE = 136.57 - 0.65\,(M_1\,CH)$$
months

crown height

Fig. 5.1. The linear and quadratic regressions of age on $M_1$ crown height in the known-age sample of wapiti, plotted along with the mean (vertical line), range (horizontal line), and standard deviation (open bar) of $M_1$ crown height in successive yearly age cohorts. The number of measured specimens in each cohort is in parentheses. Note that mean $M_1$ crown height declines systematically with age, but variability (as reflected in the standard deviation) does not. For additional discussion see the text.

We regard our analysis based on crown heights in known-age animals as basically more reliable. Assuming that our results of little or no difference in wear rate between the sexes is the generally correct one, it is also opportune, since it is usually impossible to determine the sex of fossil ungulate teeth, including those of wapiti.

The general form of the linear and quadratic regression lines is illustrated in figure 5.1, using the lines calculated for age on $M_1$ crown height. The figure also includes the mean (vertical line), range (horizontal line), and standard deviation (open bar) of $M_1$ crown heights for each age class in the

known-age sample. The number of measured $M_1$ teeth in each age class is in parenthesis.

The absolute and relative merits of the various regressions can be evaluated from statistical parameters listed in table 5.2 and from examination of the prediction errors ('residuals') as displayed in figures 5.2 and 5.3. Particularly significant in table 5.2 are the coefficients of determination ($r^2$) and the standard errors of estimate (SEE). The first is a measure of the amount of variation in age 'accounted for' by crown height. The second is a measure of average prediction error.

The $r^2$ values are uniformly greater than 0.80, indicating that there is indeed a strong relationship between (advancing) age and (decreasing) crown height. However, the SEE values are quite large, particularly for the molars, indicating that crown height is not a very accurate predictor of individual age. The seeming contradiction is explained by the fact that variation in crown height within each age class is substantial, even though mean crown height declines systematically with age (these facts are illustrated for $M_1$ in figure 5.1).

The high SEE values only constitute a problem, however, if the goal is to predict individual age quite precisely. In archaeology, placement of an individual within a relatively broad age class is usually sufficient for interpretative purposes. The age class we find most useful is 10% of potential ecological longevity. For any given species this results in a sufficient number of classes (10) to define the basic shape of an age profile, which is what we focus on in interpretation (see below). The selection of 10% of potential life span has the further advantage that it permits direct comparisons among age profiles for species with different potential life spans.

Wapiti/red deer as old as 20 to 22 years are known, but they are rare individuals whose survival was probably made possible by human intervention, either direct or indirect. Mitchell *et al.* (1977) state that wild red deer do not live long after their first molar crown has worn away. Applied to our known-age wapiti, this would suggest a potential ecological longevity for wapiti/red deer of somewhat more than 14 years, in close agreement with the 15 to 16 years suggested by Flower (1931). We have taken 16 years (192 months) as the correct figure here, from which it follows that 10% of potential life span would be 19.2 months.

Figures 5.2 and 5.3 allow a visual assessment of the extent to which the regressions will place wapiti individuals in their correct 19.2 month age class. In each figure the true ages are plotted against prediction errors ('residuals'), calculated by subtracting predicted age from true age. An individual whose age has been perfectly predicted by a regression will lie directly on the '0' prediction-error line. An individual whose age has been underestimated will lie above this line, while one whose age has been overestimated will lie below it. An individual which has been placed in its correct 19.2 month life span segment will lie within 9.6 months ($\pm$ 19.2 $\div$ 2 months) of the '0' line. To aid visual assessment, the $\pm$ 9.6 month band has been shaded.

The figures show that the various regressions are in fact

## ROCKY MOUNTAIN ELK (*Cervus elaphus canadensis*)

AGE=32.40 - 0.23 (dP4 CH) months
AGE=36.686 - 0.345 (dP4CH) + 0.00069 (dP4CH)2 months
dP4
RESIDUALS (months)
AGE (months)

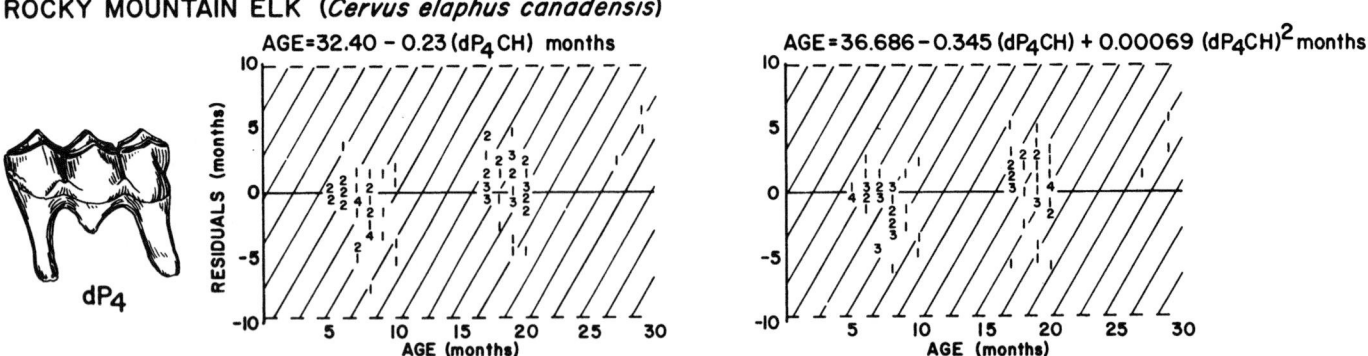

Fig. 5.2. True age plotted against true age minus estimated age ('residuals'), using a linear regression (left) and a quadratic regression (right) to estimate age from $dP_4$ crown height. Individuals whose ages were underestimated lie above it. All individuals which lie within the shaded bands had their ages estimated to within ±9.6 months of true age. For additional discussion see the text.

AGE = 136.57 - 0.65 (M1CH) months
AGE = 168.362 - 1.214 (M1CH) + 0.0022 (M1CH)2 months
M1
AGE = 186.45 - 0.69 (M2CH) months
AGE = 210.159 - 1.115 (M2CH) + 0.0016 (M2CH)2 months
M2
AGE = 207.73 - 0.70 (M3CH) months
AGE = 215.436 - 0.812 (M3CH) + 0.00039 (M3CH)2 months
M3
RESIDUALS (months)
AGE (months)

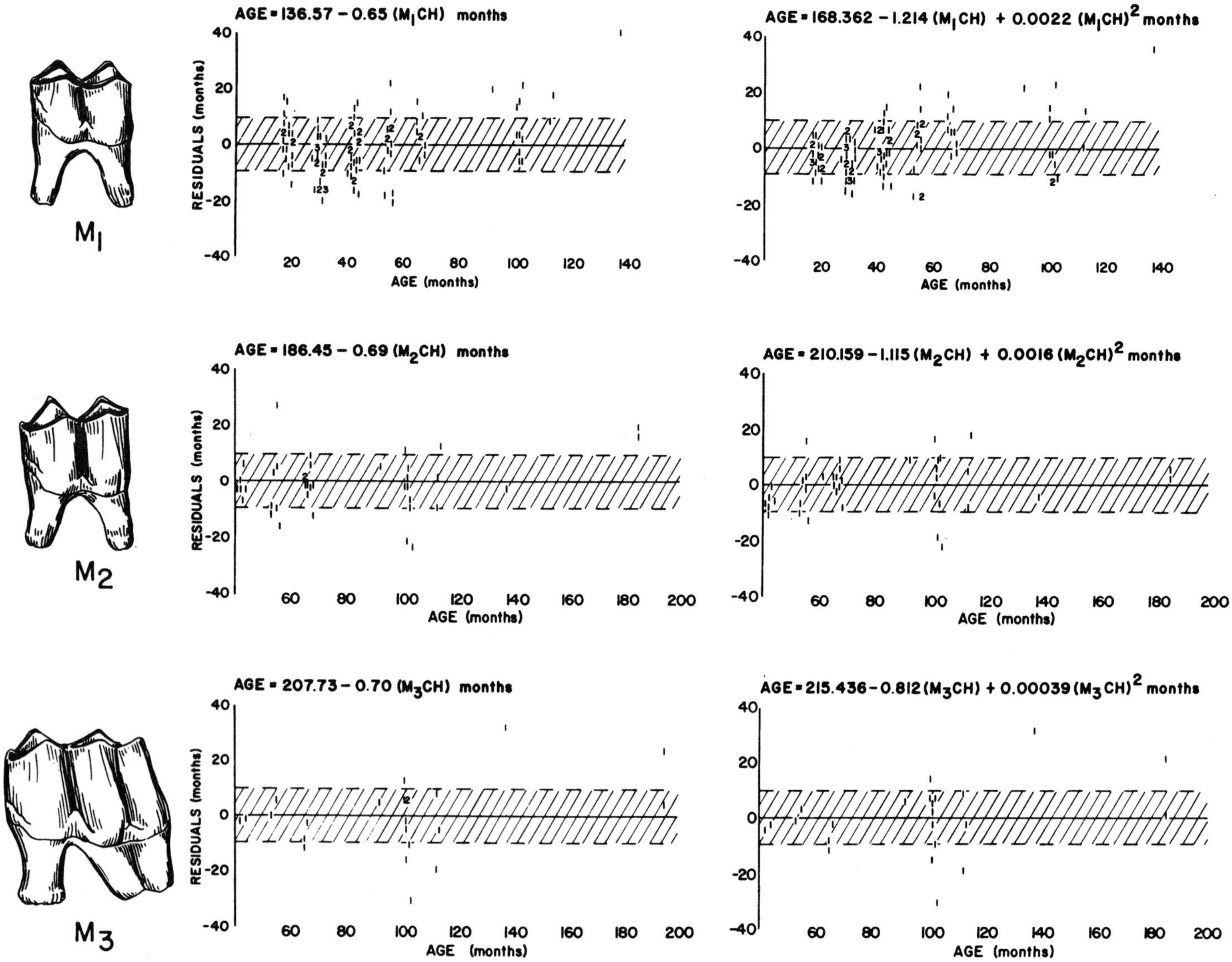

Fig. 5.3. True age plotted against true age minus estimated age ('residuals'), using linear regressions (left) and quadratic regressions (right) to estimate age from the crown heights of $M_1$, $M_2$, and $M_3$ respectively. Individuals whose ages were overestimated by the regressions lie below the 'O' line. Those whose ages were underestimated lie above it. All individuals which lie within the shaded bands had their ages estimated to within ±9.6 months of true age. For additional discussion, see the text.

Table 5.2. *The mean age, mean crown height, standard deviation of age, standard deviation of crown height, coefficient of determination (r²), standard error of estimate (SEE), and sample size associated with the linear and quadratic regressions of age on crown height discussed in the text*

|  | dP$_4$ | M$_1$ | M$_2$ | M$_3$ |
|---|---|---|---|---|
| Mean age (months) | 13.33 | 46.35 | 81.00 | 97.83 |
| Mean crown height (mm) | 8.28 | 13.84 | 15.26 | 15.81 |
| Standard deviation of age (months) | 6.46 | 26.86 | 35.64 | 37.40 |
| Standard deviation of crown height (mm) | 2.57 | 3.77 | 4.93 | 5.00 |
| Coefficient of determination (r²) |  |  |  |  |
| Linear regression | 0.84 | 0.84 | 0.92 | 0.86 |
| Quadratic regression | 0.84 | 0.86 | 0.93 | 0.87 |
| Standard error of estimate (SEE) (mths) |  |  |  |  |
| Linear regression | 2.60 | 10.85 | 10.48 | 14.07 |
| Quadratic regression | 2.59 | 10.07 | 9.53 | 14.35 |
| Sample size | 83 | 105 | 39 | 23 |

*Note*: the regressions and associated parameters were all calculated using the sub-programme REGRESSION from *Statistical Package for the Social Sciences* (Nie *et al.* 1975), as available on the University of Chicago's Amdahl 470 computer.

quite successful at placing individuals within their correct 19.2 month (10% of life span) age intervals. For dP$_4$, not a single individual was misplaced by either the linear or quadratic regressions. For the molars, however, misplacements do occur with both kinds of regression, and there is a general tendency for the proportion of misplacements to increase with age. This reflects the fact that as mean crown height decreases with age, variability in crown height does not (see figure 5.1 where this is quite clear for M$_1$). In other words, older individuals are relatively more variable in crown height than younger ones, progressively reducing the accuracy of crown height as an age estimator. It is important to note, however, that virtually all individuals which are not assigned to their correct age class are assigned to an immediately adjacent one. Equally important, the chances of over-prediction appear to be about the same as those of under-prediction, so that in large samples prediction errors would tend to cancel each other out. The figures certainly suggest no way in which the use of crown heights to estimate age could alter the basic shape of an age profile in a sample large enough to calculate one to begin with. And it is on basic profile shape that we focus in interpretation (see below).

Figure 5.2 suggests that it makes little difference whether a linear or quadratic formula is used to estimate age from dP$_4$, as long as the goal is simply correct assignment to a 19.2 month age class. However, figure 5.3 indicates that the quadratic formulae may be preferable for the molars, in that these formulae are less likely systematically to under-predict the ages of older individuals. This is exactly the result we would expect if the rate of dental attrition slows in old age, as

Spinage has suggested. It is probable that the quadratic regressions would have been clearly superior to the linear ones in both r² and SEE values, if our samples had included a larger number of older individuals.

**Comparison of the theoretical and regression equations**

The regressions for age on crown height in wapiti dP$_4$, M$_1$, M$_2$ and M$_3$ can be directly compared to the theoretical age-estimation formulae in table 5.3. The theoretical formulae were calculated assuming that wapiti potential ecological longevity is 192 months, that dP$_4$ is shed at 26 months, and that M$_1$, M$_2$ and M$_3$ erupt at 6, 12 and 30 months respectively (Quimby and Gaab 1957; Lowe 1967; Mitchell 1967). Initial (unworn) crown heights were taken as 14.0, 27.0, 29.2 and 31.0 mm for dP$_4$, M$_1$, M$_2$ and M$_3$ respectively. The figures were entered into the calculations without their decimal points (i.e. in tenths of a millimetre).

The table shows that the various regressions are generally quite similar to the corresponding theoretical formulae in the constants by which crown height (or crown height squared) is multiplied. The principal difference lies in the value for age when crown height is '0'. It will be remembered that in calculating the theoretical formulae this was automatically taken to be age shed for dP$_4$, and potential ecological longevity for the molars.

The differences in the value for age at crown height '0' are particularly striking for M$_1$, not only between each regression and its corresponding theoretical formula, but between the regressions themselves. The problem almost certainly derives from the fact that M$_1$ is the first of the molars to erupt and the lowest crowned. As a consequence, it becomes heavily worn long before potential ecological longevity and thereafter wears very slowly, as Spinage's wear model predicts. In other words, among the three molars, it is the one to which the assumption of a constant (linear) rate of wear is least applicable, leading to potentially serious age-estimation errors. The theoretical linear formula will seriously and systematically over-predict the ages of all (particularly younger) animals, while the linear regression will seriously and systematically under-predict those of older ones. For M$_1$ it is clear that age estimation is far more appropriately based on the quadratic model.

The choice for M$_2$ is less clear-cut. Because M$_2$ erupts later and is higher crowned than M$_1$, its rate of wear remains more nearly constant into advanced individual age. Therefore, for all but the very oldest individuals, the linear model will probably provide reasonable age estimates. The same is probably true for M$_3$, although final judgement on this should probably be deferred, given the relatively small number of measured M$_3$ teeth on which the regressions are based. From an archaeological perspective, the situation with regard to M$_3$ in wapiti is academic in any case, since the tooth erupts only after the deciduous teeth are shed. This means it may not be used in any attempt to construct a complete age profile. For this we must rely on M$_1$ and M$_2$.

Table 5.3. *Left. The linear and quadratic regressions of age on crown height in wapiti* $dP_4$, $M_1$, $M_2$, *and* $M_3$. *Right. The corresponding 'theoretical' age-estimation formulae, assuming constant and variable rates of wear respectively*

| Regressions | Theoretical Formulae |
|---|---|
| $dP_4$ | |
| $AGE = 32.4 - 0.23\,(CH)$ | $AGE = 26 - 0.19\,(CH)$ |
| $AGE = 36.69 - 0.345\,(CH) + 0.00069\,(CH)^2$ | $AGE = 26 - 0.371\,(CH) + 0.0013\,(CH)^2$ |
| $M_1$ | |
| $AGE = 136.57 - 0.65\,(CH)$ | $AGE = 192 - 0.68\,(CH)$ |
| $AGE = 168.36 - 1.214\,(CH) + 0.0022\,(CH)^2$ | $AGE = 192 - 1.378\,(CH) + 0.0026\,(CH)^2$ |
| $M_2$ | |
| $AGE = 186.45 - 0.69\,(CH)$ | $AGE = 192 - 0.61\,(CH)$ |
| $AGE = 210.16 - 1.115\,(CH) + 0.0016\,(CH)^2$ | $AGE = 192 - 1.216\,(CH) + 0.0021\,(CH)^2$ |
| $M_3$ | |
| $AGE = 207.73 - 0.70\,(CH)$ | $AGE = 192 - 0.52\,(CH)$ |
| $AGE = 215.44 - 0.812\,(CH) + 0.00039\,(CH)^2$ | $AGE = 192 - 1.045\,(CH) + 0.0017\,(CH)^2$ |

For $dP_4$, both regressions suggest that '0' crown height would only be achieved if the tooth remained in the mouth beyond the age (26 months) when it is generally shed. Assuming a constant rate of wear, the linear regression in fact suggests that '0' crown height would only be reached at 32.4 months. It will be remembered that 'age at crown height = 0' plays a role in the calculation of the constant(s) by which crown height is multiplied. In our earlier paper, we pointed out that substituting 32.4 months for 26 months in calculating the theoretical linear formula changes the constant by which crown height is multiplied to 0.23. In other words, the theoretical formula becomes identical to the linear regression. Now, 32.4 months is approximately 25% greater than 26 months. Since it is likely that a comparable difference between 'age shed' and 'age at crown height = 0' characterizes deciduous teeth in various species, we suggested that the theoretical formula for predicting age from $dP_4$ crown height might be better given as:

$$AGE = 1.25\,AGEs - (1.25\,AGEs/CHo)(\text{crown height})$$

It is tempting to use the regressions for the molars to correct the corresponding theoretical formulae in a similar way. The basic rationale for this would be that the regressions provide more accurate estimates of the age when the crown height of each molar will approach '0'. The regressions make it clear that this happens substantially earlier in $M_1$ than in $M_2$ or $M_3$, an observation which is readily verified by direct examination of wapiti jaws.

However, we do not feel that the regressions are sufficiently well founded to warrant using them to refine the theoretical formulae. This is particularly true for the regressions of age on crown height in $M_2$ and $M_3$, which are based on relatively few specimens. More importantly from an archaeological perspective, it is not vital to develop theoretical formulae that predict individual age as accurately as possible. Rather we will be satisfied with ones that will reveal the basic

age structure or profile of a sample of individuals. It will be recalled that the regressions do this quite well when estimated ages are grouped into 10% of life-span classes. For the most part, the theoretical formulae are similar enough to the regressions to argue that they will provide the same basic profile shape. The only theoretical formula which may be seriously flawed in this respect is the linear one for $M_1$, and we do not recommend its usage.

We see no reason to choose between the linear and quadratic formulae for $dP_4$, either of which will probably provide reasonable results, when estimated ages are grouped into 10% of life-span classes. Generally speaking, the quadratic formulae for $M_2$ and $M_3$ are perhaps preferable to the linear ones, since they implicitly reflect the variable rate of wear which is probably characteristic of all hypsodont ungulate teeth. However, the linear formulae (based on the assumption of a constant rate of wear) will probably provide basically the same profile shape in most cases. The exceptions will be samples in which there are large numbers of lightly worn crowns (wearing more rapidly than average) or heavily worn ones (wearing less rapidly). In such cases, the linear and quadratic formulae might provide quite different results, and only the quadratic one should probably be used. A further point this raises is that no age profile should be presented without the crown heights on which it is based. This will permit a reader to evaluate the likelihood that a formula used to convert crown heights to ages has seriously distorted basic profile shape.

**The construction and interpretation of age profiles**

Kurtén (1953) and Voorhies (1969) laid the foundations for the construction and interpretation of age profiles for hypsodont ungulates in fossil samples. There have been many fruitful applications of the methodology, of which the best known archaeological examples are undoubtedly those involving bison at a series of prehistoric sites in western North

America (Frison 1978, with references). One of us (R.G.K.) has applied the methodology to a wide variety of African ungulates (Klein 1978, 1979, in press (a) and in press (b)) for which age profiles were based on estimates of age from crown height using the theoretical formulae discussed in this chapter.

As examples of age-profile construction and interpretation here, we offer data on red deer from levels 4 and 6 at the Magdalenian III site of El Juyo, near Santander in northern Spain (Freeman and Echegaray, in prep.), and from the famous Mesolithic (Maglemosian) site of Star Carr, North Yorkshire, England (J.G.D. Clark 1954, 1972). The red deer ages in each sample were estimated from $dP_4$ and $M_1$ crown heights, using the theoretical quadratic estimation formulae for each tooth. Crown heights in the El Juyo samples were measured by R.G.K.; those in the Star Carr sample by K.A. On analogy with extant red deer, the age estimation formulae were derived on the assumption that $dP_4$ was shed at about 26 months, $M_1$ erupted at about 6 months, and potential ecological longevity was about 192 months. Initial $dP_4$ and $M_1$ crown heights were taken as 12.4 and 23.1 mm for El Juyo and as 9.3 and 22.5 mm for Star Carr. The difference reflects the fact that the Star Carr deer were significantly smaller on average than the El Juyo ones. The ages estimated from crown heights were grouped into 19.2 month (10% of life span) classes. The number of individuals represented in each of the two youngest classes, for which both $dP_4$ and $M_1$ provided estimated ages, was taken to be the larger number, whether suggested by $dP_4$ or $M_1$.

The resulting age profiles and the crown height measurements on which they are based, are presented graphically in figure 5.4. The profiles from the two El Juyo levels are essentially identical. In both, individuals in the first 10% of life span predominate, and there are progressively fewer individuals in each succeeding life span segment. This is reminiscent of the age structure of a stable live population of large mammals, referred to by Voorhies (1969) as 'catastrophic', since it is what would result if the entire population were suddenly wiped out by a great flood, volcanic eruption, epidemic disease, or similar catastrophic event. In an archaeological context, a catastrophic age profile suggests a hunting method which did not discriminate among individuals on the basis of their age. In the case of a gregarious ungulate like the red deer, the most likely method is driving into corrals, deep snow, or some other trap where all individuals in a group could be dispatched at once. Given the shape of the age profiles, we hypothesize that the El Juyo Magdalenians obtained red deer primarily, if not exclusively, by driving.

If the El Juyo people had obtained red deer mainly by stalking individuals, the archaeological age profiles would probably be much richer in old individuals (beyond 40 or 50% of potential life span) and poorer in prime-age adults (between 10% and 40–50% of life span). This is because stalking is inherently more likely to net the weakest or least wary individuals – the old and the very young. Voorhies has referred to an age profile dominated by the very young and

the old as 'attritional', because it is what results from accidents, endemic disease, day-to-day predation and other essentially attritional causes of mortality in a population of large mammals. One of us (R.G.K.) has documented attritional profiles in samples of ungulates from African archaeological sites (Klein 1978, 1979), but we have been unable to locate a clear example of an attritional profile in archaeological red deer. We have presented an idealized or theoretical attritional profile in the upper right-hand corner of figure 5.4, where its relationship to a catastrophic profile is also illustrated.

It is important to emphasize that 'catastrophic' and 'attritional' as we have used them here (following Voorhies) refer to overall profile shape and not to the precise numerical content of the age classes within a profile. Different species, even populations within a species, will vary in the precise content of the age classes, depending on their reproductive pattern and the causes of mortality to which they are exposed (Caughley 1966). Equally important, both chance variation ('sampling error') and the inaccuracy inherent in our age-estimation method are far more likely to affect the precise number of individuals in a particular age class than the fundamental shape of an age profile.

The Star Carr profile is interesting because it is neither 'catastrophic' nor 'attritional'. It bears some resemblance to a catastrophic profile, except that there are relatively few individuals in the first 10% of life span. We have observed similar profiles in other fossil samples, where the poor quality of bone preservation suggests that the jaws of the youngest animals may have been selectively removed by post-depositional leaching, profile compaction, etc. However, the Star Carr bone is well preserved, and there is no reason to suspect differential destruction of very young jaws. Bay-Petersen (1978) has shown that similar profiles characterize red deer at a variety of Mesolithic sites in Denmark, and has suggested that they reflect a subsistence strategy in which the very young were deliberately conserved. This is a possibility, but there is no clear advantage to conserving the very young, many of whom must die in any case if a population is not to outgrow its resource base. If the hunter's (or herder's) goal is to maintain ungulate numbers, it makes better sense to conserve reproductively active adults, particularly females.

Based on its geomorphic context and artefact sample, Pitts (1979) has argued that the area excavated at Star Carr functioned as a specialized locus for processing hides and manufacturing antler artefacts. The red deer dentitions at the site may thus derive mainly from skulls brought there for their antlers. We think this explains the relative paucity of individuals in the first 10% of life span when most males would either lack antlers or have relatively insubstantial ones. Very young females would of course be even less likely to be present in an antler-working area.

### Seasonality and crown heights
Kurtén (1953) was probably the first to point out that the crown heights of a seasonally breeding ungulate can be

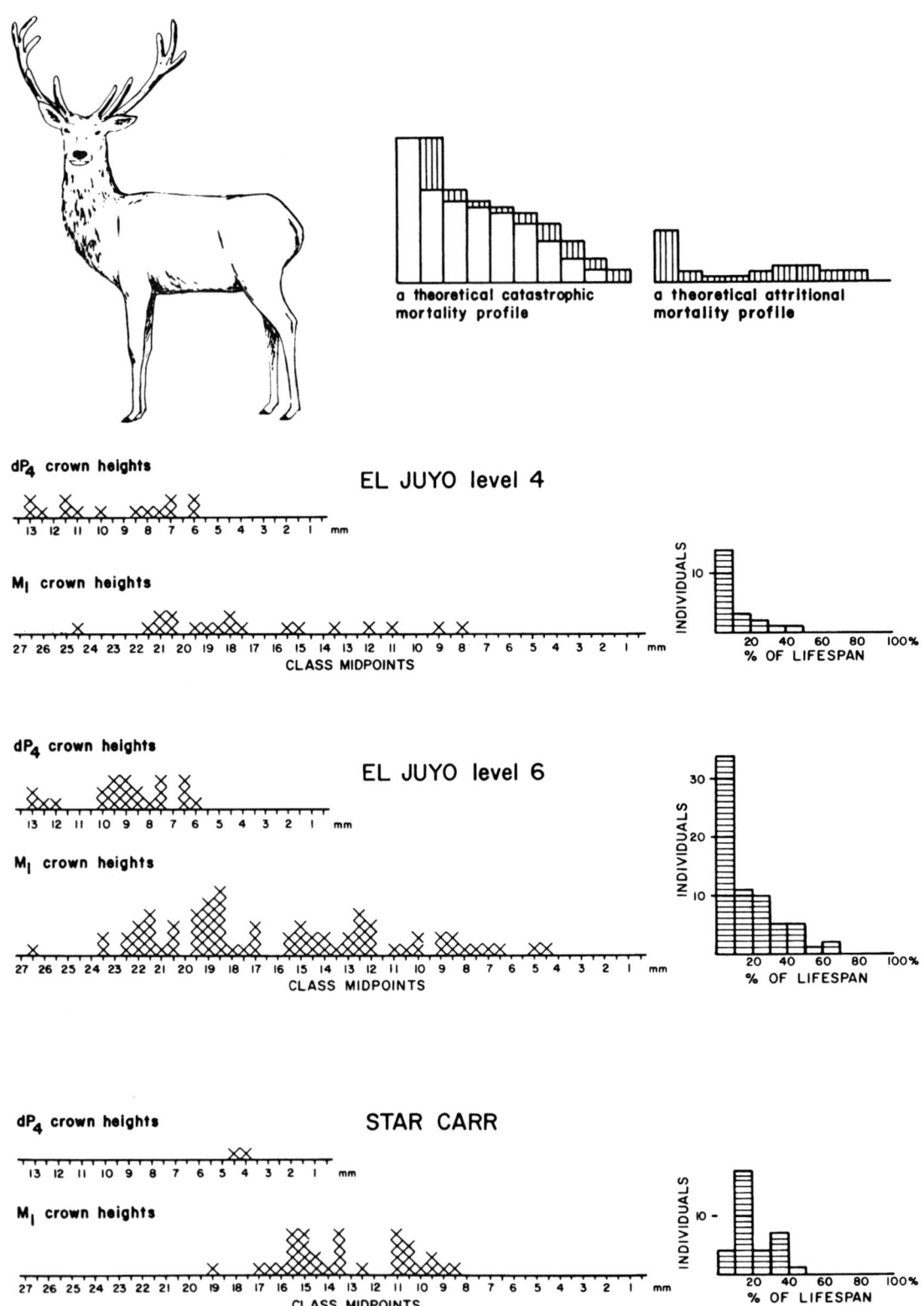

Fig. 5.4. Upper right: theoretical catastrophic mortality profile (white bars) and attritional mortality profile (striped bars) for a stable population of large mammals, such as wapiti/red deer. Lower left: dP$_4$ and M$_1$ crown heights in the red deer samples from El Juyo levels 4 and 6 and from Star Carr. Measurements made to the nearest tenth of a millimetre have been grouped into 0.5 mm classes. Lower right: mortality profiles derived from the corresponding crown heights, using the formulae for estimating age from crown height discussed in the text.

used to determine whether bone accumulation at a fossil site was seasonally restricted or whether it was spread throughout the year. In the case of seasonally restricted bone accumulation, the crown height distribution will exhibit several distinct modes, each separated by more or less equidistant gaps from adjacent ones. The modes will reflect the mean crown heights of successive cohorts of individuals all born at about the same time. The gaps will reflect periods of the year when individuals of each cohort were elsewhere, so that mortalities were unrepresented at the site. The number of actual or potential modes should be equal to the potential ecological longevity of the species, minus the time between birth and eruption of the tooth whose crown heights are being examined.

Probably the most fruitful application of the method in archaeology has been to confirm that bison drives at several sites in the western United States were seasonal events (Frison 1978, with references). Otherwise the method has been little used. Our known-age wapiti data illustrate one reason why. The individuals involved were almost all born in late May or early June, and they almost all died between October and December. Yet there is no distinct multimodal pattern in a plot of their crown heights (fig. 5.5).

The explanation may be found in figure 5.1. While successive yearly age cohorts do differ from one another in mean $M_1$ crown height, it is also clear that they overlap very extensively in this character. Under the circumstances, a multimodal pattern, clearly reflecting the underlying seasonality of birth and death, would only emerge in a truly enormous sample of wapiti teeth, far larger than any archaeologist is ever likely to obtain. It is probable that vast samples would also be necessary to demonstrate seasonal site occupation from crown heights of the conspecific red deer, and we conclude that the lack of readily discernible multimodality in the El Juyo and Star Carr $M_1$ plots (fig. 5.4) is *not* evidence for year-round occupation at each site.

Generally speaking, wapiti/red deer are unsatisfactory for documenting seasonal occupation from crown heights because they are low-crowned relative to potential life span. This means that individuals in any given age cohort lose relatively little crown height each year, so that the difference between mean crown heights in adjacent cohorts tends to be small. The result is that crown height modes are closely packed

and difficult or impossible to discern, except in very large samples. It is probable that the study of cementum annuli has far more potential than crown heights for documenting seasonal occupation (or its absence) from species like wapiti/ red deer (Spiess 1976, 1979). In a European context, the most promising species in which to search for seasonality in crown height plots are probably bovids, especially the ibex (*Capra ibex*), which is characterized by a particularly high crown height to life span ratio.

### Summary and conclusion

Our data on wapiti indicate that the relationship between age and crown height is both close enough and systematic enough to estimate age from crown height, when the goal is simply to determine the broad age structure of a group of individuals. Our data further suggest that the basic shape of an age profile may be reasonably approximated by estimating age using a set of theoretical assumptions about the relationship between age and crown height, when this cannot be established empirically. These assumptions will probably provide meaningful age profiles for most hypsodont ungulates, particularly for cervids and bovids, all of which have teeth that are very similar to those of wapiti in shape and structure.

We particularly recommend the use of the following theoretical formulae, first suggested by Spinage:

For a deciduous tooth:     $AGE = AGEs[(crown\ height - CHo)/CHo]^2$
For a permanent tooth:     $AGE = (AGEpel - AGEe)[(crown\ height - CHo)/CHo]^2 + AGEe$

where AGEs is the age when a deciduous tooth is shed, AGEe is the age when a permanent tooth erupts, AGEpel is the age past which few or no individuals survive in the wild (potential ecological longevity), and CHo is initial (unworn) crown height.

In most instances, for $dP_4$, $M_2$ and $M_3$, the following somewhat simpler linear age-estimation formulae will also provide adequate results:

For a deciduous tooth:     $AGE = AGEs - (AGEs/CHo)(crown\ height)$
For a permanent tooth:     $AGE = AGEpel - [(AGEpel - AGEe)/CHo](crown\ height)$

These simpler formulae should not be used, however, when a sample contains a large number of very lightly worn or very heavily worn teeth. Whichever formulae are used, we recommend grouping estimated ages into fairly broad age classes. We have found an age class based on 10% of potential ecological longevity to be particularly useful.

Although crown height is admittedly an imperfect means of estimating age, it is almost certainly the best means available for archaeological ungulates. The major obstacle that most archaeologists will face in trying to develop interpretable age profiles from crown heights will not be the inaccuracy inherent in the technique, but the small size of most archaeological faunal samples.

*Acknowledgements*
We thank the National Science Foundation for financial support and T.P. Volman for critical comments on a preliminary draft.

YELLOWSTONE

$M_1$ crown heights

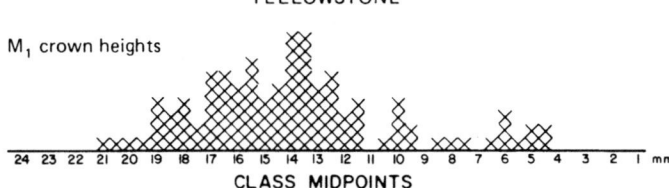

CLASS MIDPOINTS

Fig. 5.5. The distribution of $M_1$ crown heights in the known-age sample of wapiti. Measurements originally made to the nearest tenth of a millimetre have been grouped into 0.5 mm classes. Note the total absence of patterned multimodality, in spite of the fact that the sample comprises individuals which were born and which died during restricted parts of the year. For additional discussion see the text.

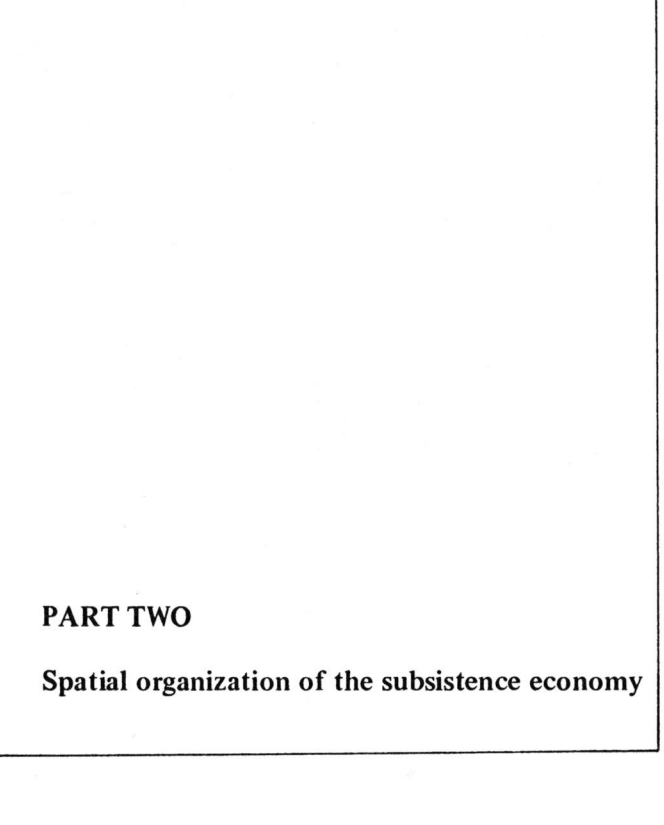

PART TWO

Spatial organization of the subsistence economy

Chapter 6

Editorial

The notion that hunters and gatherers tend to move about over extensive areas and use a number of camp sites or settlements in the course of their annual subsistence activities has gained wide currency in recent years. This has been accompanied by a growing commitment in archaeological analysis to the problem of defining the spatial dimension of prehistoric subsistence economies, and to recognition of the need to place the materials recovered from individual archaeological sites into a broader spatial and geographical framework.

These movements are generally thought of as seasonal moves linking discrete areas or resource zones into an annual round. The area so encompassed can be referred to in archaeological work as the *annual exploitation territory* (Vita-Finzi and Higgs 1970; Higgs and Vita-Finzi 1972; Jarman *et al.* 1982) or the *home range* (Foley 1976) of a human group. Such moves may also involve shifts of the annual range from one area to another from year to year or at longer intervals, leaving particular tracts of country unoccupied or only intermittently used for years at a time. This larger area can be equated with the concept of lifetime range used in animal behaviour studies, although it is open to question as to whether it would be possible to distinguish effectively between home ranges and lifetime ranges in the reconstruction of prehistoric behaviour.

Binford (1980) has emphasized the importance of making a further distinction between *residential mobility* and *logistical mobility*. Residential mobility consists of movements of the residential group from one settlement to another as resources become available in different areas at different seasons. The pattern of land use is essentially one in which people move – or 'map on' – to resources, a strategy described as 'foraging'. Logistical mobility refers to circumstances where two or more sets of resources of critical importance in the subsistence economy become available simultaneously but in widely separated areas. Since the residential base can obviously only be located near one set of resources, special task groups have to make planned trips to bring in the other resources from the outlying areas. These may be partially processed at the point of extraction before being transported back to the residential base. In this 'collecting' strategy it is the resources that are moved to the residential group rather than the other way around. Collecting strategies are thus characterized by fewer residential moves, a proliferation of archaeological 'locations' such as butchery camps, storage caches or lookout posts, and a greater emphasis on food preservation and storage techniques. As Binford emphasizes, foraging and collecting may be combined in varying mixes within a single exploitation strategy (see also chapter 3).

Hunter-gatherer subsistence economies, then, can be classified along two somewhat different axes. One axis represents a continuum between long-distance mobility and sedentism, the other between foraging and collecting. This raises two separate issues in the analysis of spatial organization. The first is the size of the annual exploitation territory and the range of movements necessary for its exploitation. Ethnographic examples suggest that these may range from an annual round trip for the residential group of up to about 1000 km at one extreme, to essentially sedentary situations at the other extreme, where annual food requirements can be met from within a sufficiently circumscribed area to permit permanent occupation of a single settlement. The second issue is the way in which people organize their exploitation of the annual territory, whether by foraging, collecting or some combination of the two, and hence the way in which they integrate the use of individual sites with complementary functions into regional site systems.

Theoretical interest centres on the circumstances which give rise to these differing patterns of mobility and resource integration. Binford (1980) emphasizes environmental variables and supplies ethnographic evidence suggesting that collecting strategies become more prevalent in colder environments with a short growing season. Other factors, however, can affect patterns of mobility, for example variations in population density or social organization. This imposes a strong requirement in archaeological analysis to devise adequate methods for achieving two objectives: the identification of site systems comprising groups of linked sites with complementary functions; and the reconstruction of the palaeoenvironments with which these site systems were associated.

A technique which is capable of contributing to both these objectives is site catchment analysis. Since all the following four chapters employ some variant of this technique, a brief introduction to the underlying concepts is called for. Site catchment analysis has generated considerable confusion in the literature, in part through a failure of its critics to comprehend the objectives for which the technique was first devised, and in part through a failure of the early publications (e.g. Vita-Finzi and Higgs 1970) to clarify the distinction between site catchments and site exploitation territories (Jarman *et al.* 1982, Bailey and Davidson in press).

Site catchment analysis results in empirical statements about the sources of origin of the various materials recovered in the excavation of a site. These materials may be food remains, the raw materials from which the artefacts are made, natural constituents of the deposit such as sediments or pollen, or other materials of interest. These different materials may be derived from different areas of origin and accumulated by a variety of agencies, both human and non-human. The *economic catchment*, strictly defined, of a given site, is the actual area from which are derived the food resources which people eat while they are in residence at that site. Economic catchments may thus vary in shape and size according to the specific features of the resource in question, the function of the site and the exploitation strategies of the site occupants. Other catchments, such as the geological catchment of raw materials from which the discarded artefacts have been made, may cover a very different area from the economic catchment. Clearly the accuracy with which an economic catchment can be defined by site catchment analysis in this sense will depend on the techniques available for tracing the food remains in the site back to specific points of origin in the surrounding environment. Flannery's study (1976) of the early farming village of San José Mogoté in the Oaxaca valley is a useful example of site catchment analysis in this strict sense of the term.

The *site exploitation territory*, in contrast, is a theoretical statement about the area around a site which is *assumed* to have been habitually used for subsistence by the inhabitants of the site. The boundary of the site exploitation territory is defined in accordance with least-cost principles as the maximum radius of travel on foot over which people would normally tend to move in the course of daily subsistence activities. The radii most commonly employed are 10 km (or 2 hours' walking time) and 5 km (or 1 hour's walking time), depending on the nature of the resources and their exploitation requirements. Radii of 1 km (or 10 minutes' walking time) are also frequently used, especially in the analysis of farming economies, where the most productive resources are also likely to be both labour-intensive and land-intensive, and therefore concentrated within the immediate vicinity of the site (Higgs 1975; Flannery 1976). The definition of these boundaries is of course based on assumed norms of behaviour, and examination of the economic potential of resources lying within these boundaries offers no more than a statement, at best, of what

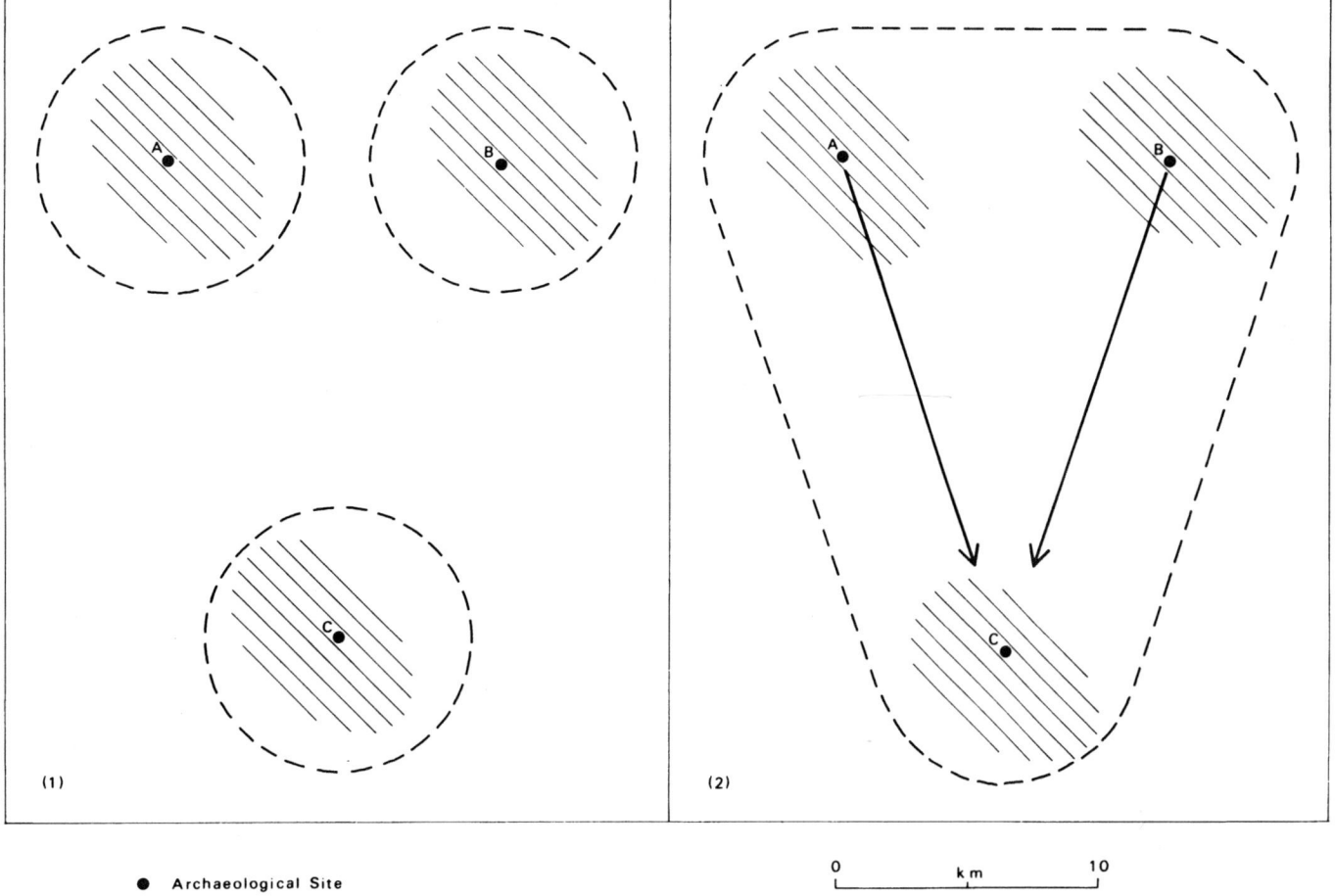

● Archaeological Site

0       k m       10

Fig. 6.1. Diagrammatic illustration of variation in size of economic catchment under different systems of exploitation. In (1), three discrete patches of resources are exploited from three residential camps (A, B and C), with mutually exclusive economic catchments. In (2) only the economic catchment of site C is shown. In this case sites A and B are used as satellite camps for the partial processing of the adjacent resources and their transfer to the main camp C, resulting in the enlargement of its economic catchment. See text for further explanation.

was potentially available to the site occupants. This type of analysis is properly described as site territorial analysis, although it is often subsumed under the label of site catchment analysis.

It may be objected that the economic catchment and the site exploitation territory are overlapping terms without a clear conceptual distinction. An economic catchment after all is simply an empirical statement of the site exploitation territory, while the site exploitation territory represents a hypothetical assessment of the economic catchment. The degree to which one can legitimately refer to the economic catchment of a site rather than its site exploitation territory will simply be a matter of the confidence one can attach to the definition of spatial limits to the subsistence activities practised from the site. Definition of catchments, although largely empirical, may involve an element of hypothesis, because of the uncertainties that may accompany attempts to source materials to precise points of origin. Conversely, site territorial analysis, although based on assumed norms of behaviour, usually also has an empirical component. Despite this overlap,

it is nevertheless useful in the interests of analytical rigour to maintain a distinction between site catchments and site exploitation territories, and these terms and definitions are now a matter of widespread convention among field practitioners.

The importance of distinguishing the economic catchment from the site exploitation territory is illustrated in figure 6.1. Two simplified systems of exploitation are shown, each dependent on the same mix of three staple resources and producing the same gross annual output of food. In the first system, the resources are available in different seasons and are exploited by a foraging strategy with a sequence of residential moves between seasonally occupied settlements. The economic catchment of each settlement is coterminous with its theoretically defined site exploitation territory. The annual exploitation territory thus comprises a series of mutually exclusive economic catchments (or site exploitation territories). In the second example, the resources are exploited by a collecting strategy in which only one site is now used as a residential base. The other sites are now used by task-specific groups or individuals for the exploitation of the outlying resources, which are then transferred after some preliminary on-the-spot processing back to the residential base. In this case the annual exploitation territory is still essentially the same as before, and it still comprises a series of mutually exclusive site exploitation territories. However, the economic catchment of the residential base has now been extended to include the site exploitation territories of the outlying camps. In effect the site catchment is identical with the annual exploitation territory. This is, of course, a greatly simplified example, and other factors would probably complicate the picture. However, the example should be sufficient to illustrate the point that a given set of resources may be exploited by different strategies, resulting in different economic catchments and hence a different representation of food remains within the deposits at individual archaeological sites.

In chapter 8, Davidson provides a clear example of the use of site catchment analysis in this way to identify variations in the extent of annual exploitation territories. He also draws attention to the ambiguities inherent in observed changes of food remains in the sequence of an individual site. These may reflect changes in the function of the site in relation to the exploitation of a given set of resources, rather than economic transformations of a more fundamental character (see also part 3). Davidson further suggests that it may be useful to make a distinction between 'tactics' — activities carried out at a particular site — and 'strategy' — the combination of tactical manoeuvres that characterize the regional settlement/subsistence system. Thus in Davidson's terms the changes in food remains, apparent at individual sites with a shift of subsistence behaviour of the type shown in figure 6. 1, would represent a change in tactics rather than a change in strategy.

One obvious uncertainty in site territorial analysis is the accuracy of assumptions about distance limits. Ethnographic examples of people travelling more or less than the expected limits are sometimes quoted. However, much depends on the purposes of the archaeological analysis. One way in which site territorial analysis is used in all four chapters in this part is as a measuring device. Here the aim is to assess in a systematic way *relative* differences or similarities between the economic potential of sites, rather than to define the absolute spatial limits of subsistence activity. Moreover, it will be apparent that different distance limits may be imposed to accommodate any uncertainties about the precise figures that applied in the past depending on the particular needs of the problem under study. Bailey *et al.* (chapter 7) use 20-km circles and 2-hour boundaries, as well as detailed assessments of features in the immediate vicinity of sites. Davidson (chapter 8) uses 2-hour, 1-hour and ½-hour boundaries as well as empirically defined catchments, Clark (chapter 9) employs 3-km circles, and Rowley-Conwy 10-km, 5-km and 2½-km circles (chapter 10).

Ideally a site territorial analysis should be complemented by a site catchment analysis in every case, thus allowing some assessment of the relationship between what was potentially available and what was actually exploited. However, the food

species commonly found in archaeological sites are often not traceable with any accuracy to specific locations or areas in the surrounding environment. In other cases, notably with plant foods, it may be suspected that food resources important in the site economy are under-represented in the on-site data. Indeed it was precisely because of these uncertainties that site territorial analysis was first devised, namely as an alternative means of providing some assessment of the site economy. However, where the aim is to go beyond the reconstruction of subsistence economy and to provide some theoretically valuable statement of the relationship between environmental potential and subsistence behaviour, it is obviously essential to have evidence of past activities that is independent of the reconstructions supplied by site territorial analysis. A number of approaches is developed in this section. Typically, variations in economic potential as measured by site territorial analysis are compared with variations in patterns of on-site data, such as intensity of occupation, faunal diversity, representation of anatomical elements, or the nature of artefact assemblages. Analyses of this type contribute to one of the major objectives of spatial analysis, that is, the definition of variations in site function and the testing of hypotheses about the ways in which sites are linked together to form site systems.

The chapters in this section fall into two groups. Bailey *et al.* and Davidson both deal with last glacial environments (in north-west Greece and south-east Spain respectively), and with evidence suggesting subsistence economies that tend towards the highly mobile and logistical ends of the spectrum. Bailey *et al.* re-examine the field data from Epirus, scene of one of the early archaeological attempts to reconstruct long-distance patterns of seasonal mobility. They discuss the problems of using locational and site territorial data to test hypotheses about seasonality and about the nature of the exploitation strategies used in prehistoric deer economies. Davidson examines the problems of comparing on-site and off-site data in animal-based economies, and of identifying links between widely separated sites. He also discusses some of the problems of interpreting time trends, which anticipates issues dealt with at greater length in Part 3.

Two general points emerge from both these studies. The first is that it may often be possible to establish useful relative differences between sites — for example differences in the intensity of occupation, length of sequence, or the faunal and artefact assemblages, without being able to place the sites in some pre-existing scheme of functional classification. The second point is the importance of acquiring independent evidence about the natural environment and the subsistence activities that were practised in that environment. Bailey *et al.* note the potential circularity of argument that may arise from using territorial data to infer patterns of subsistence, while Davidson emphasizes the pitfalls of the reverse procedure in which archaeological evidence of subsistence is used to identify variations in the natural environment. A third point implicit in both studies is the problem of how large an area should be taken into account in regional analyses of hunter-

gatherer subsistence systems. Bailey *et al.* note the potential
and limitations of using complementary resource zones linked
by transhumant routes in the modern landscape as a hypothetical guide to annual exploitation territories in prehistory,
while Davidson is able to utilize site catchment data. Both
approaches present difficulties, but it is clear from both studies
that the area which needs to be taken into account when
interpreting the material from an individual site may be far
more extensive than the area commonly deemed appropriate
in the design of archaeological field research. The question of
the appropriate scale for regional analyses is taken up again in
Part 4.

The chapters by Clark and Rowley-Conwy deal with
early Holocene coastal environments and with evidence
suggesting sedentary or sedentary-cum-mobile subsistence
economies. Clark proposes three alternative models of settlement patterning for the Asturian shell middens of Cantabria,
and makes use of a wide variety of on-site and off-site tests,
concluding that the middens probably represent residential
bases (see also chapters 12 and 13). The off-site analyses are
of particular interest in presenting some detailed proposals for
extrapolating patterns of prehistoric environment and vegetation from present-day conditions. The possibility that the
coastal settlements may be complemented by seasonal use of
sites in the hinterland with typologically quite different
artefact assemblages is also examined.

Rowley-Conwy introduces his analysis of the Danish
Erteb∅lle with a general discussion of sedentism among hunters
and gatherers. He suggests that sedentary hunters may represent a special variant of Binford's logistical category (see also
Yesner 1980), albeit a variant characterized by a sufficiently
distinctive set of economic, social and technological features
to justify the definition of a separate category of 'complex'
hunters. Here too a combination of off-site indicators is used

to support the conclusion that the Erteb∅lle shell mounds
represent essentially sedentary residential bases.

It is interesting to note the similarities as well as the
contrasts between the Danish and Cantabrian sites. In both
areas the coastal shell middens appear to be more or less
sedentary residential bases supported by task-specific sites for
the exploitation of specific resources at some distance from
the residential base. In Cantabria these outlying sites appear to
have been formed in the course of exploiting red deer in the
hinterland. In Denmark they are mainly other coastal middens
used in the exploitation of specific coastal resources such as
wildfowl or seals, a difference which probably reflects the
greater productivity of the Danish coastal environment as compared with Cantabria.

These analyses of Mesolithic coastal economies anticipate
the question of whether they, along with their analogues in
other parts of the world, represent a 'stage' in the evolution of
hunter-gatherer subsistence economies, transitional between
the classic patterns of Palaeolithic hunting and gathering and
the development of 'Neolithic' agriculture (e.g. Osborn 1977,
Perlman 1980). Rowley-Conwy suggests that sedentary hunting is associated with a specific combination of environmental
factors. So far from treating this as a relatively recent adaptation, we ought to find evidence of similar patterns wherever
the appropriate environmental factors are present, regardless
of time period. He further suggests that sedentary coastal
economies may not provide the favourable preconditions for
the development of plant cultivation as has sometimes been
supposed. On the contary they may indicate a resource base of
sufficient security and productivity to negate the advantages
of arable farming, at least in the conditions of north-west
Europe. The question of long-term economic trends and their
causes is dealt with further in Parts 3 and 4.

Chapter 7

Epirus revisited: Seasonality and inter-site
variation in the Upper Palaeolithic of north-west
Greece
Geoff Bailey, Pat Carter, Clive Gamble and
Helen Higgs

This chapter examines the hypothesis of long-distance seasonal
transhumance between complementary resource zones served by
seasonally occupied home-base sites, which was proposed for the
Palaeolithic rockshelters of Epirus in the 1960s. The assumptions that
underpin this hypothesis are made explicit, as are the assumptions involved in the use of site exploitation territories as a method of testing
hypotheses about prehistoric settlement and land use. The seasonal
hypothesis is reconsidered in the light of more detailed territorial
studies and analysis of material collected in the original excavations.
Variation in the faunal and cultural material between sites is used as a
basis for re-examining the site locations in relation to their environmental setting. Alternative hypotheses of relations between sites
within a regional setting are proposed, and their implications for the
interpretation of deer exploitation strategies are briefly discussed.

### Introduction

Investigations of Palaeolithic settlement in Epirus were
initiated by E.S. Higgs in 1962 to establish a climatic and
chronological sequence which would allow correlation with
adjacent regions in Europe, south-west Asia and North Africa
(Dakaris *et al.* 1964). This work led to the discovery of a
number of rockshelter and surface sites of Middle and Upper
Palaeolithic date (fig. 7.1), and to the excavation of the
Kokkinopilos surface sites and the rockshelters of Asprochaliko
and Kastritsa (Higgs and Vita-Finzi 1966; Higgs *et al.* 1967;
Vita-Finzi 1978: 139). As the project developed, the aims
shifted from chronological correlations between individual
sequences on a continental scale to the study of spatial
relationships between sites at a regional scale and to the
reconstruction of regional landscapes and patterns of land use.
This culminated in the interpretation of Asprochaliko and
Kastritsa as seasonally complementary home-base sites in a
single system of exploitation extending from the coast to the
heights of the Pindus Mountains.

This shift from 'vertical' to 'horizontal' thinking was in
line with other projects of the time, notably that of MacNeish
(1964), and anticipated a more general reorientation of
research design towards a regional framework in archaeological
studies of hunter-gatherer subsistence (e.g. Carter 1970; J. G.
D. Clark 1972; Jochim 1976; Gamble 1978a; Parkington 1980;
Part 2, this volume). It is now commonly recognized that
hunter-gatherer groups are often highly mobile with large
annual territories, and that archaeological research designs
should be adjusted accordingly.

The Epirus work also provided a model for palaeoeconomic field studies carried out elsewhere in the Mediterranean and beyond. These were characterized by reliance on
three distinctive concepts. The first is the concept of the 2-
hour site exploitation territory, and the associated techniques
of site territorial and site catchment analysis as a systematic
means of relating sites to their local environments (Vita-Finzi
and Higgs 1970). The second is the concept of the 'close man—
animal relationship', and the third the closely related concept
of the 'optimum exploitation of resources' (Higgs and Jarman

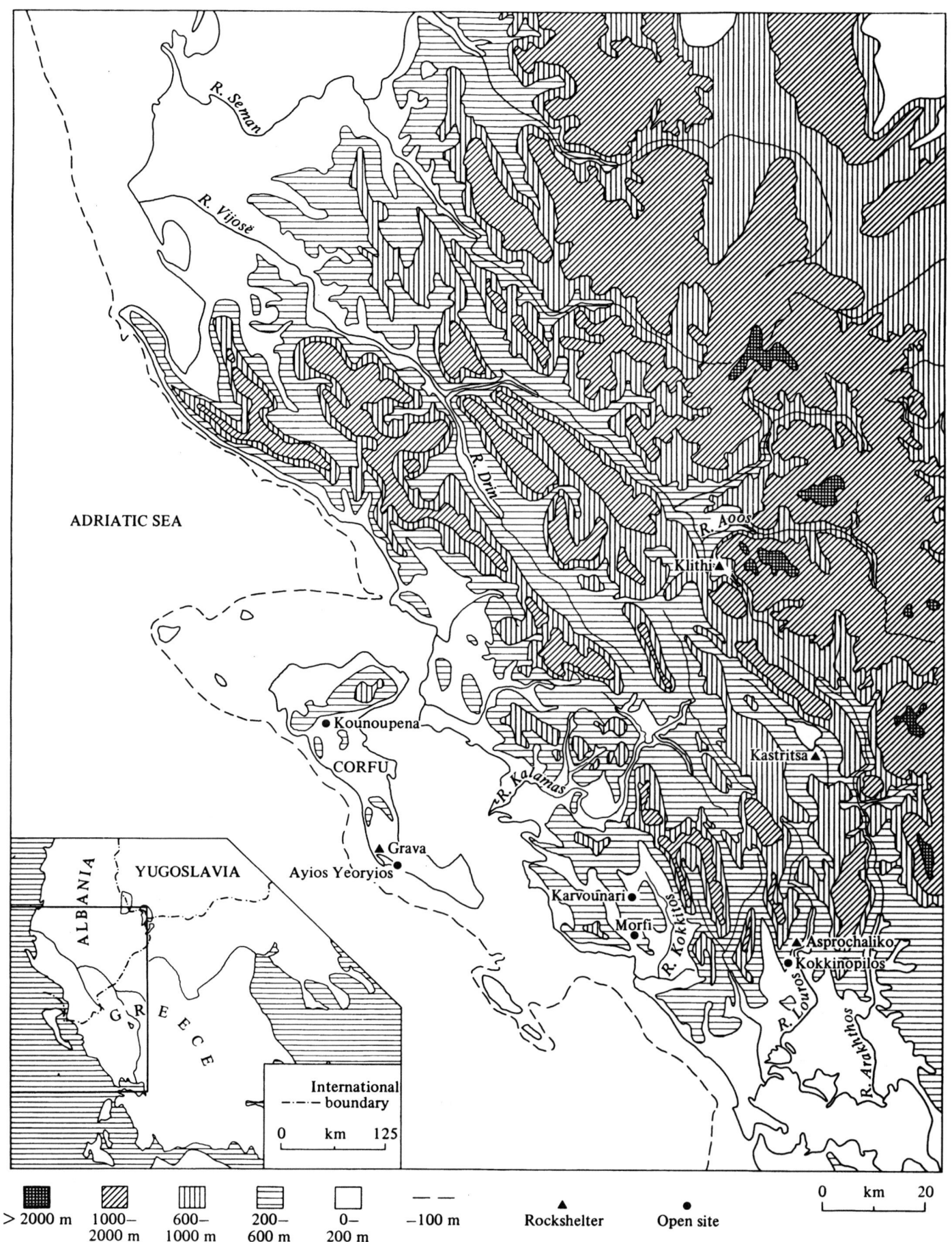

ADRIATIC SEA

CORFU

Kounoupena

Grava
Ayios Yeoryios

Karvounari

Morfi

Kastritsa

Klithi

Asprochaliko
Kokkinopilos

R. Seman

R. Vijosë

R. Drin

R. Aoos

R. Kalamas

R. Kokkitos

R. Louros

R. Arakhthos

ALBANIA

YUGOSLAVIA

GREECE

International
boundary

0    km    125

> 2000 m    1000–    600–    200–    0–    − − −    − 100 m    ▲    ●
             2000 m   1000 m  600 m  200 m                      Rockshelter    Open site

0    km    20

Fig. 7.1. Topography of north-west Greece and southern Albania, showing selected archaeological sites.

1969; Higgs 1972, 1975; Jarman 1976). An optimum exploitation was held to be the norm on prehistoric time-scales, and was defined as the maximum food yield sustainable in the long term under given conditions of environment and technology. These latter two concepts, sometimes described under the label of 'husbandry', embody the twin conceptions of conservation and manipulation of resources, and were seen as a replacement for the concept of 'hunting' with its connotations of a 'random' or 'catch-as-catch-can' existence.

Our reconsideration of the Epirus field data suggests that some of the basic assumptions of this palaeoconomic approach now require critical re-examination and modification.

### A strategy for reconstructing prehistoric land use

An ideal procedure for reconstructing land use in animal-based economies according to the principles implicit in the original Epirus work would involve the following:

#### (a) Model building

(1) Look at the regional pattern of land use at the present day with particular emphasis on ecological limiting factors that may influence the seasonal distribution of grazing resources. Use recent or present-day transhumant routes linking seasonally complementary grazing areas as a guide to hypothetical patterns of seasonal mobility and regional economic integration in the prehistoric past.

(2) Project these patterns on to the prehistoric landscape, allowing for any climatic and environmental changes.

(3) Reinforce the hypothesis of seasonal mobility by assuming that human population densities will rise to the optimum level – in effect that populations will overcome seasonal food shortages by movement to a seasonally complementary resource zone, thereby maintaining a higher overall population density than would be the case for sedentary populations, whose numbers would be limited by the least available resource in the worst season of the year.

#### (b) Model testing

(1) Plot the distribution of archaeological sites on the landscape and compare with the routes of seasonal movement linking complementary resource zones. Examine the seasonal potential of resources within site exploitation territories.

(2) Examine the aspect of individual sites, combined with 24-hour temperature readings (Higgs and Webley 1971; Legge 1972), on the assumption that sites with a southerly aspect will be more favourable for use in winter than in summer, and vice versa.

(3) Consider alternative models such as sedentism supported by storage of food or by the exploitation of a variety of resources available in one locality at different seasons.

### Problems of model building

The steps in model building outlined above represent a series of simplifying assumptions of a uniformitarian nature. They assert a belief that there are certain uniformities or universals in the relationship between site location/subsistence and environment. These can be projected into the past as a fixed and coherent framework of relationships against which variation in behaviour can be measured. The assumed universals in this case are the ecological limiting factors operating in a given environment (subject to variation through palaeoenvironmental control), the behavioural response of animal species such as red deer or sheep to these ecological limiting factors, and the demographic tendency of human populations to stabilize around an optimum density which achieves a full exploitation of the available food resources.

All the above universals can of course be challenged on the grounds that they are liable to a much wider range of variation than is implied in the initial model. Like other uniformitarian projections from present to past, such an exercise raises a number of difficulties, all of which stem from an underlying uncertainty as to which features of ethnographically and historically derived patterns of land use are fundamental universals of human economic behaviour, and which are subject to variation according to the particular circumstances of time and place.

Some of these difficulties can be illustrated by the use of Sarakatsani transhumance as a model for seasonal mobility in the Epirus environment. The Sarakatsani engage in long-distance transhumance, moving their flocks of sheep and goats from winter grazings in the coastal lowlands to summer pastures on the high Pindus (Campbell 1964). These movements can be used as a guide to seasonal exploitation territories in the prehistoric past.

However, like many other Mediterranean transhumants (Lewthwaite 1981), the Sarakatsani are closely tied in with a wider market economy, providing an inexpensive cheese supply. This is a role that is possible only because of the demand created by large sedentary populations and the existence of a cash economy and transportation network that permits rapid transfer of labour and product. Sedentary villages supported by forestry are found both on the coast and in the hinterland in a patchwork of sedentary and sedentary-cum-mobile economies. Without the stimulus of an extensive market economy, it is possible that smaller flocks would have been kept, with correspondingly less need or incentive to undertake long-distance movements in search of seasonal pasture. It could thus be argued that the development of Sarakatsani transhumance is not uniquely determined by the climate and physical relief of Epirus, but represents the development of a highly specialized economic niche brought into being by a combination of environmental and socio-historical factors.

Ingold (1980, 1981) has made the point in a more general way by emphasizing that what constitutes an optimum level of exploitation or an ecological limiting factor is not uniquely determined by the potential of the natural environment. Even the harshest and simplest environment is likely to offer scope for different patterns of exploitation. Since the economic system may be determined in part by social factors working independently of environmental variation, different economic systems in the same natural environment may be sensitive to different ecological limiting factors and define different optima of exploitation. Bender (1978,1981) has also emphasized the potential role of social factors such as the integration of local subsistence economies into wider exchange or marketing networks, and the ways in which these social factors can boost levels of local subsistence output and population density independently of environmental factors. The question of what constitutes an optimum exploitation of available resources, and whether populations would tend to stabilize around some optimum level on prehistoric time-scales, is also open to considerable debate (Bailey 1981b). In short, it would seem to be impossible to measure the optimum level of exploitation in a given environment without some prior or independent knowledge of the economic system under study (see also Part 4 for discussion of social factors).

The above issues have come into focus largely as a result of the introduction of social theory drawn from anthropological knowledge of contemporary societies into discussion of prehistoric economy. The result, however, has often tended to be a somewhat abstract polarization between the 'ecological rationality' of palaeoeconomy and the 'social rationality' of the alternatives (Sheridan and Bailey 1981), rather than a set of practical proposals for alternative methods of studying prehistoric subsistence economies. The difference between these two poles of thought is to some extent a difference of emphasis – on the limits imposed by the natural environment on the one hand, and on the variation possible within those limits on the other. These ought to be complementary concerns. But it is clear that both approaches can be carried to extremes – palaeoeconomy by so insisting on the determining effect of environment as virtually to deny the possibility of any independent variation at all, social theory by so emphasizing the unfettered potential of human creativity as to suggest that variation is limitless. The tendency towards abstract polemic might be further avoided if it were more clearly appreciated that the apparent techno–environmental determinism of palaeoeconomy is not so much a matter of ideology but of methodology, that is to say that it provides an initial framework without which coherent analysis of the prehistoric record cannot even begin.

### Problems of model testing

All of these problems inherent in the classic palaeo-economic prescription would be less serious if the proposed archaeological tests were truly independent of the assumptions built into the initial model. However, quite apart from the intrinsic ambiguities and poor resolution of much archaeological data, one of the most strongly advocated tests, namely the use of site territorial analysis, is itself dependent on a uniformitarian premise that is derived from a limited number of ethnographic examples. The use of concentric circles (or time boundaries), inspired as it was by the mongongo-eating !Kung Bushmen and the arable farmers of von Thünen's isolated state (1875), implies a radial pattern of

daily movements from a centrally located home base, a model appropriate for plant-food exploitation, but less so for animal-based economies. With plant foods, as with other sedentary resources, a major factor is transportation costs, which may be expected to increase in proportion to increasing distance from the residential base. With mobile animal resources, however, the unpredictability of their movement from year to year and their fluctuating population numbers – especially in extreme environments with a tendency to ecological specialization (Gamble 1978a) – means that the central problem facing the consumer is one of locating the prey and securing its capture rather than the cost of transporting the dead carcase. Sturdy (1972, 1975) was the first to show that some of the major European Upper Palaeolithic sites, so far from being centrally located in relation to the distribution of the reindeer whose bones dominate their archaeological faunas, are asymmetrically located on the edge of major blocks of reindeer grazing terrain. He proposed the term 'extended territory' to cover cases where the catchment of resources supporting the subsistence economy of a given site extended beyond the 2-hour boundary of the hypothetical site exploitation territory, and suggested that the steep topography associated with the asymmetrical location of the major sites offered advantages in predicting and controlling the movements of the herds, with a consequent reduction of effort and risk in their exploitation. Binford's (1980) exposition of the differences between 'foraging' and 'collecting' strategies supports the notion that specialized, animal-based economies tend to be associated with widely spaced residential bases supported by extensive economic catchments and a logistically organized network of small camps used for special purposes such as game watching or overnight shelter at some distance from the main base.

Another problem with site territorial analysis, whatever the radius of the territorial boundary employed, is that the area so enclosed can only provide a statement of resource *potential*. In making the hypothetical leap from what is potentially available to what was actually exploited, the analyst necessarily has to make some assumptions about which features of the environment are to be considered as significant to the prehistoric occupants of the site. There is a danger that, in reaching this decision, the analyst will rely on precisely the same assumptions as those built into the original model – assumptions which it is the purpose of the site territorial analysis to test!

The classic answer to this dilemma is to argue that potential resources close to the site should be given priority over those further away, in accordance with least-cost principles, and that a suitable system of weighting within the hypothetical site exploitation territory should narrow down the possibilities – ideally to a single possibility uniquely determined by the location of the site in relation to the surrounding environment. However, as indicated above, the particular dynamics of animal-based economies may lead to considerable spatial modification of the least-effort principle.

Animals of importance in the site economy may actually live at some distance from the site, either because the territory where they spend the greater part of the year is geographically remote from the point at which they are killed for human consumption, or because the carcases are transferred from remote areas via butchery camps.

The above criticisms do not necessarily imply that the hypothesis of seasonal mobility for prehistoric Epirus is incorrect. It can still be regarded as a strong hypothesis supported by an inter-meshing of corroborative evidence which is not solely dependent on the validity of the Sarakatsani ethnographic model or the assumptions of site territorial analysis. However, with the benefit of hindsight two major weaknesses can be identified.

The first is the emphasis on seasonal mobility as a sufficient characterization of an economic system. At the time when the seasonal hypothesis was proposed, it represented an innovative exercise in lateral thinking, challenging archaeologists to emerge from the bottom of the deep excavation trenches into which they had dug themselves in the interests of constructing chronological and typological frameworks, and to look at the surrounding landscape. Since then, however, the mobility of hunters and gatherers has become virtually a truism, while sedentism and the conditions which give rise to it has become the interesting exception in need of explanation (see chapter 10). The emphasis on seasonal mobility as the important similarity between the Sarakatsani transhumants and the red deer hunters of Asprochaliko and Kastritsa (assuming the hypothesis to be correct in the latter case) may mask differences of far greater significance for understanding the underlying principles of economic behaviour.

This emphasis on similarities and continuities is further symptomatic of a second critical weakness, and that is the vulnerability of the classic palaeoeconomic approach to self-fulfilling predictions in which the universals built into the initial framework of study are recycled with minimal modification as the conclusion of investigations, resulting in arguments that do not fall far short of circularity. The emphasis on continuity defined by the determining effect of unchanging environmental limitations — amounting to a virtually synchronic and ahistorical view of human behaviour — partly accounts for another classic feature of early palaeoeconomic work, and that is the relative neglect of on-site data, discussion of which in many cases was confined to little more than the evidence of the site locations themselves and statements about the prevalence of red deer as the dominant species in excavated faunal assemblages.

Further advance in understanding clearly depends on more detailed examination of alternative hypotheses, as well as improved analytical methods and research designs. The latter is, perhaps, the more crucial requirement. For, as we have indicated, the major problem is not so much the correctness or otherwise of the assumptions employed in the initial framework, but the problem of finding archaeological tests

which are truly independent of these assumptions and which therefore have some chance of exposing any weaknesses in them. We shall briefly illustrate some possibilities of development along these lines, with particular reference to the maximum of the last glacial period in Epirus and adjacent regions. The major excavated evidence of human activity during this period comes from the rockshelters of Asprochaliko and Kastritsa (Bailey *et al.* in press). These sites provide a composite sequence extending throughout much of the last glacial period with stone industries ranging from Middle Palaeolithic to late Upper Palaeolithic. However, only Upper Palaeolithic occupation is recorded at Kastritsa, and this is further confined to the period *c.* 20 000 to 13 000 b.p. We shall therefore deliberately exclude discussion of temporal trends in order to focus more clearly on spatial and geographical relationships.

### The last glacial environment

There is marked variation of relief, with limestone ridges extending in a north-west to south-east direction and rising to a maximum elevation of 2500 m (fig. 7.1). Intervening depressions contain Tertiary flysch consisting of shales, marls and sandstones. Valley bottoms and lake basins are filled with Quaternary alluvium. The major thickness of the alluvium consists of red beds of the Kokkinopilos Formation, locally up to 50 m thick (Vita-Finzi 1978; Macleod and Vita-Finzi 1982). Deposition, already in progress by 24 000 b.p., had ceased by about 7000 b.p., and is attributed to erosion of *terra rossa* soils from the limestone uplands by short-lived, violent rainfalls and seasonal frost activity working on a thinly-vegetated surface. A later series of buff-coloured alluvial deposits up to 5 m thick was accumulated in historical times by erosion of Kokkinopilos deposits and, in part of the Louros basin, of brown Mediterranean soils formed on flysch or on chert and shale bands in the limestone (Macleod and Vita-Finzi 1982).

The −100 m bathymetric contour is used as an approximation of the coastline at the maximum of the last glacial (following Vita-Finzi 1978; see also van Andel and Shackleton 1982; Bailey, chapter 13 this volume). The resulting extension of the coastal plain would clearly have greatly increased the area of available lowland grazing.

During the maximum of the last glacial (*c.* 20 000 b.p. to 16 000 b.p.) the permanent snowline is estimated to have descended to about 2000 m (Vita-Finzi 1978), and there was a general lowering of temperature and precipitation. In the Ioannina Lake basin, it is estimated that summer and winter temperatures may have been as much as 10°C below the present, with values of 13°C to 17°C and −3.4°C to −4.9°C respectively (Bottema 1974; Vita-Finzi 1978). The surrounding vegetation was mainly open *Artemisa* steppe, with a narrow zone of scattered trees at about 700 m to 900 m, and alpine meadows above 900 m (Bottema 1974). The coast is thought to have enjoyed a more even temperature because of its proximity to the sea (Vita-Finzi 1978).

Table 7.1. *Total number of identified faunal specimens at Asprochaliko and Kastritsa*

**Asprochaliko**

| Stratum | Cervus no. | Cervus % | Dama no. | Dama % | Capreolus no. | Capreolus % | Bovid no. | Bovid % | Caprine no. | Caprine % | Equid no. | Equid % | Sus no. | Sus % | Total |
|---|---|---|---|---|---|---|---|---|---|---|---|---|---|---|---|
| Upper Palaeolithic | 38 | 38 | 15 | 15 | 7 | 7 | 0 | 0 | 36 | 36 | 0 | 0 | 4 | 4 | 100 |
| Upper Palaeolithic/ Micro-Mousterian | 2 | 67 | 0 | 0 | 0 | 0 | 0 | 0 | 1 | 33 | 0 | 0 | 0 | 0 | 3 |
| Micro-Mousterian | 144 | 33 | 170 | 39 | 34 | 8 | 11 | 3 | 59 | 14 | 0 | 0 | 14 | 3 | 432 |
| Micro-Mousterian/ Basal Mousterian | 13 | 45 | 2 | 7 | 6 | 21 | 2 | 7 | 5 | 17 | 0 | 0 | 1 | 3 | 29 |
| Basal Mousterian | 128 | 53 | 44 | 18 | 18 | 7 | 6 | 2 | 44 | 18 | 0 | 0 | 4 | 2 | 244 |
| Uncertain | 195 | 49 | 103 | 25 | 50 | 12 | 7 | 2 | 43 | 11 | 0 | 0 | 4 | 1 | 402 |
| Totals | 520 | 43 | 334 | 28 | 115 | 9 | 26 | 2 | 188 | 16 | 0 | 0 | 27 | 2 | 1210 |

**Kastritsa**

| Stratum[a] | Cervus no. | Cervus % | Dama no. | Dama % | Capreolus no. | Capreolus % | Bovid no. | Bovid % | Caprine no. | Caprine % | Equid no. | Equid % | Sus no. | Sus % | Total |
|---|---|---|---|---|---|---|---|---|---|---|---|---|---|---|---|
| Upper Palaeolithic 1 | 1424 | 77 | 6 | 0.3 | 52 | 3 | 41 | 2 | 30 | 2 | 254 | 14 | 41 | 2 | 1848 |
| Intermediate 2 | 171 | 83 | 0 | 0 | 4 | 2 | 1 | 0.5 | 3 | 2 | 27 | 13 | 0 | 0 | 206 |
| Upper Palaeolithic 3 | 1873 | 64 | 0 | 0 | 33 | 1 | 224 | 8 | 21 | 1 | 748 | 26 | 32 | 1 | 2931 |
| Intermediate 4 | 392 | 63 | 1 | 0.2 | 7 | 1 | 73 | 12 | 2 | 0.3 | 144 | 23 | 3 | 0.5 | 622 |
| Upper Palaeolithic 5 | 3238 | 86 | 3 | 0.1 | 30 | 1 | 188 | 5 | 20 | 0.5 | 251 | 7 | 27 | 1 | 3757 |
| Intermediate 6 | 220 | 95 | 0 | 0 | 3 | 1 | 3 | 1 | 1 | 0.4 | 5 | 2 | 0 | 0 | 232 |
| Upper Palaeolithic 7 | 194 | 95 | 0 | 0 | 0 | 0 | 6 | 3 | 0 | 0 | 3 | 2 | 1 | 0.5 | 204 |
| Intermediate 8 | 15 | 71 | 0 | 0 | 0 | 0 | 2 | 10 | 1 | 5 | 3 | 14 | 0 | 0 | 21 |
| Upper Palaeolithic 9 | 58 | 82 | 0 | 0 | 0 | 0 | 7 | 10 | 0 | 0 | 4 | 6 | 2 | 3 | 71 |
| Uncertain | 2115 | 75 | 5 | 0.2 | 49 | 2 | 164 | 6 | 44 | 2 | 392 | 14 | 49 | 2 | 2818 |
| Totals | 9700 | 76 | 15 | 0.1 | 178 | 1 | 709 | 6 | 122 | 1 | 1831 | 14 | 155 | 1 | 12710 |

[a] Strata 1, 3, 5, 7 and 9 represent a continuous sequence of excavated layers. Strata 2, 4, 6 and 8 represent mixtures of material from adjacent layers. Thus stratum 2 combines material from strata 1 and 3, stratum 4 material from strata 3 and 5, etc. For further details see Bailey *et al.* (in press).

## Seasonality reconsidered

The original seasonal model was based on the proposition that red deer populations would move between the coast and the interior because of seasonal environmental constraints. Seasonal movement by the human population in response to these deer migrations was held to be demonstrated by the dominance of red deer bones in the faunal assemblages, by the modal altitude of terrain within each site exploitation territory, and by the aspect of each site.

In re-examining this seasonal hypothesis, it is useful to consider how far these three sources of data originally quoted in its support can be held rigorously to exclude the alternatives. The most obvious alternative is that the coastal and interior areas supported essentially independent subsistence economies of a sedentary or sedentary-cum-mobile type, or at any rate economies with smaller annual exploitation territories than originally hypothesized.

Although the actual scale of red deer movements during the maximum of the last glacial is open to question, it seems likely that there would have been some degree of seasonal movement of the deer between high altitude and low altitude grazing, given the relatively short growing season and the relative severity of winter conditions. It follows that an alternative to the seasonal hypothesis of human exploitation would have to meet one or more of the following three conditions:

(1) that there is sufficient variation of altitude over relatively short distances to provide seasonally complementary deer grazing within economic reach of a single settlement;

(2) that a sufficiently large number of deer can be killed in the season when they are available to provide a surplus of food which can be stored for use later in the year;

(3) that alternative food resources are available during the seasons when the deer are absent from the area.

## Fauna

Table 7.1 shows a number of contrasts in the representation of ungulate species at the two sites. Data from a number of levels are shown to provide some comparison and control on interpretation. It is assumed that the majority of the ungulate fauna was accumulated as human food refuse. At Kastritsa red deer (*Cervus elaphus*) consistently dominate the assemblages, accounting for 76% of the identified ungulate remains. However, at Asprochaliko there is a more even spread of species, with red deer accounting for only 38%. Also caprines, which account for only 1% at Kastritsa, are present at Asprochaliko in virtually identical quantities to red deer. Fallow deer (*Dama dama*), roe deer (*Capreolus capreolus*) and pig (*Sus scrofa*) are also relatively common at Asprochaliko, while bovid and equid (mostly *Bos primigenius* and *Equus* sp.) (the next most common species at Kastritsa) are entirely absent. Data from other levels at Asprochaliko confirm this general tendency. The Grava rockshelter (fig. 7.1) provides some additional hints about the nature of faunal exploitation in the coastal region. A small test excavation yielded red deer, roe deer and fallow deer, pig, large bovid and equid, although there is no information about relative proportions (Sordinas 1969). Thus the general impression is of a similar range of ungulate species on the coast and in the interior, but with rather different proportions of species represented at individual sites.

It could be argued that these differences are related in part at least to differences in the local environments. Asprochaliko (fig. 7.2) is in a narrow gorge, with steep rugged limestone slopes on either side where caprines might be found in some numbers, while red deer would probably spend most of their time feeding in the broader alluvial valleys to north and south. The milder climate attributed to the coastal region, by allowing the growth of a wider variety of plants and shrubs, could also be invoked to explain the better representation of browsers like roe and fallow deer, or the omnivorous pig. However, pollen data are not available to test this possibility. In any case one might expect these species to be equally at

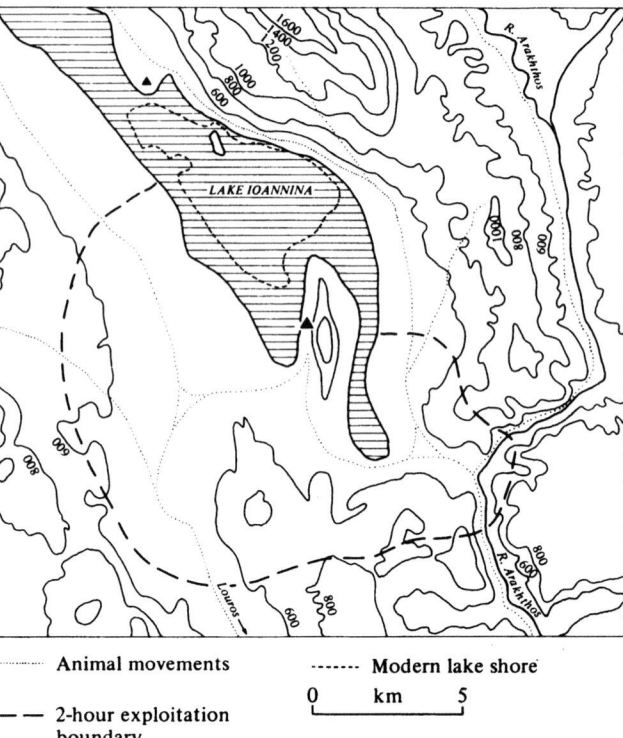

Animal movements          ------ Modern lake shore

— — 2-hour exploitation boundary

0          km          5

Fig. 7.3. Topographic setting of Kastritsa (centre triangle). Also shown is the cave of Perama. Contours are at 200 m intervals.

home around the marshy margins of the Ioannina Lake, with some additional browse from the scattered stands of trees which were demonstrably present in the vicinity (Bottema 1974). However, Kastritsa is located in the middle of an extensive alluvial lake basin with virtually no rugged terrain in its immediate vicinity (fig. 7.3), and this might account for the scarcity of caprines in the excavated fauna. Similarly the absence of caprines at Grava and the presence of bovid and equid can be attributed to the more open topography around the site (fig. 7.4).

The more even proportions of species at Asprochaliko (and perhaps also at Grava) could be further taken to indicate the availability to the human population of alternative resources that would have weakened if not wholly removed any need for year-round dependence on the seasonally mobile red deer. Conversely it could be argued that the predominance of red deer bones at Kastritsa suggests specialized mass slaughter with the possibility of storing the surplus to provide supplies of venison over the winter.

### Site exploitation territories

For this analysis we shall include the site of Klithi (figs. 7.1 and 7.5) to extend the range of comparison. This site has not yet been excavated but it is in an inland/upland location which poses a number of contrasts with the other site locations. It is also a very large rockshelter with a substantial talus deposit and numerous surface indications of prehistoric occupation.

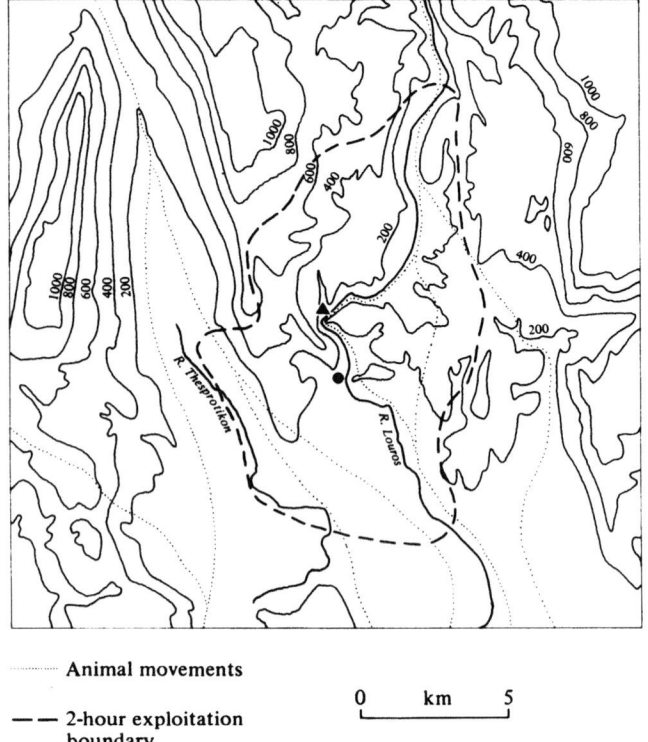

Animal movements

— — 2-hour exploitation boundary

0          km          5

Fig. 7.2. Topographic setting of Asprochaliko (triangle). Also shown is the site of Kokkinopilos (circle). Contours are at 200 m intervals.

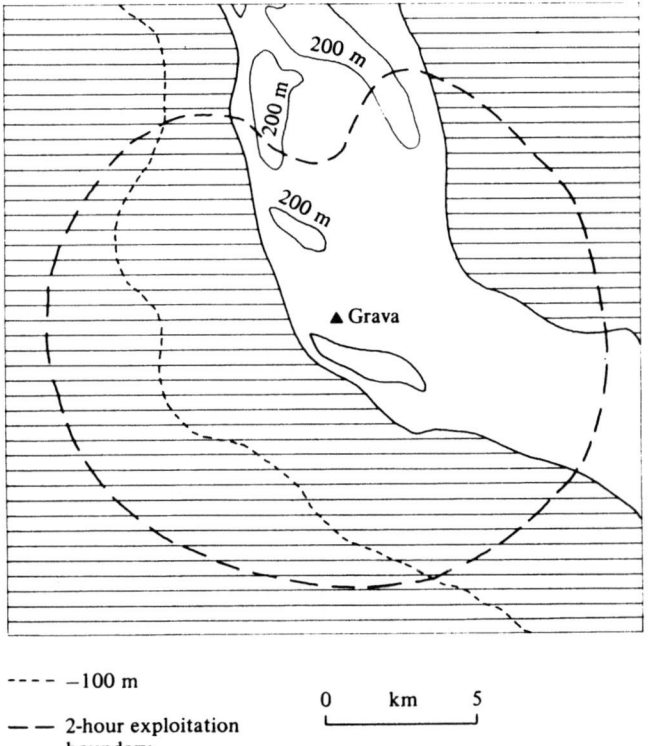

---- −100 m

— — 2-hour exploitation
boundary

0    km    5

Fig. 7.4. Topographic setting of Grava.

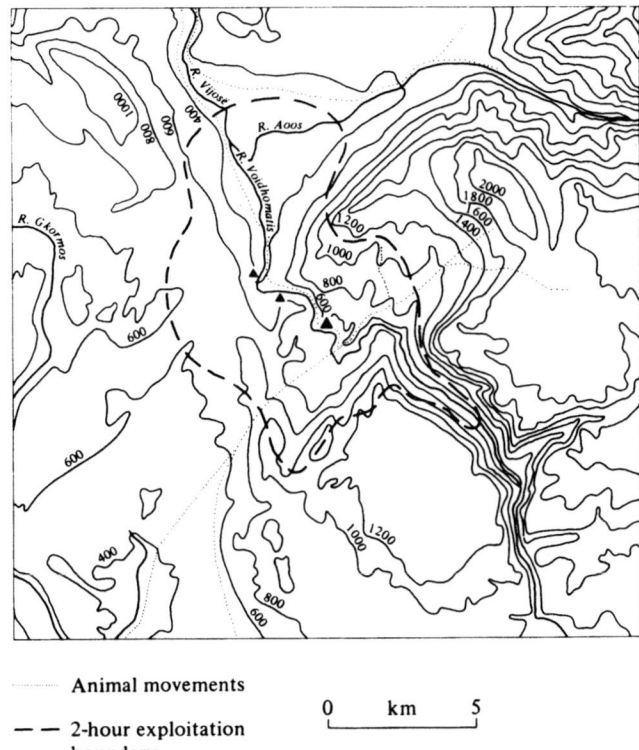

·········· Animal movements

— — 2-hour exploitation
boundary

0    km    5

Fig. 7.5. Topographic setting of Klithi (the largest of the three
sites shown). Contours are at 200 m intervals.

Any exercise in site territorial analysis depends on two
sorts of initial assumptions: the size of territory to be analysed;
and the landscape features to be employed in the assessment
of economic potential. For territory size we have used 2-hour
boundaries, following the recommendations of the original
study (Vita-Finzi and Higgs 1970), and 20-km circles. There
are four reasons for adopting the latter figure. First, it covers
a sufficiently large area to cope with the possibility that sites
might be asymmetrically located in relation to their major
food resources. Secondly, it provides an alternative set of
figures as a cross check on any interpretation of relative
differences between sites. Thirdly, it gives a reasonable
estimate of the maximum economic catchment likely to be
used in a hunting economy in which outlying resources are
incorporated into the subsistence of the home base via extended hunting trips and use of butchery camps (or by the
control of extended territories). Finally, the distance between
Klithi and Kastritsa, and between Kastritsa and Asprochaliko,
is about 40 km in each case. Grava is somewhat further from
its nearest neighbour. Whether the regularity in spacing is
fortuitous or not, at any rate it is clear that 20-km circles
define broadly contiguous but mutually exclusive areas around
each site.

Two types of calculation have been made to divide the
territories into land use categories. The first is based on
altitudinal limits. Higgs *et al.* (1967) suggested that the 600 m
contour defines a significant boundary between winter and
summer deer ranges, and we accept this as a useful indication
of differences in the seasonal potential of site exploitation

territories. The use of 200 m and 1000 m contours is also
included to give a more detailed pattern. A second set of
categories is based on surface geology and sediments, differentiated into alluvium, limestone and flysch. Although
some alluvium has been deposited since the maximum of the
last glacial, the major part of the alluvial deposits would
already have been in place, and we have assumed that subsequent alluviation has not radically altered the areal extent
of the alluvium. Similarly we have assumed that the character
of flysch landscapes with thin soils and heavily dissected topography can be projected into the last glacial period, although
it is possible that the present-day appearance may be due in
part to relatively recent erosion. We have made the further
assumption that these three categories can be ranked in terms
of their grazing productivity and economic potential, at least
as far as the larger ungulates are concerned, and red deer in
particular. This is necessarily a very preliminary assessment,
and we fully recognize the many unresolved problems arising
from such an attempt to equate surface geology, soil type,
vegetation and animal communities. But our concern at this
stage is less with reconstructing the precise economic potential
of any given site in isolation, than with establishing a general
and widely applicable regional framework for detecting broad
relative similarities or differences between sites as a basis for
testing hypotheses about the economic exploitation of deer
populations. Clearly further refinement combined with
additional geomorphological work, especially on the now
submerged coastal plain, is desirable.

The 2-hour territories are generally severely distorted

Table 7.2 *Topography of site exploitation territories*

| | 0–200 m | | 200–600 m | | 600–1000 m | | > 1000 m | | Total |
|---|---|---|---|---|---|---|---|---|---|
| | km² | % | km² | % | km² | % | km² | % | km² |
| **Klithi** | | | | | | | | | |
| 2-hour | – | – | 30 | 40 | 43 | 57 | 2 | 3 | 75 |
| 20 km | – | – | 460 | 37 | 428 | 34 | 368 | 29 | 1256 |
| **Kastritsa**[a] | | | | | | | | | |
| 2-hour | – | – | 83 | 70 | 36 | 30 | – | – | 119 |
| 20 km | – | – | 476 | 38 | 564 | 45 | 216 | 17 | 1256 |
| **Asprochaliko** | | | | | | | | | |
| 2-hour | 53 | 56 | 38 | 40 | 4 | 4 | – | – | 95 |
| 20 km | 420 | 33 | 536 | 43 | 176 | 14 | 124 | 10 | 1256 |
| **Grava**[a] | | | | | | | | | |
| 2-hour | 184[b] | 96 | 8 | 4 | – | – | – | – | 192 |
| 20 km | 688[b] | 97 | 20 | 3 | – | – | – | – | 708 |

[a] Areas of open water are excluded from the calculations.
[b] Includes land between 0 and −100 m.

Table 7.3 *Surface geology/sediments of site exploitation territories*

| | Flysch | | Limestone | | Alluvium | | Total |
|---|---|---|---|---|---|---|---|
| | km² | % | km² | % | km² | % | km² |
| **Klithi** | | | | | | | |
| 2-hour | 36 | 48 | 19 | 25 | 20 | 26 | 75 |
| 20 km | 796 | 63 | 280 | 22 | 180 | 14 | 1256 |
| **Kastritsa**[a] | | | | | | | |
| 2-hour | 24 | 20 | 32 | 27 | 63 | 53 | 119 |
| 20 km | 864 | 69 | 240 | 19 | 152 | 12 | 1256 |
| **Asprochaliko** | | | | | | | |
| 2-hour | 6 | 6 | 68 | 72 | 21 | 22 | 95 |
| 20 km | 380 | 30 | 596 | 48 | 280 | 22 | 1256 |
| **Grava**[a] | | | | | | | |
| 2-hour | 33 | 39 | 12 | 14 | 40 | 47 | 85 |
| 20 km | 40 | 20 | 40 | 20 | 120 | 60 | 200 |

[a] All areas of open water are excluded from the calculations, including areas between 0 and −100 m at Grava.

and reduced in size by steep topography. Two-hour boundaries also tend to discriminate against the steeper and higher terrain. If we consider land below and above 600 m (table 7.2), there is a clear separation between the lowland sites of Asprochaliko and Grava, and the inland sites of Klithi and Kastritsa. This reinforces the idea of a seasonal separation between the two zones. But there remains a fairly substantial area of terrain below 600 m within the 20-km circles of the inland sites (37% and 38%), and the percentage is even higher in the 2-hour territories (40% and 70%). Thus winter occupation in the hinterland is not unequivocally excluded. On the other hand high-level summer grazing is relatively poorly represented at Asprochaliko (a maximum of 24%), and not at all at Grava, although this is offset to some extent in both cases by the more varied pattern of faunal exploitation already noted. The more detailed breakdown of topographic categories indicates a progressive shift in the modal altitude of terrain as one moves from Grava to Klithi, and this might be taken as evidence that the sites were linked together as a series of complementary grazing territories in an annual round. However, there is little

in these territorial results, especially in combination with the faunal data, that positively excludes the existence of localized inland and coastal economies.

Similarly the geological data (table 7.3) show a broad separation between the coastal and hinterland sites, with the most productive category (alluvium) better represented on the coast, and the least productive category (flysch) inland, although the differences are not such as to suggest clear support for a seasonal hypothesis. Again it may be noted that the 2-hour territories tend to minimize the disadvantage of the inland sites in this respect. The site exploitation territory of Grava (fig. 7.4) is difficult to assess, since most of it is under water. But if the percentage figures for the present-day land surface are representative, then the Grava exploitation territory at the maximum marine regression could have been one of the most productive for terrestrial resources.

In summary, the territorial data suggest a gradient of increasing economic productivity from the hinterland to the coast, but little unequivocal evidence of a clear-cut separation between the two zones.

### Vegetable and aquatic resources

So far the argument has been presented in terms of the terrestrial ungulates. However, two other sets of resources need to be considered. Plant foods are difficult to assess, since the sites were excavated before the development of systematic flotation techniques, while the site territorial data are essentially uninformative about the potential availability of edible plant foods. In the absence of any other indication we can only fall back on indirect inferences from the available pollen data (Bottema 1974). Given an environment dominated by *Artemisia* steppe, it could be argued that plant foods would have provided no more than a minor supplement to the diet. At best we might postulate the availability of small quantities of edible roots and greens in the marshy environs of the Ioannina Lake, and perhaps also along the river courses. The Kastritsa site might thus have had some minor advantage because of its lake-side location.

Exploitation of aquatic animals is a more serious possibility, at least on site territorial and locational grounds. During the last glacial the level of Lake Ioannina was higher than at present, presumably because of reduced evaporation rates, and the lake would have dominated the immediate surroundings of the site (fig. 7.3). Despite this, fish bones are entirely absent from the excavated fauna, although the deposits were carefully sieved. Bird bones, however, are frequently recorded, and may indicate an exploitation activity enhanced by the lake-edge environment and an additional, if relatively minor, source of food.

The site of Grava would have included some sea shore within its 2-hour site exploitation territory, even at the maximum regression (fig. 7.4). The contribution of marine resources is relatively difficult to assess, because here as elsewhere most of the evidence for such exploitation is likely to have been deposited at sites now submerged. However, one would expect some trace of such activity to be preserved at sites such as Grava. As it is, Grava has yielded no evidence whatsoever of marine remains, not even mollusc shells. This contrasts with Cantabrian deposits in a comparable situation (chapters 12 and 13). Indirect sources of evidence do not encourage the hypothesis of a heavy dependence on marine resources either. The anadromous sturgeon (*Acipenser spp.*) is found today in rivers on the Adriatic coast, and the monk seal (*Monachus monachus*) is also present in the Mediterranean (Ekman 1953). Eels (*Anguilla anguilla*) and trout (*Salmo trutta*) are also present. But sea fish are mainly pelagic species such as mackerel (*Scomber scombrus*) and the bluefin tuna (*Thynnus thynnus*) and therefore relatively difficult of access. The ecological productivity of the Mediterranean is also relatively poor under present-day conditions, because nutrients formed on the sea bottom tend to be trapped in deep water by high surface-water temperatures, or to be carried out of the Mediterranean basin by bottom currents. It is conceivable that conditions would have been better with the lower temperatures and low sea levels of the last glacial period. But the steep-sided nature of the basin and the relatively restricted tidal inflow suggest that it would have always have been relatively unproductive compared with Atlantic waters, and it is unlikely that there were any resources equivalent to the Atlantic salmon (see chapter 19). Thus exploitation of marine resources is a possibility, but there is no basis for suggesting that it would have provided more than a minor advantage in the occupation of coastal areas.

### Aspect

Temperature readings under present-day conditions demonstrate that Kastritsa, facing north-west, is relatively unsuitable for use in winter, while the reverse applies to the south-facing Asprochaliko, which becomes uncomfortably hot during the day in summer (Higgs and Webley 1971). The south-facing Grava is similar to Asprochaliko in this respect. However, the conditions at Kastritsa would not totally discourage winter occupation if there were good economic reasons for staying in the locality and no other natural shelter available. Alternatively the south-facing Perama cave on the opposite side of the lake (fig. 7.3) could have been resorted to, or open sites with artificial shelters could have been created. Similarly at Asprochaliko it could be argued that the unpleasantly hot daytime temperatures would not be relevant to the presumably cooler summer climate of the last glacial period. Moreover Klithi, as an inland site, fails to fit the expected pattern, since it faces south. Here, however, one could argue that the extra warmth would have been desirable during the last glacial even in summer, since the site would have been close to the permanent snowline on the mountains immediately to the north-east. In any case other rockshelters with a different aspect and evidence of Palaeolithic occupation are available at the mouth of the Klithi gorge (fig. 7.5). Here too, then, the data are equivocal in their seasonal implications.

### Inter-site variation

The main outcome of the preceding discussion is to demonstrate the inherent ambiguity of the data on seasonality. A more useful approach at this stage is to consider in more detail variations between the sites themselves, rather than treating them as points on a map. It has been implicitly assumed so far that the sites are home bases, equivalent in every respect except for the possibility of differential season of occupation and some minor differences of local topography and environment. However, recent work demonstrates that hunter-gatherers may use sites for a variety of purposes and that locations of good archaeological preservation do not necessarily indicate the former presence of residential bases (Binford 1978a, 1980; Gould 1980). Moreover, our analysis of the excavated materials shows that there are considerable differences in the rate of accumulation of cultural material, suggesting differences in intensity of use, and by implication differences of function.

### On-site data

In table 7.4 gross quantities of stone and bone are expressed in terms of the volume of deposit from which they

Table 7.4. *Densities of Upper Palaeolithic artefacts and fauna in selected trenches at Asprochaliko and Kastritsa*

|  | Asprochaliko | | | Kastritsa | | | |
|---|---|---|---|---|---|---|---|
| Excavation area[a] | R2 | R3 | R42 | R2 | R3 | R11 | R12 |
| Excavation layers | 4, 7, 10 | | | 1–15 | | 11–15 | |
| Time span (kyr)[b] | 12.7 | 12.7 | 12.7 | 7.0 | 7.0 | 3.0 | 3.0 |
| Mean layer area (m$^2$) | 1.12 | 1.29 | 1.67 | 1.97 | 1.80 | 3.00 | 3.00 |
| Total finished tools[d] | 215 | 54 | 14 | 1907 | 2261 | 287 | 595 |
| Total waste[d] | 5071 | 1499 | 427 | 17714 | 21646 | 2625 | 8119 |
| Total manufacture | 5286 | 1553 | 441 | 19621 | 23907 | 2912 | 8714 |
| Finished tools:waste | 1/24 | 1/28 | 1/30 | 1/9 | 1/10 | 1/9 | 1/14 |
| Time density (manufacture/m$^2$/kyr) | 371 | 95 | 81 | 1423 | 1897 | 323 | 968 |
| Adjusted for shelter size (× 120/75)[c] | 594 | 152 | 33 | 1423 | 1897 | 323 | 968 |
| Mean time density | | 260 | | | | 1153 | |
| Identified bones | 15 | 2 | 2 | 204 | 522 | 157 | 352 |
| Identified teeth | 10 | 6 | 3 | 143 | 365 | 85 | 250 |
| Total fauna | 25 | 8 | 5 | 347 | 887 | 242 | 602 |
| Tooth:bone | 1/1.5 | 1/0.33 | 1/0.67 | 1/1.4 | 1/1.4 | 1/1.9 | 1/1.4 |
| Mean tooth:bone | | 1/0.83 | | | | 1/1.5 | |
| Time density (fauna/m$^2$/kyr) | 1.76 | 0.94 | 0.24 | 25.2 | 70.4 | 26.9 | 66.9 |
| Adjusted for shelter size (× 120/75)[c] | 2.81 | 0.78 | 0.38 | 25.2 | 70.4 | 26.9 | 66.9 |
| Mean time density | | 1.32 | | | | 50.8 | |

[a]Estimates have been adjusted to take account of rockfalls and areas of disturbed or collapsed deposit.
[b]From 26 100 to 13 400 b.p. at Asprochaliko; 20 400 to 13 400 b.p. at Kastritsa.
[c]Shelter size adjustment is in proportion to the available living area and assumes that the Asprochaliko shelter was not occupied to capacity.
[d]For details of definitions see Bailey *et al.* (in prep.).

were excavated and its rate of deposition. Only selected trenches, representing those areas of the excavation with the densest material and/or the longest sequence of deposits, have been used in the calculations. Ideally one would also wish to allow for within-site variation as well as the total areal extent of the occupation zone. For example, a rockshelter with a confined living area might give rise to uniformly high densities of material, whereas a more spacious site might yield lower and more variable densities because of the greater opportunity for dispersal of activities, even though both sites were consistently used by the same number of people performing similar activities over a comparable span of time. As a check on this we have estimated the total potential living surface at Kastritsa and Asprochaliko as 75 m$^2$ and 120 m$^2$ respectively. The Asprochaliko figures have been adjusted upwards accordingly, to allow for the possibility of greater dispersal of materials. Even so the density of total manufactured material per unit time at Kastritsa is about 247% higher than at Asprochaliko. Since there are various uncertainties about the calculation of these figures, we are reluctant to read too much significance into this difference, although it suggests that Kastritsa was the more intensively used site. The ratio of finished tools to other artefact categories provides a more striking contrast (table 7.4). Finished tools are two and three times more common at Kastritsa than at Asprochaliko, and this strengthens the hypothesis of some sort of difference in function between the two sites.

Faunal quantities are strikingly different, with a rate of accumulation at Kastritsa 3332% higher than at Asprochaliko. However, we are hampered here by lack of data on unidenti-fiable fragments. Moreover, since bone is vulnerable to total destruction, it is possible that part of the difference is due to post-depositional factors. The rate of accumulation of sediment is rather slower at Asprochaliko. Thus material might have remained on an exposed surface for longer, with greater risk of damage or destruction before burial (Gifford 1978). Teeth to bone ratios can provide a general indication of preservation conditions (see chapter 4) and show only a slight difference between the two sites. It is conceivable that this comparison is misleading and that these figures have been distorted by differential butchery practices. For example, it may be that skulls and mandibles were introduced into one of the sites more rarely than other parts of the skeleton. We can only say on the evidence analysed so far that there is no support for a hypothesis of differential preservation, and that the differences in rates of bone accumulation at the two sites appear to reflect genuine differences in their use as bases for animal exploitation.

We recognize that these differences might be the product of at least three behavioural variables: population size; total duration of stay (whether seasonal or permanent, repeated from year to year or more intermittent); and the activities performed at the site (butchering of carcases, equipment manufacture and maintenance etc.). The resolution of the available data does not allow us to distinguish these variables with any confidence, and we therefore prefer to avoid speculative attempts to place the sites within absolute categories, such as residential base or butchery site, while emphasizing that the measurable *relative* differences between them provide a useful basis for further analysis.

This discussion of relative intensity of site usage can be

extended to the other two principal Palaeolithic rockshelters of the region. Sordinas (1969) estimated the potential living surface at Grava to be about 70 m², very similar to Kastritsa. Cemented and partially eroded deposits apparently resting on bedrock yielded about 1000 Upper Palaeolithic artefacts, and the faunal remains mentioned above. These data are not strictly comparable to the other sites because only a small test pit was excavated. But even allowing for the possibility of erosion, the cultural deposits appear to have been of limited thickness and extent, and the available data suggest relatively sparse or intermittent occupation.

At the other extreme is the site of Klithi. This is a spacious rockshelter with a potential living area of 700 m² and an immense cone of deposition with numerous Palaeolithic flints scattered on its surface. There is no doubt that the site is a large one in terms of the number of people it can accommodate. Initial indications are that it was also the scene of relatively intensive use. However, the latter point is at best hypothesis and its accuracy must await the results of excavation.

While the regional pattern of relative site usage suggested by the above observations is admittedly hypothetical in view of the limited data available from Grava and Klithi, there are several other indications in its support. First, there is clear evidence of Upper Palaeolithic occupation in two rockshelters at the mouth of the gorge within which the site of Klithi is situated and some 2 to 3 km distant from it (fig. 7.5). This suggests that the area as a whole was relatively attractive to human settlement regardless of the specific function of individual sites within the group. In the Ioannina Lake basin, in contrast, apart from Kastritsa there is only the site of Perama (fig.7.3), where the evidence of Palaeolithic occupation is in doubt; and a handful of surface flints found near the crest of the ridge to the north. At Asprochaliko there are the nearby Kokkinopilos surface sites (Dakaris *et al.* 1964). Most of the finds here are Mousterian, although Upper Palaeolithic artefacts were found in one exposure. At Grava no clear evidence of Upper Palaeolithic material has been found in the near vicinity.

Secondly, extensive areas in the region at large have been surveyed for sites, and a number of potentially habitable rockshelters lacking evidence of occupation is known. Many surface sites have also been discovered, notably the red bed (Kokkinopilos Formation) occurrences at Kokkinopilos, Karvounari, Morfi and on Corfu (fig. 7.1), with clear evidence of Upper Palaeolithic material in at least the first two cases. It is difficult to assess intensity of occupation of these open sites, both because of poor chronological control, and because the spatial dispersal of material in an open context as compared with the superpositioning of material in the confines of a rockshelter would make quantitative comparison between the two types of site uncertain. However, even allowing for all the uncertainties of dating surface material by its technological features, it appears that the Upper Palaeolithic finds at Kokkinopilos and Karvounari are both fewer and more localized in extent than the Mousterian artefacts. Moreover,

these surface sites are also predominantly in the coastal areas, and this cannot be attributed merely to differential exposure or investigation, since red bed deposits apparently similar to those on the coast are found inland and have been intensively surveyed without result.

All these indications add up to a picture not simply of relative differences between individual sites, but between areas, suggesting the hypothesis of a hierarchical site distribution at the regional scale (see also chapters 8, 13, 15 and 18); with relatively few but intensively used sites in the coastal lowlands, and perhaps one dominant site (Klithi) forming the apex of the hierarchy. While this hypothesis needs further testing through excavation and survey, it has interesting implications for the pattern of land use. First, it is almost exactly the reverse of what would be predicted from the territorial data examined above, which suggest that the most productive resource zones, and by implication the most intensively used sites, ought to have occurred in the coastal areas. Secondly, it implies that the on-site data cannot be explained solely in terms of the resources within economic reach of the site (however large the assumed radius of the site exploitation territory), but may be influenced by the relationship of the site to other sites within a wider context of regional intergration. While we accept that there are many remaining deficiencies in the available on-site data, the indications of a hierarchical pattern are sufficiently strong to suggest that it is worth exploring the off-site data in these terms, with a view to resolving some of the apparent contradictions between potential economic productivity and relative intensity of site use.

### Off-site data

In exploring further the evidence of site locations in relation to their environmental setting, we shall retain the basic assumption that red deer were the major staple resource, an assumption which is difficult to avoid in view of our previous discussion of likely alternatives. We shall also assume that their exploitation was conducted within a least-cost framework (Keene 1979; Bettinger 1980; Earle 1980), and that a major consideration of economic strategy was to reduce the effort and risk involved in their location and capture. A further point to bear in mind is that a successful location for deer exploitation is likely to be a compromise between two factors which are to some extent in opposition: sufficient proximity to large numbers of animals to ensure ready access to them; yet sufficient distance from them to ensure that they are not disturbed and dispersed by human presence (Sturdy 1972, 1975; Binford 1978a: 489). This does not mean that we propose to ignore alternative food resources. On the contrary the availability of even small quantities of alternative supplies may provide a crucial insurance in specialized deer economies, even to the point of exercising an important limiting effect on the overall level of economic success. Other resources such as shelter, water or fuel may also have a critical limiting effect if they are in short supply or irregularly distributed. In this respect the diversity and predictability of the alternative resources available at a given location may be as important as the potential abundance of the major staple.

A feature of the immediate topography at three of the four main sites is that it provides excellent conditions for the interception of animals. Asprochaliko is in a classic 'hour-glass' location in a short narrow gorge which opens out into broader valleys at either end (fig. 7.2). Animals could easily be trapped with little means of escape against the natural barriers presented by the river or the steep slopes on either side. Klithi is similarly in a narrow gorge (fig. 7.5), while Kastritsa is at the foot of a steep ridge which converges on the shore of the expanded Ioannina Lake (fig. 7.3). Grava has the least favourable location in this respect (fig. 7.4).

The attractions of a given site also depend on the frequency and predictability with which animals may be expected to converge on that location. A site that is far removed from the main grazing areas or routes of movement of the herd animals may be at a disadvantage, regardless of the opportunities for interception provided by the immediate topography. A site in the middle of a featureless plain, for example, would be easily bypassed, unless its occupants practised such labour-intensive techniques as driving and rounding-up of animals from a large area, construction of extensive artificial fencing, or close herd control. Grava is essentially in this situation, which may further account for the sparse evidence of its use.

The Louros valley, within which Asprochaliko is located, is a major route between the coastal plain and the Ioannina Lake basin, and might therefore be expected to channel deer movements towards the site to some extent. However, there are major alternative routes through valleys to the west (the Thesprotikon) and to the east (the Arakhthos). Even for animals entering the Louros valley there are several alternative routes which bypass the site over low and easily traversed hills up to 8 km to the east, beyond the 2-hour boundary (fig. 7.2). Moreover, there is little seasonally complementary grazing in the area, and the Asprochaliko gorge would probably always have been, at best, a routeway, with the deer moving fairly rapidly out of economic reach to north or south depending on the season. The unpredictability or short duration of deer movements within the vicinity of the site could explain not only the relatively sparse evidence of its use, but also the greater reliance on other ungulate species. It can be argued that even small groups of people staying at the site for relatively short periods would have to resort to these other species as a necessary back-up when the deer failed to use that particular route in the expected numbers.

Kastritsa, in contrast, is well placed to catch animals moving into the eastern end of the Ioannina Lake basin from the Louros and Arakhthos valleys. Some deer might bypass the site by continuing northwards up the Arakhthos. However, this route leads into an extensive upland region of deeply dissected flysch landscapes which would probably have offered relatively unattractive summer grazing compared with the

south-facing limestone slopes that ring the northern edge of the lake basin (fig. 7.3). The site has three other important advantages. First, it is in an area with extensive high and low altitude grazing, where deer might be expected to remain within economic reach for some considerable period of the year. Secondly, the site is not directly on the routes of animal movement, but sufficiently close to the main grazing areas that deer could be diverted or driven relatively easily into the natural topographic trap adjacent to the site. Thirdly, there are the small additional advantages of the lake-shore resources — the birds, and perhaps also marsh plants and fish, although archaeological evidence for the latter two is lacking. These features could explain both the relatively intensive use of the site and the relatively high proportion of red deer remains, compared with Asprochaliko.

The immediate vicinity of Klithi, in its narrow limestone gorge with steep, rugged terrain rising to the north, suggests similarities with Asprochaliko. This, and the proximity to the permanent snowline of the last glacial, suggests that the site would be a good base for the exploitation of ibex and/or chamois, especially in autumn and winter when the animals would be driven down to a lower altitude by the winter snows. However, the site location is also similar to Kastritsa in terms of red deer exploitation, although it is rather more asymmetrically located in relation to the major grazing areas. Lowland and highland grazing are both abundant as at Kastritsa. Similarly, deer on the Konitsa plain, to the north-west, could remain out of reach of the site by moving to the north-east, but would find their way on to the limestone pastures of the high Pindus blocked by the steep scarp slopes along the banks of the Aoos, with relatively unattractive flysch country to the north (fig. 7.5). Moreover, animals could be relatively easily diverted into the Klithi gorge, and the small rockshelters at its mouth may perhaps represent bases used for this purpose. Any tendency for deer in the western end of the Ioannina Lake basin to move to higher pastures would inevitably bring them about 1 km to the east of the site, where they could easily be caught, since this is the only possible route on to the high Pindus from the south (fig. 7.5). We might then predict that excavation at Klithi should yield evidence of relatively intensive site use, and a high proportion of red deer in the faunal remains, as at Kastritsa, albeit with relatively more emphasis on caprines.

The above interpretations do not depend on the assumption that deer would have made large-scale, long-distance seasonal migrations. However, it is worth noting that the relative differences between the various sites would have been enhanced in these circumstances. In particular Kastritsa and Klithi would have gained in importance through their control of major routes between the coastal lowlands and the interior uplands. Klithi stands out in this respect, since it lies at the convergence of a whole series of valleys which fan out to all the major areas of coastal plain that would have been available during the maximum marine regression (fig. 7.1). The Vijosë and the Drin valleys lead down to the Albanian coast, the Kalamas and the Kokkitos to the area around Corfu, and the Thesprotikon and the Louros to the south. Regardless of whether or not the deer moved over these distances, Klithi would have been well placed to serve as a regional focus for the integration of scattered human populations, who might meet together in the Klithi locality for marriage ceremonies or other communal rituals and the exchange of goods and information (see Part 4). This suggests further predictions about the nature of the materials that ought to be recovered in excavation, for example exotic items such as sea shells brought in over long distances. Rather than suggesting a simple pattern of long-distance movements by whole social groups, the available on-site and off-site data suggest as a more realistic alternative a seasonal rhythm of aggregation and dispersal by the human population. The major aggregations would be in summer in the hinterland at sites such as Kastritsa and Klithi, where resources would be predictably available in abundance. In winter there would be a dispersal into small units scattered over a very large region, mainly in the coastal areas, but perhaps with some small groups remaining in the hinterland to live off stored food or the occasional ungulates available there throughout the winter.

### Man—animal relationships

The above analysis has some further implications for the interpretation of the 'man—deer' relationship. The concepts of close man—animal relationships, symbiosis and husbandry (Higgs and Jarman 1969, 1972; Jarman 1976) arose in part in response to the belief that a year-round association with red deer implied by the seasonal model, and persisting for thousands of years, would necessarily have resulted in a high risk of overkill without some measure of control and conservation. Such a belief rests on the assumption that regional patterns of exploitation might be sufficiently complete and intensive to make the threat of overkill an imminent possibility. Our re-examination of the Epirus data raises serious doubts about the validity of this basic assumption. Subsequent discussions have emphasized the inherent ambiguity of the archaeological data, and the difficulties of drawing a neat line between 'random' and controlled exploitation, and between fortuitous and intentional husbandry (Jarman *et al.* 1982). Other authors have pointed out that 'random' slaughter, involving whole social groups, may be quite harmless to the prey species as a whole, provided that there is a dispersed population in the region at large acting as a reservoir to replenish local losses (Klein 1978, 1979; chapters 4 and 5 above). The Epirus data suggest that there would have been extensive tracts of country where dispersed populations of deer could have remained free of human predation, or where they could easily bypass major centres of human settlement. Whether this situation was due to the difficulties of gaining access to the deer in areas lacking suitable topographic checks on their movement, or to some other limiting factor holding the human population density below a level at which it might begin to exert pressure on the regional deer

population, is difficult to say. Either way there would have been little need or incentive for the human population to switch from 'opportunistic' to 'controlled' patterns of exploitation (Bailey 1981b). The term 'control' here is susceptible of further clarification since it may be used in two different senses. In one sense it means greater efficiency (in terms of the ratio between food returns and labour input) in predicting the location and securing the capture of animals. Manipulation of animal movements aided by topography may form a part of such patterns. Here control is largely a matter of increased efficiency of slaughter. Control, however, may be used in a different sense to indicate a greater concern with the livelihood of the animals, for example through selective slaughter intended to conserve the breeding stock, winter feeding, or deliberate movement of the herds between pastures to ensure the most efficient use of available grazing. While admitting all the ambiguities of the evidence, we suggest that prehistoric exploitation patterns in Epirus were controlled in the former sense but not in the latter.

### Conclusion

If our general conclusions about the regional integration of settlement and subsistence are necessarily tentative, they nevertheless indicate that it may be quite misleading to try and resolve the nature of occupation at individual sites or in particular areas in terms of a choice between mutually exclusive hypotheses of seasonality or sedentism. Our analysis suggests that it may be more productive to compare sites in terms of the relationship between the on-site and off-site data in each case, and that such a comparative perspective may stimulate further analysis of both sets of data. Detailed examination of relative differences in the on-site data can give greater focus to the analysis of the environmental setting by posing specific questions and suggesting alternative scales of measurement. The use of 2-hour boundaries may provide a reasonable order of magnitude for purposes of initial analysis, but will not necessarily or automatically reveal all the important features of the site—environment relationship. Examination of the immediately adjacent terrain as well as the position of the site in relation to a broader regional setting may add important additional information. Conversely the off-site data can provide a coherent framework for further on-site analysis and excavation. In this respect excavation at Klithi will be of crucial importance for further interpretation, not only as a test of predictions derived from comparison with other sites, but because it should clarify the nature of Middle Palaeolithic exploitation patterns. We have avoided consideration of long-term trends, partly to focus on the spatial variables in the Epirus environment, but more importantly because almost nothing is known about the nature of Middle Palaeolithic occupation, if any, in the hinterland. In contrast to Asprochaliko, the sequence at Kastritsa does not extend back before about 22 000 b.p. Deposits below this level are mainly beach deposits or lake silts and suggest that the site would have been unusable in earlier periods because of its low-lying lake-side position. Evidence from other regions of Europe (Parts 3 and 4) suggests that there may have been major changes in economic strategy during the Upper Palaeolithic period. There are also major disagreements about how such changes should be explained. Whether the pattern we have suggested for last glacial Epirus can be traced back into earlier periods, and what sort of modifications it underwent during the late glacial and early postglacial, are questions which can only be answered with further field work.

*Acknowledgements*

We are grateful to the British Academy and the research funds of the Universities of Cambridge and Southampton for financial support; to the British School at Athens, the Ministry of Culture at Athens, the Ioannina ephorate and the staff of the Ioannina Museum for their cooperation in allowing our re-examination of the data; to Mike and Heather Jarman, Andy Garrard and Marsha Levine for faunal identifications; and to Katy Edgcombe for computer assistance.

Chapter 8

# Site variability and prehistoric economy in Levante
Iain Davidson

The author discusses concepts and methods in the study of prehistoric economies for fisher-gatherer hunters and shows the operation of these in a detailed case study in the Levante region of eastern Spain. Data are presented from the Palaeolithic cave sites of Parpalló, Les Mallaetes, Volcán and other sites of southern Valencia province used between 30 thousand and 10 thousand years ago. He discusses the sites in their spatial and environmental context and uses the analysis of the site catchments and site exploitation territories together with analysis of faunal remains in terms of relative abundance of species and body-part distributions to outline important features of economic change at local and regional level. He is explicitly concerned with the effects of sampling on the variability in archaeological remains within sites, and on the regional interpretations which are made possible by differential site preservation or detection. The author emphasizes that it is only possible to study prehistoric economy when there is information about site systems involving more than one site, independent evidence about the local and contemporary environments and about interrelations between these as they change through time.

## Introduction
The study of the economy of hunter-gatherers in pre-history has generally been carried out through the interpretation of faunal and, more rarely, macrofloral remains. I have argued previously that more is involved than the simple description of faunal and plant remains. The study of prehistoric economy must be carefully conceived in terms of the choices of resources by considering the range of available resources as well as the residues of the exploited resources. This must entail the study of several sites. In this chapter I will discuss some aspects of my recent study of prehistoric economy in the late Palaeolithic of eastern Spain (Davidson 1980), to illustrate the way in which this more complex conception may be realized.

In my previous discussion of the theory of studying economy for fisher-gatherer-hunter archaeological sites I argued that such studies were only possible provided three individual aspects were included: studies of site systems involving more than one site, studies of independent evidence about the environment, and the study of change through time (Davidson 1981). This discussion demonstrated that in terms of archaeological data it is often easier to identify the main features of economic organization by detecting relative changes through time, rather than by reconstructing in detail the economy of a particular period.

Change through time at particular sites is not a sufficient indication that economic change is taking place, for two main reasons. First, there is uncertainty about within-site variability, produced by spatial segregation of different activities (Dennell 1972; Binford 1978a; Rigaud 1978), and therefore uncertainty as to how much of the temporal variability in a stratigraphic sequence is due to such contextual variation, and how much represents genuine economic change. Secondly, much of the environmental information, essential to a study of economy as a relationship with environment, is derived from the same site. It may, therefore, be biased by the presence of the site and its occupants at the time of deposition of the environmental assemblages.

Some further insight may be gained by comparing diachronic sequences from sites in different environments. But even this improvement may not be sufficient to define relations with environment, since the environmental information from any one site will necessarily be influenced to some degree by human selection. It is therefore necessary to incorporate diachronic studies of environmental change into the study in order to control this variable.

The final requirement for any satisfactory study of prehistoric economic change is to consider the way in which site systems as studied by the previous criteria change in their distribution through time. This approach will lead only to studies which show broad long-term changes in prehistoric economies, unless there is rigorous control over chronology so that it can be established that sites were indeed occupied contemporaneously. In this situation it may be possible to establish some features of the contemporary economy for a group of sites.

These conditions are rarely met. Here I will show some of the results of my analysis of sites in eastern Spain, where some of the conditions are met with sufficient detail to establish some of the outlines of the regional economy and some specific interpretations for individual sites (Davidson 1980). I shall draw on the methodological and theoretical distinction between site catchments and site exploitation territories. A *site catchment* refers to the empirically determined range of forays from a given site for resources of all types including food and raw materials. The *site exploitation territory* is an arbitrarily defined area around a given site within which it is assumed that the daily exploitation of food resources habitually occurs. I shall be concerned less with justifying the accuracy of these concepts for defining the absolute spatial limits to activity from a given site, than with their utility as measuring devices for detecting relative changes – between sites or between periods of time – in the relationship of subsistence exploitation to environment. I shall also use a distinction between tactics – short-term methods of exploitation at a particular location – and strategy – the combined patterning of tactical methods over a wider area and a longer period (Davidson 1980).

I will, first, explore the information about the site catchments of the sites, and the implications for the understanding of regional exploitation strategies. Then I will discuss some of the evidence for local exploitation tactics in the relations with the large mammals. I will conclude with some observations about the nature of the evidence available for interpretation of prehistoric economies. Support for this set of requirements is provided by the recent work of Binford. He has shown that there is spatial patterning to the distribution of refuse within sites although this may not always be simple (Binford 1978b). Such results have been used effectively to show the difficulties with normative interpretations of artefact assemblages as indicators of 'cultures' (Rigaud 1978). Varia-

bility between assemblages from different layers sampled at a single site may be a result of a shifted locus of activity (cf. Jones 1980), rather than any change in the organization of exploitation strategies.

Moreover, in logistically organized (or 'collecting') exploitation strategies (Binford 1980; chapters 3 and 18, this volume) there is a great variety of site types, and consequent variability between sites in the materials discarded (Binford 1978a). Binford (1978a: 482) has argued that such considerations may account for much of the selective bias in specific faunal assemblages which might otherwise be interpreted as selective exploitation of species leading to economic management (cf. Jarman 1972a). This supports my contention that local economies can only be studied by an analysis of the integration of activities between sites.

Foraging strategies (Binford 1980) would result in residues at sites which reflect the local environment of the site, and, so long as the strategy of foraging remained unchanged, environmental change as a result of climatic or geomorphic change would be reflected in the diachronic patterning of residues in individual sites, provided also that the same type of activity areas in the sites were being sampled throughout the sequence. Such diachronic patterning could not be interpreted as economic change. In foraging strategies, the expectation would be that diachronic patterning would show similar trends in different sites, although the particular mix of species would depend on the local site environment in each case. If there were a great difference between the species from environment to environment this might produce different patterns of archaeological residues. But this would be due to differences in the way particular food resources were processed rather than real differences in economic exploitation between the sites.

In logistically organized systems, some of the patterning of the remains is the result of the tactical advantages in the exploitation of different species, and the fit between the diachronic patterning of residues at individual sites and the fluctuations in environment would not be so close. Moreover, there would also be a greater range of patterns of relationship between residues and environment from site to site.

The difference between foraging strategies and logistic strategies is a major economic difference, and would only be revealed in archaeological studies by analysis within a diachronic framework of more than one site, of residues in relation to environmental change, and of spatial distributions of site systems. It is, however, important to remember that the opposition between foraging and logistic systems is not clear-cut, in the sense that exploitation strategies are purely one or the other. In Binford's (1980) type examples, the activities at the dispersed summer residences of the modelled Nunamiut system included foraging activities, although the system as a whole must be characterized as logistically organized. It is however, difficult to argue that there is an element of logistical organization involved in the exploitation of the resource patches of the modelled G/wi foraging system. Only

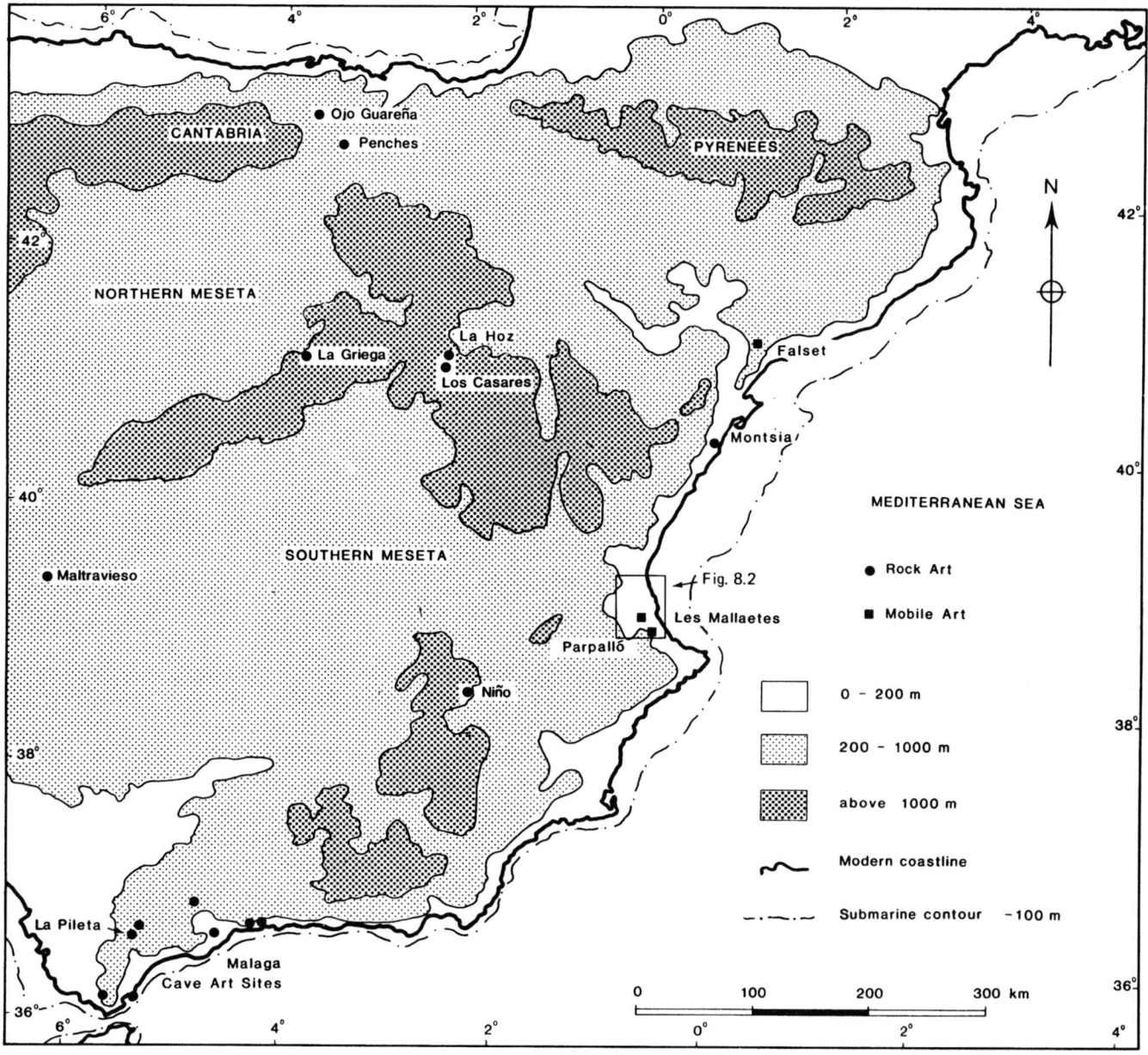

Fig. 8.1. Map of eastern Spain showing study area and distribution of Palaeolithic art sites which are outside the Cantabrian region.

analysis of settlement patterns and the associated subsistence evidence allows the nature of the adaptation to be adequately described.

### The sites

The archaeology of eastern Spain is dominated by the studies made by workers at the Servicio de Investigacion Prehistorica (S.I.P.) de Valencia, notably in the studies of the late Palaeolithic. Studies in other areas have been made but the finds are nowhere as abundant, nor as appropriate for the interpretation which I am advocating (see map, fig. 8.1). The reasons for this variation between regions are a suitable subject for future studies.

The study of the late Palaeolithic in Valencia province became the object of wider interest with the excavation by Pericot (Pericot 1942) of the cave of Parpalló (see for example Coles and Higgs 1969) which became one of the so-called classic sites because of the similarities between the artefact sequence there and the better-known sequences in France. Pericot excavated all of the deposits in the cave in three seasons of excavations from 1929 to 1931. Subsequent exploration in other parts of southern Valencia province has shown that Parpalló was one of many sites used in the same general period, but was still nevertheless uniquely rich in stone and antler artefacts, in art, and in faunal remains (fig. 8.1). My own research concentrated on the analysis and interpretation

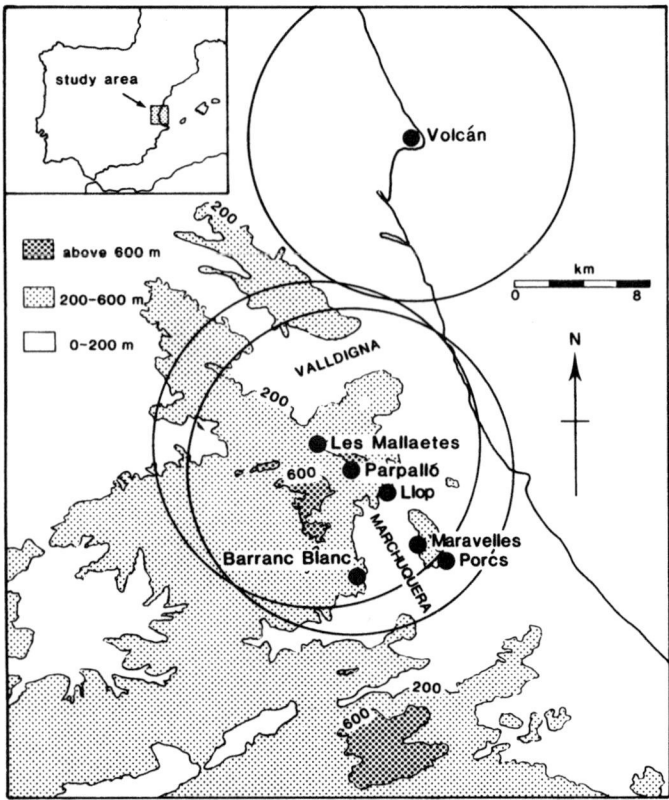

Fig. 8.2. Map of study area showing main sites and geographical features.

Table 8.1. *Age estimates, in thousand C14 years b.p., for important typological boundaries, from calculations for Les Mallaetes*

| Typological boundary | Age estimate | Error estimate |
|---|---|---|
| Base of Solutrean | 21.573 | 0.371 |
| Appearance of barbed and tanged arrowheads | 18.777 | 0.496 |
| Last *puntas de muesca* | 14.922 | 0.782 |

*Source:* Bofinger and Davidson 1977; Davidson 1980.

Table 8.2. *Site use in southern Valencia province*

|  | Les Mallaetes | Parpalló | Llop | Maravelles | Barranc Blanc | Porcs | Volcán |
|---|---|---|---|---|---|---|---|
| After *puntas de muesca* | ? | √ | – | – | – | – | √ |
| *Puntas de muesca* | √ | √ | – | ? | √ | √ | √ |
| Barbed and tanged arrowheads | √ | √ | – | ? | √ | ? | √ |
| Solutrean | √ | √ | √ | √ | √ | ? | √ |
| Gravettian | √ | √ | – | – | – | – | – |
| Before gravettian | √ | – | – | – | – | – |

*Note:* for fullest available details see Fortea 1973; Fullola 1979; Aparicio 1977.

of the faunal collections from this site, and from others in the region (fig. 8.2).

The site of Parpalló is a cave in the extensive karst system of the Cretaceous limestone massif of Mondúver, west of Gandía in Valencia province. The cave is at 450 m above the present level of the Mediterranean Sea, which is now only 8 km to the east. Only 3 km from Parpalló, on the same mountain, is the cave of Les Mallaetes, at a height of about 600 m above modern sea level (Fortea and Jordá 1976). These two sites are the best-documented and best-dated sites in all of eastern Spain (Bofinger and Davidson 1977). The third site which is of interest to the present study is that of Volcán, on the coast near Cullera. This site is at about 120 m above the present sea, in the limestone hill which stands out of the flood-plain of the River Júcar, north of the estuary of that river and south of the fresh-water lagoon of the Albufera. This site, which has been the subject of several preliminary reports but no definitive studies (Aparicio and Fletcher 1971; Davidson 1972), is only about 20 km from the sites of Mondúver. At least five other sites all close to Gandía, have been excavated, at different times and by different methods. The results of these excavations are not suitable for detailed incorporation into this study, except in the most general way. This is possible, to a limited extent, because the chronology provided by the analysis of C14 dates (Bofinger and Davidson 1977) from Parpalló and Les Mallaetes enables us to identify type fossils in the artefact

assemblages. Some of the typological stages at these two sites can be identified at Volcán and the other five sites. Typological stages at these sites are indicated in table 8.1. At Volcán, Aparicio notes a *punta de muesca* (notched point) found in 1971, and a barbed and tanged arrowhead found in 1972 (Aparicio 1973: 80). My detailed analyses of mammal bones from this site were undertaken during these seasons of excavation, and therefore may be taken to span the occurrence of these two artefact types in Parpalló layers 6 and 7 (of my terminology) and the named layers of Les Mallaetes.

The chronology of the artefact stages used in this analysis is presented in table 8.2. The previous statistical analysis showed that for the main part of the sequences Parpalló and Les Mallaetes were contemporary (Bofinger and Davidson 1977). This analysis also demonstrated that the sedimentation rates could be considered as linear. This showed that the depth estimates for the beginning of the Solutrean and for the appearance of barbed and tanged arrowheads were respectively within 2 cm and 8 cm of Pericot's estimate. I take this as support for Pericot's excavation methodology, and observation of uniform, horizontal stratification (Pericot 1942).

In addition to these estimates, the Les Mallaetes sequence includes earlier dates and industries, back to about 30 thousand years ago. In another trench there is a layer with a C14 date of about 10 thousand years b.p., and layers above with stone industries, fauna and pottery. The stratigraphic relations between the two trenches are not clear, because of the sparseness of the industries at the top of the deep trench, but Fortea has argued that there was a stratigraphic break earlier than 10 thousand years b.p. (Fortea and Jordá 1976). Parpalló has a date of about 14 thousand years b.p. from this interval with industries characterized by abundant antler projectile points. This industry, and especially the antler points, is absent from the sequence at Les Mallaetes. At Parpalló the later phases of occupation are effectively undated, and the latest parts of the sequence were removed or disturbed before the beginning of the scientific investigation. This discussion will, therefore, be concerned with the period of contemporary use of these sites, from about 22 000 b.p. to about 15 000 b.p.

## The environmental context

This period coincides with the maximum of the last glacial, maximum regression of the sea, and probably maximum aridity. Geomorphological study of the region has concentrated on the classification of exposed surfaces and land forms, and there is rather little study of the processes involved and no studies with precise dating by either radiometric or archaeological techniques (see Davidson 1980: 9.19 for detailed discussion and references). In the most detailed study, the exposed sediments of the major valleys of the area, including the Júcar, Valldigna and Marchuquera, rest on deposits which would usually support a similar vegetation to that on the existing exposed sediment. The exception to this generalization is the zone affected by the recent dune formations, against which the marsh soils of the Albufera have formed (Goy n.d.). On the other hand, consideration of the heavy amounts of erosion from the limestone slopes which accounts for the deposition on the alluvial plain of the Júcar (Rosselló 1972) suggests that the slopes may at some time in the past have supported patches of thicker soil and hence more abundant vegetation. Whatever the detail of the geomorphic changes over the period of the final stages of the last glacial, there seems no doubt that the environment of Volcán was much wetter than the environment of the other sites. There was a major permanent river, and probably a marsh which was more than seasonal, formed by the springs which now feed the Albufera.

Unfortunately the information from more direct and detailed studies at Les Mallaetes is not yet available (Dupre, pers. comm.; Fumenal, pers. comm.). In the first stages of the pollen study, Dupre (1978) argued that the pollen from the lower layers showed fluctuations in relative abundance which could be interpreted as climatic changes. Because of the continuing presence of Mediterranean species, most changes were interpreted as changes in aridity, and not primarily in temperature. Precise identification of pollen zones must await Dupre's definitive study, as hasty interpretation cannot allow for the difficult problem of vertical movement of pollen in the loose sediments of the cave.

The most detailed study of past climatic changes in the relevant period in southern Spain is the pollen analysis from Padul (Florschütz, Menéndez and Wijmstra 1971). The pollen core was from a peat bog at 1000 m above modern sea level, and below the slopes of the Sierra Nevada in Granada province. The site is so high that Mediterranean species are largely absent from the cold episodes, which are dominated by *Artemisia*, while in interstadials pine pollen predominates in a spectrum with higher frequencies of arboreal pollen. *Quercus* pollen is only common in the late glacial period, and the evergreen oak, *Quercus ilex*, typical of Mediterranean vegetation, only appears at about 10 000 b.p.

The mammals of major importance to this study are Spanish ibex (*Capra pyrenaica*), red deer (*Cervus elaphus*), aurochs (*Bos primigenius*), horses and asses (*Equus* spp.) and rabbits (*Oryctolagus cuniculus*) (see Davidson 1972; and Freeman 1973a for discussion). Of these, the first two species are clearly most abundant, and at Parpalló and Les Mallaetes most of the variability in the relative abundance of species can be expressed in terms of these. There is no strong reason why these species should be affected by the climatic, geomorphic and vegetational changes we have been discussing, but I have argued previously that there is some influence on relative abundance and on the sizes of male and female members of the species (Davidson 1980), although the lack of independent local evidence of climatic change means that this is only a preliminary, and imprecise, observation. In a later section I will discuss how the economic choices of the inhabitants of the caves may be distinguished from the external effects of environmental change. Before that we will look at the evidence for the changing use of the site catchments of the three main sites, and the implications of these observations.

## Site catchments

Information about the extent of the site catchments of the sites of southern Valencia province is limited by the lack of knowledge about sources of raw materials. Flint in particular might be an indication of the range from which raw materials might have been gathered, but the information is scanty. Certainly no local flint sources are known. Indeed at the time of scientific discovery of Parpalló, that cave was the source of tinder flints for the local village of Barig (Pericot 1942). Local geologists suggested that flint should be found in the Jurassic limestones (Robles, pers. comm.). They did not know of any local sources, and my own searches in the sierras between Mondúver and Cullera, which are the only local Jurassic limestones, proved fruitless. There is, therefore, some suggestion that the stone raw material was obtained from remote quarries. All the animals whose bones constitute the food wastes, and the raw material for antler points, were available within the site exploitation territories of the sites.

The only finds which provide information about the size of site catchments, therefore, are marine shells. As the occupations of the sites occurred during the maximum depression of the sea level, these shells indicate frequency of contact with a distant resource, whether direct or indirect (e.g. through trade or exchange), and also some of the responses to the changes in the distance to that resource with changes in sea level. The quality of the information from the shells from these three sites is very uneven because of the different attention paid to marine molluscs during the excavations. The most complete

Table 8.3. *Distribution of shells at three sites*

| Parpalló | | Les Mallaetes | |
| --- | --- | --- | --- |
| Age | No. of shells | Age | No. of shells |
| 11.893 | 212 | | |
| 12.959 | 111 | | |
| 15.232 | | 14.922 | 3 |
| 16.555 | 18 | | |
| 17.221 | 5 | 17.172 | 15 |
| 17.887 | 70 | | |
| 18.886 | 148 | 18.777 | – |
| 20.218 | 150 | 19.230 | 22 |
| 21.550 + | 2 | 21.573 | |
| | 2 | 22.026 | 3 |
| | | 26.861 | 2 |

| | Volcán | | | | | | | | | | | | | | | |
| --- | --- | --- | --- | --- | --- | --- | --- | --- | --- | --- | --- | --- | --- | --- | --- | --- |
| Species | Spit | | | | | | | | | | | | | | | |
| | 2 | 3 | 4 | 6 | 7 | 10 | 11 | 12 | 20 | 21 | 22 | 23 | 24 | 25 | 26 | 27 |
| *Cardium echinatum* | | | | | | √ | | | | | | | | | | |
| *Nassa sp.* | | | | | | | √ | | | | | | | | | |
| *Dentalium sp.* | | | | | | | | | √ | | | | √ | √ | √ | |
| *Chlamys opercularis* | | | | | | | | | | | √ | | | √ | | |

*Note:* Shells from Volcán identified by Cuerda and Gasull (1971) from 1968 excavations. The spit numbers have only general relationship with spit numbers for later years.

report is by Vidal (Vidal 1947; see also Pericot 1942: 269) on the shells from Parpalló, and there is an unpublished report on the shells from Volcán (Cuerda and Gasull 1971). The only data on the marine molluscs from Les Mallaetes is the enumeration which I undertook of the shells included in the bone collection (see also more detailed discussions for all three sites in Davidson 1980: 7.6–7.8, 7.72–7.74, and 8.6–8.7). This uneven quality prevents any detailed comparison between the sites. Nevertheless, it emerged from the analysis by Vidal that the collection included many edible species, some shells which were used as ornaments, some which had traces of red paint, and some which, because they must have been collected from the beach when dead, were presumably collected for curiosity. It seems likely that shells may have been used in the same ways at all three sites. The horizontal distribution of marine molluscs at Volcán shows that these, unlike the shells of terrestrial molluscs, are all distributed in the area of concentration of food wastes, suggesting that these may have been primarily intended as food at Volcán, and that many of the snails were not.

Inspection of the stratigraphic distribution of the shells shows an uneven distribution (see table 8.3), but one which is consistent between sites. In particular the stratigraphic distribution at Les Mallaetes and Volcán suggests that the shells were most abundant at the time when the sea shore was most distant. We may argue that there is a similar pattern at Parpalló also, despite the sampling problems.

Sea-level changes over this time period show a similar patterning between the west Mediterranean (Aloïsi *et al.* 1978) and other areas. Maximum regression of the sea corresponded

to the period of maximum cold, and there was a steady increase in the height of the sea from these low levels to a level possibly 2 m above the present level at about 4.5 thousand years ago. Recent studies show that sea level at maximum regression was lower than 60 m below the modern level (e.g. Blackwelder *et al.* 1979) but the local picture is complicated by isostatic subsidence of the Valencia coast (Rosselló 1971). In the absence of local evidence of the dating of such subsidence no estimate can be made of the exact extent of the coastal plain at the time these shells were brought back across it to the hill and mountain caves. The effect of recent subsidence would be that the last glacial coast would now be at a greater depth than the amount of eustatic depression of the sea level, and may be represented without exaggeration by the −100 m bathymetric contour. This would suggest that the shore was at least 30 km from Parpalló at the last glacial maximum, which in turn indicates a rate of transgression of about 3.75 km for every millennium of the period of warming from the maximum of the last glacial period.

The marker of cold climate at Les Mallaetes and at Parpalló (see Fortea and Jordá 1976; and Davidson 1980:5.13) can be dated at both sites to about 19 000 b.p. There is no such information from Volcán, and the only chronological information is the vertical excavation unit numbers, which are unrelated to any vertical stratigraphy. Nevertheless, it is possible to relate gross chronological features of the artefact typology at the well-dated sites to the few published artefacts from Volcán. The cold marker occurs, at both Les Mallaetes and Parpalló, between the two layers with maximum abundance of shells. At Volcán, all the marine shells occurred below the *bastón de mando* (Fletcher and Aparicio 1969) in the original season of excavation, with the exception of one shell in later deposits. The earliest specimen of a *punta de muesca* from this site occurs two spits above the *bastón*. The abundance of marine shells, therefore, appears to occur at the same level in all three sites, and to be around the time of the maximum regression of the sea. Shells do not disappear from Parpalló but they are much less abundant than in the cold layers, until the reappearance in the top, mixed, layer. The top of Volcán contained a shell midden with Bronze Age pottery, over a sterile layer which I have interpreted as representing a phase when the mountain of Cullera was isolated by the transgressing sea.

This evidence seems to be paradoxical, and contrasts with the least-cost interpretation suggested for Francthi cave in Greece, where marine shell abundance appears to vary directly with the proximity of the approaching shore in the final stages of the Pleistocene (Shackleton and van Andel 1980; see also chapter 13, this volume). In southern Valencia, in the layers when the sea was at its most distant the shells were at their most abundant. As the sea began to return to modern levels, and therefore to get closer to the sites, shells became less abundant, until after the sea reached Volcán, when the marine molluscs were intensively exploited as a food source at the cave. Here is clear evidence of change in the pattern of

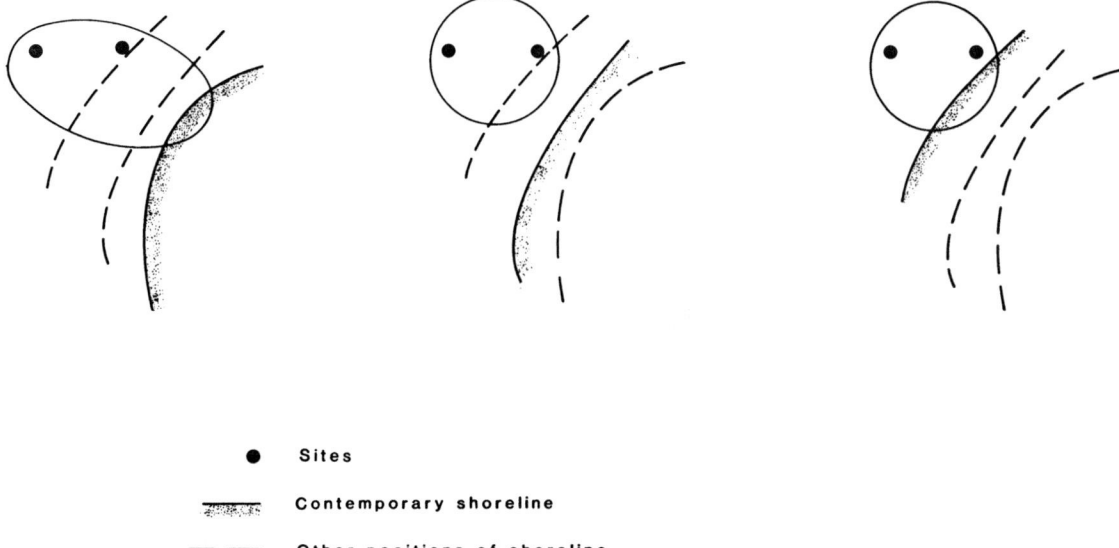

● **Sites**

━━━ **Contemporary shoreline**

— — **Other positions of shoreline**

Fig. 8.3. Schematic model of site catchments at three stages of marine transgression. The site catchments change in size with the three different positions of the shoreline. The model has no scale but is the same for the three phases shown.

human behaviour, at a time when environmental change was taking place, which was not a simple response to that environmental change. This feature emerges from analysis of imperfect evidence, but is not likely to have been biased during the collection or analysis to favour this result. It should, of course, be treated as a hypothesis to be tested in future research. Figure 8.3 shows the schematic representation of this situation.

The data thus suggest that at the time of maximum cold, maximum aridity and maximum regression of the sea, the size of the catchment from which resources were drawn was rather large, at least up to 30 km across, but that this catchment contracted rather rapidly as soon as the climate began to ameliorate, after about 17 000 b.p. Thus, while the contraction of catchment is the opposite of what would be expected from a least-effort interpretation (c.f. Shackleton and van Andel 1980), it would be consistent with environmental change insofar as the amelioration of climate would have resulted in an increase in resource density within the catchment, and therefore, a reduction in the need to obtain resources from more distant areas such as the sea shore. Nevertheless, this is a clear case where the nature of the changing economy can only be discerned by analysis of several sites, emphasizing not only change through time in the residues which are left at the site, but also the relationship between available resources and patterns of exploitation. Some further information about this hypothesis can be obtained from the study of the mammal remains at the sites, and the way in which the patterns of exploitation and discard of these remains changed through the sequences.

### Relative abundance of species

The unequal quality of the excavations of the three sites and of the collection methods applied to the faunal remains means that it is impossible to investigate the possibility that some non-human agency introduced bones to the caves. The lack of gnawing on the bones suggests that carnivores were not a significant agent of deposition or of deletion of bones. I have therefore assumed that all mammal bone was introduced by humans, although I have reservations about the rabbit bones.

The unequal quality of excavation and collection also means that it is not possible or appropriate to present all of the data from the three sites in the same form. We cannot calculate percentages at Parpalló because we know that at least the rabbit bones are largely missing; some calculations for Les Mallaetes are inappropriate because the sample sizes are very small; and the estimation of diachronic trends at Volcán is vitiated by the lack of chronological information in general, but specifically by the lack of information on the relationship between the arbitrary excavation units (spits) and the natural stratification. Table 8.4, therefore, shows the distribution of remains from the four major species at Parpalló with estimated C14 ages. The table shows numbers of post-cranial (PC) bones, and estimates of Minimum Numbers of Individuals (MIND) which must have died to create the assemblage. These estimates of MIND are calculated by taking account of the ages at death of the animals, and the sides of the body of the specimens. I continue to use the abbreviation MIND to distinguish this estimate from the minimum number used by Binford (MNI) which is an estimate of the number of anatomical segments represented, and takes no account of the side of the animal (Binford 1978b; Straus 1977a).

Table 8.5 shows the distribution of specimens from the Palaeolithic layers at Les Mallaetes. For this table I have used the grouping of layers by Fortea (pers. comm. and Fortea and Jordá 1976), but I have also calculated statistics for the situa-

Table 8.4. *Parpalló: stratigraphic distribution of post-cranial elements, and relevant calculations of MIND for four major species.*

| Layer | Depth in metres | Age | Ibex PC | Ibex MIND | Deer PC | Deer MIND | Bos PC | Bos MIND | Equus PC | Equus MIND |
|---|---|---|---|---|---|---|---|---|---|---|
| 1 | 1–1.5 | 13.225 | 220 | 71 | 214 | 35 | 17 | 1 | 38 | 6 |
| 2 | 1.5–2 | 13.891 | 250 | 33 | 226 | 33 | 39 | 5 | 49 | 5 |
| 3 | 2–2.75 | 14.557 | 160 | 24 | 151 | 23 | 28 | 3 | 24 | 4 |
| 4 | 2.75–3.5 | 15.556 | – | 15 | – | 3 | – | – | – | – |
| 5 | 3.5–4 | 16.555 | – | 1 | – | – | 1 | – | – | – |
| 6 | 4–4.5 | 17.221 | 280 | 26 | 163 | 27 | 52 | 4 | 28 | 4 |
| 7 | 4.5–5.25 | 17.887 | 227 | 12 | 97 | 9 | 22 | 2 | 88 | 6 |
| 8 | 5.25–6 | 18.886 | – | 24 | 4 | 2 | 1 | – | 5 | 4 |
| 9 | 6–7.25 | 19.885 | 1232 | 140 | 571 | 39 | 100 | 4 | 152 | 7 |
| 10 | 7.25 + | 21.550 | | | | | | | | |

*Note:* ages calculated from statistics in Bofinger and Davidson (1977), in thousands of years. PC = post-cranial, MIND = Minimum Number of Individuals.

Table 8.5. *Les Mallaetes: stratigraphic distribution of post-cranial elements, and relevant calculations of MIND for four major species.*

| Layer | Age | Ibex PC | Ibex MIND | Deer PC | Deer MIND | Bos PC | Bos MIND | Equus PC | Equus MIND |
|---|---|---|---|---|---|---|---|---|---|
| S–G | | 3 | 2 | 5 | 1 | – | – | – | – |
| 1 Puntas de muesca | 14.922 | 6 | 3 | 2 | 1 | – | – | – | 1 |
| 2 Barbed/tanged arrowheads | 17.172 | 7 | 2 | 6 | 1 | 1 | 1 | 1 | 1 |
| 3 Sterile | 18.777 | – | 1 | – | – | – | – | – | – |
| 4 Solutrean | 19.230 | 39 | 11 | 13 | 2 | 2 | 1 | 1 | 1 |
| 5 Atypical | 21.573 | 1 | 1 | – | 1 | – | – | – | – |
| 6 Gravettian | 22.026 | 9 | 1 | 34 | 2 | – | – | – | 1 |
| 7 Aurignacian | 26.861 | 2 | 1 | 6 | 1 | – | 1 | 1 | – |

*Note:* ages calculated from statistics in Bofinger and Davidson (1977), in thousands of years. PC = post-cranial, MIND = Minimum Number of Individuals.

Table 8.6. *Volcán: all bones and teeth*

| | Spit 18 | 19 | 20 | 21 | 22 | 23 | 24 | 25 | 26 | 26A | 27 | 27A | 27B | 27C | 28 | 28A | 28B | 29 | Total |
|---|---|---|---|---|---|---|---|---|---|---|---|---|---|---|---|---|---|---|---|
| Caprine | – | 1 | – | – | – | 1 | – | 3 | 6 | – | 1 | 1 | – | 4 | 4 | – | – | 1 | 22 |
| *Cervus* | 16 | 13 | 29 | – | 4 | 9 | 12 | 23 | 13 | 12 | 3 | 15 | 8 | 18 | 25 | 4 | 16 | 12 | 232 |
| antler | 11 | 7 | 9 | – | – | – | – | 2 | – | 3 | – | 1 | 1 | 10 | 3 | 1 | 5 | 1 | 54 |
| *Equus* spp. | – | 4 | 2 | – | – | 1 | 1 | 8 | 1 | – | – | – | 3 | 3 | 4 | 1 | – | 1 | 29 |
| *Bos* | – | – | – | – | 1 | – | – | 2 | 6 | – | 2 | 1 | – | – | – | 1 | – | – | 13 |
| *Sus* | – | – | – | – | – | – | – | – | – | – | – | – | – | 1 | 1 | – | – | 1 | 3 |
| Lagomorph | 148 | 221 | 523 | 4 | 53 | 60 | 97 | 132 | 309 | 204 | 205 | 191 | 236 | 295 | 269 | 113 | 149 | 331 | 3540 |
| Hedgehog | – | 1 | 1 | – | 1 | – | – | – | 2 | 1 | – | – | – | – | 1 | 1 | – | 1 | 9 |
| Carnivore | 2 | 3 | – | – | – | – | 1 | 2 | 15 | 2 | – | – | – | 2 | 20 | – | 1 | 4 | 52 |
| Other | | | | | | | | | a + b | | | | | | | | | | |
| Totals | 177 | 250 | 564 | 4 | 59 | 71 | 111 | 172 | 352 | 222 | 211 | 209 | 248 | 333 | 327 | 121 | 171 | 352 | 3954 |

*Note:* a + b = *Crocidura* cf. *russula* + *Mus musculus.*

tion which arises if the few finds from the upper layers of one of the trenches, labelled S–G, are included with the layer from the deep trench in which were found *puntas de muesca*. Fumenal (pers. comm.) suggests that there is some corroboration of this interpretation from her detailed sedimentological studies. These results should be taken as more accurate estimates than the previously published figures (Davidson 1976a).

Data from Volcán are shown in table 8.6. This is the only one of the excavations for which I was able to assess the collection of the bones, and I can therefore be certain that all of the rabbit bones and tiny splinters were collected. In table 8.7 I show the figures for post-cranial bones from Volcán. It is not possible to calculate the MIND when there is uncertainty about the groupings of spits. Moreover the same lack of information prevents the addition of chronological information on these tables.

In my previous published account of Les Mallaetes I

Table 8.7. *Volcán: Cervus elaphus post-cranial bones*

| Spit | No. specimens |
|------|---------------|
| 18 | 12 |
| 19 | 12 |
| 20 | 22 |
| 21 | 1 |
| 22 | 4 |
| 23 | 8 |
| 24 | 8 |
| 25 | 14 |
| 26 | 10 |
| 26A | 11 |
| 27 | 3 |
| 27A | 8 |
| 27B | 3 |
| 27C | 15 |
| 28 | 18 |
| 28A | 2 |
| 28B | 13 |
| 29 | 9 |

Table 8.8. *Ratio of post-cranial elements for Spanish ibex and red deer*

| Parpalló | | Les Mallaetes | |
|----------|--|---------------|--|
| Age | Ratio ibex/deer | Age | Ratio ibex/deer |
| 13.225 | | | |
| 13.891 | 1.03 | | |
| 14.557 | 1.06 | | |
| 15.556 | 1.06 | 14.922 | |
| 16.555 | – | | (3.00) 1.43 |
| 17.221 | – | 17.172 | |
| 17.887 | 1.72 | | 1.17 |
| 18.886 | 2.34 | 18.777 | |
| 19.885 | – | 19.230 | |
| 21.550 + | 2.16 | 21.573 | 3.00 |
| | | 22.026 | |
| | | 26.861 | 0.265 |
| | | | 0.33 |

| Volcán | |
|--------|--|
| Spits | Ratio ibex/deer |
| 18–21 | 0.02 |
| 22–24 | 0.05 |
| 25–26A | 0.22 |
| 27–29 | 0.141 |

*Note:* ages in thousands of years.

suggested that the important trend shown by the faunal specimens was an increase in relative abundance of Spanish ibex, and decrease of red deer (Davidson 1976a), whatever the manipulations of the primary data. This trend was particularly evident when the upper layers, which are primarily postglacial, were included. It is now possible to examine the trends during the Palaeolithic period in more detail and to compare them with the other sites. Moreover, since the preparation of that previous publication, we can also consider these trends on a radiometric time-scale.

The sample sizes dictate that comparisons between the abundance of Spanish ibex and red deer will be the most useful. This is also indicated by a consideration of the problems associated with the different collection methods, particularly for Parpalló. The relative absence of rabbit bones, despite the observation that they were so abundant (Pericot 1942, 1968), shows that there was some selection of bones by size at the time of excavation of Parpalló. The presence of labels indicating selection of large bones suggests that this may not have been accidental. It is therefore only possible to assess relative abundance for species which would have been treated in the same way in this selection process, and this is probably true for the ibex and deer. It is particularly fortunate that these are also the most abundant species at all of the sites. The broad picture that emerges from Palaeolithic layers at both Les Mallaetes and Parpalló is one in which there is a relative increase in ibex followed by a relative decrease, over the same time period. However there are several qualifications to this observation.

If we calculate the ratio using MIND it is impossible to compare all three sites, because we cannot calculate MIND for Volcán, and the small numbers at Les Mallaetes make the ratio erratic. Nevertheless, I showed in the previous consideration of Les Mallaetes that the trends of the ratio were preserved whatever the manipulation of the data. I have also shown that the same is true at Parpalló (Davidson 1980: 7.67) by using z-scores of the various ratios. In that analysis, MIND ratios behave in a very similar fashion to ratios of post-cranial elements, and only ratios of crude bone numbers behave erratically. I attribute this to the changing importance of horn and antler raw material, and to differential fragmentation of jaws. I have, therefore, continued to use the ratio of post-cranial elements as an indicator of relative dietary importance of these two species.

Table 8.8 shows the ratios of red deer to Spanish ibex for the three sites, and the ratios are plotted in figure 8.4 for the dated sites. Les Mallaetes has very low values in the bottom two layers of the sequence – that is more deer than ibex – but the ratio increases in the Solutrean to about three ibex for every deer. This is just above the value for the bottom layers at Parpalló. The values at the two sites converge in the next layer above, which gives ratios between 2 and 3 for both sites. The two sites then appear to diverge. In the upper layers at Parpalló the ratio is near to 1, but at Les Mallaetes the ratio in the layer with *puntas de muesca* is 3.0. The layer of Les Mallaetes designated S–G in the tables could not be linked, either by typology or by relative stratigraphic position, to either the layers with *puntas de muesca* or the layer below that. I, therefore, considered the results if the bones from the S–G layer were combined with either of these two alternative layers (Davidson 1980: 7.87). Linking with the *puntas de muesca* layer changed the ratio so that the contemporary layers at the two sites again nearly coincide. The divergence is more apparent than real. The alternative dating accentuated the

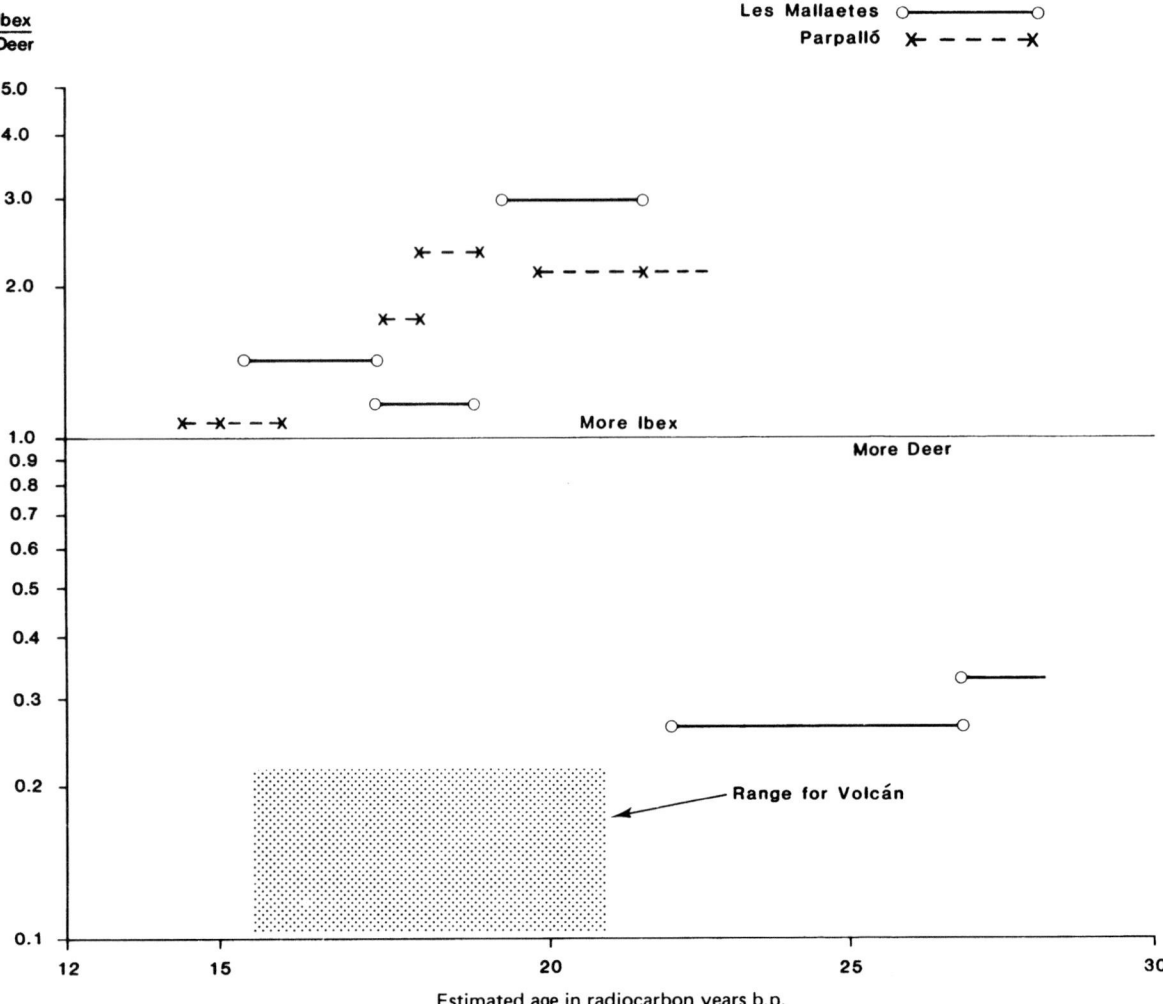

Fig. 8.4. Ibex/deer ratios at Parpalló and Les Mallaetes calculated from numbers of post-cranial specimens.

divergence. Later discussion with Fumenal about the sedimentology suggested that the first interpretation is likely on the basis of the similarity of interpretation of the climatic circumstances of deposition of the two layers.

This is a remarkable result. It seems to suggest that, although the two sites had different environments, the species exploited from two sites showed a similar pattern of change through time in relative abundance. I have argued that the two sites were probably used at different seasons (Davidson 1976), and had different tactical roles in the regional exploitation strategy (Davidson 1980); and that the tactical advantages can be appreciated by a consideration of the site exploitation territories within half an hour of the sites. Despite this, the variation in the ratio of deer to ibex was the same at the two sites. This may be taken to suggest that the range of habitual exploitation from the two sites was much larger than that within which tactical advantage could be perceived. Table 8.9 shows the areas of site exploitation territories for the three sites, which demonstrates that the 2-hour territories have very

Table 8.9. *Site exploitation territories areas by different methods of calculation*

|  | Parpalló | | Les Mallaetes | | Volcán | |
|---|---|---|---|---|---|---|
|  | Area | % | Area | % | Area | % |
| 10km (ideal) | 314 | 100.0 | 314 | 100.0 | 314 | 100.0 |
| 2-hr | 44.9 | 14.3 | 31.3 | 10.0 | 286 | 91.1 |
| 2-hr shared | 24.6 | 55 | 24.6 | 78.6 | | |
| 2hr unshared | 20.2 | 45 | 6.7 | 21.4 | | |
| 5km (ideal) | 78.5 | 100.0 | 78.5 | 100.0 | | |
| 1-hr | 7.8 | 9.9 | 8.6 | 11.0 | | |
| 1-hr shared | 2.5 | 32.1 | 2.5 | 29.1 | | |
| 1-hr unshared | 5.3 | 67.9 | 6.1 | 70.9 | | |
| 2.5km (ideal) | 19.6 | 100.0 | 19.6 | 100.0 | | |
| ½-hr (unshared) | 1.6 | 8.5 | 1.4 | 6.9 | | |

*Note:* percentages indicated for 2-hour territory are percentages of ideal territory size, while the percentages for shared and unshared territory are the percentages of the 2-hour territory size. The same conventions apply for other sizes of territory.

great overlap. A site exploitation territory of the order of two hours in radius may be of the right order, as Bailey (this volume, chapter 13) has shown also for the sites of Cantabria. This result might be taken to indicate that the primary cause of variation in the relative abundance of deer and ibex was environmental change, and not human choice. If this were so then we might expect a similar trend in the data from Volcán.

Table 8.8 shows the ratios of post-cranial bone of the two species for grouped spits from Volcán. The sample sizes for the ibex are very small, but there seems to be a change in the ratio of ibex to deer, with an initial rise in the ratio and a very steep decline thereafter, from the presumptively older group of spits to the later group. Aparicio has indicated that this selection of spits may include the transition between the phase with barbed and tanged arrowheads, and the subsequent phase with *puntas de muesca* (Aparicio 1973: 80). In this transitional phase at the other two sites the ratio also declines. If this is to be taken as corroboration of an environmental interpretation for the data from Les Mallaetes and Parpalló, then it is necessary to show that the environmental conditions at Volcán were similar. In this respect it is important that the amount of time travelled in habitual exploitation from Volcán must have been more than the half hour which provided tactical advantage in the mountain sites, and closer to the two hours which we have used for the site exploitation territory calculations there.

Situated at the summit of the eastern part of a small hill, Volcán has a much larger proportion of its ½-hour site exploitation territory dominated by the hilly terrain preferred by ibex than of its 2-hour territory. This is especially true now that the alluvial plain comes so close to the site, but even before that alluvium was all deposited, a small site exploitation territory would have favoured a greater abundance of ibex, rather than deer. The overwhelming abundance of deer at Volcán cannot be explained by a small site exploitation territory. Consideration of the nature of the environment within the 2-hour site exploitation territory of Volcán shows important differences from the site environments of the other two sites.

If any part of the variation in the ibex:deer ratio at Les Mallaetes and Parpalló is attributable to climatic change, it would be because climatic changes caused shifts in the altitudinal distribution of vegetation and zones of tolerable temperatures. While there is sufficient altitudinal variation in the vicinity of Les Mallaetes and Parpalló to entertain this hypothesis, this is less likely at Volcán, which is on a low hill with little variation of altitude in the surrounding terrain. Another environmental factor that might be relevant at Volcán is the progressive deposition of the alluvium, which was taking place during the occupation of the site. It is conceivable that this could have affected the relative abundance of ibex and deer in the environment, but it is unlikely that it could account for a relative increase in red deer followed by a relative decrease.

A third factor that needs to be considered is seasonality.

I argued that Volcán was probably used in summer, on the basis of limited evidence from the bird bones (Eastham pers. comm.), and because the river and the marsh would have been constant sources of water for deer in the dry summers of a more arid glacial period. Some other evidence indicates that the site was also used in winter, and in spring (see Davidson 1980, table 9.4, reproduced here as table 8.10). If the site of Volcán was used in summer, then it may be suggested that this was partly because deer descended to the flood-plain in the arid summer for water available at the river and marsh, and for shade from the trees which would have grown along the river banks. Ibex would be seeking cooler pastures at this time in the cooler mountain tops. This separation of the species at this season might account for some of the difference of emphasis between the mountain sites and Volcán.

Simple interpretation of these data in terms of environmental change might postulate that changes in the ibex:deer ratio should be parallel at all sites. The data suggest, however, that the similarities are despite differences in the environment and environmental change. It would be tempting, therefore, to conclude simply that environmental change was not the primary cause of variability in relative abundance of these species. A more detailed consideration of the relationships between the species and the environment, and of the ways in which environment changed over the time period suggests, however, that some of the variability is due to environmental change, but in complex ways. At the same time human behaviour is interacting with the environment, and human behaviour is itself changing. Only by attempting to assess the interactions between humans and their environments, allowing for tactical differences between the exploitations from

Table 8.10. *Summary of evidence for seasonality*

**Les Mallaetes**

*Generally summer*
antler only in Gravettian and 'barbed and tanged'–absence implies summer
male ibex
foetal or neonate caprines except in *puntas de muesca* and Aurignacian
absence of early wear states on deciduous dentition
little evidence for hearths

**Parpalló**

*Winter*
massacred antler
many hearths
*No season*
general distribution of wear stages in deciduous teeth

**Volcán**

*Summer*
swifts, ?lark, ?some ducks, neonate caprines
*Winter*
(gyr falcon – top only), massacred antler
*Spring*
eggshell

Table 8.11. *Parpalló: Capra pyrenaica, Spanish ibex. Body-part summaries; numbers of bones*

| | Layer | | | | | | | | |
|---|---|---|---|---|---|---|---|---|---|
| | 1 | 2 | 3 | 4 | 5 | 6 | 7 | 8 | 9 + 10 |
| All fore-limb | 61 | 81 | 46 | – | – | 97 | 88 | – | 427 |
| All hind-limb | 20 | 19 | 11 | – | – | 16 | 45 | – | 400 |
| All extremities (ex. toes) | 111 | 89 | 67 | – | – | 57 | 42 | – | 223 |
| All toes | 3 | 23 | 7 | – | – | 2 | – | – | 21 |
| All axial | 25 | 38 | 29 | – | – | 108 | 52 | – | 161 |
| All cranial | 340 | 228 | 137 | 63 | 6 | 135 | 118 | 99 | 913 |
| Totals | 560 | 478 | 297 | 63 | 6 | 415 | 345 | 99 | 2145 |

*Note:* Fore-limb: scapula, humerus, radius, radius/ulna, ulna. Hind-limb: pelvis, femur, tibia, patella, lateral malleolus. Extremities (ex. toes): metapodial, metacarpal, metatarsal, lateral metapodial, astragalus, calcaneum, navicular-cuboid, tarsals and carpals. Toes: phalanges. Axial: atlas, axis, vertebrae, sacral. Cranial: maxilla, mandible, skull, horn/antler.

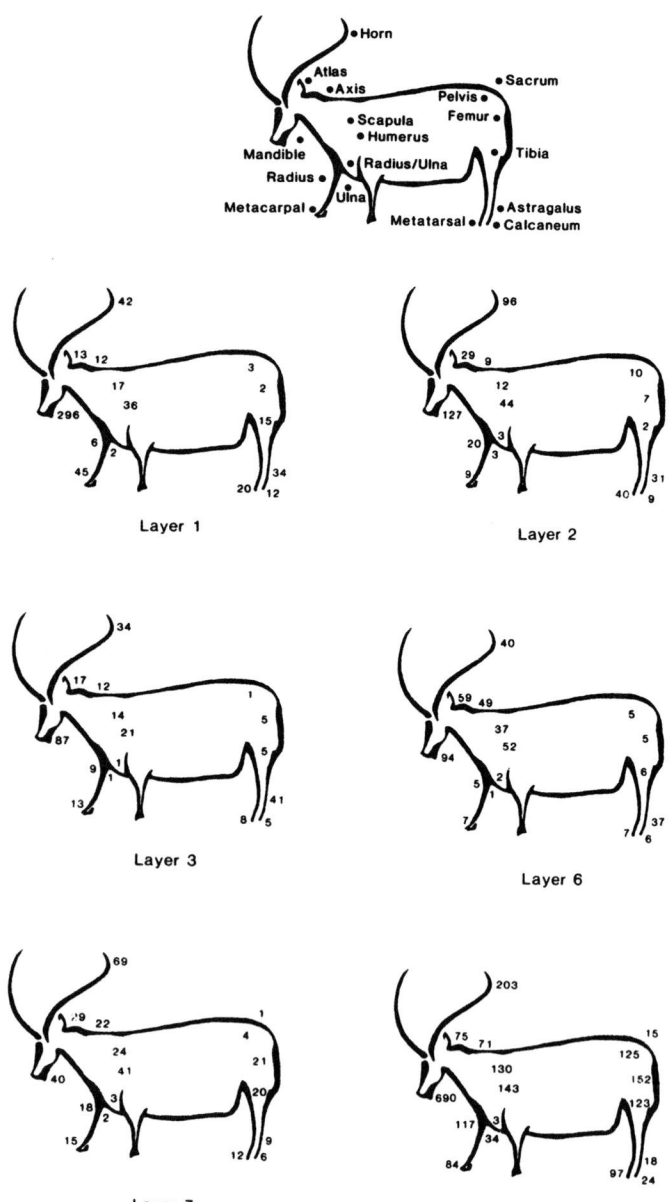

Fig. 8.5. Parpalló: bone numbers of *Capra pyrenaica.*

different sites, can this complicated set of interrelationships be analysed. Much would be gained by local studies of the changing environments contemporary with these human behaviours. Some further light on the variability of behaviour at these sites can be derived from analysis of the distribution of different anatomical segments there.

**Body-part distributions**

Patterns of exploitation of species involve not just the relative abundance of different species, but also the different butchery practices. Binford calls this economic anatomy, by which he refers to the different perceptions of economic importance of different skeletal elements, and anatomical segments (Binford 1978a). I have not yet used Binford's methodology on these data, but present here a consideration of the distribution of body parts for different species at the three sites. Table 8.11 shows the distribution of body parts of ibex from Parpalló and this is shown in more detail in figure 8.5. Full details of the discussion of distribution of body parts is given in my thesis (Davidson 1980: 7.17– 7.37). Distribution of body parts of other species at Parpalló is given in tables 8.12 to 8.14 and figure 8.6.

Many processes operate on bones between their presence as structural elements within a living animal and their appearance as statistics in an archaeological report. Some of these processes are summarized in table 8.15. In both ibex and deer there are variations in the relative abundance of fore-limbs and hind-limbs, and although for both species the excellent preservation of distal humerus and astragalus suggests that the relative scarcity of other anatomical elements may be due in part to differential destruction of elements other than these, this was not the only factor operating.

I considered together the ibex and deer as medium-sized animals, and the equids and cattle as large-sized animals. Because of their similarity in body and bone size, post-depositional attritional processes might be assumed to have acted in similar ways on ibex and deer, and on cattle and equids, but in different ways on medium and large animals. Demonstration that the patterning of distribution of body parts is not the

Table 8.12. *Parpalló: Cervus elaphus, red deer. Body-part summaries; numbers of bones*

| | Layer | | | | | | | | |
|---|---|---|---|---|---|---|---|---|---|
| | 1 | 2 | 3 | 4 | 5 | 6 | 7 | 8 | 9 + 10 |
| All fore-limb | 57 | 55 | 24 | – | – | 45 | 25 | 0 | 199 |
| All hind-limb | 29 | 26 | 34 | – | – | 32 | 25 | 1 | 124 |
| All extremities (ex. toes) | 108 | 121 | 78 | – | – | 82 | 44 | 1 | 214 |
| All toes | 15 | 20 | 5 | – | – | 0 | 1 | 1 | 9 |
| All axial | 5 | 4 | 10 | – | – | 4 | 2 | 2 | 25 |
| All cranial | 357 | 156 | 120 | 7 | 23 | 153 | 26 | 26 | 455 |
| Totals | 571 | 382 | 271 | 7 | 23 | 316 | 123 | 31 | 1026 |
| Cranial without maxilla | 219 | 118 | 84 | – | 6 | 104 | 21 | 14 | 225 |

*Note:* see table 8.11. for anatomical elements included in these categories.

Table 8.13. *Parpalló: Bos primigenius, aurochs/cattle. Body-part summaries; numbers of bones*

| | Layer | | | | | | | | |
|---|---|---|---|---|---|---|---|---|---|
| | 1 | 2 | 3 | 4 | 5 | 6 | 7 | 8 | 9 + 10 |
| All fore-limb | 1 | 5 | 2 | – | – | 7 | 3 | – | 11 |
| All hind-limb | 1 | 6 | 6 | – | – | 7 | 4 | – | 19 |
| All extremities (ex. toes) | 6 | 16 | 12 | – | 1 | 22 | 8 | 1 | 33 |
| All toes | 9 | 12 | 8 | – | – | 16 | 7 | – | 27 |
| All axial | – | – | – | – | – | – | – | – | 10 |
| All cranial | 2 | 4 | 9 | – | 1 | 18 | 3 | – | 57 |

Table 8.14. *Parpalló: Equus, spp., horses and asses. Body-part summaries; numbers of bones*

| | Layer | | | | | | | | |
|---|---|---|---|---|---|---|---|---|---|
| | 1 | 2 | 3 | 4 | 5 | 6 | 7 | 8 | 9 + 10 |
| All fore-limb | 1 | 1 | 2 | – | – | 6 | 10 | 3 | 19 |
| All hind-limb | 2 | 4 | 5 | – | – | 8 | 17 | 1 | 18 |
| All extremities (ex. toes) | 22 | 19 | 8 | – | – | 5 | 19 | 1 | 44 |
| All toes | 13 | 35 | 9 | – | – | 9 | 27 | – | 70 |
| All axial | – | – | – | – | – | – | 5 | – | 1 |
| All cranial | 88 | 53 | 15 | – | 3 | 10 | 9 | 60 | 63 |

same for ibex and deer, and not the same for cattle and equids, shows that the post-depositional processes were acting on assemblages which had already undergone some other process of differential selection. I suggest tentatively that one of the factors which had changing importance through the sequence of occupation of the site was the attention paid to fore-limbs and hind-limbs. I further suggest that, in the case of the deer, this was partly due to an increasing importance of antler as a raw material for 'bone' points.

Expansion of the discussion to the other sites is again hampered by the small samples, but the figures for Les Mallaetes are shown in table 8.16, and for the deer from Volcán in table 8.17. Moreover, the differences between the methods of collection and post-excavation treatment of the collections from Parpalló and the other two sites means that some further qualifications must be applied to inter-site comparisons. In particular, the number of small bones, such as phalanges, from the recent excavations, is what would be expected from the greater care in collection methods. Nevertheless, the relative abundance at Volcán is difficult to attribute entirely to this factor. Limb bones are also very scarce at Volcán, and if the relative abundance of limb bones and phalanges had originally been the same at Parpalló as at Volcán then 250 phalanges from my layer 1 at Parpalló and 175 from my layer 2 would have had to have been lost during the collection at the time of excavation. I find this large figure unlikely, and suggest that post-depositional factors cannot explain all of the variation between the sites.

At Les Mallaetes there is little similarity in the trends of relative body-part distribution to the contemporary trends at Parpalló and there is no similarity between the distributions for ibex and for deer. In addition there is some support for my hypothesis of seasonal use of Les Mallaetes from the generally low representation of cranial elements of deer. This would be the expected result if Les Mallaetes were used in summer when the deer had antlers in velvet which were soft and useless for manufacture of tools. The few fragments of antler in these deposits could be pieces which were brought to the site after preliminary preparation elsewhere, rather than the remains of antlers of freshly killed carcasses brought to the site for initial processing.

Unsatisfactory though the evidence may be because of factors largely beyond control at the time of analysis, there is a strong suggestion here that the carcasses were being treated differently at the different sites. My hypothesis would be that this results from the different economic anatomy at different seasons and at sites in different tactical situations within the annual exploitation strategy.

### Discussion

I have shown that the evidence from these three sites may be interpreted in terms of prehistoric variability within the sequence of use of sites, and between sites, and in terms of a changing relationship between the prehistoric inhabitants of the sites and the changing environment. Some of the variability is difficult to interpret because of the unsatisfactory control over the samples, but detailed analysis of the diachronic trends at sites suggests that not all can be attributed to

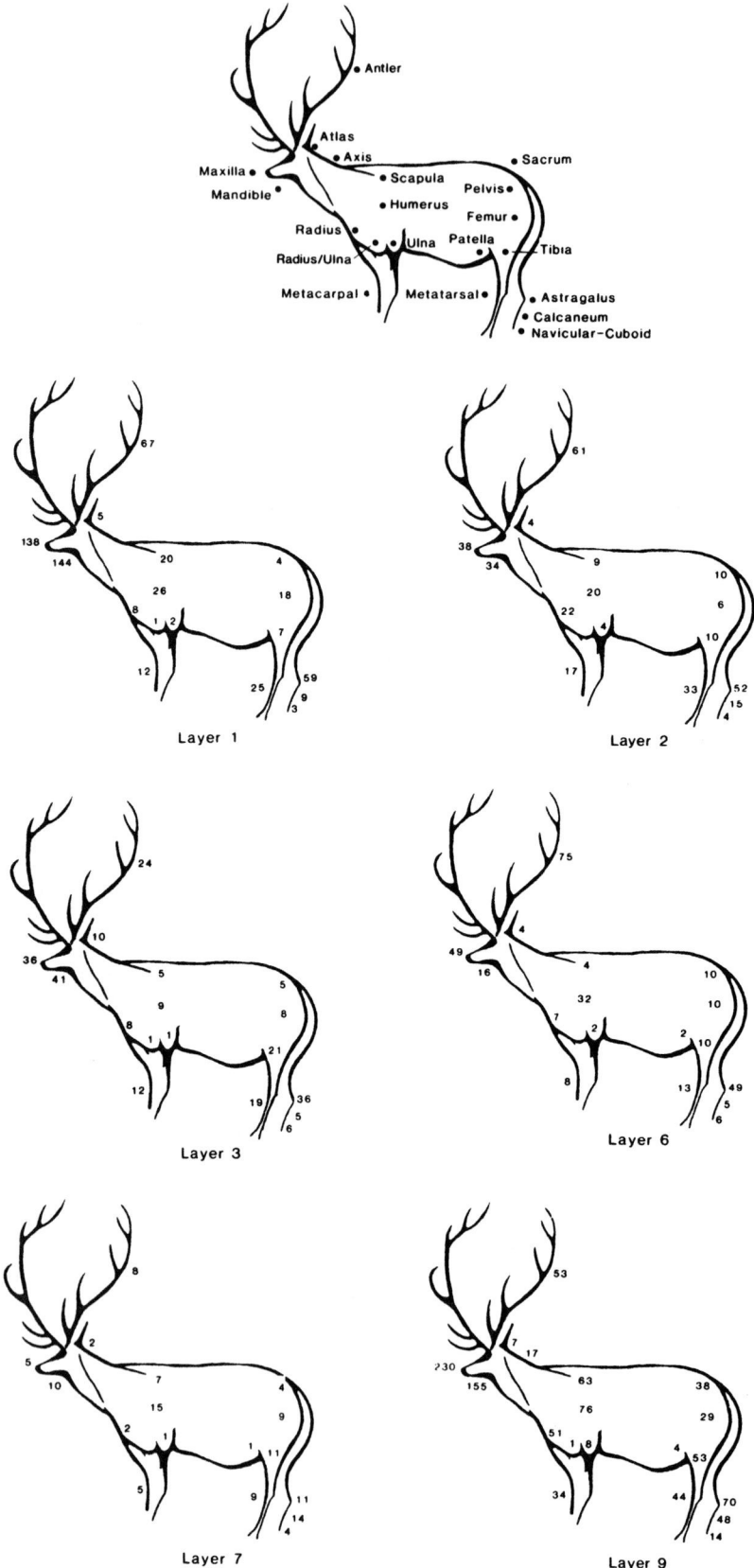

Fig. 8.6. Parpalló: bone numbers of *Cervus elaphus*.

Table 8.15. *Factors affecting body-part representation*

| | Cranial | Axial | Fore | Hind | Foot | References |
|---|---|---|---|---|---|---|
| Economic anatomy | little food cache protectors | much food | seasonal | best | poor Schlepp | Binford & Bertram 1977 Yellen 1977; Serjeant 1976 |
| Artefacts | horn and antler for tools | no | little | possibly esp. tibia | metapodials? | J.G.D. Clark 1953 |
| Scavenging | yes | yes | yes | yes | yes | Brain 1969; Binford & Bertram 1977; A.P. Hill 1976, 1978 |
| Preservation/storage | no | no | seasonal not usual | yes | discarded | Binford & Bertram 1977 |
| Chemical & mechanical post-deposition | summer antler soft jaws break | good | scapula fragile | pelvis fragmented | good | Brain 1969; Binford & Bertram 1971 |
| Excavation sample | good | unknown | unknown prob. good | unknown variable | some v. good size effect | Payne 1972 a,b |
| Analysis | good | mostly not analysed | good | fragments difficult | good | |

Table 8.16. *Les Mallaetes: body-part summaries for red deer and Spanish ibex*

| | Red deer | | | | | | Ibex | | | | | | |
|---|---|---|---|---|---|---|---|---|---|---|---|---|---|
| | | 1 | 2 | 4 | 6 | 7 | | 1 | 2 | 4 | 5 | 6 | 7 |
| Layer | S–G | PdM | B + T | Solut. | Gravet. | Aurig. | S–G | PdM | B + T | Solut. | Atyp. | Gravet. | Aurig. |
| Fore-limb | – | 1 | – | 2 | 2 | 1 | – | 1 | 2 | 7 | – | 1 | 1 |
| Hind-limb | 2 | 1 | 1 | 1 | 1 | – | – | 1 | 1 | 4 | – | 3 | – |
| Extremities | 3 | – | 1 | 4 | 14 | 3 | 1 | 4 | 2 | 8 | 1 | 3 | – |
| Toes | – | – | 1 | 6 | 12 | 1 | 1 | – | 2 | 13 | – | 1 | – |
| Axial | | | | | | | – | – | – | 1 | – | 1 | – |
| Cranial | – | – | 3 | 2 | 4 | – | 1 | – | – | 9 | – | – | 1 |
| Lower teeth | 1 | – | – | 2 | 4 | – | 3 | 3 | 4 | 27 | – | 1 | 1 |
| Upper teeth | – | – | 1 | 3 | – | – | 1 | 1 | 1 | 22 | – | 3 | 1 |
| Totals | 6 | 2 | 7 | 20 | 38 | 5 | 7 | 10 | 12 | 91 | 1 | 13 | 4 |

*Note:* PdM = *puntas de muesca*, B + T = barbed/tanged arrowheads.

Table 8.17. *Volcán: deer, body-part summaries. Spit numbers from excavations of 1971, 1972*

| | Layer | | | | | | | | | | | | | | | | | |
|---|---|---|---|---|---|---|---|---|---|---|---|---|---|---|---|---|---|---|
| | 18 | 19 | 20 | 21 | 22 | 23 | 24 | 25 | 26 | 26A | 27 | 27A | 27B | 27C | 28 | 28A | 28B | 29 |
| Fore-limb | – | 1 | 1 | – | – | – | 3 | 1 | – | 1 | – | – | – | 1 | 1 | – | 1 | 1 |
| Hind-limb | 2 | 3 | 3 | – | 1 | – | – | – | – | 3 | – | – | – | 1 | 1 | – | 1 | – |
| Extremities | 6 | 2 | 10 | – | 1 | 5 | 4 | 8 | 2 | 6 | 3 | 8 | 2 | 3 | 12 | 2 | 6 | 4 |
| Toes | 4 | 6 | 8 | – | 2 | 4 | 1 | 7 | 8 | 2 | – | – | 1 | 10 | 4 | – | 5 | 4 |

this factor. Many of the conclusions must, however, be presented as hypotheses for testing elsewhere in the region and in other regions. Nevertheless, some conclusions may be presented in terms of the means of assessing prehistoric economies which I outlined at the outset, and in terms of the operation of the prehistoric economy in southern Valencia province during the later stages of the last glacial period.

I have shown in this discussion that it is very difficult to interpret the remains from an individual site in terms of the relative importance of human choices and environmentally induced changes. However, interpretation is possible when there is a clearer understanding of the environmental changes taking place at the time of the human use of several sites, and when it is possible to compare the different sequences of

residues related to the environmental changes. The discussion of these features is made simpler by the distinction between site catchments and site exploitation territories, and between the tactical use of particular sites, and the exploitation strategy by which they were related. In principle, at least, it would be possible to interpret the relationships between the activities performed at different sites, such as those discussed in this chapter, as part of a set of activities performed during an annual round at a group of linked sites, provided there was adequate control of the chronology. I have attempted such a synthesis, despite the inadequacies of the evidence from these sites, and the still greater inadequacies of information about the other sites of the local region. Part of the purpose of this speculative approach is to show the sorts of hypothesis which might account for the apparent abundance of Palaeo-lithic sites in this part of Valencia province in comparison with other regions in eastern Spain. It is my intention to present my conclusions in the form of hypotheses which future research should be able to test and revise.

Inspection of the list of sites occupied at different periods, and of the hypotheses about the extent of site catchments at different periods, suggests that in the initial phases of use of the region, say around 30 thousand years ago, there were rather few sites, with hunting camps and no particular integration of activities between the sites which have survived. This pattern could be said to be typical of that which would be expected in a foraging economy, with encounter hunting of animals by small groups of hunters. By 25 thousand years ago there is some evidence of the tactical use of sites in a seasonal round, and perhaps, therefore, of more logistical organization of activities. This pattern of organization was extended, so that about 20 thousand years ago there were extensive visits to a distant shore, and a greater number of sites in use. This period may also be one when dispersion into the hills and tablelands to the west took place seasonally, producing sporadic sites such as Cueva del Niño (see Davidson 1980, chapter 10 and Davidson in press). This pattern continued through the following five millennia, but the frequency of visits to the shore began to decline, and eventually almost ceased, despite the fact that this was a period in which the shore was itself moving closer to the caves as a result of eustatic rise in sea level. The apparent reduction of numbers of sites which were used corresponds to the period of reduction in size of the site catchments, and to the intensification of use of the antlers of deer as raw material for the manufacture of increasingly important artefacts. Other changes in patterns of exploitation are also indicated, particularly at Volcán, where ibex became less abundant in the faunal remains. The remains from Volcán also suggest that there may be some human deletion of parts of the upper limbs of red deer from the collection, or that bones of upper limbs of red deer were not brought to the site. There is a suggestion that an exactly complementary process operated at Parpalló, though this will remain for ever unproven because of the uncertainty about the collection methods. Such practices might be associated with drying or curing of meat, though more evidence will be needed to assert this confidently.

Throughout this chapter I have been preoccupied with the effects of sampling within sites, and little with sampling of sites within regions. The conclusions may seem appropriate descriptions of a single site system with the investigated sites representing typical tactical roles in a local exploitation strategy. It should not be forgotten, however, that caves are fixed in space, and are particularly visible archaeologically, partly because they produced highly localized stratified deposits and partly because archaeologists have looked there. Many activities which were not carried out at caves will not be so readily investigated archaeologically. This problem becomes particularly important when any attempt is made to suggest the integration of activities between sites. In

the present case, it may be that the inhabitants of Parpalló visited Volcán, and that we are dealing essentially with only one group of people and one system of exploitation. On the other hand we may well be sampling a range of activities by several groups. But this may not be disastrous at this stage of analysis. The important point in the present case is that we have sites with a range of activities. This may be taken as an indication of the range of activities in a site system. Such a range could, however, arise by chance and give a completely distorted indication of the scale of spatial organization in the particular prehistoric situation as is illustrated schematically in figures 8.7 and 8.8.

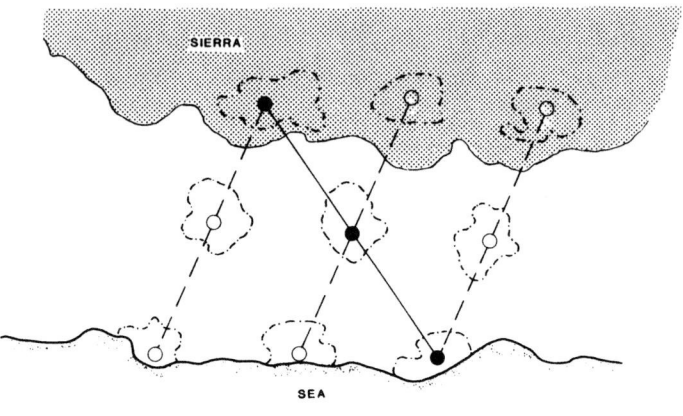

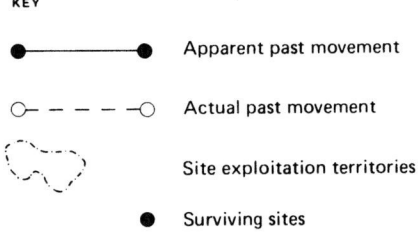

Fig. 8.7. Simple model of site systems and interpretation based on surviving archaeological sites.

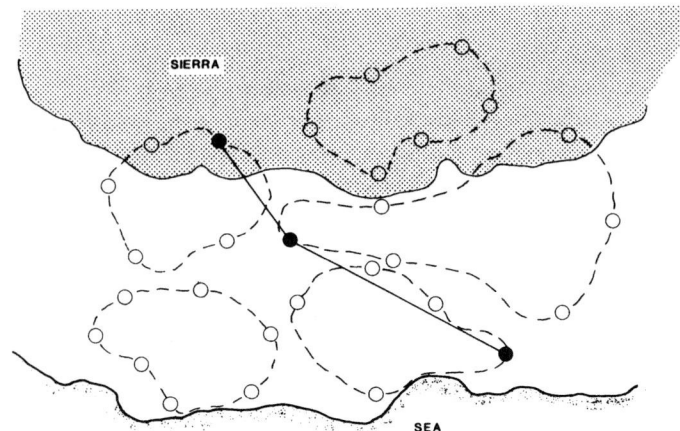

Fig. 8.8. Complex model of site systems and interpretation based on surviving archaeological sites. Key as for fig. 8.7.

Figure 8.7 shows a simple model of inter-site integration. Three simple systems of seasonal site use are shown in which the general exploitation strategy involved movement between three sites in an annual round to exploit resources as they became suitable for exploitation in particular spatial locations. In the situation which I have illustrated three sites have been found, and six are lost for one reason or another (see e.g. Hamond 1978). Quite by chance the three happen to show a range of activities which indicate diversity at different seasons, and we interpret the complementarity as indicating past association. Figure 8.8 shows an alternative model, in which the same set of data are produced by an entirely different system of exploitation. Given the culture history of the region and the likely result of post-depositional attritional processes operating on sites, the real situation is just as likely to approximate this more complex model, involving the sampling of complex groupings of sites within a greater number of site systems. The purpose of this hypothetical example is to illustrate the scope of the problem, and the difficulties which may arise from inadequate interpretive models.

There are two means of escaping from this problem. All of my interpretations have been based on the material usually included in 'economic' interpretations, namely faunal data and site locations. Indeed, it is one of the criticisms of many economic interpretations that they ignore other evidence, as I have appeared to ignore the evidence of the stone and antler artefacts, and of the art (but see Davidson 1980: 9.35–9.38). Study of such materials is urgently needed to distinguish the stylistic links between objects which may have been used within one, rather than another, site system. The social territories indicated by the distribution of distinctive art and artefacts are an essential element in the understanding of the range of resources available to human groups (J.G.D. Clark 1975; see also Part 4 below).

The second escape is less appropriate for the elucidation of detailed culture histories and seeks to avoid the problem by aiming at a more general objective, in which the focus is on the range of past relationships, rather than the specific articulation of the component parts of particular systems. The delineation of a range of activities within a region gives a general idea of the strategies involved in the exploitation of a particular environment. The fact that we may have three complementary parts of different systems does not prevent us from inferring the type of circumstances in which particular tactics were employed. In terms of the interpretation of exploitation strategies this remains an important general conclusion, even though we may not be able to get any information about the complete systems within which those individual sites were used. In particularly favourable circumstances, the investigation of site catchments can show that particular localized resources were being used in common by occupants of different sites, and then the linking of site catchments may indicate a social relationship between the occupants of different individual sites. The resources which can be used to indicate such relationships would normally have to be much more localized than the sea shells used as an example here. In this example, however, the common response to the same environmental change may indicate a similar use of the site catchment.

In conclusion, therefore, I would suggest that we can understand much about the range of past relationships with environment, but that the information which we obtain may not correspond in a simple way with familiar models of site systems and exploitation strategies. Such inferences require more sophisticated analysis than has been undertaken hitherto. It is, however, necessary to pursue the inquiry by the rather abstract means advocated here in order to establish the framework within which the more sophisticated analyses may be undertaken.

*Acknowledgements*
Much of this chapter is included in my doctoral thesis, and therefore all the many people acknowledged there should be acknowledged here. I must single out from that larger group Geoff Bailey, Eric Higgs, Luis Pericot, Domingo Fletcher and Bob Chapman for their special support and encouragement. Luke Godwin read and commented on an earlier draft and his helpful criticisms have been incorporated. Doug Hobbs did the drawings, and Wendy Chappell typed tables and bibliography. All of these people have no responsibility for my own individual view of prehistory and the prehistory of Spain. That is mine alone.

Chapter 9

## Boreal phase settlement/subsistence models for Cantabrian Spain
Geoffrey A. Clark

Since it has been suggested that coastal adaptations are distinct from those of inland peoples, that coastal adaptations share common features, and that culture/ecological models for pre-agricultural coastal economies should be developed, an effort is made here to characterize coastal environments in terms of relative productivity, and to outline the assumptions which bear upon their exploitation by pre-agricultural societies (Lawrence 1969; Perlman 1980; Yesner 1980; G.A. Clark 1981a). Three alternative settlement/subsistence models for a Spanish Boreal phase coastal assemblage called the 'Asturian of Cantabria' (Vega del Sella 1914; Clark 1975b, 1976a,b) are then presented and evaluated. The assumptions upon which these models are based are made explicit, a 'grammar' for converting present-day resource distributions to those characteristic of the Early Holocene is developed, and the relative adequacy of the models is assessed using a quantified site territorial methodology. Because the integrity of the Asturian as a distinct culture /stratigraphic unit has recently been called into question on chrono-logical grounds (Straus 1979b), an attempt is made to examine the consequences of possible contemporaneity between some Asturian and Azilian sites in terms of the models noted above. While this effort stops short of a formal test, an alternative scenario for Early Holocene human adaptation in Cantabria is presented and discussed.

### Introduction
Archaeological research on pre-agricultural coastal adaptations has been stimulated in recent years by the publi-cation of topical studies concerned with aspects of subsistence change and the relative efficiency of different subsistence strategies in coastal environments (Thomas *et al.* 1975; Perlman 1980); resource diversity and 'niche width' (Hardesty

1975; Hespenheide 1975, 1980; Christenson 1980a); cost/ benefit analyses and decision models (Bettinger 1980; Earle 1978, 1980) and (natural) variability in coastal productivity (Braun 1974; Odum and Copeland 1974). One consequence of these studies has been the realization that coastal environ-ments and adaptations can be considered distinctive from those of non-coastal pre-agriculturalists (e.g. Lawrence 1969), and that there is a need to develop cultural—ecological models which are tenable for pre-agricultural coastal econo-mies in general (see also chapter 10, this volume).

While such comprehensive models are clearly in the future, the fresh perspective generated by these studies has allowed for the identification of most of the factors which influence contemporary research designs applied to pre-agricultural coastal adaptations. Some of these are argued to be valid for prehistoric subsistence change in general, whereas others are restricted to particular environments, technologies and/or subsistence strategies. Causality in an ultimate sense remains a hotly debated topic, and is attributed (1) to subsistence stress caused by population growth (Boserup 1956; Binford 1968; Spooner 1972; Cohen 1975, 1977); (2) to environmental and (3) to technological change (Braun 1974; Parmalee and Klippel 1974; Thomas *et al.* 1975; Botkin 1980; Coombs 1980; Reidhead 1980); and (4) to changes in social organization (Lees 1973; Cowgill 1975a,b; Earle 1978). Resouce stress owed to regional population growth is favoured as the principal determinant of changes in the subsistence economy in Late Pleistocene/Early Holocene Cantabria (cf. chapter 12, this volume; Straus *et al.* 1980, 1981), but no position is taken here on the general adequacy of stress models as causal factors. It is evident, though, that changes in regional population density can at times directly affect changes in subsistence, and for that reason demographic stress variables should be taken into consideration on a case-by-case basis regardless of the outcome of discussions about causality in general.

### Coastal environments and their exploitation: some assumptions

Assumptions about hunter-gatherer behaviour in general, and about the nature of coasts, coastal resources and associated aspects of the terrestrial environment (e.g. estuaries, the tidal zone, the coastal plain, coastal relief, biotic communities) constitute biases in the models discussed below. These assumptions are related (1) to aspects of Cantabrian coastal geomorphology, (2) to hunter-gatherer subsistence practices in coastal environments, and (3) to human economic activity in general.

For the purposes of this chapter, the Cantabrian coast is considered to be a 'moderate productivity' coast (Inman and Nordstrom 1971). Although not characterized by the wide coastal shelf typically associated with the highest coastal productivities (Odum 1971), the accidented nature of the strand, and the presence of numerous inlets and estuaries, results in an environment with a 'patchy' distribution of densely populated, high diversity eco-niches which compensates to a certain extent for sparsely populated expanses of rocky, wave-stressed shoreline with low species diversity indices. Because the continental shelf off Cantabria is both steep and very narrow, it is suggested that even during glacial maxima, with sea-level depressions in excess of 100m, the shoreline would have been displaced only about 8-10km north of its present location (Defense Mapping Agency Hydrographic Center 1977). Thus the Cantabrian situation is an unusual one, in that assumptions about the location and accessibility of different kinds of marine and terrestrial resources in relation to prehistoric sites and to features of the regional landscape are justifiable to a greater extent than would be the case in coastal situations with wide-shelf environments. Moreover, the Cantabrian coast is tectonically stable, so that for the Late Pleistocene/Early Holocene time ranges of interest here, it can be safely assumed that the position of the shoreline did not differ markedly from that of the present (cf. chapter 13 below).

As is true of most such studies, statements about human economic and decision-making behaviour are incorporated in the present essay. So-called cost-risk minimization principles are basic assumptions. In hunter-gatherer contexts, people are expected to minimize both effort (measured by energy or time inputs) and risk (measured by the probability that resource requirements will not be satisfied) (Perlman 1980: 260-1).

Over the long term, those environments which allow for effort-risk minimization will be occupied first, and will continue to be occupied and exploited according to cost-risk minimization principles so long as the social and technological sub-systems are sufficiently flexible to accommodate stochastic variation in the resource base, and so long as calamitous macroclimatic change and/or demographic stress do not force a system-wide re-articulation of the elements of the regional predation cycle.

The assumption of cost-risk minimization has a number of consequences for hunter-gatherer economic behaviour, some of which can be observed or at least monitored in archaeological contexts. It is taken as given that morphologically modern hunter-gatherers (i.e. *Homo sapiens sapiens*) efficiently utilize easily recognizable and exploitable resources in their environments, and that they are typically aware of differentials in relative nutritive value, reliability, procurement efficiency, yields per unit weight and per unit cost, seasonal variation in availability and relative transport costs (Thomas *et al.* 1975). Thus the notion of increased Terminal Pleistocene 'living in' to an environment (i.e. becoming increasingly familiar with its spectrum of economic resources) (Braidwood and Howe 1962; Braidwood 1975) has no meaning for post-Neanderthal hunter-gatherers because an intimate familiarity with available and potential resources can be assumed. This does not imply, however, that all hunter-gatherers are *equally* efficient in their patterns of predation, nor that differences in efficiency cannot be detected for given regions over time.

If these statements are accepted, the optimal solution to resource procurement will be the one which produces the highest overall return whilst simultaneously minimizing both effort and risk (Perlman 1980: 260, 273). Departures from the optimal solution should be able to be deduced on logical grounds or arrived at empirically, if adequate archaeological data are available. Without resorting to value-laden and untestable assertions about the relative appeal of different kinds of foods (e.g. Cohen 1975, 1977), consideration of factors which result in increased effort and/or risk would allow for the identification of sub-optimal procurement patterns. Sub-optimal strategies have been discussed by ecologists (e.g. MacArthur and Pianka 1966; Emlen 1966; Emlen and Emlen 1974) and by archaeologists (e.g. Cohen 1977; Perlman 1976, 1980). When considered in relative terms (and ideally across time), selection for smaller prey sizes, selection for dispersed, uniformly distributed low-density species, highly mobile forms, species which are more difficult to locate, capture and process; species which involve increased transport costs in general, more dangerous species, and a greater diversity of (especially low-yield, high-risk) species all indicate situations in which some factor or factors is acting to bring about the implementation of a sub-optimal procurement strategy.

Estuarine environments above 40° latitude on high-relief coasts have been identified as those which entail the lowest risks and the least effort for the acquisition of subsistence resources (Clarke 1976; Perlman 1980). This is because of their pronounced ecotonal character (especially marked in

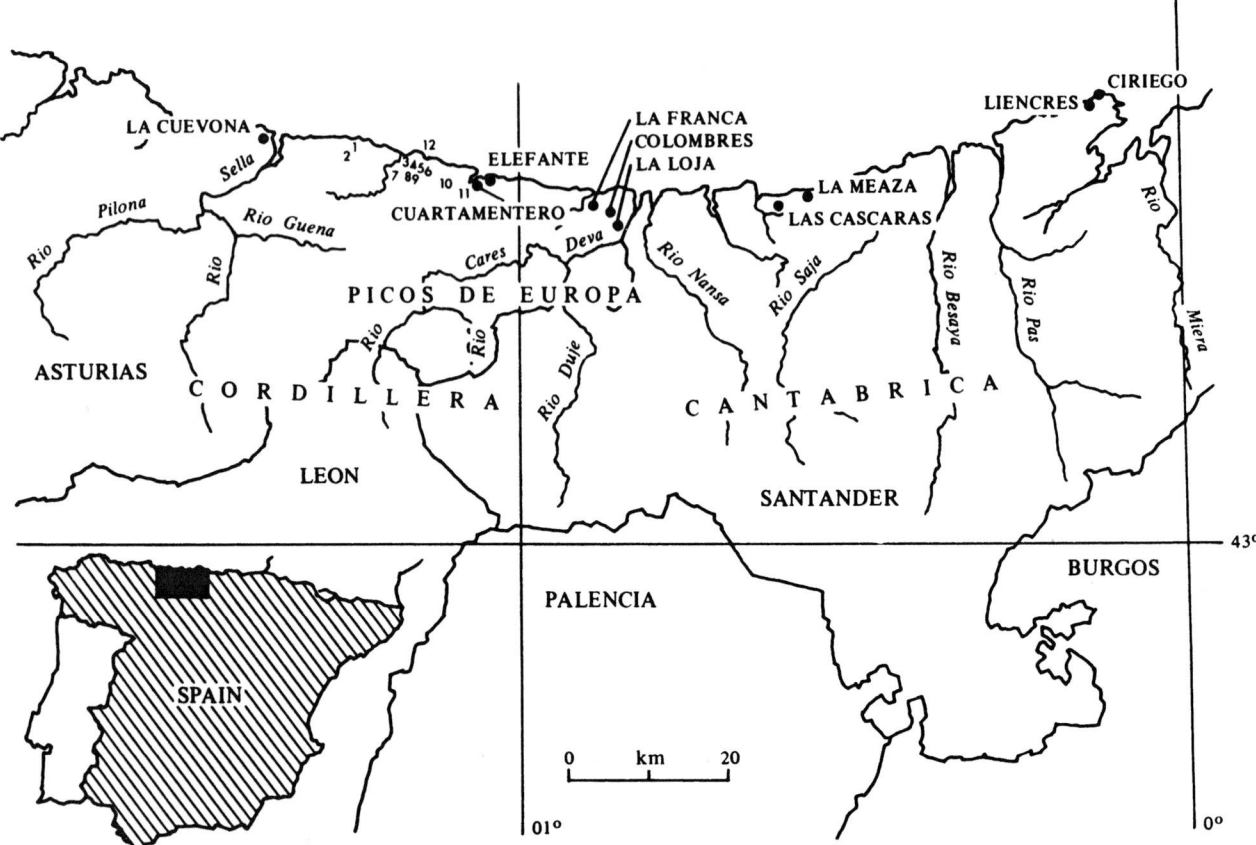

Fig. 9.1. Major topographic features in the Cantabrian provinces of Asturias and Santander with the distribution of Asturian sites indicated. Numbered sites: 1. Cuevas del Mar, 2. Penicial, 3. Bricia, 4. Cueto de la Mina, 5. La Riera, 6. Tres Calabres, 7. Coberizas, 8. Arnero, 9. Lledías, 10. Balmori, 11. Allorú, 12. Fonfría.

Cantabria, where sharp vertical relief compresses resource zonation in a narrow coastal strip often no more than 10 km wide) which in turn encourages a high species-diversity index for the region as a whole. Woodland and woodland margin niches rich in nuts and deer, rivers in which freshwater and anadromous fish abound, estuaries with abundant shellfish and waterfowl (and, in Cantabria, alpine niches with caprid populations located within 2–5 km of the sea) all combine to provide a subsistence base that acts to minimize effort (because mobility is minimized, due to the proximity of different biotopes) and risk (because of the buffering effect of moderate-yield, low-risk shellfoods, because of the high density of dietary staples (e.g. deer, nuts) located in close proximity to one another, and because the diversity of food resources allows for maximum flexibility in procurement strategies) (Hewes 1948). Estuarine environments should also allow for greater sedentism; other wave-stressed coastal environments and interior zones should be occupied in lower densities and be exploited less intensively than estuarine zones (Perlman 1980).

### Cantabrian landscapes
In central Cantabria, the remains of hunter-gatherer

groups living between 8650 and 6800 b.p. are concentrated in some density. These archaeological residues tend to occur in the mouths of caves and are usually assigned to the Asturian culture/stratigraphic unit, first defined by the Count of Vega del Sella (1914, 1916, 1923, 1930). The 28 known Asturian sites are confined to the adjacent provinces of Asturias and Santander, and are especially dense in the area of Llanes, in eastern Asturias (fig. 9.1). Although not apparent from figure 9.1, there is a tendency for sites to proliferate in clustered groupings so that the site territory may have been capable of supporting a larger population than could have been accommodated within the confines of a single cave or rockshelter (Bailey 1978, Conkey 1980; see also this volume, chapter 13). The most intensive occupations appear to have been centred near the coast where shellfish were readily available, and, along with red deer (*Cervus elaphus*) probably provided the protein base for daily subsistence. Nothing is known of plant resources collected prehistorically, although oak (acorns), beech (beech-nuts), hazel (hazelnuts), juniper and a variety of cereal grasses are known to have been present in the region and were probably utilized during the Early Holocene (Leroi-Gourhan, pers. comm.; Clark and Menéndez Amor 1975).

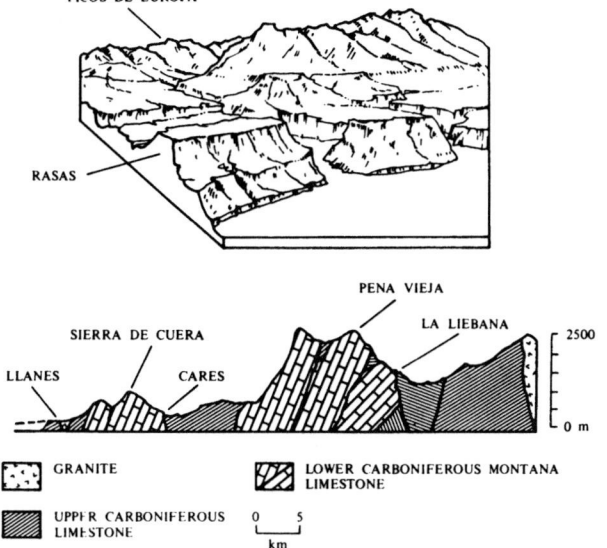

GRANITE

UPPER CARBONIFEROUS LIMESTONE

LOWER CARBONIFEROUS MONTANA LIMESTONE

0    5
|___|
km

Fig. 9.2. Block diagram and section of the region south of Llanes, eastern Asturias, indicating location of coastal ridges (*rasas*), coastal valleys, Cordilleran foothills and intermontane valleys (after Houston 1967:181, 182).

The landscape in central Asturias consists of five major structural components, created by Mesozoic orogeny and folding and faulting of Carboniferous date (fig. 9.2). While most apparent along a north–south transect in the region of Llanes, these landforms are replicated to various degrees along much of the Cantabrian coast. They consist of (1) a series of low (50–100 m) ridges and platforms which parallel the coast and which usually occur within a kilometre of the present shoreline; (2) a narrow coastal plain, extending at most some 15 km inland; (3) low (300–1300 m) ranges of foothills distributed in broken east–west trending chains from central Asturias east to the Vizcayan border; (4) the intermontane valleys and (5) summits of the Cordillera, which attain a maximum elevation of over 2600 m in the Picos de Europa, a scant 27 km from the sea (Martínez Alvarez 1965: 95–129; 1975: 135–58; Houston 1967: 180–5). Superimposed on these structural elements are a variety of life zones the distributions of which are dependent upon variations in the moisture and temperature regimes, altitude, vegetation, microtopographic conditions, and the proximity of the sea.

The region is drained by a regular lattice of short, north–south flowing rivers, which have their headwaters in the Cordillera and which transect the east–west trending ranges of mountains and hills, and the coastal plain. Spaced at intervals of 10 to 15 km, these water courses provide natural avenues of north–south transit in a region which is often quite rugged topographically and difficult of access. Straus (1975a: 41–58) has suggested that the Cantabrian river valleys were sheltered locales during the rigorous climatic conditions of pleniglacial times, and also provided natural routes of north–south migration, presumably utilized seasonally by both men and animals as part of an annual round.

Climate today is equable, although there is evidence of Pleistocene glaciation in the Picos de Europa and in several other Cordilleran centres. Significant snowfall is confined at present to elevations above 1500 m. Average yearly rainfall along the coast reaches or exceeds 120 cm; there is no real dry season. The landscape has been much altered by man. Natural climax vegetation apparently consisted of a mosaic of mixed deciduous/coniferous forest and open grassland in the first century B.C. at the time of initial Roman colonization. Predominant arboreal species included several kinds of oak (*Quercus*) and pine (*Pinus*), with chestnuts (*Castanea*), beech (*Fagus*) and birch (*Betula*) in association (Mayor and Diaz 1977; Guinea Lopez 1953: 220–8). Systematic deforestation beginning in Roman times became much accelerated during the Middle Ages, so that the predominant cover today is artificial grassland (*prado*) with isolated but at times quite extensive plantations of eucalyptus and Monterrey pine, introduced late in the last century as part of an extensive reforestation programme. Only in comparatively isolated intermontane valleys (e.g. those of the Ríos Dobra, Cares, Dujé) do traces of the original climax vegetation survive (Clark 1976a: 27–31).

The sites assigned to the Asturian phase are regarded as trash heaps associated with base camps occupied by a local group or a major part thereof on a fairly continuous (perhaps even perennial) basis, and representing the residues from a wide variety of procurement, processing, maintenance and disposal activities. In light of the assumptions about coastal ecology and human subsistence behaviour outlined above, and when the particulars of the regional landscape are taken into account, there is considerable *a priori* evidence to support this notion (e.g. sites are optimally situated to exploit estuarine, forest, forest margin and montane resources; site locations minimize 'cost' factors (especially moving, transport) because they are approximately equidistant from major resource zones which are themselves located in close proximity to one another). However, the statement that Asturian sites are middens associated with base camps is regarded here as a hypothesis to be tested, rather than an *ad hoc* assertion. It is further assumed that resource procurement was done on a transient basis (cf. Binford 1978b, 1980). Trips were made to coastal, estuarine and inland resource areas, and foodstuffs and raw materials were brought back to the home site. This would have been the case if the sites were occupied seasonally or perennially.

### The archaeological data
Asturian sites have been identified with the formation of a particular kind of shell midden. These accumulations, called 'concheros', are artificial deposits composed of variable quantities of sediment, bone fragments and marine shells. Concheros have formed since earliest Solutrean times in Cantabria (20–21 000 b.p.) (Straus, Clark and González 1978; Bailey, chapter 13 below) and may be more or less cemented into breccia-like deposits, depending upon the extent of percolation by carbonate-charged waters and upon subsequent microclimatic conditions in the area of accumulation.

Table 9.1. *Major variables used*

1  Biotopes probably present prehistorically:
   Alpine
   Forest/forest margin
   Estuarine
   Marshes
   Open Country
   Sea

2  Percentage of biotopes probably present prehistorically

3  Ranked percentages of biotopes present prehistorically

4  Mean linear distance to each biotope in site exploitation territory

5  Ranked mean distances to each biotope in site exploitation territory

6  Fauna:
   Terrestrial fauna theoretically present by biotope
   Terrestrial fauna actually represented archaeologically
   Percentage of usable meat/species
   Marine fauna theoretically present by biotope
   Marine fauna actually represented archaeologically

7  Archaeological remains present:
   Débitage
   Small tools
   Heavy-duty tools

Table 9.2. *Conversion of present-day environments into a reduced series of Early Holocene environments*

| Present-day environments | Prehistoric environments |
| --- | --- |
| Alpine | Alpine: elevation 200 m or greater than 100 m with steep gradient (greater than 40°). |
| Forest/forest margin | Forest/forest margin: land less than 100 m elevation, excluding marshes, estuaries, sand and open coast; unforested areas may also be included. |
| Estuarine | First 500 m of river flood-plain. |
| River valley flood-plain | Forest/forest margin: mixed deciduous/coniferous woodland; deciduous species dominant. |
| Marsh | Marsh |
| Open country | Forest/forest margin or open country: open country if above 100 m, relatively flat, no higher than 200 m. |
| Pasture land (*prado*) | Forest/forest margin: between 0–100 m; more than 500 m back from shoreline and not anything else. |
| Agricultural land | Forest/forest margin or open country. |
| Monte bajo | Forest/forest margin if 0–100 m in elevation and at least 100 m from coast. Open country if between 100–200 m and relatively flat. |
| Monte alto | Forest/forest margin if 0–100 m in elevation and at least 100 m from coast; otherwise open country. |
| Open coastline | Open coastline: 0–100 m from shoreline. |
| Sea | Sea: It is assumed that the coastline has not fluctuated significantly since the Boreal period. |

Normally, little stratigraphy is present in them and artefact density is low. Concheros probably represent nothing more than big garbage heaps. They are not inferred to be living sites, which were probably located in the open air in close proximity to the caves.

Sites are classified as Asturian if they (1) contain concheros with or without substantial industrial remains in which modern variants of limpet (*Patella* spp.) and topshell (*Trochocochlea crassa* or *Monodonta lineata*) predominate, and in which the so-called Pleistocene limpet variant (*Patella vulgata sautuola*) and the winkle (*Littorina littorea*) are absent, and (2) if the deposits contain the characteristic Asturian pick in primary depositional context.

In this study an effort was made to utilize as much information about the environment as possible, while attempting to avoid unrealistic assumptions about the precise location and importance of particular resources, given the necessity for extrapolation from present-day conditions. It is necessary to draw a fine line between what might theoretically be possible, given optimum information about Early Holocene Asturias, and what is really legitimately possible, given the considerable inadequacies of the data actually available. If an experiment can be designed using variables which are gross enough to be realistic (given present knowledge and available archaeological data), yet fine enough to provide some insight into differences and similarities among Asturian sites and their exploitation territories, then no (or little) violence will be done to assumptions built into the model.

Variables used here can be divided into four major groups, which reflect (1) gross biotopes present prehistorically in the vicinity of each site, (2) distance and access measures,

(3) faunal resources potentially available and actually recovered, and (4) archaeological remains present (table 9.1). It is reasoned that a settlement/subsistence model derived from knowledge of present regional ecology may enable us to suggest a settlement/subsistence system which would have been efficient in the past. However, before such a model can be constructed, it is necessary to transform contemporary classifications of environmental life zones into one which might be argued to have been present prehistorically (table 9.2). I suggest that the mechanism for conversion presented here is at least a reasonable one, given present knowledge of Early Holocene palaeoenvironments and a realistic appreciation of the scale at which it is defensible to operate. Notice, however, that a 1:1 equivalence is not provided in every case. If it is granted that much Early Holocene topography in Cantabria consisted of a forest/open country mosaic, then a means must be found for making unambiguous 'on the ground' assignments of present zones which could have been either forested or grassland to one or

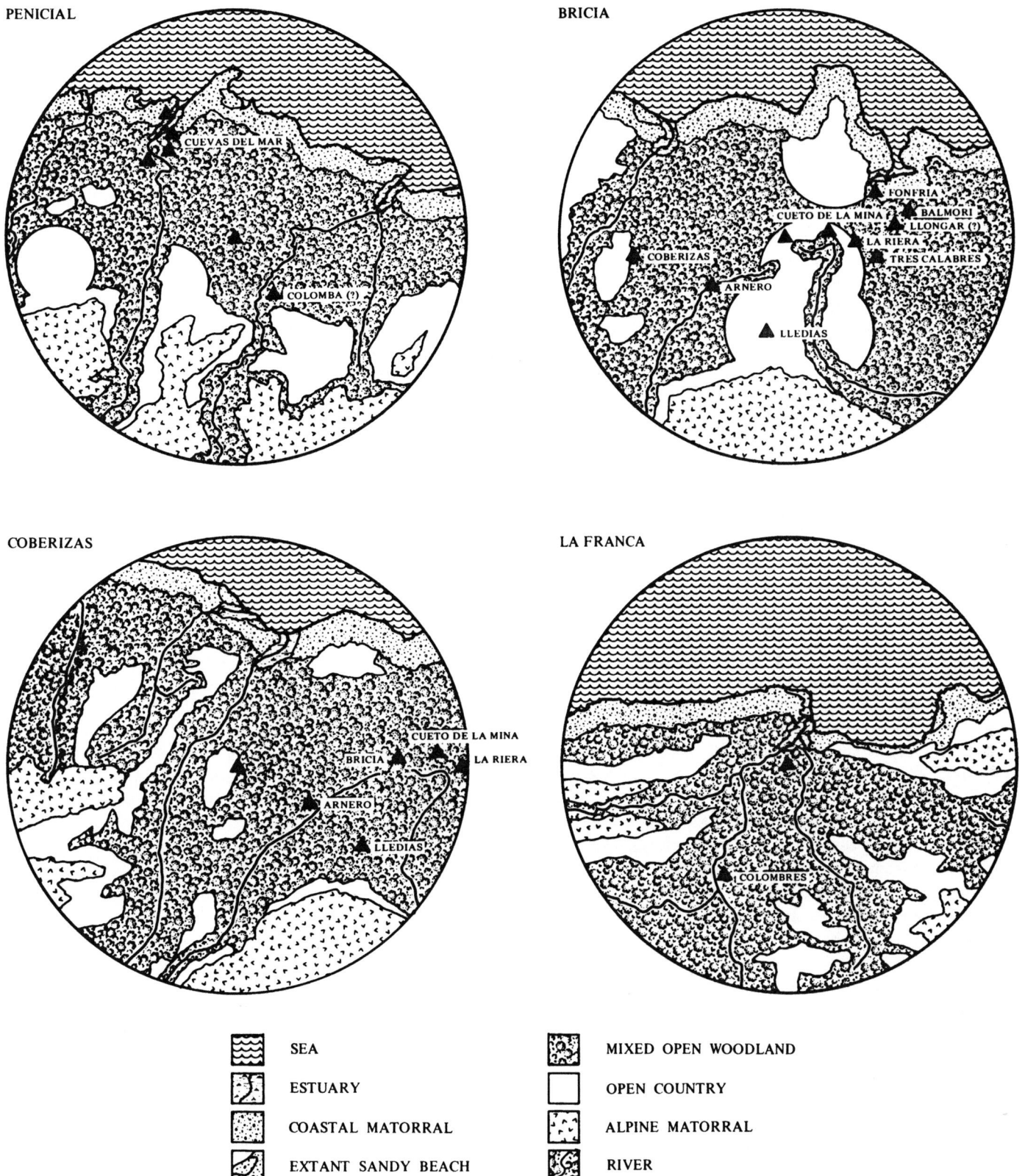

Fig. 9.3. Site exploitation territories for the Asturian sites of Penicial, Bricia, Coberizas and La Franca (Mazaculos II).

the other category. Subject to certain constraints, this can only be done on a random basis using knowledge of present ratios of forest to open country biotopes in relatively undisturbed areas (Clark and Lerner 1980).

### Methodological considerations

A circular site exploitation territory was first imposed around each of the 28 sites. The circles were designed with a 3 km radius which, given the zonal compression and the rugged terrain characteristic of this portion of the north Spanish coast, was considered to be an adequate estimate of the distance an entire group would be likely to be willing to travel in one day to attain a particular resource without the necessity for transient camp sites. As a preliminary step, the 12-part classification of present-day biotopes given in table 9.2 was used to make a record of the distributions of life-zones surrounding each site. These were subsequently transformed into the 7-part classification of past life zones (table 9.2). This was a straightforward procedure, except for the ambiguity inherent in the realization that a mosaic of forest and open country was present in the Early Holocene. We had no way of distinguishing those areas which were forested from those which were covered with open scrub and grassland vegetation.

If it is legitimate to assume that the ratio of grassland to woodland biotopes has remained fixed since the Early Holocene for undisturbed portions of the region as a whole, even if distributions of biotopes have changed, then a conversion can be accomplished using parts of the eastern half of Asturias as a basis for computation. This section of the province was examined and the ratio of present-day open country to woodland was determined to be approximately 38 : 62. After transformation according to the rules given in table 9.2, the area of combined wooded/open country was determined for each circle, and areas designated open country were located using a random selection process within those portions of the circle assigned to the combined biotopes. This was done until a 4 : 6 ratio of open country to woodland was achieved.[1] This process accounts for the partially circular character of some open-country biotopes in figure 9.3. Site exploitation territories 'transformed' in this manner provided the basic data for the remainder of the analysis. A number of access and distance variables were then computed.

Resource accessibility was monitored by computing the mean distance from each site to each biotope class. A mean distance had to be used because biotopes were often irregular in shape and discontinuous in distribution. The linear distance to each patch of a given biotope class was taken, the distances summed and divided by the number of distances taken. The process was repeated for each biotope class in each of the 28 site territory circles. Both mean distances to resources and ranked mean distances were analysed using a battery of nonparametric statistics.

Potential and actual resources were then considered; this aspect of the analysis was confined to fauna. I was concerned to get some kind of an index of species available within each site exploitation territory which could then be compared with species actually found archaeologically. The larger species of terrestrial mammals are generally mobile and flexible in their habitat requirements, and so typically crosscut several biotopes (Thomas *et al.* 1975 : 7). Thus it is difficult to assess their subsistence importance solely in terms of the relative frequencies of preferred habitats in a site exploitation territory. In table 9.3 the principal game species potentially available to Holocene hunters are listed, along with live weights derived from north Spanish data (Noval 1976 : 13 −28, 43−59) and the proportion of usable meat per species. Although 13 species are potentially important, there is archaeological evidence for systematic exploitation of only six of them (red deer, roe deer, chamois, ibex, and to a much lesser extent, boar and horse) (Clark 1971b: 1246). Red deer are by far the most important species prehistorically in Cantabria, both in terms of numbers of individuals represented and in terms of meat yield. This is true not only for the Asturian culture stratigraphic unit (Clark 1971b: 1244−57), but for the Magdalenian and Solutrean periods as well (Freeman 1973a: 3−44; Straus 1975a: 381−420).

The other major component in the Asturian diet for which there is archaeological evidence was shellfood. There are no less than 140 species of shellfish on the Asturian coast today (Clark 1971a: 595−613; 1976a: 330−48). However, only about a dozen occur in archaeological contexts assigned to the Asturian period, and only three are commonly found in great numbers. These are the European topshell (*Trochocochlea crassa = Trochus lineatus = Monodonta lineata*) and two limpets (*Patella vulgata, Patella intermedia*), which together account for almost 95% of identified shell. All are estuarine and intertidal species, exposed twice daily by the action of the tides. The limpets in particular are often found concentrated in great numbers (12−30/square metre) and can be collected by anyone with comparative ease. While these species were of undoubted economic importance, just how important they were as a staple is difficult to assess. Certainly their combined dietary contribution *vis-à-vis* red deer was minimal,[2] and they must represent either (1) dietary supplements accumulated over the long term either seasonally or perennially, or (2) an insurance resource exploited intensively only when other staples were unavailable or of diminished productivity. A seasonal pattern of collection is suggested by preliminary analysis of oxygen isotope ratios from Asturian shell samples from the La Riera cave which indicate collection during the winter months (Shackleton, pers. comm.; Bailey *et al.* in press).

The co-occurrence of limpets and topshells in shell middens is a phenomenon peculiar to the Early Holocene in Cantabrian Spain; other midden deposits which pre- and postdate the Asturian are composed of different but equally distinctive spectra of molluscan species (Clark 1976a: 215−36; 1976b). Reasons for these systematic changes involve both long-term macroclimate change (mean annual sea-water temperature increased during the Asturian period, and declined somewhat after about 6000 b.p.) and increased concentration

Table 9.3. *Mammals potentially available as game animals to Early Holocene hunters in Cantabrian Spain*

| Order, genus and species | Common name | Average live weight | % usable meat | Preferred habitat |
|---|---|---|---|---|
| **Artiodactyla** | | | | |
| *Cervus elaphus* | red deer | 180–330 | 50 | open deciduous woodland, woodland margins; matorral, parklands |
| *Capreolus capreolus* | roe deer | 15–32 | 50 | deciduous woodland, woodland margins; *monte alto* |
| *Capra ibex* | ibex | 80–110 | 50 | alpine zones above tree line (summer); rocky areas with matorral |
| *Rupicapra rupicapra* | chamois | 22–35 | 50 | alpine zones above tree line (summer); rocky areas with matorral; forest |
| *Sus scrofa* | boar | 100–275 | 60 | *monte bajo, monte alto;* open montane woodlands and forest margins |
| *Bos primigenius* | aurochs | 625–750 | 60 | open parklands, grasslands; open deciduous woodland |
| **Perissodactyla** | | | | |
| *Equus caballus* | horse | 275–300 | 60 | open woodland, woodland margins (browser); heathland, grassland (grazer) |
| **Carnivora** | | | | |
| *Ursus arctos* | brown bear | 105–155 | 70 | woodland margins, open deciduous woodland; mixed deciduous/coniferous woodland |
| *Lutra lutra* | otter | 6.8–10.7 | 70 | river banks, lake-shores, estuaries |
| **Lagomorpha** | | | | |
| *Oryctolagus cuniculus* | rabbit | 1.2–1.5 | 50 | *monte bajo;* woodland margins |
| *Lepus europaeus* | brown hare | 2.3–3.8 | 50 | *monte bajo,* open grasslands; woodland margins |
| **Pinnepedia** | | | | |
| *Phoca vitulina* | harbour seal | 80–140 | 70 | coastline, rocky coastal cliffs; estuaries |
| *Halichoerus grypus* | Atlantic grey seal | 125–360 | 70 | coastline, rocky coastal cliffs; estuaries |

Data from Noval (1976), Corbet (1966), Van den Brink (1967), Morris (1965), Altuna (1972), Straus (1975a, 1977a), Jochim (1976), Freeman (1973a) and White (1953).

over time on estuarine and more open, moderately wave-beaten intertidal zones for exploitative purposes (Clark 1971a: 428–60: 1971b: 1253–6; 1976a; Straus *et al.* 1980; chapter 12, below). Human predation on these zones had become so intensive by the end of the Pleistocene that mean limpet size within species declines significantly during and after the Azilian as a consequence of over-exploitation (Straus *et al.* 1980; chapters 12 and 13, below).

#### Settlement/subsistence system models

Hypothetical settlement/subsistence system models should take into account (1) particulars of regional topography, (2) probable resource distribution (in part a function of regional topography) and (3) cyclical or periodic variation in resource availability and in the use/occupation of particular loci in the site system. However, the extent to which we can control for these factors is limited by very imperfect knowledge of Early Holocene vegetation and climate, and restricts us to the three alternatives, designated models A, B and C, outlined in figure 9.4, referring to single river systems.

Model A proposes the existence of two base camps, one located near or on the coast and the other somewhat more inland, perhaps in one of the valleys of the east–west-trending foothill ranges which parallel the Cordillera. Assuming significant seasonal movement along the north–south-trending river valleys which transect the coastal plain, it would perhaps be advantageous to have a bipolar system, entailing an autumn/

winter encampment in close proximity to seasonally more accessible montane resources like ibex and chamois, yet situated at a low enough elevation (and in a sheltered valley) so that the occupants themselves would not suffer from the effects of the altitudinal gradient. The other base camp would be occupied in the spring and summer, would be situated on or near an estuary, and would be oriented towards the exploitation of lowland cervids and shellfish. In support of this model is the observation that some Asturian sites are considerably more inland than others (fig. 9.1); remains of alpine species are quite commonly found, indicating systematic utilization of that life zone and alpine caprids do in fact descend to lower elevations during the winter months, so that they would be more accessible to human predation at that time. Test implications for model A would entail demonstration of a bimodal pattern of life zone distributions, and of species present and potentially available. It is also reasonable to expect that artefact spectra would be distinct in this situation. Limited activity sites located in intervening areas may be identified in statistical comparisons of site exploitation territories and resources.

Model B proposes a single base camp located on the coastal plain or in the valleys of the coastal hill range adjacent to it. Presumably occupied by at least a portion of a local group on a perennial basis, such a camp would be strategically located to take advantage of the demonstrated mainstays of the Asturian diet: red deer and shellfish—both concentrated

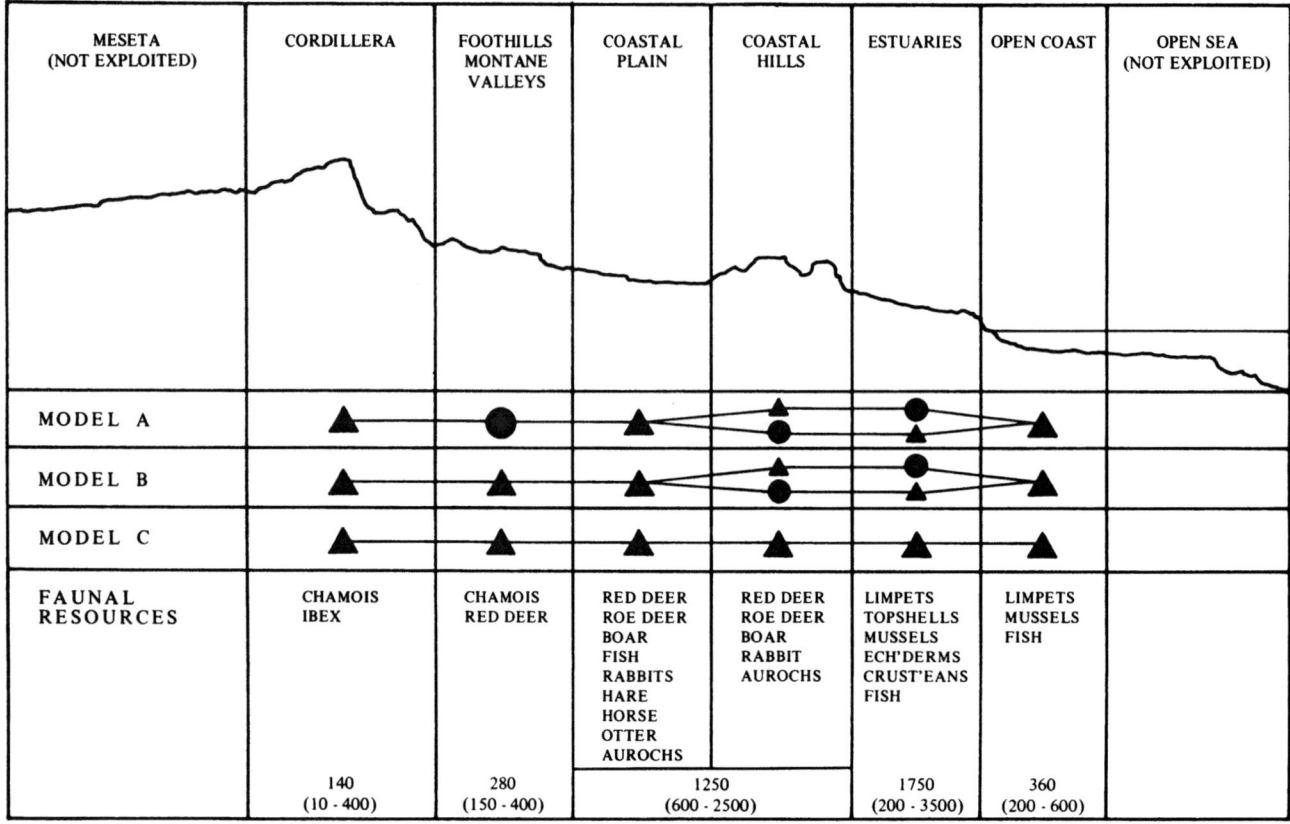

| MESETA (NOT EXPLOITED) | CORDILLERA | FOOTHILLS MONTANE VALLEYS | COASTAL PLAIN | COASTAL HILLS | ESTUARIES | OPEN COAST | OPEN SEA (NOT EXPLOITED) |
|---|---|---|---|---|---|---|---|
| MODEL A | ▲ | ● | ▲ | ▲ ● | ● | ▲ | |
| MODEL B | ▲ | ▲ | ▲ | ▲ ● | ● ▲ | ▲ | |
| MODEL C | ▲ | ▲ | ▲ | ▲ | ▲ | ▲ | |
| FAUNAL RESOURCES | CHAMOIS IBEX | CHAMOIS RED DEER | RED DEER ROE DEER BOAR FISH RABBITS HARE HORSE OTTER AUROCHS | RED DEER ROE DEER BOAR RABBIT AUROCHS | LIMPETS TOPSHELLS MUSSELS ECH'DERMS CRUST'EANS FISH | LIMPETS MUSSELS FISH | |
| | 140 (10 - 400) | 280 (150 - 400) | 1250 (600 - 2500) | | 1750 (200 - 3500) | 360 (200 - 600) | |

●   Base camp sites
▲   Limited activity sites

Fig. 9.4. Schematic representation of three alternative settlement/subsistence models for the Cantabrian Asturian. Numbers are net primary productivity ranges and means for major types of ecosystems expressed in grams per square metre per year (modified from Perlman 1980: 272).

the year round on the wooded lowlands and in the coastal estuaries which cut across them. Resources located at some distance from the camp would be obtained by hunting and gathering parties sent out from the home site on a periodic basis. The reader should keep in mind that life zones in eastern Asturias are defined more by altitudinal differences than by anything else, and are compressed from north to south into a narrow band from 7 to 12km wide. Thus a hypothetical single base camp located near the coast is in fact a viable alternative to the bipolar model discussed above. Distances are not so great nor (north–south) movement so difficult nor alpine resources so important that they could not have been obtained by hunting parties detached from a perennially occupied home site. Test implications for model B would entail demonstration of an essentially unimodal pattern of life zone distributions, species present and potentially available. If limited activity sites are present, they should be recognizable by distinctive faunal and perhaps lithic components (e.g. a high incidence of chamois, ibex) and by distributions somewhat inland of presumed base camps, following north–south-trending river courses (e.g. Río Bedón/Cabras).

Model C is a 'no base camp' model. It proposes move-

ment, in the course of an annual round, by an entire local group, up and down the major river courses with transhumance more or less confined in each case to a single drainage system. A test of this model is difficult to operate for two reasons. First, it assumes that the only differences amongst sites will be in terms of the resources found in them; no base camp/limited activity site distinction is to be made. Also, in order to conclude anything about whether it involves a single group or several groups, it is necessary to control for stylistic variation beforehand, and to be able to compare stylistic variables within and between river systems. Unfortunately there is nothing in the restricted spectrum of Asturian artefacts which is both sufficiently numerous and also likely to be a good indicator of stylistic variability. So we cannot demonstrate that a single group is involved in any case, which thrusts us back upon the more general models A and B. While the notion of extended family bands moving up and down the major valley systems exploiting resources as they become available has a certain intrinsic appeal, it is impossible to demonstrate one way or the other given data presently in hand or likely to become available. Confirmation of a model C type situation would depend almost entirely upon the degree of distinctive-

Table 9.4. *Proportional representation of life zones within site exploitation territories and distance from sites*

| | Percentage zone by site | | | | | | Distance from site in Kilometres | | | | | | | |
|---|---|---|---|---|---|---|---|---|---|---|---|---|---|---|
| | Woodland | Open country | Alpine | Coastline | Sea | Estuarine | Woodland | Open country | Alpine | Coastline | Sea | Estuarine | River | Beach |
| Bricia | 46.0 | 13.7 | 8.8 | 11.5 | 19.0 | 0.9 | 0.05 | within | 2.0 | 1.0 | 1.8 | 2.0 | 1.3 | 2.0 |
| Cueto de la Mina | 45.0 | 13.8 | 7.1 | 13.2 | 19.7 | 1.3 | within | 0.7 | 2.2 | 0.8 | 1.5 | 2.2 | 1.4 | 1.9 |
| La Riera | 45.7 | 10.5 | 6.7 | 16.2 | 20.4 | 0.7 | 0.5 | within | 2.0 | 1.0 | 1.5 | 2.2 | 1.1 | 1.4 |
| Tres Calabres | 49.7 | 9.5 | 13.0 | 11.5 | 16.4 | | within | 1.6 | 2.5 | 0.7 | 1.3 | | 1.8 | 1.6 |
| Coberizas | 52.0 | 15.4 | 14.8 | 8.1 | 6.9 | 2.8 | within | 1.5 | 1.6 | 1.5 | 1.8 | 1.6 | 0.5 | |
| Allorú | 48.6 | 14.1 | 1.3 | 9.2 | 25.2 | 1.3 | within | 0.9 | 2.5 | 0.5 | 1.3 | 2.2 | 2.2 | 1.4 |
| Vidiago | 16.8 | 10.9 | 7.4 | 11.7 | 37.1 | 2.8 | within | 1.5 | 1.8 | within | 0.5 | 1.1 | 1.0 | |
| Balmori | 45.0 | 11.1 | 2.1 | 14.6 | 27.2 | | 0.7 | within | 2.8 | within | 0.8 | | 2.0 | |
| Lledías | 43.9 | 17.9 | 31.0 | 4.3 | 1.4 | 1.4 | within | 1.3 | 0.6 | 2.3 | 2.6 | 2.3 | 1.2 | |
| Fonfría | 40.5 | 13.3 | 1.4 | 13.5 | 30.3 | 0.9 | within | 0.8 | 2.6 | 0.1 | 0.5 | 2.6 | 1.5 | 1.4 |
| Arnero | 34.0 | 25.9 | 20.1 | 9.1 | 7.3 | 3.8 | within | 1.1 | 1.8 | 2.0 | 2.5 | 1.5 | 1.4 | |
| Penicial | 35.6 | 15.9 | 11.3 | 16.0 | 18.1 | 2.8 | within | 1.1 | 2.5 | 1.0 | 1.4 | 1.7 | 0.8 | 1.8 |
| Colomba | 48.0 | 11.0 | 17.4 | 9.3 | 10.4 | 2.5 | within | 1.16 | 1.3 | 1.6 | 2.1 | 2.3 | 1.5 | |
| Cuevas del Mar | 32.9 | 5.7 | 7.0 | 11.2 | 41.6 | 1.5 | within | 1.5 | 2.0 | within | 0.5 | along | 1.5 | 0.2 |
| La Franca | 34.0 | 12.7 | 6.3 | 11.0 | 34.0 | 1.6 | within | 1.2 | 1.5 | 0.3 | 0.8 | 0.3 | 0.3 | |
| Colombres | 38.8 | 29.6 | 14.2 | 12.3 | 3.8 | 0.8 | within | 1.1 | 2.0 | 1.8 | 2.4 | 2.0 | 0.6 | |
| Infierno | 45.0 | 23.3 | 10.4 | 11.7 | 7.4 | 2.3 | 0.6 | within | 2.0 | 2.0 | 2.5 | 2.3 | 1.2 | |
| Cuartamentero | 51.8 | 10.5 | 5.3 | 9.5 | 21.6 | 1.2 | within | 1.8 | 2.2 | 0.4 | 0.9 | 1.0 | 0.8 | |
| Elefante | 39.7 | 14.5 | 1.7 | 8.9 | 34.3 | 1.0 | 0.8 | 1.5 | 2.8 | within | 0.01 | 1.0 | 0.8 | |
| Cueva del Rio | 56.4 | 6.5 | 2.1 | 14.8 | 16.9 | 3.2 | within | 2.1 | 2.5 | 0.2 | 0.6 | 0.7 | 0.8 | 1.3 |
| La Cuevona | 40.6 | 8.3 | 1.7 | 11.7 | 33.5 | 4.4 | within | 1.7 | 2.6 | 0.2 | 0.7 | 0.3 | 0.2 | 0.6 |
| La Lloseta | 42.8 | 17.4 | 6.0 | 11.8 | 19.8 | 2.2 | within | 1.2 | 2.5 | 0.8 | 1.25 | 1.2 | 0.9 | 1.0 |
| Liencres | 38.2 | 6.4 | | 13.4 | 40.9 | 1.1 | 0.9 | 1.3 | | within | along | 1.2 | | |
| Ciriego | 32.3 | 7.3 | | 11.4 | 47.8 | 1.2 | 0.9 | 1.14 | | within | 0.1 | 1.7 | | |
| Las Cáscaras | 31.5 | 21.9 | 14.2 | 14.6 | 14.8 | 3.0 | within | 0.4 | 1.0 | 1.3 | 1.8 | 2.2 | 1.1 | 2.8 |
| La Meaza | 57.8 | 25.4 | 7.4 | 5.3 | 1.7 | 1.4 | within | 0.7 | 2.2 | 2.4 | 2.8 | 2.5 | 3.0 | 2.7 |
| Mésé | 38.5 | 2.4 | 59.0 | | | | within | 0.1 | 2.2 | | | 2.5 | 3.0 | 2.7 |
| Llongar | 46.4 | 10.8 | 3.0 | 11.4 | 28.0 | | within | 0.8 | 2.5 | 0.1 | 0.5 | | 1.5 | 1.6 |

ness of the different resources to be derived from each of the six life zones shown in figure 9.3. As there is a considerable degree of overlap in resource distributions, the probable result is likely to be confounded with the test implications for model B (i.e. a unimodal pattern of life zone distributions, species present and potentially available).

### Analysis and results

Analysis consisted of tests for homogeneity over (1) the proportional representation of life zones and (2) the ranks of the proportional representation of life zones across all sites listed in table 9.4. Proportional representation is given by the percentage of total area per exploitation circle of each life zone represented in that circle. Both percentages and ranks were used because percentage representation gives a more accurate picture of overall life zone similarity across sites than does the simple rank of the various life zones. However, the ranks provide an additional measure of difference/similarity which is not so sensitive to random variation in the actual area represented. The number of sites is rather small, and, because the exploitation territories themselves are small, it is expected that they would vary considerably amongst themselves (table 9.4).

### Homogeneity tests

Data from table 9.4 were used to plot the percentage representation of life zones for each site exploitation territory and the resultant graphs were first compared visually. Although it was possible to group sites impressionistically by overlaying pairs of cumulative percentage graphs which appeared to be similar to one another, when all the sites were examined together no clear sub-group definition was evident. A Kolmogorov—Smirnov test was then performed on the percentage data from all possible pairs of sites (Siegel 1956: 127—36; Blalock 1972: 262—5). A Kruskal—Wallis 'H' test, a non-parametric approach which is analogous to the one-way analysis of variance model, was used to evaluate the ranks (Siegel 1956: 184—93; Blalock 1972: 349, 350). In both cases, the null hypotheses ($H_0$) are non-directional:

$H_0$ (Kolmogorov—Smirnov test): the proportional representation of environmental zones is the same or similar across all (pairs of) sites.

$H_0$ (Kruskal—Wallis H test): the ranks of the proportional representation of environmental zones are the same or similar across all sites.

The corresponding alternative hypotheses ($H_1$) are simply that the areal percentages and their ranks are not the same (i.e. that they deviate by an order of magnitude greater than that attributable to chance variation alone). Acceptance of the null hypothesis in either case would indicate that the sites are all basically similar so far as their locations are concerned, which would tend to support models B and C.

The Kolmogorov—Smirnov test indicated that the sites

formed a homogeneous set with respect to life zone composition, individual differences in site exploitation territories falling within the range expectable due to chance variation. The Kruskal—Wallis test over the ranked life zone data produced similar results. The H statistic was 21.27, with k−1, or 27 degrees of freedom. The probability associated with a value for H ≥ 21.27 is approximately 75%. In both cases the null hypothesis is accepted, and it is concluded that Asturian site exploitation territories are not significantly different amongst themselves with respect to life zone representation.

The distance to the various life zones across sites is regarded as a measure of resource accessibility. An overall index of accessibility is derived by ranking the mean distances to resource zones by site, and then comparing the ranks across all sites using a rank-order statistic (the Kruskal—Wallis test). The null hypothesis is again non-directional:

$H_0$ The ranks of the mean distances to resource zones is the same or similar across all sites.

$H_1$ The ranks of the mean distances to resource zones are not the same across all sites (i.e. they deviate by an order of magnitude greater than that attributable to chance variation).

Again, homogeneity implies similarity of location *vis-à-vis* different life zones, and, by extension, functional equivalence amongst the sites evaluated. The H statistic in this case was 25.87, with 27 degrees of freedom. The probability associated with a value for H ≥ 25.87 lies between 50% and 70% and by interpolation is approximately 53%. The null hypothesis is consequently accepted, with a probability of Type I error equal to 0.05.

The results of the tests for homogeneity are quite consistent; they support the notion that Asturian sites are generally located in similar environmental circumstances with comparable resource zone accessibility indices. As noted, this tends to support model B, which postulates the existence of coastally situated base camps, although model C is not conclusively refuted either. Model A, a bipolar hypothesis with inland and coastal base camps, seems to be rather unlikely, although it should be kept in mind that inland Asturian sites may exist but have simply not been identified as such. It should also be noted that little information is provided by the homogeneity tests about what particular variables are important in determining site location; all that has been shown so far is that site location is reasonably consistent.

### Multivariate analyses

In order to refine the examination of possible differences amongst Asturian sites, and ultimately to identify those variables which are important in site location, cluster and discriminant function analyses were performed on the data, using (1) mean distances from sites to life zones, (2) percentage representation of life zones, (3) potentially available and archaeologically documented fauna, and (4) stone artefacts as variables (table

Table 9.5. *Major and minor variables used in the cluster and discriminant function analyses*

1  Mean distance from site to life zone for 8 life zones:
    to open country
    to mixed open woodland
    to alpine matorral
    to coastal matorral
    to estuaries
    to all rivers
    to sea
    to (sandy) beaches

2  Percentage representation of 8 life zones in site exploitation
    territories:
    open country
    mixed open woodland
    alpine matorral
    coastal matorral
    estuaries
    river valleys
    (sandy) beaches

3  Economically important faunal resources:

| *Oryctolagus cuniculus* | rabbit |
| *Lepus europaeus* | hare |
| *Sus scrofa* | boar |
| *Cervus elaphus* | red deer |
| *Capreolus capreolus* | roe deer |
| *Equus caballus* | horse |
| *Rupicapra rupicapra* | chamois |
| *Capra ibex* | ibex |
| *Lutra lutra* | otter |
| *Phoca vitulina* | seal |
| *Patella vulgata* | limpet |
| *Trochocochlea crassa* | topshell |

4  Stone artefacts:
    débitage
    heavy-duty tools
    small tools

Table 9.6. *Summary table of variable entry sequence*

| Variable code number | Rank | Variable name | F statistic to enter |
|---|---|---|---|
| 22 | 1 | ibex | 17.0689 |
| 19 | 2 | roe deer | 9.4679 |
| 21 | 3 | chamois | 7.6447 |
| 11 | 4 | % alpine zones | 6.7208 |
| 5 | 5 | mean distance to estuaries | 6.3285 |
| 23 | 6 | otter | 5.6298 |
| 13 | 7 | % estuarine zones | 4.2469 |
| 15 | 8 | hare | 3.1206 |
| 10 | 9 | % woodland zones | 3.0021 |
| 7 | 10 | mean distance to sea | 2.7173 |
| 2 | 11 | mean distance to woodland | 2.1188 |
| 3 | 12 | mean distance to alpine | 1.6540 |
| 14 | 13 | % sea | 1.5938 |
| 26 | 14 | heavy-duty tools | 1.4060 |
| 24 | 15 | harbour seal | 1.3571 |

9.5). The cluster analysis (see Clark & Lerner 1980 for details) allowed for an arbitrary division into five groups of sites at about the 50% level of overall similarity. The fact that group formation was not obvious or clear cut underscores the observation made earlier on the basis of the homogeneity tests — that really marked differences amongst the sites are not apparent. Only a few pairs of sites have really high similarity coefficients (e.g. Cueto de la Mina and La Riera) and these are generally located near one another in closely similar environmental settings.

    The groups defined by inspection of the cluster analysis dendrogram were further evaluated using a discriminant function. The discriminant analysis programme used here (BMDP 7M) is a 'stepwise' version, which means that variables are entered one at a time according to their decreasing capacity to discriminate the criterion groups. Inspection of the variable entry sequence indicates those variables which are probably significant determinants of site location (table 9.6). Variables are ordered by their F statistics from most to least important; variables which enter the equation after rank 7 are considered negligible in terms of their contributions to the discriminatory

power of the equation. What is immediately evident from an inspection of table 9.6 is that three of the first four variables consist of, or are related to, the exploitation of alpine resources (i.e. ibex (ranked first), chamois (third), percentage of alpine zone present (fourth)). Woodland adapted roe deer (ranked second) are a principal secondary contributor to the resource base, but one which is not uniformly found in all Asturian sites. Mean distance to and areal percentage of estuarine life zones (ranked fifth and seventh respectively) are also variables of some significance, underscoring the importance of accessibility to shellfish-gathering zones, and parenthetically the importance of shellfoods themselves in the Asturian diet. The other distance measures, however, are of comparatively minor significance — an observation owed to (1) the proximity of alpine zones (ranked twelfth) to the coast, (2) an absence of evidence for the exploitation of marine resources (ranked tenth), and (3) the ubiquity of forested patches (ranked eleventh) in the reconstructed Early Holocene environment. It is significant that the Asturian dietary staples (red deer, limpets and topshells) do not figure at all in the list of site location determinants. This underscores the fact that these resources are found in all Asturian sites, and so presumably would have little or no discriminatory value for differentiating amongst them.

    In resumé, it appears that the results of the statistical analyses are most consistent with model B, which postulated that Asturian sites are the remains of base camps situated in the hills and along the estuaries near the coast. In support of this conclusion are (1) the apparent near homogeneity of Asturian sites with respect to proportional, distance and access measures of life zone categories, which in turn implies that the Asturian sites so far known are functional equivalents; (2) the overall similarity in resources potentially available in those life zones, and in resources represented archaeologically; (3) the absence of any Asturian sites situated in the foothills and intermontane valleys of the Cordillera which might represent the inland base camps postulated by model A, and (4) the apparent absence of inland limited activity sites postulated by model C. It is recognized that the detection of limited activity sites is a major problem with the analysis, given the kinds of data on hand or likely to become available in the near future. Only in the case of the Santander strand line knapping station of Liencres can a strong case be made for functional differentiation, and that case could have been made anyway on the basis of unrelated *a priori* knowledge (Clark 1975a, b; 1979a, b; Scheitlin and Clark 1978).[3] A systematic failure to distinguish limited activity sites, failure to assign them to their correct chronological position and/or identify them as pertaining to a single settlement/subsistence system could all seriously prejudice the credibility of the analyses presented here (cf. below).

If, however, the data analysed are considered representative of a settlement/subsistence system operative in eastern Asturias between 8650 and 6800 b.p., then a pattern like that postulated by model B makes sense in terms of resource accessibility and efficiency in the expenditure of energy, given the topography of the region and the north–south compression of environmental zonation. Sites located near the coast are ideally situated (1) to exploit both forest and forest-margin staples (red and roe deer); and high-yield parkland/grassland ungulates (aurochs, horse); (2) to take advantage of seasonally available alpine resources (ibex, chamois) and (3) to exploit estuarine limpets and topshells either as permanent dietary supplements, or as 'emergency' foods in times (or seasons) of relative scarcity. While it is argued that Asturian sites so far known are most compatible with base camp components in a model B type situation, it is important to stress that movement by task groups of variable size and composition (Freeman 1968a), and with various objectives, up and down the north–south-trending watercourses, is certainly not precluded. It is rather a question of archaeological visibility, and the collection of the right kinds and quantities of data, which makes detection of these camps so difficult. Ephemeral hunting and collecting stations, occupied for a few days at most, would be nearly invisible archaeologically, even if deposition took place in cave or rockshelter contexts. If encampments were in the open air, only special, fortuitous geological circumstances (e.g. blowouts, stream erosion) or the massive excavations associated with large-scale public works would lead to their discovery and excavation.

### Mesolithic adaptations

In the analysis just presented it is assumed (1) that the Asturian is an assemblage which represents (in an imperfect way) the entire spectrum of variability in human adaptation to central Cantabrian environments during the Boreal period and (2) that all sites evaluated are at least roughly contemporaneous. In the classic literature, Asturian assemblages were believed to post-date those assigned to the Azilian, which was usually considered to date to the last cold phase of the Tardiglacial (cf. García Guinea 1975b). The relative temporal ordering of the two assemblages was based on the 1916–8 excavations

of the Conde de la Vega del Sella in the entrance to La Riera cave (Asturias) where an Asturian conchero directly overlies a typical Azilian midden with flat harpoons and bladelets (Vega del Sella 1930: 11–25). While some Spanish prehistorians have questioned this straightforward interpretation because of the 'primitive' nature of Asturian assemblages, assigning them to the Lower Palaeolithic (e.g. Jordá 1963a, 1975), Asturian-type concheros overlie Magdalenian, Azilian and undifferentiated Upper Palaeolithic levels at Coberizas, Bricia, Cueto de la Mina and a number of other sites (Clark 1976a, b), although the case is most secure at La Riera and has been confirmed by recent work there (Clark and Straus 1977a; Straus and Clark 1978a; Straus *et al.* 1980, 1981).

The two assemblages are very different in terms of composition, comprising mainly heavy-duty quartzite tools (cobble picks, choppers; flake sidescrapers, notches and denticulates) in the case of the Asturian, and flint microlithic industries, with lots of small endscrapers and backed bladelets but few heavy-duty tools in the case of the Azilian. The dubious notion of 'degeneration', so pervasive in the European Mesolithic literature, was sometimes invoked to explain the contrast between Upper Palaeolithic-like Azilian industries on the one hand, and rudimentary cobble-tool dominated Asturian industries on the other. A re-investigation of the Asturian (1969–72) was successful in augmenting the size and probable representativeness of the sample of Asturian lithic artefacts. It showed that bladelets, retouched bladelets and other artefact types which are expected components of Late Pleistocene/Early Holocene collections elsewhere were also to be found in Asturian concheros, albeit in very low frequencies (Clark 1975a; 1976a, b). Excavation of the open-air site of Liencres, considered Asturian because of the presence of unifacial picks, produced a collection which was dominated by small flint flakes and bladelets, and which stood in marked contrast to the Asturian of the caves. The differences between the two kinds of assemblage were explained in functional terms (Clark 1975a, b; 1979). Liencres excepted, however, the impression remained that Asturian industries were generally crude and varied little from site to site, a curious homogeneity which I attributed in part (and possibly erroneously) to post-excavation selection in the curation of museum pieces. Based on the results of a limited testing programme, it was recognized that the Asturian concheros were not themselves living sites, but rather trash heaps associated with living sites (Clark 1971b). Efforts to locate undisturbed Asturian living floors proved fruitless until 1977, when González Morales located one at the base of a typical conchero under the overhang at Mazaculos cave (La Franca) in eastern Asturias (González Morales and Marquez 1978; González Morales 1978).

Although the amount of compositional variability which could be assigned to the Asturian increased somewhat as a result of work in the early 1970s, it now appears (1) that our conceptions of meaningful analytical units might have artificially constrained our notions of the amount of expected intra-

Table 9.7. *Cantabrian Mesolithic radiocarbon dates*

| Site level | Laboratory number | Age (b.p.) | Reference |
|---|---|---|---|
| *Asturian* | | | |
| Bricia/conchero | GaK−2908 | 6800 ± 160 | Clark 1976a: 235 |
| Coberizas/level B1 | GaK−2907 | 7100 ± 170 | Clark 1976a: 235 |
| Mazaculos II (La Franca)/level 3 | GaK−8162 | 7280 ± 220 | Kigoshi: pers. comm. |
| Penicial/upper cave (conchero) | GaK−2906 | 8650 ± 180 | Clark 1976a: 235 |
| La Riera/level B1 (conchero) | GaK−2909 | 8650 ± 300 | Clark 1976a: 235 |
| Mazaculos II (La Franca)/level 3.3 | GaK−6884 | 9290 ± 440 | González Morales 1978: 380,381 |
| *Azilian* | | | |
| Urtiaga level C | CSIC−63 | 8700 ± 170 | Cava 1978: 170, 171 |
| Los Azules/level 3a | CSIC−216 | 9430 ± 120 | Fernandez-Tresguerres 1976: 288 |
| Ekain/base level 4 | I−9239 | 9460 ± 185 | Cava 1978: 170, 171 |
| Los Azules/level 3d | CSIC−260 | 9540 ± 120 | Fernandez-Tresguerres 1976: 288 |
| Zatoya/lower level 2 | Ly−1399 | 11480 ± 270 | Cava 1978: 170, 171 |
| Zatoya/level 3 | Ly−1400 | 11840 ± 240 | Cava 1978: 170, 171 |
| Ekain/level 3 | CSIC−171 | 12750 ± 250 | Barandiarán and Altuna 1977: 52 |
| Ekain/level 5 | CSIC−172 | 13350 ± 250 | Barandiarán and Altuna 1977: 52 |
| *Post-Azilian* | | | |
| Zatoya/upper level 2 | Ly−1398 | 8180 ± 220 | Cava 1978: 170, 171 |
| Arenaza I/level 2/bed D | CSIC−173 | 9600 ± 180 | Cava 1978: 170, 171 |
| Arenaza I/level 3 | CSIC−174 | 10300 ± 180 | Cava 1978: 170, 171 |

assemblage variability (i.e. the analytical universe might have been inappropriately chosen and was in any event determined by poorly defined culture/stratigraphic unit boundaries); (2) that at least *some* early Asturian and some late Azilian industries, identified as such by index fossils, might be approximately contemporaneous rather than sequent phenomena; and (3) that Azilian and other Cantabrian microlithic industries might best be explained as the remains of hunting technologies first developed in the area around 16–17 000 b.p.

The hypothesis that Asturian and Azilian assemblages might be complementary in functional terms is owed to Lawrence Straus (1979b) and is based in part upon weak radiocarbon evidence published since 1975 (table 9.7). Perhaps more compelling than the dates are the fundamental compositional differences between the assemblages, and the observation that there may be no functional significance between the artefacts found in concheros and their faunal components beyond that of 'bulk-garbage disposal behaviour' (Straus 1979b: 320, 321). In other words, picks and other easily manufactured heavy-duty tools were discarded along with large bones, shell and other bulky debris in cave mouths which, by Boreal times, were no longer suitable (or required in the milder, postglacial environment) for human habitation.

The fact that the Asturian, like many coastal Mesolithic 'cultures', is poorly defined (by shell middens with a certain composition, a single artefact type), lends credence to the possibility of a complementary relationship between these assemblages and the Azilian. In the scenario proposed by Straus, Asturian sites are the remains of a suite of activities centred on the exploitation of plant resources (cf. also Clarke 1976), as well as estuarine, riverine and coastal fish and shellfish, and deer. There is (scant) evidence for the processing of

plant foods in grinding-stone fragments from Liencres, Colombres and Balmori (Clark 1976a: 133–214). The Azilian sites, which have a more inland distribution (n = 17, x̄ = 12.6 km, s = 8.1) than those assigned to the Asturian (n = 25, x̄ = 1.2km, s = 0.8), would represent residues associated primarily with the hunting and processing of cervids and caprids (figures from Straus 1979b: 322). Microliths in general are believed to be the replaceable elements in a light-weight, multicomponent technology in which they functioned as weapon and tool tips and edges mounted in wooden or antler armatures (Clarke 1976). Thus unnamed Pleistocene/Holocene boundary microlithic assemblages found in sites in the Basque provinces of Vizcaya and Guipúzcoa (e.g. Marizulo) may be the functional complements of Asturian base camps.

While not evaluated formally, this conception of Boreal-phase adaptations complements the present study insofar as it might supply the missing limited activity stations postulated in models A and B (cf. also Bailey 1973). If this is so, and if Asturian sites are garbage dumps associated with base camps, one would expect that (1) hunting stations would tend to have a more inland distribution than centrally located base camps; (2) the evidence of caprid and cervid remains would be proportionately higher in 'Azilian' (and other microlithic) sites than in 'Asturian' ones (caprids would be more prevalent in the higher, alpine terrain of the Cordilleran foothills); (3) 'Azilian' sites would be smaller (which is difficult to test because most 'Asturian' living areas apparently were destroyed or remain undiscovered) and (4) 'Azilian' sites would contain a more limited spectrum of artefact types than would 'Asturian' middens. If mid-latitude European hunter-gatherers favoured 'logistical' settlement/subsistence strategies (i.e. those which procure food by means of special task groups, field process it and then transport it back to residential sites), as Binford (1980) has recently suggested, then (5) some evidence of storage facilities should be found in residential sites (e.g. base camps); (6) base camps should be located to minimize distance to a 'most critical' resource (red deer, in this case); and (7) sites related to the exploitation of secondary resources should be located within easy transport distance of residential camps.

Because Cantabrian data are not yet sufficiently fine-grained to allow us to have much confidence that we have recovered a representative sample of a settlement/subsistence system operative at a given point in time, the tenability of Binford's ethnoarchaeologically-grounded generalizations cannot for the moment be assessed. Only a much improved radiocarbon chronology and better data pertinent to both seasonality and the exploitation of plant resources will eventually allow for a conclusive evaluation. Straus's conception of a complementary relationship between the 'Asturian' and the 'Azilian' is compelling on logical grounds, and has the advantage that it can be partially tested using data on hand. Ultimately, however, Mesolithic adaptations must be viewed from a long-term diachronic perspective as they represent an artificially bounded segment of time in a continuum of change in subsistence strategies, the broad outlines of which are discernible as far back as the Mousterian (Freeman 1973a) and which extend up in time to the regional Neolithic and beyond (cf. Straus *et al.* 1980; chapters 12 and 13, this volume; Altuna 1980).

*Notes*

1. The formula for converting present-day to past cover, and for the random location of patches of open country uses an 'Areagraph' dot-counter, which gives areas for irregular shapes in square inches. (1) Area in square inches is converted to area in square centimetres by multiplying by 6.45 (1 in² = 6.45 cm²). (2) Total area in square centimetres of combined forest and open country is multiplied by 0.38 (proportion of open country in E. Asturias) to get the proportion of open country for each circle. (3) Select a number greater than 3 but less than 10 from a random-numbers table. (4) Divide the the proportion of open country in square centimetres by the number obtained in 3 above to get the area of *each* open country circle. (5) Insert that number in the formula for the area of a circle and solve for the radius: $A = \pi r^2$; $r = \sqrt{A/\pi}$. (6) Set the dividers at the value for the radius (which will be 1.37 cm in this case). (7) Use the random-numbers table to select two sets of angles such that one set consists of numbers between 0 and 100, and one consists of numbers between 100 and 200:

| $x_1$ | 55 | 42 | 82 | 39 | |
|---|---|---|---|---|---|
| $x_2$ | 148 | 132 | 108 | 179 | etc. |

(8) Plot these pairs of angles on the overlay from a baseline tangential to the catchment circle; the intersect gives the centre of the open country circle. (9) Use the dividers to draw each circle of randomly located open country. N.B. If the angle intersect falls in the ocean or off the map, open country is not plotted for that particular intersect.

2. Bailey (1973: 74) has estimated that a single red deer provides the caloric equivalent of about 20 000 shellfish.

3. Liencres is an open-air chert scatter with typical quartzite Asturian picks which owes its existence to the presence of scarce flint sources nearby (cf. Clark 1975b, 1979a; Scheitlin and Clark 1978). Ciriego describes a region adjacent to Liencres where Carballo (1960: 146) encountered surface finds of Asturian picks in the 1940s and 1950s.

Chapter 10

## Sedentary hunters: the Ertebølle example
Peter Rowley-Conwy

Sedentary hunter-gatherers are examined and found to be sufficiently different from band-scale societies to warrant the term 'complex hunters'. Recent examples are often found in particular types of environment. Demographic, ecological, social and other aspects are examined in further detail, and a model is put forward for the development of complex hunters. The shell middens of the Ertebølle culture in the western Baltic are in a suitable environment for complex hunters. An area is examined in detail. On the basis of site size, economy location and the presence or absence of overlying Neolithic deposits, the sites are found to divide into permanent bases and temporary camps. The ecological basis for such systems leads to the conclusion that complex hunters are not a late specialization, but that hunters may be expected to take advantage of favourable environmental circumstances whenever they appear.

### Hunter-gatherers: some general considerations

#### Nomadic and sedentary hunters
The last 10 or 15 years have seen a great deal of study of hunters[1]; much interesting work has been done, and our knowledge has been much increased. Hunting is normally regarded as having been the only way of life throughout almost the whole of human history, and so it is not surprising that many generalizations have been presented concerning this, the 'most primitive' mode of human existence.

#### Note
1. Following the lead of Lee and DeVore (1968b), the term 'hunters' is used to designate all hunter-fisher-gatherers. It is a term of convenience, not a definition.

The most famous of these generalizations is perhaps the 'nomadic style' put forward by Lee and DeVore (1968b). They write: 'We make two basic assumptions about hunters and gatherers: (1) they live in small groups and (2) they *move around* a lot' (1968b: 11, my italics). A number of things follow from these assumptions. Mobility prevents the accumulation of much personal property, so society is basically egalitarian; the nature of the food supply prevents the agglomeration of large groups of people except perhaps on a seasonal basis; local groups do not ordinarily maintain exclusive rights to resources, and a more flexible organization caters for variability in the food supply; food surpluses are rare; and groups do not usually become strongly attached to any single area.

Many other generalizations emphasize the same points. Service, for example, writes that 'most obvious and probably most crucial in its effect on the culture generally is the *nomadism* required by the foraging economy' (1966: 7, my italics), particularly in the fields of technology and social organization. Sahlins states that, because food resources near a camp sooner or later become depleted, 'the solution is, of course, to go somewhere else. Thus the first and decisive contingency of hunter gathering: it requires *movement* to maintain production on advantageous terms' (1974: 33, my italics). Because of this, technology is necessarily simple and portable— 'if the gross product is trimmed down in comparison with other economies, it is not the hunter's productivity that is at fault, but his *mobility*' (1974: 33, my italics).

These generalizations are typical of much recent thinking. It is clearly common ground among the authorities quoted here that *mobility* is the most important factor in the shaping of the general nature of hunting societies. This is a relatively recent development – many earlier discussions emphasized the threat of starvation and the ceaseless nature of the food quest. Much recent work has served to dispel this view (e.g. Lee 1968, 1979; Woodburn 1968). Mobility has replaced starvation as a more powerful causative influence. Archaeologists, having updated their concepts in parallel with this, have often assumed that, because nomadic hunting is the most simple way of life known to ethnography, prehistoric hunters were therefore automatically of nomadic type. There are, however, other factors to be taken into account. Hunters not conforming to this nomadic norm are well known to ethnography, as all the authorities quoted above make clear. Other options do sometimes seem to be available to hunters, and these should be examined before all prehistoric hunters are assumed to conform to the recently held nomadic norm.

What characterizes the recent hunters who do not conform to the nomadic norm is not that they diverge with regard to one or a few of the characteristics noted above; they usually do so with regard to most or all of these characteristics. Technology is usually much more complex and developed, frequently including items not associated with hunters – sometimes pottery, occasionally even metallurgy, also pecked or polished stone tools, dwelling structures of some permanence, and a great proliferation of food-getting technology. Social structure is also generally more complex. Mechanisms are usually available for the storage of wealth, and some form of ranking is frequently found. The hereditary, ranked aristocracy of the Northwest Coast Indians is the most developed and best known example. Demographically these groups diverge from the nomadic norm in that larger social units exist on a permanent basis. Villages exist which are often many times larger than the hunting band, and although a variety of temporary camps is used for specific tasks, these villages are occupied by at least some of the people all of the time. Overall population density is frequently higher. Territoriality is marked. Specific groups and individuals do maintain rights to specific resources. In general these hunters are therefore characterized by a greater complexity of their arrangements, and may be termed 'complex hunters' to distinguish them from the more simply organized nomads.

The features mentioned above as typifying nomadic hunters spring directly from their nomadism; correspondingly, many of the features common among complex hunters arise from their sedentism. The correspondence between sedentism, population growth and social complexity has been noted (Dumond 1972a; Lee 1972b; Binford and Chasko 1976; Harris 1977; and see below). The absence of the constraints imposed by nomadism is the major difference between the two kinds of hunter, so that sedentism has as formative an influence on the basic features of complex hunters as mobility does on nomadic hunters. The question is thus why some hunters are nomadic and others are sedentary.

*The environmental context of nomadism and sedentism*

Various authorities have emphasized that mobility on the part of hunters should be seen in ecological terms, and that many factors ensure that mobility is maintained. Lee stresses the lack of internal mechanisms for resolving disputes among the Bushmen – the egalitarian nature of their society means that the only alternative is 'to vote with their feet, to walk out of an unpleasant situation' (Lee 1972a: 182). Group fissioning because of this serves to maintain mobility; fissioning usually occurs before food resources in a particular area become depleted, so that 'this mobility has a profound ecological adaptive significance . . . By stabilising numbers at a lower level through a behavioural spacing mechanism, the population is buffered against a wide range of variation in the abundance of food resources' (Lee 1972a: 182–3).

Annual and longer-term fluctuations in food supply are clearly of the greatest importance for an understanding of the mobility of nomadic hunters. Binford (1980) has drawn attention to the influences exerted by differences in the nature of the food supply. He points to the range of variation between the relatively frequent and generalized residential moves of hunters in warmer climates (*residential mobility*); and the less frequent moves of hunters in cooler, more seasonally variable environments – the moves being, however, more specifically directed towards one or a combination of seasonally available resources appearing at different places. Special purpose extractive camps, resource storage, and transport of resources from extractive camp to base camp are all characteristic of this adaptation (*logistic mobility*) (see also Rowley-Conwy 1980). It is clear that some of the arrangements of the 'logistic' variant do not tally so well with the models (such as those outlined at the start of this chapter) frequently used by archaeologists. Low latitude, 'residential mobility' groups have played a disproportionate part in the generation of such models.

Examination of recent complex hunters leads to the conclusion that the sedentism of these groups is linked to the nature of their food supply, just as the varied mobility patterns of nomadic hunters are linked to theirs. A brief survey has been made of some of the literature dealing with four sets of complex hunters: the Northwest Coast Indians (Forde 1934; Goddard 1934; Drucker 1951, 1965; Suttles 1968; Oberg 1973); the Bering Strait Eskimo (Nelson 1899); the North Alaskan Eskimo (Spencer 1959); and the Ainu (Watanabe 1968, 1972). These groups all live in *areas where several species of migratory mammals, birds and fish appear in places closely adjacent to one another – but at different times of the year.* These resources may then be exploited from a single home base, a variety of briefly occupied special-purpose camps also being used. Table 10.1 details some of the subsistence activities described by the authorities mentioned above, and distinguishes between those activities carried out from the

Table 10.1. *Procurement activities of some recent complex hunters*

| | Jan | Feb | Mar | Apr | May | Jun | Jul | Aug | Sep | Oct | Nov | Dec |
|---|---|---|---|---|---|---|---|---|---|---|---|---|
| **Northwest Coast** | deer | | trout | | | | sea fish | | | deer, goat → | | |
| | fur | | fur | | | | | bear | | | fur animals → | |
| | | | cod | | | birds' eggs | | | | cod | | |
| | shellfish | | | | | | | | | shellfish → | | |
| | | | halibut | – – – – – – – – – | | | | dog salmon | | | | |
| | | | | seaweed | | | | | | | | |
| | | salmon (offshore) | | | | | coho salmon – – – | | | | | |
| | | | | | | sockeye salmon – – – | | | | | | |
| | | | | sea mammals – – – – – – – – – | | | | | | | | |
| | | | | | plants – – – – – – – – – – | | | | | | | |
| | herring – – – – | | | | | | | | | | | |
| | | | herring eggs | | | | | | | | | |
| | | | candlefish – – – – – | | | | | | | | |
| | | | | waterfowl – – | | | | | | | | |
| **Bering Strait Eskimo** | | fur animals | | | | herring | | wildfowl | | | fur | |
| | seals – – – – | | | | | | salmon – – – | | seals | | | |
| | | | | | | | | blackfish | | | | |
| | | | | | | | | shellfish | | | | |
| | | | tomcod, sculpin | | | | | | | | | |
| | | | caribou – – – – – – – – – – – – – – – – – – – – – | | | | | | | | | |
| | | | | | | | | whales | | | | |
| | ptarmigan | | | | | | | | | ptarmigan → | | |
| **N. Alaskan Eskimo** | tomcod | | | | bowhead whale | | | whales | | | tomcod → | |
| | seals | | | | | seals | | | | | seals → | |
| | | | | | caribou | | | | | | | |
| | | | | | | | walrus | | | | | |
| | | | | | | | candlefish | | | | | |
| | | | | | | | freshwater fish | | | | | |
| | | | | | | | wildfowl – – – – – | | | | | |
| **Ainu** | | | bear – – – – – | | | | – – – – – | | | | bear – – | |
| | deer | | deer – – | | | cherry salmon | | | | deer | | |
| | | | | hucho | | | | | | dog salmon | | |
| | | | | | sea fish – – | | | | | sea fish – – | | |
| | | | | | | plants | | | | | | |
| | | | | | | swordfish – – – – | | | | | | |

*Note:* solid lines represent activities carried out from permanent settlement, dotted lines activities carried out from temporary camps.

home base and those carried out from temporary camps. The schemes are incomplete and generalized, and ignore the variability within any one area. The Northwest Coast groups, for example, are spread over a great length of coastline, along which significant variations occur. Watanabe makes clear the differences between the Ainu of the coast and those of the interior. Not all groups within the area carried out all the activities listed.

The significance of the exploitation of migratory resources is twofold. *First,* by exploiting a species which *concentrates seasonally* at one point within its annual range, a human group is effectively exploiting the whole of the annual range of that species. If several animal species are involved, then several annual ranges are exploited in this way. As the animals are concentrated, unusually high kills may be made in a short time. This gives rise to two further activities often associated with complex hunters: large-scale storage of resources to cover those times of the year when no migratory resources appear; and large-scale transport of resources from the procurement camps (when such are necessary) to the home base.

*Secondly,* when several migratory species are exploited, *differential seasonality* of these species enables each to be exploited in turn. A particularly notable example is the series of salmon species exploited on the Northwest Coast and by the Ainu — the various species do not run at the same time, so their overlapping seasonality ensures that salmon may be caught over several months and a sufficient quantity stored. Concentration on migratory species also means that permanently residing native species (e.g. non-migratory deer, plants, shellfish) may be left alone for parts of the year, and can be utilized alongside stored food during the periods of the year when no migrant visitors are available.

Complex hunters thus fall outside the classification established by Binford (1980 — see above). They represent a development beyond that of his 'logistic' variant. While 'logistic' groups move their base camps periodically, complex hunters do not need to do so. The full spectrum of necessary resources may be exploited from a single residential base and its attendant special purpose camps. This is not Binford's 'Garden of Eden principle', in other words 'that things were so "wonderful" at certain places in the environment that there was no need to move' (1980: 19). Rather, the different areas exploited from the different 'logistic' base camps are for complex hunters all superimposed in one place.

The conclusion at this stage is, therefore, that recent complex hunters appear to have just as good reasons for their mode of existence as nomadic hunters do for theirs. It is therefore unjustifiable to assume that all prehistoric hunters fulfilled the nomadic model.

### Further examination of complex hunters

If these considerations are to be relevant to archaeology, it is necessary to do more than point to an ecological basis for the sedentism of some recent complex hunters; we must

attempt to see whether this ecological basis has general predictive value. The above examination of recent complex hunters leads to the suggestion that overlapping seasonality of useful resources within a limited area is the main condition for the development of complex hunters. Before this is accepted, however, further consideration is necessary. Various possible objections to complex hunting are examined in the following sections.

### Demographic factors

Nomadic hunters of small group size and low population density could obviously make a living in any of the areas occupied by the above-mentioned complex hunters. It will be argued here, however, that there are reasons why complex hunters may be expected to appear in environments where such systems are feasible.

Studies of the demography of nomadic hunters indicate the maintenance of population at a low level. The problem is, put simply, how nomadic hunters manage to produce so few children. Lee (1972b) points out the importance of mobility in increasing the degree of spacing between childbirths. His argument is well known: to carry more than one child creates difficulties for the mother. A four-year spacing is therefore optimal because with this spacing it is never necessary to carry more than one child. Children are breast-fed for up to 3½ years, and among the Bushmen lactation suppresses ovulation. Mobile hunters usually have no soft foods available for the earlier weaning of children. As Lee points out, 'settling down removes the adverse effects of high fertility on individual women' (1972b: 39), and births among recently sedentary Bushmen are indeed spaced closer together. The availability of milk and other soft foods in an agricultural system may contribute to the earlier weaning of children (Lee 1972b).

A population increase is thus likely to follow the development of sedentism, a point also noted for the Nunamiut Eskimo by Binford and Chasko (1976), who examine various aspects of the problem. Lactation is discussed, and the point is again made that mobile hunters usually have no soft foods suitable for weaning children. The usual method of softening foods is to boil them, which requires some kind of container. Pottery is ideal (Binford and Chasko 1976), but is almost invariably absent from the technological repertoire of nomadic hunters due to its weight and fragility. Technology thus plays a part in the demographic aspects under discussion, and the high correlation between pottery and permanent settlement needs no emphasis.

These points are important for the present argument. No adaptation is perfect, and periodic disasters due to resource failure can hit hunters of all kinds, mobile or sedentary. Among the complex hunters discussed above, for example, Nelson (1899) mentions that several villages of Bering Strait Eskimo were wiped out in 1879–80, and Watanabe (1972) mentions the death of 200 Ainu in 1725. The significant point is that, given their closer spacing of births, *sedentary hunters will be able to recover quicker from disaster and will thus be in a*

*position to out-compete more mobile groups.* This is an
important point in the argument that sedentism is likely to
develop among hunters where this is feasible. The degree of
variability within any one culture would ensure ample scope
for the operation of such selective pressures. It is not argued
that a series of catastrophes are a necessary factor in the
emergence of sedentary hunters; rather that they could be a
relevant factor. Other factors need to be considered also.

### Work effort

One argument against the likelihood of permanent
settlement being adopted might be that it would run counter
to the least-effort principle — as Lee says of the Bushmen,
'the larger the group, the more work the individuals in it will
have to do' (1972a: 181). To assume that all complex hunting
necessarily involves greater work input than all nomadic
hunting would, however, be to adopt too rigid a viewpoint.
What does seem to be true is that complex hunters, in taking
and storing large quantities of a briefly available migratory
resource, are likely to be involved in bursts of work punctuated by periods of relative inactivity. Such a pattern, it might
be argued, could inhibit the development of sedentism. This
would, however, be to regard work effort in isolation, rather
than as 'the intervening variable between population and food
supply' (Lee 1972a: 180). A low threshold of maximum work
effort is, as mentioned above, of ecological significance among
the Bushmen. Signs of a progressively depleted environment
will be felt at an early stage, and consequent camp movement
ensures that the environment will be protected against over-
exploitation. It can be envisaged that there might, in different
circumstances, be an advantage in a higher threshold of maximum desirable work effort. Figures of 'average work effort'
can be misleading if the range of variation they cover is ignored
— Lee's (1968) famous figure of 15 hours work per week per
adult !Kung Bushman covers a range of 0 to 32 hours among
the men alone. Such a range would give ample scope to the
operation of any selective pressure.

These are somewhat abstract arguments, and of perhaps
greater interest is the problem of whether sedentism was
initially *perceived* as involving more work. There are grounds
for believing that the option may first have been taken up
because it appeared to involve less work. The starting point
for this model will be a situation involving nomadic hunting
groups approximating the band level of group size (average 25),
with a low overall population density and relatively widely
spaced childbirths. The next stage will be to suppose that an
environmental alteration takes place, making permanent
settlement feasible. The phrase 'making permanent settlement
feasible' means that existing resource procurement levels may
now be maintained from a single residential site, without an
increase in work effort. It now takes less effort to stay in the
same place than to be mobile, as the effort put into mobility
is no longer expended. This might be the state of affairs if,
for example, a new series of migratory resources began to
appear at the same point (e.g. at a sea coast) at different times
of the year. Settlement on the coast would thus have access

to both the terrestrial and the marine zones. So far, no population increase need have occurred.

Smith (1979) has examined the question of limiting
factors on hunters, and comes to the conclusion that even
hunters not limited by the amount of work they do and who
have lots of free time, would reduce their work time still
further if they could do so while maintaining existing resource
procurement levels. Smith suggests that they would do this
in order to increase their energetic efficiency, and so leave
more time for obtaining mates, maintaining social networks
etc. It seems unnecessary, however, to invoke so rigidly
optimizing a mechanism; after all, if work input is already low,
why should a further increase in energetic efficiency mean so
very much? A rather more parsimonious explanation is the
desire to increase leisure time. Thus the Yir Yoront of northern
Australia, when presented with steel axes to replace their stone
ones, used the new axes neither to increase productivity and so
improve their lot (as the missionaries who supplied the axes
had hoped) nor to intensify inter-group contact (as Smith
would predict). The Yir Yoront took advantage of the situation
to spend more time asleep (Sharpe 1952).

There seems thus to be little difficulty in accepting the
proposition that mobility will be avoided if the rate of resource
procurement could at the same time remain unchanged. Once
sedentism occurs, however, many of the restraints maintaining
population at its former level will be removed, and in particular
the frequency of births may be expected to increase along the
lines suggested by Lee and by Binford and Chasko. Although
Binford and Chasko (1976) were unable to demonstrate it, it
also seems reasonable to assume that a greater proportion of
children could be reared to adulthood. An immediate consequence of sedentism seems certain to be, as documented for
the !Kung and for the Nunamiut, a rise in population. Not
until this population increase made itself felt would an intensification of the food quest be necessary. An increase in work
effort would, in this model, *follow* sedentism, and thus not
prevent sedentism from occurring in the first place.

The course intensification would be likely to take would
reinforce the dependence of the sedentary group on migratory
resources. Non-migratory, evenly spread resources would
deteriorate to a greater extent than they would around a
temporary camp, as they would be continuously exploited in a
more intensive manner. It would be necessary to travel further
in order to procure plant foods, while mammals would also
decline in numbers and move away as hunting and disturbance
increased. On the other hand, seasonally concentrated marine
resources, for example, would not be affected in the same way:
an increase in the capture of fish would be unlikely to affect
total stocks, and fish caught in any area would rapidly be
replaced. Given a constant technology, yields per unit of
labour would not diminish as would those of non-migratory
resources.

### Group size

In a recent study, Wobst (1976) examined aspects of the

spacing of hunters organized in bands. He concluded that a human mating network would have to encompass a minimum of about 475 people, if every individual were to be sure of gaining a mate on maturity (see Part 4). If band size is 25, then 19 bands would form a minimum mating network. Each band would thus have to maintain contact with 18 other bands. An open, hexagonally organized pattern of evenly spaced bands, in which each band is the centre of its own unique network, would be the most likely. In such a system the average distance between any band and its 18 contact bands would be minimized (see fig. 10.1).

The further the system is from a hexagonal one, the more distance costs increase. The most extreme type of system would be a linear one (such as would be the case if the bands were arranged along the coast), and Wobst therefore regards the coasts as unlikely areas for settlement (except by specialists late in the prehistoric period), because of the increased distance costs such linear settlement would involve.

This conclusion may be challenged. Groups like the recent complex hunters mentioned above were after all able to cope with the various problems that their mode of settlement presented them. Another view is that complex hunters practise an alternative and different system of settlement to that of the nomadic groups, not just a more problematic and specialized version of it.

If we assume for the sake of argument that the bands in Wobst's hexagonal system are located 10km apart, then it can be calculated that the average distance from any band to the 18 other bands with which it must maintain contact is 15.6km. Wobst's suggestion that a linear arrangement would be unlikely is highlighted by the fact that 19 bands would, given the same spacing, extend over 180km of coastline. The average distance between any band and its 18 contact bands would be 50 km. The inland group clearly has the advantage if these figures are taken at face value.

There are two ways of reducing distance costs on the coast: either distance between groups must be reduced, or group size must be increased. In the calculations below the following figures will be used:

| hypothetical inter-band spacing | 10km |
| average distance cost, inland | 15.6km |
| average distance cost, coast | 50km |
| normal band size | 25 |

To reduce coastal distance costs to inland levels, the distance between bands would have to be reduced to:

$$\frac{15.6}{50} \times 10\,\text{km} = 3.1\,\text{km}$$

At this spacing, the average distance from any band to its 18 contact bands becomes the same as that in the inland hexagonal arrangement. (The figure of 3.1 km is of course as hypothetical as the original 10km from which it has been calculated.) Given the limitations on places suitable for settlement sites, however, a tendency towards larger settlements seems more likely than one of closely spaced bands. If the distance between settlements is kept at 10km, the number of people in each group must be increased to:

$$\frac{50}{15.6} \times 25\,\text{people} = \text{about } 80$$

Given this group size, individuals only have to travel an average of 15.6km because there are more individuals within each settlement. Each group need only be in contact with five other groups if each numbered 80. (The average distance to other groups is in fact 18km but the difference is made up by the greater number of people on the individual's own settlement.)

If 25 is a 'mystical number' close to which nomadic hunters group themselves, then around 80 may be the counterpart for complex hunters. The range of 15 to 75 mentioned by Wobst (1976) for mobile bands gives a corresponding range of 48–240 for complex hunters. The crucial point is, of course, whether the environment can support groups of this size; if so, then the locational pressures which combine to produce one norm among nomadic hunters may produce another norm among permanently settled complex groups.

*Vulnerability and risk*

It could be argued that, once set in motion, population increase among complex hunters might continue beyond safe limits, resulting in dangerous dependence on the most productive resource in the spectrum. There seems, however, no reason why complex hunters should not stabilize their numbers within a favourable range of variation, just as nomadic hunters have done.

The degree of annual fluctuation in the availability of migratory resources would be a factor working against a heavy reliance on only a single species. The variability of each resource would make it likely that dependence on the most productive one would not go beyond the point where other resources could make up the shortfall in the event of failure. Thus the bowhead whale was the most important resource hunted by the North Alaskan Eskimo and killed during its

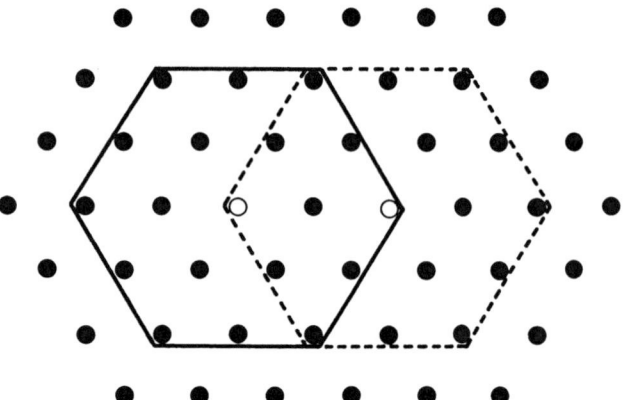

Fig. 10.1. Wobst's model of an open, hexagonally arranged system in which each band is the centre of its own, unique network of 18 other bands.

spring migration. Poor whale kills occurred every six or seven years, however, and although this could mean hardship, autumn whaling or winter sealing would be intensified to make up the shortfall (Spencer 1959).

Technological factors are important in this context. Nomadic hunters, by maintaining a low level of population, can cope with shortage of a resource by diversification and flexibility of response: secondary resources are often available as alternatives. It might be argued that this option would be less likely to be available to complex hunters because of their usually greater numbers. Complex hunters have an advantage, however, in that they are able to store bulky technological items on their settlements. Although some nomadic groups do leave specific items behind at points on their seasonal round, the complex hunter is clearly much better situated in this respect. The complex groups mentioned above all kept large nets, 20 m or 40 m in length, for catching birds, although even migratory species were never of more than secondary importance in their economies. By maintaining the technology, and practising the techniques at a low level of intensity, complex groups were maintaining a reserve strategy which could be intensified for a season if necessary. Nomadic hunters would be much less likely to maintain such normally inessential items, and the constraints set by mobility are also important. It is mentioned of the Yahgan of Tierra del Fuego that they knew neither nets nor fishtraps although subsisting in large measure on fish (Service 1971). Complex hunters are thus not necessarily more vulnerable to resource fluctuation than nomadic groups; once again an alternative solution is available.

### Social factors

A major difference between nomadic and complex hunters is the absence among the former of dispute-solving mechanisms. Fissioning after disputes is a major reason for the mobility of nomadic hunters. All the complex groups mentioned above have more developed social institutions capable of resolving disputes without recourse to fissioning, and, while inter-group mobility among complex hunters may be considerable, a higher threshold of group fissioning would clearly be advantageous among permanently settled groups.

Dispute-solving often involves an individual with sufficient authority or prestige to act as mediator, and to come to a decision acceptable to both sides. Herero cattle herders fulfil this role among newly sedentary Bushmen (Lee 1972a). One way in which prehistoric hunters might evolve such a mechanism for themselves is by means of the identification of individuals with particular resources, a feature of complex hunters (see above). It is possible that an individual controlling a particularly productive or predictable resource point might be in a position to acquire sufficient status; and larger group size does imply greater social complexity (see chapter 19).

The ease with which hunters might be able to develop such a mechanism has been debated — Bender (1978: 208) has suggested that sedentism among hunters would be unlikely because of 'the social problems involved in continuous contact — gatherer-hunters have few mechanisms for controlling strife other than splitting up and moving on'. All the recent complex hunters discussed here do, however, have such mechanisms; and as most of the world does now live in permanent settlements, the situation must have arisen and the problem must have been solved many times in the past. Meillassoux (1973) cites the case of the Mbaka pygmies, at present settling down and adopting agriculture, who have developed more compact, long-lasting work and family groups, show an increase in polygyny, bridewealth marriage, councils of elders and the accumulation of personal wealth. These are all foreign to a system of nomadic hunting, and are associated with a farming way of life; Meillassoux emphasizes that the appearance of these features is 'not due to imitative processes, but to the requirements of their new activities' (1973: 197). An alternative view is thus that social attributes seem to have considerable flexibility, and would be unlikely to prevent permanent settlement.

Bender also criticizes 'techno-environmental' theories of the origin of sedentism on other grounds. Building and storage costs would increase; stagnant water and poor hygiene would encourage disease; stored food might perish or be stolen; concentration on fewer resources might be risky; and work patterns would have to be reorganized to involve periods of intense activity. Bender sees social pressures as more important: due to resource variability, alliances would be likely to develop in which groups would be forced to over-produce at certain times. If redistribution of the excess resources were delayed, 'clearly there is a pay-off in staying put and creating permanent storage facilities' (Bender 1979: 213).

Pressure cannot be measured, and it is unclear why such social pressures should be stronger than 'techno-environmental' ones. The last two of the above-mentioned objections to 'techno-environmental' explanations have been dealt with in the foregoing, and the others may be briefly discussed. Many nomadic hunters build several structures in the course of a seasonal round, and investment in a single albeit more substantial one need not be a problem. Farmers and complex hunters all do it. Energy saved on annual migrations may be redeployed in this direction. Disease might be a risk, but epidemics among hunters (complex and nomadic) are usually introduced by outsiders, often Europeans. Clean water would obviously be an influence on the original location of the settlement; and, once again, why social rather than other causes of sedentism should make hunters more hygienic in their habits is not clear. Storage, finally, may be a problem; equally, peoples all round the world, using a variety of foodstuffs and techniques, do solve the problem. It would appear, therefore, that the objections to a 'techno-environmental' explanation of sedentism are apparent rather than real, and indeed the 'social' explanation involves problems of rather greater magnitude. One wonders whether alliances strong enough to force people to over-produce and stay put if they did not wish to would be very likely to appear in a nomadic

situation — might this not be to demand for pre-sedentism a
level of organization and coercion more likely to be found in
sedentary systems?

*Conclusions*

I suggested that the overlapping seasonal apperance of
various migratory resources was the crucial factor in the development of sedentism among hunters, and examined various
possible problems and objections to this suggestion. The conclusion is that, if there are logical aspects in the behaviour of
nomadic hunters, then there is a corresponding but alternative
logic in the arrangements of complex hunters. It is thus postulated that complex hunters are likely to develop where a
suitable array of migratory resources is available. This suggests
that complex hunters need not be some kind of late, specialized
offshoot, and that not all archaeologically visible hunters need
be nomadic. The next stage is to see whether sedentary hunters
are visible in the archaeological record where suitable constel-
lations of migratory resources would have been available.

**Sedentary hunters in the archaeological record: the
Erteb∅lle example**

This section examines the Mesolithic Erteb∅lle culture
(*c.* 5800–5200 b.p.) of eastern Denmark within its regional
setting of the western Baltic. I will suggest that parts of the
western Baltic region saw the appearance, at different times
of the year, of a variety of migratory resources, and that there
are grounds for believing that the Erteb∅lle represents a sedentary system, comprising permanently occupied base camps and
seasonal special-purpose camps.

Little attention has hitherto been paid to any evidence
for the existence of larger, more complex demographic units in
the Erteb∅lle. Any discussion of such factors would be incon-
clusive given the present state of research. The following
discussion therefore restricts itself to questions of sedentism,
on the assumption that at any rate some of the complex
attributes of modern sedentary hunters are likely to characterize their prehistoric counterparts as well.

*The western Baltic as an environment for sedentary
hunters*

It is a basic fact of ecology that estuarine and coastal
zones are among those with the highest primary productivity
— the mean net primary productivity is about 1800 dry g/m$^2$
per year (table 10.2). This is surpassed only by swamps and
marshes, and by tropical forests, with the slightly higher mean
value of 2000 g/m$^2$ per year. Temperate forest is well down
the scale with 1250 g/m$^2$ per year (Whittaker 1975), and
furthermore much of the productivity here is in the form of
wood and leaf growth, not much use to human beings. Humans
cannot directly exploit the base of the estuarine ecological
pyramid (the plankton), but can exploit many organisms at
the subsequent levels. These may be immensely productive —
for example, Yonge (1949) states that 1 hectare of musselbed
may yield some 7.4 million kcal a year. At 2500 kcal a day,

Table 10.2. *Net primary productivity of the world's ecosystems*

| Ecosystem type | Net primary productivity per unit area (dry g/m$^2$/yr) | |
| --- | --- | --- |
| | Mean | Normal range |
| (a) relevant to the Danish Mesolithic | | |
| Temperate forest | 1250 | 600–2500 |
| Swamp and marsh | 2000 | 800–3500 |
| Lake and stream | 250 | 100–1500 |
| Continental shelf | 360 | 200–1000 |
| Algal beds, reefs, estuaries | 1800 | 500–4000 |
| (b) other | | |
| Boreal forest | 800 | 400–2000 |
| Woodland and shrubland | 700 | 250–1200 |
| Savanna | 900 | 200–2000 |
| Temperate grassland | 600 | 200–1500 |
| Tundra and alpine | 140 | 10–400 |
| Desert and semi-desert | 40 | 0–250 |
| Cultivated land | 650 | 100–3500 |
| Open ocean | 125 | 2–400 |
| Tropical forest | 2000 | 1000–3500 |

*Note:* rearranged after Whittaker 1975: 226.

this is almost 3000 man-days' food supply, or the annual
calorific requirements of over eight people. Although variation
will be great depending on species composition, type of coast,
techniques of exploitation etc., it is important to stress that
the system is frequently one under which man will not be 'left
out'. The influence of this high productivity on human settlement is thus likely to be considerable.

There is a high degree of variation in all the figures listed
in table 10.2, and some of the factors affecting estuarine and
coastal productivity must be discussed.

*Latitude* is highly important. Cushing (1975) emphasizes the dichotomy between temperate and subtropical/trop-
ical coastal productivity. In general, warmer seas have a more
or less even productivity and population level of plankton — a
low-amplitude cycle. By contrast, temperate seas have a high-
amplitude cycle, with a spring growth burst of phytoplankton
starting in March and reaching a peak in April. After this
numbers decline drastically due to the increase of zooplankton
and other organisms which feed upon the phytoplankton
(fig. 10.2). This seasonality has major effects at subsequent
stages of the food chain: warmer seas (like land surfaces) are
characterized by a high number of species at a relatively low
degree of concentration, while the reverse — fewer species in
greater concentration — is typical of temperate seas. As an
example, the smallest fish in the food chain (5–10 cm in length
and a few grams in weight) may be mentioned. In temperate
waters these fish are herring, and modern trawl nets in areas of
high concentration can catch hundreds of tons per hour. The
warm-water equivalents occur in densities as low as 1 per
1000 m$^3$ of sea-water. A trawl with a 20 × 20 m mouth would
thus take only some 4000 per hour — a total weight of only
60 kg. Further up the chain, in temperate regions, shoals of
larger fish move predictably between breeding, nursery and

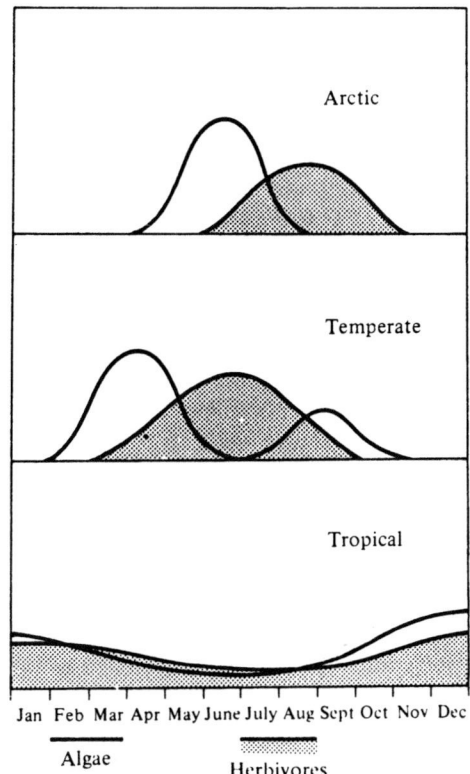

Jan Feb Mar Apr May June July Aug Sept Oct Nov Dec

Algae
Herbivores

Fig. 10.2. Plankton production cycles in various regions (after Cushing 1975).

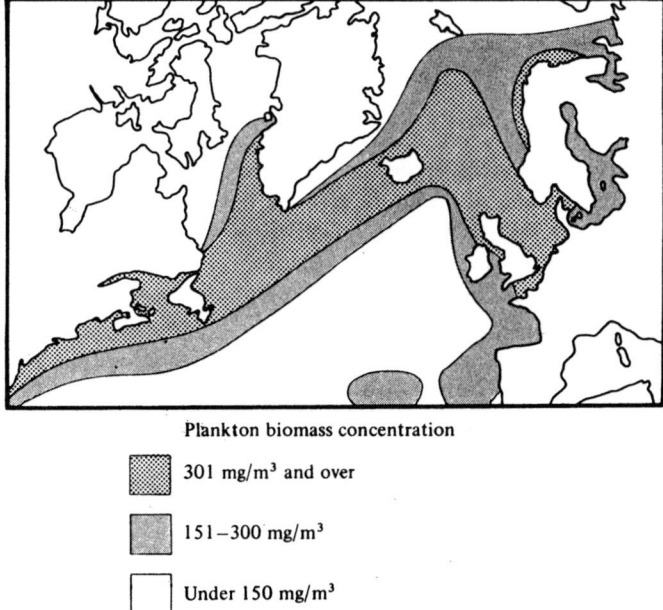

Plankton biomass concentration

301 mg/m³ and over

151–300 mg/m³

Under 150 mg/m³

Fig. 10.3. Plankton biomass zones in the North Atlantic (after Coull 1972).

feeding grounds, and this has had a great effect on the development of fisheries (Cushing 1975).

*Mixing of nutrients* from deeper levels of the sea is important (Coull 1972). This is inhibited in warmer seas by the thermocline: the sun heats the top layer of the water, and this therefore continues to float on the underlying layers of cooler water (tropical areas where currents and winds combine to produce upwelling are an exception to this). In temperate waters the thermocline is less pronounced, resulting in more mixing. The result of this is a band of high plankton productivity. Figure 10.3 shows this zone in the north Atlantic, where the densest area has mean plankton biomass values of over $300\,mg/m^3$, peaking seasonally at up to $2000\,mg/m^3$. The shallow seas of the continental shelf areas are believed to contain twice as much plankton as all the rest of the oceans put together; winter storms in shallow seas ensure much mixing of nutrients from the seabed, utilized in the subsequent spring growth explosion (Coull 1972).

*Tidal action* is important, serving to increase nutrient circulation. Tidal movements in the western Baltic today are minimal. In the late Mesolithic, however, various factors (changes in the configuration of the bed of the North Sea, the presence of more and wider links between the North and Baltic Seas) would have meant a much more tidal and saline western Baltic (Nielsen 1938). The zone of highest plankton productivity now reaching the eastern coast of Denmark (fig. 10.3) would therefore probably have extended further into the Baltic. Coull (1972) notes that plankton productivity is higher in the Baltic than the Black or Mediterranean Seas because the Baltic is less affected by thermoclines, and because it receives many nutrients from water carried into it from the melting snows, just in time to be utilized by the spring growth explosion.

This discussion has emphasized the seasonally highly productive nature of the temperate coastal ecosystem. The overlapping of seasonally useful resources within a limited area, so important to complex hunters, is thus likely to occur at some points within the temperate zone. Some coastal areas are particularly likely candidates. The Ertebølle area satisfies the conditions for high seasonal productivity set by latitude, nutrient mixing, sea depth and tidal action. The multiplicity of islands and coastal indentations form a vast length of coastline, and the local topography makes access to the shore no problem over most of the area. The overlapping seasonality of useful species would have been marked: local terrestrial resources would have been most useful in summer and autumn, and sea fish (e.g. cod, mackerel) are also available at this time of year. Eels concentrate in large numbers in autumn for their return to the sea (Davies 1944), and harp seals may also have been available at this time (Møhl 1970a). In winter, a lean time for terrestrial resources, migrating and breeding sea mammals were available (Møhl 1970b), and migratory birds (swans, ducks, geese and others) were present in large concentrations. The spring gap, before the reappearance of the summer resources, would probably have been the major period of exploitation of the oyster (of which many Ertebølle middens largely consist) which would be at its most nutritious at this time (Rowley-Conwy 1980).

The Ertebølle area thus stands a good chance of having been able to support a complex hunting system. It is thus fortunate that geological circumstances are such that the Late Mesolithic coastline is now above sea level so that coastal settlement may be studied.

*Site evidence*

Shell middens round the world, past, recent and present, fit into a variety of economic systems, performing a variety of economic roles in a variety of ways. They may be base camps or short-term stations, each of which categories may be further subdivided according to time and length of occupation, size of population unit, purpose etc. (Bailey 1978). Such is the diversity that the term 'shell midden' has little value other than the purely descriptive: a midden of shells may be the only common factor between two otherwise very different sites.

If it is assumed that a site system used by complex hunters consists in part of permanent sites and in part of temporary camps, certain expectations may be put forward regarding the nature of the two site types. Erteb\o{}lle site visibility is largely restricted to coastal settlements, as these are the ones which consist of shell middens and are thus much easier to find. Apart from mixed surface scatters of flints, inland sites have yet to be found, with the notable exception of Ringkloster (S.H. Andersen 1974).

The area of Jutland chosen for study is presented in figure 10.4, and a number of Erteb\o{}lle sites is plotted. Many more sites are known, but those mapped here are the ones that have yielded the best data regarding their size and stratigraphy. Denmark during the late Atlantic period was tilting about a line running roughly N.W.–S.E.; coastlines north–east of this line are now above sea level. The maximum extent of the Litorina Sea is indicated in figure 10.4 (after Jessen 1920; Mertz 1924).

*Site size.* Site size may be important in facilitating a distinction between permanent and temporary sites. Although many factors may affect midden size, the largest middens may generally be expected to accumulate near the permanent sites. This was indeed the case for the Northwest Coast – Drucker (1943) was able to divide sites into permanent villages and temporary camps on the basis of midden size, and had the added advantage in some cases of being able to confirm his ascriptions by asking the local Indians what the sites had been used for.

The calculation of site size in the present case presents some problems. In no cases should the given sizes be regarded as anything more than a rough approximation, as most authorities give only the length, breadth and average thickness of the middens. Norslund is one of three sites covering a 500m stretch of coastline (Anderson and Malmros 1965: 35, fig.1); the excavators state that 'a whole complex of settlements lay on the fiord's edge . . . One gets the impression that the whole area formed a large complex of settlements' (p. 36, my translation from the Danish). Quarrying has removed much of the area, but one of the three sites is known to have contained a shell midden of 100 – 200m$^2$, and artefacts were recovered

from a futher 600m$^2$ of the surface. We are thus probably justified in assuming that the site complex was very large. Dyrholm II does not consist of a shell midden; the finds were recovered from a shallow gravel layer covering an area of some 90 × 33 m. This, however, represents the maximum scatter of worked flint. Areas of dense concentration of worked flint, as well as finds of pottery and axes, suggest a more limited area, perhaps in the order of 1000 – 2000m$^2$ (see Mathiassen 1942, maps 2 – 4). Figures of volume and area are not directly comparable to those of the shell middens. Brabrand is not a shell midden; the finds were redeposited in a series of marine layers (Mathiassen 1942). Site size thus cannot be estimated, although the large number of artefacts recovered does suggest that the site could have been of some size.

Table 10.3 lists the sites in order of volume. A wide range of variation is visible. Area and depth do broadly speaking co-vary (figure 10.5), showing that greater area is not just the result of a more dispersed occupation. If it is true that the smaller sites are likely to have been the temporary camps, briefly occupied for the procurement of specific resources, then they should exhibit some form of economic specialization.

*Site economy. Brovst* and *Havn\o{}* are located on small islands, 2.5km$^2$ and 0.25km$^2$ respectively, at distances of 600m and 1000m from their respective areas of mainland. It is unlikely that either could have supported populations of red deer, roe deer and wild pig (the Erteb\o{}lle period's most common ungulates): Mellars's (1975) figures of 1000–2500 kg/km$^2$ for ungulate biomass in mixed deciduous woodland suggest ungulate biomass figures of 250–625kg for Havn\o{} island and 2500–6250kg for Brovst island. The Havn\o{} fauna includes aurochs as well as the other three species (Winge, in Madsen *et al.* 1900), and any single aurochs probably weighed more than the total ungulate biomass the island could support. The Brovst fauna is not published; even if the island were to have supported only red deer, the maximum biomass figure would (at 200 kg per deer) permit a population of only some 31 animals. The presence of other species, the occurrence of bad years, periodic overhunting etc. make it unlikely that the island could have supported permanent ungulate populations. The Hebridean island of Oronsay may be mentioned in comparison. This island, with six shell middens, had an area of about 3.5 km$^2$ and lies some 10–12 km offshore; bones of land mammals in the middens are rare, more suggestive of the transport of specific bones to the island than of a resident population (Mellars 1978). The appearance of ungulates in the island faunas in Denmark is thus likely to indicate sporadic or specialized forays onto the islands by the hunters rather than permanent occupation.

*Aggersund* contains unusual quantities of bones of Whooper swan (*Cygnus cygnus*), and M\o{}hl suggests that the killing of swans may have been the main reason for the existence and location of the settlement. All seasonal evidence points to the winter (M\o{}hl 1978).

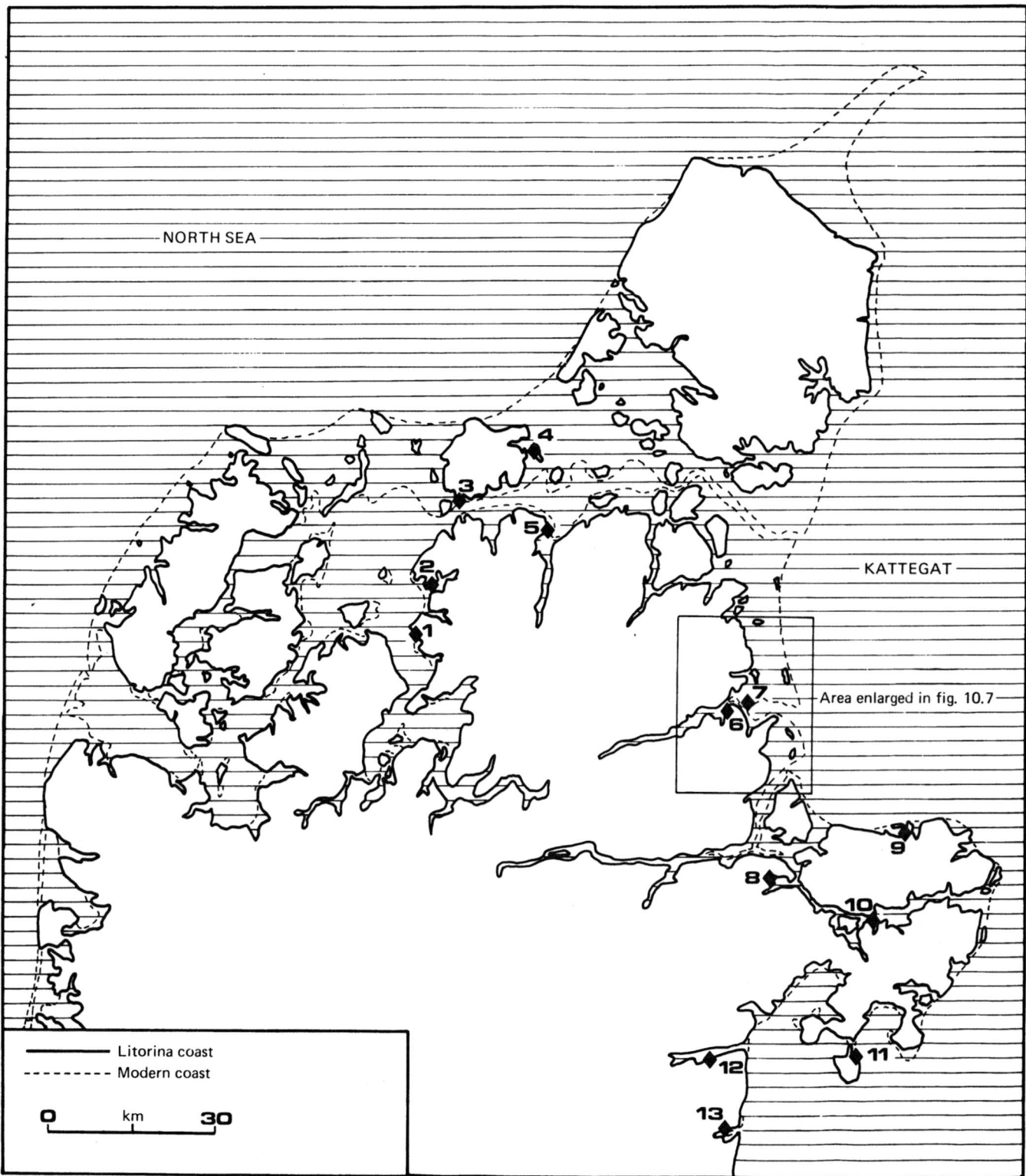

Fig. 10.4. Erteb∅lle sites chosen for study. See table 10.3 for site listing. The position of the Litorina coast is based on Jessen (1920) and Mertz (1924).

Table 10.3. *Size of Erteb$\phi$lle deposits*

| Site | Volume of Erteb$\phi$lle level (approx) m³ | Area of Erteb$\phi$lle level (approx) m² | Maximum depth of Erteb$\phi$lle level m | Whether early Neolithic level also present |
|---|---|---|---|---|
| *Smaller sites* | | | | |
| (3) Aggersund | 10 | 70 | 0.4 | yes |
| (4) Brovst | 15 | 200 | 0.3 | no |
| (11) Vænge S$\phi$ | 10 | 100 | 0.3 | no |
| (10) Kolind III | 150 | 480 | 0.5 | yes |
| (5) Sebber | 250 | 1000 | 0.35 | yes |
| (8) Dyrholm II | – | under 2000 | – | yes |
| (7) Havn$\phi$ | 500 | 1500 | 0.5 | yes |
| *Larger sites* | | | | |
| (6) Åm$\phi$lle | 1850 | 1850 | 1.2 | no |
| (9) Meilgaard | 2000 | 3100 | 1.45 | no |
| (1) Erteb$\phi$lle | 2000 | 2800 | 1.9 | no |
| (2) Bj$\phi$rnsholm | 5000– 8000 | 6000– 12000 | over 1.0 | no |
| (13) Norslund | large (see text) | – | – | no |
| (12) Brabrand | unknown | – | – | no |

*Note:* Numbers in brackets refer to location of sites in figure 10.4.
*Sources:* Madsen *et al.* 1900; Mathiassen 1942; Andersen and Malmros 1965; Andersen 1969, 1975,1978; Bailey 1978.

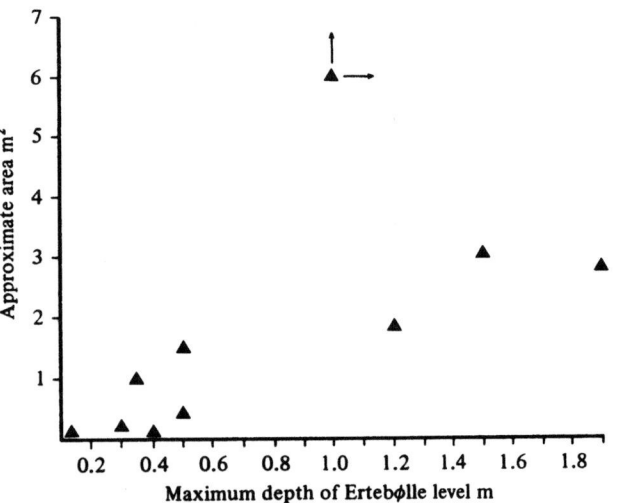

Fig. 10.5. Approximate area and maximum depth of Erteb$\phi$lle shell middens.

*Vænge S$\phi$* has produced only a small bone sample. Many of the bones were of whale, however (Andersen 1975), and the site was located on a small islet a few metres from the shore of a wide shallow bay which would have been suitable for the stranding of whales (Rowley-Conwy 1980).

*Dyrholm* was likewise located on an islet a few metres offshore, overlooking the interior part of a fiord (Mathiassen 1942). Migratory birds and pig-tooth eruption indicate that occupation took place in autumn and early winter. It is conjectured that the site may have been used for the catching of eels, as the season is correct and the location suitable (Rowley-Conwy 1980). One piece of artefactual evidence might offer

some support to this suggestion: the bone tools from Dyrholm include a uniquely high proportion of items described as awls (Mathiassen 1942: 21, and fig. 11). Some Northwest Coast groups used similar tools for skinning eels (Kroeber and Barrett 1960, pl. 20). Identity of form does not of course imply identity of function, but taken together with the seasonal and locational evidence does lend the possibility of eel catching some support.

Of the seven smaller sites put forward in table 10.3, therefore, evidence from five supports the suggestion that they were seasonal camps. Of the remaining two, *Kolind* is in a broadly similar location to Dyrholm and also has unusually large numbers of 'awls' among the bone tools, and so may possibly have been the same type of site. *Sebber* was sampled in 1908 and little information has ever been published (Mathiassen 1942).

This is not the place for a discussion of data from other sites. However, summary of seasonal specializations from Erteb$\phi$lle camps throughout Denmark may be given, along with suggested season of occupation.

Table 10.4. *Evidence for seasonality of exploitation*

| Probable | | conjectural |
|---|---|---|
| small whales (winter) | (M$\phi$hl 1970b) | eels (autumn, early winter) |
| seals (winter) | (M$\phi$hl 1970b) | land mammals (any time) |
| cod (probably summer) | | mackerel (summer) (Becker 1939) |
| fur animals (winter) | (Andersen 1974) | |
| newborn deer (spring) | | |
| pigs (winter, spring) | | |
| swans (winter) | (M$\phi$hl 1978) | |
| ducks (winter) | (Skaarup 1973) | |
| harp seal (autumn) | (M$\phi$hl 1970a) | |

*Source:* Rowley-Conwy 1980, 1981 where not otherwise indicated.

To demonstrate that the larger sites were not seasonally abandoned is more difficult. None of them display evident specialization, some sites have both summer and winter visitors among the birds (Winge, in Madsen *et. al.* 1900), and where adequate samples of pig jaws are available from large sites, no obvious seasonal pattern emerges (Rowley-Conwy 1980).

*Site location.* Location may be further considered. Seasonal camps are likely to be directed towards the exploitation of a particular resource, and may thus be in rather 'specialized' locations. It is notable that Brovst and Havn$\phi$ were on small islands, Dyrholm and Vænge S$\phi$ on small islets and

Table 10.5. *Percentage of sea within circles of various radii around Erteb¢lle sites*

| Site | % sea within: | | |
|---|---|---|---|
| | 2½km | 5km | 10km |
| **(a) small sites** | | | |
| Aggersund | 69 | 59 | 58 |
| Brovst | 65 | 63 | 72 |
| Vænge S¢ | 68 | 69 | 75 |
| Sebber | 63 | 51 | 44 |
| Havn¢ | 72 | 58 | 40 |
| Kolind III | 41 | 28 | 13 |
| Dyrholm II | 33 | 22 | 24 |
| **(b) uncertain size** | | | |
| Brabrand | 17 | 10 | 19 |
| **(c) large sites** | | | |
| Åm¢lle | 30 | 25 | 24 |
| Meilgaard | 37 | 42 | 46 |
| Erteb¢lle | 52 | 62 | 50 |
| Bj¢rnsholm | 57 | 51 | 49 |
| Norslund | 26 | 29 | 40 |

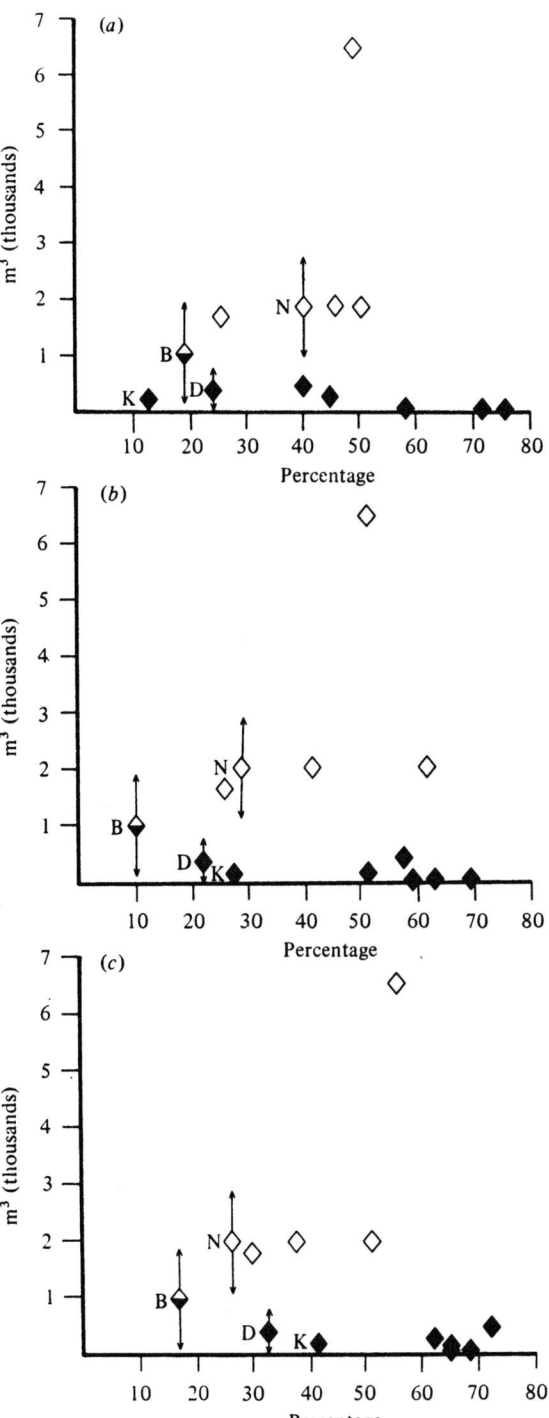

Fig. 10.6. Percentage of sea within reach of Erteb¢lle sites. Horizontal axis: percentage of sea; vertical axis: volume of midden. (a) 10 km radius; (b) 5 km radius; (c) 2½ km radius. Open diamonds are suggested permanent sites, closed diamonds are suggested temporary camps. N = Norslund; B = Brabrand; D = Dyrholm; K = Kolind.

Kolind and Aggersund on the ends of headlands. Permanent sites are, on the other hand, unlikely to be located for the exploitation of a single, seasonally available resource, but should have a more 'generalized' location. Transport of resources from temporary camp to permanent site would have been important in the model put forward here. This would be easiest by water, so it is not surprising that, if there are permanent sites, they should be among the coastal shell middens as suggested above. Shelter would have been an important consideration, suggesting a location on fiords and inlets rather than on open coasts or headlands. This ties in with the fact that estuaries are highly productive ecologically (see above): Danish fiords are not deep rifts in the geological formation, but are shallow and gently shelving, with easy access to the sea shore. In ecological terms they may, in fact, be regarded as estuaries. The probability that such areas were foci of Mesolithic settlement has been emphasized (Clarke 1976; Paludan-Müller 1978). It was suggested above that the oyster may have been important in the late winter and spring, and Nielsen (1938) mentions that the fiord interiors would have been the best places for oysters. That the permanent sites should be located close to the resource bridging the lean time of the year seems not unlikely.

The large sites of Erteb¢lle, Bj¢rnsholm, Åm¢lle, Meilgaard and Norslund all lie in more generalized locations, the first two overlooking a widening in the Limfiord, the last three on the interior shores of smaller fiords. Brabrand, of unknown size, is similar to the last three. The two site types thus display different locational tendencies.

It is of interest to see whether the different locational tendencies exhibited by the two suggested site types can be directly measured. The percentages of sea around the sites are listed in table 10.4, using circles of 2½, 5 and 10km radius. These values are plotted in figure 10.6. It is apparent that no obvious correlation exists between site type and percentage of sea — there is a wide spread of values in each case.

Among the smaller sites, Dyrholm and Kolind stand out as having a considerably more terrestrial orientation than the others. (These sites are marked D and K in figure 10.6.) These sites were, however, located on the interior parts of a long fiord system (see fig. 10.4). If a fully terrestrial location was desired, clearly the sites need not be located on fiords at all. The fact that the sites are on the fiord therefore suggests that some particular resource was produced from the fiord (perhaps eels, as suggested above). This seems to be a case in which formal site territorial analysis is of little help, as the relatively terrestrial orientation of these two sites implied by the method is probably more apparent than real.

These two sites may thus be exceptional among those suggested as having been seasonal camps. If they are ignored, hints of a tendency may be visible: the smaller sites tend to group towards the top end of the range of percentages of sea.

This tendency would fit the proposed model. As the special purpose camps available for study will be those exploiting specific marine resources (as shell middens they are more easily visible than other types of camp), a higher percentage of sea around them might be expected. Permanent sites, in more generalized locations, might be expected to tend towards less specifically marine orientations.

One of the problems involved with site territorial analysis is the question of circle size, and whether indeed different types of site might not be better measured by circles of different sizes. It could be argued that special purpose camps, located as close as possible to the exploited resource, would

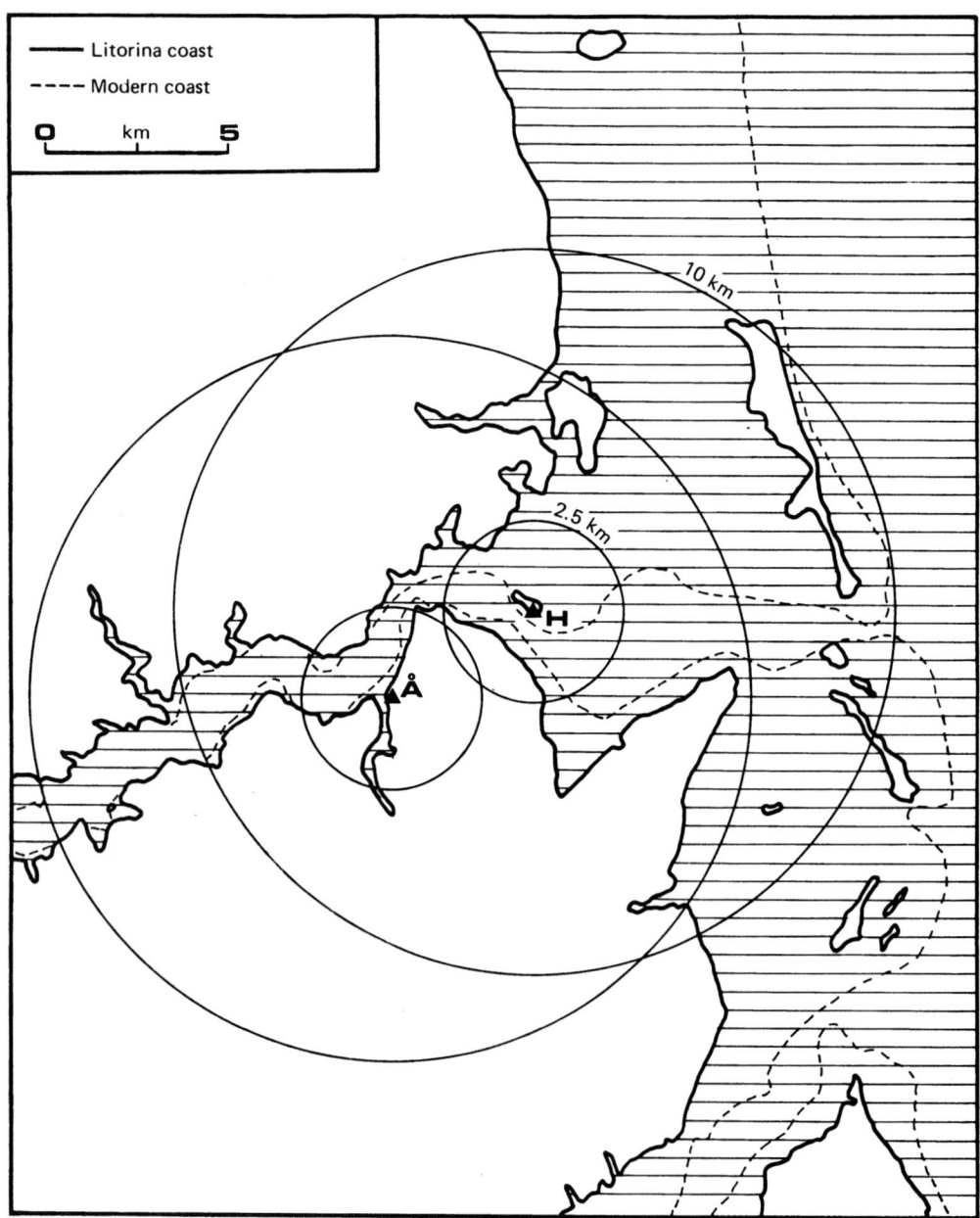

Fig. 10.7. 2.5 km and 10 km exploitation territories of Amølle and Havnø.

be best measured by a small circle; while a larger circle might be more appropriate to a permanent, more general purpose site. Closely adjacent sites are mapped in figure 10.7, with 10 km and 2½ km circles in each case. Although the sites are close together, the coast is such that they are in very different locations. Use of the 10 km circle for both sites tends to blur this difference. In figure 10.6, the best separation of the sites (except Dyrholm and Kolind) is at the 2½ km level. If the 2½ km and 10 km circles are taken together, however, it is seen that all large sites have under 50% sea within a 10 km circle; while all small sites have over 60% sea within a 2½ km circle (still excepting Dyrholm and Kolind).

Site territorial analysis is thus rather problematic in the present case. Particular problems (such as those pertaining to Dyrholm and Kolind) must be taken into account, and varying the circle size causes demonstrable changes. However, if the technique is used as one aspect of a larger series of arguments it can, as here, offer support to observed tendencies in the data. It would not, in the present case, have been possible to argue only on the basis of site territorial analysis.

*Neolithic levels.* Also listed in table 10.3 is the occurrence of early Neolithic levels on the sites. It can be seen that none of the larger sites have Neolithic occupation levels, while of the seven smaller sites, five do have Neolithic levels. In other words, those sites suggested to have been seasonal camps are more likely to have Neolithic levels as well. (It must be emphasized that we are here referring only to regular Neolithic levels, not to the occasional presence of a few Neolithic artefacts on the surface of the Mesolithic midden.)

Skaarup (1973) has demonstrated that shell middens of Neolithic date are to be seen as hunting or fishing stations used by the farmers, not as evidence of hunters surviving alongside immigrant farmers. In the model presented here, it can be seen why particular shell middens were likely to continue in use in the Neolithic. Seasonal camps, for the procurement of a specific resource, often continued in use as the resources were integrated with the farming economy. Permanently occupied Mesolithic sites would not be so well located regarding individual resources, and so the farmers, living (presumably) further inland, would have no use for them; it was these sites, therefore, that were abandoned. The presence or absence of Neolithic levels on these sites thus lends support to the model. It is interesting that Brabrand, of unknown size but resembling the larger sites in terms of location, should also follow them in lacking a Neolithic level.

*Discussion*

The suggestion is thus that the Ertebølle sites mapped in figure 10.4 may be divided into larger sites, which were abandoned in the Neolithic; and smaller sites, many of which continued in use in the Neolithic, and which exhibit economic and/or locational specialization. These two site categories, it is suggested, correspond to permanent sites and temporary camps respectively. Many factors have not been taken into account

here, for instance the length of time the individual sites were occupied within the Ertebølle time-span. Many other sites are known in the area, and as they are excavated the situation will doubtless come to appear more complex; given the considerations discussed above, however, it seems unlikely that the pattern will become completely obscured.

If these considerations are correct, it would seem that many aspects of the Ertebølle resemble in their complexity what we normally associate with farmers rather than hunters. The idea that sedentary hunting may permit social and demographic developments parallel to those of the first European farmers receives support from a consideration of the spread of farming across Europe. Radiocarbon dating has shown that the speed at which farming spread varies from area to area. Farming is now seen to have spread relatively fast over much of central Europe; when farming approached the south-western Baltic, however, a considerable delay occurred before it spread further. This was first noted by J.G.D. Clark (1965) and has since been amply documented by Ammerman and Cavalli-Sforza (1971). The Bandkeramik date of 6440 ±100 b.p. (Bln—119) from Korlat in Hungary may be compared with that from Eitzum in north—central Germany of 6310 ±200 b.p. (Bln—51) (Ammerman and Cavalli-Sforza 1971). These two sites are about 1000 km apart. The site of Lindebjerg, 400 km north of Eitzum on Zealand, is dated to 5010 ±100 b.p. (K—1659) (Tauber 1973) and represents the first *reliable* evidence of farming in Denmark.

The delay in the penetration of farming into the western Baltic area is clear. In view of what has been argued above, one strong possibility is that the west Baltic environment may have made farming a relatively unattractive option. Farming systems, in their move to the north—west, had to make considerable adjustments to the new environments they faced. New varieties and techniques had to be developed, so that at any stage of its spread farming near its northern boundary is likely to have been less reliable and more problematic than elsewhere. It is not surprising, therefore, that the stable and productive economy based on the natural resources of the western Baltic should remain a viable alternative to farming for so long. It is sometimes suggested that more sedentary fishing groups are, because of their sedentism, somehow predisposed to make the change to farming more easily than more nomadic hunters, so that farming should spread quicker in areas of sedentary fishing groups than in areas of nomadic hunters (Waterbolk 1968). The above considerations cast doubt on this view. The European evidence, showing farming spreading quickly across areas probably occupied by nomadic hunters and coming to a halt only when it approached areas occupied by complex hunters, argues strongly that this view should be rejected.

How might the Ertebølle data fit other models? Brief absences from the sites here claimed to be permanently occupied might not be visible archaeologically. However, there seems no overriding reason why these sites should be abandoned for a short period. If storage played the role it does among recent complex hunters, then the need to watch over stored items would render such abandonment unlikely. It has been suggested (Paludan-Müller 1978) that estuaries might have been permanently occupied, while other areas might have seen a mobile system, the two systems comprising separate populations. This seems less likely than the radial model proposed here. The ethnographic information discussed above suggests that the integration of seasonal camps and permanent settlements into a single system would be more likely. The fluctuations in resource availability within the estuaries would suggest the likelihood of other resources being exploited by the estuary dwellers in due season; and the absence of storage facilities among nomadic hunters would render a mobile system more vulnerable to resource failure. Paludan-Müller's conclusions about the productivity and use of the various resource areas are, however, accepted as correct.

All in all, therefore, the Ertebølle seems on present evidence most likely to fall into the category of complex hunters, erected above on the basis of expectations derived from ethnographic studies. Much work is being done on the various Scandinavian Mesolithic groups, and it will be interesting to see whether this will develop the arguments put forward here and whether they are applicable to other areas as well.

### Concluding remarks

I have tried to predict some of the situations in which complex hunters might be expected, and concluded that the Ertebølle area was one such situation. An examination of the archaeological data lends support to the model.

It is therefore argued that there is no need to assume that hunters in prehistory automatically resembled modern nomadic groups. A complex system such as that put forward here is one alternative. Others may also exist. Rick (1980) has suggested that hunters with population only at band level were sedentary in parts of the Andes, and this kind of alternative

has not been examined here (although in the Andean case — in which Rick emphasizes the low geographical and seasonal variation of the vicuna, the principle food source — a system of non-seasonal movement, caused by progressive increase in procurement costs as more animals in an area were killed, could perhaps have produced the same pattern). The logic behind the operation of the various alternatives should be examined before they are rejected as possible models for prehistory.

The implication is that nomadic hunting need not be given the status of a 'stage' from which human behaviour emerged at a particular time. The Ertebølle example is from relatively late in the prehistoric period; what has been repeatedly emphasized in the above, however, is the ecological rather than the temporal basis for the nature of the system. The possibilities of Palaeolithic sedentism are beyond the scope of this discussion; suffice it to point out that Klein (1980a) mentions that 'the archaeological record. . . could be used to argue that some Upper Palaeolithic peoples were organized in "tribes" or even simple "chiefdoms" ' (pp. 209–10). A wide variety of changing situations is likely to have meant a variety of changes from nomadism to sedentism and vice versa at different times and places. Sedentism may, in short, be viewed as running parallel to nomadism, not as a new development bringing an old era to a close. Finally, it must be stressed that, if we have here dwelt on ecological aspects, this in no way 'denies the humanity' of mankind; rather, in pointing to the ability to manage a flexible response in the face of varied opportunities, this humanity is emphasized.

*Acknowledgements*

I should like to thank Glynis Jones, Paul Halstead, Jim Lewthwaite and Robin Torrence for reading the manuscript and offering me the benefits of their comments.

PART THREE

Long-term economic change: demographic and environmental factors

Chapter 11

Editorial

With the shift in emphasis to temporal trends, we move into a far more complex area of debate. Many of the issues examined previously in isolation now recur in combination. Notable links with preceding chapters are the use of faunal data and site locations to make inferences about strategies of animal exploitation, functional analyses of assemblage variability, and assessments of exploitation territories and economic catchments as clues to patterns of mobility and economic integration. Attempts to analyse change in each of these indicators relative to the others is compounded by the problem of controlling for change in the natural environment, and this inevitably creates many additional complexities in analysis as well as ambiguities of interpretation.

A first problem is to determine what exactly we mean by 'change' when applied to human economies or human adaptations. It seems useful here to recognize at least four different components that may contribute to a pattern of change, all of which are implicated in the interpretation of long regional sequences.

*Functional change* refers to lateral shifts in the location of various activities, giving the appearance of temporal change at a given location, even though there is no change in overall subsistence strategy. The commonest manifestation of this is at the intra-site level of analysis, especially on large sites where there would have been scope for the performance of different activities in different parts of the site. Bahn, for example, shows that in some of the large Pyrenean sites, it is possible to demonstrate that excavations in one area of a site have produced a different faunal sequence from the excavation of a contemporaneous sequence of deposits in another area of the site. Similarly, where different sites are linked together in a single site system, variations in the functions of the sites relative to each other may give the appearance of change within the deposits of any one site, even though there is no change in the regional subsistence strategy (see chapter 8). Detecting functional change of this sort is essentially a matter of adequate sampling procedures and adequate control over the lateral and spatial components of variability in subsistence behaviour.

*Environmental change* may alter the resources available for exploitation, or lead to changes in their productivity or accessibility. As discussed by Bailey, environmental changes may have both direct and indirect effects on subsistence strategy.

*Tactical change* is a term suggested by Davidson (chapter 8) to describe changes in the way people achieve a given goal, for example by altering their patterns of mobility or settlement, as distinct from changes in the goals aimed for. For example, a shift from foraging to collecting in response to environmental changes affecting the seasonal availability and accessibility of resources might be described as a tactical change (see Part 2). This use of the term 'tactical' is admittedly ambiguous in that there is no clear definition of the point at which changes of tactics become changes of strategy. The shift from foraging to collecting, for example, would represent for many analysts a change of strategy rather than of tactics. Nevertheless, it seems useful to distinguish changes in the organization of subsistence strategies which are essentially small-scale and potentially reversible, from the changes described below.

*Intensification* refers to an increased rate of exploitation occurring independently of any of the other changes already described. It may take the form of a more intensive exploitation of existing resources, or the addition of new resources to the subsistence which, despite their availability, were previously neglected. The characteristic features of this type of change are that it is directional, usually in the direction of increased population size or density, and that it appears to be irreversible (or reversible only at considerable cost, through the shedding of excess population by starvation or emigration, for example). Again it is difficult to draw a neat boundary between this category of change and the preceding one. A shift from foraging to collecting that occurred independently of any environmental change, for example in response to new social or demographic pressures, might be seen as a process of intensification rather than of tactical reorganization.

Clearly part of the problem in archaeological analysis is to disentangle these various components and to identify which are recorded in the evidence of changing site locations and material residues. Assuming that this can be established, a second problem to be faced is the question of why changes

occur. The solution to this problem obviously depends to some extent on the type of change under study. The reasons for functional or environmental change, assuming that they are accurately identified as such, should be relatively straightforward. However, changes in the organization of exploitation strategies, especially those regarded as examples of intensification, raise additional questions of causation, which lead into discussions of demography, technology (including organizational techniques and skills as well as material equipment), and social organization. Demographic issues dominate the arguments in this section, in line with the widespread popularity enjoyed in recent years by population-pressure theories as sources of unified explanations for global developments such as the origins of agriculture (Binford 1968; Flannery 1969; Higgs and Jarman 1975; Harris 1977; Cohen 1977; Jarman *et al.* 1982).

The essence of Cohen's argument, which represents perhaps the most comprehensive and widely quoted exposition, is that human populations naturally tend to grow beyond the carrying capacity of existing food supplies, and that the resulting stress caused by such periodic imbalances provides the stimulus for territorial expansion and economic intensification. This premise raises a number of difficulties both of theory and of practical application, many of which are recognized by Cohen himself (see also Bender 1978; Bailey 1981b). These difficulties are more fully elaborated in this section. But it may be useful as a preliminary to emphasize two general points about population-pressure theories.

The first point is that there is not one single theory but at least two opposed theories. In the first, population pressure is assumed to be virtually a constant over the long time-periods of the archaeological record, and therefore an ever-present stimulus. Somewhat different implications may be drawn from this initial premise. But, given the apparently slow rate and discontinuous pattern of economic change apparent in the Late Pleistocene record, it is difficult to argue from this premise that population pressure offers a sufficient explanation of specific instances of economic change, even though it may be a necessary precondition for such change. Thus other factors have to be brought in as part of any overall explanation, such as developments in technology. On the other hand this theory avoids the problem of explaining why population pressure occurs, since this is seen as an ever-present condition.

A second type of theory rests on the very different premise that population pressure is a variable phenomenon in the long term, that is, it is present during some periods but absent, or less obviously present, in others because of long-term fluctuations in birth and death rates. In this case, population pressure may be accepted as a sufficient explanation of particular instances of economic change, but leaves unanswered the further question as to why population pressure should become manifest at some points in the archaeological record but not at others.

It should be added that there are some grounds for doubting either type of population-pressure theory as a basis for explaining economic intensification. It can be argued that the degree of population pressure that would be tolerable before population cutbacks came into play, such as a reduction in the birth rate, would be insufficient to provide the stimulus for intensification. Cases have also been claimed where economic intensification appears to have occurred without the aid of any exceptional degree of population pressure (Bender 1978). The most important factor cited in this context as an addition or an alternative to population pressure is social organization, and the ways in which this can affect subsistence patterns, either directly, or indirectly through its effects on decisions about reproduction (Rowley-Conwy, this volume; Part 4).

There is no simple means of deciding between these alternatives solely on *a priori* theoretical grounds, and the ultimate choice must depend on the discriminatory power of the archaeological data that can be brought to bear on these issues. This brings us back to a practical point about population-pressure theories, and that is the question of identifying population pressure in the archaeological record. Cohen (1977) has suggested 14 potential archaeological indicators, while emphasizing that all are susceptible to alternative explanations. An important distinction to bear in mind in the context of the data presented in this section is the distinction between pressure on the exploiting population (of humans), and pressure on the exploited populations (of animals and plants). Evidence of one type of pressure does not necessarily indicate the presence of the other. For example evidence of increased stress on the human population, such as the smashing of bones to obtain marrow, may indicate greater irregularity in the supply of meat because of changes in the availability or accessibility of animals, changes in the hunting strategies by which they are exploited, or changes in the availability of other resources that fill the gaps between successful hunting trips. It does not necessarily imply that the animal populations are under imminent threat of over-exploitation because of increased demands by a growing human population. Conversely, evidence that a particular resource has come under heavier predation pressure, such as a size decrease in mollusc shells (an issue much discussed in the following pages), might indicate only that people were collecting more molluscs because the human population had increased or was spending more time near the coastline. It is not unequivocal evidence that people were engaged in mitigating the effects of stress caused by a previous imbalance between their population numbers and their existing food supplies. A further problem has to do with the point at which increased predation exceeds the capacity of the prey to reproduce its numbers. Many species can tolerate relatively high cropping rates of sexually immature juveniles, many of whom would in any case be lost through natural mortality (see chapter 5). Increased exploitation is not necessarily evidence of over-exploitation. Determination of the point at

which a shift in the age-structure of the exploited organism might indicate that its continued survival was under threat depends on detailed information about its biology and ecology (e.g. Parkington 1976). This is not to deny that a good case can be made for the use of such evidence as indications of population pressure, but emphasizes the need for careful consideration of the various factors that may be involved.

Clark and Straus (chapter 12) and Bailey (chapter 13) offer very different perspectives on the Middle and Upper Palaeolithic sequence of Cantabria. Clark and Straus base their interpretation on the detailed sequence of data made available by their recent excavations at La Riera, backed up by more general data from other sequences in the region. They place particular emphasis on the palaeoenvironmental framework supplied by cave sediments and pollen and draw attention to the apparent discrepancy between climatic oscillations and faunal trends. This evidence, combined with other indications suggesting an overall growth in human population, suggests that the sequence of economic changes amounts to a process of progressive economic intensification. This is further explained in terms of periodic disequilibrium between human populations and their resources, resulting in the application of new techniques of exploitation, such as large-scale slaughter of red deer by mass driving techniques, and the increased exploitation of fish and shellfish, culminating in the concentrated shell middens of the early post-glacial Asturian culture. They also present detailed data on variability in artefact assemblages, which recall some of the issues discussed by Torrence (chapter 3). They note that there is an alternation of two basic tool-kits throughout the sequence, which cross-cut the conventional cultural boundaries defined on stylistic criteria, and which they identify with different sets of activities.

Bailey takes a different view of environmental change, and emphasizes the importance of identifying key environmental limiting factors and plotting their changing geographical distribution in relation to site locations. Particular emphasis is placed on changes in sea level and their likely impact on a narrow coastal plain. He further argues that changes in these environmental factors may account for rather more of the observed palaeoeconomic changes than allowed for in the interpretations of Clark and Straus. Several environmental hypotheses are explored, including the possible direct effects of environmental change on the availability of different species, and more subtle or indirect environmental effects. He suggests that some of the changes in site distributions and patterns of faunal exploitation may reflect 'tactical' changes in response to climatically induced variations in the productivity and seasonal availability of the resources, rather than evidence of economic intensification, and that the alternating expansion and contraction of the total resource base that may accompany extreme fluctuations of climate and environment can exacerbate the tendency to population disequilibrium.

Straus and Clark's comments on this environmental

approach underline the point that so much of the crucial evidence required in the analysis of long-term trends is unavailable, or a matter of hypothesis rather than established fact. Independent evidence about variations in the availability of resources is especially difficult to establish, and critical tests that might discriminate between alternative hypotheses are clearly called for. An important missing element in Cantabria as on other coastlines is any evidence about the environment and human occupation of the submerged shelf that would have been exposed as dry land during the maximum marine regression. This general gap in the Late Pleistocene record has stimulated much recent discussion about the development of underwater techniques of environmental mapping and archaeological survey (Masters and Flemming 1983), and this may offer a new line of inquiry in Cantabria, as elsewhere.

Finally in this section, Bahn examines the evidence of Middle and Upper Palaeolithic economies in the Pyrenees, which offer a number of parallels and contrasts within the Cantabrian evidence. He emphasizes the evidence of changing patterns of site location in relation to faunal evidence, using a distinction between site locations with relatively open site exploitation territories suitable for generalized or eclectic hunting, and site locations in gorges or restricted topography favouring specialized hunting or herding. While noting the general similarities with Cantabria in faunal trends, he sees these as variations on an underlying theme imposed by the very specific constraints of the mountain environment. He discounts the effects of changing sea levels or demographic trends emphasized in Cantabria, and suggests that such long-term changes as can be identified are, at best, trends towards a greater degree of control over the herd animals. A point clearly brought out in his analysis is the potential bias inherent in reliance on evidence from caves or rockshelters. The discovery of an open-air Mousterian site with faunal and locational features quite different from other Mousterian sites, and more like those found in the Upper Palaeolithic, emphasizes how dependent is the interpretation of long-term trends on the degree of control over spatial and geographical variations in subsistence behaviour.

Chapter 12

## Late Pleistocene hunter-gatherer adaptations in Cantabrian Spain
Geoffrey A. Clark and Lawrence G. Straus

Archaeological research in Cantabrian Spain over the past 15 years has allowed for increasingly sophisticated control of palaeo-environmental variables and for the detection of palaeoclimatic oscillations of Late Pleistocene/Early Holocene date. However, despite significant methodological advances and the accumulation of quantities of reliable archaeological data, the traditional culture/stratigraphic framework for the regional Upper and post-Palaeolithic continues to provide the basic analytical units employed by most researchers. We suggest that this approach is unnecessarily restrictive and limits possible explanation of observed phenomena to only a few of many possible factors. The adoption by some Anglo-American workers of a regional perspective emphasizing palaeoecology and 'functionalist' interpretations of data can be detected after about 1965. This transformation of the paradigm for Cantabrian research, while admittedly incomplete, has already allowed for the development of alternative interpretations of settlement patterns, inter-assemblage variability, site functions and activity variants which often have little to do with the 'classic' culture/stratigraphic analytical units. Research embodying the pursuit of such 'functionalist' objectives is reviewed here both for the region as a whole, and in the context of substantive results of the La Riera Palaeoecological Project in Asturias. We suggest that the approach can lead to novel insights about prehistoric behaviour when applied to data obtained through the implementation of a fully integrated functionalist research design.

### Introduction
Since the end of the Middle Palaeolithic (c. 35 000 b.p.) until the initial appearance of domestication (*c.* 4500 b.p.) (Altuna 1980), hunter-gatherer populations in Cantabria have responded to often severe macroclimatic changes, and to regional demographic pressure by systematic adjustments in modes of subsistence linked to changes in settlement patterns. While such adjustments are seldom if ever immediately apparent archaeologically, it is the task of the palaeoanthropologist not only to determine their existence and to place them in time, but also to try to understand *why* these transformations took place. To achieve this, key environmental and behavioural variables must be identified and monitored in the archaeological record, and be convincingly related to the systemic and behavioural contexts from whence — ultimately — they were derived (Schiffer 1976). Because of the relatively poor resolution possible at these remote time ranges and because of the likelihood of sampling error and the magnitude of intervening climatic change, modern approaches to the study of Palaeolithic behaviour must emphasize 'man—land' relationships (Butzer 1971a). Man—land relationships have a major role in structuring a social system's ordering of space. This is particularly true in pre-agricultural contexts in which the intimate relationship with the environment typical of hunter-gatherers is not mitigated by other factors. Although it is acknowledged that 'man—man' relationships have also played a role (e.g. Wobst 1976), they seldom become *determinants* of the distributions of prehistoric population aggregates until after the appearance of domestication economies (Roper 1979).

The placement of archaeological sites, then, and their changing roles within the larger framework of a settlement/ subsistence system, are not independent variables to be studied in isolation, but represent instead ordered and rational accommodations between human groups and their environments. Reconstruction of the regional economy occupies a central place in studies of this kind (Higgs and Jarman 1969: 40).

The recent change in orientation is attributed to widespread recognition of the shortcomings of the 'normative' characterizations of archaeological assemblages typical of the research of the era from 1960 to 1970 (Binford 1962, 1964; Binford and Binford 1966; Freeman 1964, 1968a). Founded on the Bordesian notion that an industry or 'culture' could be described by a relative frequency distribution of standardized morphological types (Bordes 1953, 1961a; de Sonneville-Bordes and Perrot 1953), archaeological research tended to become reduced to the sterile practice of classification, with the resulting entities – allegedly the tangible remains of actual cultures (de Sonneville-Bordes 1963, 1966) – then organized into unilineal or bilineal evolutionary schemata (Bordes 1968) in which successive phases were ordered extra-regionally (i.e. outside south-west France) in accordance with their positions in a few long established and deep stratigraphic sequences first recorded in the Périgord (e.g. Laugerie-Haute, La Madeleine, La Ferrassie). Explanation of these regularities was confounded with the description of supposed central tendencies in tool-type distributions in a closed logical system which held that archaeological assemblages were direct manifestations of extinct 'cultures' (identity-conscious social groups) and, although lip service was occasionally paid to the study of human behaviour, most work was in fact concerned with the time–space systematics of industries considered in isolation (Barker 1973). Settlement patterns, inter- and intra-assemblage variability, differences in site function and activity variants were, with few exceptions, either ignored in the search for broad industrial similarities or 'explained' by reference to the normative phylogenetic paradigm which dominated European prehistory since the time of Breuil.

The development of Spanish prehistory can be shown to be closely allied to that of France, and this has been the case since the inception of work in Cantabria in the 1870s. Although a synopsis of changing trends in Cantabrian archaeological research designs is beyond the scope of this chapter, historical overviews are given by Madariaga (1972) and García Guinea (1975b: 13–32). A short résumé in English has been published by the authors (Straus and Clark 1978b: 292–7). Below we focus on some recent work which has influenced the ways in which archaeologists perceive stability and change in the Cantabrian archaeological record. This research, in part an outgrowth of developments in the theoretical aspects of the discipline over the past 15 years, has had a significant impact on our conceptions of the research process in general, and on the design of the La Riera Palaeoecological Project in particular.

## A functionalist perspective in Cantabrian archaeology

Post-1965 investigations by English and American scholars have focused on two major issues: (1) whether assemblage variability can best be explained by functional or 'cultural' factors; and (2) whether changes in subsistence can best be accounted for by linked changes in environment or by stress engendered by the complex interaction of demographic factors. The first issue has been most extensively addressed; the major elements of recent 'functionalist' approaches are outlined below. The second issue is part of a current discipline-wide debate (cf. Cohen 1975, 1977; Perlman 1980; Yesner 1980); in Cantabria, it has only recently been the subject of sophisticated inquiry (cf. González Echegaray and Freeman 1971, 1973; Bailey 1973, 1978; Straus 1975a, 1977a; Straus et al. 1980; Clark 1981; Klein et al. 1981). It should be kept in mind that both subsistence and palaeoenvironmental data were extremely inadequate until quite recently, so that research designs for examining subsistence and environmental perturbations were not really feasible at all until about 1975. On a regional scale these data are still very incomplete. As will become obvious below, we tend to favour demographic stress explanations for changes in human subsistence behaviour – simply because at present we can detect no strong, positive correlation between such changes and changes in the natural environment. We acknowledge, however, that the issue is not resolved, nor will it be resolved until much additional palaeoenvironmental information is acquired which can be ordered in time by an improved, regional framework of radiocarbon determinations.

### Mousterian

With few exceptions, research embodying the pursuit of functionalist objectives in Cantabria has been identified with the so-called 'American school' (González Echegaray 1976), dominated by scholars affiliated with the Department of Anthropology at the University of Chicago. The present phase of investigations began with the dissertation research of Leslie Freeman on the Cantabrian Mousterian. Although conventional morphological tool types constituted the units of analysis (Bordes 1961a), Freeman was able to demonstrate that they were associated across sites in ways consistent with functional interpretations of the Mousterian facies defined earlier in France. Clusters of tool types thought to be related to shredding/scraping activities, to cutting and to shaving cylindrical objects, were identified using factor analysis and, since time, stylistic variation and sampling error could supposedly be controlled or eliminated as factor determinants, Freeman concluded that the factors might correspond to generalized Middle Palaeolithic 'tool-kits' appropriate to different broadly defined task spectra. He went on to suggest that there was also a certain degree of correspondence between these hypothetical tool-kits and some of the conventional French Mousterian facies of Bordes (1961b). 'Cultural' explanations favoured by French prehistorians were rejected because of the improbability that traditions manifested in stone-tool morphology and frequency could have persisted essentially unchanged over such vast areas and time ranges. The integrity of the Mousterian facies themselves, defined on the basis of a limited sample of French sites, also came under critical scrutiny for the first time (Freeman 1964, 1966, 1967, 1968b, 1973b).

Freeman, in collaboration with the Spanish prehistorian Joaquín González Echegaray, pursued many of these same research directions at Cueva Morín, in Santander, tested in 1966 and excavated in 1968–9. The Cueva Morín project was the first large-scale international multidisciplinary research endeavour of the post-war era, and eventually resulted in the definition of 22 well-defined natural strata, including seven superimposed Mousterian deposits, some with indisputable fragments of living floors. The earlier part of the Upper Palaeolithic sequence was also well preserved there (seven levels), which is rare in Cantabria. Published to date in three comprehensive volumes (González Echegaray and Freeman 1971, 1973, 1978), and in a number of articles, the project emphasized carefully controlled horizontal excavation, a methodological novelty in Spain at the time, which allowed for the definition of features and for the recovery of important contextual and associational data which had previously been ignored.

*Solutrean*

Perhaps the most comprehensive 'functionalist' re-evaluation of a major culture/stratigraphic unit is the work of Lawrence Straus on the Cantabrian Solutrean (Straus 1974a, b; 1975a–c, 1976a–c, 1977a–f, 1978a–c, 1979c, d; 1980b). Beginning with his doctoral dissertation research in 1973, and continuing until the present, Straus has examined lithic and faunal collections, and the geographic and topographic distributions of 36 Solutrean sites with respect to resources exploited in an effort to try to reconstruct the total settlement/subsistence system operative in Cantabria between 21 000 and 17 000 b.p. Rejecting over-fine 'index-fossil' based chronological schemes for subdividing the Cantabrian Solutrean as not supported (and in fact * contradicted) by independent radiometric dating or stratigraphy (Jordá 1955, 1977; Corchon 1971), Straus was able to define two basic types of Cantabrian assemblages. One was rich in endscrapers, sidescrapers, notches and denticulates, and classic Solutrean points, and was typical of sites in Asturias and Santander. The other was poor in Solutrean points, but contained relatively many burins, truncated pieces and backed bladelets; it was generally found at sites in the more rugged mountainous terrain of the Basque country (Vizcaya, Guipúzcoa) and in extreme south-west France. Differences in the artefact inventories were correlated using principal components analysis with differences in the make-up of the faunal assemblages, dominated by red deer (*Cervus elaphus*) and with substantial numbers of horse (*Equus caballus*) and large bovines (either *Bos* or *Bison*) in the relatively flat, woodland/grassland mosaic environments of coastal Asturias and Santander, but characterized by a high

incidence of alpine caprids (especially ibex (*Capra ibex*) and chamois (*Rupicapra rupicapra*)) in the mountainous, cliffside Basque Solutrean sites. The clear-cut geographic correlates of the dichotomous variability observed among Solutrean collections was explained in functional terms; because of marked regional topographic differences between the eastern and western sites, which also contained distinctive faunas, differences in artefact assemblages were attributed to differences in site function, related ultimately to differences in the kinds of animals most frequently killed and processed in the two areas. Straus has detailed evidence for regular patterns of Solutrean site location, generally along major river courses and indicating systematic exploitation of mountainous interior and coastal habitats. Some sites were evidently chosen for their strategic locations (at gorges, box canyons etc.) while others seem to have been selected for the protection afforded by centrally located coastal-plain caves. In addition, Straus has indicated possible regional stylistic differences, based on analyses of Solutrean foliate points (1977d, e).

*Magdalenian*

Research on the Cantabrian Magdalenian has also benefited from adoption of a functionalist perspective. Since it was recognized almost 20 years ago that the Cantabrian Magdalenian could not be classified in strict accordance with the six- or seven-part French sequence (González Echegaray et al. 1963), post-1965 research efforts can be dichotomized by reference to a 'Cantabrian Lower Magdalenian' (17 000 to 13 000 b.p.) which lacks harpoons, and a 'Cantabrian Upper Magdalenian' (15 000 to 10 000 b.p.) which has them (Straus 1980b). Before innovative new work on 'Magdalenian' systematics could be undertaken, however, it was first necessary to dismantle the powerful normative characterization of these industries which had developed in the literature since the early 1960s. This has resulted in the identification of similar 'Upper' and 'Lower' Magdalenian assemblages, and in the isolation of assemblage types which defy correlation with *any* single culture/stratigraphic unit.

The Lower Magdalenian (or Magdalenian III of González Echegaray (1960) and subsequent authors) is best documented at lowland coastal sites in Santander and Asturias, where it is recorded in at least 15 levels at nine sites, including the 'key' sequence (six thick, artificial levels) at the cave of El Juyo in Santander (Janssens et al. 1958; González Echegaray 1960, 1971). While precise similarities with French Magdalenian III assemblages at Laugerie-Haute, Le Placard and other sites cannot be documented (González Echegaray 1960; Utrilla 1974, 1976; Moure 1975), there are nevertheless some broad resemblances in tool-group indices (Clark and Clark 1975) and a (coincidental) concordance of two early radiocarbon dates from El Juyo (15 300 ± 700 b.p.) and Altamira (15 500 ± 700 b.p.) with those from the French Magdalenian III (González Echegaray 1973). The Cantabrian assemblages are defined by a high incidence of thick (nosed, carinate, nucleiform) endscraper types and by the supposedly diagnostic presence of quadrangular-section bone points. Backed bladelets might also be relatively important in some levels (Janssens and González Echegaray 1958; Utrilla 1976; Jordá 1977). This broad definition has been used uncritically by some workers so that assemblages which lack Solutrean and Upper Magdalenian diagnostics, and which are in approximately the correct stratigraphic position, are sometimes classified by default as Magdalenian III.

While there are no known instances of stratigraphic inversions at a single, well-dated site (suggesting that the presence/absence of harpoons does have some gross temporal significance), there are indications (1) that some Lower Magdalenian assemblages are very similar in overall composition to some Solutrean, Upper Magdalenian and even Asturian ones (e.g. La Riera 17 (Sol.) and 18, 19 (Mag.); El Cierro (Sol., Mag.); El Juyo (Mag.); Altamira (Sol., Mag.); Tito Bustillo 1, considered Magdalenian III (1969) until it produced a harpoon (1975); Balmori E1 (Ast.), E5 (Mag.)) (Straus 1974a, 1975a, b; Straus and Clark 1978a, b; García Guinea 1975; Moure and Cano 1976; Clark 1974, 1976a; Clark and Clark 1975); (2) that there is an Upper and post-Palaeolithic assemblage type dominated by thick endscrapers, denticulates and notches, and with variable frequencies of dihedral burins, backed bladelets and sidescrapers which persists through time and which cross-cuts several traditional culture/stratigraphic units; and (3) that some Solutrean and Lower Magdalenian levels, and some Upper and Lower Magdalenian levels, can be considered essentially contemporaneous if comparative age is based upon an assessment of radiocarbon dates and their error ranges (Utrilla 1976; Straus et al. 1977, 1978, 1980). The combined evidence for contemporaneity and for similarity in lithic and faunal assemblage composition implies a persistent functional equivalence for these assemblages, regardless of any significance which might be attached to the presence/absence of (rare) archaeological 'index fossils'. These questions should be resolved to some extent when recent re-excavations at Rascaño (Santander), a site with stratified Lower and Upper Magdalenian levels (González Echegaray 1979a), and El Juyo, with a long and apparently homogeneous sequence of 'Lower Magdalenian' living floors dating in part to c. 14 000 b.p. (Klein et al. 1981) are published. A date of 14 570 ± 300 b.p. has recently been reported for a so-called Magdalenian III/IV level at Erralla Cave in Guipúzcoa (Mariezkurreña 1979: 240).

So far as the 'Upper' Magdalenian is concerned, the work of Alfonso Moure at Tito Bustillo cave (Ribadesella, Asturias), where a small 'Upper' Magdalenian living floor was excavated, is noteworthy for its concern with careful horizontal exposure, and for a multidisciplinary research design, with rapid publication of palaeontological, palynological and malacological analyses, in conjunction with conventional descriptions of the artefact assemblages and stratigraphy (Moure 1975; Moure and Cano 1976). The single-component

occupation at Tito Bustillo is chronometrically dated to about 14 440 b.p. (mean of eight determinations but with a range of 15 400 to 13 500 b.p.) and suggests substantial temporal overlap between some supposedly sequent 'Upper' and 'Lower' Magdalenian assemblages.

Engraved Magdalenian bone and antler industries from Cantabria have been studied recently by Margaret Conkey, who has been concerned to isolate an axis of variability which can be attributed exclusively to style, to design a method for the description of a pan-Cantabrian Magdalenian design system, and to use it to define different kinds of identity-conscious social units there (Conkey 1978a, 1978b, 1980). Central to her approach is the thesis that truly symbolic communication systems (expressed in language, art) make their appearance only with the advent of morphologically modern man. If this is so, and if adequate samples of Palaeolithic artwork can be obtained for a given region and time period, then it should be possible to monitor different kinds of social interaction in which group boundaries are expressed, maintained and reinforced symbolically. Since it is commonly acknowledged that a pattern of aggregation/dispersion is characteristic of most hunter-gatherers, she suggests that evidence for prehistoric hunter-gatherer aggregation and dispersion can be found in the relative diversity of categorized design structures on worked bone at different kinds of Cantabrian Magdalenian sites, and that hypothetical aggregation sites (e.g. Altamira) should be characterized by statistically greater diversity of design elements than would be typical of other kinds of (Magdalenian) occupation and limited activity stations. An analysis of structural diversity in packages of design elements using engraved bone artefacts from Magdalenian levels at Altamira and El Juyo (Santander), and El Cierro, Cueto de la Mina and La Paloma (Asturias), does demonstrate such a differential, although the sample sizes are small and the crucial question of contemporaneity cannot be satisfactorily resolved (Conkey 1980; Clark 1980; Straus 1980a).

*Azilian and Asturian*

Recent excavations of Azilian or predominantly Azilian deposits are confined to the long-term projects at Los Azules (Fernández-Tresguerres 1976, 1979) and Cueva Oscura (Perez 1977)(Asturias); El Piélago (Santander)(García Guinea 1975b) and Ekain (Guipúzcoa)(Barandiarán and Altuna 1977); in no instance has more than a preliminary report been published. A thorough comparison of the old and recent literature undertaken by Straus (n.d.) complements earlier partial efforts by García Guinea (1975b) and Clark and Richards (1978). It indicates that there are marked similarities in the overall composition of many Azilian and Upper Magdalenian assemblages such that it is difficult, if not impossible, to distinguish them except by recourse to (rare) harpoon index fossils (cylindrical in section for the Upper Magdalenian; flat or ovoid for the Azilian)(cf. also Straus and Clark 1979; Groupe de Travail de Préhistoire Cantabrique

1979). Whether or not it is possible to assign a collection to one or the other unit because of the fortuitous discovery of a harpoon, it is evident that both kinds of assemblage often have substantial numbers of small endscrapers (including 'thumbnail' types), practically all are dominated by microliths (especially backed bladelets) and have variable quantities of non-diagnostic 'micro-points' (e.g. 'Azilian' points, microgravettes (which are not typologically distinct)), while only a few have geometric pieces (the exceptions are Ekain 2 and 3, Piélago)(García Guinea 1975). This similarity in assemblage composition lends support to the existence of a sophisticated and specialized (hunting?) technology in which 'compound tools' composed of disposable microlithic elements mounted in (curated?) wooden or antler hafts played an important part (cf. Clarke 1976; Rozoy 1978). It also implies a functional equivalence between at least some Upper Magdalenian and Azilian assemblages which overlap to a certain extent in time, spanning the late tardiglacial and Preboreal periods.

The Asturian, an assemblage type found in shell-midden contexts in cave mouths which supposedly follows the Azilian, which is stratified above it at La Riera yet which is very distinct from it typologically, was recently studied by Clark (1971a, b; 1975a, b; 1976a, 1979a, b; this volume; Clark and Richards 1978). He described the broad outlines of crude lithic and faunal assemblages from 29 Asturian sites in Asturias and Santander, and was able to establish a (contested) Preboreal/Boreal boundary age for them, based on radiocarbon dates and stratigraphy (Jordá 1963a, 1975; Clark 1971b, 1976a). More recent work has been concerned with intra-site spatial analysis at the unique and functionally distinct open site of Liencres (Santander) (Clark 1975a, b; 1979a, b) and with the construction and evaluation of alternative models for resource utilization in Early Holocene Cantabria (Clark, this volume; Clark and Lerner 1980; Bailey 1973, 1978, this volume). In particular, it has been possible to demonstrate that all known Asturian stations except Liencres are basically similar phenomena so far as their lithic and faunal contents, and their locations relative to critical resources are concerned. If the Asturian is considered as the analytical universe (cf. below), Bailey's (1973) hypothesis of seasonal transhumance involving a bipolar settlement pattern (summer in the mountainous uplands, winter on the coast) might require modification. A marked pattern of seasonality in the collection of a single resource (e.g. shellfish) does not necessarily imply that a site was abandoned during the rest of the year (cf. chapter 9). Whether the Asturian should be considered as a temporally distinct culture/ stratigraphic unit, however, has recently been called into question.

In the light of an early radiocarbon date from an Asturian living floor at Mazaculos (9290 ± 440 b.p.)(González Morales and Marquez Uría 1978), and demonstrable overlap with Late Azilian dates from Los Azules (9430 ± 120, 9540 ± 120), Urtiaga C (8700 ± 170), Ekain 4 (9460 ± 185),

Erralla (post-10 580 ± 270), La Riera (post-10 630 ± 120) and Morín (pre-9000 ± 150)(Straus *et al.* 1978; Mariezkurreña 1979), it seems reasonable to propose at least partial contemporaneity between these two supposedly sequent assemblage types. These observations have led Straus (1979b) to suggest that at least some Asturian and Azilian assemblages might represent different functional and/or depositional facies of a single settlement/subsistence system. The Azilian sites, which typically have a more inland distribution, might represent the remains of hunting stations (a notion supported by their rich microlithic technologies) while the purely coastally distributed Asturian sites, generally acknowledged to be refuse dumps rather than actual living areas (the living floor at the base of the Mazaculos midden excepted), might represent the residues associated with (winter?) exploitation of shellfish and plant resources (Straus 1979b).

In sum, recent comparative evaluations of Upper Palaeolithic assemblages which ignore fossil director-based culture/stratigraphic distinctions have allowed for the definition of at least two major kinds of Cantabrian assemblage types which appear to persist and recur throughout the entire Cantabrian Würm tardiglacial and postglacial period. These assemblage types are dominated on the one hand by scrapers, denticulates and notches and crude core and flake heavy-duty tools, and on the other by retouched (especially backed) bladelets and burins (Straus n.d.). While possible correlations with faunal remains, categories of débitage and site locational data remain to be established, the dichotomous variability observed suggests the existence of two rather generalized and flexible technologies which persist over fifteen millennia and which probably reflect in some imperfect way two distinct sets of activities or behaviours related to the procurement and processing of plant and animal resources. The periodicity in their occurrence might ultimately be explained by recurrent shifts in adaptation, initiated or influenced by climatic change, changes in the distribution and availability of 'key' resources and the efficiency with which they were exploited, and changes in regional demography – at present the best candidate for a single causal factor – or they may simply reflect changes in site 'use'. While we do not deny the existence of Late Pleistocene social groups, we submit that much of the variability observed in archaeological collections cannot be accounted for as (or in most cases even related to) an axis of stylistic variation, and, while the presence/absence and relative frequency of some 'index-fossil' tool type might have some limited temporal significance, it seems injudicious to restrict possible explanation of more widely observed regularities in assemblage composition to changes through time in the 'ethnic' affiliations of these groups as monitored by rare (and not necessarily stylistically sensitive) type fossils.

**The La Riera project: research design**
Much of the research perspective just discussed is embodied in the activities of the multidisciplinary,

multinational La Riera Palaeoecological Project, directed since 1976 by the authors. The La Riera project was designed to generate and test hypotheses about Late and post-Pleistocene ecosystems in Cantabrian Spain. These hypotheses, which are reported in detail elsewhere (Straus and Clark 1978b: 297–301), examine possible relationships amongst food resources, site location and macroclimatic change, test for periodicity of prehistoric occupation (i.e. whether (or when) occupation of the cave was seasonal or perennial) and examine patterns of covariation in artefact (retouched pieces, débitage) and faunal (species, body parts) categories. The overall objective is to isolate changes in adaptation recoverable from the archaeological record at the cave and at other sites of comparable antiquity in the region, even if the relationship between residues and activities is not necessarily direct (Binford 1978a, b). Primary variables recognized by the human activity. Time is regarded as a reference variable against which to measure change attributable to other causes and is controlled by radiometric dating and by stratigraphy. Investigation takes place simultaneously on the site and regional levels, although ultimately it is from the regional context that significant causal factors must be derived (Vita-Finzi and Higgs 1970; Jarman 1972b; Smith 1976; Part 2 below).

Recent studies by Freeman (1973a), Bailey (1973, 1978, this volume); Clark (1971a, b; 1975b; 1976a; Clark and Lerner 1980), Davidson (1976b, this volume); Straus (1975a; 1976a, c; 1977a, c; 1979b) have all proposed models of Upper Palaeolithic and Mesolithic settlement/subsistence systems for Cantabrian Spain to account for changes in technology and faunal assemblages. Immediate objectives of the project include attempts to test these hypothesized regional models against La Riera data, to monitor and explain changes in patterns of utilization of the surrounding landscape, in the role of the cave in these natural and behavioural systems over time, and in the technologies employed in the adaptive process. Adaptation is considered to be a regional pheno-menon, and is defined as the repertoire of collective social responses related to the procurement and processing of the plant and animal resources necessary for group maintenance and survival.

**Cantabrian Spain past and present**

Cantabria, which comprises the northern Spanish coastal provinces of Guipúzcoa, Vizcaya, Santander and Asturias, is essentially a long (c. 350 km) and narrow (c. 45 km) rectangle, bisected by the 43° 15′N latitude, and bounded

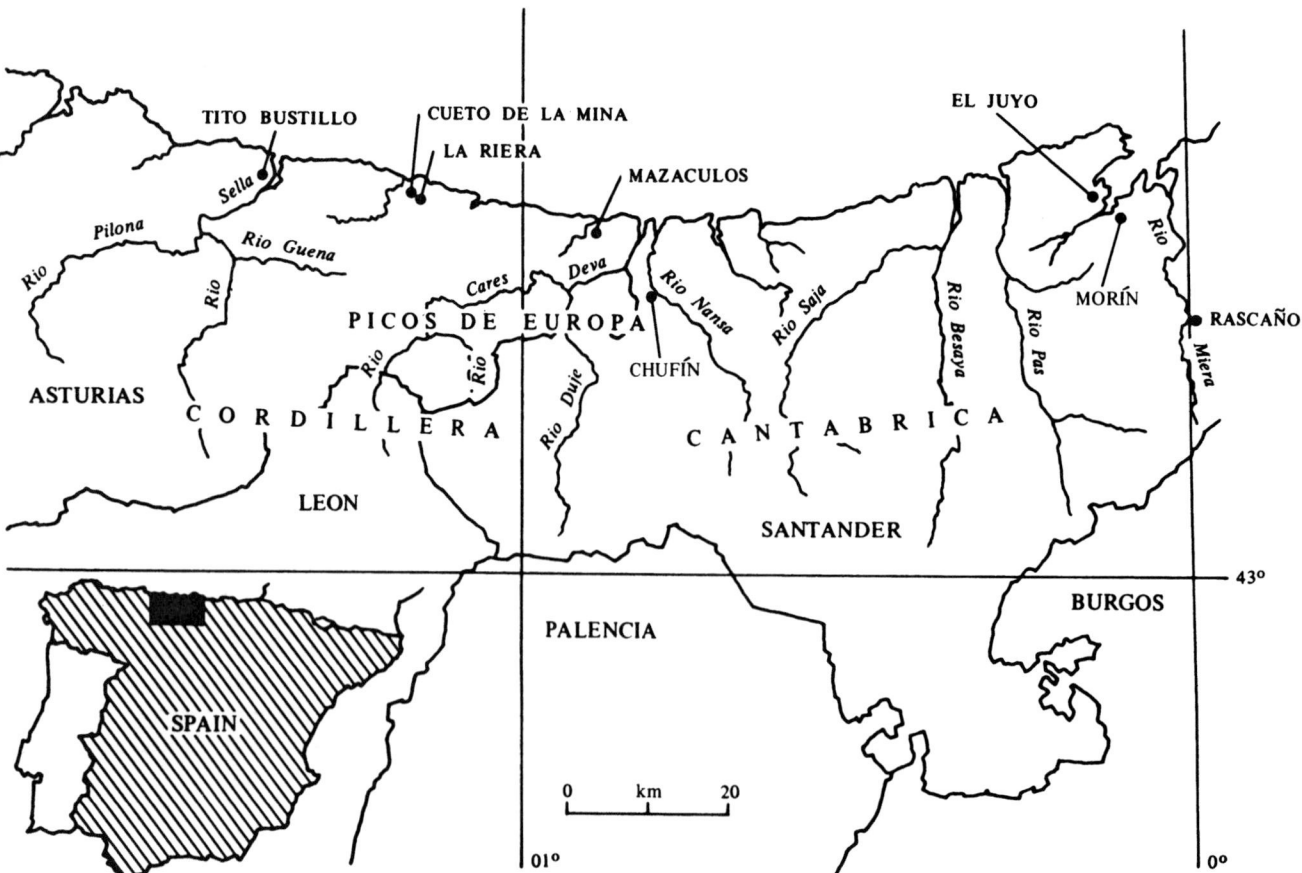

Fig. 12.1. Central Cantabria showing topographical features and major sites mentioned in the text.

on the north by the Cantabrian Sea (Bay of Biscay), on the south by the Cantabrian Cordillera (which separates the region from the rest of Spain) and on the east by the western Pyrenees (fig. 12.1).

The landscape in eastern Asturias, where Late Pleistocene sites are concentrated in great density, consists of the five major structural components described earlier (cf. chapter 9). Superimposed on these structural elements are a variety of life zones, the occurrence and distribution of which are determined by local moisture and temperature regimes, altitude, and the proximity of watercourses and the sea.

The equable present-day climate differs markedly from that of the Late Pleistocene, known from dozens of pollen and sediment samples taken in columns from controlled stratigraphic contexts at La Riera cave and at other sites in the region. Although depositional hiatuses and occasional conflicting dates in the radiocarbon chronology complicate the interpretation of both La Riera series, the analyses nevertheless allow for a reasonably consistent description of the broad outlines of palaeoclimatic change in the region of Llanes during the interval between *c.* 21 000 and 8650 b.p. (cf. below). La Riera data thus complement those from the stratigraphic sequence at Cueva Morín (Santander) where prehistoric occupation extends back well into the Middle Palaeolithic, and where a long series of early Upper Palaeolithic deposits are also preserved (> 35 000–9500 b.p.). Climates markedly colder than those of the present, with landscapes almost totally devoid of arboreal vegetation and with evidence of intensive frost weathering (e.g. much *éboulis*, cryoturbation pockets) are indicated at both lowland coastal sites, along with dry and humid warm episodes, conditions like those of the present and evidence for shifts in the periodicity of precipitation (Butzer 1971b, 1973; Boyer-Klein 1980; Leroi-Gourhan 1971a, b). Similar fluctuations are also documented from the long sequence at El Pendo and from shorter stratigraphic columns at Chufín, Rascaño and Piélago, at the multi-cave complex at El Castillo (all in Santander) and at Tito Bustillo (Asturias)(García Guinea and Puente 1975; Butzer 1981).

### The La Riera project: substantive results

Although many of the 'functionalist' reinterpretations of Cantabrian data discussed earlier might be regarded by a sympathetic reader as more adequate or satisfactory explanations of patterned assemblage variability than those of previous decades, a critic might observe that these advances are more apparent than real — that this notion of improved adequacy could be accounted for by post-1965 changes in the paradigms which govern archaeological research in England and in the United States (Clarke 1973; L.R. Binford 1973; S.R. Binford 1972; Clark 1981b, 1982). Ultimately, the credibility of these claims will only become firmly established, and critics won over, by demonstrations that the new paradigm actually works — that is, that it can lead to novel

insights about prehistoric behaviour when applied to new data obtained through the implementation of a fully-integrated 'functionalist' research design. The La Riera research design has already been described; below we outline some of the salient contributions which the project has made so far, and point to those areas which might repay future 'functionalist' research.

### Chronology and Palaeoclimatic change

The work at La Riera is distinguished by unusually 'fine-grained' control of regional palaeoclimatic change, measured with a radiocarbon chronology which at present is one of the longest and most complete on the Iberian Peninsula (tables 12.1 and 12.2). Use/occupation of the cave begins during a wet, temperate episode prior to 21 000 b.p., and terminates with the accumulation of the Asturian midden around the Preboreal/Boreal boundary (8650 b.p.). The complex sequence of moisture and temperature oscillations summarized in table 12.2 is discussed elsewhere (Straus *et al.* 1980, 1981). Although there are discrepancies in the interpretation of the pollen and sediment records, and occasional inversions in the sequence of radiocarbon dates, agreement is about as good as might be expected, given that the separate analyses monitor distinct kinds of data. Sampling error and differences in laboratory methods, analytical precision and the like; natural agencies not directly related to prevailing macroclimatic conditions (e.g. percolation of fine sediments through fissures in cave walls, ceiling; microenvironmental factors relating to the particular setting of the cave) and disturbances owed to the intensive human activity concentrated in the cave mouth (Straus 1979a) can all affect agreement between sedimentological and palynological monitors of palaeoclimatic conditions. The remarkably good correspondence with named and dated climatic phases in the Aquitaine (Laville 1975) was frankly somewhat surprising, given differences in topography and latitude in the two regions (table 12.2). However, the significance of the La Riera palaeoclimatic sequence does not lie in its degree of correspondence with climatic phases defined elsewhere, but rather in its potential to allow us to use it to control for the major factor of macroclimatic change as a possible causal agent for changes in other aspects of the La Riera data base (e.g. artefact, faunal assemblages). It is clear from tables 12.1 and 12.2 that there is very little correlation between changes in conventional culture/stratigraphic unit designations and fluctuations in the regional moisture and temperature regimes.

### The industries

Given the relatively small size of La Riera, and the limited area excavated, the four field seasons produced enormous quantities of stone artefacts, bone and shell. The 55 000 + lithics were classified and weighed according to 28 raw material categories, supplemented by petrographic analyses of the most common types. Débitage (15 types),

Table 12.1. *La Riera radiocarbon determinations*

| Level | Period | Laboratory number | Age b.p. Libby ½-life | Range at one standard deviation |
|---|---|---|---|---|
| Conchero | Asturian | GaK-2909 | 8650 ± 300 | 8350–8950 |
| Conchero (top) | Asturian | GaK-3046 | 6500 ± 200 | 6300–6700 |
| 27 | Azilian/Magdal. | BM-1494 | 10 630 ± 120 | 10 510–10 750 |
| *(27 | Azilian/Magdal. | GaK-6985 | 14 760 ± 400 | 14 360–15 160)* |
| 24 | Upper Magdal. | GaK-6982 | 10 890 ± 430 | 10 460–11 320 |
| 23 | Upper Magdal. | Ly-1646 | 10 340 ± 560 | 9780–10 900 |
| 20 | Lower Magdal. | Ly-1645 | 12 360 ± 670 | 11 690–13 030 |
| *(20 | Lower Magdal. | GaK-6980 | 17 160 ± 440 | 16 720–17 600)* |
| Hiatus indicated by palynological, sedimentological data | | | | |
| 19 | Lower Magdal. | Q-2116 | 15 230 ± 300 | 14 930–15 530 |
| 19 | Lower Magdal. | Q-2110 | 15 520 ± 350 | 15 170–15 870 |
| 19 | Lower Magdal. | GaK-6448 | 16 420 ± 430 | 15 990–16 850 |
| 17 | Upper Solutrean | GaK-6445 | 16 900 ± 200 | 16 700–17 100 |
| 17 | Upper Solutrean | GaK-6444 | 17 070 ± 230 | 16 840–17 300 |
| 16 | Upper Solutrean | GaK-6983 | 18 200 ± 610 | 17 590–18 810 |
| 15 | Upper Solutrean | UCR-1272 | 17 225 ± 350 | 16 875–17 575 |
| *(15 | Upper Solutrean | GaK-6449 | 15 600 ± 570 | 15 030–16 170)* |
| 14 | Upper Solutrean | UCR-1271A | 15 690 ± 310 | 15 380–17 000 |
| 12 | Upper Solutrean | GaK-6446 | 17 210 ± 350 | 16 860–17 560 |
| 10 | Upper Solutrean | GaK-6447 | 19 820 ± 390 | 19 430–20 210 |
| 8 | Upper Solutrean | GaK-6981 | 20 690 ± 810 | 19 880–21 500 |
| * (8 | Upper Solutrean | GaK-6450 | 15 860 ± 330 | 15 530–16 190)* |
| 4 | Upper Solutrean | GaK-6984 | 20 970 ± 620 | 20 350–21 590 |
| 1 | Pre-Solutrean | UCR-1270 | 19 620 ± 390 | 19 230–20 010 |
| 1 | Pre-Solutrean | Ly-1783 | 20 360 ± 450 | 19 910–20 810 |
| 1 | Pre-Solutrean | BM-1739 | 20 860 ± 410 | 20 450–21 270 |

*dates in brackets are not in accord with the stratigraphic position of the sample at $\bar{x} \pm s$.

manuports (4 types) and retouched tool (92 types) components were analysed separately by computing their respective proportions in each of 36 natural strata. Some 300 bone/antler artefacts were classified by M. González Morales according to the typology of Barandiarán (1967).

Although we believe that normative characterizations of industrial assemblages have validity only as very general descriptive devices, various strata at the site can be assigned to classic culture/stratigraphic units on the basis of fossil-director artefact types. Levels 2–17 are Upper Solutrean, containing characteristic foliate and/or shouldered points, invasively retouched flakes and flat thin chipping debris. The lowest of these levels dates to c. 21 000 b.p. – surprisingly early for a so-called 'Upper' Solutrean deposit (Straus, Cabrera et al. 1978a). Level 24 is by definition Upper Magdalenian, as it yielded fragments of a cylindrical harpoon, while level 28, below the Asturian conchero (level 29), contained a classic flat Azilian harpoon like one found by Vega del Sella in the 1916–18 excavations. The uppermost

shell midden (level 29) yielded quantities of Asturian cobble picks to the Conde (Vega del Sella 1930) as well as to Clark (1974; Clark and Richards 1978) in his 1969 excavations of the conchero.

Other strata are not so easily assignable. The basal level (1) contains a scanty Upper Palaeolithic industry with only 57 retouched pieces. A few large blades with scalar retouch and some thick endscrapers recall the Aurignacian. Levels 18, 19 and 20 (16–17 000 b.p.) are heavily dominated by backed bladelets (62–74%)(as is Solutrean level 17) and probably pertain to the so-called Cantabrian Lower Magdalenian. Although both Upper Magdalenian and Solutrean levels at La Riera contain a few quadrangular-section bone 'points', most of these supposedly typical Lower Magdalenian diagnostics do in fact come from levels 19 and 20. The close similarity between levels 18–20 and level 17, detailed in earlier publications, reinforces the conclusion based on reinvestigation of old collections that certain Solutrean and certain Lower Magdalenian assemblages in Cantabria can be

Table 12.2. *La Riera: tentative sequence of macroclimatic change based on pollen and sedimentological evidence*

| Level | Period (Aquitaine sequence) | Climate |
|---|---|---|
| 30 | Boreal | |
| 29 | Pre-Boreal/Boreal boundary | Warmer |
| 28 | Pre-Boreal | |
| 27 | Dryas III | |
| 26 | Dryas III | Cold/wet |
| 25 | Dryas III | |
| 24 Top | Brief temperate episode (lots of ferns, possibly introduced?) | |
| 24 Main | Dryas III or known cool episode within Allerod | |
| 23 | Allerod | Warmer |
| 22 Top | Allerod begins (lots of juniper) | |
| 22 Main | Dryas II | |
| 21 | Dryas II | Cold/dry |
| 20 | Dryas II | |
| | Hiatus (Bolling, Dryas I?) | |
| 19/20 | Lascaux | |
| 19 | Lascaux | Warm/humid |
| 18 | Lascaux | |
| 17 | Lascaux | Warm/dry |
| 16 | Würm IV (Perigord I/Laville) | Cold/dry |
| 15 | Laugerie | |
| 14 | Laugerie | |
| 13 | Laugerie | |
| 12 | Laugerie | Warm/wet |
| 11 | Laugerie | |
| 10 | Laugerie | |
| 9 | Laugerie | |
| 8 | Würm III ends | |
| 7 | Würm III | Cold/dry with warm |
| 6 | Würm III | humid episodes |
| 5 | Würm III | |
| 4 | Würm III | |
| 3 | Würm III | |
| 2 | Würm III | Cold/humid |
| | Hiatus | |
| 1 | ?? | Temperate/humid |

differentiated only by the presence or absence of Solutrean points (Straus 1975b, 1978b, 1979d; Clark 1974, 1975b; Clark and Clark 1975). The overall industrial similarities suggest general functional similarities among the different cave occupations.

Combined levels 21–23 represent a thick bed of silty clay with only scarce cultural remains. Although lacking in fossil directors, the lithic industry, with equally large percentages of burins and endscrapers, could be classified as Upper Magdalenian, which agrees well with dates of about 11 000 b.p., from the top of level 23 and level 24.

Assignment of materials from levels 25–27 is likewise problematical, as meaningful distinction between Final Magdalenian and Azilian industries in Cantabria is dubious in default of the characteristic harpoons. Like Azilian level 28 *and* Upper Magdalenian level 24, these levels have large percentages (*c.* 40%) of backed bladelet types, including

'Azilian' points, and some 'thumbnail' endscrapers. Level 27 dates to about 10 000 b.p., making it either an early 'Azilian' or a very late 'Magdalenian'. The earlier impression of continuity between final Pleistocene and Early Holocene Cantabrian lithic industries (Carballo 1960) is thus fully confirmed at La Riera, underscoring the arbitrary nature of the classic culture/stratigraphic unit designations.

A notable feature of the La Riera data is the inverse relationship between backed bladelet and notch/denticulate-dominated levels. In general, the denticulate group far outnumbers the backed bladelet group in the lower part of the sequence (levels 1–15) while the upper levels (17–28) are heavily dominated by backed bladelets, with generally few denticulates. In levels 4, 5, 16 and 21/23, the two groups are in proportional equilibrium. Either this basic difference is a reflection of some major differences among activity and/or disposal patterns in the cave, or it indicates the functional replacement of flake denticulates by serrated implements composed of hafted backed bladelets. However, a unilineal developmental trend is not universally supported by the facts. While the appearance of large numbers of backed bladelets in Cantabrian assemblages is generally believed to be a Magdalenian phenomenon (Jordá 1977), both some early and late Solutrean assemblages at La Riera (levels 4, 5, 17) have substantial numbers of these microliths, as do several other Cantabrian Solutrean assemblages (e.g. Aitzbitarte, Ermittia, Bolinkoba, Morín, Chufín)(Straus 1974b, 1975a, 1978b, 1979d). Other Solutrean assemblages, in contrast, have high proportions of denticulates, suggesting that activity differences probably lie at the heart of the basic assemblage distinctions observed at La Riera (table 12.3; figs. 12.2, 12.3).

While it is apparent that patterned differences and similarities exist among the La Riera artefact collections, it is also clear that such patterning seldom corresponds to the traditional culture/stratigraphic units to which the assemblages may be assigned. The characteristics of the large débitage fraction (95%) were also examined, both by themselves and in relation to the retouched tool inventory, as it was thought that débitage might be regarded as a more direct monitor of past human activity than the sometimes scarce retouched tools.

Flaking debris was classified into a number of types which fall into two basic groups: primary and secondary. Primary waste consists of various core types, plain and decortication flakes, edge and platform renewal flakes, blades and bladelets. Secondary débitage consists of trimming flakes, shatter and burin spalls. While on an average there are 20.1 knapping by-products for every finished tool, the range of values extends from as few as 8 (levels 2, 3, 24) to as many as 40 (level 15), indicating a wide disparity among the levels in the extent to which knapping was done *in situ* during the individual occupations (fig. 12.4). Similarly, while the average ratio of primary to secondary debris is nearly one (0.96), the range extends from 0.22 (level 10) to 2.12 (levels 21–23) (fig. 12.5). In some levels relatively much secondary retouching

Table 12.3. *Percentages of major tool groups, La Riera, 1976—9*

| Levels | Total number of tools | % total endscrapers | % thick endscrapers | % side-scrapers | % total burins | % dihedral burins | % truncation burins | % backed bladelets | % denticulates + notches | % Solutrean points | % perforators |
|---|---|---|---|---|---|---|---|---|---|---|---|
| 1 | 57 | 15.8 | 3.5 | 0 | 15.8 | 14.0 | 1.8 | 1.8 | 33.3 | 0 | 1.8 |
| 2/3 | 51 | 21.6 | 9.8 | 2.0 | 7.8 | 5.9 | 0 | 2.0 | 33.3 | 5.9 | 2.0 |
| 4 | 106 | 5.7 | 0 | 2.8 | 14.2 | 12.3 | 1.9 | 14.2 | 11.3 | 26.4 | 0.9 |
| 5 | 68 | 7.4 | 0 | 0 | 7.4 | 5.9 | 0 | 14.7 | 17.6 | 23.5 | 1.5 |
| 6 | 39 | 0 | 0 | 0 | 10.3 | 10.3 | 0 | 2.6 | 23.1 | 46.2 | 0 |
| 7 | 149 | 13.4 | 3.4 | 4.7 | 9.4 | 9.4 | 0 | 5.4 | 25.5 | 18.8 | 2.0 |
| 8 | 116 | 17.2 | 0.9 | 4.3 | 7.8 | 5.2 | 0 | 4.3 | 35.4 | 5.2 | 4.3 |
| 9 | 107 | 9.3 | 0 | 7.5 | 14.9 | 13.1 | 0.9 | 0 | 47.7 | 0.9 | 2.8 |
| 10 | 71 | 25.4 | 5.6 | 0 | 7.0 | 7.0 | 0 | 0 | 32.4 | 7.0 | 4.2 |
| 11 | 65 | 9.2 | 4.6 | 6.2 | 12.3 | 7.7 | 1.5 | 3.1 | 49.2 | 0 | 3.1 |
| 12/13 | 65 | 9.2 | 1.5 | 6.2 | 10.8 | 10.8 | 0 | 3.1 | 56.9 | 0 | 1.5 |
| 14 | 316 | 13.6 | 3.2 | 10.4 | 11.1 | 9.2 | 0.3 | 2.9 | 38.9 | 1.0 | 2.5 |
| 15 | 76 | 11.9 | 4.0 | 7.9 | 6.6 | 5.3 | 0 | 11.8 | 22.4 | 1.3 | 1.3 |
| 16 | 181 | 7.2 | 2.8 | 3.3 | 12.7 | 10.5 | 0.6 | 23.8 | 22.1 | 0 | 2.8 |
| 17 | 151 | 6.0 | 3.3 | 1.3 | 4.6 | 4.6 | 0 | 70.9 | 8.6 | 0.7 | 1.3 |
| 18 | 225 | 6.7 | 6.2 | 0 | 4.4 | 4.0 | 0.4 | 69.3 | 8.4 | 0 | 0.4 |
| 19 | 219 | 7.3 | 5.3 | 0.5 | 7.8 | 6.9 | 0.5 | 61.9 | 10.5 | 0 | 1.4 |
| 19/20 | 78 | 6.5 | 3.9 | 1.3 | 1.3 | 1.3 | 0 | 74.4 | 7.7 | 0 | 1.3 |
| 20 | 203 | 6.5 | 3.5 | 0.5 | 6.0 | 4.0 | 1.0 | 63.1 | 6.0 | 0 | 4.0 |
| 21/23 | 61 | 18.0 | 8.2 | 0 | 19.7 | 14.8 | 1.6 | 16.4 | 19.7 | 0 | 6.6 |
| 24 | 202 | 17.3 | 5.4 | 2.5 | 6.9 | 4.5 | 1.5 | 54.0 | 3.0 | 0 | 0.5 |
| 26 | 52 | 11.5 | 0 | 1.9 | 1.9 | 1.9 | 0 | 38.5 | 7.7 | 0 | 0 |
| 27 | 105 | 17.1 | 2.9 | 3.8 | 7.6 | 7.6 | 0 | 43.8 | 15.2 | 0 | 1.9 |
| 28 | 32 | 3.1 | 0 | 0 | 9.4 | 6.3 | 3.1 | 62.5 | 9.4 | 0 | 0 |

was done; in others, very little, suggesting that finished tools were brought into the cave from elsewhere. Levels with relatively little knapping debris usually have many more pieces of primary than secondary debris, whereas levels with much debris in general tend to be heavily dominated by secondary débitage (Straus and Clark 1978a, b).

Systematic regularities were also observed in the analysis of the weights of 28 lithic raw material types. Level 1 (Aurignacian?) is dominated by one kind of dark grey quartzite (type I) whereas Solutrean levels 2–5 contain a variety of flint and quartzite types no one of which is dominant, suggesting a wide-ranging procurement strategy. Levels 6–17 are again dominated (> 50%) by type I quartzite, implying selectivity in procurement. Magdalenian levels 18–24 have fairly large proportions of white type B flint, smaller amounts of a variety of other flints (especially types Q (yellow), A (red)) and about 30% type I quartzite. Azilian

and Asturian levels 26–29 have about 15% type A flint and about 50% type I quartzite, with traces of other types. Except for levels 2–5 (the probable remains of functionally specialized Solutrean hunting camps), the shifts in raw material procurement generally correspond to breaks between culture/stratigraphic units, possibly related to changes in the settlement/subsistence systems within which lithic procurement strategies may have been 'embedded' (Binford 1979a). That the Azilian and Asturian levels should have similar procurement patterns lends support to the hypothesis that these two kinds of assemblage might represent distinct yet partially contemporary activity/disposal facies.

When raw material is considered in relation to artefact types, it is evident that heavy-duty tools (choppers, denticulates, notches, sidescrapers) tend to be made of quartzite (ratio by weight 1.6 : 1.0) whereas flints were selected for the manufacture of smaller items (6.9 : 1.0). Thus,

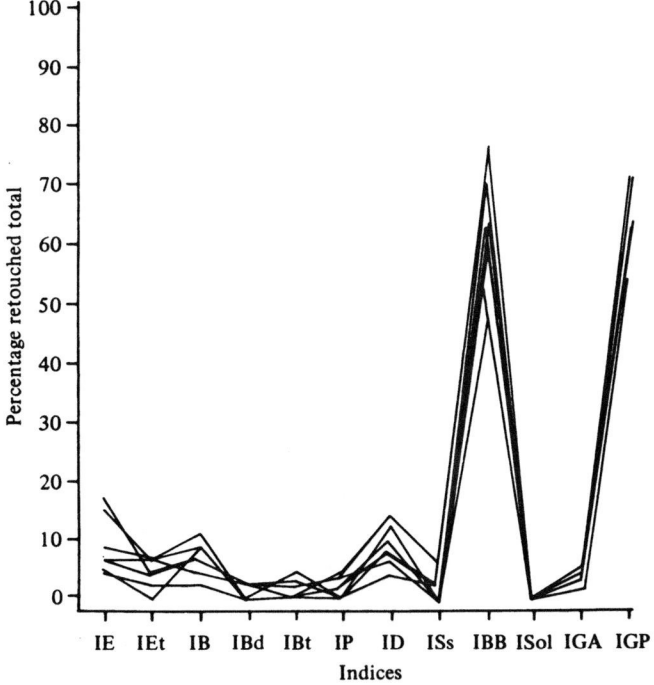

Fig. 12.2. La Riera: plot of major tool group indices for backed bladelet dominated levels (17–20, 24, 27, 28). Key: IE = endscrapers, IEt = thick endscrapers, IB = burins, IBd = dihedral burins, IBt = truncation burins, IP = perforators, ID = denticulates/notches, ISs = sidescrapers, IBB = backed bladelets, ISol = Solutrean index, IGA = Aurignacian index, IGP = Perigordian index (type definitions conform to those of de Sonneville-Bordes and Perrot).

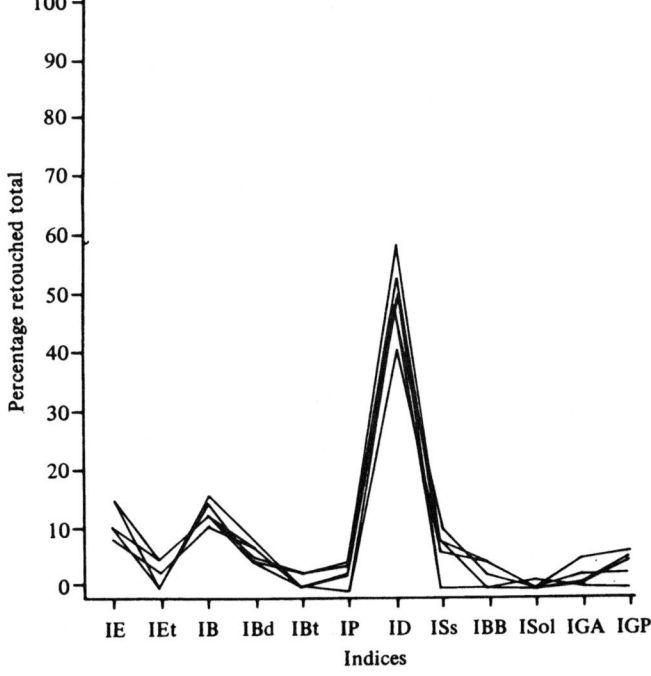

Fig. 12.3. La Riera: plot of major tool group indices for denticulate/notch dominated levels (9, 11–14). Groups as in fig. 12.2.

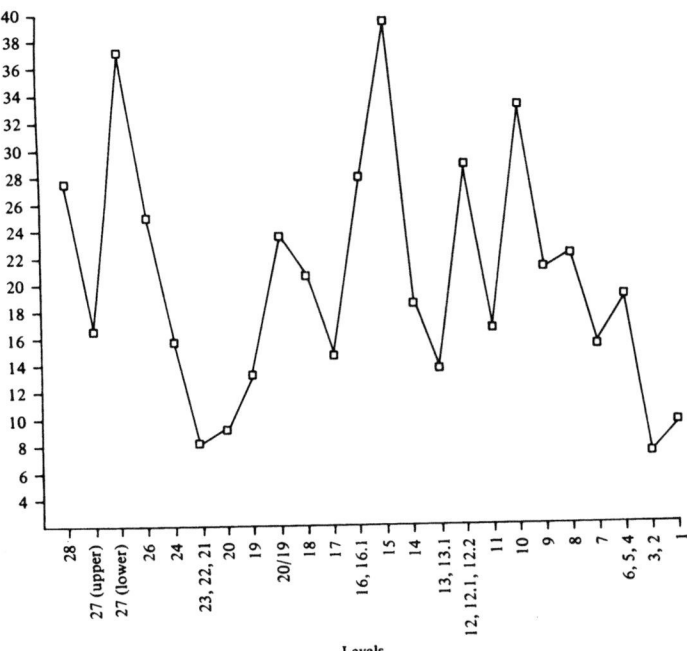

Fig. 12.4. La Riera: plot of ratios of débitage + cores to retouched pieces by levels.

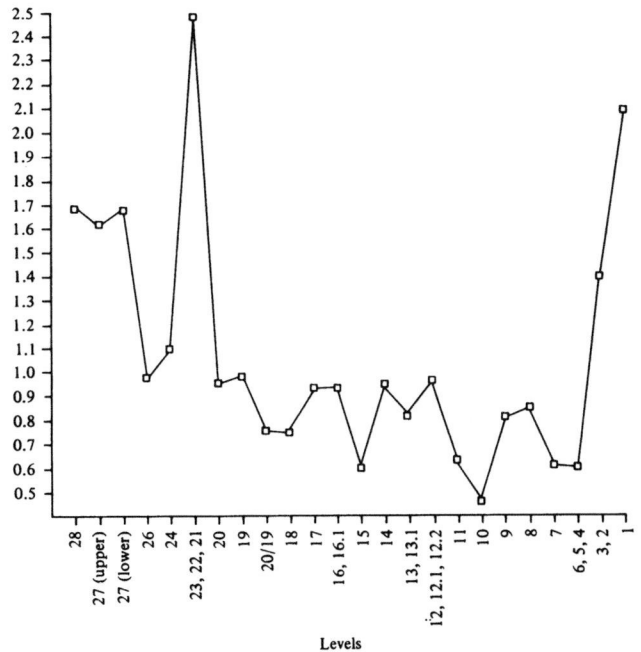

Fig. 12.5. La Riera: plot of ratios of primary débitage to secondary débitage by levels.

while there is a correspondence between notch/denticulate dominated levels and a high incidence of quartzite (and an implied functional distinction between these levels and those dominated by smaller flint tools), whether quartzite was selected for the production of heavy-duty tools or whether it was simply the most commonly prevalent raw material is a moot point. However, the La Riera flints occur only as

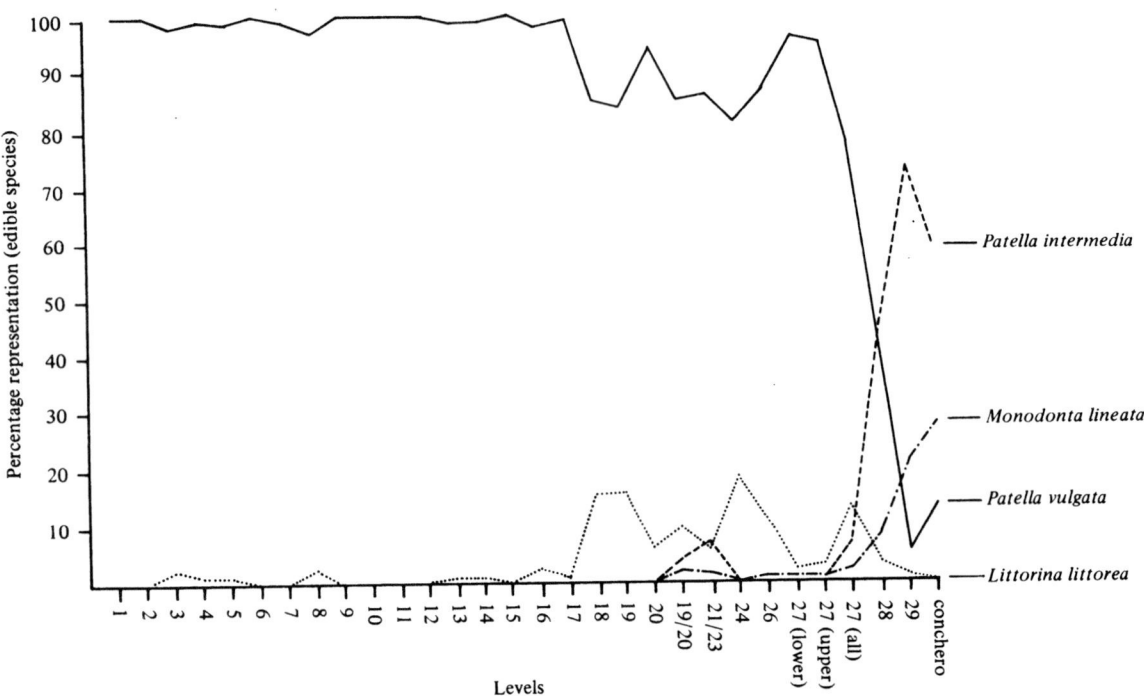

Fig. 12.6. La Riera: plot of relative frequency of four edible species of shellfish.

small nodules and pebbles, perhaps restricting the size and number of artefacts made from this raw material (cf. Straus 1980b).

*The fauna*

In contrast with patterns of variability in the procurement of lithic raw material, the rich marine and terrestrial faunas of La Riera defy any simplistic correlation with changes in climate or changes in culture/stratigraphic unit affiliation.

Over 19 000 relatively intact molluscs representing 21 species were collected, weighed and identified (by J.A. Ortea). Edible molluscs make up 97.5% of the total, while 'ornamentals' and other types represent only 2.5%. Overall 92% of the edible total are limpets (*Patella* spp.); 5.6% are periwinkles (*Littorina littorea*) and 2.4% are topshells (*Monodonta lineata*). The samples examined indicate exploitation of two different gathering zones: (1) rocky, moderately wave-beaten littoral, defined by the presence of *P. intermedia*, *M. lineata* and sea urchins (*Paracentrotus lividus*); (2) sheltered locales (probably the rocky shores of estuaries), defined by the presence of *P. vulgata* and *L. littorea*. The absence of limpet (and other) species typical of high-energy shorelines suggests that systematic exploitation of shellfoods did not extend to heavily wave-beaten open coastal niches.

During the earlier occupations (levels 1–20), gathering took place only in sheltered zones, probably estuaries, where large specimens of *P. vulgata* and *L. littorea* were collected. In and above level 20, *P. intermedia* occurs in the samples.

Its presence in increasing frequency in the upper part of the site sequence (levels 20–30) indicates that gathering was extended to the open, moderately wave-beaten shore, possibly in response to an increase in population density which required the acquisition of a broader range of food resources. Topshells (*M. lineata*) and sea urchins (*Paracentrotus lividus*) appear first in level 19/20, and mussels (*Mytilus edulis*) are added in level 24. These species, along with *P. intermedia* and crabs (*Carcinus* sp.), comprise a distinctive faunal assemblage which is best represented in the Asturian conchero (level 29)(fig. 12.6).

Expansion in the number and diversity of zones exploited is accompanied by a significant decline in the size of the limpets collected, and by an increase in the relative importance of shellfoods (as indicated by shell: bone weight ratios) through time (figs. 12.7, 12.8). While size is more or less constant in levels 1–19, the average limpet diameter declines steadily after level 20 as the larger estuarine *P. vulgata* gets smaller (probably because of systematic over-exploitation) and the smaller coastal *P. intermedia* is collected with increasing frequency. (Ortea (pers. comm.) notes that *P. vulgata* reaches very large dimensions today in polluted harbours where they are not collected intensively.) The cold-loving periwinkle *L. littorea* sheds some light on ambient sea-water temperature for it is found throughout the sequence except in levels 9–15 (which probably correspond to the warm, wet Laugerie Interstadial) and level 29 (the Preboreal/Boreal boundary Asturian conchero). The appearance of significant numbers of thermophile mussels and topshells in level 29 confirms exploitation of warming Postglacial seas.

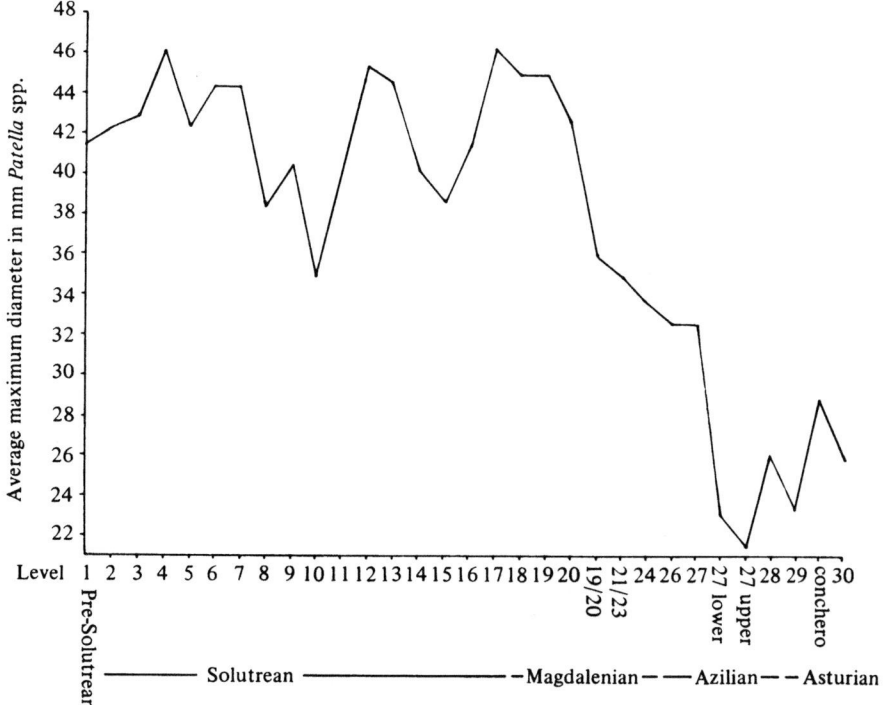

Fig. 12.7. La Riera: plot of maximum limpet size through time.

Winter collection of shellfish at La Riera is documented by oxygen isotope analyses of limpet and gastropod cross-sections in samples from levels 24, 29 and the Asturian conchero suspended from the cave roof (M. Deith, pers. comm.; Bailey *et al.* 1982).

Remains of fish (mostly vertebrae) were recovered from levels 4–28 and were identified by M.M. de la Hoz. While never numerous (due to factors of preservation, a lack of emphasis on fishing, or both), fish bones increase dramatically in numbers above level 26, perhaps marking increased emphasis on the procurement of marine resources beginning some time in the Azilian. Anadromous salmonid species (*Salmo salar, S. trutta trutta, S. trutta fario*) are present throughout the sequence, an indication of fishing in estuarine and/or riverine waters. The specimens of salmon (*S. salar*) are all large-sized adults, suggesting that this species was taken in the winter and spring extrapolating from present-day migration patterns. Remains of marine species (Sparidae) first appear in level 24, marking the initiation of open coastal fishing and confirming malacological indicators of an expansion in the exploitation of aquatic resources during the late Magdalenian. Sole (*Solea* sp.) appears in the conchero.

While changes in the nature and diversity of aquatic faunas perhaps serve best to document increasing stress on the inhabitants of La Riera over time, the enormous ungulate fauna identified by J. Altuna provides a more direct indication of the nature of the subsistence base. The 1976/9 excavations provided 31 480 identifiable bones of vertebrates (excluding fish); of these, 31 336 (99.5%) were mammals, and 31 125 of

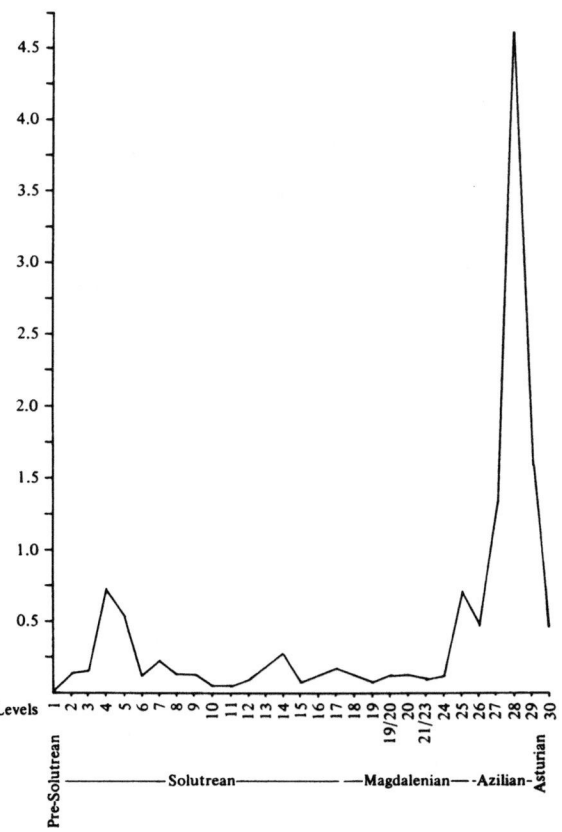

Fig. 12.8. La Riera: plot of ratio of shell to bone weight through time.

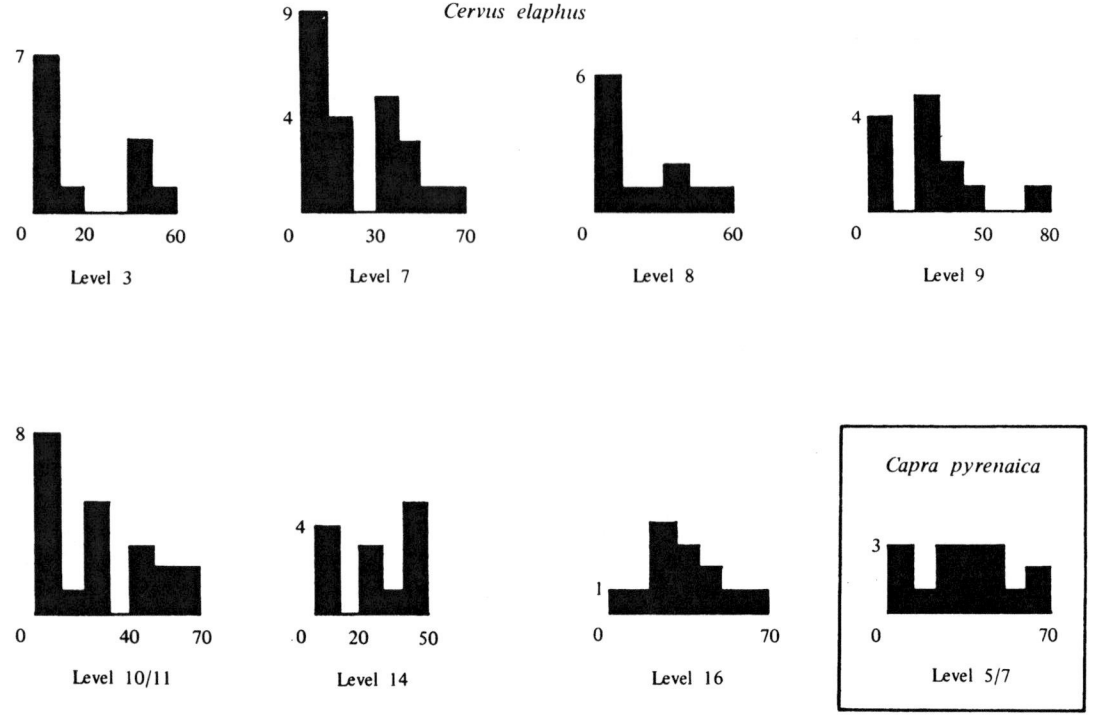

Fig. 12.9. La Riera: age structures from largest collections cervid and caprid dentitions based on crown height measurements of $dP_4$ and $M_3$ (1976–1979). The vertical axis gives the number of individuals; the horizontal axis the percent of lifespan by 10% increments.

the mammals (99.3%) were ungulates — clearly the principal source of animal protein throughout the sequence. Identifiable remains were weighed by species, and the minimum number of individuals (MNI) was calculated by the method of Brain (1976) in order to give a clearer indication of the amount of meat provided than could be obtained from a simple bone count. It was also possible to determine the season of death of juvenile and sub-adult red deer and ibex based on the eruption cycles of deciduous and permanent dentitions.

The horse (*Equus caballus*) dominates in levels 1–3, although bovines (*Bos* or *Bison*) equal it both in weight and in MNI count in level 1. While present throughout, these large ungulates have minimal importance in the rest of the sequence. However, the major representation of these species in level 1 is significant in that this Upper Palaeolithic stratum appears to predate the Solutrean, when faunas overwhelmingly dominated by red deer first appear in Cantabria (Straus 1977a). Pre-Solutrean faunas are generally composed of only small numbers of red deer, with the much larger, meatier horses and bovines usually represented by a few individuals per level.

Ibex (*Capra pyrenaica*) dominate in levels 4–6 in MNI and in numbers of remains, although red deer (*Cervus elaphus*) are also common (and in fact outweigh ibex in levels 5, 6). In all of the remaining strata (7–30), red deer is the dominant species by all three indices; it clearly provided the bulk of the

animal protein throughout the sequence despite major climatic perturbations which evidently had little direct effect on its availability in the vicinity of the cave. The presence of ibex in most levels can be explained by the proximity of nearby alpine niches in the rocky escarpment of the Sierra de Cuera, only 1.5 km to the south of the cave.

Hunting of cervids seems to have concentrated on herds composed mainly of hinds and fawns, as indicated by the large numbers of juvenile deer in the sample (144 out of 360 individuals)(cf. also Altuna (1976) regarding a similar pattern at Tito Bustillo where the prominence of hinds is positively indicated by metrical studies). Deer hunting may — as argued below — have involved mass drives or surrounds, and took place the year round, although there are indications of summer and summer/autumn exploitation of deer (and ibex) during some of the occupations forming levels 15–27. The incidence of juveniles goes up sharply in levels 24–28, perhaps indicating a possible shift in hunting strategies. Of the 13 ibex whose age at death could be determined, 11 were killed shortly after birth (around May), since their milk dentition had not yet begun to wear. Perhaps the hunting strategy consisted of surprising females while separated from the herd to give birth. On the scant evidence available, ibex hunting would appear to have been mainly a spring and summer activity.

Following the methodology (and assumptions) of

Klein (1978, 1979; Klein *et al.* 1981, this volume) dP$_4$ and M$_3$ dental crown heights of red deer and ibex from all the principal La Riera levels were measured and analysed by Straus in order to characterize the age profiles of the game killed by prehistoric hunters. As with the new Magdalenian collections of red deer from El Juyo (Klein *et al.* 1981)(and the old Solutrean and Magdalenian Obermaier collections from Altamira, also in Santander (Allwarden, pers. comm.)), the La Riera Solutrean and Magdalenian collections indicate the killing not only of substantial numbers of young individuals, but also of prime-age adults (fig. 12.9). There are few if any truly old individuals represented by the M$_3$ specimens recovered from La Riera. Klein *et al.* (1981, this volume) argue that such age profiles of kills essentially replicate the profile of a stable live population, suggesting that they represent 'catastrophic mortality', affecting not just the weakest age grades of a natural population, as would be the case with 'attritional mortality' (such as by 'selective' wolf predation on the very young, very old and infirm). In essence, it is the presence of substantial numbers of prime-age adults which points to some non-selective, mass form of human predation. As red deer (particularly hinds with their young) are gregarious, one explanation for the 'catastrophic' nature of the age profiles of the archaeological death assemblages could be the prehistoric use of drives ('battues') or surrounds to procure substantial numbers of deer from herds at one time. Such techniques (perhaps specifically involving the driving of groups of animals upslope towards hidden hunters, by taking advantage of their natural escape pattern) may also have been used to procure large numbers of ibex as well (particularly in the lower La Riera Solutrean levels, where there are many prime age adults as well as several juveniles represented).

Additional support for the proposition of sizeable Solutrean and Magdalenian red deer (and ibex) slaughters can be derived from the 'maximal' MNI calculated by Altuna. Despite the relatively small area excavated at La Riera (at most 15–20% of the inhabitable cave entrance) and the thinness of the archaeological levels, the MNI figures for red deer in particular are often quite high. Fifteen to twenty individuals are not uncommon even for fine-level subdivisions. Taking into account the restricted size of the remnant surface area available for excavation, the numbers of individual red deer (and, in some cases, ibex) must have originally been much larger, even if some of our level subdivisions are in reality palimpsests formed by a few successive human occupations of the cave. Similarly high numbers of red deer characterize the Magdalenian levels from the recently excavated sites of Tito Bustillo (Altuna 1976) and El Juyo (Klein *et al.* 1981, this volume). The old Cantabrian faunal collections studied by Freeman (1973a) and Straus (1977a) showed the initial presence of large numbers of red deer (and ibex) with the Solutrean and/or Early Magdalenian. The data from Tito Bustillo, El Juyo, Rascaño, La Riera and other modern excavations in the region support the evidence for systematic,

massive kills of red deer and ibex beginning as early as 20 000 b.p.

Red deer are, however, almost always present in archaeological deposits antedating the Solutrean, but in much smaller numbers. An important question is whether the appearance of large numbers of *Cervus* and *Capra* in levels dating to the last 10 000 years of the Würm was due simply to some environmental change favouring an increase in regional deer and ibex population size, or to a change in human subsistence practices and animal procurement strategies. A similar kind of question has been answered by convincing recourse to environmental arguments with regard to fluctuations between clear-cut browsers and grazers (mainly bovids of several genera) from the end of the Middle Pleistocene in South Africa's Cape Province (Klein 1980b), but can such an explanation also work for the increase in archaeological representations of red deer in Cantabrian Spain around 20 000 b.p.?

It has long been held that red deer is primarily a woodland species, and it has been used by Cantabrian prehistorians as an indicator of environmental change (i.e. increases in red deer = increases in trees = increases in temperature and humidity, and vice versa)(e.g. Freeman 1973b). Recent palynological analyses of Würm sediments from a number of sites by Leroi-Gourhan (1971a, b; n.d.) and Boyer-Klein (1976, 1980)(sometimes supported by sedimentological analyses) indicate the existence of major climatic oscillations, marked by significant fluctuations in arboreal pollen and changes in the composition of the non-arboreal pollen fraction. What is relevant here is the fact that red deer generally dominate the faunal assemblages at coastal-plain sites like El Juyo, La Riera and Tito Bustillo (whereas ibex dominate mountain sites like Rascaño) regardless of the dominant vegetation type (or climate) for the period from about 20 000–10 000 b.p. and into the Preboreal, Boreal and Atlantic phases of the Holocene. Red deer at La Riera, for example, are generally numerous and dominant in all strata above level 6 under climatic conditions which ranged from cold/dry to temperate/humid (or even warm/wet) (cf. table 12.1) and with landscapes at times apparently nearly devoid of trees, at others characterized by parklands with scattered thickets or woods, and at still others (notably the Early Holocene) dominated by deciduous forest. During virtually treeless stadial episodes, the non-arboreal vegetation was alternately dominated by heaths, grasses or composites. That *Cervus* should be so well represented under such a variety of conditions in the Upper Pleistocene should not be surprising, as a recent review of the North American and European literature on the habitat and diet of *Cervus elaphus/canadensis* (Straus 1981a) indicates extreme catholicity on the part of this species. Widely distributed throughout the northern temperate zone of the eastern and western hemisphere, *Cervus* tends in fact to be a *grazer*, although it certainly can and does make use of browse, particularly when snow covers the grasses, sedges and other flowering plants which constitute its more

Table 12.4. *Incidence of Cantabrian sites adjusted for time*

| Culture/stratigraphic unit | Number of sites | Approximate temporal duration | Number of sites per millennium |
|---|---|---|---|
| Acheulean | 3 | 100 000 | 0.03 |
| Mousterian | 13 | 65 000 | 0.20 |
| Aurignacian/Perigordian | 18 | 15 000 | 1.20 |
| Solutrean | 33 | 3000 | 11.00 |
| Lower/Middle Magdalenian | 35 | 3000 | 11.67 |
| Upper Magdalenian | 36 | 3000 | 12.00 |
| Azilian | 33 | 3000 | 11.00 |
| Asturian | 28 | 2000 | 14.00 |

usual diet. Red deer/elk also take refuge in woods and thickets when available in winter for shelter from storms, as well as for browse. They are by no means, however, strictly woodland creatures as several modern case studies clearly show (e.g. the deer of the Scottish Highland heaths described by Darling (1963)).

With such an incredibly diverse set of dietary and habitat ranges, it is not surprising that red deer should have thrived in a wide variety of sequential Cantabrian environments. The climate and vegetation of northern Spain fluctuated in much the same way throughout the earlier Würm as they did in the later Würm and Early Holocene, based on palynological and sedimentological analyses of the early Upper Palaeolithic and Mousterian deposits at Cueva Morín (Leroi-Gourhan 1971a; Butzer 1971b, 1973). The constituent species of both Early and Late Würm Cantabrian faunas are essentially the same (Altuna 1972). There would seem, therefore, to be no *a priori* reason for a dramatic increase in Late Würm red deer (or ibex) population densities as reflected by the archaeological faunal assemblages of the Solutrean, Magdalenian and Mesolithic periods. Cantabria seems to have been a region well suited to these species, and may well have served as a major refuge for *Cervus* during the last glacial (Altuna 1972, 1979). It is worth stressing that red deer, bovines and horses are present in Mousterian and early upper Palaeolithic faunal assemblages, as well as in those of the late Upper Palaeolithic. The significant difference lies in the absolute and relative increase in the numbers of *Cervus* individuals represented archaeologically. This increase cannot be explained by invoking environmental change, since conditions before and after 20 000 b.p. seem to have fluctuated to similar, radical degrees, while the faunal spectrum seems to have remained essentially the same (compare chapter 13). The explanation for the increase may, therefore, lie in the adoption of the kinds of specialized mass-hunting techniques suggested above by later Upper Palaeolithic and post-Palaeolithic hunters (perhaps armed with more effective weapons such as atlatls, traps, or even bows, as suggested by the presence of gracile bone, antler and lithic shouldered points). Red deer (and ibex) were being more systematically cropped at the same time that new resources

(e.g. fish, shellfish, boar) were being added to the regular subsistence base; traditional food sources (e.g. horses, bovines) continued to be utilized when available. The most generally satisfactory explanation for these seemingly related developments is simply increased human need, easy to comprehend given Cantabria's highly constrained, limited topography and long history of human occupation. A sharp increase in regional population growth rates is suggested by the marked increase in site frequency after the end of the early Upper Palaeolithic (table 12.4).

The La Riera ungulate bones are much triturated (in fact, they are the most fragmented faunal remains of the 11 Cantabrian samples studied by Altuna to date (pers. comm.)). Some 200 000 bone splinters were recovered overall, and even compact marrowless bones (e.g. astragali) were broken in antiquity, suggesting that ungulate carcasses were maximally utilized (e.g. for grease, marrow extraction), and/or that the bone was subjected to an (unusual?) amount of predepositional trampling prior to incorporation in the archaeological context. The occasional occurrence of intact joints, however, lends support to the first suggestion, implying a degree of subsistence pressure on human populations in the region. Except for an under-representation of heads, there is little clear-cut selectivity in the anatomical parts present, suggesting that nearly whole carcasses were often transported more or less integrally to the cave from nearby kill sites. This would have been feasible, for most of the game bag consisted of small- to medium-sized ungulates. The faunal samples from basal levels 1–3 (dominated by horse and bovine bones and teeth) are too small to allow for meaningful inferences about selectivity in butchering practices, except to note that the carcasses are much more incompletely represented than is the case with red deer and ibex.

The remaining ungulates (reindeer, roe deer, chamois, boar) have only minimal economic importance at La Riera. There is an increase in roe deer (*Capreolus capreolus*) after level 20, perhaps coinciding with the terminal Pleistocene trend toward climatic amelioration. Boar (*Sus scrofa*) is found only in the upper levels (21/3, 26–28). An increase in the incidence of boar and roe deer is typical of Cantabrian sites of Pleistocene/Holocene boundary date, and may reflect an increase in wooded biotopes (roe deer) and, in the case of boar, development of a technology (and the need) for hunting these large and dangerous animals (Freeman 1973a). Reindeer (*Rangifer tarandus*), a certain indicator of cold climate, is represented in levels 21/3 and 24, and there by only seven pieces of identifiable bone. In contrast with France, reindeer were never common in Cantabria, despite evidence for periglacial conditions in both regions.

### Concluding remarks

The La Riera data are instructive in several important respects. So far as the lithic assemblages are concerned, we believe that considerably more behaviourally sensitive information has been obtained by *ignoring* classic culture/

stratigraphic subdivisions than by using them as a basis for analysis. It has been possible to define two basic kinds of assemblage which alternate throughout much of the cave's long history of use and occupation: (1) those dominated by notches and denticulates, with a relatively high incidence of sidescrapers (e.g. levels 9, 11–14), and (2) those dominated by backed bladelets with variable numbers of burins (e.g. levels 17–20, 24, 27, 28). As indicated earlier, these two major assemblage types may have some currency elsewhere in Cantabria, and clearly vary independently of culture/stratigraphic unit affiliation. Insofar as the form of the defining retouched tool groups is distinctive, a functional interpretation is implied with backed bladelet rich assemblages perhaps representing a broad spectrum of activities related to hunting contexts in which the microliths functioned as disposable weapon points and edges, the notch/denticulated dominated assemblages perhaps related to processing activities in general, including the processing of vegetal matter for which we have no direct archaeological evidence. The large débitage fractions (always over 95%) also indicate possible behavioural differences. Certain levels contained relatively much evidence for secondary retouching, whereas others had very little, suggesting that, during the latter episodes, tool manufacture and/or repair was of minimal importance, and that tools made elsewhere were being used and/or discarded in the cave. That patterns of variability in the débitage and retouched tool components do not coincide is not surprising, as both classes of artefacts monitor distinct (and not necessarily directly related) sets of activities. In neither case could correlations with episodes of climatic change be established, which strongly suggests that whatever behavioural factors are monitored by the various axes of assemblage variability which we have described, they are in no sense directly determined by or responsive to shifts in the prevailing regional macroclimate. With some notable exceptions, changes in the relative abundance of lithic raw material types were shown to correspond to breaks between culture/stratigraphic units — a correlation which could perhaps be related to changes in the overall settlement/subsistence systems of which lithic procurement strategies were a part. It is interesting to note that no truly exotic raw materials occur at La Riera, so that there is at present no evidence for intra-regional exchange (Esbert *et al.* n.d.), although the ibex hunters of level 4–6 might have been 'based' elsewhere, and used La Riera only as a temporary camp-site.

While most studies of faunal material emphasize their value for climatic interpretations and for the establishment of relative chronologies, we controlled for both these factors independently (by using sediment and pollen data to monitor climate, and radiocarbon dates to control for time). This allowed us to examine other possible causes for the complex ecological information encoded in the abundant La Riera malacological and ungulate faunas. Analysis of the ecological requirements of four economically important shellfish species allowed for the identification of two exploitation zones

(estuaries, moderately open coast) which were used with different degrees of intensity by the occupants of the cave through time. The exploitation of species typical of moderately wave-beaten coastal habitats only becomes evident fairly late in the sequence, and is regarded as an extension of earlier estuarine collecting into zones where edible species were smaller, less densely concentrated and more perilous to acquire. As no climatic factors were adduced to account for this change, and as measurements of limpet diameters indicated over-exploitation of estuarine species through time, we suggest that the inhabitants of the area were moved to increase the diversity of their subsistence base (even to the extent of collecting 'less desirable', lower-yield, higher-risk foods), by an increasingly dense local population which was fast outstripping its 'traditional' resources. The hypothesis of demographic stress is supported by increases in gross site numbers per culture/stratigraphic unit over time (cf. Straus 1977a: 71, 72; Clark, this volume), and by other categories of faunal evidence which themselves cannot be explained by recourse to climatic change arguments. (1) While anadromous salmonids are taken throughout the sequence, marine fish show up for the first time late in the sequence, as do sea urchins and birds (all in level 24) and, later, crabs; (2) in level 25 and above, there is a marked increase in the ratio of shell to bone, indicating relatively more intensive use of shell foods; (3) after level 20 there is an increase in the killing of newborn deer, implying eventual disequilibrium in and the beginnings of possible over-exploitation of cervid populations; and (4) evidence of increasingly maximal utilization of ungulates in general, with the addition of boar and roe deer as these species became more prevalent in the environment.

### Postscript

We believe that an understanding of the dynamics of change in extinct sociocultural systems must ultimately be sought in terms of human behaviour (Jochim 1979), that sociocultural systems represent ordered, functionally differentiated and integrated adjustments to their natural and cultural environments, and that our approach contains within it reasonable and defensible monitors of the behavioural variables which we wish to examine. While we believe, in the absence of evidence to the contrary, that causal priority must for the present be accorded to increasing stress over time on the resources available to the prehistoric Cantabrians (Binford 1968), and that a general tendency on the part of human populations to increase might ultimately be responsible for that stress (Dumond 1972b; Cohen 1977), it is important to recognize that the orientation of a piece of research determines not only how it is organized, what variables are considered relevant to monitor in the 'archaeological context', what form (if any) hypothetical relationships amongst variables might take, but also, and most important, the *adequacy* of any proposed explanations (Clark 1981b). While recognizing that many of our hypotheses remain to be confirmed (or disconfirmed) with data from future excavations, we hope at least to have indicated some of the potential benefits which might be derived from interdisciplinary palaeoecological research efforts like the one presented here. It is our belief that an understanding of Late Pleistocene/Early Holocene hunter-gatherer adaptations in Cantabria and in south-west Europe in general will best be achieved through pursuit of an 'ecological approach to prehistory' which emphasizes a diachronic perspective, the analytical autonomy of diverse classes of archaeological and natural science data, and which avoids the circular reasoning characteristic of many current studies of prehistoric time—space systematics.

*Acknowledgements*

We wish to acknowledge the continuing support of the National Science Foundation (grant no. BNS76-08382), our respective institutions (Arizona State University, University of New Mexico), the Subdirección General de Excavaciones Arqueológicas of the Spanish Ministry of Culture, and our French, Spanish, English and American colleagues and natural science collaborators. The contributions of J. Altuna (Palaeontology Laboratory, Museo de San Telmo, San Sebastián), J.A. Ortea and M. Menéndez de la Hoz (Department of Zoology, University of Oviedo), H. Laville (Quaternary Institute, University of Bordeaux) and A. Leroi-Gourhan (Palynology Laboratory, Musée de l'Homme, Paris) were of exceptional importance; without the collaboration of these individuals, this chapter could never have been written.

## Chapter 13

### Economic change in Late Pleistocene Cantabria
Geoff Bailey

The problem of identifying the relationship between changes of natural environment and long-term subsistence trends is here examined. Special attention is directed to the analysis of changing spatial relationships between site location and major topographic variables such as change in sea levels and snowlines. The effect of sea-level change on a narrow coastal plain is emphasized. It is suggested that subsistence trends may have been affected in a complex manner, either directly or indirectly, by environmental changes, and that disentangling the relative influence of environmental and cultural variables on subsistence trends is further complicated by changes in patterns of refuse disposal.

### Introduction

The interest of the Cantabrian data is that they present evidence for subsistence changes which are apparently independent of any environmental changes that might explain their occurrence (Freeman 1973a; Straus 1977a; Straus *et al.* 1980), in so far as environmental change has been measured by pollen, sediments or other palaeoenvironmental indicators (Leroi-Gourhan 1971b; Boyer-Klein 1980; Butzer 1981). The most frequently championed hypothesis is a demographic one, invoking human population increase and resulting pressure on the pre-existing resource base as the primary stimulus to change. This hypothesis has been expounded both in global terms (Cohen 1977) and in relation to the Cantabrian data (Bailey 1982; chapters 12 and 14, this volume). However, despite the attractions of this population-pressure hypothesis, one has to admit that it is not without difficulties. The main difficulties are, first, that archaeological evidence of population increase, for example an increase in the number of settlement sites, is at best evidence that population increased, and gives no indication as to whether the population increase was the cause or the effect of any associated economic changes. Secondly, since the hypothesis is arrived at as much by elimination of environmental factors as by positive corroboration from other sources, the question is raised as to how effectively environmental change has been eliminated as a possible cause of subsistence change. Thirdly, if population increase is seen as the stimulus to change, this raises the further question as to what caused the population increase.

I therefore propose to approach the problem from an alternative perspective, namely the point of view of the null hypothesis which specifies that subsistence changes are the result of environmental changes unless proved otherwise. In adopting this view it is important to emphasize that environmental change may have both direct and indirect effects on subsistence economy. The direct effects will be those which involve environmentally induced changes in the type or relative proportions of the available food species. Indirect effects stem from changes in more subtle and elusive properties of the environment such as the productivity (biomass per unit area per unit time) of the available resources, or their accessibility. For example, one might view the environmental changes induced by Late Pleistocene fluctuations of the continental ice sheets as a series of alternations between 'better' conditions (i.e. with more abundant or easily available resources) and 'worse' conditions (when the same resources were less abundant or less easily available). One might further envisage an expansion of human population during the 'better' periods, followed by a situation of increased population pressure with the change to 'worse' conditions, when population would be forced to contract by emigration or adjustment of birth and death rates, or to intensify exploitation of the environment, for example by turning to previously neglected food resources (see chapter 19). In the latter case we might say that environmental change was the ultimate cause of subsistence changes, even though population pressure was the proximate cause. These distinctions between direct and indirect environmental effects and between ultimate and proximate levels of causation are crucial to an understanding of the argument that follows, even though they pose very considerable complexities of analysis and interpretation.

This emphasis on environmental factors may seem an extreme position, but I have adopted it quite specifically to counteract two tendencies in interpretation. The first is rooted in the fear that over-emphasis on environment will raise the charge of environmental determinism, with the result that environmental factors may be treated rather superficially as referring to a vague and homogeneous entity which can be adequately summarized by one or two general indicators (such as mean annual temperature of the percentage of tree cover). With such an approach it is not difficult to find evidence that the prehistoric environment could have remained constant during a period of subsistence change, or vice versa. The reality is likely to be far more complex, since most environments are a composite of many factors, not all of which will necessarily be closely correlated or changing at the same rate, and some of which will have had a greater impact on human subsistence than others. The view that environmental explanations are too 'simple' in the context of human behaviour and should be eschewed in favour of more 'exciting' cultural explanations can become a serious deterrent to effective research.

The second tendency is to assume that all long-term trends in subsistence are necessarily progressive ones – towards intensification of resource exploitation, higher overall population densities, greater organizational complexity, and so on. This in its turn is part of an underlying assumption that the 'past' (as seen from our present point of view) must necessarily be seen as in some way leading up to the present, a view that may be no more than a trick of our distorted time perspective (Bailey 1981a). Thus in the context of the Late Pleistocene, the temptation is to see any evidence of economic change as tending towards the development of the agricultural and livestock economies that became widespread in the Early Holocene.

The approach adopted here, then, is a methodological one, designed to encourage the critical search for relevant environmental data, and should certainly not be taken to imply a belief that prehistoric subsistence behaviour can be wholly explained in environmental terms. It is certainly not the intention to deny that there may have been independent demographic, cultural or social trends towards the development of more powerful and productive economic systems over time. Rather the point is that we are unlikely to be able to place much confidence in such interpretations unless we have effective control over the palaeoenvironmental framework.

A general problem of interpretation is the problem of identifying the 'effective' environment – the environment perceived by the human population as being relevant to its subsistence needs. The dangers inherent in the concept of an 'objective' environment constituted independently of the people who lived in it have been widely recognized in archaeological interpretation (Childe 1958; J.G.D. Clark 1975; Ingold 1980). There is no guarantee that the available palaeoenvironmental techniques will necessarily reflect environmental changes of relevance to a given subsistence economy. These techniques may identify apparently major changes which are nevertheless of little relevance to subsistence, or leave undetected quite subtle changes of crucial impact. A further problem is that some palaeo-environmental techniques, notably the use of cave pollen and cave sediments, were originally devised, and continue to be used, primarily for chronological correlations (Laville *et al.* 1980), rather than for the reconstruction of 'effective' environments. An important task then is to identify those features of the environment that would have had an important limiting effect on the distribution of human populations and the organization of subsistence economies. Here I shall use the evidence of site locations and their relationship to the geographical distribution of key environmental constraints at different time periods, as a complement to palaeoeconomic and palaeoenvironmental data incorporated in archaeological sequences.

### The prehistoric landscape

The main characteristics of the Cantabrian environment are described in chapters 9 and 12. Two features in particular are likely to have exerted a major limiting effect on subsistence exploitation at all periods. The first is the winter climate and especially the extent of snow cover. There is no permanent snowline under present-day conditions, but in winter snowfalls render much of the terrain above about 1000 m impassable for humans and most ungulate species (Gilbert and Beckinsale 1941). This enhances the relative productivity of the coastal plain, which, with its low altitude and proximity to the ameliorating influence of the Gulf Stream, benefits from a relatively mild winter climate and very infrequent snow cover. This seasonal polarity between coast and interior has contributed to a seasonally mobile element in the traditional pastoral economy (de Terán 1947), although extrapolation of such seasonal patterns to the prehistoric past should be treated with caution (see chapter 7).

The climate of the last Glacial was generally colder and

drier than at present (Kopp 1965; Butzer 1981), although there were minor fluctuations of temperature and precipitation, not necessarily in phase with each other. Assuming synchroneity with the continental ice sheets, the Cantabrian glaciation would have reached its maximum extent between about 21 000 b.p. and 17 000 b.p. (Denton and Hughes 1981), although Butzer (1981) suggests an earlier date. The permanent snowline descended to a level between about 1200 m and 1500 m, and sediments and pollen indicate that at its coldest the last Glacial landscape would have been predominantly open steppe, with Periglacial phenomena such as cryoturbation down to near sea level (Butzer 1981). Minor oscillations are indicated by variations in sediments and the proportion of tree pollen in cave sequences. These have been equated with minor interstadial events in French deposits (Boyer-Klein 1980; Laville *et al.* 1980; chapter 12, above), although climatic interpretation in some cases is controversial (see below). The lower limit for terrain impassable under winter snow cover would presumably have been considerably lower than at the present day, although it is difficult to estimate because of a number of factors. These include uncertainties about the proportion of snowfall to total precipitation and the effects of varying precipitation on snow cover. The Gulf Stream also probably shifted away from the Cantabrian coastline during the glacial maximum (CLIMAP 1976). Nevertheless, the proximity of the ocean would have continued to have had some ameliorating effect on the immediate coast relative to winter temperatures further inland, and this is likely to have maintained a degree of seasonal polarity between coast and hinterland, with the coastal plain representing a relatively favourable winter zone.

A second limiting factor is the generally rugged topography, with mountains rising to maximum heights of 2700 m above sea level only 25 km from the sea shore. This reinforces the effect of climatic differences over short distances and confines the coastal plain to a relatively narrow strip. If the 200 m contour is taken as a rough guide to the inner margin of the coastal plain, it will be apparent that the latter varies in width from less than 5 km in eastern Asturias to a maximum of about 20 km in central Santander (fig. 13.1). The topography has a further limiting effect in constraining the routes of access between the coast and the interior. It should, however, be noted that the effects of topography are not wholly negative. The sharp altitudinal gradient produces a range of resources within a relatively small compass, especially in eastern Asturias, while the barriers imposed by steep terrain could have been used to advantage by human populations in the prediction and control of animal movements.

*Sea-level variation*
A major consequence of the glacial climate, especially important in this region because of its impact on the width of coastal plain, would have been glacio-eustatic variation in sea level. This can be estimated from submerged shoreline features (Emery and Milliman 1970); emerged coral reefs (Bloom

*et al.* 1974; Chappell and Veeh 1978); 0–18 abundance ratios in deep sea sediments (Shackleton 1977); and maximum ice volumes (Denton and Hughes 1981). 0–18 ratios give a continuous record and the most detailed curve of relative sea-level variation, although low average sedimentation rates may result in poor discrimination of short-lived fluctuations on a time-scale of about 1000 years or less. The 0–18 record is also thought to give good estimates of the actual depth of sea-level drop implied by the troughs in the curve of isotopic variation, but a poor estimate of the actual height of sea-level rise implied by the intermediate peaks. Shoreline features are subject to displacement by tectonic or isostatic movements. The New Guinea coral reefs are thought to provide reliable estimates of high sea-level stands, although the curve of relative variation is a simplified one, being based essentially on the connection of relatively few dated points by straight lines. Ice volume estimates provide a useful check on the date and extent of the maximum regression but few other reference points. Figure 13.2 shows curves of sea-level variation according to 0–18 and coral-reef data. The period of most relevance to this chapter is from about 40 000 b.p. to 5000 b.p., and several points within this time-span can be fixed with some confidence. Emerged reefs give good evidence of two periods of relatively high sea level (although well below the present level) of about – 40 m at about 40 000 b.p. and 28 000 b.p., with a brief intervening regression. This compares closely with the Hengelo and Denekamp interstadials defined in European pollen cores (Woillard 1979) and is also consistent with the 0–18 record. After 28 000 b.p. sea level dropped to a very low level. Both the isotope record and the measurement and dating of maximum ice volumes indicate that the sea-level drop was about 150 m below the present level, that this low sea-level stand lasted with little variation for at least 4000 years between about 21 000 b.p. and 17 000 b.p., and that this was lower than any other regression during the last glacial period (Shackleton 1977; Hughes *et al.* 1981). Sea level probably remained low until about 14 000 b.p., and then rose steadily to reach approximately the present level at about 6000 b.p.

Additional interstadial events of relatively minor duration or intensity have been recorded in pollen and sediment sequences in the caves of the Perigord and Cantabria, notably the Würm III/IV or 'Laugerie' Interstadial at about 20 000 b.p. (Laville *et al.* 1980; chapter 12 above). There is no clear record of this in the sea-level curve. This could be because the apparent climatic amelioration is peculiar to conditions in south-west Europe and represents local or regional events which had no impact on a global scale. However, the actual magnitude of climatic change that can be inferred from cave sequences is subject to considerable uncertainty. Laville *et al.* (1980: 349–50) note that sedimentological analyses 'do not inform upon palaeoclimatological conditions in terms of absolute scales of humidity and temperature, but only in terms of their relative amplitude' and that in connection with pollen it

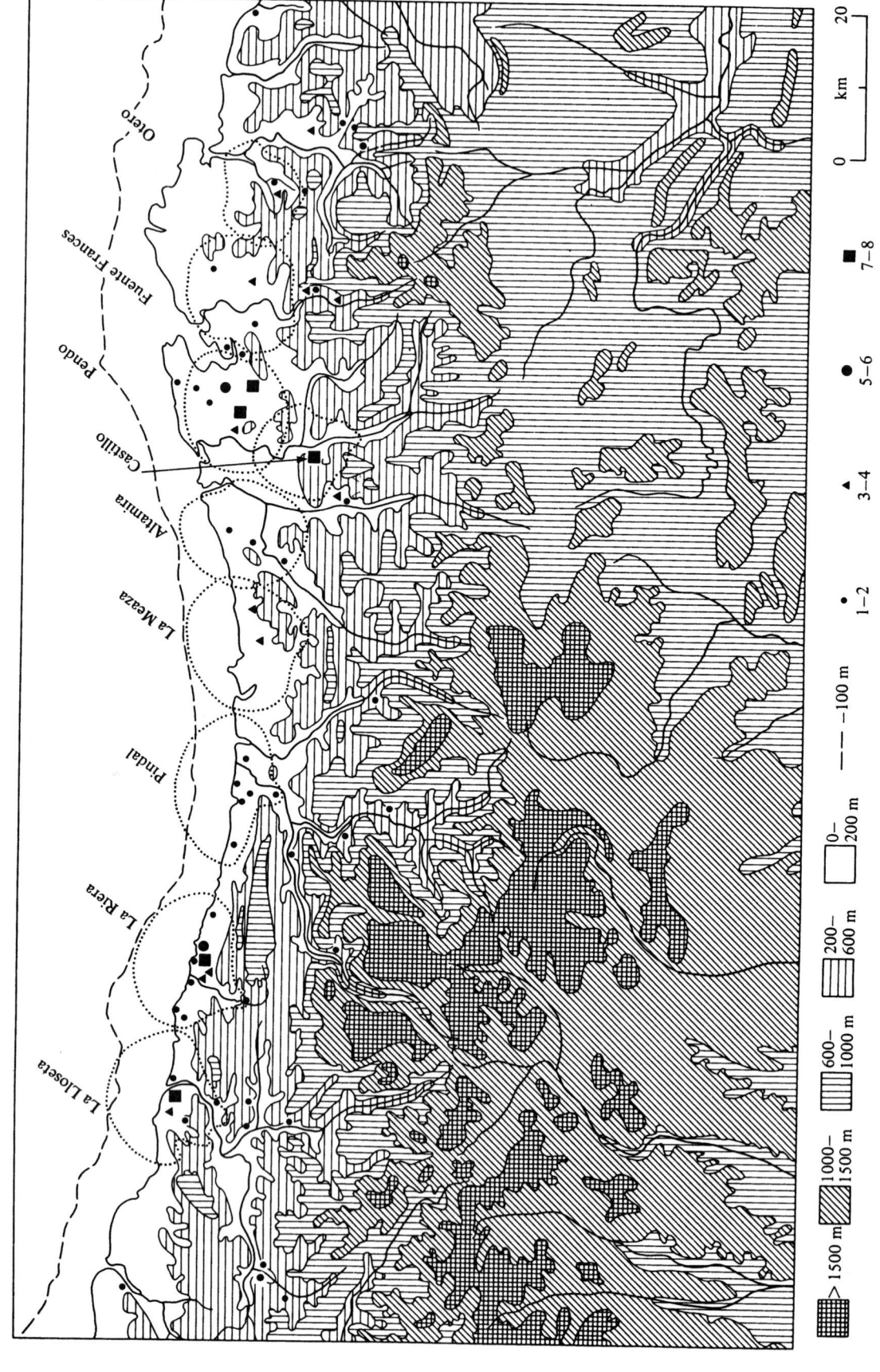

Fig. 13.1. Topography and archaeological sites of Cantabria (eastern Asturias and Santander). Sites are weighted according to the number of periods represented, and are then listed in table 13.1. from north to south and from west to east. Closely adjacent sites are represented by a single symbol on the map and are grouped separately in the table. Dotted boundaries represent 2-hour site exploitation territories of major sites.

Table 13.1. *Representation of Palaeolithic and Mesolithic occupation at sites in eastern Asturias and Santander, by archaeological period*

| Site name | Acheulean | Mousterian | Aurignacian | Gravettian | Solutrean | Lower Magdalenian | Upper Magdalenian | Magdalenian* | Azilian | Asturian | Total |
|---|---|---|---|---|---|---|---|---|---|---|---|
| *Asturias* | | | | | | | | | | | |
| Valdediós | — | — | | | — | — | — | x | — | x | 2 |
| Aviao | — | — | Unspecified Upper Palaeolithic | | | | | | — | — | — |
| Ferran | — | — | | | | | | x | — | — | 1 |
| Collareu | — | — | Unspecified Upper Palaeolithic | | | | | | — | — | — |
| Cova Rosa | — | — | | | x | x | | | — | — | 2 |
| Cierro | — | — | x | | x | x | | | — | — | 3 |
| Lloseta | — | — | | | — | x | | | — | x | 2 |
| Cuevona | — | x | | | — | x | | | — | — | 2 |
| Viesca | — | — | | | — | — | | x | — | — | 1 |
| Río de Ardines | — | — | | | — | x | | | x | — | 2 |
| Tito Bustillo | — | — | | | — | — | x | | — | — | 1 |
| San Antonio | — | — | | | — | — | | | — | x | 1 |
| Villa | — | — | Unexcavated | | | | | | — | — | — |
| Los Azules | — | — | | | — | — | | | x | — | 1 |
| Buxu | — | — | | | x | — | | | — | — | 1 |
| Collubil | — | — | | | — | x | | | x | — | 2 |
| Penicial | — | — | | | — | — | | | — | x | 1 |
| Cuevas del Mar | — | — | | | — | — | | | — | x | 1 |
| Meré | — | — | | | — | — | | x | — | x | 2 |
| San Antolín | — | — | | | — | — | | | — | x | 1 |
| Coberizas | — | — | | | x | — | | x | — | x | 3 |
| Arnero | — | x | x | | — | — | | | — | x | 3 |
| Fonfría | — | — | | | — | — | | x | — | x | 2 |
| Lledías | — | — | | | — | — | | x | — | x | 2 |
| Bricia | — | — | | | — | — | x | | — | x | 2 |
| Cueto de la Mina | — | — | | x | x | x | x | | x | x | 6 |
| La Riera | — | — | x | | x | x | x | | x | x | 6 |
| Tres Calabres | — | — | | | x | — | | | — | x | 2 |
| Balmori | — | — | | | x | x | x | | x | x | 5 |
| Bulnes | — | — | | | x | — | | x | — | — | 2 |
| Herrerías | — | — | | | — | — | | | — | x | 1 |
| Vidiago | — | — | | | — | — | | | — | x | 1 |
| Sel | — | — | | | x | — | | | — | — | 1 |
| Hermida | — | — | | | — | — | x | | x | — | 2 |
| La Franca | — | — | | | — | — | | | — | x | 1 |
| Colombres | — | — | | | — | — | | | — | x | 1 |
| La Loja | — | — | Unspecified Upper Palaeolithic | | | | | | — | — | — |
| Pindal | — | — | | | — | — | | x | — | x | 2 |
| | 0 | 2 | 3 | 1 | 10 | 9 | 6 | 9 | 7 | 21 | 68 |
| *Santander* | | | | | | | | | | | |
| La Mora | — | x | — | — | — | — | — | — | — | — | 1 |
| Unquera | — | x | — | — | — | — | — | — | — | — | 1 |
| Chufín | — | — | — | — | x | — | — | — | — | — | 1 |

Table 13.1. (Continued)

| Site name | Acheulean | Mousterian | Aurignacian | Gravettian | Solutrean | Lower Magdalenian | Upper Magdalenian | Magdalenian* | Azilian | Asturian | Total |
|---|---|---|---|---|---|---|---|---|---|---|---|
| La Meaza | – | – | – | – | – | – | – | x | x | x | 3 |
| Las Cáscaras | – | – | – | – | – | – | – | x | x | x | 3 |
| Carranceja | – | – | – | – | x | – | – | x | – | – | 2 |
| Altamira | – | – | – | – | x | x | – | – | – | – | 2 |
| Cuco | – | – | – | – | – | x | – | – | – | – | 1 |
| San Felices de Buelna | x | – | – | – | – | – | – | – | – | – | 1 |
| Hornos de la Peña | – | x | x | – | x | x | – | – | – | – | 4 |
| La Pasiega | – | x | – | – | x | x | – | – | – | – | 3 |
| Las Monedas | – | x | – | – | – | – | – | – | – | – | 1 |
| Castillo | x | x | x | x | x | x | x | – | x | – | 8 |
| Cobalejos | – | x | – | – | x | – | x | – | – | – | 3 |
| Pendo | – | x | x | x | x | – | x | – | x | x | 7 |
| Juyo | – | – | – | – | – | x | – | – | – | – | 1 |
| Peña Castillo | – | – | – | – | – | x | – | – | – | – | 1 |
| Liencres | – | – | – | – | – | – | – | – | – | x | 1 |
| Peña del Mazo | – | – | – | – | x | – | x | – | x | – | 3 |
| Morín† | – | x | x | x | x | – | x | – | x | – | 6 |
| Astillero | x | – | – | – | – | – | – | – | – | – | 1 |
| Los Moros | – | – | – | – | – | – | – | – | x | x | 2 |
| San Vitores | – | x | – | – | – | – | – | – | – | – | 1 |
| Mar | – | – | x | – | – | – | – | – | – | – | 1 |
| Fuente Frances | – | x | – | – | – | x | x | – | – | – | 3 |
| Rascaño | – | x | – | – | x | – | – | – | x | – | 3 |
| Bona | – | – | – | – | x | – | – | – | – | – | 1 |
| Salitre | – | x | x | – | x | – | – | – | x | – | 4 |
| Otero | – | – | x | – | x | – | x | – | x | – | 4 |
| Chora | – | – | – | – | – | – | x | – | – | – | 1 |
| Cobrantes | – | – | – | – | – | – | – | x | – | – | 1 |
| Valle | – | – | – | – | – | x | x | – | x | – | 3 |
| Venta de la Perra | – | Unspecified Upper Palaeolithic | | | | | | | | | – |
| Sotarriza | | Unspecified Upper Palaeolithic | | | | | | | | | – |
| La Haza | – | – | – | – | x | – | – | – | – | – | 1 |
| Mirón | – | – | x | – | x | – | – | – | – | – | 2 |
| Covalanas | | Unspecified Upper Palaeolithic | | | | | | | | | – |
| Peña del Cuco | | Unspecified Upper Palaeolithic | | | | | | | | | – |
| Total | 3 | 11 | 8 | 3 | 15 | 9 | 9 | 4 | 11 | 5 | 81 |
| | 3 | 13 | 11 | 4 | 25 | 18 | 15 | 13 | 18 | 26 | 149 |

*These are levels where the material is insufficient to allow division into Lower or Upper Magdalenian.

†Chatelperronian industries are also present at this site.

Sources: Alcalde del Rio et al. 1911; Hernández-Pacheco 1919; Vega del Sella 1923; Obermaier 1925; González Echegaray 1952; González Echegaray and Ripoll Perelló 1953; González Echegaray 1957; Hernández-Pacheco et al. 1957; Hernández-Pacheco 1959; González Echegaray et al. 1963; Jordá Cerdá 1963b; González Echegaray et al. 1966; Clark 1971b; Fernández-Tresguerres 1976; Cabrera and Bernaldo de Quirós 1977; Clark 1979b.

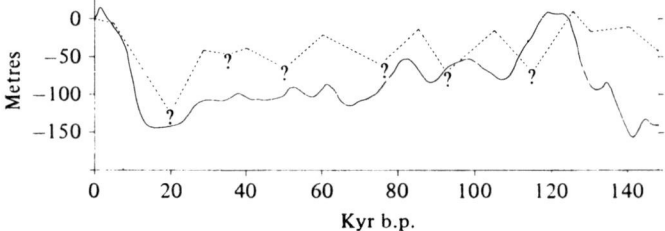

— Smoothed 0–18 curve
----- Reef data    ? Sea-level minimum uncertain

Fig. 13.2. Late Pleistocene sea-level variation. After Bloom *et al.* 1974, Shackleton *et al.* in prep.

cannot yet be determined 'precisely how much local biotopes in the vicinity of individual sites may skew the evidence for more general shifts in regional vegetation'. Writing about the Würm III/IV interstadial, they note that it is not represented in the loess sequences of northern France, and 'that this interstadial reflects convention more than climate and that, unlike its predecessors, it is characterized by neither pedogenesis nor erosion in cryoclastic deposits anywhere in France. In fact, there exist earlier phases of climatic amelioration (such as the first three mild oscillations of Würm I) which have not been given interstadial status even though they witnessed even more temperate conditions' (Laville *et al.* 1980: 316).

In plotting the probable position of the prehistoric Cantabrian shoreline at the maximum regression by reference to modern bathymetric contours, tectonic stability has been assumed. Tectonic uplift took place during the Tertiary and early Quaternary. But any minor effects that may have persisted into more recent periods are of negligible significance in estimating variations of the prehistoric shoreline during the past 50 000 years from modern bathymetric contours. Accumulation of sediment on the sea floor can also probably be discounted as a distorting factor, if the maximum sedimentation rate of 11 cm/1000 years quoted by Emery and Milliman (1970) can be taken as a guide. A more serious potential source of error is the hydro-isostatic depression of the ocean floor and continental shelves by the extra weight of sea water during high sea levels. The sea-level rise relative to the land since the maximum regression, allowing for hydro-isostatic deformation, has been estimated as 90 m (Mörner and Dreimanis 1973) and about 100 m (Hughes *et al.* 1981), although the effect could vary in different parts of the globe (Clark *et al.* 1978). The − 100 m contour is thought to provide a reasonable approximation of the maximum extension of the Cantabrian coastal plain, taking all these various factors into account. Van Andel and Shackleton (1982) have recently suggested that − 130 m may be a closer approximation.

### General features of site location

In relating site distribution to topographic features, attention is confined to sites of Palaeolithic/Mesolithic date in the province of Santander and in eastern Asturias (fig. 13.1).

The sites are weighted in terms of their relative importance as judged by the number of archaeological periods represented (table 13.1). This is obviously a crude device, given uncertainties about relative chronology, lack of comprehensive data about the rate of accumulation of cultural material at different sites, and the possible distortion involved in relying on a pattern composed almost entirely of cave and rockshelter sites. But it does give a useful general indication of preferred areas of occupation during the prehistoric period.

One point that is clearly apparent is that the major evidence of settlement is concentrated below 200 m, and especially on the coastal plain. This emphasizes the importance of the limiting factors discussed above in restricting the main centres of population to the relatively narrow coastal zone, and further enhances the likely impact of sea-level variation on the extent of this zone. As can be seen from the position of the − 100 m contour, the maximum regression would have had the effect of almost doubling the width of the coastal plain, especially in eastern Asturias.

Also shown in figure 13.1 are the 2-hour exploitation territories of some of the major coastal sites. These sites have been selected on the basis of their long sequences or evidence of abundant occupation. In some cases there are a number of sites so close together that one can refer to site clusters, all the sites within a given cluster having virtually identical site exploitation territories. In the interpretation that follows it is assumed that each site cluster represents a residential base, even though it is not usually possible to identify with confidence the specific function of individual sites within a cluster. It could be that all the sites were used simultaneously as residential bases because of the large size of the resident population. Or only one site may have been used at any one time, the others being occupied at other times on some rotational basis. Or one site may have served as the residential base, the others as short-term sites used for specific tasks. Straus (1977a) has plausibly argued that the smaller inland sites were probably used as short-term hunting camps for exploitation of ibex.

A point of interest is that the eight major site clusters on the coastal plain are distributed so as to form almost contiguous site exploitation territories. This spacing effect cannot be attributed to the availability of limestone caves. Other cave sites would have been available, for example midway between the Riera and Lloseta clusters, and between Riera and Pindal. But these contain no evidence of occupation prior to the accumulation of shell middens during the early Postglacial, when the special circumstances of intensive shell-gathering may have imposed a different set of locational constraints (see below). Nor can the spacing be attributed solely to the availability of major river valleys, since some of these have relatively little or no evidence of prehistoric occupation, while some of the major site clusters are not in river valleys at all.

While this spacing effect provides interesting corroboration of the 2-hour distance limit as a reasonable order of magnitude for site exploitation territories, it will be noted that there is also considerable overlapping in some cases, notably in the case of Pendo, Morín and Cobalejos (the territorial boundaries of the latter two are omitted from figure 13.1 for the sake of clarity). While there is a substantial measure of archaeological contemporaneity between these sites (table 13.1), no available dating technique can demonstrate true contemporaneity. It is therefore possible that these sites were used on some rotational basis. Nevertheless the 'packing' of sites in this part of the coastal zone suggests that it was a strongly preferred area with a relatively intensive exploitation of resources. In other cases occupation seems to have been relatively sparse, notably at La Meaza and Pindal.

The three areas centred on the sites of Lloseta, La Riera and Castillo, respectively, seem to have been particularly favoured areas. As I have argued in greater detail elsewhere (Bailey 1982), these locations probably owe their importance to the fact that they control the main routes of access between the coastal plain and the few areas of relatively productive and extensive hinterland resources. Thus, at least during some part of the prehistoric sequence, these sites could have formed the focal centres of major site systems linked together in an integrated exploitation of coastal and interior resources. Castillo is relatively far inland because of the greater width of the coastal plain at this point, and should probably be regarded as forming a joint focus with the large sites nearer the coast such as Morín and Pendo. The presence at Castillo of marine shells brought in from the Catabrian seashore 15–22 km away demonstrates links with the coast, as well as showing that the economic catchment of Castillo was larger than its hypothetical 2-hour site exploitation territory (see Part 2 above). Contact with the coast is also suggested by the well-known similarities of the engraved deer heads from Castillo and Altamira (Ucko and Rosenfeld 1967: 63). Castillo, nevertheless, has a central role in this system, since it is located at the confluence of major routes connecting the coastal plain with the valleys of the hinterland. Also the main valley that passes in front of the cave offers one of the easiest routes across the watershed and onto the *meseta* (interior plateau). There is no certain evidence of last Glacial occupation on the northern *meseta* (Clark *et al.* 1975), and it is doubtful that any food resources available there were of major or regular significance in Cantabrian subsistence strategies. However, there are traces of Palaeolithic art, and this, together with the reported presence of a Mediterranean shell species in the Azilian level at Castillo (Fischer 1925), is suggestive, albeit equivocal, indication of occasional contact or movement between Cantabria and the *meseta*. Even without the *meseta* connection, however, Castillo by virtue of its location could have formed the node of a wide-ranging network of contacts and may represent an aggregation site in Conkey's (1980) terminology, at least during some part of the prehistoric sequence. To the west in Asturias, there seem to have been similar site systems centred on Lloseta and La Riera, but of more limited areal extent and with the focus of integration displaced seawards by the more mountainous interior.

### Time trends

In comparing temporal trends in site location and faunal exploitation, it is necessary to bear in mind the obvious deficiencies of both sets of data. In the case of the locational data presented in table 13.1 and figure 13.1 some periods may be over-represented because of the widespread occurrence of distinctive type-fossils, other periods under-represented because of greater use of open-air settlements, while detailed chronological resolution is lacking from all but a handful of sites (see chapter 12). Similarly the faunal data presented in table 13.2 are patchy, with better studied data at some sites than others. With these qualifications in mind, the main objective must necessarily be to focus on general temporal and spatial trends that can be detected with fairly crude data from a large sample of sites. For these reasons I shall analyse the overall sequence in terms of three major chronological units: (1) Mousterian and early Upper Palaeolithic (pre-35 000 b.p. to *c.* 20 000 b.p.); (2) late Upper Palaeolithic (*c.* 20 000 b.p. to 10 000 b.p.); and (3) Mesolithic (*c.* 10 000 b.p. to 7000 b.p.). This is necessarily somewhat arbitrary. But the units are sufficiently broad to include reasonably large samples of sites, while not being so broad that they are insensitive to major temporal trends. The boundaries between the units also apparently coincide with major changes in the faunal sequence.

### *Mousterian*

With so many uncertainties about the chronology of Mousterian sites and their relationship to changes in climate, sea levels and snowlines, it is difficult to say much in detail about the Mousterian other than to use it as a baseline for comparison with later periods. The faunal data suggest an eclectic (and probably opportunistic) exploitation focused on the large mammals that would have been found on the coastal plain (bovids, horse and red deer). Similarly site locations are predominantly in the coastal lowlands, and this might suggest that the resources of the sea shore and the uplands were of little interest at this time (fig. 13.3). But this is belied by the evidence, albeit meagre, of Mousterian shellfish exploitation at Morín (Madariaga 1971), and by the site of La Mora, admittedly of uncertain date (see chapter 14), which is clearly in a highland location, and was probably used for ibex hunting (Altuna 1972). The overwhelming impression of Mousterian exploitation patterns in comparison with later periods is not that they represent a radical difference of relative emphasis on different resource zones so much as a generally far less intensive exploitation overall.

Although one might expect a break in exploitation patterns at the Middle–Upper Palaeolithic transition, there is little indication of this either in site locations or faunal data. Close examination suggests that, taking into account the time-spans involved, faunal exploitation may have become

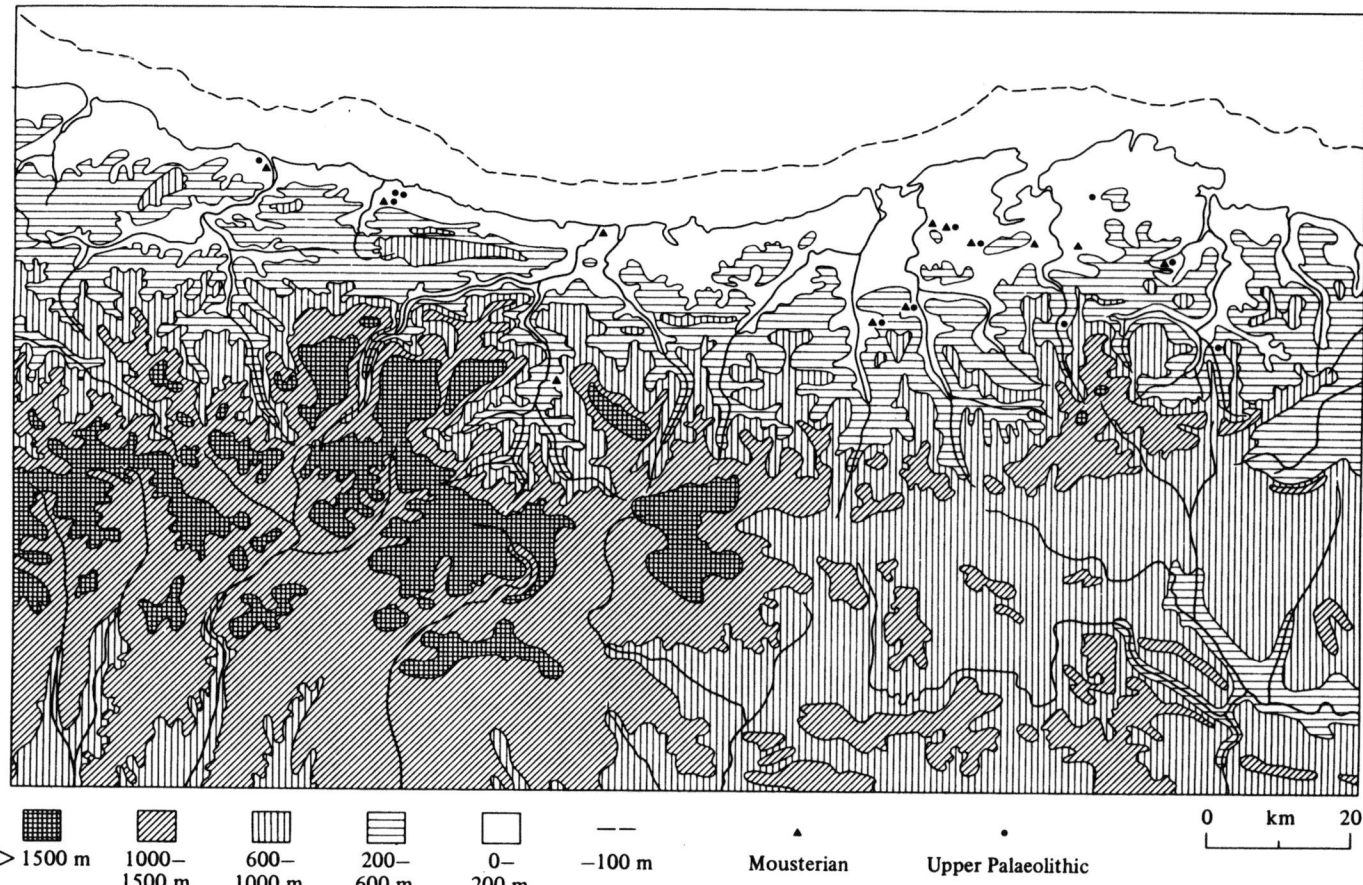

Fig. 13.3. Distribution of Mousterian and early Upper Palaeolithic sites in Cantabria.

more intensive (table 13.2). However, both Freeman (1973a) and Straus (1977a) have stressed the continuity in faunal patterning, and it would seem that any change is poorly represented by the fairly sparse available data, and is in any case greatly overshadowed by the more striking changes later in the sequence.

*Late Upper Palaeolithic*

With the Solutrean period, beginning at about 20 000 b.p. and continuing into the Magdalenian period, there are a number of indicators suggesting a shift in exploitation patterns, probably associated with higher population densities. There are more sites in the coastal lowlands, with red deer accounting for a higher percentage of the faunal remains, and more sites in highland locations, indicating an increased emphasis on ibex (table 13.2; fig. 13.4). As indicated in the previous section, it is not this polarity between coastal plain and uplands that marks the divergence from earlier patterns, so much as the apparent increased activity in both zones.

The differentiation and delimitation of the various Solutrean and Magdalenian phases is subject to a number of uncertainties on both typological and chronological grounds. Radiocarbon dates suggest a span of *c.* 21 000 b.p. to 16 000 b.p. for the Solutrean, *c.* 17 000 b.p. to 13 000 b.p. for the Lower Magdalenian: and *c.* 15 000 b.p. to 10 000 b.p.

for the Upper Magdalenian (chapter 12 above; Stuckenrath 1978). The overlaps might be genuine, or they might indicate the poor resolution of the radiocarbon sequence and/or the uncertainties of typological separation (especially between Lower and Upper Magdalenian)(chapter 12). In any case it seems reasonable to suppose that the bulk of the data in table 13.2 and figure 13.4 refers to a period about the maximum of the last Glacial, when sea levels and snowlines would have been at or close to their maximum descent. This correspondence between the archaeological and the environmental evidence gains in significance from the probability that both sea levels and snowlines would have undergone a significant lowering during the period from about 28 000 b.p. to 20 000 b.p., although the resulting alteration in landscape would not have been as dramatic as that implied by a difference between full interglacial and maximum-glacial conditions. This, in itself, indicates a strong *prima facie* case for the investigation of environmental influences, although the precise nature of the link between environmental change and subsistence/settlement patterns remains to be established.

The increased emphasis on the hunting of ibex and chamois could be related at least in part to environmental change. Both species prefer rugged terrain and range up to the snowline in summer. The lowered snowlines of the last

Table 13.2. *Representation of fauna in archaeological assemblages of eastern Asturias and Santander*

| Archaeological Period | Sites N | Duration kyr* | Bovid | | | Equus | | | Cervus | | | Capra | | | Rupicapra | | | Capreolus | | | Sus | | | Total | |
|---|---|---|---|---|---|---|---|---|---|---|---|---|---|---|---|---|---|---|---|---|---|---|---|---|---|
| | | | M | % | R | M | % | R | M | % | R | M | % | R | M | % | R | M | % | R | M | % | R | M | R |
| Mousterian/ Chatelperronian | 2 | 50 | 16 | 23 | 0.3 | 17 | 24 | 0.3 | 31 | 44 | 0.6 | 2 | 3 | 0.04 | 0 | 0 | 0.0 | 3 | 4 | 0.06 | 1 | 1 | 0.02 | 70 | 1.4 |
| Aurignacian | 1 | 5 | 14 | 6 | 2.8 | 12 | 15 | 2.4 | 27 | 4 | 5.4 | 4 | 5 | 0.8 | 2 | 3 | 0.4 | 13 | 6 | 2.6 | 3 | 4 | 0.6 | 75 | 15 |
| Gravettian | 1 | 5 | 5 | 10 | 1.0 | 8 | 16 | 1.6 | 19 | 38 | 3.8 | 6 | 12 | 1.2 | 2 | 4 | 0.4 | 9 | 18 | 1.8 | 1 | 2 | 0.2 | 50 | 10 |
| Solutrean | 10 | 5 | 17 | 9 | 3.4 | 33 | 17 | 6.6 | 102 | 52 | 20.4 | 16 | 8 | 3.2 | 16 | 8 | 3.2 | 9 | 5 | 1.8 | 4 | 2 | 0.8 | 197 | 39 |
| Lower Magdalenian | 3 | 4 | 13 | 8 | 3.3 | 14 | 8 | 3.5 | 121 | 71 | 30.2 | 6 | 4 | 1.5 | 2 | 1 | 0.5 | 12 | 7 | 3.0 | 2 | 1 | 0.5 | 170 | 43 |
| Upper Magdalenian | 2 | 5 | 6 | 6 | 1.2 | 13 | 13 | 2.6 | 50 | 50 | 10.0 | 18 | 18 | 3.6 | 10 | 10 | 2.0 | 3 | 3 | 0.6 | 2 | 2 | 0.4 | 102 | 20 |
| Azilian | 1 | 2 | 2 | 18 | 1.0 | 1 | 9 | 0.5 | 5 | 45 | 2.5 | 1 | 9 | 0.5 | 0 | 0 | 0.0 | 1 | 9 | 0.5 | 1 | 9 | 0.5 | 11 | 6 |

*Dates are approximate and there is probably some overlapping of periods.

M = minimum number of individuals
R = minimum number of individuals per unit time (1 kyr)

*Sources:* Klein *et al*. 1981; Moure Romanillo and Cano Herrera 1978; Straus 1977a.

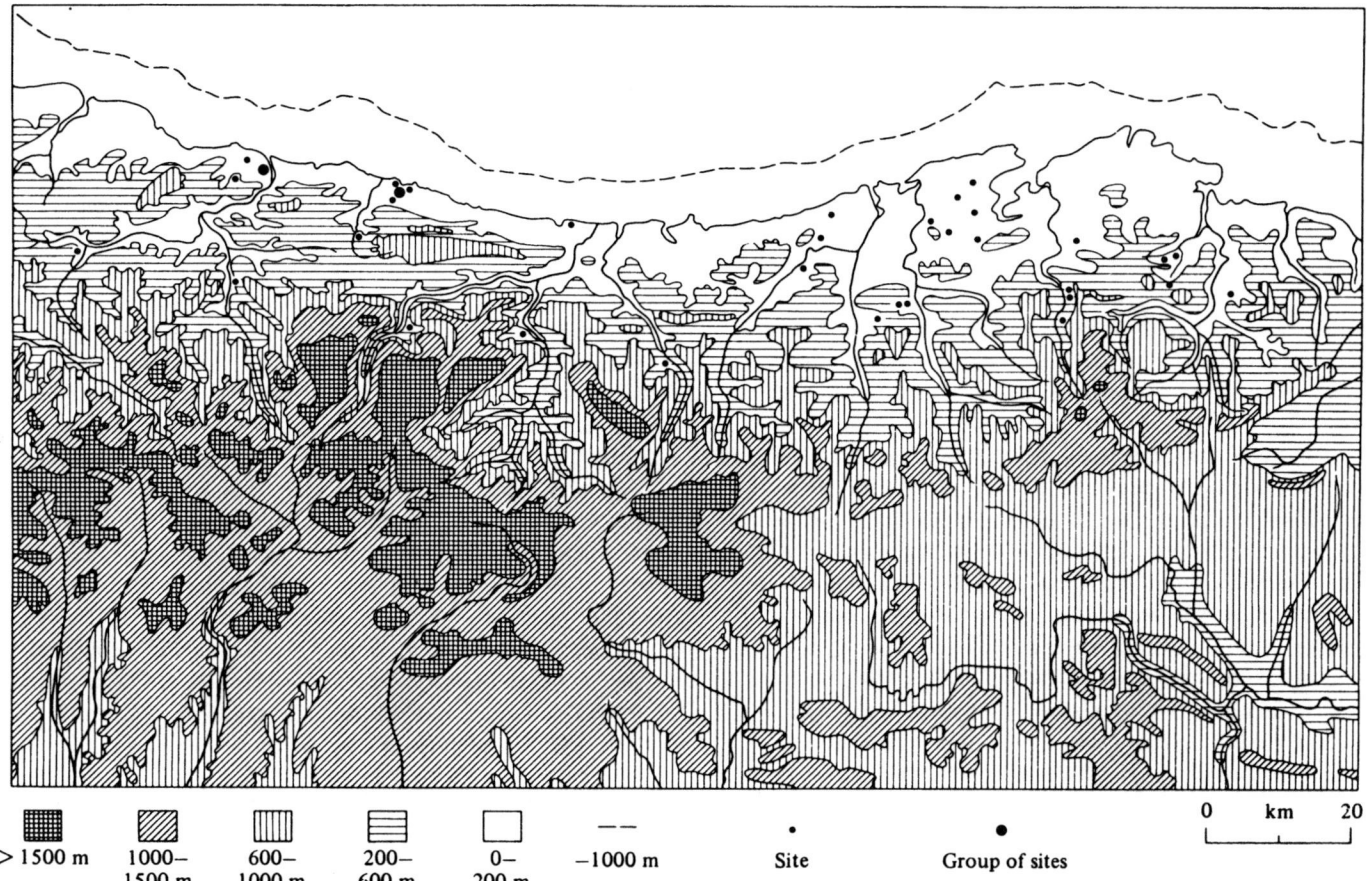

Fig. 13.4. Distribution of Solutrean and Magdalenian sites in Cantabria.

> 1500 m   1000– 1500 m   600– 1000 m   200– 600 m   0– 200 m   −1000 m   Site   Group of sites   0   km   20

glacial would have led to a greater overlap between their ranges and existing human exploitation territories, especially in winter, so that the animals would have been more easily accessible from the large settlements on the coastal plain, or from special upland camps at no great distance from the coast, which could easily be reached by hunting parties travelling inland.

The increased emphasis on red deer, however, is less easily explained, since it appears to go against the trend of any known climatic fluctuations (chapter 12 above; Freeman 1973a). If anything one might expect colder temperatures and fewer trees at the maximum of the last glacial, quite the reverse of conditions that might be invoked as favouring red deer at the expense of horse and bovids. In seeking to resolve this apparent contradiction it is important to note the implications of the quantitative data in table 13.2. The percentage representation of horse and bovids may have declined, but their absolute frequency actually appears to have increased, while the absolute frequency of red deer increased dramatically. Whatever factor contributed to the increased representation of red deer appears to have favoured the other large ungulates also, albeit to a lesser extent.

The extension of the coast by lowered sea level is clearly of significance in this respect. It is true that the coastal plain

in the period between 40 000 b.p. and 28 000 b.p. would not have been as narrow as at the present day, since the sea level, though relatively high, would have remained lower than at present. However, there would have been a drop in sea level of between 60 m and 90 m, according to the figures discussed above. Thus the regression from about 28 000 onwards would have added substantial areas to the lowland habitat of the larger ungulate species, especially on the more constricted stretches of the coastal plain, and it should be re-emphasized that the sea level between about 21 000 b.p. and 17 000 b.p. would have been lower than at any other time during the last Glacial. The change would certainly have had a significant impact on individual site exploitation territories. Sites which today are virtually on the sea shore would scarcely, if at all, have had their site exploitation territories impinged upon by the glacial sea shore (fig. 13.1).

The extension of the coast, however, does not by itself account for the disproportionate increase in red deer exploitation. An important factor here is the seasonal implications of an extended coastal plain, the main impact of which would have been to extend the area of available winter grazing. Together with a reduced growing season resulting from the lower temperatures and the lower and more seasonally restricted precipitation (Kopp 1965), this in its turn would have put a greater emphasis on complementary areas of summer grazing in the more broken topography of the adjacent hinterland. Red deer, with their broad dietary tolerances and adaptability to varied topography and vegetation would be well suited to take advantage of these conditions and to maintain higher populations through the combination of dispersed seasonal grazing resources than would otherwise be possible. Their capacity for middle-range migratory movements is well known. Moreover, their tendency to form herds in the seasonal moves between spatially discrete pastures is accentuated by human predation and makes them particularly amenable to techniques of interception, especially in areas of sharp topographic relief with limited routes of access.

Many of the larger sites are reminiscent of the situation first described by Sturdy (1972, 1975) in Germany, where Magdalenian reindeer sites are optimally located to make use of topographic barriers as aids in the prediction and control of herd movements, while minimizing the disturbing effects of human proximity during crucial periods such as the breeding season. Castillo, for example, is located at the junction of a series of broad valleys leading south to the watershed. Much of the terrain in a southern arc around the site, and extending well beyond the limits of the site exploitation territory, is effectively ringed by natural barriers to form an extended territory. Thus the human occupants could leave the deer virtually undisturbed during the summer in the knowledge that their only possible route for the autumn migration to the winter territories on the coast would be via Castillo. Similarly the large coastal site-clusters centred on La Lloseta and La Riera together control the major routes of access between the coast and a large area of inland grazing (fig. 13.1). This extensive series of intermontane valleys is not completely encircled by natural barriers, and the small sites around its edge could be considered as blocking sites (in Sturdy's terminology), or they may have served a variety of purposes, including observation of deer movements, ibex hunting, or caching of meat as part of a logistic exploitation strategy incorporating the sites of the coast and the hinterland in a single site system (see also chapter 7).

Another environmental factor that may have contributed to the proportional increase of red deer in Cantabria is the effect of climatic changes in south-west France. Here, the onset of extreme glacial conditions resulted in the increase of reindeer at the expense of red deer, and it is thus possible that Cantabria served as a refuge area for red deer populations during the maximum glacial (see chapter 12).

In summary it is argued here that environmental changes of potential impact on the human economy did occur at about the time when the archaeological data indicate changes in subsistence and settlement. The hypothesis is advanced that these environmental and behavioural changes are closely interconnected. In particular it is suggested that the increase in deer exploitation may be related to ecological specialization under deteriorating climatic conditions which favoured the adaptable red deer over other species (cf. Gamble 1978a), together with an actual increase in deer carrying capacity because of the extended coastal plain. Similarly it can be suggested that the changes in site patterning are related to a greater accentuation of logistic exploitation strategies necessitated by the more ecologically specialized environment (see Part 2 above). It is thus argued that the archaeological evidence for a change in subsistence strategies represents a response to environmental changes, rather than a case of economic intensification occurring independently of environmental change. It must be admitted, however, that given the imperfections of the available data — notably poor chronological resolution and imperfect qualitative data about subsistence changes — the latter hypothesis cannot be excluded.

The evidence for marine exploitation, on the other hand, seems more suggestive of intensification in the above sense, since marine resources, and especially molluscs, would appear to have been equally available in earlier periods. Apart from the appearance of occasional salmonid vertebrae, there is also an increased representation of marine remains, including mollusc shells and occasional seal bones (Straus 1977a; chapter 12 above). The small quantities hardly indicate an intensive exploitation. The quantities described (cf. chapter 14) represent at most a few bag-loads of mollusc shells, and there is nothing in the available stratigraphic or chronological data to indicate whether these were deposited all at once or as a series of smaller collections brought in at separate intervals over a period of weeks, months, years or even decades. The surviving quantities, however, could be misleading, since the known sites would have been some distance from the contemporaneous shoreline, and much of the processing of marine foods might have taken place at sites now submerged or otherwise lost to view. Nevertheless, the evidence, though comparatively slight, is greater than for preceding periods, and this is all the more significant in that it occurs at a time when the sea shore would have been further away from the sites rather than closer. This runs counter to the usual arguments about the effects of the time—distance factor on the exploitation and transportation of food resources (Bailey 1978, in press), and might be considered particularly good evidence for an intensification of resources that were equally available in earlier periods. Here too, however, alternative hypotheses can be proposed.

If we accept that there was a general increase in human population in response to the improved conditions for ungulate exploitation, then it would indeed be reasonable to expect a concomitant increase in complementary food supplies such as fish and shellfish. Alternatively, the increased representation of marine food remains, even at some distance from the coast, might reflect an enlargement of site catchments with the shift to a greater emphasis on logistic exploitation strategies (Part 2 above). During the Solutrean and Magdalenian periods, there is an increased tendency for materials of all kinds to be moved over large distances. Castillo,

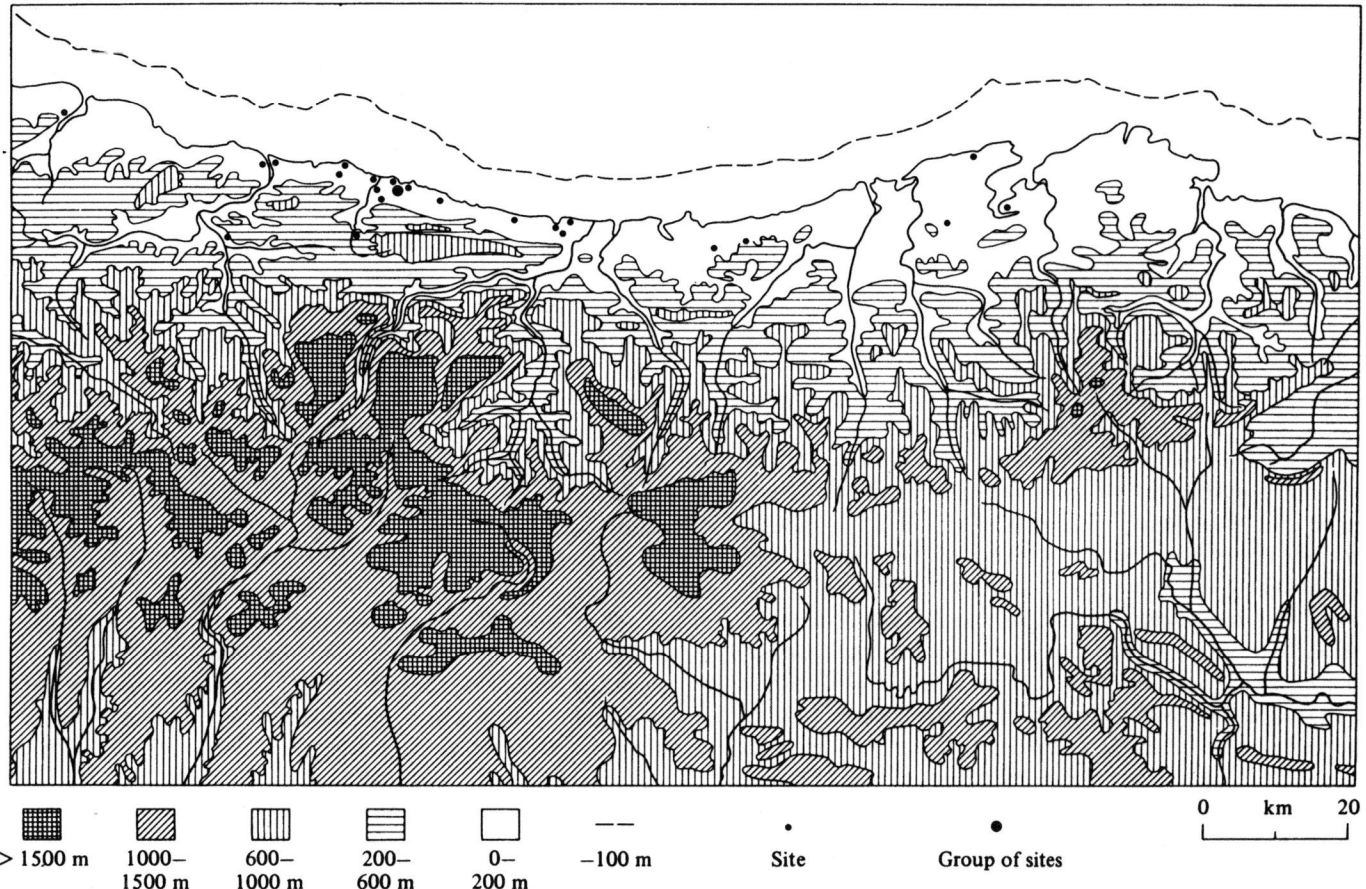

Fig. 13.5. Distribution of Mesolithic (Asturian) sites in Cantabria.

> 1500 m     1000–     600–     200–     0–     –100 m          Site          Group of sites
            1500 m    1000 m   600 m   200 m

0    km    20

on the evidence of its molluscan fauna and artistic remains, may have had a site catchment extending from the Catabrian sea shore to the Mediterranean. As Davidson suggests for Valencia (chapter 8), such evidence may reflect the tactical reorganization of exploitation strategies in response to the more extreme climatic conditions at the maximum of the last glacial, with the development of larger annual territories, greater dispersal of activities, more widespread inter-group contacts, and movements of individuals and small parties over longer distances, rather than an intensification of overall exploitation strategies (see also Part 4, below).

*Mesolithic*

The most striking feature of the periods *c.* 9000 b.p. to 7000 b.p. is the increase in coastal sites associated with the Asturian culture (fig. 13.5). The majority of these are shell middens with large quantities of mollusc shells, remains of sea urchins and occasional bones of sea fish (Clark 1971b; chapter 9 above). There is also an apparent decrease in evidence of inland occupation (fig. 13.5). The impression of a subsistence economy dominated by marine resources is, however, belied by faunal data and site locations. Bones of terrestrial mammals continue to be well represented, although

data that would allow comparison with earlier periods in terms of minimum numbers of individuals are not available. Qualitative data and counts of fragments from limited test excavations (Clark 1971b) suggest that red deer continued as the predominant species. Small quantities of pig, roe deer, cattle, chamois and ibex are also present and suggest a faunal spectrum quite consistent with environmental conditions of temperate woodland and varied relief.

Estimates of the relative dietary contribution of marine and terrestrial food resources are beset with difficulties. But I have previously argued (Bailey 1973, 1975, 1978) that marine resources are greatly over-represented by the apparent bulk of their archaeological remains. The emphasis on terrestrial resources is further emphasized by the probable existence of a significant inland component to the Asturian economy. Recent radiocarbon dates suggest that some part of the Azilian represented in inland sites may have overlapped with the Asturian, and that so-called Azilian sites may be the complement of the coastal middens (Straus 1979b; chapter 9 above). Only one inland site in the area examined here can be placed in this category. Other inland Azilian sites are known (table 13.1), but no dating evidence is yet available from them to test the possibility of contemporaneity with the coastal shell middens. Until such data are available, it would be fruitless to speculate further about the detailed pattern of hinterland exploitation, although it seems reasonable to postulate some sort of complementarity with the coast, and probably a more intensive exploitation than that implied by the one site in figure 13.5.

Whatever the doubts about the contribution of marine resources, the shell middens clearly represent a far vaster accumulation of mollusc shells than in any preceding period, and suggest a much greater relative emphasis on marine exploitation. Moreover, there is no known environmental trend that might be invoked to account for a change in the availability of molluscs on the scale required to explain the increase in archaeological quantities. The predominant species, as in earlier periods, are gastropods, mainly limpets, characteristic of rocky shore habitats. It is unlikely that any of the known changes of climate and sea level would have so altered the shoreline topography as to have had a dramatic effect on the gross overall quantities of available gastropods, although they probably affected some of the changes in species representation. The case for intensification appears a strong one, and this is reinforced by several other details of the molluscan data, notably the decrease in size of limpet shells (suggesting heavier predation pressure), which marks the culmination of a trend extending back to late Magdalenian times, and the increased representation of less easily accessible molluscan species (Straus *et al.* 1980; chapter 12 above).

Other suggestive features are the details of site locations (fig. 13.5). Many of the middens are located near earlier deposits or stratified above them, and form clusters of sites with virtually identical site exploitation territories, suggesting a strong element of continuity in settlement location. But there is also an increase in the number of sites within individual site clusters, which might be taken as evidence of a more intensive use of pre-existing site exploitation territories. In the site cluster centred on the sites of La Riera and Balmori, for example, there are some 10 rockshelters with evidence of Asturian occupation, compared with a maximum of six for any preceding period. There is also some infilling of areas between existing site clusters, suggesting that the actual, as opposed to hypothetical, site exploitation territories were smaller than previously. Whereas earlier settlement appears to have concentrated on the most favourable locations for integrating productive coastal and inland resource zones, the overall impression of Asturian site distributions is of more densely packed settlement along the full length of the coastline (Bailey 1982).

An important factor here is the rise in sea level, which would have closely approached the present level during the Asturian period. If the extension of the coastal plain by marine regression had the beneficial effects claimed in the previous section, then the reduction of the coastal plain by marine transgression might be expected to have had a correspondingly deleterious effect. The faunal data (table 13.2) are at least suggestive here, in that they indicate a progressive reduction in the Upper Magdalenian and Azilian periods in

the absolute representation of ungulate remains and in the proportional representation of red deer, as might be expected with a contraction of the coastal plain with rising sea level after the maximum regression. Comparable quantitative faunal data are unfortunately not available at present for the Asturian. It would thus be tempting to see in this marine transgression a powerful environmental force bringing pressure to bear on the pre-existing economy, thus providing the dynamic for intensification of previously neglected resources such as molluscs, and a plausible explanation of the apparent trend of economic changes. It is suggestive that the majority of shell middens are on the narrow Asturian coastal plain, where the stress resulting from the loss of lowland terrestrial resources would have been most marked.

However, none of these indicators is unequivocal. The increased quantities of mollusc shells might simply be a function of reduced distance to the sea shore resulting from glacio-eustatic sea-level rise. Thus it could be argued that any intensive shell-gathering that might have occurred during periods of lowered sea level, especially during the maximum regression, would have resulted in the consumption or processing of most of the catch at ephemeral sites now submerged, with relatively few intact molluscs being carried back to settlements which would have been nearly 10 km or more inland (fig. 13.1). The apparent increase in shell quantities could be quite illusory, indicating a change in patterns of refuse disposal rather than an intensification of shell-gathering, while the concentration of shell middens in Asturias might simply reflect the fortuitous proximity of the postglacial sea shore to locations which had long been the scene of repeated settlement because of their suitability for terrestrial exploitation (Bailey 1978, in press). Similarly, the less easily accessible gastropod species, such as *Patella intermedia* (see chapter 12), could be present in the midden deposits because the reduced distance to the sea shore had made the extra effort involved in their collection worthwhile, or because of minor changes in shoreline morphology (cf. Shackleton and van Andel 1980).

The earlier sea level stands at about 28 000 b.p. and 40 000 b.p. (fig. 13.2), although relatively high, were slightly lower than during the Asturian period. The critical distance thresholds for bulk transportation of molluscs are probably of the order of $\leqslant 5$ km, and could be as low as $\geqslant 1$ km. But unfortunately it is not possible to estimate these limits with sufficient precision to determine whether the mid-Würm sea-level stand (between about 40 000 to 28 000 b.p.) would have been high enough to bring the intertidal zone within easy economic reach of sites near the present-day shoreline, or whether the lack of shell middens in the late Mousterian and early Upper Palaeolithic indicates a genuine absence of intensive shell-gathering. High sea levels comparable to the postglacial level are not encountered in the record until about 120 000 years ago, and there are too many uncertainties about the archaeological material, if any, of this early date to permit any confident comparison with the postglacial.

As for changes in the size of mollusc shells, the difficulty here is that size decrease could reflect altered growth rates resulting from climatic or environmental changes, rather than an increased proportion of younger specimens resulting from increased predation (Swadling 1976). Many terrestrial animals undergo a size decrease in response to the major climatic changes of the late-glacial/postglacial transition (Jarman 1969; Klein n.d.), and there is a reasonable likelihood that many marine organisms would have been similarly affected. In order to eliminate the environmental hypothesis it would be necessary to show that the size change in Cantabrian limpets could be wholly accounted for by a shift in the age-structure of the exploited mollusc populations, but this is a test which has yet to be undertaken. The hypothesis of increasing exploitation pressure on the molluscs remains plausible but unproven. Even if it were to be demonstrated, it would not necessarily follow that this indicated increased stress on the human population. It might simply show that the limpets were being collected more frequently because of their greater proximity to pre-existing residential bases during a period of high sea level.

Interpretation of changes in site locations involves equally complex considerations. An increase in site density could only be accepted as evidence of increased population density if three conditions could be established: first, that the sites had similar (rather than complementary) economic functions; secondly, that the sites were strictly contemporaneous; thirdly, that the average number of inhabitants per site remained unchanged. The first condition probably holds for the Asturian. Although some of the shell middens might have been special-purpose camps used primarily for consuming or processing molluscs at some distance from settlement sites, it should be noted that the majority of investigated middens contain remains of terrestrial fauna. This, together with Clark's analysis of land-use categories within site exploitation territories (chapter 9), strongly suggests that most middens had similar functions as settlement sites supported by a mixed subsistence economy.

The other two conditions are less easy to establish. Chronologies in particular are simply not available, or likely to be available with existing techniques, with the necessary resolution to test contemporaneity of occupation in other than very broad terms. However, two hypotheses may be proposed to account for the observed changes in settlement pattern without requiring either a population increase, or a situation of population pressure on pre-existing resources. The first is a general hypothesis relating changes in settlement strategy to changes in general features of the environment. It depends on a distinction between generalized environments with a high plant and animal biomass and a broad spectrum of evenly distributed resources, and specialized environments with fewer and less predictable resources with a greater tendency to form widely-spaced aggregations (Gamble 1978a; Binford 1980; chapter 3 above). The former are typically associated with small settlements dispersed across the landscape in a patchwork of small annual and site exploitation territories, the latter with larger exploitation territories and more widely spaced settlements serving as the focus for relatively large aggregations of people at least on a seasonal basis. This hypothesis is certainly suggestive in that the environmental changes leading to the development of temperate woodland during the Asturian period would have been changes in the direction of a more generalized environment.

A more specific hypothesis depends on an assessment of the economic potential of marine molluscs. It is likely that shellfood, while not contributing a large quantity of food relative to other resources, was important for people living near the sea shore as a predictable day-to-day supplement gathered on a regular basis. At the same time local supplies of limpets might be rapidly depleted, necessitating visits to more distant shorelines. The high costs of transporting molluscs, already mentioned, might be sufficient in these circumstances to shift the focus of settlement along the coastline over quite small distances of a kilometre or so, even though the new location would make little difference in terms of access to terrestrial resources. On this hypothesis the overall settlement strategy would have been a rotational one in which only a limited proportion of the total number of sites would have been in use at any one time. In effect the larger number of sites might simply reflect an increased emphasis on 'foraging' strategies with a greater frequency of residential moves within the year, as compared with the logistic strategies which may have been more prevalent during the Upper Palaeolithic period (see Part 2 above).

As to the effects of a reduced coastal plain, the minimum estimate for the duration of sea-level rise from the maximum regression to about the present level would be about 4000 years. If we make the generous assumption that the coastal plain supplied 100% of the food supply and that 75% of this was lost by marine transgression, this would mean an average reduction in food supply of about 1.9% per 100 years, or about 1% per human generation. While the impact of such a loss would presumably vary, depending on the absolute size of the initial population and the degree of population pressure already existing, it seems doubtful whether much emphasis can be placed on the allegedly stressful consequences of an environmental change which would have had a scarcely perceptible impact on the available food supply within the lifetime of a single individual. Moreover, the loss of coastal plain would have been compensated for by other changes associated with the return to temperate conditions. It is true that red deer densities appear generally lower in woodland than in open environments at the present day (de Nahlik 1959), and that in Cantabria ibex and chamois may have become less accessible as they moved into more remote mountain retreats with the rise of the snowline. But pig and roe deer would have been favoured by the new conditions, and the climatic amelioration would have reduced the severity of seasonal restraints and allowed an increase in the overall plant biomass, including most probably an increase in plant foods suitable for human consumption.

## Discussion

Considerable interest has been generated in the idea that population growth has been more or less continuous during the Pleistocene, and that recurrent episodes of increased population pressure, created when population growth exceeds some pre-existing ceiling on resource availability, have provided the principal stimulus to economic intensification and subsequent population growth, leading ultimately to the development and spread of agriculture (Higgs and Jarman 1975; Cohen 1977). While such a model has a general appeal on a global scale and in the time perspective of tens or hundreds of thousands of years, it needs to be closely examined in the light of the problems of interpretation posed by regional sequences. At the theoretical level recent discussions have emphasized the ambiguities inherent in 'population pressure' arguments, and in particular the importance of clarifying the distinction between population pressure, which may be virtually a constant over long time-spans, and sustained population increase, which evidently occurred only rarely or intermittently (Bailey 1981b; Jarman *et al.* 1982). At the practical level it appears from the Cantabrian data that there are two sorts of uncertainty: precisely what are the economic changes implied by the archaeological data; and what were the underlying causes of those changes.

With some features of the evidence, it has been argued that the apparent archaeological evidence of economic change may be misleading, indicating a change in patterns of settlement behaviour and refuse disposal, rather than an intensification of particular resources. Thus the apparent increase in marine remains in Upper Palaeolithic deposits might reflect an enlargement of the economic catchments associated with residential bases, representing a reorganization of exploitation strategies in response to climatic change. The growth of shell middens in the early Postglacial might simply indicate the greater proximity of the sea shore to existing centres of preferred human habitation, and the shift to a foraging strategy with more numerous and more closely-spaced residential bases.

Even if we allow that economic intensification was the long-term outcome of 30 thousand years and more of human occupation, and that human population densities were higher at the end of the sequence than at the beginning, many of the economic changes appear closely related, either directly or indirectly, to environmental changes, and there remain considerable difficulties in the way of disentangling the environmental factors from the demographic, social and cultural ones – of determining what were the causes and what were the effects. Let us suppose that the evidence of marine exploitation is taken at its face value as suggesting two episodes of intensification, one after about 20 000 b.p. and the

second in the early Postglacial. Even on this supposition a case can be made for the indirect effects of environmental change, in the earlier period because of expansion of the coastal plain allowing population growth, and in the later period because of contraction of the coastal plain and consequent reduction of pre-existing staple resources in relation to the pre-existing population level. Changes affecting populations outside the region of study may have had an additional impact. For example, local population pressure may have been augmented by the influx of populations displaced southwards by the advance of the north European ice sheets (see chapter 19). However, it is open to question as to whether the rate of advance of the continental ice sheets, any more than the rate of sea-level rise, would have been sufficiently rapid to put much strain on the relationship between population and food resources in Cantabria.

One of the major problems in comparing the different stages of the Cantabrian sequence is that one is not comparing similar environments. Thus it is very difficult to hold environmental factors constant as one would wish in order to focus better on the other variables in the economic equation. One solution to this dilemma would be to concentrate on indicators of exploitation pressure which are to some extent independent of environmental change. Variation in the population structure of exploited mollusc populations is one such potential indicator, which should be detectable regardless of the actual quantities of shells that happen to be incorporated in surviving midden deposits, and regardless of any environmentally induced changes in shell size. However, inter-individual variation in growth patterns of limpet species, especially *Patella vulgata*, suggests that these may not be very suitable for this type of analysis (Lewis and Bowman 1975; Bailey *et al.* 1982). Studies of bone fragmentation offer another source of potential evidence (chapter 12). Another aid to interpretation would be archaeological data from the last interglacial, when the conjunction of high sea level and temperate climate would have been similar to the early postglacial. However, such evidence is not yet available in Cantabria. In any case it is doubtful whether the terrestrial faunal resources of the last interglacial period, and hence the economic response to them, would have been precisely similar to the postglacial period, because of the presence of animal species – either as available prey or competing predators – that subsequently became extinct. Indeed it is doubtful whether the ideal control situation of two identical environments could ever be found. Given the time scale of Pleistocene perspectives and the widespread environmental effects of climatic change, environmental factors present a pattern of virtually continuous variation, and the evolution of human subsistence economies is scarcely separable from the evolution of the landscape and its natural resources. At any rate it is clear that a much finer resolution of data and probably a longer sequence will be required if long-term economic trends are to be disembedded from their environmental matrix. As it stands, the available evidence of major changes in settlement and subsistence strategies in Cantabria suggests organizational changes in response to changing environmental opportunities rather than an independent cumulative, directional process of economic intensification and population growth. As such the record is a testament, not so much to the determining effect of the natural environment on human activity, as to the economic opportunism of past populations in responding to changing environmental conditions.

### Acknowledgements

I am grateful to Clive Gamble, Geof Clark and Larry Straus for comments on an earlier draft, and to Nic Shackleton for discussion of sea-level data and for supplying the oxygen isotope data for figure 13.2.

Chapter 14

**Further reflections on adaptive change in Cantabrian prehistory**
Lawrence G. Straus and Geoffrey A. Clark

Bailey's contribution (chapter 13) on the causes of subsistence change in prehistoric Cantabria was written partly in response to our contribution (chapter 12). We agree that terminal and post-Pleistocene sea-level transgression could have exacerbated the subsistence situation for Mesolithic hunter-gatherers, but we wish to take issue with Bailey on a number of other points.

(1) The general pattern of faunal changes with increased exploitation of red deer and ibex after 20 000 b.p. is consistently represented at a number of Cantabrian sites. Recent analysis of the long sequence of Middle and Upper Palaeolithic assemblages at El Pendo (Santander) confirms the pattern (Fuentes 1980). It shows intensified exploitation of red deer (and ibex) in the Upper Palaeolithic along with the continued hunting of small numbers of horses and bovines. Mass hunting of red deer and ibex in the Solutrean and Magdalenian has been documented by dental studies of the age structure of the killed animals at Tito Bustillo (Altuna 1976), La Riera (Straus *et al.* 1981), El Juyo (Klein *et al.* 1981; this volume) and Rascaño (Altuna 1981). Subsistence diversification is also part of the picture at El Pendo and elsewhere, with the first consistent representation of boar, chamois and roe deer. Shellfish are most abundant by far in the El Pendo Magdalenian (Madariaga 1980a). We disagree with Bailey on the effect of changes in the physical environment versus that of demographic factors in causing these subsistence trends.

There is no evidence that red deer were less abundant in the Cantabrian environment prior to 20 000 b.p. Red deer is an extremely flexible species (Strauss 1981a) and we think it unlikely that its numbers were significantly affected by the climatic and vegetational changes during the last glacial period. The record from La Riera (and elsewhere) indicates that there is no apparent relationship between climatic oscillations, as recorded by sediments, pollen, rodents and molluscs, and the frequency of red deer bones. We also find it unlikely (based on the available evidence) that variations in the width of the coastal plain would have affected the abundance of red deer to the extent suggested by Bailey. In particular we do not believe that the coastal plain would have been that much narrower in the Early Würm upper pleniglacial or lower pleniglacial (when only relatively small numbers of red deer were being hunted) than in the late upper pleniglacial.

(2) The increased representation of molluscs beginning early in the Solutrean occurs at the maximum sea-level regression, and is, in our view, a clear indication of intensification. Substantial amounts of molluscs were brought back to La Riera, then some 10 km from the shore (as opposed to 1.5 km today). Levels 4 and 5 are thin and localized, yet each has over 9 kg of large shells of *Patella vulgata*. Level 7, sampled in an area of about 15 m$^2$, yielded over 10 kg of shells. This suggests that marine resources were already assuming a certain importance, despite the relatively wide coastal plain

present at that time. If the La Riera evidence indicates, as Bailey suggests, an enlargement of site catchments, then that implies, in our view, greater energy expenditures, and we see this in its turn as a further indication of subsistence pressure. Thus we argue that such catchment enlargement is one of many methods used by late Upper Palaeolithic peoples to alleviate a food problem ultimately caused by an imbalance between regional population size and the types of food gathering practised until that time (see also Clark 1981a).

(3) We reiterate our view that the increasing diversity of marine resources through time and the corresponding decrease in limpet size seems to indicate the existence of subsistence pressures on a growing human population during the late Glacial. Madariaga (1980b: 705) explicitly states that the size decrease 'indicates over-exploitation and the collection of young limpets'. Recent surveys (Gavelas 1980) have also increased the number of known Asturian sites in Asturias and Santander to a total of 77. This reinforces our conception of high site densities in the Early Holocene.

(4) Reference by Bailey to the little-known site of La Mora in the Picos de Europa as an example of montane ibex hunting by Neanderthals is questionable. A pit dug in this site revealed a partly jumbled stratigraphy containing a small number of small flakes and blades of quartzite, slate, limestone and oligist (González Echegaray 1957). There is little reason to believe that this is a Mousterian assemblage. Quartzite industries have often been labelled 'Mousterian' simply because of their 'crude' appearance (see discussion in Strauss 1977f, 1978c; Clark 1979b).

In conclusion, while we agree that rising sea-level could have had an impact on the Early Holocene resource base, we do not believe that earlier subsistence changes were influenced by environmental changes. Clearly stadial conditions existed during the Middle and early Upper Palaeolithic, but did not provoke the kinds of diversification and specialized procurement methods we have documented. We suggest that the new variable in the equation was a denser regional population and we believe that the site numbers we have presented are at least a *partial* reflection of that condition (see Straus (1981b)).

Chapter 15

Late Pleistocene economies of the French
Pyrenees
Paul G. Bahn

The development of subsistence practices is traced from the Lower
Palaeolithic to the Azilian, and is illustrated with some key examples.
Evidence provided by site locations and contents is examined in order
to assess whether economies were generalized or specialized, and
whether/how herds may have been under some sort of control. Middle
and Upper Palaeolithic economies are compared; the use of mountain
resources, small game and plants is highlighted; and some conclusions
are discussed in relation to data from Cantabria. Economic
developments are placed against the background of environmental
change, including the retreat of the sea and of the glaciers; and the
very sparse evidence for population increase is evaluated.

### Preamble

In this chapter I attempt to trace economic developments
in the Middle and Upper Palaeolithic of the French Pyrenees
through the interpretation of faunal assemblages and an
examination of site locations. The emphasis is on long-term
economic changes and how far they can be attributed to
environmental and demographic trends.

The first part of the study comprises a brief exposition
of the faunal, environmental and locational data in
chronological sequence, and highlights some evidence for
seasonal mobility. At the same time it contrasts sites with
circular or unspecialized site exploitation territories (those
which lie in areas suitable for generalized, uncontrolled
exploitation of mobile resources) with those which have
distorted territories offering little to the eclectic hunter but
comprising topographic features that would be of great
advantage to economic strategies involving the interception
or corralling of herds.

The second part shifts the focus to a more detailed study
of individual factors: the use made of different resources;
site location; and the sparse evidence for population trends.
In doing so it compares the Pyrenean evidence with similar
studies in neighbouring Cantabrian Spain.

### Introduction

The Pyrenees have long been a region of great interest
to the prehistorian, not only because of the richness of the
cultural material from certain periods, but also because of the
geographical features of the chain (see Bahn, 1979a). They lie
across one of the two land 'exits' leading south from the main
body of Europe, and stretch from the Atlantic to the
Mediterranean, but have never formed an effective barrier:
even during periods of glaciation the two extremities of the
chain could be crossed without difficulty.

The structure of the French Pyrenees comprises an
axial zone of crystalline massifs and, to the north, long parallel
folds of secondary limestones in which the majority of
Pyrenean prehistoric sites have been sought and found.

The chain, some 400 km in length, and with an average
height of a little less than 2000 m, descends gently in the west;
the Mediterranean extremity descends relatively steeply from
high, wide plateaux to the coastal plain. Between the two

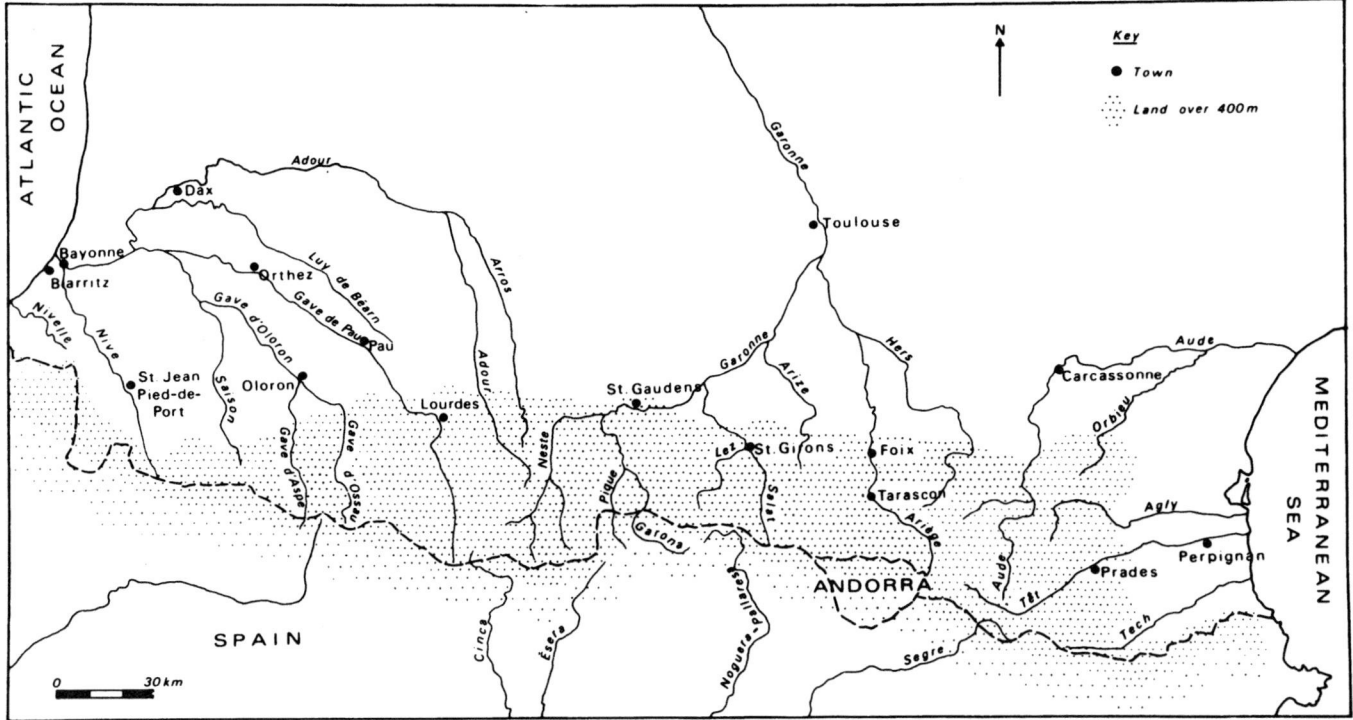

Fig. 15.1. The French Pyrenees. Relief and drainage.

lie the massive Central Pyrenees with their deep valleys and surviving glaciers (fig. 15.1).

The region therefore contains a series of climatic and vegetational zones from the Atlantic to the Mediterranean, together with an environment which changes rapidly within the abrupt ascent from foothill to high mountain. This pattern clearly had some effect on the patterning of material culture in both prehistoric and historic times: each extremity seems to have undergone different influences, while the central area tended to be rather conservative despite the absorption of some new ideas. In addition, lateral communication was almost impossible between many of the parallel valleys, a fact which must have enhanced the individuality and economic self-reliance of their human occupants.

Opinions differ slightly as to the location of the limits of permanent snow in the Pyrenees during the glacial period; in the east, which had no glaciers below 2300 m, the snowline was at 2000–2200 m (it is over 2800 m today); and in the west, which had small glaciers on 1500 m peaks, the snowline was probably down to *c.* 1400 m (it is at 2500–2800 m today). One may assume that the orographic structure of the area has remained constant since the periods considered here, and it is known that the present, basic morphology of the valleys was already well established by at least Magdalenian times, and probably long before (Méroc 1953). Only a small stretch of land was exposed at either coast by the glacial drop in sea level owing to the narrow continental shelf.

According to Gaussen (1933) the last glaciation probably lowered vegetation limits by *c.* 700 m. Temperature

and precipitation will not have altered their basic pattern of geographical and seasonal variation during the Late Pleistocene, but obviously absolute figures will have fluctuated. No single, uniform, climatic sequence is valid for the whole area. The factors of longitude, proximity to the coast, altitude and exposure all affect local conditions. This may be one reason for the different economic specializations which arose in the Upper Palaeolithic.

The Pyrenees suffer from a surfeit of cave sites, since this is where the earliest excavations were concentrated, caves being easy to locate and inherently likely to yield some evidence of early human occupation. Open-air sites of all periods are scarce, and largely confined to surface scatters; a tiny minority have been excavated, but preservation of organic remains is usually poor or non-existent, so that their information for the economic prehistorian is very limited. Therefore the study which follows will inevitably rely heavily on cave and rockshelter sites, and, wherever possible, will use data from recent reliable excavations, while clinging to the hope that the faunal remains encountered by the excavators are representative of the prehistoric economic strategies despite differential preservation and sampling.

### Economic developments
#### The Middle Palaeolithic

This period is poorly known in the French Pyrenees, and there are few sites of any importance. It has been argued (Méroc 1953) that those Mousterian sites which are found at high altitude (e.g. the cave of Bouichéta (Ariège), at 800 m) or whose faunal assemblages show a complete absence of reindeer should be assigned to an interstadial or, more probably, to the last interglacial period. Studies in other parts of southern France (e.g. de Lumley 1971) have suggested that Mousterian open sites are common in Early Würm, but that the cold maximum of Würm II forced man to abandon these and to inhabit caves and rockshelters. This observation may be valid for the Pyrenees, but here the factor of altitude plays a role; so that in the warmer phases of pre-Würm and Early Würm, Mousterian man could inhabit open sites in the foothills, but could also occasionally exploit the higher reaches of valleys by resorting to caves where necessary.

An important point is that Mousterian and even pre-Mousterian material has been recorded in the Pyrenees at high altitudes, both in caves and as surface finds, the highest being two axes from 1010 m (Miquel 1931); no doubt many traces have been erased by subsequent glacial activity. Such finds, attributed to warm phases, may perhaps be compared with similar high-altitude material in the Alps (Dellenbach 1935). Moreover, the high Alps were visited in Magdalenian/Azilian times specifically for the exploitation of the marmot and other fur-bearing creatures (Deffontaines 1948) and, intriguingly, the highest Pyrenean Mousterian cave, L'Estelas, at over 900 m contained a great abundance of marmot (Roule and Regnault 1895) as well as the large herbivores which

seem to have been the staples of the period. Most Mousterian sites, however, are located in the foothills, where Mousteroid artefacts are found on numerous hills and ridges.

Two important sites in the Pyrénées Atlantiques are the collapsed rockshelter of Olha and, farther east, the great cave of Isturitz (see fig. 15.2); the date of their long Mousterian occupations is uncertain, but on typological grounds the two are thought to be broadly contemporaneous (Delporte 1974), and they are associated with fairly humid, cool/temperate conditions, a steppic environment, and moderate percentages of arboreal pollen.

Until the faunal material from recent excavations at Olha II is published, the only evidence from Olha is the original work of Passemard (1920, 1935/6); unfortunately most of this information in unquantified. The site comprises three habitation layers separated by thick sterile layers of rockfall, and this stratigraphy is thought to span at least several millennia, but shows remarkably little change in subsistence over time: red deer, bovids and horses predominate throughout (table 15.1).Red deer account for the majority of bones, but horses and bovids are always well represented; in fact red deer are never overwhelmingly predominant except perhaps in Fi-2 (the richest layer), and it should be remembered that horses and bovids offer far more meat than the cervid; one bovid is roughly equivalent in carcase weight to four red deer. Faced

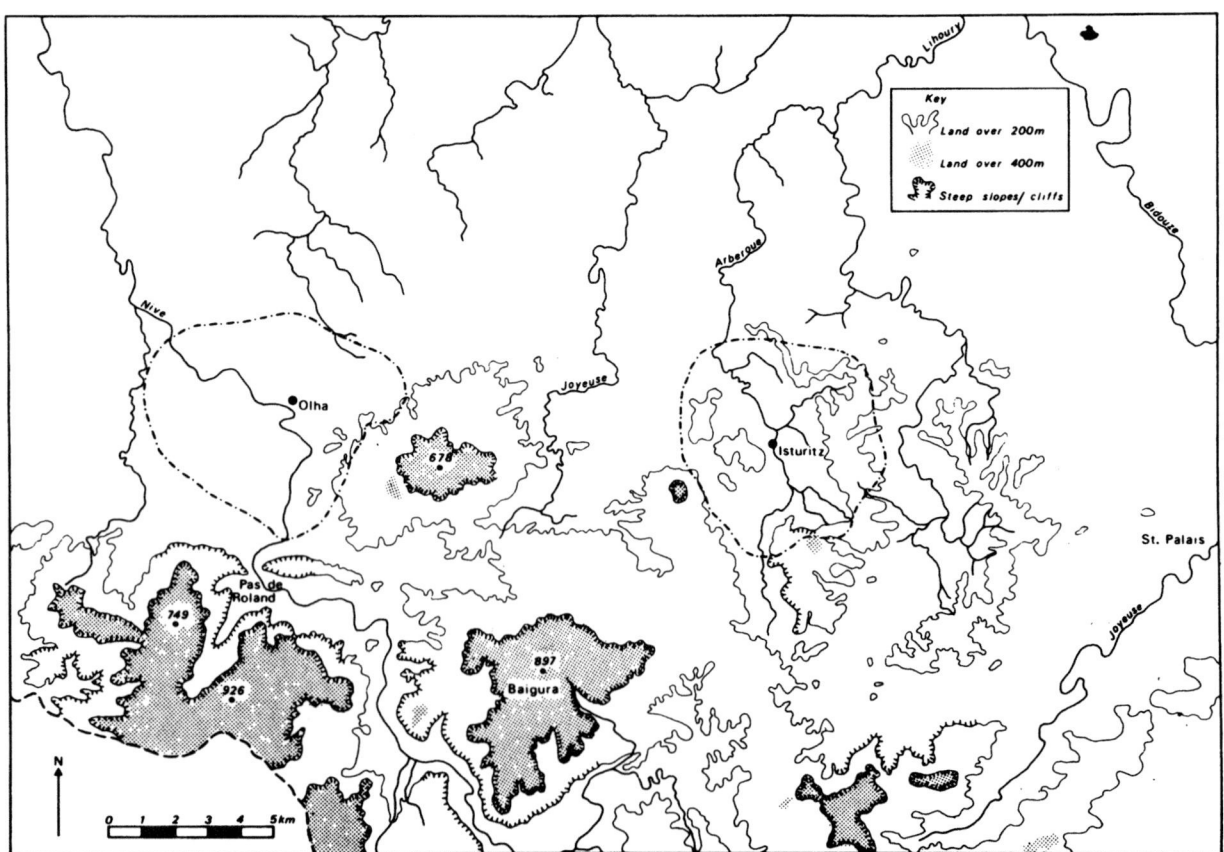

Fig. 15.2. Location and 1-hour site exploitation territories of Olha and Isturitz.

Table 15.1. *The Olha fauna*

| | Foyer inf.−4 | Foyer inf.−3 | Foyer inf.−2 | Foyer inf.−1 | Foyer moyen | Foyer sup. |
|---|---|---|---|---|---|---|
| *Rangifer tarandus* | | | | | 1 tooth | fragments |
| *'Cervus elaphus'* | *c.* 20 fragments | *c.* 100 fragments/ teeth | CCC | CC | CC | CC |
| *Capreolus capreolus* | 2 fragments? | 'a few teeth' | 'a few fragments' | | | |
| Big bovid | 3 teeth | 11 teeth, + fragments | C | C | C | C |
| *Rupicapra pyrenaica* | | 'a few teeth' | | | | |
| 'Small ruminant' | | | 'a few fragments' | | 'a few fragments' | |
| *Equus caballus* | 1 tooth | 11 teeth | C | C | R/C | R/C |
| *Elephas primigenius* | | | | | | 2 teeth, + fragments |
| *Rhinoceros tichorhinus* | | | | | 1 tooth? | 'a few teeth' |
| *Dicerorhinus merckii* | | 4 teeth | C | | | |

R/C = present
C = common
CC = very common
CCC = extremely common

*Note*: Like Freeman (1973a) I have arbitrarily excluded rodents, insectivores, carnivores and hominids from the dietary lists in this table and those that follow; but I have included elephants and rhinos.

with a similar situation, Lantier (1974) suggested that the bovids and equids were exploited for meat, the cervids primarily for skins, antler, sinew, etc. It can be seen from table 15.1 that the diversity of prey species is rather limited at Olha, and the economy can be regarded as a generalized one based fairly equally on three large herbivores.

Olha (fig. 15.2) must have been of importance in a local area largely bereft of caves. It was immediately adjacent to the River Nive; a cliff on the opposite bank affords a remarkable view over a wide area, and particularly southwards. The distance which can be reached on foot from the site in one hour is substantial, but a '2-hour territory' would be greatly restricted in the south and east by massifs and would include the Pas de Roland, the point where the Nive finally emerges from a narrow, steep-sided gorge onto the plain. This river, one of the most important of the region, also provides a major route into the uplands which was undoubtedly utilized by man and prey alike. One can therefore speculate that Olha was an advantageous base from which to intercept herds along the Nive. Unfortunately there is no evidence concerning seasonality at Olha I.

The middle Palaeolithic stratigraphy of the nearby cave of Isturitz has analogies with that of Olha (Passemard 1922, 1944; de St Périer and de St Périer 1952): both, for example, begin with very small, separate hearths, poor in fauna, which suggest short stays by a small number of people. The list of species (table 15.2) is similarly restricted, with a dependence on the same trio of herbivores. Both faunas are considered temperate, but a few fragments of reindeer appear towards

the end of the Mousterian occupation of both sites. Isturitz is the only major cave for many miles around, and it clearly served as a base and regional focus throughout the Palaeolithic; as at Olha, however, no information is available concerning possible seasonality in the Mousterian.

Farther east in the Pyrenees, the few Mousterian sites with any faunal information (e.g. Gargas, Les Abeilles, Roquecourbère − see Bahn 1979a) seem to have similar faunal lists to those mentioned above. In some cases, where meat weight is taken into account, the bovids provide up to two-thirds of the usable meat represented. This seems to hint at more specialized exploitation, and that is precisely what has been found recently at Mauran.

An open site of several hundred square metres, Mauran lies on a small plateau overlooking the River Garonne. Its rare tools are a mixture of quartzite pebbles and denticulate flints (Girard *et al.* 1975). Occupied in a warm, humid phase according to pollen and sedimentology, it has evidence of toolmaking, butchering and skinning (tool-types and flint-marks), and cooking. In the small portion excavated, thousands of bone fragments were found, representing a minimum number of 73 bovids of all ages and a very few horse remains. Some bones were still in connection, and the site was obviously the killing and butchering camp of a Mousterian group which was very heavily dependent on bovid meat. Unfortunately one cannot estimate whether this was the staple throughout the year, or whether the site merely represents an occasional mass cull. It is interesting that an open site with a similar fauna and stone industry has also been excavated at Livernon

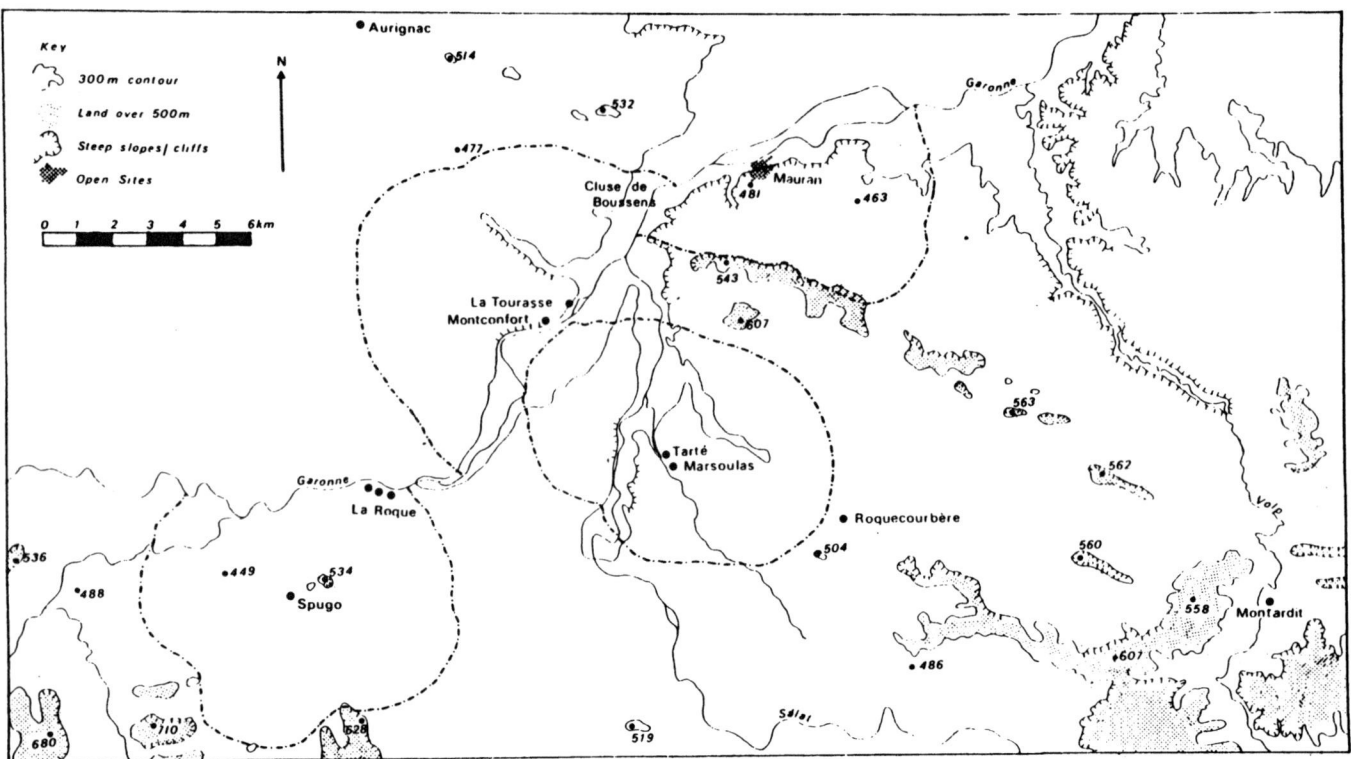

Fig. 15.3. Combined 1-hour site exploitation territories of the principal Garonne sites.

in the Quercy, to the north; this suggests that such specialized camps are by no means rare in the Middle Palaeolithic of south-west France.

Figure 15.3 shows that Mauran has a semi-circular 1-hour territory, if one assumes that the Garonne was not habitually crossed; the river presents a formidable obstacle in this region, and would certainly have been a useful barrier in the driving of cattle, which presumably thrived in the water-meadows along the river. The location is important because it is close to the Cluse de Boussens, which is not only the point where the Garonne breaks through the ridge of the 'Petites Pyrénées', but also lies close to a major ford across this imposing river. The positioning of an open site is far more a matter of choice than is the occupation of a cave, and Mauran's 'half-territory' and its excellent view both northwards and along the valley suggest that it was a specially chosen vantage-point from which to intercept bovid herds. It therefore provides a contrast to Mousterian sites with circular, unspecialized territories and generalized economies, like those discussed above. It might be argued that sites like Mauran were merely task-specific outposts from the base-camps, and future analysis of the remains may help to resolve this issue.

The principal Mousterian site of the Eastern Pyrenees is the cave of Le Portel (Ariège) which, in places, is filled to the roof with material of the period. The stratigraphy suggests a stable and long-lasting culture; the faunal information available is rather disparate (see Bahn 1979a, table 20), but combines to form a picture of the usual restricted range of

species, and an economy based on the trio of bovids, horses and cervids. However, there is a marked change from the base of the fill where red deer are abundant and reindeer rare, to the summit where the ratio is reversed. Such a switch probably had an environmental cause, and this hypothesis is supported by sedimentology at the site (Vézian 1971). Nevertheless, it should be noted that, despite numerical importance, reindeer were still no more than equal to bovids and horses in terms of meat weight.

*The early Upper Palaeolithic*

Soon after the end of the Mousterian period, Le Portel was abandoned until the Magdalenian; whereas it is in the Aurignacian period that the nearby cave of St Jean de Verges was first occupied (Vézian and Vézian 1966). Obviously one cannot envisage a shift of settlement by the same group, but nevertheless the move seems significant in the context of environmental and economic change; for Le Portel has an almost circular territory (see fig. 15.4), and a location with little potential for the interception of herds, since it does not lie on a major or transverse river. St Jean de Verges, on the other hand, has very clear potential for interceptions of this kind, and a circular territory only if the Ariège was habitually crossed — which would be difficult in the spring (March–June) maximum flow. Like Le Portel the cave is located in the Plantaurel ridge, but in this area the ridge rises as an impassable cliff, and is crossed by the Ariège in two gorges, the first immediately north of Foix (see fig. 15.4 for cluster of minor

Table 15.2. The fauna of Isturitz

(a) 'Mousterian' to 'Gravettian/Upper Aurignacian'

| | P/SV (St M) 'Early Moust.' | Bear layer ('Moust.') | SIV (St M) 'Typ. Moust.' | M (St M) 'Typ. Moust.' | SIII (St M) 'Typ. Aurig.' | A (Ist. + St M) 'Typ./Mid. Aurig.' | SII (St M) 'Mid. Aurig.' | V (Ist.) 'Mid. Aurig.' | IV (Ist.) 'Upper Aurig./ Grav.' | FIII (Ist.) 'Upper Aurig./ Grav.' |
|---|---|---|---|---|---|---|---|---|---|---|
| *Rangifer tarandus* | | (2 fragments) | R | RR | 2/25% C | R | 3/33.3% C | 2–3/25% C | 20–22/ 39.3% | C |
| *Cervus elaphus* | R/C | | C | C | R | R | 1/11.1% R/C | 2/16.7% R/C | 4/7.1% CC | C |
| *Cervus megaceros* | 1 fragment | | | | 1/12.5% 1 fragment | | | 1/8.3% fragment 1 | 2/3.6% fragments 2 | C |
| *Capreolus capreolus* | R/C | | | | | | | | 2/3.6% fragments 3 | |
| Big bovids | R/C | | C | CC | 2/25% | C | | 1–2/16.7% C | 12–14/25% CC | CCC |
| *Capra ibex/ pyrenaica* | | | | | | | | 1/8.3% | | |
| *Rupicapra rupicapra* | | | | 1 fragment | 1/12.5% | R/C | 2/22.2% (2 fragments) | 2–3/25% | 6–7/12.5% (8 fragments) | |
| *Sus scrofa* | | | | R/C | | | | | | |
| *Equus caballus* | R | | R/C | CC | 2/25% CCC | CCC | 3/33.3% CCC | CCC | 4–5/8.9% CCC | CC |
| Total | | | | | 8 | | 9 | 12 | 57 | |
| *Elephas primigenius* | | | | | | | | | | |
| *Rhinoceros tichorhinus* | | | 2 fragments | R/C | 1 fragment | R/C | | 1 fragment | 3–4 | R/C |
| *Lepus timidus* | | | | R/C | | | 1 (4 fragments) | 1–2 (4 fragments) | 2 fragments 2 | R/C |
| Birds | | | | R | | C | R | R/C | R/C | R |
| Molluscs | | | | | 73 (*L. littorea*) | | | | 65 (*L. littorea*) | |

(b) 'Epigravettian/Final Aurignacian' to 'Final Magdalenian'

| | III (Ist.) 'Epigr.'/Final Aurig.' | C (Ist.) 'Epigr./Final Aurig.' | IIIa/b (Ist.) 'Solutr.' | FII (Ist.) 'Solutr.' | SI (St M) 'Magd. IV' | E (Ist/St M) 'Magd. IV' | II (Ist.) 'Magd. IV' | I (Ist.) 'Magd. V/VI' | FI (Ist.) 'Magd. V/VI' |
|---|---|---|---|---|---|---|---|---|---|
| *Rangifer tarandus* | 4/16.7% CC | R/C | C? | C | CC | CC → CCC | CC | CC → CCC | CCC |
| *Cervus elaphus* | 1/4.2% CC | | | | 5 fragments | R/C | C | CC | C → CC |
| *Capreolus capreolus* | 6/25% (11 fragments) | | | | 2 fragments | | 5 fragments | 2 fragments | |
| Big bovids | 2/8.3% CC | CC | C? | CC | C | C | C | C | C |
| *Capra ibex/ pyrenaica* | | | | | R/C | | 2 fragments | | |
| *Rupicapra rupicapra* | 5–6/25% C | | | | C | | | | |
| *Saiga tartarica* | | | | R/C | 1 fragment | | C | C | |
| *Sus scrofa* | | | | | 1 fragment | | | 2 fragments | |
| *Equus caballus* | 4/16.7% CC | C | C? | C | CCC | CC → C | CCC | CC | CC |
| Total | 24 | | | | | | | | |
| *Elephas primigenius* | | | | | 1 fragment | R/C | | | |
| *Rhinoceros tichorhinus* | | | | | 4 fragments | R/C | | | |
| *Lepus timidus* | 1 fragment | | | | | | | | |
| Seal | | | | | | Teeth | | | |
| Fish | | | | | c. 20 vert. | | 7 vert. | | |
| Birds | R | | | R/C | C | | C | C | |
| Molluscs | 6 (*L. littorea*) | | | | C (incl. 31 *L. littorea*) | | CC (132 *L. littorea*) | R (14 *L. littorea*) | |

Where given, absolute figures are MNI and percentage of individuals.

Ist. = Salle Isturitz/Grande Salle/North Salle
RR = very rare
R = rare
R/C = present

St M = Salle St Martin/South Salle
C = common
CC = very common
CCC = extremely common

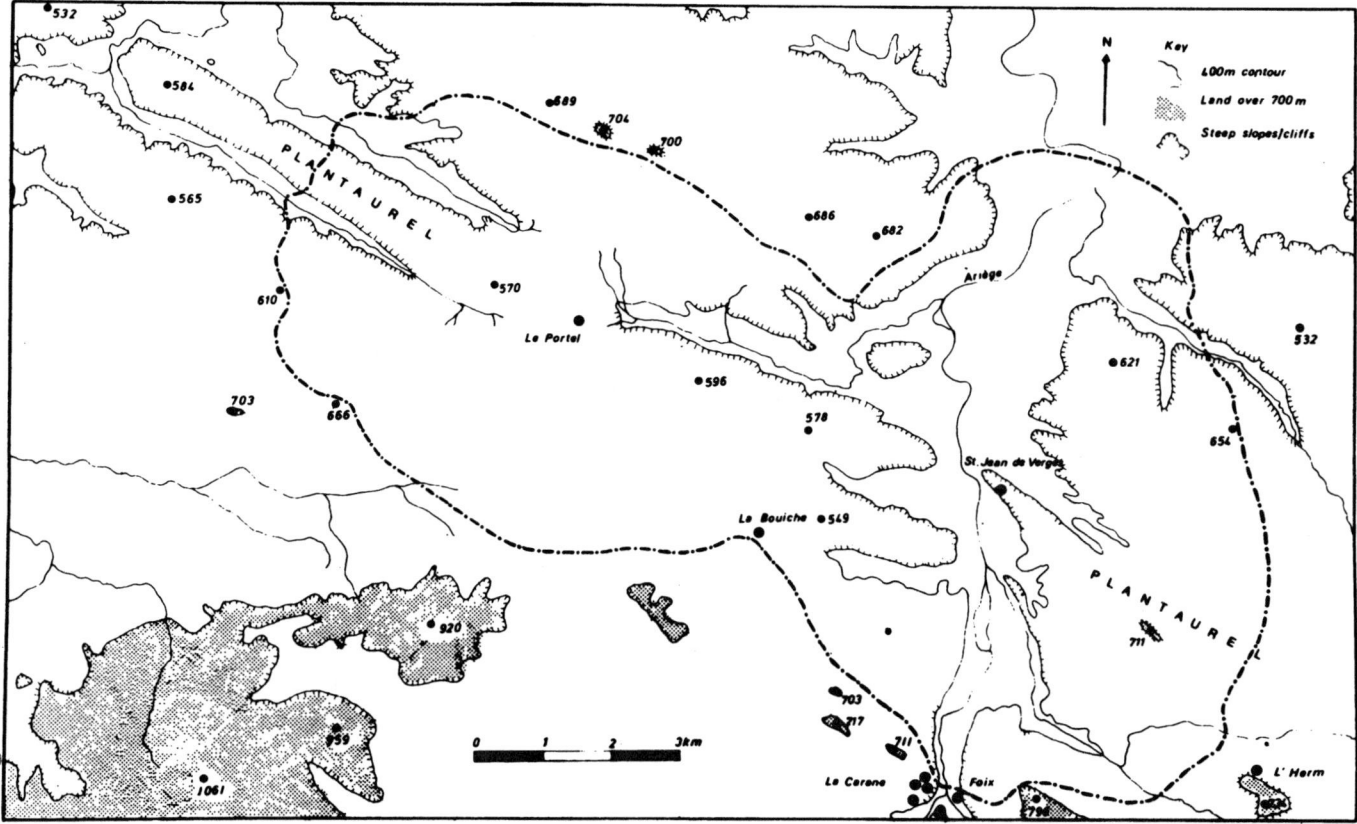

Fig. 15.4. Combined 1-hour site exploitation territories of Le Portel and St Jean de Verges.

sites at this point) and the second at St Jean de Verges. Between the two the valley widens. The cave has excellent views of Foix, as well as west and northward, and its position was ideal for the control and corralling of moving herds. Hence it is no surprise that in its fauna (table 15.3) bovids and horses are still of importance but reindeer appears to predominate.

The fauna as a whole, together with the sediments, suggest cool but not harsh conditions, and this picture is repeated in other Central Pyrenees Aurignacian sites such as Gargas, Tarté and Aurignac itself. Another feature of this period shared by these sites is a broadening of the diversity of species exploited, which now regularly include roe deer, boar, small game and birds. Nevertheless, most sites other than St Jean de Verges continue the Mousterian pattern of a heavy reliance on bovids and horses, merely supplemented by cervids. Indeed at Gargas, in a small sample, bovids account for about two-thirds of the meat (Bouchud 1958; Bahn 1979a, tables 10 and 11). As only Verges is dated (to *c.* 22 000 b.p.) it is difficult to know whether its dominance of reindeer has any climatic/chronological significance. However, it is not the only site with a specialized economy: the rich Aurignacian layers of Isturitz in the west show a cold, humid climate, and a similar broadening of the faunal spectrum, but horse bones are extremely abundant (St Périer and St Périer 1952: 223;

Passemard 1922), a fact which is completely masked by Bouchud's figures (1966). The economy is dominated by horses throughout, and certainly the cave is well suited to their exploitation: its 1-hour territory is quite circular, it has a fine view in all directions, and, located at the junction of the lowest foothills and the plain, it dominates a series of closed valleys and a basin which provides excellent grazing on slopes leading from the Arberoue River to plateaux that stretch for miles; although forested in historical times, these would have had their present bleak moorland aspect in Würm III times. Herds of horses may have been exploited by stalking, coursing, game drives or even loose herding – even today, the little Pyrenean horses of the area are 'ranched' by the peasants who leave them to roam and breed freely.

One final point worthy of mention is that, in the original excavation of Aurignac, Lartet (1861) noticed and stressed that the fragmentation of herbivore bones for marrow was done by smashing rather than with the method and precision seen in the later period. Similar observations were made elsewhere, for example at the Grotte des Rideaux at Lespugue (de Saint-Périer 1924), where the reindeer fragments were bigger than those of the Magdalenian, and the same is even discernible from the Early to the Late Magdalenian of Isturitz (de Saint-Périer 1936: 11). Is this to be interpreted in cultural terms, or does the development of a systematic and thorough

Table 15.3. *The fauna of Mauran, Aurignac and St Jean de Verges (Tuto de Camalhot)*

| | Mauran (Mousterian) | Aurignac (Aurignacian) | | St J. de V. (Aurignacian) | | St J. de V. (Gravettian) |
| --- | --- | --- | --- | --- | --- | --- |
| | | No. of fragments | MNI/% | No. of fragments | MNI/% | MNI/% |
| *Rangifer tarandus* | | | 10–12/25% | CCC | 25/59.5% | 1/11.1% |
| *Cervus elaphus* | 1 | | 1/2.1% | C | 3/7.1% | 1/11.1% |
| *Megaceros hibernicus* | 1 | | (1) | | | |
| *Cervus (Dama) somonensis* | | | | 4 | 2/4.8% | |
| *Capreolus capreolus* | | | 3–4/8.3% | | | |
| Big bovids | CCC | | 12–15/31.3% | 12 | 2/4.8% | 3/33.3% |
| *Capra ibex/pyrenaica* | | | | 27 | 3/7.1% | 1/11.1% |
| *Rupicapra rupicapra* | | | | 4 | 2/4.8% | 1/11.1% |
| *Sus scrofa* | 2 | | 1/2.1% | 1 | 1/2.4% | |
| *Equus asinus* | | | (1?) | | | |
| *Equus caballus* | R | | 12–15/31.3% | > 20 | 4/9.5% | 2/22.2% |
| Total | | | 48 | | 42 | 9 |
| *Rhino. tichorhinus* | | | 1 | | | |
| *Rhino. sp.* | | | | 1 | | 1 |
| *Elephas primigenius* | 2 | | 1 | | | |
| *Lepus (timidus?)* | 1 | | 1 | > 4 | 3 | |
| Birds | | | 10 | 18 | 10 | 2 |
| Seashells | | | | 60 | | |

R = rare
C = common
CCC = extremely common

processing of bone, analogous to that of some Eskimos (see Delpech and Rigaud 1974) perhaps indicate a growing need to extract the maximum nutrition from available resources?

### The later Upper Palaeolithic

For this period pollen and sediments in the western Pyrenees suggest a change from the fairly mild and humid climate of the Aurignacian to very cold and dry, steppic conditions in the Gravettian, and then back again in the Solutrean, which is thought to coincide with the Würm III/IV interstadial. Certainly the Gravettian fauna of Isturitz seems 'cold', with large numbers of reindeer, while mammoth, woolly rhino, the great white owl and numerous arctic foxes are also present. The fauna at Gargas shows a decline of the horse and an increase of reindeer, whereas at Isturitz (table 15.2) horses remain abundant but both bovids and reindeer also regain importance so that the occupants seem to have returned to a Mousterian type of broad-based economy which continues in the ensuing Epigravettian phase. As David (1973: 281) pointed out, this contrasts sharply with the dependence on reindeer found in many Gravettian sites to the north. However, it is the reindeer remains of this period which provide the first concrete evidence of seasonality in the Pyrenees, in that antlers and dentition point to cold-season occupation of both Isturitz and Gargas (see Bouchud 1966; Bahn 1979a). Despite lack of additional evidence, it seems reasonable to assume that some herds, and possibly some human groups, will have spent the summer in the Pyrenean uplands (Bahn 1977).

The economies of the Solutrean period are very poorly known in the Pyrenees, since occupations of caves at this time appear sporadic and short, even at Isturitz. In some cases this semi-abandonment may be due to excessive humidity within the caves, as in the Mesolithic – for example Passemard (1922: 17) encountered clay deposits above and below his Solutrean layer at Isturitz, and it may be no coincidence that this is the only phase of the Upper Palaeolithic during which hearths occur *outside* one of the Lespugue caves, at Les Harpons (de Saint-Périer 1928: 17). As one might expect, the Solutrean fauna of sites like Les Harpons and Roquecourbère shows a reduction in importance of reindeer, and a dominance of horse, while at Isturitz the trio of herbivores maintain their role.

The most intriguing economic feature of the Pyrenean Solutrean is the rise of fish exploitation; most of the evidence is indirect, for instance engravings of fish at Isturitz, and, in one of the outdoor hearths at Les Harpons, a thin polished bone blade (de Saint-Périer 1928: 17) which closely resembles objects used by Eskimos in salmon-fishing. It is noteworthy that identical objects abound at Laugerie-Basse, Le Placard and the Solutrean of Laugerie-Haute. The only direct clues to fish exploitation are the trout vertebrae from the late Solutrean cave of Embulla in the eastern Pyrenees (Sacchi and Abelanet 1980: 24). The sudden appearance of an interest in fish at this time is intriguing: even if salmon runs were affected by glacial conditions, one can hardly assume that all Pyrenean rivers were totally devoid of fish until the Solutrean, and certainly sea fish would have been available earlier. It would be too easy and unrealistic to claim that pre-Magdalenian fish bones have simply not been preserved at any Pyrenean site.

Table 15.4. *The fauna of Gourdan*

| | 'Mousterian' | 'Solutrean' Cervid layer | 'Mid. Magd.' | | 'Upper Magdalenian' | | 'Azilian' |
| --- | --- | --- | --- | --- | --- | --- | --- |
| | | | Aurochs layer | Horse layer | Reindeer layer | Red deer layer | Transition |
| *Rangifer tarandus* | R/C | R | R/C → C | C | CCC | CC → R/C | RR |
| *Cervus elaphus* | | C | C | R/C | R/C | CC | CC |
| *Alces sp.* | | | R | | R | | |
| Big bovids | | C | C | C | R | | R/C |
| Ovicaprids (including *Capra primig.*) | | | | R/C | R/C | | |
| *Capra ibex/pyrenaica* | | R/C | R/C | R/C | R/C | R/C | |
| *Rupicapra rupicapra* | | R/C | R/C | R/C | R/C | R/C | |
| *Saiga tartarica* | | | R | R | | | |
| *Sus scrofa* | | | | | | R/C | R/C |
| *Equus caballus* | | C | C | CC → C | R/C | | R/C |
| *Elephas primigenius* | R/C | | R | | | | |
| Lagomorphs | | | | | R/C | R/C | |
| Birds | | R/C | R/C | R/C | C | C | |
| Fish | | | | | | R/C | R/C |
| Molluscs | | | | | | | CC (*Helix*) |

RR = very rare　　　　C = common
R = rare　　　　　　　CC = very common
R/C = present　　　　CCC = extremely common

### The Magdalenian

There are far too many major sites and there is far too much economic evidence in the Pyrenean Magdalenian to be adequately described here. Several important caves, such as Les Espélugues (Lourdes), lower Massat and Enlène, were dug in the last century by a number of scholars, but each excavator encountered a different pattern of faunal specialization (which is unsurprising in view of the size of these caves), and so their information is of little use here. As was pointed out in the Introduction, one is unlikely to find identical faunal oscillations from site to site, and area to area, for topographic and climatic reasons; and the results of the old excavations underline the role played by sampling. It is therefore difficult to assess how far a Magdalenian site's faunal record is due to economic strategy, and how far to natural fluctuations in the availability of each species.

That the faunal record alters radically through the Magdalenian even at individual sites was already made clear by Piette (1889) who subdivided the Magdalenian of both the Grotte de Gourdan (Haute Garonne) and the right bank of the Mas d'Azil into four levels characterized by the most abundant species (see tables 15.4 and 15.5).

(1) A basal, bovid level. At Gourdan, in fact, this layer seems to have a roughly equal abundance of bovid, horse and reindeer remains; whereas at the Mas d'Azil it contained whole aurochs skulls, and its bone material was less fragmentary than that of later layers, thus supporting the point made above.

(2) This was followed by a 'horse layer' — in fact, at Gourdan, it showed little change other than a decline of bovids and an increase in reindeer. However, at the Mas d'Azil, the horses, already abundant in the bovid level, constituted most of the mass of this layer.

(3) Above this was a 'reindeer level' in which the bones of this species were superabundant: at Gourdan they constituted most of the layer's mass, and Piette estimated that he had found over 3000 reindeer in the portion of the cave which he dug (see Bahn 1977). These three layers saw the gradual decline of bovids and the concomitant rise in reindeer.

(4) Finally in the 'red deer layer' he encountered the gradual decline of the reindeer and the rising dominance of the red deer which characterizes the postglacial period of much of southern Europe.

This sequence, obviously, is not valid for every Pyrenean Magdalenian site; nevertheless, there are regularities in that red deer become dominant in the final Magdalenian or shortly afterwards in most sites; and apart from the late 'ibex sites' of the eastern Pyrenees (see below), many Magdalenian sites tend to show a predominance of horse or reindeer or both: for example the short 'Magdalenian IV' occupation of Le Portel, dated to 12 760 b.p., has a clear predominance of reindeer; the Middle and Late Magdalenian of several caves around the basin of Arudy (Pyrénées Atlantiques) show a predominance of horses — with possible evidence for a selection of age and sex (see Bahn in press (a)) — supplemented by reindeer; while the Middle Magdalenian phases at the various

Table 15.5. *The fauna of the Mas d'Azil*

| | Right bank | | | | | | Left bank | | | | | | | |
|---|---|---|---|---|---|---|---|---|---|---|---|---|---|---|
| | Bovid layer (Early Mgd.) | Horse layer (Mid. Mgd.) | Reindeer layer (Mid. Mgd.) | Red deer layer (Late Mgd.) | Transition layer | 5th Mgd. layer | 4th Mgd. layer | 3rd Mgd. layer (B) | 2nd Mgd. layer (D) | Top Mgd. | F (Azil.) | G (Arisian) | H (Neol.-Br.A-GR) | I |
| *Rangifer tarandus* | R | R/C→ | CC | C→R/C | | | R/C | R/C | R | RR | (RRR) | | | |
| *Cervus elaphus* | | | R/C | CC | CC | R/C | R/C | | C/CC | CC | CC | CC | C | R/C |
| *Saiga tartarica* | | R/C | | | | | | | | | | | | |
| *Capreolus capreolus* | | | | | | | | | R/C | R/C | R/C | | R | |
| Bovids | CC | R/C | R/C | R/C | | | R/C | R/C | R/C | R/C | R/C | R/C | R/C | R/C |
| *Capra ibex/ pyrenaica* | | R/C | R/C | R/C | | | | | R/C | R/C | R/C | | | |
| *Rupicapra rupicapra* | | | R/C | C | | | | | R/C | | R/C | | | |
| *Capra primigenia* | | R/C | R/C | | | | | | | | | | | |
| Ovicaprids | | | | | | | | | | | | | R/C | R/C |
| *Sus scrofa*/Suids | | R/C | R/C | C | | | | | R/C | | CC | CC | C | R/C |
| *Equus caballus* | C | CC→ | C | R/C | | | | R/C | R/C | | R/C | R/C | RR | |
| *Lepus/Oryctolagus* | | R/C | R/C | R/C | | | | | R/C | | R/C | | R/C | |
| Birds | RR | R/C | C | CC | | | | | R/C | R/C | C | R/C | | |
| Fish | | | | C | | | | | ? | ? | R/C | R | | |
| Frogs | | | | | | | | | | | R/C | | | |
| Seashells | | R/C | R/C | R/C | | ? | ? | ? | R/C | R/C | R/C | R/C | R/C | |
| Freshwater shells | | | | | | | | | | | R/C | R/C | R/C | |
| Snails | | | | | | | | | | | | CCC | C | |

RRR = extremely rare    C = common
RR = very rare    CC = very common
R = rare    CCC = extremely common
R/C = present

Table 15.6. *The fauna of Duruthy: number and percentage of ungulate fragments*

| | Layer 5 'Magd. III' | Layer 4 'Magd. IV' | Layer 3' 'Magd. V' | Layer 3 'Magd. VI' | Layer 2 'Azil.' | 3b (Inf.) 'Azil,' | 3a (Sup.) 'Azil.' |
|---|---|---|---|---|---|---|---|
| *Rangifer tarandus* | 24/7.45% | 353/25.12% | 11/23.91% | 4306/71.71% | 15/24.19% | 5/33.3% | 2/14.28% |
| *Cervus elaphus* | | 26/1.85% | | 972/16.18% | 34/54.83% | 9/60% | 9/64.28% |
| *Capreolus capreolus* | | | | 2/0.03% | 2/3.22% | 1/6.66% | 1/7.14% |
| Big bovids | 99/30.74% | 628/44.69% | 3/6.52% | 564/9.39% | 1/1.61% | | |
| *Capra pyrenaica* | | | | 13/0.21% | 1/1.61% | | 1/7.14% |
| *Rupicapra rupicapra* | | 2/0.14% | | 3/0.04% | | | |
| *Sus scrofa* | | | | 1/0.01% | 2/3.22% | | 1/7.14% |
| *Equus caballus* | 199/61.80% | 396/28.18% | 32/69.56% | 143/2.38% | 7/11.29% | | |
| Total | 322 | 1405 | 46 | 6004 | 62 | 15 | 14 |
| *Oryctolagus cuniculus* | | | | 1 fragment | | | |
| *Tursiops tursio* | | 2 teeth | | | | | |
| *Salmo salar* | | | | 51 fragments | | | |
| *Salmo fario* | | | | 1 fragment | | | |
| Birds | | | | 126 fragments (including 57 of *Nyctea scandiaca*). | 1 fragment | | |

Lespugue caves (Haute Garonne) have faunal samples dominated by horse, by reindeer or by both (Bahn 1979a).

It would be dangerous and naive to draw too many conclusions from the fauna in these early excavations, and to refer to horse or reindeer economies without due regard to the other species present; but it can be seen that in the Magdalenian, despite the great diversity of species available, there is a shift from the previous generalized economies to a very heavy dependence on only one or two herbivore species. This situation is clearest in the very full information from the cave of Isturitz (table 15.2(b)) and the rockshelter of Duruthy (table 15.6).

*Isturitz and Duruthy* (*west Pyrenees*). There is no gap between the Solutrean and the Magdalenian of the Pyrenees, yet the earliest phases of the latter are typologically equivalent to phases III and IV of Breuil's sequence. At Duruthy, the start of the Magdalenian coincides with that of Würm IV, and the sediments indicate cold and humid conditions, with a subsequent cold and dry oscillation, which coincides with palynological evidence for a very open steppic landscape (see Arambourou 1978). The end of this phase has been dated to 14 180 b.p., and its faunal remains, measured in number of fragments, show that the horse is very dominant, with bovids fairly abundant and reindeer comparatively rare. Unfortunately, no indication of the minimum number of individuals or of the extent of fragmentation has been given for the site by Delpech (1975). It appears that the economy was based jointly on equids and bovids.

The Middle Magdalenian ('phase IV') is well represented at both Isturitz and Duruthy. At Isturitz both pollen and sediments indicate a cold and dry climate, though it should be noted that the site's published pollen analysis (Leroi-Gourhan 1959) is untrustworthy (Leroi-Gourhan, pers.

comm.). At Duruthy, on the other hand, the evidence points to a series of humid and temperate phases separated by colder episodes. At Isturitz, Passemard (1922: 20) found that bovids and equids were very numerous, but stressed that reindeer increased in importance until, by the end of the phase, it was predominant. De Saint-Périer, on the other hand (1930: 21; 1936: 13) found that horse was predominant throughout, with reindeer in second place. The discrepancy may indicate that the layers of the two excavators were not precisely equivalent or synchronous, but may also be due to sampling, since there is a great deal of lateral variation in both bones and cultural material in this enormous cave, showing a clear localization of activities; for example, there are accumulations of worked and unworked antlers, while the vertebrae and ribs of large herbivores are common around the cave entrance but not farther inside (de Saint-Périer 1936: 11).

The Isturitz economy in 'Magdalenian IV' (table 15.2(b)) does not seem to have undergone a great change since the earlier part of the Upper Palaeolithic: the usual trio of species dominate, with others playing a very minor, supplementary role. The one new development, already heralded in the Solutrean, is the exploitation of fish on an apparently minor scale.

The horse bones represent animals of all ages including many 'young animals' and even some newborn specimens (de Saint-Périer 1930: 21; 1936: 13). The presence of the latter is intriguing, in view of my earlier speculations concerning some sort of management of horses from this site. Ethnographic data (Jarman and Wilkinson, 1972: 95) suggest that it is unlikely, although by no means impossible, that hunters would kill a heavily pregnant mare, let alone a newborn foal, since this kind of exploitation would endanger the future of the species. The heavy reliance on horse for many millennia which is evident at Isturitz suggests very strongly that exploitation

was careful and efficient (compare Levine, this volume).
It is intriguing also that the Magdalenian of this site yielded
a fractured reindeer metacarpal which points to protection
by man (Bahn 1978a) as well as one of the many possible
examples of a Pyrenean Palaeolithic dog (see Bahn 1979a).

It is quite clear that Isturitz was primarily a winter site:
the intensified exploitation of reindeer is accompanied by a
greater use of antlers. De Saint-Périer (1930: 22; 1936: 14)
found that almost all the big (i.e. male) antlers were shed,
while the female specimens were mostly unshed. A similar
conclusion was reached from antlers at Lespugue (de Saint-
Périer 1920) and Gourdan (see Bahn 1977).

The 'Magdalenian IV' period is well dated at Duruthy,
to 13 840 b.p. (base) and 13 510 b.p. (top). Burnt sand-
stone from the layer has been dated to 14 500 by thermoluminescence. The faunal material indicated a rather cold
and open environment; at first sight, this clashes with the
data from pollen and sediments which pointed to a relatively
temperate and humid period with cold episodes; but in fact
the bones simply reflect the fact that this site too was
primarily occupied in the winter.

Parts of the site have bad bone preservation, and so
there is some bias in favour of the identification of bovids
and horses. Where preservation is good, reindeer are sometimes
dominant. The most recent figures for this layer (table 15.6)
show that bovids are dominant, with horse and reindeer in
second place, and other species of minimal importance. When

meat weight is taken into account, these figures seem rather
similar to those of the Gravettian of Isturitz: up to two-
thirds of usable meat probably came from the bovids, which
may constitute some kind of specialization. The reindeer
is far less important than in the same period in the Dordogne.
Unlike Isturitz, Duruthy has no fish remains in this phase.

The group of rockshelters around Duruthy are in an
excellent position for winter occupation; the cliff faces
south-west and reflects sunlight throughout most of the day,
so that even in January this locality enjoys very mild
temperatures; as at Isturitz, the proximity to the coast ensures
that an oceanic climate dominates, with mild winters. A
further advantage of the location (fig. 15.5) is the nearby ford,
and the presence of a series of narrow passages between
rivers and very steep slopes, useful for the interception of
herds crossing the ford (see Bahn 1979a).

Evidence for 'Magdalenian V' is sparse at both sites. At
Isturitz in the Late Magdalenian (V/VI), Passemard (1944)
found that reindeer increased in predominance, horses were
still very abundant, and bovids and red deer were well
represented. Bovids and horses had decreased in numbers
since the Middle Magdalenian, and the red deer increased
markedly at the top of the layer (1922: 24). This picture
was confirmed and enhanced by de Saint-Périer (1936: 13)
who found that horses were still abundant, and that red deer
were more frequent than in the Middle Magdalenian and 'took
over' from reindeer at the top of the layer. In short, the

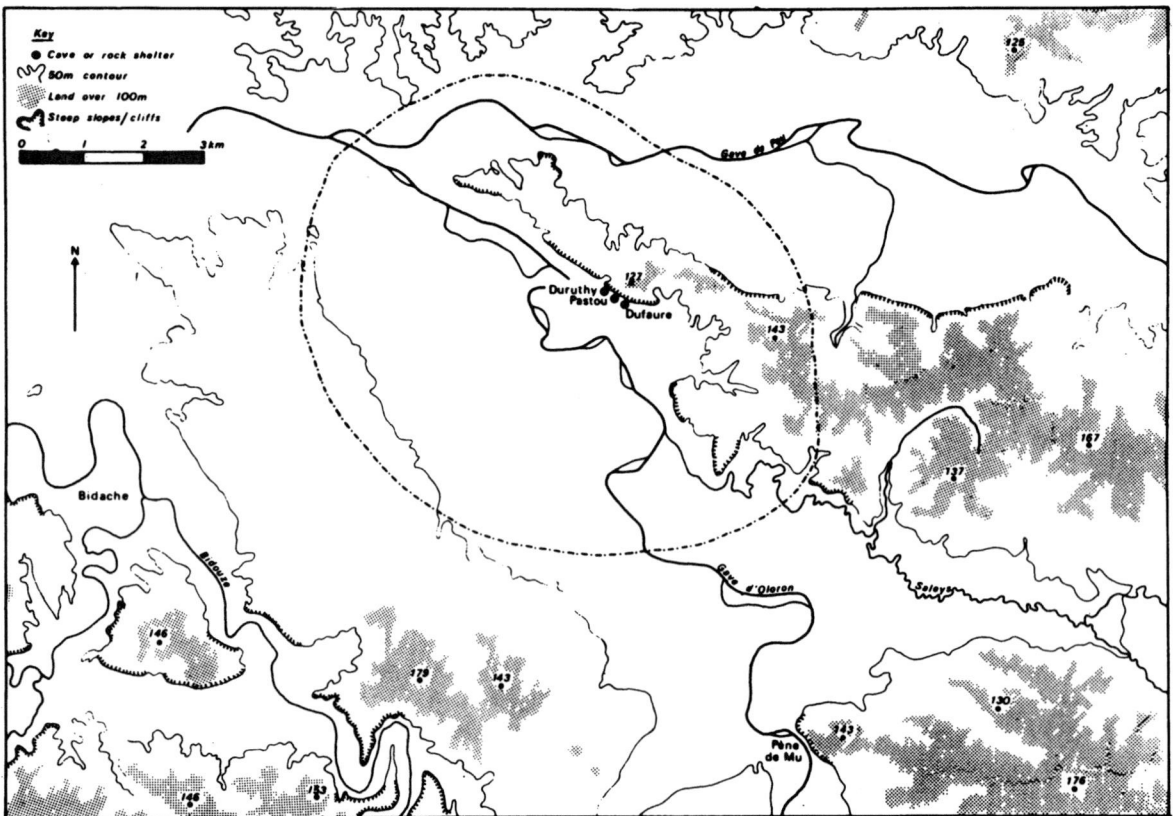

Fig. 15.5. One-hour site exploitation territory of the Duruthy group of rockshelters.

indications are that reindeer gained in importance until, as the climate grew milder, exploitation switched to red deer, while the interest in small resources, first seen in the Middle Magdalenian, was developing steadily.

The same picture can be seen in even more detail on the left bank of the Mas d'Azil where Piette (1895) found a total of five superimposed Upper Magdalenian levels whose material culture was the same, but whose faunal record showed the gradual disappearance of reindeer and the rising dominance of the red deer, together with a growing reliance on small resources. Occupation continued at the Mas d'Azil throughout the Magdalenian because, like the major sites in the west, it was well suited to both large-herbivore and cervid economies. Its 1-hour territory is fairly circular, and comprises several small basins which would be excellent grazing for the large herbivores. But there are additional advantages: the River Arize crosses three parallel limestone ridges; in the first and last of these it formed a gorge, while in the middle ridge it made the tunnel of the Mas d'Azil. Hence these gorges, together with the steepness of other slopes, help to form potential natural corrals, such as the basin between the cave and the ridge to the south. The gorge through that ridge is dominated by caves with minor Magdalenian traces which were most probably lookout posts or control sites within the economic strategy of the occupants of the major site (see Bahn 1979a).

Some of the best information concerning the Late Magdalenian comes from Duruthy, where layer 3 (phase VI) has yielded rich quantities of faunal material (table 15.6). Pollen and sediments suggest a very complex sequence of oscillations from cold/humid to temperate/humid. The environment carried considerable woodland. The base of the layer is dated to 12 640 b.p., the top to 11 150 b.p., while thermoluminescence gave 11 300 b.p. This level seems to end during the Allerod climatic phase.

The faunal information concurs with that of Isturitz: that is there was a decline in the importance of horses and bovids, and a notable intensification of reindeer exploitation followed by a change to red deer as the mild woodland environment took hold. It is noteworthy that, as this layer has more bone fragments than any other, so more species are represented than before. Nevertheless, the vast majority of specimens belong to the usual three species (reindeer, bovid, horse) plus the red deer. The thousands of reindeer fragments clearly demonstrate the increased importance of that species, but its overall dominance is diminished when meat weight is taken into account, for bovids probably gave almost as much meat as reindeer. The period can therefore be seen as one of 'reindeer people', but with caution. It also sees a rise in the use of small resources, including the first appearance of fish in the site, together with some perforated and engraved carnivore canines which de Saint-Périer (1928: 19), by analogy with the Eskimos, thought to be baits for fishing.

The reindeer antlers and jaws point to occupation of the site between August and March (Arambourou 1978).

The humidity and the development of woodland is underlined by the numbers of water-loving trees in the pollen, and the first appearance of boar, roe deer and rabbit on the site. Despite the still harsh, glacial winters, conditions were clearly improving, and the high humidity may be one fact in the decline of the horse, which dislikes marshy conditions, while bovids thrive on wet grazing.

*Ibex sites (east Pyrenees).* I have described and assessed elsewhere (Bahn 1979a and b) some of the ibex sites of the later Magdalenian in the eastern Pyrenees; the layers of the cave of La Vache (Ariège), for example, span several centuries, from 12 850 b.p. to 12 540 b.p. while a brief occupation at nearby Les Eglises is dated to *c*. 12 900 b.p. These sites and others are clustered around the basin of Tarascon which, apart from the Mousterian evidence at Bouichéta mentioned earlier, does not seem to have been available for occupation before the Magdalenian. The basin is at the junction of two of the most deeply penetrating valleys in the Pyrenees (the Ariège and Vicdessos) which offer relatively easy access to the frontier area. Although well inside the Pyrenees it lies at only 460 m, and has a sheltered, dry and sunny microclimate. The valleys are extremely narrow and steep-sided immediately upstream of the basin (see fig. 15.6), and thus the sites are in a location with great potential for the interception or control of animal herds; La Vache, in particular, is situated at the most strangulated part of the Vicdessos valley. The ibex was found to be the dominant animal in the modern excavations of La Vache and, more recently, at Les Eglises – indeed at the latter it is almost the only large mammal present (Delpech 1975), and its bones are often found in connection. At La Vache the faunal list is more varied, but ibex account for up to 90% of herbivore fragments, and their abundance implies a successful long-term exploitation of the species in the form of heavy seasonal culls and/or some sort of animal control. The ease with which the animal can be manipulated and the apparent stability of the economic relationship led Davidson (1976: 497) to suggest that some type of loose herding of ibex could be envisaged at Les Mallaetes in eastern Spain (see also chapter 8), and the same could be argued here.

It can be seen from figure 15.6 that the exploitation territories of La Vache and the others are the most restricted of all Pyrenean Palaeolithic sites, and would be even more restricted if the rivers formed an effective barrier in the spring melt. La Vache lies above a scree slope and below a cliff – its environment of abrupt, rocky mountains is ideal ibex country, and very suited to the type of exploitation described above, while highly unsuitable for a more generalized economy. I have argued (1979a and b) that factors such as the probable position of the snowline and the altitudinal movements of the ibex make it likely that these sites were occupied in the winter, or at least in the late autumn and early spring. The diet was supplemented with a few other herbivores, lagomorphs and fish, but especially with lagopeds (i.e. willow grouse and

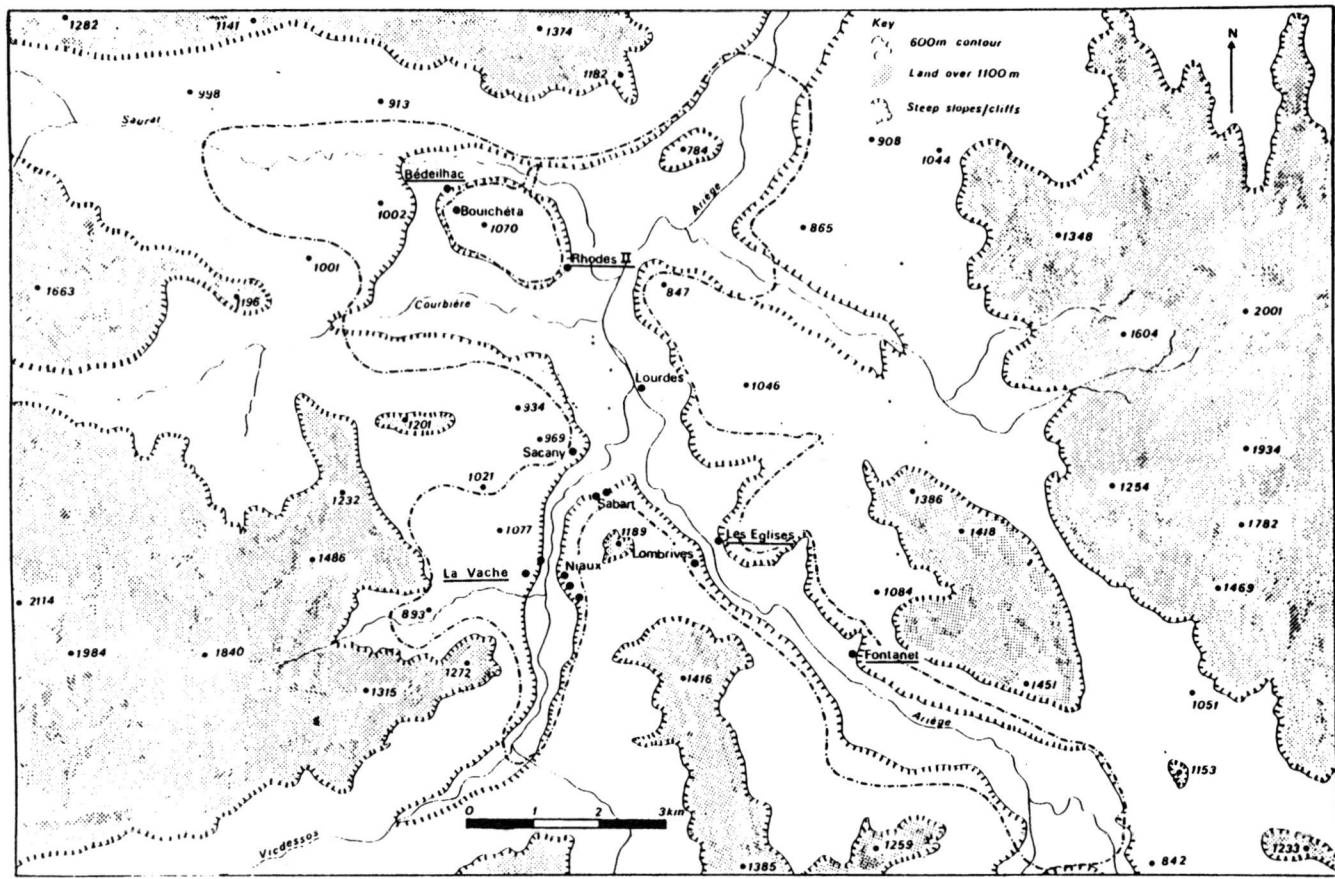

Fig. 15.6. Combined 1-hour site exploitation territories of La Vache, Bédeilhac, Les Eglises, Fontanet and Rhodes II.

rock ptarmigan). La Vache yielded a minimum of 245 individual lagopeds, and although their dietary contribution was tiny in comparison with that of the ibex, they represent an easy catch and a change of diet. Their great abundance also points clearly to cold-season exploitation, since they too make altitudinal movements in order to avoid excessive snow cover. J.G.D. Clark (1952) has argued that the presence of large numbers of lagoped bones in archaeological sites implies the use of snares during the season of snow cover, and this is supported by ethnography.

Finally, further to the east, two other ibex sites are known: the Grotte de l'Oeil comprises a small and short-lived occupation with an economy, based on both ibex and isard (the Pyrenean chamois), which reflects the mountainous terrain nearby. Its cultural material provides further analogies with the more important site of the Cauna de Belvis: this cave, at 960 m in a small calcareous ridge on the Plateau de Sault (Aude), has four layers of 'Magdalenian VI' totalling only 28 cm; the material is homogeneous, showing no development, and suggests that occupation of the site was short-lived; it has been dated to 12 270 b.p. (Sacchi 1976). Ibex is very dominant in the fauna, with isard second, and the pollen indicates very harsh and dry conditions.

In terms of assemblage, period, fauna and duration the cave has obvious analogies with Les Eglises. Its territory

seems less suited to the exploitation of ibex herds, as the cave dominates a flat plain ringed by hills and mountains. However, only 3 km to the south there is an imposing series of gorges, and the whole region is full of such gorges, cliffs and cul-de-sac valleys. Exits from the plateau could have been controlled easily. It should be noted, however, that Belvis is at a much higher altitude than Tarascon, and whereas the latter has a mild and dry microclimate, that of the Plateau de Sault is harsh and wet, with abundant snow in the winter. One might therefore speculate that the ibex, isard and 'cold birds' descended further than this in the winters of Würm IV, and hence the site is most likely to have been occupied in the summer or late spring/early autumn.

The foregoing account has shown that from the Mousterian far into the Upper Palaeolithic there is great continuity in the economic base, albeit with localized variations, but that the picture changes in the Magdalenian. It is now necessary to take a closer look at the development of some of the variables involved in order to assess their importance.

### The exploitation of resources
*Large herbivores*

The picture which has emerged from similar studies of other areas of southern Europe (e.g. Freeman 1973a; Barker

1975; Straus 1977a; chapters 12 and 13, this volume) is one
of a generalized economy in the Middle Palaeolithic, based
on several forms of large herbivore, no one species greatly
outnumbering the others. This is followed, in the Upper
Palaeolithic, by a shift to heavy dependence on two, or even
one species. The Pyrenean evidence produced a similar
conclusion, but with some qualifications. In broad terms
one can see the Middle Palaeolithic economies as fairly
homogeneous, based on a trio of bovids, horse and red deer,
the large lowland herbivores. However, it has been stressed
above that the open site of Mauran is a highly specialized site
devoted to mass culls of bovids. This reliance on three species,
with an occasional concentration on bovids, can also be seen
in Cantabrian Spain (Straus, 1977a), and, as in Spain, most
of the major Pyrenean Mousterian sites are located in positions
advantageous for generalized economic strategies. Mauran is
an important exception.

The Upper Palaeolithic economies became increasingly
heterogeneous. Thus, while some sites persist with a Mousterian
type of strategy during the Aurignacian, others show signs
of a specialization in reindeer (St Jean de Verges) or in horse
(Isturitz), and the smaller, supplementary resources are present
more often and in greater numbers. This period also sees the
first appearance of seashells which, together with other
imported materials (e.g. at Verges), may be linked with the
growing importance of migratory cervids.

The Gravettian and Solutrean in the French Pyrenees
have poor faunal evidence, which points only to a basic,
broadly based economy, though with occasional emphasis
on one species (e.g. the bovids at Isturitz). In the Magdalenian
of course, as was shown above, these broader economies are
replaced in the early phases by heavy concentrations on
reindeer, horse or ibex. In Cantabrian Spain (Straus 1977a)
it seems there is no clear evidence of Aurignacian specialization,
better evidence for some specialized economies in the
Gravettian and Solutrean, and a Magdalenian similar to the
Pyrenean, though with concentrations on red deer, as well
as on alpine herbivores in the rugged Basque country. As has
been stressed above, and as can be seen from the tables, the
late Magdalenian is the period with the broadest range of
exploited prey: for example, it is at this time that Pyreneans
seem to have included fish, freshwater molluscs, land snails
and possibly even toads in their diet; yet it also has the greatest
number of economies that are heavily concentrated on single
biotopes (e.g. the alpine) or single herbivore species. It will
be recalled that this is also the time when bones seem to have
been processed to the extreme in order to extract the maximum
nourishment.

### Mountain herbivores
The isard is represented by isolated finds in the
Mousterian of Olha, Isturitz, Le Portel, etc. and the ibex first
appears in the Chatelperronian of Gargas. Thus, as in Cantabria,
the alpine biotope was not systematically exploited at this
time. The two species are consistently present in small numbers

throughout the Upper Palaeolithic, especially, as one might
expect, in the sites at the junction of mountain and foothill.
Their presence may indicate an exploitation aimed at procuring
skins. They are only of real importance in the Late Magdalenian
sites of the rugged country of the east Pyrenees.

### Forest herbivores
The roe deer, pig and giant deer are all present, though
very rare, in the Pyrenean Mousterian. The giant deer occurs
sporadically until its apparent decline in the middle of the
Upper Palaeolithic, whereas both roe deer and pig persist until
the Magdalenian, although never appearing to be of great
economic importance. This is no doubt due to their solitary
and elusive life-style, the pig being also quite dangerous.

### Dogs
Dogs are only considered here as possible contributors
to the diet in the role of hunting or herding aids. There have
been many claims for Palaeolithic dogs in the Pyrenees since
Lartet's in 1861, based on bones or on tooth marks. All have
been ignored in the past, but since modern excavations are
now yielding dog bones in various parts of Palaeolithic Europe
and elsewhere (e.g. Musil 1970; Davis and Valla 1978; Bosinski
and Evers 1979: 63–5), it seems worth issuing a reminder of
the possible examples at eight or nine Magdalenian sites in the
Pyrenees (see Bahn 1979a).

### Small game and birds
Lagomorphs first appear sporadically in the Aurignacian
(e.g. at Gargas) and Gravettian (Isturitz), and remain rare
throughout the Upper Palaeolithic. It cannot be proved that
they were exploited by man; nevertheless it may be significant
that the bones of hare are of numerical importance (106
fragments) in the final Magdalenian of La Vache.

Birds, like other small resources, are totally absent from
the occupation material at Olha: this cannot be attributed to
lack of preservation, since bird bones are abundant in the
rockfall layers between the occupation levels; moreover,
birds are present, though rare, in the Mousterian of Isturitz.
Once again, however, one cannot be sure of exploitation by
man. Bird bones increase in number, and in their range of
species, through the Upper Palaeolithic; corvids, lagopeds and
water birds are the most characteristic forms, although the
great white owl is frequently present in cold phases. At Isturitz
the birds seem more important in the Magdalenian than in
the Solutrean (de Saint-Périer and de Saint-Périer 1952: 73),
while at Gourdan Piette noticed (1889: 10) that they became
increasingly abundant through the Magdalenian, and were
especially common in the 'reindeer layer'. This increase in
the exploitation of birds at the end of the Palaeolithic has
been linked not only with dietary needs but also with a greater
use of feathered arrows. The culmination of the trend, of
course, is the apparently common snaring of lagopeds at the
ibex sites, as described earlier, in the final Magdalenian.

### Water resources

It was mentioned earlier that the first evidence — vertebrae, engravings and a possible decoy — for an interest in fish occurs in the Solutrean of the French Pyrenees, and it is noteworthy that fish make their first appearance in Cantabrian sites during the same period (Straus 1977a: 64–5). In the Pyrenees, some fish bones occur in the mid-Magdalenian (e.g. at Isturitz), but at most sites (e.g. Gourdan, Lespugue, Mas d'Azil, Duruthy) they first appear only in the final Magdalenian. Some of the specimens, notably salmon and pike (Lespugue, Gourdan) are enormous, bigger even than the largest in France today. It is worth noting that, according to J.G.D. Clark (1952: 28), pike vertebrae threaded on reindeer gut are still a favourite toy among Lapp children in northern, Finland. Another point of interest is that the fish remains of the Pyrenees are frequently associated with the well-known Magdalenian 'harpoons', and at several sites the two first appear at the same time. This cannot always be a coincidence, although experimentation and ethnography suggest that only some of these barbed points were suitable for fishing.

Sieveking (1976) believes that fish were an important resource in the Magdalenian (see also chapter 19) and has claimed that very little fish-bone debris is known from Pyrenean caves because 'in the early excavations fragile fish bones (were) either ignored or missed'. This statement itself omits the fact that Piette, amongst others, often mentions the finding of fish vertebrae. Certainly many Pyrenean rivers are known to have been very rich in fish during the historical period (and especially in trout and salmon); but since the cave sites seem to have been occupied chiefly in the colder seasons, it is possible that many of the salmon vertebrae may have been brought in as decorative objects from elsewhere. Unlike Sieveking, therefore, I do not consider fish a particularly important resource in the Palaeolithic at inland sites. It is true that fish offer certain dietary elements which are lacking in small game; and in any case, Magdalenian people undoubtedly exploited them from time to time in order to vary the diet; but the paucity of remains suggests that they represent a minor and subsidiary resource. There is also evidence that marine fish were largely ignored in the Upper Palaeolithic (see Bahn 1977).

Sea shells first appear in the Châtelperronian (Gargas), and are regularly present from the Aurignacian onward; I have argued elsewhere (Bahn 1977) that their purpose was decorative rather than nutritional. Freshwater molluscs and toad make an appearance in the Middle and Late Magdalenian at one or two sites, as do land snails, foreshadowing their great increase in the Postglacial.

### Plants

The evidence for plant exploitation is limited but varied (Bahn in press (b)). Artefactual remains range from a possible grinder in the Mousterian of Olha, to grinding stones in the final Magdalenian of Duruthy, thought to have been used in the preparation of wild grain, and found together with hundreds of backed bladelets bearing a gloss caused by the cutting of straw (Arambourou 1978). There are several artistic depictions in the Magdalenian which are thought to represent plants, and notably the famous sculpted 'cereal ears'. Human remains, including those of children, from several Upper Palaeolithic sites display very worn teeth which may be due to considerable consumption of plant food; and finally, macro-remains include chestnuts, hazelnuts, walnuts, acorns and fruit-stones at a series of Late Magdalenian sites (see Bahn 1979a). At Aurensan, the pioneering excavators processed some samples of the Magdalenian layer by a crude but effective method of flotation, and discovered carbonized seeds of raspberry and strawberry (Frossard and Frossard 1880: 32).

In short, despite an ever-increasing contribution by various small resources to the diet, it is clear that the Palaeolithic occupants of the Pyrenees were always heavily dependent on the gregarious herbivores. In the absence of detailed faunal information, the principal guide to the exploitation methods used is the topographic position of the sites.

### Site location

It is improbable that water or fuel were ever hard to come by in the Palaeolithic Pyrenees, and so these are unlikely to have been important determining factors in site location, and the same is probably true of non-mobile edible resources. I have argued elsewhere (1978b) that the numerous thermal springs may have played a key role, but in ritual rather than economy. Fords are likely to have been important, and some examples (Mauran, Duruthy) have been mentioned above.

The fall and rise in sea level had no detectable effect on the Pyrenean Palaeolithic, since the gain/loss of land surface would have been small, and any coastal sites will have been drowned. The glaciers and the lower snowline, however, had a more noticeable impact; for apart from the Mousterian incursions up to at least 1000 m as mentioned earlier, and a Châtelperronian level at Belvis (960 m), there is no trace of the Palaeolithic in the mountains until the Solutrean, and even here (e.g. at lower Massat) the finds are disputed (see Méroc 1953; Clottes 1976). Nevertheless, it is quite possible that Solutrean groups could have visited the uplands, since this period in the Pyrenees coincides with the mild and humid Würm III/IV interstadial, and it is thought (Leroi-Gourhan 1967) that deglaciation began around 18 000 b.p. However, as one would expect, it is in the Magdalenian, and particularly in its later stages, that upland sites spring up — most noticeably around the Tarascon basin. It was shown above that in earlier periods some of the foothill or plain sites seem to have been occupied in cold seasons, and it seems reasonable to assume that animals and men sometimes ascended, in the summer, some distance into the uplands; but it is not until the Magdalenian that one finds clear evidence — for example, in the shelter of La Grazo dé l'Aspiouo (800 m) in the Ariège. This site is situated high on a steep slope, and has an imposing view. However, its exploitation territory is so heavily restricted that it could not have been more than a temporary camp. It is therefore unsurprising that it contained only a small hearth and a few tools and bones (Galy 1883); there is no trace of any kind of tool fabrication. The presence of reindeer remains and of seashells implies that this formed a summer lookout post within an exploitation system based on reindeer migrations.

The Pyrenees have several examples of a 'site switch'. This can occur within a cave (e.g. between the two 'salles' of Isturitz), and is most clearly seen at the Mas d'Azil, where, during the later Magdalenian, occupation of the right-bank warren of caves was largely abandoned in favour of the left-bank entry of the river-tunnel – a wise move since the river seems often to have overflowed into the inner caves. Even on the left bank the occupation layers alternate with sterile, laminated flood-loams. When both banks were unavailable the occupants probably resorted to nearby sites such as the shelter above the cave entry where Piette (1891, 1895) found identical material without intervening loams. These periodic floods may well be linked to the retreat of the glaciers and the improving climate.

One type of site switch, from the unspecialized Le Portel to the highly strategic St Jean de Verges, was discussed above. Another type can be traced on either bank of the Garonne (fig. 15.3) where the Middle Magdalenian sites of Montconfort and the Spugo de Ganties, both fairly high caves, are forsaken for the rockshelters of La Tourasse and La Roque respectively – sites which are rather lower, and at the river edge. In the case of Montconfort and La Tourasse, both sites have a reindeer-dominant fauna; the Spugo has a predominance of bovids as befits the lush wet pastures of that part of the Garonne, while the La Roque shelters have the usual reindeer to red deer fauna. In neither case can an increase in fishing be the reason for the move to the river edge – indeed fish are not found at La Tourasse until the Azilian, and none at all were reported from La Roque (Bahn 1979a, tables 25 and 27). One can only speculate that these shelters were not previously available, due to river level.

Some sites seem to have been suited to both unspecialized and specialized strategies; this, together with other factors, led to their being occupied more or less continuously throughout the Palaeolithic. Isturitz and the Mas d'Azil are the chief examples here. They have much in common – both huge caves, with vast accumulations of cultural material and portable art; both with parietal art. One might dub them the two known 'super-sites' of the Pyrenees – huge multi-purpose economic, cultural and socio-religious foci, at the apex of a hierarchical network of sites, in which one can envisage a large category of major habitation sites or base camps of the Gourdan type, and also a multitude of task-specific work camps and minor, transitory encampments (compare chapters 7 and 8).

Many major Upper Palaeolithic habitation sites, especially in the central Pyrenees, are in locations very unfavourable for generalized exploitation of herds – indeed some territories are so heavily distorted and restricted as to positively discourage settlement if eclectic hunting was the basis of the economy. Hence it is very probable that since occupation is repeated or continuous at these sites and since their stratigraphies argue for economies that were highly successful in the long term, the locations must have been economically advantageous, and aimed at the efficient and easy interception of mobile resources, wild or controlled, at key points. The most common location of this type is at the junction of mountain and foothill/plain, where a river emerges from a narrow upland valley; these were the points allowing recurrent and predictable contact with the ascending and descending herbivore herds. Obviously the existence of caves here is also a factor involved in the prehistoric concentrations, but open sites and surface scatters also cluster at these same points. It is noteworthy that some of these locations were already occupied in the Mousterian (e.g. Gargas and Gourdan on the Garonne).

It is possible that some sites were occupied all the year round, but the faunal and cultural material usually points to seasonality and movement, particularly in the Magdalenian, so that some people must have been absent at least in mid-winter or summer, and these junction-sites were the scene of seasonal agglomeration and dispersal. The problem of human aggregations raises the question of whether there is any evidence to link economic change with population pressure.

### Population

Demographic data are scarce and vague in the Pyrenean Palaeolithic. Cohen (1977) has argued that population pressure can be assumed where there is a switch to less palatable or previously unused resources; and it is certainly true that in the region under consideration one can see a steady broadening of the resource base, with an increase, through the Upper Palaeolithic, and especially in the Magdalenian, in the use of resources which are dangerous, small and/or elusive, and which had been totally ignored in previous periods.

Other than that, however, the evidence is poor. Within particular sites there may be some sign of increased occupation – for example, the area of occupation at Duruthy increases greatly in 'Magdalenian VI'; and in the Mas d'Azil Piette noticed that each of his Magdalenian levels covered a wider area than the one below (Piette 1891). As it would be naïve to place great faith in the significance of such facts with regard to population increase, one is left with the number of sites for each period. The figures which follow are extremely rough, and indeed minimal, since they do not include doubtful cases or any open sites other than major examples of the Mauran type. Groups of rockshelters (e.g. Duruthy, La Roque, Aurignac, Olha) have been counted as single sites. One should also take into account disruptive factors like rockfalls (e.g. the collapse of Olha) or the effects of increased humidity (abandonment of caves in the Solutrean), and the fact that attributions to a period usually rest on the presence of type-fossils which may not always be conveniently present (see Bahn 1979a).

|            | Moust. | Châtelp. | Aurign. | Gravet. | Solutr. | Magdal. |
|------------|--------|----------|---------|---------|---------|---------|
| Approx. no. sites | 26 | 12 | 26 | 17 | 16 | 72 |

In terms of time-span, the Aurignacian shows a net increase in site numbers after the long Mousterian, while the Magdalenian seems to have a population explosion. However, this leap is a little exaggerated since the figure includes half a dozen decorated caves with no known occupation debris; at least 25 Magdalenian sites have never been excavated to bedrock, and so may well have been occupied in earlier periods, which would alter the ratio still further; and of course deglaciation, and the new availability of sites which it brought in the east, is an important factor.

Thus, in view of the huge time-scale involved, and the very gradual adoption and minor role of the previously unused resources, I would judge that the region had an extremely low rate of population increase during the Palaeolithic, perhaps with a slight acceleration in the Magdalenian.

### Conclusion

Ecologically the French Pyrenees have a compressed zonation; the close proximity of winter and summer zones must have had a direct influence on the behaviour of the gregarious herbivores, and it is in the movements of seasonally-migrating animal herds that lies the key to the economic adaptations of the Pyrenean Palaeolithic.

As I have shown, environmental change sometimes replaced one species with another, as in the rises and falls of the reindeer, but overall it seems to have had little influence on the exploitation *methods* of the Pyreneans. It can be argued that population pressure was a constant spur in the long term, in that it led to the exploitation of minor resources or to the maximal extraction of bone-marrow; and of course fluctuations in climate and population, localized in space and time, may have had dramatic effects on the inhabitants.

Nonetheless it is the topography and the environmental constraints of the area which shaped the spatial distribution of sites, and the methods used to exploit migrating herds, regardless of the effects of climatic change other than the ascending snowline.

I have indicated that in its economic developments the Pyrenean Palaeolithic is closely comparable to that of Cantabrian Spain, except that it displays evidence for some site-specialization and the interception of herds in the Mousterian. In the Upper Palaeolithic, and above all in the Magdalenian, one finds clear evidence for seasonal occupation of sites and hence of greater mobility — this is tied to an increase both in heavy dependence on single species and in occupation of sites that could only have been advantageous to groups involved in the systematic interception and controlling of migratory herds. The development of control over meat sources can thus be traced right through the Late Pleistocene; and, in the Magdalenian at least, a strong case can be made for some forms of loose herding being employed, since the boundary between these and judicious, selective mass drives is so blurred as to be illusory and irrelevant.

# PART FOUR

**Social interaction and economic change: large-scale perspectives**

## Chapter 16

**Editorial**

Social factors have been referred to in passing at several points (chapters 7, 8, 10); in this section they are brought to the forefront of discussion. An interest in the social dimension of hunter-gatherer behaviour has been stimulated in recent years by three principal sources of inspiration: simulation studies of mating networks and their locational and social implications (notably Wobst 1974a, 1976); Marxist-inspired theories of social evolution, where the emphasis on social relations of production provides a point of contact between social theory and archaeological studies of prehistoric subsistence (Bender 1978, 1981; Ingold 1980, 1981); and a growing interest in the properties for symbolic communication embodied in the more obviously stylistic features of Palaeolithic material culture, such as art, personal ornament and burial ritual, and their implications for changes in social organization (Wobst 1977; Conkey 1978a, 1980). There are thus a number of varied approaches that may be grouped under the heading of social analysis. One feature they share is their emphasis on the general point that human populations interact not only with a physical and biological environment, but with a social environment which can affect ecological relationships, subsistence practices, and patterns of variability in artefact assemblages.

The social environment in question refers to the regional social unit formed by the integration of local groups through reciprocal exchanges of marriage partners, material goods or information. A number of concepts has been proposed to describe such relations. Wobst (1974a, 1976) has proposed the concept of the *mating network* as a fundamental unit of regional analysis. This is defined by the minimum number of people that have to be linked in a stable network of relations to ensure that every member will find a marriage partner on reaching maturity, and appears broadly to coincide with ethnographically observed entities such as the maximum band or the dialect tribe. Given reasonable assumptions about the demographic structure of Palaeolithic hunter-gatherers, Wobst estimates the minimum size of the mating network at about 475 people, and the ideal spatial configuration of the participating local groups as a hexagonal arrangement which minimizes the distances between them. Wobst also suggests that at low population densities groups located on the peripheries of a mating network will be at a disadvantage because of the relatively greater distances over which they have to maintain contact with their neighbours. An ideal arrangement which minimizes this edge-effect is a series of overlapping mating networks. This leads on to a distinction between *open mating networks*, in which the participant members are free to seek marriage partners from groups in a neighbouring network, and *closed mating networks*, whose members seek mates exclusively from within the one network. Closed networks are relatively risky in the sense that groups at the edge of the network are likely to lose contact and risk extinction, or else to move in towards the centre of the network, thus creating problems of resource stress or increased quarrels and disputes. Both these tendencies can be mitigated at the cost of increased investment in social rituals which help to reinforce long-distance exchanges, to symbolize group affiliation, and to create role differentiation and the emergence of authority figures who can resolve disputes, as discussed by Jochim (chapter 19, see also chapter 10).

Two further concepts are introduced in this section. Gamble emphasizes the importance of *alliance networks* as denoting enduring relations of marital or material exchange or other forms of social interaction which extend across the boundaries of mating networks, and thus define a yet larger spatial unit of analysis. Madden suggests the term *social network system* as a more all-encompassing concept which subsumes mating and alliance networks as well as other types of social interaction. She suggests that this is a more appropriate concept in archaeological work, where one can rarely identify with any confidence the particular exchange relations in operation or the specific type of social interaction, but rather variations in the degree of social interaction. While there are some differences of detail here about appropriate concepts and units of analysis, all are essentially variations on the basic idea of inter-group exchange and the existence of socially defined regional units within which local subsistence activities take place.

Madden discusses the various processes that structure interaction at a regional scale, with particular emphasis on exchange relationships and the effects of varying population density, competition for scarce resources and distance between local groups. Analysis is directed to the conditions under which closure and differentiation of social network systems occurs, and the ways in which this might be registered by changes in the patterning of artefact assemblages. She emphasizes the costs and risks of maintaining social interactions over very long distances at one extreme, or of imposing social boundaries between adjacent groups at the other, and suggests that undifferentiated social network systems are likely to be the norm among hunters and gatherers. Differentiation may occur either because of separation by geographical distance, or under conditions of increased population stress and competition for resources. In the latter case one might expect imposed social boundaries between adjacent systems, with greater internal integration and external differentiation, and corresponding developments in the stylistic features of the material culture to symbolize such changes. Analysis of the Mesolithic sequence of Norway indicates little evidence for differentiation, probably because of the relatively low population densities and maintenance of social interaction over large areas, or at best some differentiation due to the effect of geographical separation.

Gamble examines an example which lies at one extreme of the spectrum of variation analysed by Madden, that is the situation of a harsh environment which can be exploited only at very low population densities. In this case it may be necessary for the survival of the local group to maintain regular contacts with other groups over very long distances as a form of insurance against the vagaries of the local environment. Stylistic behaviour may be of considerable advantage in this situation as a means of symbolizing group affiliation and as part of an information system which keeps scattered groups informed about environmental variation over a large area. He argues that the abundant and widespread portable art of the Upper Palaeolithic is evidence for the development of such an information system designed to serve a geographically extensive system of social alliances. He further suggests that the development of such a system of social relations may have had crucial adaptive consequences in allowing continuous human occupation of the harsh periglacial regions of northern and central Europe for the first time in human history, and that this may account for the relatively early date and widespread abundance of portable art in Europe as compared with other areas.

Jochim analyses a situation which seems to combine elements of the extremes discussed by Madden and Gamble. He suggests that the changing patterns of environment and demography during the Upper Palaeolithic resulted in oscillations in some areas between periods of highly mobile exploitation patterns with low population densities and extensive group affiliation, and periods of increased population stress leading to economic intensification and more localized patterns of social interaction. He further suggests that analysis in these terms may explain the geographical restriction of cave art to southern France and northern Spain. With the onset of maximum glacial conditions, he argues that there was some displacement of population from the harsher regions of central and northern Europe, resulting in increased population stress to the south. In France and Spain, this stress was accommodated by, among other things, an intensification of salmon fishing. This may have resulted in greater sedentism, territorial exclusion and closure of social networks, with a consequent increase in rituals emphasizing group solidarity and authority figures important in the resolution of conflicts. Cave art may have played a significant role in these social developments. With the subsequent amelioration of climate, there was a rapid dispersal and expansion of population northwards, and a reversion to more extensive and open social networks.

The social behaviour discussed in these papers has implications both for the spatial organization of subsistence economy and for patterns of long-term change, and thus has a bearing on a number of issues raised in previous chapters. At the level of spatial organization the question arises as to the relationship between the concept of the annual exploitation territory and the social network system. In theory the latter should be at least as extensive as the former, and in many cases should comprise a much larger area embracing a number of related annual exploitation territories. This recalls J.G.D. Clark's (1975) suggestion of the term 'social territory' for the highest level in a hierarchical classification, with annual exploitation territories and site exploitation territories as successively lower levels. There are, however, difficulties in the way of defining the geographical limits of these various entities. All the authors in Part 4 emphasize the uncertainties of identifying stylistic behaviour in artefact design, and the problems of isolating other variables such as functional requirements, scheduling problems or raw materials (see chapters 3 and 12). The appearance of exotic items, such as raw materials imported from distant sources or marine shells in inland sites, also raises some interesting differences of interpretation. Are these evidence of large annual exploitation territories, with people carrying materials over long distances in the course of their annual subsistence round (chapters 8 and 15); or evidence of attempts by peripherally located groups in a closed mating network to strengthen their affiliation with more centrally located groups (Wobst 1976); or evidence for reinforcement of long-distance social contacts within a framework of alliances that transcend the boundaries of mating networks (chapter 18)? There is here a potentially reciprocal relationship between studies of subsistence and studies of regional social interaction, in which greater precision about the former would help to clarify the nature of the latter, just as a focus on large-scale social interactions introduces new perspectives on subsistence.

This reciprocal relationship, and the ambiguities that may stem from it, is more sharply in focus in the study of long-term changes. Here two issues are of interest. The first is a methodological one of how to demonstrate that social changes have taken place. The notion that social changes in the Upper Palaeolithic allowed human populations to make different demographic and economic responses to last glacial environmental fluctuations in comparison with their predecessors offers an attractive resolution of some of the differences of opinion aired in Part 3 about long-term demographic and subsistence trends. At the same time, however, evidence that the proposed social changes did take place consists, at least in part, of evidence for changes in demography and subsistence. This raises the familiar risk of circularity in argument, and this is a problem that all the authors in this Part are at pains to underline. Madden emphasizes the dependence of interpretations about social interaction on information about subsistence behaviour. Gamble emphasizes the ambiguities of stylistic evidence such as portable art, and suggests that changes in stylistic behaviour can only be used as evidence of change in patterns of social interaction if they are accompanied by evidence of changes in settlement and subsistence behaviour which would have been facilitated by the hypothesized social changes, independently of change in the natural environment. Similarly Jochim emphasizes the admittedly tenuous chronology of changes in cave art, and the value of changes in the environmental and demographic framework for highlighting possible social changes. His interpretation also poses some intriguing conflicts with other data sources. The suggestion of intensified salmon fishing is one for which there is no apparent supporting evidence in the regional sequences analysed in Part 3, indicating either that the archaeological data are incomplete or misleading when viewed within a small-scale regional framework, or that alternative explanations must be sought for the restricted distribution of the cave art.

The second issue is the theoretical one of why the proposed changes in patterns of social interaction in the Upper Palaeolithic occurred. From an evolutionary perspective it is possible to see in these social changes a solution to two essentially biological problems – problems of living at very low or very high population densities respectively. From this point of view the social changes could be described as biologically adaptive in contributing to the reproductive success of the human species, facilitating both maintenance of increased population densities and colonization of new territory. However, to say that social changes are adaptive is not to explain why they arise in the first place, and we do well to make a clear distinction between the causes of social change and their biological or economic consequences – between the factors that bring a particular behaviour pattern into being, and the factors which favour its adoption and establishment as an enduring and widespread feature. Jochim's analysis suggests a pattern in which changes that occur at one period may have delayed and unforeseen consequences, which then become the cause of further changes with yet further consequences, in an irreversible process of reciprocal causation between environmental, social and subsistence changes, stretched out over long time periods. We may also note the contrast between Gamble's interpretation of alliance networks as buffering mechanisms for stabilizing occupation of marginal areas, and Bender's (1978, 1981) interpretation of the same pattern of social interaction as embodying an element of social competition which may lead to progressive intensification of food production.

However, the reasons for the first appearance of the social patterns that appear to have triggered off an accelerated process of economic change from about 20 000 b.p. onwards remain elusive. Do we suppose that the demographic and environmental pressures at the maximum of the last glacial, to which Upper Palaeolithic social developments may be seen as an adaptive response, were lacking in previous periods, even though there was a latent human capacity to respond in this way? Or do we suppose that the capacity for certain patterns of social interaction was absent in earlier periods, and that environmental and demographic stress was accommodated by alternative responses involving population decline or emigration? Clearly the further back in time one pushes these questions, the more closely involved they become with the biological evolution of *Homo sapiens sapiens*. However, Gamble cautions against using biological change as an easy solution to the problem of cultural and social developments. Attempts to relate changes in human anatomy to changes in intellectual ability are unreliable and contentious. Moreover biological change cannot simply be accepted as a 'given'. It needs to be explained in its turn, and takes place within an environmental context in which social as well as physical and biological factors may participate. It appears, then, that there is no simple answer to the question of what are causes and what are effects. Causes of one set of changes may themselves appear as effects of previous and unrelated changes. Factors which are treated as constants in one type of analysis may become variables at the centre of attention in another. Much depends on the scales of observation and analysis employed in the different cases.

Chapter 17

Social network systems amongst hunter-gatherers
considered within southern Norway
Marcie Madden

The regional context of hunter-gatherer organization and the network of social linkages that structure interrelationships amongst these groups are considered here. Such linkages have potential for creating structured and enduring patterns of spatial interaction and integration. The patterning of these linkages and relationships is discussed in relation to the development of variability in the archaeological record. Three different models of the variation that might exist in the structure of these network systems are outlined and further demonstrated within the context of a particular set of archaeological data from the Mesolithic period in southern Norway.

### Introduction

In the analysis of spatial and temporal variability in the archaeological record — and especially the artefactual record — it is commonly assumed or implied that prehistoric populations of hunter-gatherers lived in spatially discrete, isolated units forming tightly bounded social, economic and cultural entities. Such a conception has proved difficult to apply in practice, particularly in the study of artefact assemblages. Moreover, on the basis of ethnographic evidence alone, it seems more likely that many hunter-gatherer populations would have resembled a network of rather loosely defined groups and communities linked by a variety of social relationships, often extending over vast regions and even entire continents (cf. Wobst 1978; chapters 18 and 19 below). Some of these relationships were clearly economic in nature or origin, whereas others would have been organized in accordance with

less overtly economic factors such as kinship relations or political and religious affiliation.

It is therefore of some importance in archaeological interpretation to consider how the distribution of populations was organized over such vast areas; what were the number, nature and arrangement of their articulated components; what sort of processes maintained this pattern of distribution and articulation; how these processes were structured and at what points discontinuities occurred; in what way these processes are related to the differentiation of sociocultural systems within a region, as manifest in the variability of the material record; and how this aspect of archaeological variability is to be distinguished from other variables related to raw materials and functional requirements (cf. chapters 3 and 12).

It is beyond the scope of this chapter to attempt to deal with all these issues. However, there is clearly a need within archaeology to develop a body of theory relevant to such questions. I shall here attempt to create a general framework appropriate to the analysis of regional variability in social and economic organization which is applicable to archaeological data. I shall further limit detailed discussion specifically to those processes which structure variation in the arrangement of social relations amongst hunter-gatherer societies. In this way a start may be made in developing a coherent framework for generating expectations about patterns of variability in the archaeological record, and for interpreting the often complex and ambiguous patterns of regional data in a consistent and productive manner.

Archaeologists have devoted considerable attention to the elucidation of spatial interrelationships based on ecological, economic and political principles, such as seasonal mobility, trade and warfare (Streuver and Houart 1972; Hodder and Orton 1976; Earle and Ericson 1977; Fry 1980; Part 2 above). However, much less attention has been given to the linkages based on social principles (for exceptions see Wobst 1974a; Hodder 1977, 1978a; Bender 1978). Yet linkages of kinship, marriage and other social relations have the greatest potential for creating structured and enduring patterns of spatial interaction and integration. Their role in structuring patterns' of communication and interaction needs to be more clearly understood and cannot be ignored in the interpretation of variability in the archaeological record.

### Towards a regional framework

Two sets of variables are designated as important in structuring the pattern of regional interrelationships: (1) the spatial organization of the subsistence economy, and (2) exchange relationships.

The first refers to the distribution and organization of populations with reference to specific factors of environment and subsistence economy, such as topography and resource distribution; and social factors such as the level of social organization. In this respect it can be observed that human populations are not distributed across a landscape in a continuous or even fashion. They are usually clumped together to form discontinuous, local population aggregates, the size and spacing of which vary in accordance with the distribution and abundance of food resources and the requirements of social structure (Peterson 1976a; Part 2, above).

The second set of variables refers to the exchange relationships between these local population aggregates. These provide the main nexus of integration at a regional level and determine the relationships between the participating groups and the nature of their sociocultural boundaries. It is this level of analysis which here forms the chief focus of discussion. Relatively little attention will be devoted to variations in the patterns of local subsistence organization, except where this is necessary to elucidate the nature of regional inter-relationships.

### Social interaction fields

Exchange relationships may involve exchange of energy in the form of food resources, other subsistence goods or services, of information (both verbal and non-verbal), and of personnel — as in marriage for example. I shall use the term 'social interaction field' to describe any such example of an exchange relationship. Amongst hunter-gatherers we may distinguish many different sets of social interaction fields,

structured according to different organizing principles. For example, we may distinguish interaction fields based on kinship relations, those based on marriage or other affinal relations, on trading, on warfare, and on religion. These may involve different mediums of exchange and different risks and obligations. Similarly the scale of the unit involved in the network may vary from a single individual to a family group, or to an entire community. Some of these social interaction fields, particularly those based on kinship or affinal relations, may not extend beyond the bounds of the local group. However, the majority usually have more extensive ramifications, and may extend over very large areas, with a network of linkages comprising myriad ties and obligations. Examples include interaction fields based on extensive kinship systems such as lineages, sodalities such as clans, and marriage alliances such as the connubium or the maximum band.

There are thus potentially many sets of interactional fields that may exist simultaneously within a region. The boundaries of these fields need not necessarily coincide with each other or with localized population aggregates or even defined 'societies'. In many cases particular fields might not even represent discrete or clearly bounded entities with strong behavioural or spatial correlates that would allow accurate recognition in the archaeological record. Moreover, the same personnel are generally involved in more than one social interaction field, resulting in the overlapping or cross-cutting of exchange networks. It would therefore be futile to try and identify the archaeological correlates of particular interaction fields, many of which would be scarcely identifiable without the verbal testimony of the people involved or direct observation of their actions.

A more useful theoretical construct from the archaeological point of view, and one which is more likely to be applicable to the material products of human behaviour, is the *social network system*. This may be defined as the sum of the overlapping sets of social interaction fields. Its boundaries may be expected to show up in the form of a marked discontinuity or reduction in the degree of social interaction with adjacent social network systems, or a marked change in the nature of the exchange relationships, as compared with the degree of internal integration. Its viability as an archaeological construct depends on the assumption that cross-cutting interaction fields, even though they are unlikely to be coterminous, will overlap sufficiently to form fairly discrete spatial units.

Social network systems should not be confused with other large social entities such as tribes (Helm 1968; Tindale 1974; Peterson 1976a), or maximum bands (Steward 1969; Wobst 1974a). These represent particular types of social interaction fields based on specific organizing principles. It is possible that, in practice, a social network system may broadly coincide with a tribe or maximum band, although this would be difficult to establish archaeologically. However, the concept of a social network system does not depend on identifying specific organizing principles such as political affiliations or marriage alliance, but rather on the nature and strength of the linkages and the degree of interaction and integration amongst the participating units.

## Three variants of social network systems

Three simple models are presented below; they examine different configurations that may occur in the organization of social network systems of hunter-gatherer societies. In each of these models variation is seen to occur both with respect to the internal organization and structure of the social network systems, and to the location and nature of their boundaries. Each of these models is considered to be conditioned by a distinctive permutation of several variables, the most important of which include: (1) population density, (2) competition for scarce resources and (3) distance between the local groups. For the purpose of these models two basic assumptions are required: (1) that a minimum number of individuals is necessary to ensure the viability of a population through time and that groups must distribute themselves across space and maintain a network of exchange relationships to allow for this minimal social interaction (cf. Wobst 1974a, 1976); (2) that the nature of the exchange relationships will be regulated in an effort to minimize costs and risks.

### Model 1: undifferentiated network system

*Conditions.* The population density in the area remains so low that linkages between local groups are necessary for the maintenance of economic and social relationships over a wide area and the distance between local groups is not great enough over any one area to prohibit the maintenance of a continuous network of linkages across the region.

*Description of network system.* Given the above conditions we would expect the development of a relatively open and undifferentiated social network system within which discrete and bounded sets of social interaction fields as such would not occur. The actual distances encompassed by such an open network system and the intensity of interaction across such a region would depend both on the nature of the region involved and the level of population density. One might expect a tendency towards tolerance of greater distances as population density decreased and the need to maintain basic social linkages over a wider area increased.

If the region was large and the distance between marginally located groups was so great that ties were not similar or constant across the entire area, then more concentrated areas of interaction might occur within the system amongst closest neighbours. However, the boundaries enscribing such sets of social interaction fields — if they existed at all — would be both vague and fluctuating. In this situation the social network system would contain a series of partially overlapping and relatively open sets of social interaction fields which supported an uneven but continuous flow of interactions across the entire system.

### Model 2: differentiated network system due to distance

*Conditions.* If the distance between interacting groups becomes so large that exchange of energy between units is infrequent and expensive to maintain, there is created the potential for a division in the social network system. The local groups may then turn inwards and the weak link with the more distant groups may be used infrequently or not at all, provided that population density is sufficiently high to ensure demographic viability. Otherwise the risks of separation may outweigh the costs of long-distance interaction, thereby ensuring the maintenance of an undifferentiated network.

*Description of social network system.* Where separation does occur a recognizable boundary within the original social network system may appear, marked by a significant discontinuity in the exchange relationships between the separated groups. Such a division or boundary in a social network system does not necessarily imply the recognition and defence of the 'distance boundary' by the separated groups. If the distance between the respective social network systems is great enough, so as to limit interaction for a lengthy period, then changes may occur within each system over time so as to create conditions which indirectly effect a more impermeable 'sociocultural' boundary between the units. However, the imposition of conscious social boundaries, identified and maintained by the bounded group, is a type of separating process that is dependent upon the presence of other conditions, to be discussed in model 3.

### Model 3: differentiated network system due to imposed social boundaries

*Conditions.* If the distance between groups in a region decreases to the point where there is much overlapping of exploitation territories and competition for finite resources, then the advantages of maintaining an open network system which offers relatively unrestricted access to personnel, services and resources across a wide area may no longer be cost efficient. In such a situation an imposed division within the social network system may occur to preserve the exclusivity of the exploitation territories and/or resources.

Such a situation may occur over time through the normal processes of population increase, under conditions of resource stress, or following the expansion of a group into an already occupied territory. Social boundaries imposed in this way are likely to be most stable under conditions where (1) the population size of the bounded groups approaches the level necessary for the maintenance of demographic viability, and (2) the economic productivity of the bounded groups is sufficient to sustain them.

*Description of social network system.* Under the above conditions a boundary in the social network system is created, not so much by a discontinuity in exchange relationships as described in model 2, but by a change in the nature of the linkages and exchange relationships themselves, usually involving the development of more formalized and structured linkages and an actual increase in the frequency of certain exchange relationships between bounded groups. Recognition and maintenance of such social boundaries would be facilitated both by increasing the internal integration and the cultural distinctiveness of the bounded groups.

Social boundaries are expensive to maintain both with respect to the risks incurred in limiting the range and flexibility of linkages, and the time and energy necessary for boundary maintenance. We may assume that in many cases there would not only be a continuation of certain social alliances across these imposed barriers (although on a more limited and structured scale), but an elaboration or development of formalized and probably extensive communication and exchange linkages of other sorts (such as trading connections and political alliances) to offset the economic risks incurred by putting limits on the social network system.

### Implications for material culture patterning

The foregoing theory has implications both for the evaluation and prediction of patterns of variability in material culture on a regional level. It is recognized that participation in a common sociocultural context has a levelling effect on certain classes of data — particularly the more stylistic elements of material culture — and that increasing internal integration and external differentiation of the sociocultural entity is probably marked by increasing symbolic/stylistic behaviour (Wobst 1977; Hodder 1977; 1978a; Conkey 1978a; Close 1978).

According to our discussed theory, the level of internal integration and external differentiation of groups within a region is probably lowest when conditions resemble those described for model 1. In such a situation we would expect minimal development of stylistic behaviour between groups and little evidence of stylistic zones within a region. On the contrary, material culture would probably exhibit a great deal of homogeneity across a wide area, with any diversity being of short duration or due to distance decay fall-off.

As conditions approached those outlined for model 2 differentiation in material culture would occur within a region, but more as a product of reduced communication due to distance between groups than as a product of consciously conceived behaviour by its members to signal or reinforce group affiliation and distinctiveness from their neighbours. In such situations cultural/stylistic idiosyncrasies in behaviours and materials might arise between groups by virtue of the discontinuity in communication between them. However, with distance preserving the exclusivity of the respective groups, there is no reason to expect a marked increase in stylistic behaviour. In fact there is probably an equal likelihood that any variability would concern technological and functional attributes as much as it would stylistic ones.

The level of internal integration and external differentiation of groups within a region would be highest as conditions approached those described in model 3. In such situations we would expect to find marked evidence of stylistic behaviour and of discrete stylistic zones in the material culture within the region.

### Social network systems in southern Norway

I now present a set of archaeological data in terms of the foregoing theory to further exemplify the outlined models and to demonstrate the usefulness of this approach to an archaeological situation.

The region considered roughly corresponds to the area of southern Norway. The time-span of the study comprises the Norwegian Mesolithic (*c.* 10 000 to 6000 b.p.) a rather loose temporal span which is supposed to reflect both the period of earliest occupation in Norway and the period when hunter-gatherers were still relatively unaffected by agricultural developments further to the south and east.

Materials attributed to the Mesolithic period in Norway are largely derived from small surface sites consisting of a few stone hearths and scattered lithic debris. This debris is comprised primarily of large quantities of waste flakes and a variety of flake tools, tanged and triangular flaked points, scrapers, burins, coarse blades and cores. Microblades and true microliths are generally absent except on some of the later sites. A variety of flake axes and, on later sites, core axes, are also known from many areas (for general discussions see Bøe and Nummedal 1936; Gjessing 1945; Freundt 1948; Odner 1966; Hagen 1967; Helskog 1974; Indrelid 1975, 1978; Mikkelson 1975; J.G.D. Clark 1975).

The majority of the Mesolithic sites are distributed along the old coastlines that lie between the Maximum *Tapes* Transgression level and the marine limit, with a range that extends from east of Oslofjord to the northern province of Finnmark and the territories of the Soviet Union (fig. 17.1). Few sites are recognized along the narrow coastal strip of Nordland which separates the northern and southern parts of the country (Freundt 1948; Gaustad 1973). Interior sites have been located in south Trondelag (Marstrander 1956), the Hardangervidda plateau in the southern mountains (Bøe 1942; Hagen 1963; Johansen 1969, 1978; Indrelid 1973), as well as in Finnmark (Helskog 1974).

Despite the absence of sufficient C14 dates, the chronology of these occupations has been established from their association with dated beach levels. However, the lack of stratification at these sites, the dearth of organic remains, and the paucity of significant features other than scattered hearths and a few questionable tent rings, makes it difficult at present to make a detailed assessment of spatial and temporal variability in the artefactual material.

Some variability has been noted on a broad scale. Materials from the earlier Mesolithic assemblages in the northern and southern parts of the country have been tentatively separated into different 'traditions' (Komsa and

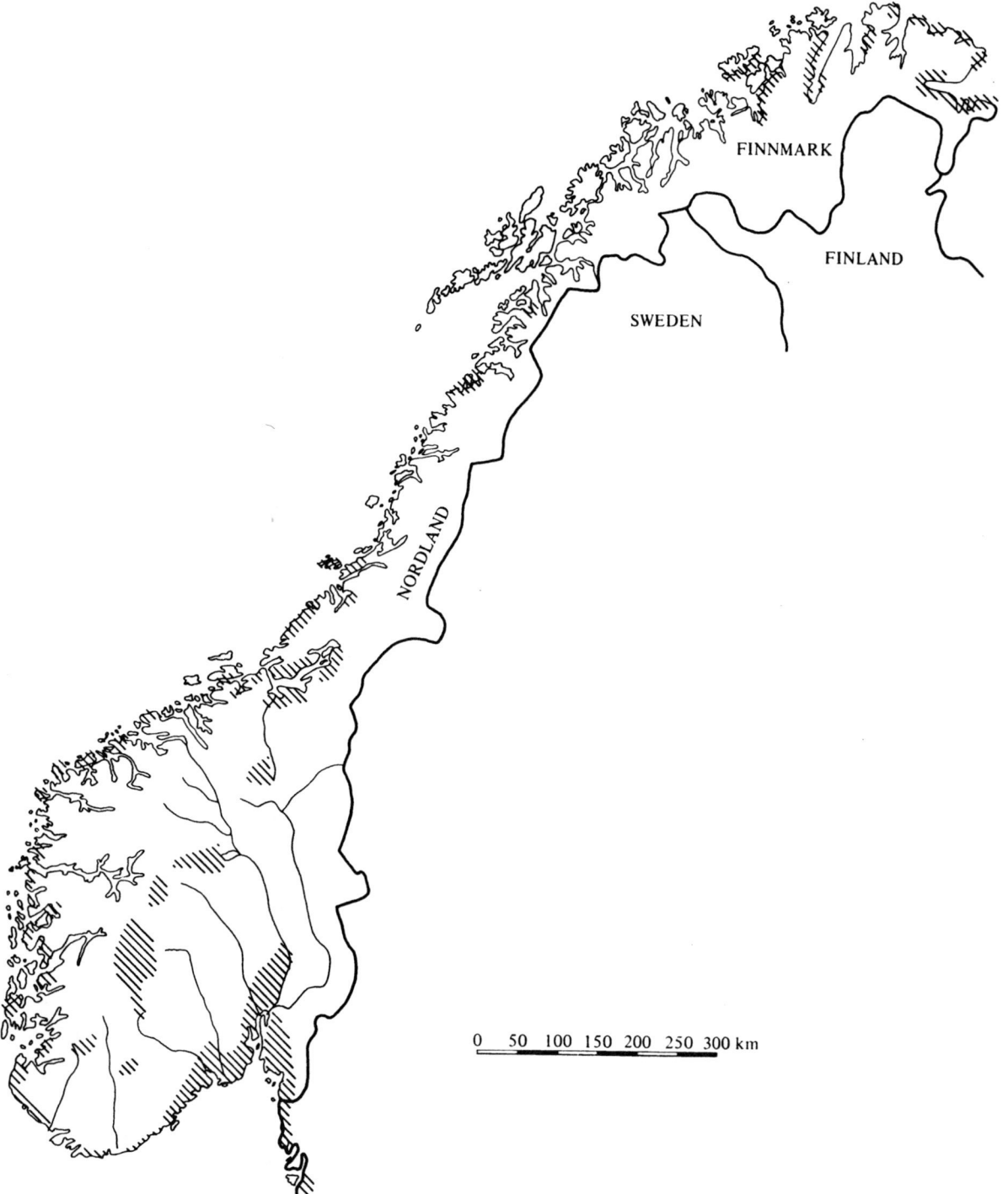

Fig. 17.1. The distribution of Mesolithic sites in Norway. Hatched areas show main concentrations of sites.

Fosna) on the basis of certain gross technological factors (cf. Bøe and Nummedal 1936; Gjessing 1945; Freundt 1948; Hagen 1967). Within southern Norway, a broad chronological division has also been made on technological grounds, between those sites dated prior to 8300 b.p., designated the 'Early Mesolithic flint tradition', and those dated between 8300 and 5000 b.p., designated the 'Microblade tradition' (Indrelid

1978). Within both 'traditions' regional differences have been discerned, particularly between sites distributed on the eastern and western coasts (Gjessing 1945; Indrelid 1975; Mikkelson 1975), and in the highlands between sites distributed in the northern and southern areas (Indrelid 1975). However, the full extent of these regional variants is not known. Nor has there been any attempt to evaluate the implications of such patterns of differentiation for the human societies involved.

I propose to use the theory outlined above to evaluate the admittedly inadequate data on regional variation in the archaeological record and to advance some tentative hypotheses about the patterns of social interaction that may have given rise to this variation. Such an assessment is certainly not intended to replace the analysis of controlled artefactual samples, work which for the most part has yet to be undertaken. However, such an approach does offer a framework for further testing and problem-oriented research in the region.

It is possible to distinguish at least three different phases in the development of the social network system in southern Norway during the Mesolithic period. The first phase corresponds to the earliest colonization period when population was still expanding into new territory and the social network system was relatively undifferentiated throughout most of the occupied country. The second phase corresponds to a somewhat later period when differentiation in the network system occurred between the northern and southern parts of the country. The third phase corresponds to the further fission and differentiation of the network system within the southern region itself.

### Phase 1 (c. 10 000 to 8000 b.p.)

Precisely when the colonization of Norway began has yet to be determined, but lithic assemblages from several areas along the coastal zone of southern Norway indicate that this area was already occupied during the Preboreal period (c. 10 000 to 9000 b.p.)(Indrelid 1978: 178). Most investigators consider that these earliest inhabitants descended from the late glacial reindeer-hunting populations of southern Scandinavia and the north European plain (cf. Indrelid 1975: 9–15; Clark 1975: 208). Migration from the continent was possible as early as the Allerød period (12 000 to 11 000 b.p.) along the route of the North Sea continent to the ice-free coasts of Norway. Two paths of migration were open during the later Preboreal period, along the North Sea to the west coast and across western Sweden to eastern Norway (Indrelid 1975: 14–15). Present consensus favours the likelihood that the earliest colonization took place during the Preboreal period via the latter two routes, although available archaeological data preclude testing of these hypotheses (Indrelid 1978; 173).

Whether or not there were one or more movements of peoples into Norway, it is apparent that having arrived they very rapidly distributed themselves along the coast and began the process of settling in to their respective areas. During the earliest periods of colonization, the presence of the glacier over the greater part of central and eastern Norway would have restricted populations to the coastal areas in south-western Norway (Indrelid 1975: 10–11). At this point population density was probably quite low and groups would necessarily have maintained a strong network of social and economic linkages across the entire occupied region. We would

therefore expect little differentiation within the social network system.

With the retreat of the glacier and the succession of new vegetation in the later Preboreal and early Boreal periods (Hafsten 1960: 437–42), new areas were made available for occupation in the north and in the central highlands. It is likely that this was the period when groups from southern Norway could have begun movement to the northern provinces. As population growth occurred and these new areas were inhabited by groups 'budding off' from their 'parent populations', we would expect a gradual expansion of the original network system to incorporate these groups in the new areas. Given the apparent rapidity of population spread, the low population density, and the similar nature of economic activities in all areas, we would expect that the actual distances encompassed by such a continuous undifferentiated network system were probably considerable during this early expansion phase. However, such a situation would probably not have been a stable one. Given the vast distances involved and the variation in topography, climate and resources across the country, we might expect a differentiation within the social network system over time.

### Phase 2 (c. 8000 to 6000 b.p.)

The earliest and most marked discontinuity in population distribution and communication, with potential for creating a division in the social network system, probably occurred between those groups occupying the southern and northern parts of the country. These regions are connected by a narrow coastal tract along which populations were very thinly dispersed throughout the entire Mesolithic period. This coastal tract would have constituted a considerable hindrance to regular communication and interaction between populations distributed in these areas. Strong linkages and relationships along this transect would have been difficult to maintain through time.

Amongst populations in the northern area communication and interaction would more easily have followed a west to east transect across the interior 'vidda' and along the coasts of Finnmark into Russia and Finland. As population density within the northern area became sufficiently high to ensure demographic and economic viability, linkages to the south may have been neglected altogether and a new series of social interaction fields might have been formed that involved greater energy exchange and transmission within the northern region.

The gap in the social network system that might have occurred between the northern and southern parts of the country may be at least partially responsible for the variation noted between the artefactual assemblages from these areas for the Mesolithic period. For the most part this variation seems to concern technological or functional attributes rather than stylistic ones. It has been noted for instance (Hagen 1967) that the earlier Mesolithic assemblages from northern Norway (Komsa) exhibit a greater frequency and variety of large and 'crude' tool forms than similarly dated assemblages from the south (Fosna). These include a number of specific forms which are completely unknown in the south, such as heavy cobble scrapers, handaxes and certain knife forms (Hagen 1967: 31). At the same time, while the south Norwegian 'Fosna' assemblages provide evidence of a well-developed microlithic industry, the frequency of microliths in northern 'Komsa' assemblages is very low (Freundt 1948: 14–15). Amongst later Mesolithic assemblages the difference between north and south becomes even more marked with the development of the so-called 'Microblade tradition' in the south – a technological 'tradition' that has no known counterpart in the north.

### Phase 3 (c. 7000 to 5000 b.p.)

Differentiation within the social network system of southern Norway itself was a process that probably began soon after the population had become established over the greater part of the country by the early Boreal period in Phase 1. This area exhibits great ecological variation, both on a regional scale and within local areas, so as to offer a variety of different habitats and zones of exploitation which would have significantly affected both the spatial organization and the exchange relationships of local populations in this area.

Southern Norway comprises a peninsula with an extensive and varied coastline that extends from the North Sea in the west to the Skagerak in the south-east. We may distinguish at least three broad zones with potential for separating populations into more localized groupings in this region: the highlands, the west coast, and the east coast.

The highlands are part of the extensive Caledonian mountain system that runs along most of the length of the country from south to north and comprises the greater part of the interior. These highlands effectively divide the southern peninsula into an eastern and western zone, with marked differences in climate, vegetation and physiography as one moves across these zones from east to west (cf. Sømme 1961).

Towards the west the mountains and high plateaux end abruptly seawards, and deep valleys and fiords penetrate far into the uplands from the coast. The western coastal zone as a consequence is very steep and dissected. Lowland areas suitable for settlement occur only as narrow strips of strandflat bordering the mountains or as offshore islands that form an outer archipelago.

Towards the east the mountains exhibit a more gradual gradient seawards, with long parallel valleys that slope gently from the highland plateaux towards the outer coast. The coastal zone in this area consequently has a relatively moderate relief with extensive lowland areas around the lower courses of the valleys and the head of Oslofjord.

A wide variety of diverse habitats and resources of potential interest to human populations were available within each of these areas. The coastal lowlands provided access to both marine and terrestrial fauna within reasonable distances.

The most important marine resources included a variety of large sea mammals such as whales and seals, as well as sea birds and fish (Indrelid 1978). In the west, red deer and wild boar constituted the primary large land species, while moose was dominant in the eastern and south-eastern parts of the country from the Boreal period onwards (Indrelid 1978: 156). In the highlands, reindeer, fish, and at certain times moose, were the main resources that attracted people to these regions (Moe, Indrelid and Kjos-Hanssen 1978: 79–81).

Archaeological evidence indicates clearly that the majority of the Mesolithic hunter-gatherer populations in southern Norway were distributed within the coastal zones for the greater part of the year. This pattern of distribution, by virtue of the differentiated coastline, would probably have been discontinuous, with a tendency towards a pattern of settlement that involved small local groupings of maritime-oriented hunter-gatherers scattered amongst the islands and along the heads of the major fiords and valleys. The economic activity and movements of most of these localized groupings for the remainder of the year appears to have involved the adjacent interior regions, rather than the coast itself, by way of the valleys and fiords that provided access to the interior forests and highlands.

On the west coast the seasonal movements of these groups are considered to have been relatively short and primarily restricted to the lowland areas (Indrelid 1978: 169). However, it should be noted that such a pattern of restricted seasonal movement can probably not be applied with equal certainty to all groups in this area, nor to the entire Mesolithic period. These deductions are based on faunal evidence obtained from sites dating to within the optimum of the postglacial warm period (c. 6000 to 3500 b.p.), when forests were extensive and supported a large and stable population of terrestrial mammals (Hafsten 1960: 442–6). The forests were not always so extensive or productive in this area. The adjacent highlands are quite near and relatively accessible. Although very steep, the routes from the inner fiords to the main plateaux can be as little as 50 km. We would therefore expect some utilization of these regions as well, at least by some groups and particularly during the first half of the Mesolithic period.

On the eastern coast the lowland areas are more extensive and offer a larger exploitation territory with less evenly distributed resources than found along the west coast. Accordingly, groups occupying this coast appear to have had a more varied and seasonally specific cycle of settlement and economic activity than that suggested for the western fiords (Indrelid 1978: 171). Mikkelson (1975: 33) has proposed a tentative model of subsistence and settlement which involves occupation and exploitation of the inland regions (water courses, forests and highlands) in the autumn and winter, and occupation and exploitation of the outer coastal zone during the remainder of the year. Although this model refers particularly to a relatively early period, it is probably applicable for most groups throughout the

Mesolithic. There is as yet no indication that either the outer coasts or the interior valleys were inhabited throughout the year during the Mesolithic period.

We may now consider how these factors of environment and subsistence might have influenced the distribution of social interaction fields in the coastal zone. On the basis of evidence so far presented it seems unlikely that there would have been the opportunity or the demand for a continuous or even network of exchange relationships along the full length of the coastal zone. In the first place the coastal zone is some 1200 km in length — not including fiords, coves and islands. While distance as such is not an insuperable barrier, the cost of maintaining exchange relationships over large distances is unlikely to be met unless there are compelling benefits by way of compensation, such as the maintenance of demographic viability for low density populations, the acquisition of supplies to make good unpredictable shortfalls in locally available food resources, or the exchange of rare and much sought after subsistence goods such as exotic raw materials. The nature of the subsistence base in the coastal areas, with a relatively abundant and diverse array of terrestrial and marine resources capable of supporting relatively dense populations, suggests that neither of the first two factors is likely to have required the maintenance of exchange relationships over very large distances. Also there is as yet no evidence for the widespread dispersal of localized resources, such as particular types of lithic raw materials.[1]

An added dis-incentive to long-distance exchange along the coastal zone is that the seasonal movements of most local groups seem to have been aligned along a coastal-inland transect centred on particular fiords and rivers, rather than as transects parallel to the coastline. Moreover, for many parts of the coast, the most easily accessible routes for transport and communication tend to be along the river systems at right-angles to the coast, rather than along the coastline. This would have been less true for the west coast where the fiords and valleys are steep and inland areas are not accessible by boat. Here, as evidenced by the presence of sites on the islands and more inaccessible reaches of the coast, boats were probably more important for travel within the island archipelago than along the inland waterways. Nevertheless, the North Sea is extremely stormy and hazardous, particularly around the southern part of the peninsula. It is therefore highly unlikely that even groups from the west coast would have ventured from their inshore waters to undertake long-distance journeys along the coastline on a regular basis.

We might therefore predict the development of a differentiated social network system due to distance in the coastal zone of southern Norway, especially if population densities in the coastal areas were relatively high. There is, however, one other possibility to be considered, and that is the use of the highland zone between the two major coastal areas. In one sense this area represents a barrier to communication between the eastern and western coastal zones.

On the other hand both zones are linked to the highlands by a network of river valleys. Moreover, there are sites present in the highland region which are usually interpreted as seasonal camps where late summer and autumn reindeer hunting constituted the main activities (Hagen 1963; Johansen 1969, 1978; Indrelid 1975, 1978). It is generally agreed that these sites were utilized by groups from both eastern and western coastal zones, although the extent and importance of this exploitation may have varied considerably in different areas and at different periods of the Mesolithic. Thus the highland region could have represented a zone of social interaction, where coastal groups from either side of the peninsula could have met periodically and maintained regular exchange relationships of various kinds, thereby unifying the whole of the southern Norway area into an undifferentiated social network system.

One particularly attractive hypothesis to account for the use of the highland zone lies in its central location in relation to the eastern and western coastal areas. Wobst (1976: 56) has argued that populations distributed at low density in linear environments, such as coastal zones, would be unable to reproduce themselves over long periods because of the distances, and hence costs, involved in participating with other groups in a mating network. If we suppose that the coastal zones of southern Norway were only capable of supporting a fairly low density of population then it could be argued that the highland region would have played a crucial role as a central area within reasonable proximity to even the most marginally located coastal groups. However, it seems unlikely that population densities were so uniformly low in the coastal areas as to require such an arrangement (see also chapter 10). The exploitation of highland resources as a seasonal supplement to offset periods of resource stress within the coastal zone seems sufficient to account for the evidence of human activity in the highland zone, without the need to invoke additional social factors in this instance.

The extent to which the exploitation of the highland zone by different coastal groups effectively offset the lags or absence in communication between them, because of their widespread distribution within the coastal zone, is difficult to assess. If, as Indrelid suggests, many groups from the western coast confined their activities to within the lowland areas during the latter half of the Mesolithic period, then for a time at least, any linkages that may have existed between eastern and western groups could not have been well developed. It may also have been possible that groups from the different coasts may have distributed themselves in different areas in the highlands when they were exploiting the area, thereby reducing the chances of contact.

The highland ranges exhibit a diverse and divided terrain with large areas of moderate slopes and plateaux that are abruptly broken by high summits, valleys, gorges and drainage systems. This dissected and diverse topography could have created conditions that probably effectively bounded reindeer aggregations and channelled herd movements (cf. Johansen

1978: 73–81), and it might have been possible that different ranges were available for exploitation by different groups. Indrelid (1975, 1978) has in fact distinguished between a northern and southern distribution of sites in the central highlands. To date these distributions have only been considered in the context of general chronological and typological questions. However, the possibility that this variation might also be related in some way to the use of different exploitation territories cannot yet be dismissed. If such a pattern of exploitation was followed it could have effectively reduced the need and incentive to develop strong and enduring social ties with more distant groups from 'the other side of the mountain', even when both coastal zones were represented in the area.

At present, however, these suggestions must remain within the realm of conjecture. Until more detailed studies of the highland sites reveal otherwise, we cannot assume a definite discontinuity in communication and interaction within this zone that could have led to a differentiation in the social network system as proposed in model 2. Within this system, however, both the nature and strength of the linkages could have varied considerably between the more widely separated groups. In this way more concentrated areas of interaction and integration may have occurred within the system, particularly within the eastern and western coastal areas.

There is as yet no reason to argue for the development of discrete social interaction fields and imposed social boundaries as described in model 3. Following initial adaptation within the coastal zone during the first half of the Boreal period, settlement and subsistence patterns appear to have remained relatively unchanged throughout the Mesolithic period (Indrelid 1978). Features which might signal levels of population density and competition capable of supporting social boundaries — such as increasing numbers of sites, occupation of more marginal areas, larger and more permanent settlements, and change or intensification in economic activity — are not indicated for any area during the Mesolithic period.

Within coastal environments, of course, the level of population density necessary to trigger excessive competition and resource stress is probably significantly higher than in less productive areas. Moreover, along the Norwegian coast, the dissected nature of the shoreline and the uneven distribution of population along its length might also have effectively preserved the exclusivity of territories and resources for a longer period. That imposed social boundaries did eventually occur within southern Norway is undisputed, as evidenced by later economic and sociocultural developements in the area. However, we must probably look to the early Neolithic period for evidence of this process.

### Some expectations for material-culture patterning in southern Norway

With respect to the archaeological material from the Mesolithic period in southern Norway, we infer that most differentiation would have occurred as a product of reduced communication rather than as a product of developing social boundaries and increasing stylistic behaviour and, as such, we would not expect to find much evidence of discrete 'stylistic clusters' in this region throughout the Mesolithic. The variation in material culture that did occur would probably be most marked between the eastern and western coasts. Within these areas we would expect that variation would exhibit a clinal distribution pattern in space. Generally speaking, given the rather ambiguous nature of the 'distance barriers' in the social network system, we would also expect a certain degree of similarity in material culture development across the entire region for the period in question.

Present evidence of the variation in artefactual assemblages in southern Norway does not appear to conflict with these expectations. There is, as would be expected, considerable agreement amongst most classes of artefacts across the entire area throughout the Mesolithic period. With certain exceptions, noted below, all areas seem to have shared a similar pattern of development in material culture in which many of the same changes occurred across a broad spectrum of data, including functional, technological and stylistic attributes.

With respect to the variation that is known to exist, it appears that the greatest variability occurs in technological and functional attributes rather than stylistic ones. Thus variation exists in the frequencies of specific tool types, particularly axes and burins, or in certain technological features such as use of raw materials and specific manufacturing techniques. On the other hand, almost no regional variability is known to occur in projectile point style, despite the fact that the temporal variability within the same class of data is considerable.

Finally, the spatial patterning of this variation does seem to reflect greater variability between, rather than within, eastern and western assemblages. Many authors, including Gjessing (1945), Indrelid (1975) and Mikkelson (1975), have noted that while many early eastern assemblages are characterized by large and well-developed microlithic industries, true microliths occur more rarely amongst most comparatively dated assemblages from the west coast. Similarly the 'microburin' technique which is considered almost diagnostic of early east Norwegian and certain west Swedish assemblages is completely unknown from western sites. Amongst sites dated to the later Mesolithic period a similar pattern of spatial variability is seen in axe material, particularly with respect to the frequency of flake versus core axes and to the finishing techniques employed in their manufacture (Indrelid 1978; Freundt 1948).

We must use considerable caution in weighing the importance of any agreement between our expectations and these observed patterns of variability in the archaeological material. In the first place no systematic comparative analysis of artefactual assemblages across a regional transect has yet been carried out for southern Norway. Furthermore, amongst these Mesolithic assemblages there is an almost total lack of those artefactual categories — such as bone and ceramic materials — which would probably be most sensitive to stylistic variation. In brief, more information is necessary before we can either assess the significance of present observations or fully test our expectations.

### Summary and conclusions

Three simplified models that consider the processes which may structure the organization and articulation of social network systems amongst hunter-gatherers have been presented. These models provided a framework for a preliminary evaluation of the social network system within southern Norway during the Mesolithic period, and for the development of some tentative expectations concerning the nature of the variability in the material culture of the area. These expectations remain to be demonstrated in the artefactual material from the area.

Within these models it was inferred that to a large extent the structure and parameters of the social network systems were dependent upon level of population density, competition for scarce resources and distances between local groups. Thus when population density and competition is low, the area and distances encompassed in a single undifferentiated network system would be most extensive. Linkages between the participating groups would be loose and flexible across the area to facilitate ease of exchange and movement throughout the larger network system.

Breaks in this network system might occur at certain points when prohibitive distance between interacting groups created a significant discontinuity in exchange. Breaks might also occur under conditions of high population density and competition. In this situation the very absence of distance factors might necessitate a change in the nature of linkages and relationships between groups so as to create an imposed social boundary to preserve the exclusivity of the resources or territory. Both these processes could give rise to definable and differentiated sets of social interaction fields within a region, but the same inferences cannot be made regarding either the internal structure or the boundary behaviour of the participating groups in each case. The specific arrangement of these networks in space, their extent, their structure and their 'boundedness' would vary considerably as a function of specific environmental, economic and social factors, to be determined for the region in question.

Amongst many hunter-gatherers in prehistory it might be argued that the inherently low productivity and instability of their subsistence economies and the nature of their social organization would have prevented the development of population densities and levels of internal integration significantly high enough to give rise to enduring social

boundaries as described in model 3. Any closure within a social network system is expensive. No doubt the long-term viability of such a system would be possible only in areas where the resource potential and/or the economic and social development of the participating groups was capable of supporting such behaviour. Such levels of social and economic development are not usually attributed to 'simple egalitarian band societies'. In such societies the most cohesive unit of association, cooperation and identity is no larger than the minimum band and other larger associations and aggregations are based on diffuse and shifting relationships derived from relatively unstructured kinship and affinal ties. Such fluid organization functions to provide extensive and flexible linkages between groups, thereby ensuring predictable alliances amongst the largest number of people within a region. Such a system works directly against both the strong integration of groups larger than the minimum band and the development of social boundaries between these groups. In such situations it might be argued that conditions of population pressure and resource stress would have been dealt with, not by a narrowing of social interaction fields and a strengthening of group boundaries, but by the dispersal or even extinction of certain groups within a region.

On the other hand, not all hunter-gatherers in prehistory should be categorized as 'simple egalitarian band societies'. As demonstrated by Wright for Natufian (1978), and King for certain California groups (1978), hunter-gatherers could have had the economic potential and the social mechanisms necessary for the integration of larger groups and the development of social boundaries between these groups. Moreover, there are indications that similar changes were occurring throughout prehistory as hunter-gatherers sought to accommodate themselves to the increasing problems of population pressure and competition for diminishing resources (cf. Bender 1978; Conkey 1978a; Jochim, this volume). Recognition of these processes in the archaeological record is important. More careful analysis of artefact assemblages along with the development of better methods to identify and measure those aspects of archaeological variability (such as stylistic attributes), which are most affected by this process, is one approach to the problem (cf. Close 1978; Conkey 1978a). However, it is also necessary to develop a body of theory which considers the regional nature of hunter-gatherer organization and the network of linkages that structure inter-relationships amongst groups. Such theory may bring us a little closer to the reality of these artefactual structures and the complex factors which generated this variability.

*Note*
1. There is some evidence for the dispersal of a locally available raw material (greenstone) within the west coast area (cf. Hagen 1967: 40–1). However, there is no evidence that this extended to the eastern side of the peninsula.

Chapter 18

**Culture and society in the Upper Palaeolithic of
Europe**
Clive Gamble

This chapter considers the problem of why Palaeolithic 'art' and
ornament first appears in northern latitudes and at a comparatively
late date after the arrival of man in that area. The discussion focuses
on the social and adaptive changes that would have been necessary in
order to maintain continuous occupation in northern Europe during
extreme glacial conditions. Primacy is given to developments in the
alliance structures of Palaeolithic hunters which were enhanced by the
information properties inherent in material culture and in particular
'art'. Settlement evidence is also used as a measure of social changes
which result in significant discontinuities in the Palaeolithic record.

Culture is an information system, where the messages are
accumulated survival information.     (David Clarke 1968: 89)

### Introduction

Recent studies of Palaeolithic art, both cave and
mobiliary, have stressed its role in the process of information
exchange (Conkey 1978a, 1980; Davidson n.d.; Gamble 1980,
1982). This reflects a recent re-emergence of interest in
concepts of style in material culture (Plog 1980; Sackett, 1977;
Wobst 1977), following a dormant period in which studies
of style were sometimes associated with over-simplistic
interpretations of ethnicity. My purpose is to look at aspects
of Palaeolithic information exchange and in particular to
consider how changes in elements of material culture, that
were involved in such a process, reflected changes in the
structure and organization of Palaeolithic society. In this
sense the chapter is not about the specific information
properties of that class of objects and representations that
have come to be termed 'Palaeolithic art'. They will instead be
used as a touchstone for discussing the development of material
culture in systems of information exchange. Furthermore they
provide a focus for a wider consideration of the significance
of variation within Palaeolithic data, which incorporates
measures provided by technology, settlement systems and
exchange networks.

Even though it is now abundantly clear that the
prehistory of humanity is not the prehistory of Europe (J.D.
Clark 1975: 176), it nevertheless still appears to hold true
that this continent can claim the earliest appearance of art and
ornament at c. 35 000 b.p. Moreover it is quite clear that art
appears at a relatively late date in the overall history of human
occupation in Europe. Thus a specific focus on the European
data raises two problems of general interest: why did art make
its earliest appearance in harsh northern latitudes; and why did
it not appear earlier?

With hindsight, might we have predicted that the addition
of art objects to the cultural inventories of Palaeolithic groups
would take place in the north, far away from the warmer
cradles of mankind to the south and centre of the globe? Is
there something about such developments which met the
adaptive requirements of populations living on the inhabitable
margins of the Palaeolithic world? If this was the case, what

were the practical advantages that such developments brought and why were they not present with the first colonizers of the European continent?

The conventional approach to these problems is to invoke specific features of hominid evolution as necessary prerequisites for the development of cultural behaviour patterns of which artistic ability forms an example. However, such explanations are inherently unsatisfactory. They are, in the first place, based on doubtful expectations about the correlation between physical evolution and cultural behaviour; secondly, they beg the further question of why the prerequisite aspect of hominid evolution did not occur earlier; and finally they fail to specify any possible reasons for the geographical bias in the earliest evidence.

An alternative approach is to examine these problems within the context of developments in social organization (Wobst 1974b: vi). In order to achieve this we need both analytical concepts and appropriate systems of measurement for the process of social evolution. The first requirement is met below by the concept of an alliance network which deals with material and marital exchanges at an extensive spatial scale. This incorporates many local or band-level interactions and provides a framework for analysing regional patterns of adaptation and variation (Bender 1981). Indications of changes in these alliance networks can be gauged from the systems of information exchange that served them. This not only had repercussions for the development of material culture – visual display, management of style – but also for other dimensions of the archaeological record where changes in human adaptations can be measured against environmental constants.

I am therefore examining two linked propositions: (a) that the visual information systems that we commonly refer to, generically, as 'Palaeolithic art' were developed in order to service some fundamental change in the structure of regional alliance networks; and (b) that these changes in the principles of organization of regionally based alliance networks played an important part in establishing continuous human occupation in regions of extreme climatic variation and unpredictability of resources.

The paradox of studies of Palaeolithic social evolution is that our starting point is the end product of a long process of social evolution which it is the purpose of archaeological study to unravel. It is all too easy to find our concepts and models tyrannized by the ethnographic present (Wobst 1978). While many aspects of human behaviour and organization can be assumed to obey uniformitarian principles, which thus unlock certain codes in the archaeological record, this cannot be claimed for more general considerations of Palaeolithic society. Demographic units and networks (Birdsell 1958; Wobst 1974a, 1976) provide one such example of using minimum estimates for the arrangement of population based on contemporary observation in order to investigate patterns of regional variation in the past (Yellen and Harpending 1972). Changes in these model arrangements can be used to predict variation in archaeological patterns. These are, however,

demographic rather than social units even though Wobst regards the maximum band level as 'the social correlate of the cultural system of hunters and gatherers' (1974a: 151). The consequences for cultural systems that stem from group closure, linear mating networks or the failure to maintain minimum population sizes at critical densities will all have great impact upon our understanding of past systems. Variation may respond to both environmental and social factors which require the differential distribution of population across the landscape. In this chapter the view is taken that the social system is dominant in the sense used by Ingold (1981), in that it establishes a system of relations for the reproduction of social and material existence which specifies the way in which the environment is to be exploited. While the set of social relations is *dominant* the environment is *determinant* in the sense that it sets limits to what is viable within the specifications set by the social system. Demographic and economic decisions are influenced by environmental constraints within a framework of social relations which are here conceived as a set of alliance structures.

This focus upon the social context of Palaeolithic behaviour patterns provides a unifying framework for the consideration of individual elements of the system. This brings into significant relationship changes in subsistence strategies and other aspects of material technology which are informing us about the status and development of social complexity. The factor of physical evolution has to be incorporated into this framework rather than placed in a dominant explanatory position.

### Biology and intelligence

This relationship is well illustrated by the conventional explanations for the appearance of Palaeolithic art. The investigation of this phenomenon has generally been firmly rooted in the technological, temporal and spatial framework of the Upper Palaeolithic. This period in Europe witnesses changes in a wide range of different behaviour patterns. Mellars (1973) lists developments in no less than eight such aspects which he groups under three main headings; material technology; subsistence activities; demography and social organization. Of these the appearance of personal ornaments and art are some of the most striking since there are few, if any, precursors to this aspect of material culture.

The Upper Palaeolithic has therefore always presented archaeologists with one of prehistory's 'big surprises' (Binford 1972b: 119) where a non-conformity in the data challenges our view of how cultures should behave. As Binford notes, reaction to such surprises generally results in explanations that invoke replacement of one population with another. This has generally been the case for explanations of the Upper Palaeolithic where support for such a view has been derived from the human fossil evidence. However, there are problems with such explanations. Bordes (1968: 147) has pointed out, for example, that this notion of population replacement brings the findings of archaeology and physical anthropology into conflict, since in his opinion it can be argued that the earliest Upper Palaeolithic stone tools are, at least in France, evolved directly from Middle Palaeolithic industries. This conflict has been partially mitigated by the recent find of a Neanderthal skull at St Césaire in association with an early Upper Palaeolithic industry (ApSimon 1980; Léveque and Vandermeersch 1980). However, a physical change, marked by the appearance of fully developed *Homo sapiens sapiens* populations, accompanies the subsequent developments of the Upper Palaeolithic period.

The appeal of biological evidence in this context lies in the fact that there are significant measurable differences of cranial morphology between the indigenous Neanderthalers and the *Homo sapiens sapiens* populations which are alleged to have replaced them (Stringer 1974). It is therefore tempting to observe with J.G.D. Clark (1946: 31) that, 'prior to the emergence of *Homo sapiens* in evolved form, the hominids were *limited by biological handicaps*' (my italics), thereby implying that the level of intelligence necessary for such cultural developments as artistic activity was lacking until a particular threshold in physical evolution had been reached.

However, it is difficult to accept the assumption that differences in cranial morphology necessarily equate with markedly different levels of intelligence. Increased levels of intelligence refer to the ability of an organism to organize behaviour in more complex ways (Wynn 1979: 372). The structure and capacity of the brain will obviously be important in such a process. Evolution took place and we can see that in the fossil record. What is lacking however in the study of fossil skulls is any means of directly assessing morphology in terms of organizational competence.

In this respect material culture is also a poor indicator of comparative thresholds in intelligence. The ambiguity of the evidence in informing us directly about such developments is shown in Marshack's (1976) study of intentionally scratched and pierced bones and modified mammoth lamellars from Lower and Middle Palaeolithic assemblages. These few pieces, of which the Pech de l'Azé specimens are the best known (Bordes 1969), have been interpreted by Marshack as part of 'a symbolised cultural complexity' (1976: 305). However, bones can be scratched and pierced intentionally without such action being necessarily organized according to a symbolic set of behaviours. The problem is that the motives for engraving on bone are not just obscure, they are, as Bordes commented upon the significance of the Pech de l'Azé material, unknown. We either accept that pre-Upper Palaeolithic groups were able to fashion art objects, but on the whole chose not to; or we can accept that their handiwork represents chance facsimiles which, because of their similarity of form, we are keen to interpret as evidence for pre-adapted behaviour.

### Society and information exchange

In order to escape from the circularity of the preceding arguments it is as well to reiterate the view that artefacts cannot be studied in isolation but must be placed within the total sociocultural system of which they once formed a part. The appearance of new forms and treatment of material culture needs to be examined in terms of the social contexts where such behaviour developed. The framework followed here is the now familiar one where culture is modelled as an information system (Clarke 1968; Flannery 1972). According to this view cultural systems are adaptive mechanisms that obtain and decode information necessary for survival. They undergo qualitative and quantitative changes that have led to more complex systems of organization. These in turn require the development of more elaborate methods to process and exchange the increased flow of information required to maintain this complexity.

This view also leads to an explicitly functional appraisal of many aspects of social behaviour that constitute such cultural systems. In particular the rather vague term *interaction* is taken to indicate the exchange of information (see chapter 17). These interactions take the form of communication through spoken language, ritual (Douglas 1970), the physical exchange of material goods (Renfrew 1975) and through the visual medium of material culture (Hodder 1978b; Sackett 1977; Wobst 1977). The functional interpretation of such interactions is well put by Wilmsen (1973: 26—7) when he notes that 'as interactions take place between bandsmen and as obligations, vows, spouses, and objects flow across boundaries, information about environmental conditions, group identification, current deployment of individuals (e.g. hunters, mates, curers) goes with them'. Central to our understanding of the changing use of material culture in information exchange is the concept of style. Style is the means by which the messages that all forms of material culture can carry are made explicit. Any set of material objects signifies that an information system of some sort is present but it is an appreciation of style that provides both qualitative and quantitative measures of that system (Wobst 1977: 327).

An example of this is provided by Wobst in a general discussion of the properties of stylistic messaging. He argues that one function of communication in this mode is that it contributes significantly to achieving predictable outcomes from social encounters. Such a benefit will only be realized in a society of a particular size where communication between socially distant persons could lead to ambiguity and the breakdown of information flow. This would occur in situations where 'the potential receivership is not partial to the most intimate life experiences and behavioural peculiarities of the message emitter' (1977: 323). If the target group for a message is no larger than close relatives and friends, then there will be little need to say-it-in-style via material culture. Thus stylistic messaging becomes important with the addition of an enlarged target population of socially distant persons with whom it is necessary to maintain the potential for communication.

Wobst's model therefore traces a link between the properties of a visual system of communication and a qualitative appreciation about the size of the society that would require such a means of information exchange. No doubt there will be differential selection of material culture to fulfil the various informational requirements. Conkey (1978a: 78–9) has for example argued that mobiliary art objects would have greater potential than either wall art or stone tools to inform on stylistic groups. This is not only due to their portability but also to the fact that some bone/ antler objects are engraved and others are not, which also adds to their utility in carrying stylistic messages.

The sudden appearance of art and ornament might also be accounted for by the rules that are inherent in stylistic messaging. Once one category of material culture is used to impart information in this way then *all* categories carry information even though, as in the case of the unengraved antler tool, they may not carry a stylistic message (Wobst 1977: 326). In contrast to a gradual development we would expect an explosion of this capacity in material culture. This would extend to stylistic messaging through stone tools, which previously had only possessed what Sackett (1977) has referred to as an active or utilitarian stylistic voice.

Changes in the size and structure of Palaeolithic society will obviously be reflected at many different levels of analysis. The depositional contexts in which the art has been found — subterranean caves, occupation sites and burials — points to a diversity of social contexts which required, and were enhanced by, the properties of this use of material culture. However, rather than assuming that because we find art we must be dealing with more complex social systems, we must turn instead to alternative means of assessing the changes that we suspect took place. This is to be done here by examining our comparative unit of analysis, the alliance network. In particular we shall look at the potential such an extensive information network possesses for modifying the determining effects of harsh environments upon the possibility of human settlement and continuous occupation.

### Alliance networks

Palaeolithic studies have lacked an analytical concept that provides a regional framework for the investigation of local variation (Wobst 1976: 49). What is required is that 'the focus of study should not be the on-the-ground band but rather that larger structure within which the band operates' (Bender 1981: 152). This requirement is met by the concept of alliance networks, which define a diverse set of social relationships where circulation and exchange of persons and goods establishes and maintains ties of variable commitment and duration.

At an extensive scale of analysis these analytical units can be investigated for particular functions. J.H. Hill (1978) has examined the role that language contact systems play in area-level adaptations. The case studies she cites demonstrate how specific language patterns are used to cope with environmental stress by providing an extensive network of contacts and facilitating 'refugee' movements from areas of periodic scarcity to those where resources are available. This analysis rests upon the point that the appropriate unit of study is the regional population unit in the ecological sense used by Rappaport (1969: 183).

A further example is provided by the name relations found among the !Kung San (Lee 1972c). Here some 70% of the population regularly use only 20 of the 69 personal names currently available. This makes it possible for any !Kung language speaker to establish a fictive kinship that extends far outside any immediate genealogical reckoning and may cover distances of over 800 km.

Comparable distances can be traced for the circulation of both goods and personnel in Australia in what Mulvaney (1976) has referred to as 'chains of connection'. Amongst other hunting groups, trading partners are a common feature (Spencer 1959), as well as more specific partnerships such as those defined through song (Balikci 1970), child adoption and spouse exchange (Damas 1972).

Alliances are therefore formed that extend ties over much larger social and spatial areas than is often implied in models of mating networks (Wobst 1974a, 1976). These mating networks, which have been modelled as hexagonal lattices containing minimum bands of about 25 persons (Birdsell 1953), have varying degrees of closure which appear to correlate with the ecological structure of resources in hunter-gatherer environments (Yellen and Harpending 1972). In many cases the borders of these networks are 'fuzzy' (Helm 1969), and Birdsell (1976) has defined a genetic isolate as any unit with more than 50% of matings occurring within its boundaries. This implies considerable flow of personnel across any boundary that might be associated with such a unit. While this mating network may approximate to a language dialect area (Damas 1969: 131; Tindale 1953), it appears, as Hill (1978) argues, that a larger unit is necessary for the investigation of long-term adaptive strategies. Peterson (1976b), for example, describes for Australia a larger population unit based on a drainage basin which encompasses a number of smaller units defined through dialect differences.

One function of these alliance networks is particularly apparent in environments where certain critical resources may be unpredictable. As Yengoyan puts it, 'populations in harsh environments, which are characterised by spatial and temporal variations in resources, require mechanisms by which all local populations are reciprocally linked to promote interaction and mobility over vast areas of highly limited resources' (1972: 8). A safety net is provided which offers some form of insurance for local groups. The foraging adaptation of the G/wi of Botswana described by Silberbauer (1972) shows how comparatively stable alliances between local groups make travel possible by granting to visitors the use of territorial resources. In this type of environment it is predictable that resource crises will occur. What is unpredictable is the timing of such crises and hence the necessity of having some form of insurance mechanism for the rapid redistribution of personnel across the environment.

It might be argued from these few examples that extensive alliance networks are a product of particular environmental conditions. This would however confuse the determinant aspect of the environment with the dominant feature of the social system. It is true that without alliance partners a group such as the G/wi would probably not be able to exist in the habitat they presently occupy. However, without a set of social relations specifying a set of extensive social and spatial alliances, there would be an even more basic obstacle to the maintenance of population in a harsh, unpredictable environment. While the development of these alliance networks made possible the extension of human settlement into such habitats, it is not necessarily the case that this aspect of social evolution owes its origins to such a simple functional requirement. However, setting aside the causes for changes in Palaeolithic social relations, it is possible to see that one consequence of these developments would be an increase in informational requirements in order to integrate and organize these alliance networks. Combined with our earlier discussion of the role of material culture in stylistic messaging it seems reasonable to suggest that Palaeolithic social evolution led to larger societies and moreover provided the opportunity to overcome particular ecological constraints.

### Mobility and settlement systems

A characteristic feature of contemporary hunter-gatherers inhabiting unpredictable environments is the degree to which risk is minimized through the acquisition and sharing of information. The principal means by which this critical knowledge is obtained is through mobility. Smith (1978) provides an example of this for the caribou-eating Chipewyan of Hudson Bay. A spatially extensive system of alliances serves to counter some of the problems posed by the unpredictability of caribou movements. These alliances are formalized through exogamous marriage ties, matrilocal residence and through visiting, which not only emphasizes kin relationships but also dispenses information about faunal abundance or scarcity. As Laughlin has noted, the Eskimo performs 'in an arena which has many high-level constraints on behaviour and which offers little guiding information. Penalties for mistakes are prompt and drastic' (1969, xiv—xv). The key to minimizing such risks is precise, accurate information about the environment and its resources, together with social contexts that allow such information to be rapidly disseminated to individual hunters. The prodigious knowledge of recent hunters, in environments where such information is critical for making correct decisions concerning exploitation, have impressed many anthropologists (Blurton-Jones and Konner 1976: 344; Binford 1979a: 257, 272; Nelson 1969: 374; Thomson 1962: 271). The extreme mobility of some groups is, Woodburn believes (1972), conditioned by the need to reaffirm social ties rather than a result of ecological imperatives. Even if this is the case it must be recognized that the pattern of alliances provides a convenient framework not only for social visiting but also for the accompanying dissemination of information about a whole range of subjects, among which the environment is likely to be a major element.

The means by which mobility contributes to environmental adaptation will vary according to the type of environment and the type of subsistence strategy. Binford (1980) has recently outlined two extremes in the spectrum of hunter-gatherer subsistence strategies: *foraging*, which is characteristic of desert or semi-desert environments and involves a heavy dependence upon plant foods, as exemplified by the !Kung San; and *collecting*, which is characteristic of high latitude environments, with a dominance of mobile animal resources, as exemplified by the Nunamiut Eskimo (see Part 2).

Foragers depend upon encounter strategies in which food is gathered daily from a residential camp. Variations in food supply are accommodated by moving consumers to resources. This results in frequent residential moves and adjustments in group size. Mobility is very high although the spatial area of the annual territory around which such groups move may be fairly compact (Silberbauer 1972).

Amongst collectors, the principal strategy is to move resources to consumers. Resources are intercepted rather than encountered. This involves a logistical strategy where considerable effort is invested in planning ahead. Critical resources, such as the caribou, are often only available for very brief periods. This *time stress* (see chapter 3) has repercussions for the organization of technology and makes storage a basic element of such intercept strategies. The residential base is moved less frequently over the course of the year. Small procurement parties set out to acquire specific resources and may not return on a daily basis. On such trips the environment is being constantly monitored and the hunters associated with a residential camp will cover a very large territory.

These two strategies result, according to Binford, in different settlement types. Foragers create sites classified as residential camps and procurement locations while collectors add to these a further three types; field camps, stations and caches. Factors of artefact deposition and site formation are also expected to further differentiate these settlement types within their respective settlement systems (Binford 1978a, 1979a).

We can now draw together some of the preceding strands in order to consider the archaeological implications of a regional analysis of information exchange among hunter-gatherers. We have seen from the study of contemporary hunter-gatherers that high risk environments will only show evidence for long-term adaptations if the groups exploiting these habitats possess a framework of extensive alliance networks. These provide, among other things, a system of safeguards where risk is minimized by permitting the free movement of personnel and information. This suggests that the main obstacle to the long-term colonization of particular habitats does not lie primarily in the field of technological advances, but rather depends upon the development of ap-

propriate social structures. These have to deal with specifying
the exploitation and distribution of widely different resources
in contrasted ecological settings. One consequence of changes
in these social structures is that the resultant networks of
alliances provide regional links between spatially scattered
groups.

The development of such structures implies an increase
in social complexity. It has been common practice to interpret
such evidence as the grave goods associated with Upper
Palaeolithic burials as a reflection of social changes (S.R.
Binford 1968a; Harrold 1980). The use and elaboration of
material culture in these contexts is often thought to point
to increases in the size and internal differentiation of
Palaeolithic society (Bender 1978). However, there are
problems with this evidence if we use it in this manner as a
direct indication of social evolution. The ambiguity of the
data makes it possible that all we have done is prove what we
wanted to prove, rather than correctly interpret the
Palaeolithic record. It could be argued that complex social
patterns evolved at much earlier times and were enhanced
by either perishable mediums, such as body painting, or by
ritual which involved no material culture at all. Much could
be made, in this respect, of the so-called Neanderthal burials,
where the association, or not, of grave goods is still contended
(Harrold 1980; Rowlett and Schneider 1974), so that the
inferences drawn from the later, Upper Palaeolithic material
are correspondingly suspect.

In the case study which follows a rather different
approach to providing a measure of changes in Palaeolithic
society will be adopted. This involves considering settlement
evidence where the processes of colonization and retreat can
be related to environmental events in the Pleistocene. The
changes in the climatic regime of Pleistocene Europe provide
a coarse measure of habitat unpredictability against which it
is possible to place the evidence of human settlement. We
would expect, in central Europe, as the climate deteriorated
with the advance of the continental ice sheets, and resources
became more unpredictable due to their greater mobility
(Gamble 1978a), that settlement would cease. In cases where
it was maintained in spite of environmental change we would
expect this to be accompanied by aspects of the 'big surprise',
such as visual display systems, changes in the organization of
technology, and evidence for innovations in information
processing. The settlement data from these harsh habitats
of the Pleistocene therefore provide an independent check upon
the evolution of more complex social structures. It will not
pin-point their origin in either time or space, but it will show
that the process of social evolution was under way and that
this had consequences for area level adaptations, and hence
for the formation of the archaeological record.

**The last ice age in Europe**
It is now possible to sketch an outline of European
climate during the last ice age, during which time art appeared

and Upper Palaeolithic blade technologies replaced the flake-
based traditions of the Middle Palaeolithic (fig. 18.1).

The evidence from $^{18}$O readings from deep-sea cores
has shown that the last interglacial was a short-lived event of
some 10–15 thousand years duration (Shackleton 1969). The
height of this warm period occurred at 125 000 b.p. as shown
by absolute dates for raised beaches in Bermuda (Harmon *et
al.* 1981). The five-part division of stage 5 in the continuous
deep-sea core record has received support from recent pollen
work at Grand Pile in north-eastern France (Woillard 1978)
where the last interglacial peak is followed by two substantial
temperate phases before the sustained onset of cold conditions.

The correlation of these pollen events with those from
the Netherlands, Denmark and northern Germany is as yet
uncertain since they appear to be earlier in age than the classic
early last glacial interstadials – Amersfoort, Brørup and
Odderade – that have been identified (van der Hammen *et al.*
1971). These interstadials all show a small increase in
temperate-Boreal elements which comes as a marked contrast
with the park tundra stadials that separate them. These three
interstadials were assigned positions on the Camp Century
$^{18}$O ice core at 75–78 000, 68–74 000 and 66 000 b.p.
respectively (Dansgaard *et al.* 1970).

Whatever the eventual correlations between the
continuous and discontinuous records of the last ice age, it
is apparent that the deep-sea core stage 5e (the last interglacial)
was followed by a series of temperate phases during which
we can see a general trend towards lower temperatures and
simpler floral communities. This gradual process ends at
65 000 b.p. Within this progressive decline it is possible to see
short-lived events when temperatures plummeted and then
rose again rapidly (Dansgaard *et al.* 1970).

This early glacial phase was then followed in northern
Europe by the pleniglacial which began with a long period of
much lower temperatures that resulted in polar desert (van
der Hammen *et al.* 1971). This was broken by a series of weak
interstadials which together make up the middle pleniglacial.
These are named after pollen localities in the Netherlands and
include Moershoofd (*c.* 48 000 b.p.), Hengelo (39–37 000 b.p.)
and Denekamp (32–29 000 b.p.). The vegetation in northern
Europe has been described as shrub tundra during these
interstadials. Temperate episodes have also been identified
from beetle assemblages in England (Coope *et al.* 1971).

After 29 000 b.p. the climate returned to polar desert
conditions. The Greenland ice cores showed a marked drop in
$^{18}$O temperature readings and a series of rapid temperature
fluctuations. During this period the ice sheets began to expand
out from the Alps and Scandinavia to reach their maximum
extent by 18 000 b.p. This date represents the maximum
lowering of sea level during the last glaciation (Peterson
*et al.* 1979, chapter 13 above). The intense dry/cold conditions
of this upper pleniglacial phase are shown by changes in the
weathering of the limestone caves in areas such as the Périgord
(Laville *et al.* 1980). In these more southerly and protected
areas a number of interstadials have been identified (e.g.

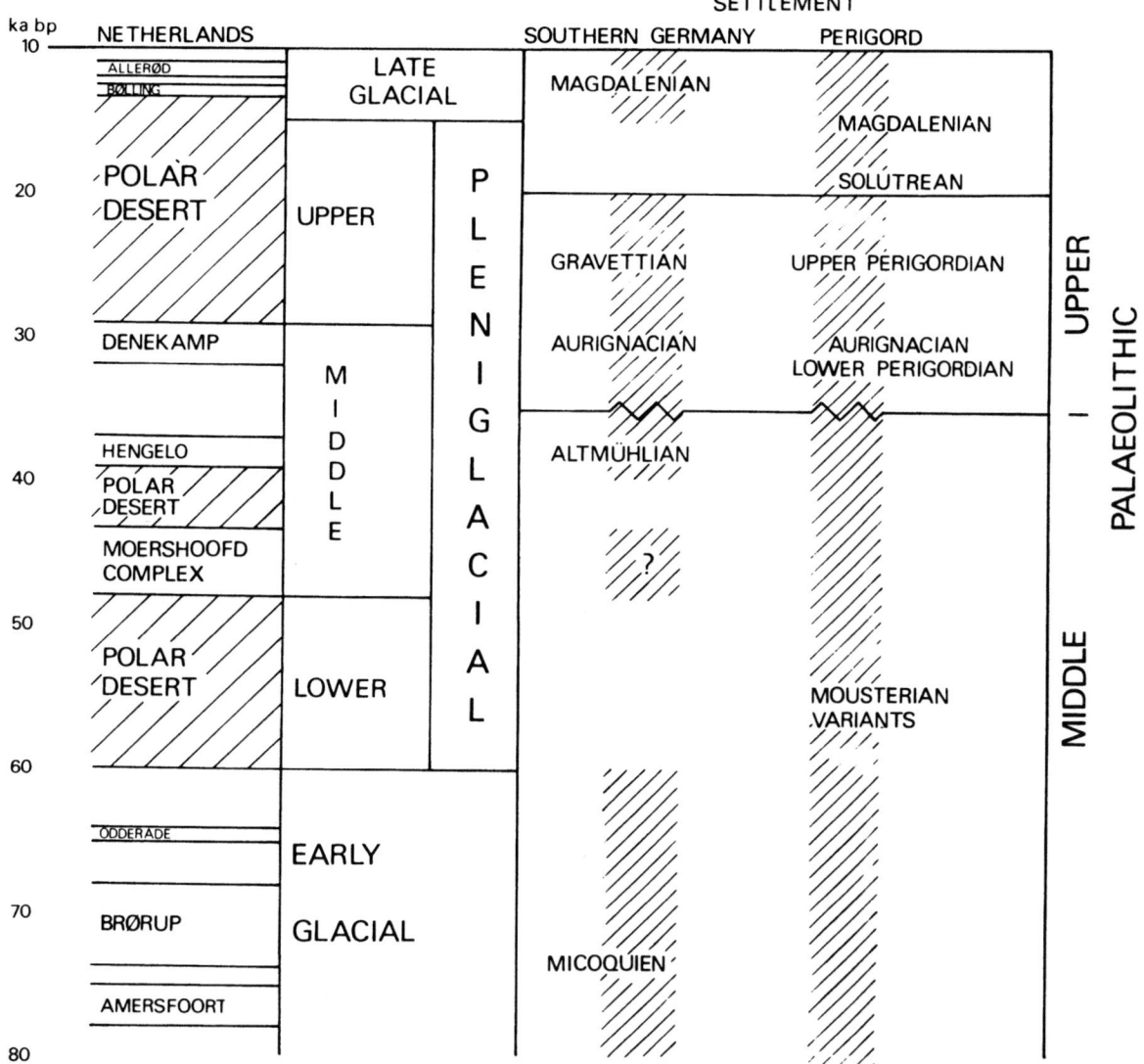

Fig. 18.1. Climatic and cultural sequences in Palaeolithic Europe.

Tursac, Laugerie and Lascaux) on the basis of pollen work within cave deposits (Leroi-Gourhan 1980; chapters 12 and 13 above).

Finally with the slow retreat of the ice sheets after 16 000 b.p. a series of temperate oscillations occur within the late glacial of northern Europe. These include the Bølling and Allerød interstadials which are sandwiched between the open vegetation conditions that characterized the cold Dryas phases.

This brief sketch emphasizes the obvious point that considerable variation in the effects of a glacial regime must have existed in Europe, and this was due to such factors as latitude and continentality. In particular those unglaciated areas of northern and central Europe were subject to intense periglacial conditions (Frenzel 1968, 1973; Kaiser 1960), and especially so in those areas caught between advancing ice fronts. In southern and western Europe these effects were considerably modified.

Although it is not possible to provide absolute figures it is reasonable to suggest that in relative terms the conditions for existence must have been more severe in the north and centre of the continent when compared to the south and west. It is not just a matter of cold, or evidence for more rigorous past periglacial activity, but rather that the end result of significant changes in factors such as these would have been to affect the resources available for exploitation by hunting and gathering groups. Less direct radiation, shorter growing seasons, late snow cover and permafrost conditions would all have combined to alter the vegetation upon which the herds of animals depended. This would have led to reductions in available numbers and biomass per unit area, altered the size of animal ranges, and influenced the degree of annual movement in search of suitable grazing. The diversity of local and regional animal communities would also have changed as these more specialized environmental conditions began to take hold. The exploitation risks for

Table 18.1. *Findspot frequency for southern Germany and south-west France*

| Period | Swabian and Frankonian limestone albs | | Périgord | |
|---|---|---|---|---|
| | sites | % | sites | % |
| *Middle Palaeolithic* (Mousterian, Micoquien) 80 000 − > 35 000 b.p. | 42 | 34 | 32 | 13 |
| *Early Upper Palaeolithic* (Chatelperronian Aurignacian Upper Perigordian/ Gravettian) < 35 000−20 000 b.p. | 21 | 17 | 98 | 40 |
| *Late Upper Palaeolithic* (Solutrean, Magdalenian) < 20 000−10 000 b.p. | 60 | 49 | 113 | 47 |

*Source*: Mellars (1973), Peyrony (1949) and Gamble (1978a, b).

Table 18.2. *Number of sites per km² in southern Germany and south-west France*

| | Swabian and Frankonian limestone albs 15 000 km² | Périgord 12 600 km² |
|---|---|---|
| Middle Palaeolithic | 0.0028 | 0.0025 |
| Early Upper Palaeolithic | 0.0014 | 0.0078 |
| Late Upper Palaeolithic | 0.004 | 0.0089 |

*Note*: Périgord area calculated from de Sonneville-Bordes (1960, fig. 1).

hunting groups would therefore have increased. Gathering would have made negligible returns and animal resources upon which groups depended would have become less predictable and hence contributed to the overall risks.

If we turn to the settlement evidence (tables 18.1 and 18.2) from two of these contrasted areas we can see that there is, even at this coarse scale of analysis, a reflection of the variable effects of climate upon recovered settlement evidence. The southern German area shows a marked decline in the number of sites that can be dated to the period during the upper pleniglacial when Germany formed part of a central European ice-free corridor. The same period in the Périgord reveals a noticeable rise in the number of findspots which have yielded evidence of human occupation during this episode of extreme cold.

These figures are not however strictly comparable since they disguise much significant variation in climate during the three time periods. A closer inspection shows that whereas Mousterian occupations are found in the Würm I and II deposits of the Périgord (Laville *et al.* 1980) there are indications that these occupations in southern Germany are generally interstadial in age (Müller-Beck 1957). Several of the south German Micoquien assemblages (Bosinski 1967) which come from well-studied contexts have been assigned a position within the Brørup interstadial of the early last glacial. This same pattern is also found in other sites in central Europe, as with the Micoquien assemblage from Königsaue, East Germany (Mania and Toepfer 1973). Not all these assemblages may eventually prove to belong to the Brørup interstadial, as it is presently defined by pollen analysis. However, it does appear to be the case that during comparable periods of polar desert in the Netherlands there was a dearth of settlement in much of central Europe. Middle Palaeolithic settlement has however been found during the interstadials of the middle pleniglacial. Most notable are the distinctive leaf point assemblages as at Mauern (von Koenigswald *et al.* 1974) in Bavaria.

The conclusion to be drawn from these rough settlement figures is that occupation was most probably continuous in south-west France while in southern Germany much greater constraints were placed on the possibility of occupation. This led to interruptions in human settlement, the latter being closely linked to the presence of favourable resource conditions.

With the evidence for Upper Palaeolithic settlement we find a rather different picture that has the added advantage of C14 determinations. In France there is a continuous distribution of sites during both the middle pleniglacial interstadials and the cold period that followed (Delibrias *et al.* 1976). The same pattern can also be seen for the C14-dated sites from southern Germany (Hahn 1976, 1977, 1981). While the number of sites from the study area is low, the most significant finding is that they were there at all during the build-up to the maximum intensity of the last ice age from 29 000 to 20 000 b.p.

However Hahn (1976: 115) has demonstrated that a hiatus in occupation existed between *c.* 20 000 and 15 000 b.p. in Germany and this corresponds to the full glacial maxima (see chapter 19). At the same time in Périgord we find Solutrean and Magdalenian assemblages. After 15 000 b.p. it is possible to see a substantial rise in the number of findspots in both areas and this broadly corresponds to occupation during the late glacial, when environmental conditions were improving again.

The earliest appearance of art occurs during the interstadials of the middle pleniglacial, and is associated with Upper Palaeolithic blade assemblages (Collins and Onians 1978). In southern Germany this includes a small human figurine, carved from a mammoth tusk, from the Stadel cave and dated by C14 to 31 750 b.p. From the neighbouring site of the Vogelherd came an important series of animal and anthropomorphic carvings (Hahn 1977; Wagner 1981) and other Aurignacian assemblages in southern Germany have also produced animal figurines (Hahn *et al.* 1977). The earliest material from France consists of engraved limestone slabs as from the Abri Blanchard, Laussel level 5 and La Ferrassie (Delluc and Delluc 1978). Bone pendants and ornaments have also been found in association with the earliest Upper Palaeolithic, as at Grotte du Renne, Arcy-sur-Cure (Leroi-Gourhan and Leroi-Gourhan 1964). Pierced ornaments and the use of decorative motifs on bone are a common feature of Aurignacian assemblages in central and eastern Europe (Hahn 1972).

It is noticeable that particular artefacts display remarkable similarities in design and stylistic treatment and that these occur over extensive areas. The so-called Venus figurines (Gamble 1982), which are known from Upper Perigordian and Gravettian contexts, are found throughout Europe between 25 000 and 23 000 b.p. At a later date a similar spatial distribution over 3000 km can be seen for schematic female profile engravings and small figurines found with late glacial lithic assemblages. Similarities in form among stone and bone artefacts have led to descriptions of techno-complexes (Hahn 1977) and social territories (J.G.D. Clark 1975) for such geographically widespread distributions.

This trend towards the development of extensive areal distributions of visually related objects can be paralleled by raw material distributions. In the Middle Palaeolithic of Germany it is a general rule that only local raw materials were used in the manufacture of handaxes and other implements (Schwabedissen 1970). During the Hengelo interstadial, and associated with Altmühlian assemblages, a much greater use of non-local raw material has been noted (Bosinski 1967: 23). The Upper Palaeolithic of central and eastern Europe saw a much greater use of non-local stone, as with the widespread occurrence of the distinctive chocolate-coloured flint from the Holy Cross mountains in Poland and obsidian from Hungary (Hahn 1977; Kozlowski 1961). The late glacial use of the Holy Cross source (Schild 1976) shows that the areal distributions of this flint were more extensive during the cold Dryas phases than during the interstadial Allerød episode.

Fossil and marine shells were also transported considerable distances from known sources. They have been found in Upper Palaeolithic contexts in the caves of south-west France (Bahn 1977; this volume) and in sites along the Don river where the origin of such objects is from the Black Sea (Klein 1969). Fossil shells from eastern England have been found in Upper Palaeolithic contexts in Belgium (Otte 1977).

These various lines of evidence point to the development of diverse chains of connection. The means by which such distribution patterns were created were no doubt varied and involved mechanisms of exchange, direct procurement and personal mobility as well as a variety of social contexts for interaction to take place. By contrast to the evidence from the Middle Palaeolithic, where such extensive distributions of materials are not found, the data suggest a more complex series of interactions together with an increase in the amount of information being processed through the system. The evidence can be placed against an environmental background of both stadial and interstadial conditions. In particular the earliest appearance of the most distinctive features, the art and ornaments, occurred during the central interstadials of the last glacial, thereby indicating that such developments were not the result of the interplay of extreme climatic conditions upon the adaptive patterns of behaviour. The progressive decline in the European climate after 29 000 b.p. does however appear to have exerted some influence over the organization of certain stylistic principles in relation to some of the objects used in information exchange (Gamble 1982).

It is not possible, therefore, to use environmental conditions as an explanation for developments in these aspects of material culture. We are instead witnessing the development of an area-level adaptation (J.H. Hill 1978) that once instituted required a series of developments in the use and organization of materials and material culture. In other words the most appropriate explanation is to be sought in the evolution of social structures which, due to different principles of organization, overcame the determining effects of the environment upon group adaptations at the regional level.

The effects of these changes can be seen in the settlement evidence. Prior to the Upper Palaeolithic the settlement of Europe can be described as a pattern of ebb and flow. When resources were predictable and abundant during interglacials and some interstadials, then evidence for occupation is often forthcoming. As resources became thinned out during glacial stadials then the exploitation territories of groups would have increased in size, populations would have become more dispersed, and as a result there would have been problems of integration. In many instances the reaction was for groups to cease exploiting areas where the disposition of resources did not permit low-cost integration. In terms of social changes these earlier social forms did not possess the structures that specified how such resources could be exploited and at the same time sustain and reproduce a social system. The environment did indeed determine the continued presence of human groups since at certain thresholds it imposed insuperable limits to the existing social system.

This ebb and flow of settlement is particularly apparent in an area such as central Europe. We have already seen how the pattern of Middle Palaeolithic settlement was particularly sensitive to changes in resources. Furthermore, at the height of the last glacial (20 000 to 15 000 b.p.) there is no evidence for the continued occupation, by Upper Palaeolithic groups, of the same area, even though such evidence is forthcoming for the glacial stadial prior to this event.

This evidence might however be used to argue against the adaptive contribution that changes in Upper Palaeolithic material culture made to regional populations. It could be

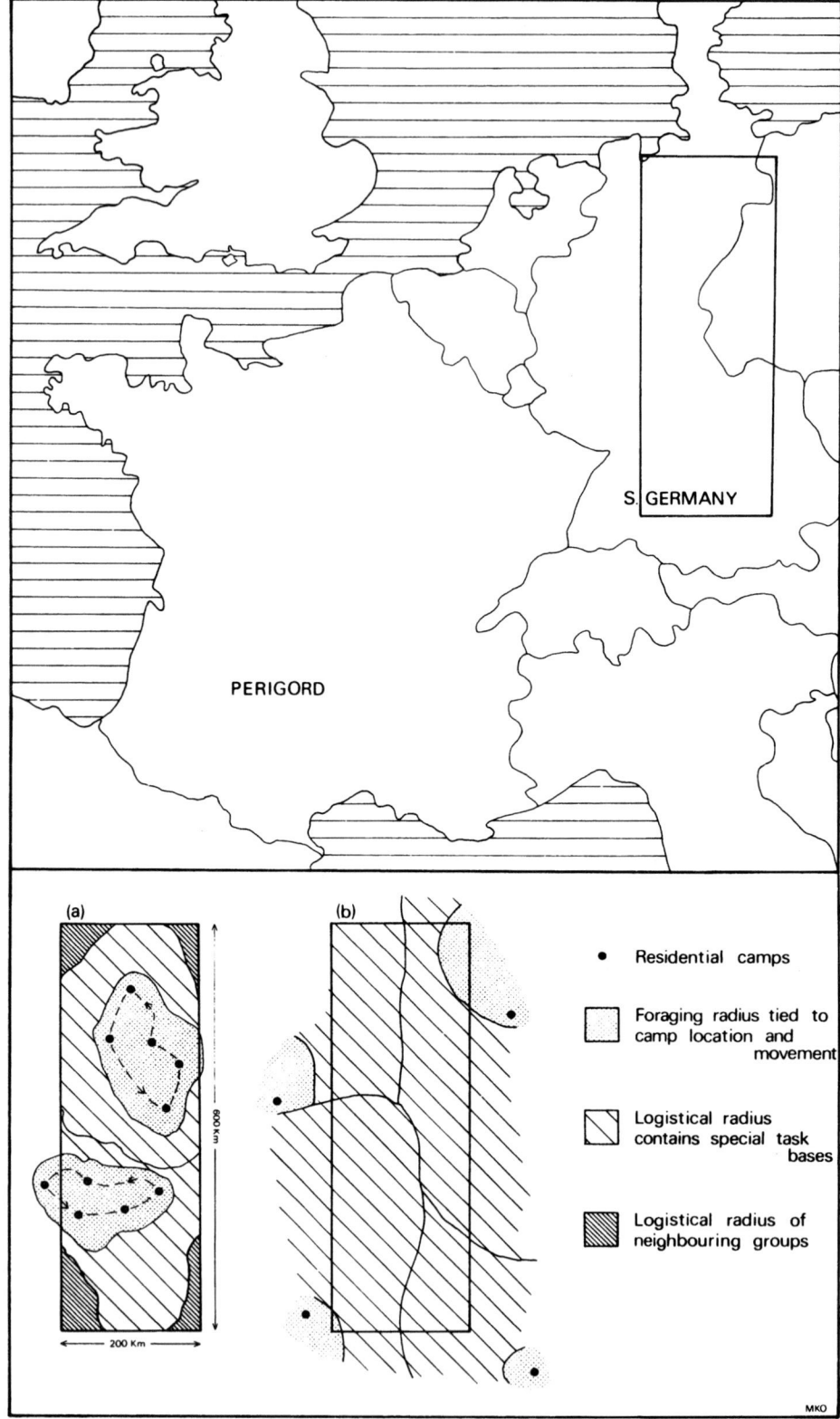

Fig. 18.2. Settlement record in an arbitrarily defined region of 120 000 km². (a) *complete,* which includes the seasonal movements of a residential base; and (b) *partial,* where only sites concerned with exploitation in the logistical radius are present and the residential bases lie outside the study region. The region of 120 000 km² is roughly equivalent to the unglaciated area of upper pleniglacial Germany. The model situation demonstrates how patterns of regional exploitation condition the formation of the archaeological record.

said that a decrease in the number of sites, as shown in the German data for the early Upper Palaeolithic, is hardly convincing evidence for major social changes that led to more complex sociocultural systems. Although the reverse of this pattern occurred in the Périgord, are we to conclude that social evolution and the origins of more complex systems must be sought solely in areas that offered relatively better environmental conditions?

The reason that this is not the case lies in the scales of analysis that are involved. These illustrate how one consequence of social change lay in regional adaptations. For an area the size of Germany it has previously been assumed (Gamble 1978a) that the archaeological remains relate to aspects of a *complete* settlement record. This view implies that within such a large geographical region we should discover a series of home bases which served as foci within seasonally contrasted exploitation zones. However, rather than approach the problem with such a home-base model (Vita-Finzi and Higgs 1970), we should briefly consider the more complex models of collector-type settlement systems (Binford 1980) where logistical principles of organization result in a highly differentiated pattern of environmental exploitation as reflected in the formation of sites. Using this model we would suggest that an area such as Germany, caught between two ice sheets, represented the outer logistic ring of the exploitation zone of groups whose residential camps lay well outside the area. In other words the settlement traces from the early Upper Palaeolithic represent only a *partial* settlement record. This is set out in figure 18.2, where the notional block of land is $120\,000\,km^2$, which is the lifetime territory size of a modern group of Arctic hunters (Binford 1983). According to the partial settlement record model we would expect specialist work camps to be created in the German study area. This could be tested by the study of site structure, and the analysis of assemblage variation and artefact deposition. Trips would only have to be made to such an area during stadial conditions for specific purposes. This should result in redundancy (in Binford's (1978a) terminology), i.e. repeated use of specific site locations and invariant lithic and bone-tool inventories. These differences should be apparent at a regional level when comparisons are made with the artefact inventories from ecologically preferred areas such as Périgord. It must be emphasized that the model has still to be tested in this manner. However it is possible to see at this stage how it can account for regional variation in some coarse measures such as the number and distribution of findspots in time and space. Moreover it can be seen that in recognizing some of the correlates of a logistically based system we are forced to consider questions of scale and adaptation and place

this within a diachronic framework. The conclusion must be that within the Palaeolithic of Europe we can find evidence for increases in the spatial and informational requirements of society even though this may not have resulted in increases in population size and density, which has, on occasion, been regarded as an outcome of technological development. The European evidence points to the conclusion that the development of logistically based collecting systems, that are characteristic of contemporary northern hunters, was dependent in the first instance upon social solutions to environmental problems, rather than technological innovations.

### Conclusion

We have examined a number of themes; information, social change, settlement systems and area adaptations in relation to Palaeolithic data from Europe. We began with two questions focused upon the appearance of a class of objects commonly referred to as Palaeolithic art, which have here been used to illustrate the discussion of these themes. There should be no surprise that the earliest art appears in the harsh northern latitudes of Pleistocene Europe. Since it is part of an information system, and these northern environments under Pleistocene conditions were particularly stressed, we can see that it would fill a functional role. In reply to the second question, the reason that art makes a late appearance in the Palaeolithic record is not because high risk environments only existed for the first time at 35 000 b.p., but rather that changes were required in the set of social structures which governed exploitation of such areas. Neither of the questions has therefore received an explanatory answer. It is understandable to find that Europe's claim as the world's 'premier salon' proved as illusory as pinning down the origins of agriculture to one of any number of hearths. It is the process rather than the question of origins which ultimately is of interest. This process is here conceived as that of social evolution, and any full answer to these and other questions must address the problem of why the principles that structured Palaeolithic society changed. This question has not been tackled here. Instead I have hopefully disentangled it from other lines of investigation dealing with exploitation, adaptation and variation in the Palaeolithic record, since it is through these inquiries that the necessary means of measurement for a sociohistorical study of the past will emerge.

*Acknowledgements*

I would like to thank Geoff Bailey, Barbara Bender, Robin Dennell, John Pfeiffer and Robin Torrence for all their comments on earlier drafts of this paper.

Chapter 19

Palaeolithic cave art in ecological perspective
Michael A. Jochim

Elaborate portable and parietal artwork has often been cited as the outstanding characteristic of the west European Upper Palaeolithic. Rarely, however, have the limited and changing spatial and temporal distributions of this artwork been investigated, and it is here suggested that these patterns of distribution may be fruitfully examined in their environmental and demographic contexts. Specifically, the parietal and portable art may represent manifestations of different social responses to processes of climatic deterioration, population movement, and economic change. The archaeological and environmental records of northern, central, and south-western Europe suggest numerous inter-regional contrasts in both ecological context and cultural response.

## Introduction

Among the most impressive features of the European Upper Palaeolithic are its works of art, which include decorated implements, portable sculptures and engravings, and above all, paintings, engravings, and sculptures on the walls of caves and rockshelters. Such features, which play a prominent role in general discussions of cultural evolution and world prehistory, are quite restricted in space and time. Although the Upper Palaeolithic spans the period of approximately 35 000 to 10 000 b.p., most of the finds under consideration are confined to the period between 25 000 and 10 000 b.p. Moreover, both categories of art, portable and parietal, became much more abundant towards the end of the Upper Palaeolithic. In addition, the geographic distribution of such finds is quite limited. Whereas various forms of portable

art were, at times, widespread throughout Europe, wall art was limited, with few exceptions, to south-western France and northern Spain (fig. 19.1). Although this Palaeolithic cave art has been the subject of a number of excellent surveys and analyses, the problem of its restricted temporal and spatial distribution has not been adequately addressed (Leroi-Gourhan 1965; Ucko and Rosenfeld 1967; Naber *et al.* 1976; Sieveking 1979).

Interpretations of the artistic pre-eminence of Franco-Cantabria have suggested greater sophistication of this region's inhabitants, but since the reasons for this sophistication have not been offered, such explanations are not very satisfactory. Occasionally, broader contexts of the art have been considered, for example by linking artistic production to the greater leisure resulting from a more successful economy. Recent ethnographic work, however, has stressed the great amounts of free time available to hunter-gatherers even in quite marginal environments (e.g. Lee 1969) and, although one should avoid a new stereotype of affluent hunter-gatherers, it would seem that leisure is an insufficient explanation. Recently suggestions have been put forward that such art be examined in terms of its functions within cultural systems dependent upon the cooperative hunting of herds of big game animals (Hammond 1974). Such cooperative endeavours as herd interception may have required large temporary work forces drawn from several neighbouring local groups, which otherwise might have

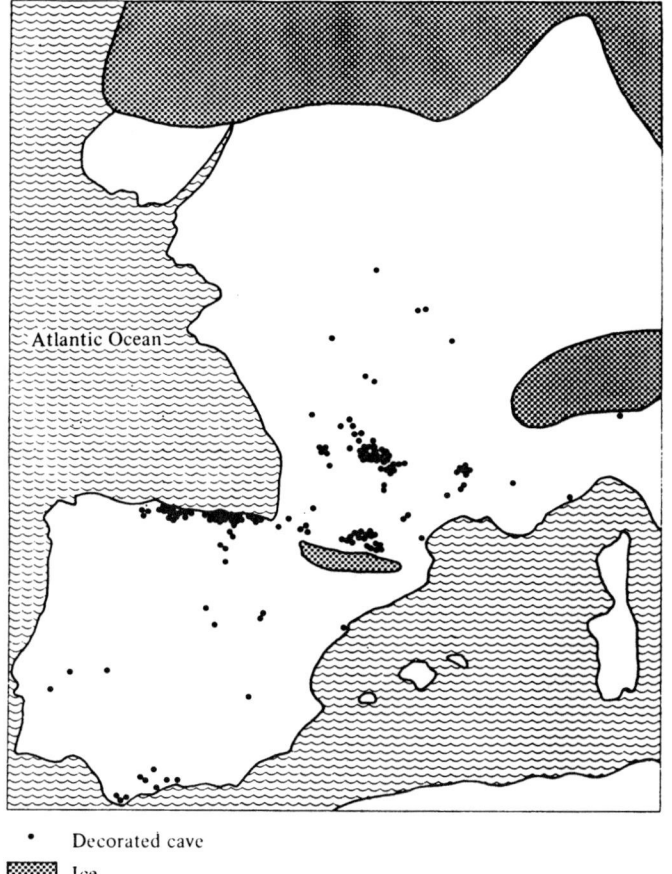

* Decorated cave

▨ Ice

Fig. 19.1: The distribution of parietal art in Western Europe, excluding Italy (after Naber *et al.* 1976).

Table 19.1. *Sequence of cultures and art styles in Franco-Cantabria*

| Years b.p. | Cultural period | Artistic style |
|---|---|---|
| 12 000 |  | IV |
|  | Magdalenian |  |
| 17 000 |  | III |
|  | Solutrean |  |
| 22 000 |  | II |
|  | Upper Perigordian |  |
| 27 000 |  | I |
|  | Aurignacian |  |
| 32 000 |  |  |

of France and Spain. The criteria for their definition include style of retouching stone tools, presence or absence of certain tool types, frequencies of different stone-tool categories, and the typology of bone artefacts. Various patterns of association and co-variation in time and space have been used to construct categories of culture and phases of development. As is true of all archaeological schemes based primarily upon lithic artefacts, the sources of variation so observed are poorly understood, and such schemes certainly measure simultaneously differences in raw material, activities, and individual and cultural style, together with their changes through time (see chapters 3 and 12). Any examination of the economic and demographic context of Palaeolithic art would ideally isolate and control these different sources of variation, but at present this framework must be used with the understanding that it forms the only available frame of reference while masking many underlying patterns of variation.

After a brief introductory phase of Lower Perigordian, the French Upper Palaeolithic consists of a long period (approximately 33 000 to 21 000 b.p.) represented by what are considered to be two alternating and in part contemporary cultures: the Aurignacian and the Upper Perigordian. Succeeding these is the Solutrean, lasting from about 21 000 to 17 000 b.p. followed by the Magdalenian until approximately 10 000 b.p.

Secondly, the art work itself must be placed within its cultural and chronological context. For the portable art this poses little problem, since the objects occur in archaeological deposits. Most of the wall art, on the other hand, is isolated from other archaeological materials, and its dating is problematic. A few decorated walls are partially buried behind deposits containing occupation debris; certain others have broken loose and occur as slabs within archaeological deposits; many more appear in the interior of caves which have archaeological occupations at their entrances; but a large number have not even this tenuous association. A chronological framework has been proposed by Leroi-Gourhan (1965) based upon stylistic comparisons

been in competition for other resources or spatially quite dispersed. The cave art and some type of associated rituals, in this view, would have served to promote necessary social cohesion in the face of competition or spatial separation.

A serious problem with this emphasis on the social ramifications of big game hunting is its inability to explain the special position of Franco-Cantabria. Concentration on herd animals characterizes the economies of most of the European Upper Palaeolithic, yet wall art is significant only in the later phases of this period, and primarily in Franco-Cantabria, while the limestone regions of eastern France, southern Germany and Moravia, for example, show no decorated caves. Valuable insights may be gained by focusing on variables of subsistence and demography, but their specific interaction must be examined as these differ between Franco-Cantabria and neighbouring regions. However inadequate the present data, intriguing patterns in the economy and population distributions can be detected.

## Chronological frameworks

A few words must be devoted to the framework used in this discussion. A series of both overlapping and sequential prehistoric cultures has been defined for the Upper Palaeolithic among wall figures and between walls and portable art, and tied to the few examples of relatively firm dating. This framework will be used, realizing the subjective nature of the assumptions of stylistic distribution and development.

The art styles as defined do not coincide with the sequence of cultural change (table 19.1). Style I is limited to rare portable sculpture and engravings during the period of about 32 000 to 25 000 b.p., coinciding with the Lower Aurignacian through Middle Perigordian. Style II contains the first wall art as well as more abundant and widely distributed portable objects including the Upper Perigordian 'Venus' figurines. This style is contemporary with the Upper Perigordian, Late Aurignacian and early Solutrean, about 25 000 to 19 000 b.p. The subsequent style III spans the later Solutrean and early Magdalenian, approximately 19 000 to 15 000 b.p.; in this style wall art becomes more abundant in Franco-Cantabria, but portable art is quite rare. Finally, style IV shows the greatest abundance of both wall art and portable objects in Franco-Cantabria, as well as the widest distribution of portable art in other parts of Europe. This style coincides with the Middle and Late Magdalenian, about 15 000 to 10 000 b.p.

### Environmental context

These sequences of culture and art occur in a context of environmental fluctuations. The entire Upper Palaeolithic spans the second half of the last glaciation. Throughout much of northern and central Europe the bulk of this period, roughly 25 000 to 14 000 b.p., consisted of the relatively cold glacial maximum, with only minor internal temperature oscillations, both preceded and followed by more significant fluctuations of greater magnitude and longer duration. In southern France and Spain, however, temperatures were less extreme during the glacial maximum, and internal fluctuations more pronounced (McBurney 1973; Part 3 above). Quite cold conditions predominated through the earlier Solutrean, but from around 19 000 to 17 500 b.p. there was a significant warming coinciding with the later Solutrean. A brief cold period followed, marking the transition from Solutrean to Magdalenian, but most of the Early Magdalenian coincided with another period of milder conditions. The bulk of the Middle and Upper Magdalenian took place during colder conditions again, although punctuated by two warm periods.

The ice sheets present throughout this period covered Scandinavia, most of the British Isles and northern central Europe, the Alps and their foothills over to the Rhone Valley, as well as the summits of the Pyrenees, Cantabrian Mountains, Massif Central, and other smaller ranges. The ice fronts fluctuated with climatic changes, but not directly in phase. Thus the maximum extent of the Scandinavian and British glaciers was reached at approximately 18 000 b.p., when temperatures were already warming in south-western France. Sea level was between 85 and 100 m lower during this time, joining Britain to the continent and causing the Seine, Thames, Rhine, and other central European rivers to drain into a North

Sea remnant or through a Channel River in the present English Channel (Flint 1971).

South-western France and Spain were more temperate and variable climatically than central and northern Europe, and this was reflected in the vegetation. Although most general reconstructions posit some type of tundra vegetation throughout most of north, central, and western Europe down into central Spain, it is clear that major variations existed. European glacial tundras in general were low-latitude tundras of greater productivity than those currently known, and clearly Franco-Cantabria was at the southern, more productive fringes of such habitats. Moreover, pollen studies have documented the constant presence of some trees in these regions, at least in sheltered valleys, throughout the last glacial period (Paquereau 1976). The regions to the north and east were increasingly subject to high winds, colder temperatures, loess deposition, and permafrosting. At the last glacial maximum, southern England was an arctic desert with scant vegetation, while eastern France and central and southern Germany were situated between the two massive ice sheets and were among the coldest parts of Europe (West 1968: 292; Flint 1971: 618). A map of general vegetational zones in Europe at the height of the last glacial is presented in figure 19.2(a).

The low-latitude tundras and park-tundras of glacial Europe were richer than any modern northern counterparts. This richness, especially in the more productive and patchy environments of south-western France, probably took the form of an unparalleled faunal diversity in glacial times. Simply in terms of large herbivores, the variety of species that appear in French Upper Palaeolithic sites is astounding, and includes mammoth, woolly rhinoceros, reindeer, horse, bison, red deer, roe deer, aurochs, ibex, chamois, saiga antelope, muskox, giant deer, wild ass, elk and wild boar. These species differed, of course, in their relative abundance and fluctuated in relative abundance with climatic changes. Reindeer, horse and bison seem to have been consistently the most numerous. In the harsher and more homogeneous conditions in glacial Germany, by contrast, it is likely that overall faunal abundance and diversity were considerably lower (Gamble, 1978a).

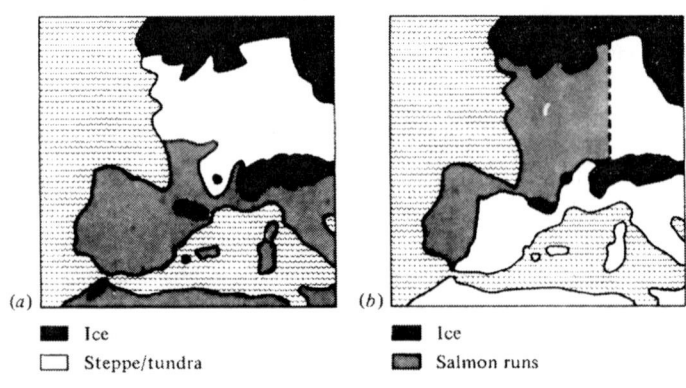

|  | Ice |  | Ice |
| --- | --- | --- | --- |
|  | Steppe/tundra |  | Salmon runs |

Fig. 19.2: (a) West European vegetational zones during the Würm maximum (after Büdel 1943). Stippled areas contain some trees. (b) location of salmon runs in glacial Europe.

In addition to features of climate, vegetation and land animals, Franco-Cantabria was characterized by one other factor during the last glacial maximum: the singular distribution of Atlantic salmon. It has long been recognized that salmon formed one component of the Palaeolithic economy in Franco-Cantabria, but the implications of this component have not been stressed. In historic times, before pollution and the construction of hydro-electric dams, salmon were widely distributed in most European rivers draining into the Atlantic, from northern Portugal up to the northern shores of the Soviet Union (Netboy 1968). One of the factors most critical in determining salmon distribution is water temperature, and the modern range is bounded at its extremes by ocean surface temperatures in summer of $2°$ to $18°C$. These temperatures are influenced to a great extent by the Gulf Stream, carrying warmer waters in a north-easterly direction along the fringes of Europe.

One of the significant features of the last glaciation was an alteration of the sea currents and surface temperatures. Temperature gradients, as reconstructed by the CLIMAP project, were not simply pushed southward, although this occurred to some extent, but, more importantly, they were compressed as the Gulf Stream came to flow directly eastward across the Atlantic (CLIMAP 1976; Gates 1976). Temperatures from $2°$ to $18°C$ ranged from southern England to the Straits of Gibraltar, with a steep thermal gradient at the latitude of northern Spain. Salmon runs would have been confined to the rivers from England to Iberia (fig. 19.2(b)).

Within this range of distribution, to judge from studies of modern salmon, there were probably significant differences with latitude (Schalk 1977). In the southern part of salmon ranges, periods of runs and spawning in the rivers tend to be rather short due to seasonally high water temperatures and the greater abundance of other species as competitors and predators. Such conditions, together with the steep thermal gradient in the glacial Atlantic, suggest that salmon were a minor component of the riverine fauna of much of Iberia south of northern Spain. On the northern fringes of salmon ranges, on the other hand, periods of runs and spawning also tend to be quite brief due to seasonal freezing and shortage of food in the rivers. Southern England and northern France may have had minor, brief runs of salmon, while there may have been somewhat larger, brief runs into the rivers of northern Germany, either through a Channel River or directly from a North Sea remnant (Payne *et al.* 1971). Utilization of salmon in such northern regions might occur during the week or two of the runs, but any more important contribution of this fish to the diet would require the technology of intensive harvesting and storage in order to spread out the super-abundance over time.

In the central portion of salmon ranges, by contrast, the fish tend to be in the rivers for considerable lengths of time. Neither intensive harvesting nor storage is necessary for these fish to become a significant part of the diet. The northern coast of Spain and the southern Atlantic watershed of France contained the potential for significant exploitation of salmon without technological elaboration. In the archaeological record of the Upper Palaeolithic there is no evidence for storage of food, nor for such cooperative techniques as weirs, traps, or large nets for catching fish. Moreover, while such intensive techniques tend to be most effective in the lower reaches of rivers where runs of fish are larger, the densest Palaeolithic occupations are along the upper parts of rivers and their tributaries, where the less intensive technique of spearing could be effective and performed on a more individual basis.

The onset of the last glacial maximum, consequently, was characterized by a number of environmental processes that would have had significant implications for the Palaeolithic inhabitants of Europe. Beginning around 25 000 b.p. was a period of climatic deterioration involving colder winters and lower yearly average temperatures. Most affected by this deterioration were northern Europe, which became a virtual arctic desert, and central Europe between the ice sheets. In each of these regions vegetational and animal productivity would have decreased significantly. As habitats for hunter-gatherers these regions became increasingly harsh and demanding (see chapter 18). The areas to the south-west of north-central Europe were much less adversely affected by these climatic changes and seem to have provided a glacial refuge for many species of plants. The abundance and variety of game, which included salmon, also appear to have been far greater in this refuge than in north-central Europe. The climate of the glacial maximum imposed strong contrasts among European environments according to their richness and security for human habitation.

### Demographic context

Because of the growing contrast among regions in their climatic severity and resource abundance, the European glacial maximum seems to have witnessed dramatic population shifts. During the main phase of the Aurignacian most of Europe free of ice shows evidence of occupation (de Sonneville-Bordes 1973). However, 'the progressive deterioration of climate in the Full Glacial seems to have brought about a cultural partition in Europe, with western and northern Central Europe coming to resemble something like a no-man's land' (Müller-Beck 1961: 444). Britain was unoccupied between 25 000 and 14 000 b.p. (Mellars 1974; Evans 1975). Belgium shows a similar gap in occupation (de Sonneville-Bordes 1973; Otte 1976). Recent surveys of the archaeological record demonstrate that much of northern and eastern France contains few sites dating to between 20 000 and 15 000 b.p. (de Lumley 1976). Germany shows a rarity or absence of occupation for the period of around 23 000 to 15 000 b.p. (Hahn 1976; Hahn and von Koenigswald 1976; chapter 18 above).

It is clear from the archaeological record in these various regions that northern and central Europe between the ice sheets was largely abandoned during the last glacial maximum. Such abandonments are understandable in terms of the climatic regimes of these regions, but little attention has been given to the fate of these regional populations. Direct movement southward would have been blocked by the Alpine glaciers. South-western France, on the other hand, seems to have been a refuge area for various plants and animals during the last glaciation; it may have been a refuge for humans as well. South-western France is the most northerly part of western Europe to show continuous dense occupation throughout the entire Upper Palaeolithic. Certainly, some of the north and central European populations may have become extinct or persisted at low densities without much archaeological visibility, but the gradual movement of many of them to the south-west must be considered as well. It is in this context that the Upper Palaeolithic economy and art must be examined.

### Implications of salmon and reindeer utilization

Resources such as salmon and reindeer differ in their implications for economic strategies of exploitation and intensification. In the ethnographic literature, for example, it has been observed that the greater the dependence on reindeer, the lower the human population density (Burch 1972). For salmon, on the other hand, ethnographic data suggest a positive correlation between use of the resource and human population density. The similarities and differences between these two resources must be further explored.

Both tend to show periodic fluctuations in overall abundance: reindeer in cycles of 35–100 years; salmon in cycles of 8–11 years. Both may be taken by individuals (spears) or, more efficiently, by groups (pounds, weirs). Both may be processed and preserved (freezing, drying, smoking). Both may occur in restricted locations (mountain passes, pools), perhaps allowing or promoting human aggregation. In terms of spatial predictability, however, these two resources differ considerably. When reindeer are quite abundant, they may occur everywhere, but otherwise they may show yearly or longer-term shifts of their migration routes, and may disappear totally from one area. Salmon, on the other hand, are restricted to rivers; they return to the same place, often at the same time each year. Thus, salmon are a much more predictable, spatially stable resource. For both reindeer and salmon, the pursuit time once they are located can be quite low, and thus they both can contribute greatly to subsistence efficiency. By contrast, search time for reindeer is variable and can be quite high, while that for salmon is minimal, and therefore their contribution to subsistence security is vastly different.

Because of the differences between these two resources, any intensification of their exploitation would have different implications. As has been frequently pointed out, an increasing reliance upon reindeer or other big game herds may lead to an increase in the size of necessary work groups on a seasonal basis, and an increased efficiency of energy capture. At the same time, this greater specialization leads to a greater susceptibility to fluctuations of the resource and puts a premium on information-sharing across regions, on the maintenance of mobility and flexibility in settlement behaviour, and on techniques of increasing the reliability of the necessary work force through affiliations with neighbouring groups (see Smith 1978).

An increasing reliance upon salmon, on the other hand, represents an increasing commitment to a spatial focus – the river and its pools and spawning grounds – and tends to promote sedentism and territorial exclusion. Size of work groups may be small if spearing is a major technique of procurement, or it may increase with the adoption of cooperative procedures using weirs or nets. Even with small work groups, however, population clustering may occur if suitable fishing locations are restricted in distribution.

### Economic and social responses

Beginning around 25 000 b.p., a number of simultaneous environmental and demographic processes start to occur: (1) climatic deterioration as the main glacial phase begins; (2) the abandonment of the northern fringes of Europe; (3) an impoverishment of resources in central Europe and, somewhat later, the virtual abandonment of this area; and (4) the influx of population into the refuge area of south-western Europe.

In this context the archaeological materials can be examined. Both in central and south-western Europe the previous ratio of population to resources would be upset, either through decline in resources or increase in population (see Part 3 above). This problem of increasing effective population pressure might prompt a variety of solutions. One such solution, potentially applicable throughout much of Europe, would be to increase the efficiency of the hunting of big game through technological innovation and social organization. Such big game animals had already formed an important economic focus, so much so that the very transition from Middle to Upper Palaeolithic and from Neanderthal to modern *Homo sapiens sapiens* has been suggested to be linked to their increasing exploitation (S.R. Binford 1968b). In this view, the need for greater potential mobility, communication, and flexibility of affiliation, together with periodic aggregations of large groups, led to fundamental changes in social arrangements and mating networks. These changes are thought to be reflected by: (1) the appearance of items of portable art and adornment to symbolize and reinforce through their exchange the broad lines of communication and affiliation; and (2) the elaboration of burial treatment to include large energy expenditures, suggesting the involvement of large groups and perhaps some degree of role differentiation.

The distribution of such items and features should be rather continuous or clinal in situations of interlocking open networks of interaction, and should become more discontinuous and discretely clumped as such networks become more closed and exclusive (chapter 17 above). The distribution of many cultural traits, including stone tools and personal ornaments during the earlier part of the Upper

Palaeolithic is relatively continuous throughout much of Europe, suggesting a situation of broad communication networks, and it is during the early part of the main glacial phase that the Perigordian Venus figurines are so widely distributed. Franco-Cantabria shares in this elaboration and relative stylistic homogeneity of portable art and ornaments, suggesting that similar processes of increasing specialization of herd animals may have been occurring here too; in fact, the differentiation and short duration of some late Perigordian phases of around 23 000 to 22 000 b.p. in this region have been linked to an over-specialization on reindeer (David 1973).

A second solution to the problems of increasing effective population pressure would be to broaden the resource base where possible. In the more extreme climates of north and central Europe this option may not have been available, leading ultimately to out-migration to the south-west, especially in the face of decreasing numbers of big game as well. In the refuge zone of south-western Europe, on the other hand, it appears that such a process did occur, beginning somewhat later than the increasing specialization on certain big game species. Quantified information is rare. In south-western France there are only hints of a gradually increasing importance of smaller mammals, birds, and fish through the late Perigordian and Solutrean (Mellars 1973; chapter 15 above). Recent faunal analyses of north Spanish sites document a progressive increase in the average number of species per site from Aurignacian through Perigordian and Solutrean, and the Solutrean shows the first significant use of fish, shellfish, and birds (Straus 1977a; see also chapters 12 and 13 above). Consequences of such economic diversification might include increased differentiation of economic roles and equipment, perhaps reflected in the progressive proliferation of new stone and bone artefact forms during the course of the Upper Palaeolithic.

A third solution, possible only in south-western France and northern Spain, would be to increase the exploitation of the relatively reliable salmon. Not only would this allow the support of larger populations, but it would also encourage greater relative sedentism and increased territorial claims to fishing grounds and the surrounding area. In south-western France and northern Spain these processes may be reflected by the progressive overall increase in material equipment and belongings and the increasing modifications of cave and shelter occupation sites in the form of walls and floors. Such processes might also be reflected by the appearance of territorially based ritual sites as land claims. Another possible result of greater sedentism might be a strain on traditional means of conflict resolution, since moving away is no longer so viable an option; increased ritual reinforcement of group solidarity and perhaps the appearance of a mediator role are possible alternative means of resolution. Decorated caves and shelters are fixed sites of apparent rituals. Role differentiation is suggested by the existence of the artists and perhaps by some of the painted figures in specialized

gear. Periodic aggregations at the important decorated caves of Altamira and Cueto de la Mina have been suggested by recent studies of faunal remains and art motifs (Conkey 1980; Straus 1977b).

Decorated walls first appear during style II times, with the beginning of the glacial maximum when the hypothesized population contraction into the south-west may have begun. By the time of the earlier Solutrean, the known archaeological sites of central and western Europe are largely confined to south-western France and Spain. Such sites are relatively large and deep and cave art is more abundant. The fact that, with a slight warming trend in the later Solutrean, the distribution of Solutrean sites spreads north to the Loire and south into the Pyrenees and beyond suggests that, indeed, population pressure existed in south-western France.

Style III art covers the later Solutrean and early Magdalenian. During this phase wall art becomes more numerous and there seem to develop regional stylistic groups in the Dordogne, the Lot Valley, the Pyrenees, and Cantabrian Spain (Leroi-Gourhan 1965). Portable art, however, becomes relatively rare in western Europe. This decline in portable art is puzzling: it may be related to the general decrease in mobility and declining need for maintaining widespread affiliation. This, together with the regionalization of the cave art styles, might reflect the formation of more closed communication networks during the Solutrean.

Wobst (1976) has speculated about the causes and consequences of closure of communication or mating networks among hunter-gatherers. Based on spatial considerations alone, he suggests that there is a certain population density threshold below which closure could not occur because potential mates are too widely dispersed. South-western Europe might have exceeded this threshold because of population contraction and the diverse economy based on both big game and salmon. Wobst has also pointed out the locational problems inherent in a closed mating network: sub-units within such a network become differentiated internally according to spatial access to mates. If not counteracted by social mechanisms, people on the edges of the network might save energy either by moving toward the centre and thereby straining both resources and the means of conflict resolution, or by attempting to form a new centre by attracting mates from the marginal populations of the adjoining societies. Possible counteracting mechanisms he suggests include increasing frequency of rituals, more society-specific and closed rituals, greater territorial symbolism and ritual, and increased exchange of exotic items, which not only facilitates communication, but also improves the position of the marginal populations, since they will have greater access to such items.

The increased abundance of style III cave art may represent such mechanisms, as may the increased appearance in south-western France during the Solutrean of exotic materials such as sea shells from both Atlantic and Mediterranean and brightly coloured quartz, jasper, and other stones (chapter 15 above). Within-group exchange items might also include the finely-made and sometimes impractically large or thin Solutrean stone points. The fact that wall art of style III tends to occur deeper within caves than that of style II may represent greater exclusiveness of the ritual symbols. In addition, the distribution of decorated caves suggests an initial development and concentration in a few centres (Dordogne, Lot, Ariège, Ardèche, Santander) supporting the idea of cave art as a response largely characterizing certain central regions in interaction networks (figs. 19.3–19.5). Moreover, if such regions comprise centres for separate interaction networks, the areal expanse of such networks may be estimated utilizing partial Thiessen polygons, giving a range of from 15 000 to 25 000 square kilometers (fig. 19.6). These speculations could be further extended to estimate population. If the minimum size of a viable mating network be assumed to be approximately 500 people (Wobst 1974a), then Franco-Cantabria would have had a population density of at least 2–3 people per hundred square kilometers during Late Solutrean and Early Magdalenian times.

The period of style IV is more complex. The climate is one of more dramatic alternation of cold and warm phases. An expansion of the Magdalenian out of south-western France into Spain, northern and central Europe begins with one of the warmer phases, but becomes more important through succeeding cold periods. This process has been called a veritable 'Magdalenian population explosion' (de Sonneville-Bordes 1973). Many of the economic trends of the Upper Palaeolithic culminate in the Middle and Late Magdalenian. In south-western France there is a continuing emphasis on reindeer until the last phases, and further increase in the use of birds and fish; a few remains of seal even occur in some sites. In the Pyrenees there is an initial dominance of reindeer along with salmon, followed by an increasing emphasis on red deer and ibex as well (Sieveking 1976; chapter 15 above). In Cantabria red deer are of increasing importance, followed

Fig. 19.5. The distribution of parietal art assigned to Style IV, given as number of sites per department.

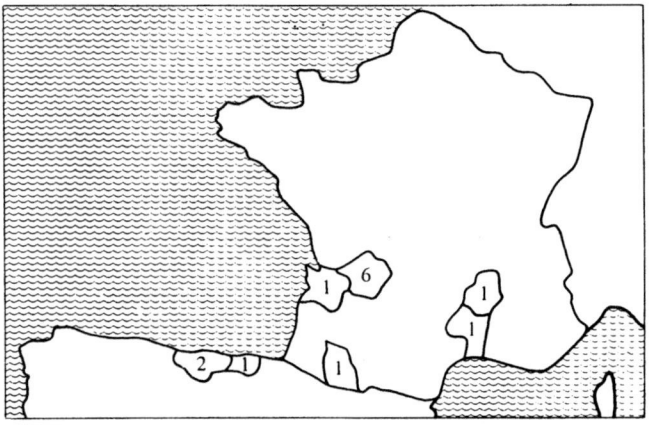

Fig. 19.3. The distribution of parietal art assigned to Style II, given as number of sites per department.

Fig. 19.4. The distribution of parietal art assigned to Style III, given as number of sites per department.

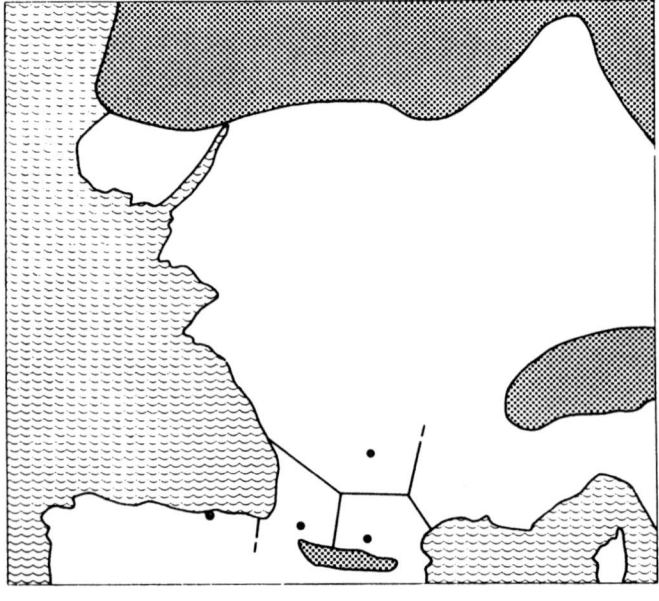

•   Centre of network

   Ice

Fig. 19.6. Boundaries of hypothetical interaction networks during the Late Solutrean and Early Magdalenian.

by sub-regional specialization on ibex, along with greater use of fish, shellfish, and hare (Straus 1977a; chapters 12 and 13 above).

Cantabria at this time seems to show evidence for a more structured bipolar settlement pattern of lowland and highland valley sites, in contrast to what may have been an earlier system of centrally located bases, and this is perhaps related to the diversification to include alpine species. In south-western France there is some tendency for site placement closer to rivers, perhaps reflecting a greater emphasis on fishing (Mellars 1973). Compared to earlier times, the number of known sites in Cantabria remains much the same, while that in the Pyrenees and south-western France increases significantly. Magdalenian or related industries appear in eastern France, Switzerland, Germany, Belgium and England, especially in the later stages.

Early in the style IV period there is a significant increase in the number of decorated caves in Franco-Cantabria, and there seems to be a breakdown in the regional stylistic groupings. Somewhat later, cave art declines and there is a tremendous proliferation of portable art. This includes elaborate decorations added to spear-throwers and batons, engraved plaques of stone and bone, and beads and pendants. In addition, burial remains become more abundant and elaborate. Many of these features show stylistic homogeneity throughout their broad area of distribution.

Many of these changes suggest further population growth leading to continued intensification of big game hunting and fishing, together with additional broadening of the resource base. The population growth itself indicates that these strategies had been successful in the past; their further elaboration along with an intensification of territorial rituals would be an expected response. Yet these strategies may have contained inherent conflicts which were aggravated by further intensification. Emphasis on big game hunting required the maintenance of flexible spatial options, especially during the increasingly variable late glacial environment. Increasing dependence on salmon, on the other hand, especially in the context of population growth, would lead to greater sedentism and territorial commitment.

This conflict in spatial strategies, together with a greater complexity of economic activities, may have overtaxed the ritual mechanisms of social organization and cohesion. The breakdown of regional groupings of cave art styles and their subsequent decrease in abundance may reflect a decline in the system of relatively closed social networks, while the population expansion and increase in portable art of wide regional homogeneity may indicate a reversion to former strategies of widespread affiliation and greater mobility. The postglacial warming, with its effects on vegetation and animals, would then have ended the concentration on herd animals and the need for such wide affiliations, reflected in the disappearance of most items of portable art. The decline of cave art, on the other hand, would seem to have begun earlier and to have been caused in part by its own success in maintaining cultural systems.

**Conclusions**

Many of the unique developments of the European Upper Palaeolithic suggest greater social complexity. These developments may represent adjustments to changes in the natural and social environments during the last glacial maximum. As a result of climatic deterioration and population shifts, Palaeolithic populations had to adapt to resource impoverishment in central and northern Europe and to increased population densities in the south-west. The refuge zone of Franco-Cantabria shows evidence for both greater energy investment in fixed locations and greater extension of social networks of interaction and integration. Population pressure may have encouraged the increase in relative sedentism, but this greater commitment to smaller areas may have posed greater risks to subsistence, requiring simultaneous social mechanisms of expanding the access to labour and resources of other areas and of integrating regional populations. The impressive cave art, the portable decorated objects, and the evidence for long-distance exchange reflect these cultural adjustments. The archaeological record of each of these features, together with the pattern of economic changes, suggests that a sequence of different responses characterized the West European Upper Palaeolithic in different regions.

**Conclusion**

Chapter 20

**Palaeolithic archaeology — some problems with form, space and time**
Martin Wobst

During the past two decades hunter-gatherer studies in general and Palaeolithic research in particular have been in a greater state of flux than most other parts of the continuum which is human prehistory. There are a number of good reasons for the intellectual excitement pervading this particular aspect of human prehistory. For example, a large part of the early effort of the so-called 'new' archaeologists was applied to Palaeolithic problems (see, for example, Binford 1972, 1973; Binford and Binford 1966; Freeman 1964; Sackett 1973) or hunter-gatherer studies in general. Many new converts, in turn, dedicated themselves to the archaeology of hunter-gatherers, if only because the entry cost was rather low. The archaeological record of hunter-gatherers is not as voluminous as that of later or more complex societies: there tend to be considerably fewer artefact categories and confounding axes of formal variation, and much less is established as 'fact' or dogma. As opposed to field research on early states or agricultural societies which might take decades to complete, a doctoral dissertation on hunter-gatherers could be compressed into the space of a few field seasons, if not a single one. Moreover, the (young) investigators might be able to assume the role of principal investigator themselves, thus allowing new perspectives to pervade the research design more fully than in the subordinate roles reserved for junior scientists within the massive field projects on more complex societies.

The initial perception of limited inherent complexity in the archaeological record of hunter-gatherers was of special appeal to those who wanted to champion new ways of dealing with the archaeological record. Complex logical arguments could be illuminated and exemplified more easily with the help of simple rather than complex archaeological data, and models, methods and approaches of the broadest and most general research appeal were easier to evaluate against an archaeological record in which a large number of variables could be held constant, if only because they had not yet evolved. Thus a disproportionate number of new methods such as factor analysis (Binford and Binford 1966), site catchment analysis (Vita-Finzi and Higgs 1970), computer simulation (D.H. Thomas 1973), linear programming (Keene 1979), and optimal diet models (Perlman 1976) all found their way into the discipline by way of hunter-gatherer archaeology.

Those ethnographers who were the most explicitly materialist in their observations and generalisations began to gain visibility exactly at that time when new perspectives were being expressed forcefully by archaeologists on both sides of the Atlantic. Materialist ethnography, in turn, had its most visible proponents in hunter-gatherer studies, finding its most effective mouthpiece in *Man the Hunter* (Lee and De Vore 1968). The stress on exchanges of matter and energy and on economic relationships in this body of literature convinced many archaeologists that ethnographic concepts could be relatively easily applied in archaeology and that there was nothing to prevent archaeologists from reversing the equation, that is, for themselves to begin contributing to general anthropological discussions through the window of hunter-gatherer archaeology. As a matter of fact, many of the more generalised inferences derived from the !Kung San (Lee 1968, 1969, 1972; Yellen and Harpending 1972) owe their subsequent use and verification primarily to hunter-gatherer archaeology. Be that as it may, the relative ease of scientific discourse between hunter-gatherer archaeology and ethnography, though not without problems (compare with Wobst 1974b, 1978), acted as an important catalyst to the development of new lines of investigation in the archaeology of hunter-gatherers.

Lastly, we should not overlook the specific impact upon hunter-gatherer studies of the explosively increasing environmental concerns and environmental doomsday predictions of the later sixties and early seventies. Post-industrial capitalism virtually invited the construction of a model society in contrast to the present one, a society not suffering from the amplification and biodegradation spirals of our time, and one in which exploitative effort as well as fear of starvation were deemed minimal. This concept of a counter culture called for modelling on a scale not heretofore fashionable in archaeology. Moreover, it required an entirely new generation of models, diametrically opposed not only to the present society but also to the dismal model of hunter-gatherers which had been so useful to the modernising world since the industrial revolution.

Hunter-gatherers have thus occupied a central role in the theoretical and methodological developments of archaeologists during the last two decades. Moreover, these developments would have been much less influential if the discipline of anthropology had been a closed scientific system, since their impact owes as much to the social organisation of the discipline and to its place in the wider world, as to their inherent logical weight or theoretical relevance. Conversely, this external environment provided a stimulus to hunter-gatherer studies and Palaeolithic archaeology, which left no aspect of this field unaffected. Moreover, the ferment in hunter-gatherer studies, along many different axes, carried over into the archaeology of more complex societies where many of the early discussions in hunter-gatherer studies are still reverberating today.

Meanwhile, the contributions in this volume bear testimony to the fact that (fortunately) a new equilibrium or orthodoxy has not yet been established in hunter-gatherer archaeology. In the context of Palaeolithic archaeology in Europe, the contributors demonstrate collectively that the study of Pleistocene populations is actively reshaping hunter-gatherer studies in general, and has much to offer to the development of general anthropological insights. Moreover, to the extent that theory, method and data are well integrated, this volume reflects the increasing maturity of problem solving in Palaeolithic archaeology. New solutions to old problems are found here not in new programmatic statements (nor, in as yet unfulfilled advertisements) but in the day-to-day interaction of archaeologists with their data. In short, these papers signify that Palaeolithic archaeologists have lost their inferiority complex and feel increasingly comfortable and welcome as active contributors to the general knowledge of archaeology and anthropology. The axes of concern to the contributors represent the major dimensions of theoretical and methodological discussion in which Palaeolithic archaeology has contributed new insights during the past two decades.

As there is no dearth of general review articles addressing the advances in Palaeolithic archaeology during the last twenty years, another review would merely add to already existing redundancy. Instead I would like to focus attention on a few select issues which the papers in this volume touch upon. In their pervasiveness or embeddedness, these issues touch upon most other aspects of Palaeolithic archaeology and hunter-gatherer studies.

### The embeddedness of formal variation

Traditional archaeology considered Palaeolithic artefacts primarily as the products of two rather unrelated behavioural domains — use function and learning context. In terms of use function, variation in the form of artefacts could be predicted if only their use in resource extraction, processing or consumption could be delimited. (Conversely, one could reconstruct this use context without further test, given the formal variation of artefacts.) Where the use context allowed for a wider range of alternative formal types than those represented archaeologically, learning theory was brought in as explanation of the conformity ('we do it this way because that is how we have learned it'). In other words, coincident form not predictable from the use context could be utilised to define the 'we' and to delineate social boundaries.

In either case, human operators could be treated as fully determined — by the learning context in which they grew up or by the environmental context which constrained use form. In this extreme environmental determinism, artefacts were merely dead ends. Although they clearly had been produced by humans, artefacts did not need to be integrated into the behavioural systems which humans articulate with, respond to and manipulate. Artefact form, like the human operators, could be treated as fully determined by factors external to social dynamics. It is little wonder that analysis of artefact form could conveniently bypass the entire social matrix within which artefacts are embedded.

The sixties and seventies brought to the fore a number of problems in this inherited set of equations. For example, traditional approaches did not allow archaeologists to deal effectively with change in artefact form through time and space, aside from those referable to changes in the natural environment (in terms of use function), or to diffusion and independent invention (in terms of learning theory). As more information accumulated on variation in artefact form through time and space, the traditional 'explanations' were found to be wanting. Once it could be demonstrated that there were differences in the degree to which artefact form was constrained and embellished, depending on the articulation of artefacts with such social variables as group size, ritual, permanence of occupation, and exchange, even within what must have been the same 'use function' and 'learning context', it became clear that the traditional explanations were insufficient to account for major parts of the observed archaeological variation (for criticisms of the inherited view, see for example, Barth 1969; Conkey 1978a; Hodder 1982; Plog 1980; Wobst 1977).

In response, the social matrix was increasingly brought in to help explain that part of formal variation which had remained unexplained by the use function of artefacts. Initially, such research merely reproduced the 'reflective' logic (Hodder 1982) of the traditional approaches. That is, aspects of the social matrix were treated, one by one, as independent variables, with artefact form (or the remainder of form unexplained by use function) as dependent variables. In other words, artefacts remained epiphenomal to behaviour, and fully determined by it. The exciting change of the last few years, however, has artefacts assuming a more active stance in social process. After all, certain kinds of social behaviour are unthinkable without the medium of artefacts and, at least in our own society, the articulation of artefacts with day-to-day behaviour is so pervasive that the question whether artefact form determines social behaviour, social context and social process or whether the reverse is true is rapidly turning into a chicken and egg dilemma.

Compared to the formal variation referable to the interaction of working edges with energy and matter, the formal variation broadly referable to information exchange is becoming an ever more profitable and urgent avenue of research. After all, the latter aspect of form is still at the base of the sorting process by which the archaeological record is usually subdivided into temporal and spatial slices. It defines the temporal and spatial dimensions of most research questions. Certainly, if we do not understand what structures the formal dimensions into which we place our research, we expose ourselves to severe logical risks. If the massive effort of Palaeolithic archaeologists to define once and for all the use function of Palaeolithic artefacts is contrasted, on the one hand, with the small proportion of artefact form which is actually interacting with matter and energy, and, on the other hand, with the massive formal differences that set apart tools of a given function in time and space, the size of our dilemma emerges all the more dramatically.

### Units of space

This book provides many good examples of the increasing sensitivity of Palaeolithic archaeologists to issues of spatial scale, beyond the level of the site, yet contrasting with the inherited notion of 'culture' in the narrowly

archaeological meaning of the term, whether it be 'social network systems' (Madden, this volume), 'alliance networks' (Gamble, this volume), 'minimal mating networks' (Wobst 1974) or a number of other partially overlapping concepts. Certainly, those archaeologists who continue to treat their site as if it existed in a spatial vacuum will be in trouble in the eighties. Similar troubles will befall those archaeologists who are interested in a regional perspective, if they merely fill a given region to capacity with look-alikes of 'their' given site.

Hunter-gatherer behaviour is regionally embedded. This realisation of the past two decades serves to underline a number of points which had been made disconnectedly by previous investigators. While there might be social affiliation with specific localities, this affiliation is primarily an ideological one which may or may not predict the actual location of individuals (see for example Williams 1974; Yellen and Harpending 1972). Obviously, many of the social dynamics are local ones for hunter-gatherers. Yet, local dynamics govern short-term interactions, while interactions over the longer term must keep open multiple options within physical and social space. If material products and precedents of behaviour do carry energy investment beyond the *ad hoc* form of utilitarian function, they should be rather sensitive to regional articulations, if only because they are a committed form and will last longer than the local use context.

The kinds of artefacts or axes of artefact variation which articulate most directly with regional processes are essentially devices which allow populations to overcome local environmental variation and constraint, much like the Hxaro exchange of the !Kung San (Wiessner 1977). Thus, it is quite conceivable that their form is essentially unrelated to environmental constraint, unencumbered by utilitarian considerations. Even artefacts which have a primarily utilitarian function will not necessarily relate closely to the environmental constraints of the local use context, if these local constraints can be overcome by generating and making use of a regional network of reciprocal obligations. In other words, both locally produced and used, and regionally articulating artefacts may not be very sensitive to environmental constraints. Instead, they should track more closely the reproduction of a set of social relations. That set of social relations, in turn, should have the fringe benefit of outwitting environmental constraints. To the extent that it does so successfully, there is no reason why its associated artefacts should covary with the environmental driving variables of the given context.

So far, most of the newly introduced archaeological entities of a spatial scale larger than the individual site are behavioural ones. On the other hand, I sense a possibility that they might become misappropriated, whether in the Palaeolithic, or in hunter-gatherer studies in general. The potential danger is that these newly coined entities, such as the minimal mating network, are treated as operational units, capable of acting in their own right. At least for most hunter-gatherers these entities have behavioural relevance only to the extent that they link *individuals* horizontally and temporally. Whether or not such entities define a congruent set of personnel and the relationships among them at any time during the Palaeolithic remains under-investigated (cf. Wobst 1976). What *can* be demonstrated is that Palaeolithic populations need to articulate with others over the spatial scale implied by the given concept, *not* that all individuals tied together by such a web of relationships actually share the same set of interacting personnel. In short, while these networks may have implications for the distribution of archaeological form on a scale as large as required by the given behavioural construct, one need not assume that an actual distribution of any given set of material culture, bounded though it may be, should be expected to circumscribe a bounded set of personnel with mutually congruent relationships.

Few reasons for behaviourally significant boundaries to hunter-gatherer interaction have yet been presented aside from colonial culture contact. It is my hunch that such reasons would have relatively little to do with environmental motivating forces. Instead, I expect them to relate more closely to manipulating, maintaining or bringing about social hierarchies or systems of ranking. Such 'vertical' complexity and its spatial correlates and variance should be a research theme particularly amenable to exploration in the context of the European Upper Palaeolithic.

### Units of time

As concern is increasing for spatial scales larger than the exploitation territories of individual sites, of necessity concern for temporal scales needs to be intensified also. The larger the spatial scale of interaction, the more time will enter simply as a by-product of the friction of distance. The more space one needs to incorporate the social context of local populations, the more time will enter simply as a function of our inability to demonstrate conclusively the contemporaneity of any two sites, particularly during the Palaeolithic. So far, quite a few of the methodological questions raised by the temporal scales of Palaeolithic research remain unresolved.

For example, the smaller the unit of time desired in one's regional research, the more one has to treat one's Palaeolithic system as being essentially in homeostasis. This is so because *shared* form is still the dating rationale by which one can generate the shortest Palaeolithic time slices. The more that formal *variation* is allowed to enter one's time slice, the more difficult it becomes to demonstrate that this variation is not due to dating error, to the fact that the system observed is changing beyond our control, or to non-representative sampling. In other words, the more formal variation one's body of regional archaeological data contains the poorer the chronological resolution. This makes it all the more difficult to put one's finger upon emergent properties, internal contradictions at the root of the system's dynamics, and upon anything that contradicts the image

of a smoothly integrated, equilibrated system which is essentially static over time spans less than the smallest time interval of one's chronological scale. We should derive little comfort from such heuristic models of homeostatic equilibrium, given the speed with which hunter-gatherer groups in the ethnographic present have undergone radical changes.

On the other hand, the control of larger time spans is increasingly vulnerable to the loss of processual sensitivity as the time span gets longer. One notable Palaeolithic example is the subdivision of time, for purposes of analysis, to parallel the cycles of Pleistocene climatic change, such as the Denekamp interstadial, the first Weichsel stadial, or the last interglacial. While these units might be easily enough identified by palaeo-environmental markers, the associated archaeological data that one might sort into the above units would not be particularly useful for further analysis. This is because the data from 'the last interglacial' and so on group together into one research universe two populations subject to rather diametrically opposed driving variables: those data from the beginning of the interglacial to its peak (subject to a warming trend with its associated environmental changes) *vs.* those from the peak of the interglacial to its waning phases (subject to the reverse climatic effects). While a set of behavioural statements could no doubt be contrived that would not be contradicted by the amalgamation of these two sets, such statements would have relatively little processual interest or relevance.

If, alternatively, one combines all archaeological data from the peak of one climatic cycle to the bottom of the next one (e.g. the height of an interstadial to the maximum of the subsequent stadial), at least one should be in a position to contrast the stress effects of climatic deterioration with those of climatic amelioration. Obviously, to work out on which side of a climatic maximum a given archaeological record is located is notoriously difficult to resolve without marker horizons. A good example of this difficulty is the continuing controversy over whether certain Early Middle Palaeolithic sites in central Europe should be placed at the beginning of the last glaciation or the end of the penultimate one (Bosinski 1967).

When it comes to cultural evolution, quite frequently one reads of comparisons between the archaeological record of two slices of time which are widely separated. Yet, without controlling the data for their specific position within a given climatic cycle, it is rather difficult to establish whether the observed difference represents directional change of a qualitative nature, or merely reversible change as a function of palaeo-environmental cyclicity (or even sampling error overrepresenting different parts of a given climatic cycle and its associated archaeological expressions).

It should prove interesting to review our textbook statements about Palaeolithic cultural evolution in this light. Much of the evidence championed in support of directional qualitative change in human cultural behaviour may simply be the result of contrasting something which is too multidimensional for stark contrast. The problem, quite frequently, is compounded even more by contrasting different points along a *spatial* transect, as for example in the fashionable progression: (1) Plio-Pleistocene hominids and Lower Palaeolithic — semi-arid lands in the vicinity of the equators, *vs.* (2) Late Lower Palaeolithic and Middle Palaeolithic — northern temperate environments *vs.* (3) Upper Palaeolithic — northern periglacial fringe. Ironically, a parallel transect placed across the ethnographic present of hunter-gatherers would show many of the same 'evolutionary' advances in the products of behaviour, as one moves from the !Kung San to the Eskimo.

In explaining cultural evolution, two more specific problems also need to be addressed in this context. The first concerns the frequent confusion in the archaeological literature about what represents an adequate explanation for emergent behaviours such as art, ritual, or the loading of artefacts with form related to information exchange rather than merely production, extraction and consumption. Frequently, the earliest *expression* of such behaviours is mistaken as evidence for the emergence of the *ability* for such behaviours. In other words, previous populations are blamed for being *unable* to do something which they did not do. Obviously, the ability to transact a given behaviour needs to precede its first transaction. Yet, these two points might be separated by a long time period. They might not necessarily respond to the same sets of stress factors, and the first transaction of a given behaviour might not relate so much to evolutionary considerations but to rather mundane and reversible causal factors. To explain the evolution of the ability for a given behaviour is a vastly more difficult logical proposition, precisely because its most visible expressions in the archaeological record may postdate by a considerable margin the emergence of the ability in question. In this context, many of the supposed evolutionary advances of Upper Palaeolithic *Homo sapiens* may not relate so much to the emergence of new abilities but to the first expression of these abilities in contexts where such expressions were sensible. This is all the more compelling because many of these behaviours are expressed first with differential pervasiveness along spatial and climatic transects, and, thereafter, vary amongst hunter-gatherers from virtual absence to the most baroque over-indulgence.

A similar mismatch between the processual context of change and its explanation is often encountered on a smaller temporal scale when it comes to the introduction of new tools in Palaeolithic (or later) material culture. Such additions to the technological repertoire are usually rationalised by contrasting the period of widespread use of the new item following its introduction, with the period in which its technological predecessors were similarly in widespread use. In other words, the new technological function is counterposed to the technological context of its predecessors, the change-over being accounted for by the technological advantage brought about by the 'new' item of technology.

As far as the actual process of introduction is concerned, this explanation might very well be off the mark, at least when compared to later and better documented introductions of new technology. Whether it be new metals, the wheel, or prehistoric weapons, their very context of introduction is rarely related closely to technological advantage. Instead, it tends to relate far more intimately to social advantage: the ability of (frequently higher ranked) individuals to bolster their position by surrounding themselves with rarefied material culture, to obligate others by giving them access to that material culture, or to shore up horizontal social interactions by ritual (made more compelling by being surrounded with unique, rarefied, contrived, yet symbol-laden items of material culture). Such new 'technological' items will enter predominantly technological spheres of articulation only after they have become so numerous that they lose their uniqueness through inflation, with a concomitant loss in their value to impress and to produce, maintain or manipulate social obligations. In other words, the process of introduction of new technology is a social one that cannot be accounted for solely by reference to technological advantage. It would be interesting to look at the introduction of Palaeolithic technology in this light: particularly tempting in that direction are the spear thrower and the bow and arrow.

Even though archaeology prides itself for being in control of large amounts of time which other social sciences lack, at present archaeology lacks processually sensitive ways of analysing large units of time. Our inherited means, such as cultural evolution, the search for origins, or the analysis of time trends in form are really only gross abstractions and temporary expedients. These concepts group units of time because of their relatedness through external form rather than internal logic. If we start our research with the expectation that the sequence of behaviour within a large time unit represents a coherent and logically interconnected behavioural unit, then we will most likely search our archaeological record for variables which are temporally congruent, that is variables which remain unchanged over the time unit in question. Or we will search for variables which gradually change in a given direction by a series of small incremental steps.

We commonly employ both procedures, often as an almost automatic byproduct of archaeological classification. We frequently define particular time units and extract them from the archaeological continuum precisely because of the temporal congruence of some aspects of formal variation. However, there is little to suggest that such a lack of formal change implies homeostasis. Rather, it follows from the laws of thermodynamics that persistent lack of change in some aspects of variation over long time periods implies disproportionate change in other aspects, if the system of which both are a part is to continue interacting effectively with its environment. Or, on the analogy of neutral genes, the persistence of a formal likeness in some features may be entirely spurious, the lack of change in their make-up being simply due to the fact that they did not interact significantly with anything of importance.

A time series of small incremental changes in archaeological form is easily created as an automatic product of archaeological sorting behaviour. What tends to happen is that we define an archaeological time slice in an arbitrary manner by reference to certain variables. Each variable is traced backwards through time along a trajectory of decreasing formal likeness to an ultimate point of origin, or projected forward in time to the ultimate point at which formal likeness with its antecedents ceases. Yet there is nothing in this procedure to suggest that the formal changes so defined are processually interconnected. Nor can it be assumed that such a long-lasting trend of change implies the continuous operation of stress factors over an equivalent time span. On the one hand, very few stress factors are conceivable which would persist over the entire period so defined (or increase in severity, to continue producing change). On the other hand, it is difficult to imagine that many (if any) of the usual archaeological variables would have sufficient elasticity to continue responding indefinitely to such a time-persistent set of stress factors. Instead, one might suppose that time-persistent stress would normally produce a response only after some threshold had been passed. If continued stress beyond that threshold evoked further response in the formal aspects of archaeological variation, there is little reason to expect that these further changes would continue in the same way or along the same trajectory as the initial response.

Whatever the reason may be for our classification procedures, whether we group time by formal likeness or by chains of incremental formal change, the chances are that this very grouping process will steer us away from the *tail ends* of formal variance — those parts of the variance which are the most exposed to change, and which should, thus, serve as the most sensitive bell-wethers of change.

## Concluding remark

In sum, we face a number of serious difficulties when it comes to the analysis of large spans of time. So far time spans have not provided us with much more than a means to talk about human evolution, whether cultural or biological, in the broadest, least processual and most formal ways, and with a relative time scale on which we can suspend those kinds and scales of question which we can already deal with operationally. Certainly research into larger spans of time should not precede research into smaller time slices, if our goal is to understand processes of change among hunter-gatherers.

My cursory look at the dimensions of time, space and form makes it quite apparent that we are most in need of research into the ways time enters into hunter-gatherer behaviour, Palaeolithic data, and archaeological concepts. In my review, I have focused primarily upon the larger scales in which these dimensions influence archaeological interpretation, primarily because the smaller scales are addressed quite cogently in pursuit of 'middle range theory' (Schiffer 1976).

*Acknowledgements*

Thanks are due to Jude who let me take a vacation from our vacation to complete this paper, and to the Department of Archaeology of Cambridge University for their hospitality and for providing me with the peace and quiet to keep my thoughts focused upon this paper. As usual, much that is interesting in this paper received stimuli from interaction with students and colleagues at the University of Massachusetts, while all that is flawed can only be blamed upon the author.

REFERENCES

Alcalde del Rio, H., Breuil, H. and Sierra, L. 1911. *Les Cavernes de la Région Cantabrique (Espagne)*, 2 vols. Monaco, Imprimerie Vve A. Cherie.

Aloïsi, J.C., Monaco, A., Planchais, N., Thommeret, J. and Thommeret, Y. 1978. The Holocene transgression in the Golfe du Lion, Southwestern France: paleogeographic and paleobotanical evolution. *Géographie Physique du Quaternaire* 32: 145–62.

Altuna, J. 1972. Fauna de mamíferos de los yacimientos prehistóricos de Guipúzcoa con catálogo de los mamíferos cuaternarios del Cantábrico y del Pirineo Occidental. *Munibe* 24.

1976. Los mamíferos del yacimiento prehistórico de Tito Bustillo (Asturias), in J.A. Moure Romanillo and M. Cano Herrera (eds.), *Excavaciones en la Cueva de 'Tito Bustillo' (Asturias): Trabajos de 1975*, 149–90. Oviedo, Instituto de Estudios Asturianos.

1979. La faune des ongulés du Tardiglaciaire en Pays Basque et dans le reste de la région Cantabrique, in D. de Sonneville-Bordes (ed.), *La Fin des Temps Glaciaires en Europe*, I: 85–95. Paris, C.N.R.S.

1980. Historia de la domesticación animal en el Pais Vasco desde sus origenes hasta la Romanización. *Munibe* 32.

Ammerman, A.J. and Cavalli-Sforza, L.L. 1971. Measuring the rate of spread of early farming in Europe. *Man* 6: 674–88.

van Andel, T.H. and Shackleton, J.C. In press. Late paleolithic and mesolithic coastlines of Greece and the Aegean. *Journal of Field Archaeology*.

Andersen, H.H. 1960. Køkkenmøddingen ved Meilgård. *Kuml* 1960: 26–35.

1969. Brovst: en kystboplads fra ældre stenalder. *Kuml* 1969: 67–90.

1974. Ringkloster: en jysk inlandsboplads med Ertebøllekultur. *Kuml* 1973–4: 11–108.

1975. En Ertebølleboplads ved Wænge Sø/Helgenæs. *Hikuin* 2: 9–48.

1978. Aggersund: en Ertebølleboplads ved Limfiorden. *Kuml* 1978: 7–56.

Andersen, S.H. and Malmros, C. 1965. Norslund: en kystboplads fra ældre stenalder. *Kuml* 1965: 33–114.

Aparicio, J. 1973. La Cueva del Volcán del Faro (Cullera) y el Paleomesolítico valenciano. *Quartär* 23–4: 71–91.

1977. Investigaciones arqueológicas en Gandía y La Safor. *Gandía* 1977: 69–76.

Aparicio, J. and Fletcher, D. 1971. La Cueva paleolítica del 'Volcán del Faro', Cullera, Valencia. *Congreso Nacional de Arqueología* 11: 175–83.

ApSimon, A.M. 1980. The last Neanderthal in France. *Nature* 187: 271–2.

Arambourou, R. 1978. *Le Gisement Préhistorique de Duruthy, Commune de Sorde-l'Abbaye (Landes). Bilan des Recherches de 1958 à 1975. Mémoire de la Société Préhistorique Française* 13.

Bahn, P.G. 1977. Seasonal migration in south-west France during the late glacial period. *Journal of Archaeological Science* 4: 245–57.

1978a. The 'unacceptable face' of the West European Upper Palaeolithic. *Antiquity* 52: 183–92.

1978b. Water mythology and the distribution of Palaeolithic parietal art. *Proceedings of the Prehistoric Society* 44: 125–34.

1979a. The French Pyrenees: an economic prehistory. Unpublished Ph.D. dissertation, University of Cambridge.

1979b. La Paléoéconomie magdalénienne du Bassin de Tarascon (Ariège). *Bulletin de la Société Préhistorique de l'Ariège* 34: 37–46.

In press (a). La paléoéconomie du Béarn. I. Epoque paléolithique. *Revue de Pau et du Béarn* **10.**

In press (b). Utilisation de ressources vegetales dans le paléolithique et le mésolithique des Pyrénées françaises. *Actes du 1ᵉʳ Colloque International sur l'Alimentation de l'Homme Préhistorique et dans les Sociétés Primitives.* Les Eyzies.

Bailey, G.N. 1973. Concheros del norte de España: una hipótesis preliminar. *Actas del XII° Congresso Nacional de Arqueologia*: 73–84. Universidad de Zaragoza.

1975. The role of molluscs in coastal economies: the results of midden analysis in Australia. *Journal of Archaeological Science* 2: 45–62.

1978. Shell middens as indicators of postglacial economies: a territorial perspective, in P.A. Mellars (ed.), *The Early Postglacial Settlement of Northern Europe*, 37–64. London, Duckworth.

1981a. Concepts, time-scales and explanations in economic prehistory, in J.A. Sheridan and G.N. Bailey (eds.), *Economic Archaeology*, 97–117. Oxford, British Archaeological Reports International Series 96.

1981b. Concepts of resource exploitation: continuity and discontinuity in palaeoeconomy. *World Archaeology* 13: 1–15.

1982. Coasts, lakes and littorals: Cantabria, in M.R. Jarman, G.N. Bailey and H.N. Jarman (eds.), *Early European Agriculture.* Cambridge University Press.

1983. Problems of site formation and the interpretation of spatial and temporal discontinuities in the distribution of coastal middens, in P.M. Masters and N.C. Flemming (eds.), *Quaternary Coastlines and Marine Archaeology.* London, Academic Press.

Bailey, G.N. and Davidson, I. In press. Site exploitation territory and topography: two case studies from Palaeolithic Spain. *Journal of Archaeological Science.*

Bailey, G.N., Deith, M.R. and Shackleton, N.J. In press. Oxygen isotope analysis and seasonality determinations: limits and potential of a new technique. *American Antiquity.*

Bailey, G.N., Carter, P.L., Gamble, C.S. and Higgs, H.P. In press. Asprochaliko and Kastritsa: further investigations of the Palaeolithic sequence in Epirus (north-west Greece). *Proceedings of the Prehistoric Society* 49.

Balikci, A. 1970. *The Netsilik Eskimo.* New York, Natural History Press.

Barandiarán, I. 1967. *El Paleomesolítico del Pirineo Occidental.* Seminario de Prehistória, Universidad de Zaragoza.

Barandiarán, J. and Altuna, J. 1977. Excavaciones en Ekain (memoria de las campañas 1969–1975). *Munibe* 29: 3–58.

Barker, G.W.W. 1973. Cultural and economic change in the prehistory of Central Italy, in C. Renfrew (ed.), *The Explanation of Culture Change*, 359–70. London, Duckworth.

1975. Prehistoric territories and economies in Central Italy, in E.S. Higgs (ed.), *Palaeoeconomy*, 111–75. Cambridge University Press.

Barth, F. (ed.)(1969) *Ethnic Groups and Boundaries*, Universitets-forlaget, Bergen.

Bay-Petersen, J.L. 1978. Animal exploitation in mesolithic Denmark, in P.A. Mellars (ed.), *The Early Postglacial Settlement of Northern Europe*, 115–45. London, Duckworth.

Beardsley, R.K. 1953. Hypothesis on inner Asian pastoral nomadism and its cultural area. *Society for American Archaeology Memoirs* 9: 24–8.

Becker, C.J. 1939. En stenalderboplads paa Ordrup Næs i Nord Nordvestsjælland. *Aarbøger for Nordisk Oldkyndighed og Historie* 1939: 199–280.

Bedord, J.N. 1978. A technique of sex determination of mature bison metapodials. *Plains Anthropologist* 23: 40–3.

Bender, B. 1978. Gatherer-hunter to farmer: a social perspective. *World Archaeology* 10: 204–22.

1981. Gatherer-hunter intensification, in J.A. Sheridan and G.N. Bailey (eds.), *Economic Archaeology*, 149–57. Oxford, British Archaeological Reports International Series 96.

Bettinger, R.L. 1980. Explanatory/predictive models of hunter-gatherer adaptation, in M.B. Schiffer (ed.), *Advances in Archaeological Method and Theory* 3, 189–255. New York, Academic Press.

Binford, L.R. 1962. Archaeology as anthropology. *American Antiquity* 28: 217–55.

1964. A consideration of archaeological research design. *American Antiquity* 29: 425–41.

1968. Post-Pleistocene adaptations, in S.R. and L.R. Binford (eds.), *New Perspectives in Archaeology*, 313–41. Chicago, Aldine.

1972a. *An Archaeological Perspective.* New York, Seminar Press.

1972b. Contemporary model building: paradigms and the current state of palaeolithic research, in D.L. Clarke (ed.), *Models in Archaeology*, 109–66. London, Methuen.

1973. Interassemblage variability – the Mousterian and the 'functional' argument, in C. Renfrew (ed.), *The Explanation of Culture Change*, 227–54. London, Duckworth.

1977a. General introduction, in L.R. Binford (ed.), *For Theory Building in Archaeology*, 1–10. New York, Academic Press.

1977b. Forty-seven trips: a case study in the character of archaeological formation processes, in R.V.S. Wright (ed.), *Stone Tools as Cultural Markers*, 24–36. Canberra, Australian Institute of Aboriginal Studies.

1978a. *Nunamiut Ethnoarchaeology.* New York, Academic Press.

1978b. Dimensional analysis of behavior and site structure: learning from an Eskimo hunting stand. *American Antiquity* 43: 330–61.

1979a. Organization and formation processes: looking at curated technologies. *Journal of Anthropological Research* 35: 255–73.

1979b. Problems/solutions. *Flintknappers' Exchange* 2: 19–25.

1980. Willow smoke and dogs' tails: hunter-gatherer settlement and archaeological site formation. *American Antiquity* 45: 4–20.

1981. *Bones: Ancient Men and Modern Myths.* New York, Academic Press.

1983. *In Pursuit of the Past: Decoding the Archaeological Past.* London, Thames and Hudson.

Binford, L.R. and Bertram, J.R. 1977. Bone frequencies – and attritional processes, in L.R. Binford (ed.), *For Theory Building in Archaeology*, 77–153. New York, Academic Press.

Binford, L.R. and Binford, S.R. 1966. A preliminary analysis of functional variability in the Mousterian of Levallois facies. *American Anthropologist* 68: 238–95.

Binford, L.R. and Chasko, W.J. 1976. Nunamiut demographic history: a provocative case, in E.B.W. Zubrow (ed.), *Demographic Anthropology: Quantitative Approaches*, 63–144. Albuquerque, University of New Mexico Press.

Binford, S.R. 1968a. A structural comparison of disposal of the dead in the Mousterian and the Upper Palaeolithic. *Southwestern Journal of Anthropology* 24: 139–54.

1968b. Early upper pleistocene adaptations in the Levant. *American Anthropologist* 70: 707–17.

1972. The significance of variability: a minority report, in F. Bordes (ed.), *The Origins of Homo sapiens*, 199–210. Paris, UNESCO.

Binford, S.R. and Binford, L.R. 1969. Stone tools and human behavior. *Scientific American* 220: 70–82.

Birdsell, J.B. 1953. Some environmental and cultural factors influencing the structuring of Australian Aboriginal populations. *American Naturalist* 87: 171–207.

1958. On population structure in generalized hunting and collecting populations. *Evolution* 12: 189–205.

1976. Realities and transformations: the tribes of the Western Desert of Australia, in N. Peterson (ed.), *Tribes and Boundaries of Australia*, 95–120. Canberra, Australian Institute of Aboriginal Studies.

Blackwelder, B.W., Pilkey, O.H. and Howard, J.D. 1979. Late Wisconsinian sea levels on the Southeast U.S. Atlantic shelf based on in-place shoreline indicators. *Science* 204: 618–20.

Blalock, H. 1972. *Social Statistics*, 2nd edn. New York, McGraw-Hill.

Blas Cortina, M., González, M., Marquez, M-C. and Rodríguez, J. 1978. Picos asturienses de yacimientos al aire libre en Asturias. *Boletín del Instituto de Estudios Asturianos* 93–94: 335–56.

Bloom, A.L., Broecker, W.S., Chappell, J.M.A., Matthews, R.K. and Mesolella, K.J. 1974. Quaternary sea level fluctuations on a tectonic coast: new $^{230}$Th/$^{234}$U dates from the Huon Peninsula, New Guinea. *Quaternary Research* 4: 185–205.

Blurton-Jones, N. and Konner, M.J. 1976. !Kung knowledge of animal behavior (or: the proper study of mankind is animals), in R.B. Lee and I. DeVore (eds.), *Kalahari Hunter-Gatherers*, 325–48. Cambridge, Mass., Harvard University Press.

Bøe, J. 1942. Til Høyfjellets Forhistorie: Boplassen på Sumtangen ved Finsevatn på Hardangervidda. *Bergens Museum Skrifter* 21.

Bøe, J. and Nummedal, A. 1936. Le Finnmarkien: les origines de la civilisation dans l'extrême-nord de l'Europe, *Institutt for Sammenlignende Kulturforskning B* 32.

Boessneck, J. and von den Driesch, A. 1978. The significance of measuring animal bones from archaeological sites, in R.H. Meadow and M.A. Zeder (eds.), *Approaches to Faunal Analysis in the Middle East*, 25–39. Peabody Museum of Archaeology and Ethnology, Harvard University, Peabody Museum Bulletin 2.

Bofinger, E. and Davidson, I. 1977. Radiocarbon age and depth: a statistical treatment of two sequences of dates from Spain. *Journal of Archaeological Science* 4: 231–43.

Bonifay, M.-F., Guerin, C. and Mourer-Chauviré, C. 1972. Etude de nouveaux restes de vertébrés provenant de la Carrière Fournier á Chatillon-Saint-Jean (Drôme). *Bulletin de l'Association Française pour l'Etude du Quaternaire* 4: 249–302.

Bonner, J.T. 1980. *The Evolution of Culture in Animals*. Princeton University Press.

Bordes, F. 1953. Essai de classification des industries 'moustériennes'. *Bulletin de la Société Préhistorique Française* 50: 457–66.

1961a. Typologie du paléolithique ancien et moyen. *L'Institut de Préhistoire de l'Université de Bordeaux Memoire* 1.

1961b. Mousterian cultures in France. *Science* 134: 803–10.

1968. *The Old Stone Age*. New York, McGraw-Hill.

1969. Os percé moustérien et os gravé acheuléen du Pech de l'Azé II. *Quaternaria* 11: 1–6.

1972. *A Tale of Two Caves*. New York, Harper and Row.

1973. On the chronology and contemporaneity of different palaeolithic cultures in France, in C. Renfrew (ed.), *The Explanation of Culture Change*, 217–26. London, Duckworth.

Bordes, F. and Prat, F. 1965. Observations sur les faunes du Riss et du Würm I en Dordogne. *L'Anthropologie* 69: 31–46.

Bordes, F. and de Sonneville-Bordes, D. 1970. The significance of variability in palaeolithic assemblages. *World Archaeology* 2: 61–73.

Bordes, F., Laville, H. and Paquereau, M-M. 1966. Observations sur le pleistocène supérieur du gisement de Combe-Grenal (Dordogne). *Actes de la Société Linnéenne de Bordeaux B* 103: 3–19.

Bordes, F., Bouchud, J., Lafille, J., van Campo, M. and Piveteau, J. 1962. Découverte d'un squelette d'enfant moustérien dans le gisement du Roc de Marsal, commune de Campagne-du-Bugue (Dordogne). *Compte-rendu Académie des Sciences de Paris* 254: 714–5.

Boserup, E. 1965. *The Conditions of Agricultural Growth*. London, Allen and Unwin.

Bosinski, G. 1967. *Die Mittelpaläolithischen Funde in Westlichen Mitteleuropa*. Köln, Fundamenta, Series A, IV.

1968. Ein Magdalenien-Fundplatz in Feldkirchen Gönnersdorf, Kreis Neuwied. *Eiszeitalter und Gegenwart* 19: 268–9.

Bosinski, G. and Evers, D. 1979. *Jagd im Eiszeitalter*. Köln, Rheinland-Verlag.

Bosinski, G. and Fischer, G. 1974. *Die Menschendarstellungen von Gönnersdorf, Ausgrabung 1968 (Der Magdalenien-Fundplatz Gönnersdorf, 1)*. Wiesbaden, Franz Steiner.

Botkin, S. 1980. Effects of human exploitation on shellfish populations at Malibu Creek, California, in T.K. Earle and A.L. Christenson (eds.), *Modeling Change in Prehistoric Subsistence Economies*, 121–40. New York, Academic Press.

Bottema, S. 1974. *Late Quaternary Vegetation History of Northwestern Greece*. Groningen University Press.

Bouchud, J. 1958. La faune de la Grotte de Gargas. *Bulletin de la Société Méridionale de Spéléologie et de la Préhistoire* 5: 383–90.

1966. *Essai sur le Renne et la Climatologie du Paléolithique Supérieur*. Périgueux, Imprimerie Magne.

1972. Les grandes herbivores rissiens des 'Abîmes de la Fage' en Corrèze (cervidés, bovidés, capridés, rupicaprines, suidés et equidés). *Nouvelles Archives du Muséum d'Histoire Naturelle de Lyon* 10: 33–59.

1975. Les grands herbivores rissiens de 'Abîmes de la Fage' en Corrèze, la conservation des restes osseux et leur interprétation climatique. *Nouvelles Archives du Muséum d'Histoire Naturelle de Lyon* 13: 119–22.

Boyer-Klein, A. 1976. Análisis polínico de la cueva de Tito Bustillo, in J. Moure Romanillo and M. Cano Herrera (eds.), *Excavaciones en la Cueva de 'Tito Bustillo' (Asturias): Trabajos de 1975*, 203–6. Oviedo, Instituto de Estudios Asturianos.

1980. Nouveaux résultats palynologiques de sites solutréens et magdaléniens cantabriques. *Bulletin de la Société Préhistorique Française* 77: 103–7.

Braidwood, R.J. 1975. *Prehistoric Men*, 8th edn. Glenview, Scott Foresman.

Braidwood, R.J. and Howe, B. 1962. Southwestern Asia beyond the lands of the Mediterranean littoral, in R.J. Braidwood and G.R. Willey (eds.), *Courses Toward Urban Life*, 132–46. Chicago, Aldine.

Brain, C.K. 1969. The contribution of Namib Desert Hottentots to an understanding of Australopithecine bone accumulations. *Scientific Papers of the Namib Desert Research Station* 39: 13–22.

1976. Some principles in the interpretation of bone accumulations associated with man, in G.Ll. Isaac and E.R. McCown (eds.), *Human Origins*, 97–116. Menlo Park, California, W.A. Benjamin.

Braudel, F. 1972. *The Mediterranean and the Mediterranean World in the Age of Philip II*, 2nd edn., revised, translated by S. Reynolds. London, Collins.

Braun, D.P. 1974. Explanatory models for the evolution of coastal adaptations in prehistoric New England. *American Antiquity* 39: 582–96.

Brothwell, D.R. and Higgs, E.S. (eds.) 1969. *Science in Archaeology*, 2nd edn. London, Thames and Hudson.

Büdel, J. 1943. Die räumliche und zeitliche Gliederung des Eiszeit-klimas. *Die Naturwissenschaften* 36: 105–12, 133–9.

Burch, E.S. 1972. The caribou/wild reindeer as a human resource. *American Antiquity* 37: 339–68.

Bureau of Land Management. 1973. *Land Use Recommendations for the Pryor Mountains*. U.S. Department of the Interior and Forest Service, U.S. Department of Agriculture.

Butzer, K.W. 1971a. *Environment and Archeology*, 2nd ed. Chicago, Aldine.

1971b. Cumunicación preliminar sobre la geología de Cueva Morín, in J. González Echegaray and L.G. Freeman (eds.), *Cueva Morín: Excavaciones 1966–1968*, 345–56. Santander, Patronato de las Cuevas Prehistóricas.

1973. Notas sobre la geomorfología regional de la parte occidental de la Provincia de Santander y la estratigrafía de Cueva Morín, in J. González Echegaray and L.G. Freeman (eds.), *Cueva Morín: Excavaciones 1969*, 269–76. Santander, Patronato de las Cuevas Prehistóricas.

1981. Cave sediments, upper pleistocene stratigraphy and Mousterian facies in Cantabrian Spain. *Journal of Archaeological Science* 8: 133–83.

Cabrera, V. and Bernaldo de Quiros, F. 1977. The Solutrean site of Cueva Chufín (Santander, Spain). *Current Anthropology* 18: 780–1.

Campbell, J.K. 1964. *Honour, Family and Patronage*. Oxford, Clarendon Press.

Carballo, J. 1960. *Investigaciones Prehistóricas II*. Santander, Diputación Provincial.

Carter, P.L. 1970. Late Stone Age exploitation patterns in southern Natal. *South African Archaeological Bulletin* 25: 55–8.

Caughley, G. 1966. Mortality patterns in mammals. *Ecology* 47: 906–18.

1977. *Analysis of Vertebrate Populations*. Chichester, Wiley.

Cava, A. 1978. El depósito arqueológico de la cueva de Marizulo (Guipúzcoa). *Munibe* 30: 155–72.

Chappell, J. and Veeh, H.H. 1978. $^{230}$Th/$^{234}$U age support of an interstadial sea level of $-40$ m at 30,000 b.p. *Nature* 276: 602–3.

Childe, V.G. 1958. Retrospect. *Antiquity* 32: 69–74.

Christenson, A.L. 1980a. Change in the human niche in response to population growth, in T.K. Earle and A.L. Christenson (eds.), *Modeling Change in Prehistoric Subsistence Economies*, 31–72. New York, Academic Press.

1980b. Subsistence change: bibliographic overview, in T.K. Earle and A.L. Christenson (eds.), *Modeling Change in Prehistoric Subsistence Economies*, 243–56. New York, Academic Press.

Clark, G.A. 1971a. The Asturian of Cantabria: a Re-evaluation. Unpublished Ph.D. dissertation, University of Chicago.

1971b. The Asturian of Cantabria: subsistence base and the evidence for post-Pleistocene climatic shifts. *American Anthropologist* 73: 1244–57.

1974. Excavations in the Late Pleistocene cave site of Balmori, Asturias (Spain). *Quaternaria* 18: 383–426.

1975a. Liencres: una estación al aire libre de estilo Asturiense cerca de Santander. *Cuadernos de Arqueología* 3: 1–84.

1975b. El hombre y su ambiente a comienzos del Holoceno en la región Cantabrica. *Boletín del Instituto de Estudios Asturianos* 85: 363–87.

1976a. El Asturiense Cantábrico. *Bibliotheca Prehistórica Hispana* 13.

1976b. L'Asturien des Cantabres: état de la recherche actuelle, in M. Escalon de Fonton (ed.), *Actes du XX$^e$ Congrès Préhistorique de France*, 84–101. Provence, C.N.R.S.

1979a. Spatial association at Liencres, an Early Holocene open site on the Santander coast, north-central Spain, in S. Upham (ed.), *Anthropological Research Papers* 15, 121–43. Arizona State University.

1979b. Liencres, an open station of Asturian affinity near Santander, Spain. *Quaternaria* 21: 249–86, 300–4.

1979c. The North Burgos archaeological survey: Bronze and Iron Age archaeology on the Meseta del Norte (Province of Burgos, north-central Spain). *Anthropological Research Papers* 19. Arizona State University.

1980. Comment. The identification of prehistoric hunter-gatherer aggregation sites: the case of Altamira. *Current Anthropology* 21: 621–2.

1981a. On preagricultural coastal adaptations. *Current Anthropology* 22: 444–6.

1981b. Confirmatory data analysis in archaeological research designs, in L. Raab and T. Klinger (eds.), *The Design of Archaeological Research*. Chicago, Aldine.

1982. Quantifying archaeological research, in M.B. Schiffer (ed.), *Advances in Archaeological Method and Theory*, 4: 217–73. New York, Academic Press.

Clark, G.A. and Clark, V. 1975. La cueva de Balmori (Asturias, España): nuevas aportaciones. *Trabajos de Prehistoria* 32: 35–77.

Clark, G.A. and Lerner, S. 1978. Multivariate analysis of Asturian site catchment data. Unpublished paper presented at the annual meeting of the American Anthropological Association, Los Angeles.

1980. Prehistoric resource utilization in early Holocene Cantabrian Spain. *Anthropology UCLA* 10 (1/2): 53–96.

Clark, G.A. and Menéndez Amor, J. 1975. Apendice II: muestras de polen de Liencre, niveles 1 y 2. *Cuadernos de Arqueología* 3: 67–70.

Clark, G.A. and Richards, L. 1978. Late and post-Pleistocene industries and fauna from the cave site of La Riera (province of Asturias, Spain), in L.G. Freeman (ed.), *Views of the Past*, 117–52. The Hague, Mouton.

Clark, G.A. and Straus, L.G. 1975. Late Pleistocene hunter-gatherer adaptations in Cantabrian Spain. Unpublished proposal submitted to the National Science Foundation.

1977a. La Riera paleoecological project: preliminary report, 1976 excavations. *Current Anthropology* 18: 354–5.

1977b. Cueva de La Riera: objetivos del 'proyecto paleoecológico' e informe preliminar de la campaña de 1976. *Boletín del Instituto de Estudios Asturianos* 91: 489–505.

Clark, G.A., Straus, L.G. and Fuentes de M., C. 1975. Preliminary site survey of the Meseta del Norte, northern Burgos Province, Spain. *Current Anthropology* 16: 283–6.

Clark, J.A., Farrell, W.E. and Peltier, W.R. 1978. Global changes in postglacial sea level: a numerical calculation. *Quaternary Research* 9: 265–87.

Clark, J.D. 1975. Africa in prehistory: peripheral or paramount? *Man* 10: 175–98.

Clark, J.G.D. 1946. *From Savagery to Civilization*. London, Cobbetts Press.

1952. *Prehistoric Europe: the Economic Basis*. London, Methuen.

1953. The economic approach to prehistory. *Proceedings of the British Academy* 39: 215–38.

1954. *Excavations at Star Carr*. Cambridge University Press.

1965. Radiocarbon dating and the expansion of farming culture from the Near East over Europe. *Proceedings of the Prehistoric Society* 31: 58–73.

1972. Star Carr: a case study in bioarchaeology. *Addison-Wesley Modular Publications* 10. Reading, Mass.

1975. *The Earlier Stone Age Settlement of Scandinavia*. Cambridge University Press.

Clarke, D.L. 1968. *Analytical Archaeology*. London, Methuen.

1973. Archaeology: the loss of innocence. *Antiquity* 47: 6–18.

1976. Mesolithic Europe: the economic basis, in G. de G. Sieveking, I.H. Longworth and K.E. Wilson (eds.), *Problems in Economic and Social Archaeology*, 449–81. London, Duckworth.

CLIMAP 1976. The surface of the ice-age earth. *Science* 191: 1131–7.

Close, A.E. 1978. The identification of style in lithic artefacts. *World Archaeology* 10: 223–37.

Clottes, J. 1976. Les civilisations du paléolithique supérieur dans les Pyrénées, in H. de Lumley, (ed.), *La Préhistoire Française*, 1214–31. Paris, C.N.R.S.

Cohen, M.N. 1975. Archaeological evidence for population pressure in preagricultural societies. *American Antiquity* 40: 471–4.

1977. *The Food Crisis in Prehistory*. New Haven, Yale University Press.

Coles, J.M. and Higgs, E.S. 1969. *The Archaeology of Early Man*. London, Faber and Faber.

Collins, D. and Onians, J. 1978. The origins of art. *Art History* 1: 1–25.

Combier, J. 1956. *Solutré. Les Fouilles de 1907 à 1925. Mise au Point Stratigraphique et Typologique*. Travaux du Laboratoire de Géologie de la Faculté des Sciences de Lyon, N.S., 2.

1970. Rapport de fouilles année 1970. Unpublished manuscript.

1973. Solutré (Saône-et-Loire). Compte-rendu des fouilles de 1973. Unpublished manuscript.

1976. Solutré. Livret-Guide de l'Excursion A8, Bassin du Rhône, Paléolithique et Néolithique. Direction J. Combier and J-P. Thevenot, *IX$^e$ Congrès de l'Union International des Sciences Préhistoriques et Protohistoriques*, 91–6, 111–17. Nice.

Combier, J. and Vuillemey, M. 1976. Bourg-en-Bress – Chalon-sur-Saône. Livret-Guide de l'Excursion A8, Bassin du Rhone, Paléolithique et Néolithique. Direction J. Combier and J-P. Thevenot. *IX$^e$ Congrès de l'Union Internationale des Sciences Préhistoriques et Protohistoriques*, 59–63, 68–81. Nice.

Conkey, M.W. 1978a. Style and information in cultural evolution: toward a predictive model for the paleolithic, in C.L. Redman, M.J. Berman, E.V. Curtin, W.Y. Langhorne Jr., N.M. Versaggi and J.C. Wanser (eds.), *Social Archeology: Beyond Subsistence and Dating*, 61–85. New York, Academic Press.

1978b. Understanding variability in Cantabrian Magdalenian bone assemblages by means of cluster analysis techniques, in M. Borillo (ed.), *Méthodologie Appliquée a l'Industrie de l'Os Préhistorique*, 143–60. Université de Provence, C.N.R.S.

1980. The identification of prehistoric hunter-gatherer aggregation sites: the case of Altamira. *Current Anthropology* 21: 609–20.

Coombs, G. 1980. Decision theory and subsistence strategies: some theoretical considerations, in T.K. Earle and A.L. Christenson (eds.), *Modeling Change in Prehistoric Subsistence Economies*, 187–208. New York, Academic Press.

Coope, G.R., Morgan, A. and Osborne, P.J. 1971. Fossil coleoptera as indicators of climatic fluctuations during the last glaciation in Britain. *Palaeogeography, Palaeoclimatology, Palaeoecology* 10: 87–101.

Corbet, G.B. 1966. *The Terrestrial Mammals of Western Europe*. London, G.T. Foulis.

Corchon, M. 1971. *El Solutrense en Santander*. Santander, Institución Cultural de Cantabria.

Coull, J.R. 1972. *The Fisheries of Europe: an Economic Geography*. London, Bell.

Cowgill, G.L. 1975a. On causes and consequences of ancient and modern population changes. *American Anthropologist* 77: 505–25.

1975b. Population and pressure as a non-explanation. *Society for American Archaeology Memoirs* 30: 127–31.

Craig, G.Y. and Oertel, G. 1966. Deterministic models of living and fossil populations of animals. *Quarterly Journal of the Geological Society of London* 122: 315–55.

Cuerda Barceló, J. and Gasull, L. 1971. Cova del Volcán del Faro de Cullera: fauna malacológica. Unpublished manuscript, Servicio de Investigación Prehistórica de Valencia.

Cushing, D.H. 1975. *Marine Ecology and Fisheries*. Cambridge University Press.

Dahl, G. and Hjort, A. 1976. *Having Herds: Pastoral Herd Growth and Household Economy*. Stockholm Studies in Social Anthropology 2. Department of Social Anthropology, University of Stockholm.

Dakaris, S.I., Higgs, E.S. and Hey, R.W. 1964. The climate, environment and industries of Stone Age Greece, part 1. *Proceedings of the Prehistoric Society* 30: 199–244.

Dalton, G. 1981. Anthropological models in archaeological perspective, in I.R. Hodder, G.Ll. Isaac and N. Hammond (eds.), *Pattern of the Past*, 17–48. Cambridge University Press.

Damas, D. 1969. Characteristics of Central Eskimo band structure, in D. Damas (ed.), *Contributions to Anthropology: Band Societies*, 116–38. Ottawa, National Museums of Canada, Bulletin 228, Anthropological Series 84.

1972. The Copper Eskimo, in M.G. Bicchieri (ed.), *Hunters and Gatherers Today*, 3–50. New York, Holt, Rinehart and Winston.

Dansgaard, W., Johnsen, S.J., Clausen, H.B. and Langway, C.C. Jr. 1970. Ice cores and paleoclimatology, in I.U. Olsson (ed.), *Radiocarbon Variations and Absolute Chronology*, 337–48. Stockholm, Amqvist and Wiksell.

Darling, F.F. 1963. *A Herd of Red Deer: A Study in Animal Behaviour*. Oxford University Press.

David, N.C. 1973. On Upper palaeolithic society, ecology, and technological change: the Noaillian case, in C. Renfrew (ed.), *The Explanation of Culture Change*, 277–303. London, Duckworth.

Davidson, I. 1972. The fauna from La Cueva de Volcán del Faro (Cullera, Valencia). *Archivo de prehistoria Levantina* 13: 7–15.

1976a. Les Mallaetes and Mondúver: the economy of a human group in prehistoric Spain, in G. de G. Sieveking, I.H. Longworth and K.E. Wilson (eds.), *Problems in Economic and Social Archaeology*, 483–99. London, Duckworth.

1976b. Seasonality in Spain. *Zephyrus* 26-7: 167–73.

1980b. Late Palaeolithic economy in eastern Spain. Unpublished Ph.D. dissertation, University of Cambridge.

1981. Can we study prehistoric economy for fisher-gatherer-hunters? In J.A. Sheridan and G.N. Bailey (eds.), *Economic Archaeology*, 17–33. Oxford, British Archaeological Reports International Series 96.

In press. *La Cueva del Niño, un Yacimiento Arqueológico con Arte Rupestre Paleolítico y Levantino: Excavaciones 1973*. *Excavaciones Arqueológicas en España*.

Davidson, I. n.d. The magnificent seven: a stingy view of fisher-gatherer-hunters in the late Pleistocene of western Europe. Paper presented at the Theoretical Archaeology Group Conference, Southampton 1980.

Davies, E. (ed.) 1944. *Denmark*. Geographical Handbook Series, Naval Intelligence Division.

Davis, S.J.M. and Valla, F.R. 1978. Evidence for domestication of the dog 12 000 years ago in the Natufian of Israel. *Nature* 276: 608–10.

Defense Mapping Agency Hydrographic Center. 1977. *Cabo de Peñas to Pointe d'Arcachon* (1 : 350 000), Region 3, No. 37030. Washington.

Deffontaines, P. 1948. Essai de classification des genres de vie montagnards. I: La vie pastorale en montagne. *Revue de Géographie Humaine et d'Ethnologie* (Paris) 1: 20–35.

Deith, M.R. and Shackleton, N.J. n.d. Seasonal exploitation of marine molluscs at La Riera. Unpublished manuscript.

Delibrias, G., Guillier, M-T., Evin, J., Thommeret, J. and Y. 1976. Datations absolues des dépôts quaternaires et des sites préhistoriques par le méthode du carbone 14, in H. de Lumley (ed.), *La Préhistoire Française*, 1499–514. Paris, C.N.R.S.

Dellenbach, M.E. 1935. La conquête du massif alpin et de ses abords par les populations préhistoriques. *Revue de Géographie Alpine* 23: 147–416.

Delluc, B. and Delluc, G. 1978. Les manifestations graphiques aurignaciennes sur support rocheux des environs des Eyzies (Dordogne). *Gallia Préhistoire* 21: 213–438.

Delpech, F. 1967. *Recherches Paléontologiques concernant Quelques Gisements du Magdalénien VI: Stations de la Gare de Couze (Dordogne), du Morin (Gironde), et de Duruthy (Landes)*. Thèse, 3$^e$ cycle, Université de Bordeaux.

1975. *Les Faunes du Paléolithique Supérieur dans le Sud-Ouest de la France*, 3 vols. Thèse, Doctorat d'Etat. Université de Bordeaux.

Delpech, F. and Rigaud, J.P. 1974. Etude de la fragmentation et de la répartition des restes osseux dans un niveau d'habitat paléolithique, in H. Camps-Fabrer (ed.), *Premier Colloque International sur l'Industrie de l'Os dans la Préhistoire*, 47–55. Université de Provence, C.N.R.S.

Delporte, H. 1974. Le Moustérien d'Isturitz d'après la collection Passemard (Musée des Antiquités Nationales). *Zephyrus* 25: 17–42.

1976. Les civilisations du paléolithique supérieur en Auvergne, in H. de Lumley (ed.), *La Préhistoire Française*, 1: 1297–1304. Paris, C.N.R.S.

Dennell, RW. 1972. The interpretation of plant remains: Bulgaria, in E.S. Higgs (ed.), *Papers in Economic Prehistory*, 149–60. Cambridge University Press.

Denton, G.H. and Hughes, T.J. (eds.) 1981. *The Last Great Ice Sheets*. New York, Wiley.

Douglas, M. 1970. *Natural Symbols*. London, Barrie and Rockliff.

Drucker, P. 1943. Archaeological survey of the northern Northwest Coast. *Smithsonian Institution, Bureau of American Ethnology*, 133.

1951. The northern and central Nootkan tribes. *Smithsonian Institution, Bureau of American Ethnology* 144.

1965. *Cultures of the North Pacific Coast*. San Francisco, Chandler.

Ducos, P. 1978. 'Domestication' defined and methodological approaches to its recognition in faunal assemblages, in R.H. Meadow and M.A. Zeder (ed.), *Approaches to Faunal Analysis in the Middle East*, 53–6. Peabody Museum of Archaeology and Ethnology, Harvard University, *Peabody Museum Bulletin* 2.

Dumond, D.E. 1972a. Prehistoric population growth and subsistence change in Eskimo Alaska, in B. Spooner (ed.), *Population Growth: Anthropological Implications*, 311–28. Cambridge Mass., M.I.T. Press.

1972b. Population growth and political centralisation, in B. Spooner (ed.), *Population Growth: Anthropological Implications*, 286–310. Cambridge, Mass., M.I.T. Press.

Dupre Ollivier, M. 1978. *Análisis polínico de sedimentos de la Cueva de 'Les Mallaetes' (Barx, Valencia)*. Tesina inédita. Facultad de Filosofía y Letras, Universidad de Valencia.

Durham, W.H. 1976. The adaptive significance of cultural behavior. *Human Ecology* 4: 89–121.

Earle, T.K. 1978. Economic and social organization of a complex chiefdom: the Halelea District, Kaua'i, Hawaii. *University of Michigan Anthropological Papers* 63.

1980. A model of subsistence change, in T.K. Earle and A.L. Christenson (eds.), *Modeling Change in Prehistoric Subsistence Economies*, 1–30. New York, Academic Press.

Earle, T.K. and Christenson, A.L. (eds.) 1980. *Modeling Change in Prehistoric Subsistence Economies*. New York, Academic Press.

Earle, T.K. and Ericson, J.E. (eds.) 1977. *Exchange Systems in Prehistory*. New York, Academic Press.

Ekman, S. 1953. *Zoogeography of the Sea*. London, Sidgwick and Jackson.

Emery, K.O. and Milliman, J.D. 1970. Quaternary sediments of the Atlantic continental shelf of the United States. *Quaternaria* 12: 3–18.

Emlen, J.M. 1966. The role of time and energy in food preference. *American Naturalist* 100: 611–17.

Emlen, J.M. and Emlen, G. 1974. Optimal choice in diet: test of a hypothesis. *American Naturalist* 109: 427–35.

Esbert, R., Ordax, J. and Suarez, L. n.d. Descripción petrográfica de siete rocas comunes de la cueva de La Riera (Posada de Llanes). Unpublished manuscript.

Evans, J.G. 1975. *The Environment of Early Man in the British Isles*. Berkeley, University of California Press.

1978. *An Introduction to Environmental Archaeology*. London, Paul Elek.

Evans-Pritchard, E.E. 1961. *Anthropology and History*. Manchester University Press.

Fernández-Tresguerres, J. 1976. Azilian burial from Los Azules I, Asturias, Spain. *Current Anthropology* 17: 769–70.

1979. L'Azilien de la grotte de Los Azules I, Asturias, in D. de Sonneville-Bordes (ed.), *La Fin des Temps Glaciaires en Europe*, 745–52. Paris, C.N.R.S.

1980. El Aziliense en las Provincias de Asturias y Santander. *Monografías del Centro de Investigación y Museo de Altamira* 2.

Fischer, P-H. 1925. Mollusques Quaternaires récoltes dans la grotte de Castillo (Espagne, province de Santander). *Journal de Conchyliologie* 68: 320–3.

Flannery, K.V. 1969. Origins and ecological effects of early domestication in Iran and the Near East. In P.J. Ucko and G.W. Dimbleby, (eds.), *The Domestication and Exploitation of Plants and Animals*, 73–100. London, Duckworth.

1972. The cultural evolution of civilizations. *Annual Review of Ecology and Systematics* 3: 399–426.

Flannery, K.V. (ed.) 1976). *The Early MesoAmerican Village*. New York, Academic Press.

Fletcher, D. and Aparicio, J. 1969. Bastón de Mando procedente de Cullera (Valencia). *Quartär* 7/8: 66–90.

Flint, R.F. 1971. *Glacial and Quaternary Geology*. New York, Wiley.

Flook, D.R. 1970. Causes and implications of an observed sex differential in the survival of wapiti. *Canadian Wildlife Service Report Series* 11: 1–71.

Florschütz, F., Menéndez, J. and Wijmstra, T.A. 1971. Palynology of a thick Quaternary succession in Southern Spain. *Palaeogeography, Palaeoclimatology, Palaeoecology* 10: 233–64.

Flower, S.S. 1931. Contributions to our knowledge of the duration of life in vertebrate animals – V. Mammals. *Proceedings of the Zoological Society of London* 100: 145–234.

Foley, R. 1976. Space and energy: a method for analysing habitat value and utilization in relation to archaeological sites, in D.L. Clarke (ed.), *Spatial Archaeology*, 163–87. London, Academic Press.

Forde, C.D. 1934. *Habitat, Economy and Society*. London, Methuen.

Fortea, J. 1973. *Los Complejos Microlaminares y Geométricos del Epipaleolítico Mediterráneo Español*. Facultad de Filosofía y Letras, Universidad de Salamanca.

Fortea, J. and Jordá Cerdá, F. 1976. La Cueva de Les Mallaetes y los problemas de Paleolítico Superior de Mediterráneo Español. *Zephyrus* 26–27: 129–66.

Freeman, L.G. 1964. Mousterian developments in Cantabrian Spain. Unpublished Ph.D. dissertation, University of Chicago.

1966. The nature of the Mousterian facies in Cantabrian Spain. *American Anthropologist* 68: 230–7.

1967. A study of Mousterian occupations in Cantabrian Spain. Proposal submitted to the National Science Foundation.

1968a. A theoretical framework for interpreting archeological materials, in R.B. Lee and I. DeVore (eds.), *Man the Hunter*, 262–7. Chicago, Aldine.

1968b. Cueva Morín: a European upper paleolithic site. *Current Anthropology* 9: 541.

1973a. The significance of mammalian faunas from paleolithic occupations in Cantabrian Spain. *American Antiquity* 38: 3–44.

1973b. El musteriense, in J. González Echegaray and L.G. Freeman (eds.), *Cueva Morín: Excavaciones 1969*, 15–142. Santander, Patronato de las Cuevas Prehistóricas.

Frenzel, B. 1968. The pleistocene vegetation of northern Eurasia. *Science* 161: 637–49.

1973. *Climatic Fluctuations of the Ice Age*. Cleveland, Case Western Reserve University Press.

Freundt, E.A. 1948. Problems of the Scandinavian Mesolithic. *Acta Archaeologica* 19: 1–68.

Fried, H.M. 1968. On the concepts of tribe and tribal society, in J. Helm (ed.), *Essays on the Problem of Tribe*, 3–23. American

Ethnological Society. Seattle, University of Washington Press.

Frison, G.C. 1978. Animal population studies and cultural inference. *Plains Anthropologist* 23: 44–52.

Frossard, E. and Frossard, C.L. 1880. *Etudes sur une Grotte renfermant des Restes Humains de l'Epoque Paléolithique découverte a Bagnerès-de-Bigorre*. 2ᵉ Edition Augmentée. Paris, Grassart.

Fry, R.E. 1980. *Models and Methods in Regional Exchange*. S.A.A. Papers 1, Washington.

Fuentes Vidarte, C. 1980. Estudio de la fauna de El Pendo, in J. González Echegaray (ed.), *El Yacimiento de la Cueva de El Pendo*, 217–37. Bibliotheca Praehistórica Hispana 17.

Fullola, J.M. 1979. Las industria líticas de Paleolítico Superior Iberico. *Trabajo Vario del Servicio de Investigación Prehistórica* 60.

Galy, O. 1883. Exploration d'un abri-sous-roche dit la Grazo de l'Aspiouo (Vallée d'Ustou). *Bulletin de la Société Ariegeoise des Sciences, Lettres et Arts* 1: 90–4.

Gamble, C.S. 1978a. Resource exploitation and the spatial patterning of hunter-gatherers: a case study, in D. Green, C. Haselgrove and M. Spriggs (eds.), *Social Organisation and Settlement*, 153–85. Oxford, British Archaeological Reports International Series (Supplementary) 47.

1978b. Animal Communities and their Relationship to Prehistoric Economies in Western Europe. Unpublished Ph.D dissertation, University of Cambridge.

1979. Hunting strategies in the central European Palaeolithic. *Proceedings of the Prehistoric Society* 45: 35–52.

1980. Information exchange in the palaeolithic. *Nature* 282: 522–3.

1982. Interaction and alliance in palaeolithic society. *Man.*

García Guinea, M.A. 1968. *Los Grabados de la Cueva de la Peña del Cuco en Castro Urdiales y de la Cueva de Cobrantes (Valle de Aras)*. Santander, Patronato de las Cuevas Prehistóricas.

1975a. *Primeros Sondéos Estratigráficos en la Cueva de Tito Bustillo (Ribadesella, Asturias)*. Santander, Patronato de las Cuevas Prehistóricas.

1975b. El mesolítico en Cantabria, in M.A. García Guinea and M. Puente (eds.), *La Prehistoria de la Cornisa Cantábrica*, 177–200. Santander, Institución Cultural de Cantabria.

García Guinea, M.A. and Puente, M. (eds.) 1975. *La Prehistoria de la Cornisa Cantábrica*. Santander, Institución Cultural de Cantabria.

Gates, W.L. 1976. Modeling the ice-age climate. *Science* 191: 1138–44.

Gaussen, H. 1933. L'histoire postglaciaire de la végétation dans le S.O. de l'Europe. *Revue Générale des Sciences Pures et Appliquées* 44: 307–12.

Gaustad, Fr. 1973. Kyst og innland i Nordland. *Tromsø Museum Skrifter* 14: 183–9.

Gavelas, A. 1980. Sobre nuevos concheros asturienses en los concejos de Ribadesella y Llanes. *Boletín del Instituto de Estudios Asturianos* 101: 675–703, 711–18.

Gifford, D.P. 1978. Ethnoarchaeological observations of natural processes affecting cultural materials, in R.A. Gould (ed.), *Explorations in Ethnoarchaeology*, 77–101. Albuquerque, University of New Mexico Press.

Gilbert, E.W. and Beckinsale, R.P. 1941. *Spain and Portugal. 1. The Peninsula*. Geographical Handbook Series, Naval Intelligence Division.

Girard, G., Hoffert, M. and Miskovsky, J-C. 1975. Contribution à la connaissance du Paléolithique Moyen en Haute-Garonne: le gisement de Mauran. *Bulletin de l'Association Française pour l'Etude de Quaternaire* 3–4: 171–87.

Gjessing, G. 1945. *Norges Steinalder*. Oslo, Norges Arkeologisk Selskap.

Gluckman, M. 1972. A band wagonload of monkeys. (A review of 'The Imperial Animal' by L. Tiger and R. Fox. Holt, Rinehart and Winston). *New York Review of Books* 19 (8): 39–41.

Goddard, P.E. 1934. *Indians of the Northwest Coast*. New York, American Museum of Natural History.

González Echegaray, J. 1952. La 'Cueva de la Monedas', nueva caverna con pinturas rupestres en la provincia de Santander. *Archivo Español de Arqueología* 25: 343.

1957. La cueva de la Mora: un yacimiento paleolítico en la región de los Picos de Europe. *Revista del Centro Estudios Montañenses* 1: 3–26.

1960. El Magdaleniense III de la costa cantábrica. *Boletín del Seminario de Estudios de Arte y Arqueología (Valladolid)* 26: 69–100.

1971. Apreciaciones cuantitatívas sobre el Magdaleniense III de la costa cantábrica. *Munibe* 23: 323–7.

1973. Nuevas aportaciones al estudio del paleolítico superior de Cueva Morín, in J. González Echegaray and L.G. Freeman (eds.), *Cueva Morín: Excavaciones 1969*, 165–220. Santander, Patronato de las Cuevas Prehistóricas.

1979a. Stratigraphie du Paléolithique final à la Grotte de Rascaño (Santander), in D. de Sonneville-Bordes (ed.), *La Fin des Temps Glaciaires en Europe*, II: 733–5. Paris, C.N.R.S.

1979b. *El Yacimiento de la Cueva de El Pendo*. Bibliotheca Praehistórica Hispana 17.

González Echegaray, J. and Freeman, L.G. (eds.) 1971. *Cueva Morín: Excavaciones 1966–1968*. Santander, Patronato de las Cuevas Prehistóricas.

(eds.) 1973. *Cueva Morín: Excavaciones 1969*. Santander, Patronato de las Cuevas Prehistóricas.

1978. *Vida y Muerte en Cueva Morín*. Santander, Institución Cultural de Cantabria.

González Echegaray, J. and Ripoll Perello, E. 1953. Hallazgos en la Cueva de la Pasiega (Puente Viesgo, Santander). *Ampurias* 15: 43–65.

González Echegaray, J., García Guinea, M.A. and Begines Ramirez, A. 1966. Cueva del Otero. *Excavaciones Arqueológicas en España* 53: 1–85.

González Echegaray, J., García Guinea, M.A., Begines Ramirez, A. and Madariaga, B. 1963. Cueva de la Chora. *Excavaciones Arqueológicas en España* 26: 1–80.

González Morales, M.R. 1978. Excavaciones en el conchero Asturiano de la cueva de Mazaculos II (La Franca, Ribadedeva, Asturias). *Boletín del Instituto de Estudios Asturianos* 93–94: 369–83.

González Morales, M.R. and Marquez Uría, M.C. 1978. The Asturian shell midden of Cueva de Mazaculos II (La Franca, Asturias, Spain). *Current Anthropology* 19: 614–15.

Goody, J.R. 1976. *Production and Reproduction*. Cambridge University Press.

1977. *The Domestication of the Savage Mind*. Cambridge University Press.

Gould, R.A. 1980. *Living Archaeology*. Cambridge University Press.

Gould, S.J. 1965. Is uniformitarianism necessary? *American Journal of Science* 263: 223–8.

Gould, S.J. and Eldredge, N. 1977. Punctuated equilibria: the tempo and mode of evolution reconsidered. *Paleobiology* 3: 115–51.

Goy Goy, J.L. n.d. *Estudio Geomorfológico del Cuaternario Litoral Valenciano*. Tesis inédita, Facultad de Geología, Universidad Complutense de Madrid.

Groupe de Travail de Préhistoire Cantabrique. 1979. Chronostratigraphie et écologie des cultures du paléolithique final en Espagne cantabrique, in D. de Sonneville-Bordes (ed.), *La Fin des Temps Glaciaires en Europe*, 713–9. Paris, C.N.R.S.

Guerin, C. 1969. Gisement pleistocène de la grotte de Jaurens (Commune de Nespouls, Corrèze): premiers résultats des fouilles 1968–1969. *Bulletin de la Société Scientifique, Historique et Archéologique de la Corrèze-Brive.*

1970. Gisement pleistocène de Jaurens (Commune de Nespouls, Corrèze) fouilles 1970. *Bulletin de la Société Scientifique, Historique et Archéologique de la Corrèze-Brive.*

Guinea Lopez, E. 1953. *Geografía Botánica de Santander.* Santander, Diputación Provincial.

Hafsten, U. 1960. Pollen-analytic investigations in South Norway, in O. Holtedahl (ed.), *Norges Geologiske Undersøkelse* 208: 434–61.

Hagen, A. 1963. Mesolittiske jegergrupper i norske høyfjell. *Universitets Oldsaks Samling Årbok* 1960–61: 109–42.

1967. *Norges Oldtid.* Oslo, J.W. Cappelens.

Hahn, J. 1972. Aurignacian signs, pendants and art objects in central and eastern Europe. *World Archaeology* 3: 252–66.

1976. Das Gravettien im Westlichen Mitteleuropa, in B. Klima (ed.), Perigordien et Gravettien en Europe. *Actes du IX$^e$ Congrès de l'Union Internationale des Sciences Préhistoriques et Proto-historiques, Colloque XV, Prétirage*, 100–20. Nice.

1977. *Aurignacien – Das ältere Jungpaläolithikum in Mittel – und Osteuropa.* Köln, Fundamenta, Series A, IX.

1981. Abfolge und Umwelt der jüngeren Altsteinzeit in Südwestdeutschland. *Fundberichte aus Baden-Württemberg* 6: 1–27.

Hahn, J. and von Koenigswald, W. 1976. Ökologischer Wandel im letzten Glazial und Postglazial. *Zentralblatt für Geologie und Paläontologie* 2: 469–72.

Hahn, J., von Koenigswald, W., Wagner, E. and Wille, W. 1977. Das Geissenklösterle bei Blaubeuren, Alb-Donau-Kreis. Eine Altsteinzeitliche Höhlenstation der mittleren Alb. *Fundberichte aus Baden-Württemberg* 3: 14–37.

Haldane, J.B.S. 1956. Time in biology. *Science Progress* 175: 385–402.

Hallam, A. 1972. Models involving population dynamics, in T.J.M. Schopf (ed.), *Models in Paleobiology.* San Francisco, Freeman.

van der Hammen, T., Wijmstra, T.A. and Zagwijn, N.H. 1971. The floral record of the late cenozoic of Europe, in K.K. Turekian (ed.), *The Late Cenozoic Glacial Ages*, 391–424. Cambridge, Mass., Yale University Press.

Hammond, N. 1974. Palaeolithic mammalian faunas and parietal art in Cantabria: a comment on Freeman. *American Antiquity* 39: 618–19.

Hamond, F.W. 1978. The contribution of simulation to the study of archaeological processes, in I.R. Hodder (ed.), *Simulation Studies in Archaeology*, 1–9; Cambridge University Press.

Hardesty, D.L. 1975. The niche concept: suggestions for its use in human ecology. *Human Ecology* 3: 71–85.

Harmon, R.S., Land, L.S., Mitterer, R.M., Garrett, P., Schwarz, H.P. and Larson, G.J. 1981. Bermuda sea level during the last interglacial. *Nature* 289: 481–3.

Harris, D.R. 1969. Agricultural systems, ecosystems and the origins of agriculture, in P.J. Ucko and G.W. Dimbleby (eds.), *The Domestication and Exploitation of Plants and Animals*, 3–16. London, Duckworth.

1977a. Alternative pathways toward agriculture, in C.A. Reed (ed.), *Origins of Agriculture*, 179–243. The Hague, Mouton.

1977b. Settling down: an evolutionary model for the transformation of mobile bands into sedentary communities, in J. Friedman and M.J. Rowlands (eds.), *The Evolution of Social Systems*, 401–17. London, Duckworth.

Harrold, F.B. 1980. A comparative analysis of Eurasian palaeolithic burials. *World Archaeology* 12: 196–211.

Hayden, B. (ed.) 1979. *Lithic Use-Wear Analysis.* New York, Academic Press.

Helm, J. (ed.) 1968. *Essays on the Problem of Tribe.* American Ethnological Society. Seattle, University of Washington Press.

1969. Discussion, in D. Damas (ed.), *Contributions to Anthropology: Band Societies*, 52. Ottawa, National Museums of Canada, Bulletin 228, Anthropological Series 84.

Helskog, E. 1974. The Komsa culture: past and present. *Arctic Anthropology* 11 (Supplement): 261–5.

Hernández-Pacheco, E. 1919. La caverna de la Peña Candamo (Asturias). *Comisión de Investigaciones Paleontológicas y Prehistóricas* 24. Madrid.

Hernández-Pacheco, F. 1959. La morrena peri-glaciar de Peña Vieja, Picos de Europa (Santander). *Trabalhos de Antropologia e Etnologia* 17: 227–34.

Hernández-Pacheco, F., Llopis Lladó, N., Jordá Cerdá, F. and Martinez, J.A. 1957. El cuaternario de la región Cantábrica. Libro Guia de la Excursion. *INQUA V Congreso Internacional.* Oviedo, Diputación Provincial de Asturias.

Hespenheide, H.A. 1975. Prey characteristics and predator niche width, in M.L. Cody and J.M. Diamond (eds.), *Ecology and Evolution of Communities*, 158–80. Cambridge, Mass., Harvard University Press.

1980. Comment: ecological models of resource selection, in T.K. Earle and A.L. Christenson (eds.), *Modeling Change in Prehistoric Subsistence Economies*, 73–8. New York, Academic Press.

Hewes, G.W. 1948. The public 'fishing and fisheries'. *American Anthropologist* 50: 238–45.

Higgs, E.S. (ed.) 1972. *Papers in Economic Prehistory.* Cambridge University Press.

(ed.) 1975. *Palaeoeconomy.* Cambridge University Press.

Higgs, E.S. and Jarman, M.R. 1969. The origins of agriculture: a reconsideration. *Antiquity* 43: 31–41.

1972. The origins of animal and plant husbandry, in E.S. Higgs (ed.), *Papers in Economic Prehistory*, 3–13. Cambridge University Press.

1975. Paleoeconomy, in E.S. Higgs (ed.), *Palaeoeconomy*, 1–7. Cambridge University Press.

Higgs, E.S. and Vita-Finzi, C. 1966. The climate, environment and industries of Stone Age Greece, part II. *Proceedings of the Prehistoric Society* 32: 1–29.

1972. Prehistoric economies: a territorial approach, in E.S. Higgs (ed.), *Papers in Economic Prehistory*, 27–36. Cambridge University Press.

Higgs, E.S. and Webley, D.P. 1971. Further information concerning the environment of Palaeolithic man in Epirus. *Proceedings of the Prehistoric Society* 37: 367–80.

Higgs, E.S., Vita-Finzi, C., Harris, D.R. and Fagg, A.E. 1967. The climate, environment and industries of Stone Age Greece, part III. *Proceedings of the Prehistoric Society* 33: 1–29.

Higham, C.F.W. 1967. Stock rearing as a cultural factor in prehistoric Europe. *Proceedings of the Prehistoric Society* 33: 84–106.

Hill, A.P. 1975. Taphonomy of contemporary and Late Cenozoic East African vertebrates. Unpublished Ph.D. dissertation, University of London.

1976. On carnivore and weathering damage to bone. *Current Anthropology* 17: 335–6.

1978. Taphonomic background to fossil man – problems in palaeoecology, in W.W. Bishop (ed.), *Geological Background to Fossil Man*, 87–101. Edinburgh, Scottish Academic Press.

Hill, J.H. 1978. Language contact systems and human adaptations. *Journal of Anthropological Research* 34: 1–26.

Hinde, R.A. and Tinbergen, N. 1958. The comparative study of species-specific behaviour, in A. Roe and G.G. Simpson (eds.), *Behaviour and Evolution*, 251–68. New Haven, Yale University Press.

Hodder, I.R. 1977. The distribution of material culture in the Baringo district, Western Kenya. *Man* 12: 239–69.

1978a. Social organization and human interaction: the development of some tentative hypotheses in terms of material culture, in I.R. Hodder (ed.), *The Spatial Organization of Culture*, 199–271. London, Duckworth.

1978b. The maintenance of group identities in the Baringo district, Western Kenya, in D. Green, C. Haselgrove and M. Spriggs (eds.), *Spatial Organisation and Settlement*, 47–73. Oxford, British

Archaeological Reports International Series 47.

1982. *Symbols in Action*, Cambridge University Press.

Hodder, I.R. and Orton, C.R. 1976. *Spatial Analysis in Archaeology.* Cambridge University Press.

Holly, B.P. 1978. The problem of scale in time-space research, in T. Carlstein, D. Parkes and N. Thrift (eds.), *Timing Space and Spacing Time, Vol. 3: Time and Regional Dynamics*, 5–18. London, Edward Arnold.

Houston, J.M. 1967. *The Western Mediterranean World: an Introduction to its Regional Landscapes.* New York, Praeger.

Hughes, T.J., Denton, G.H., Andersen, B.G., Schilling, D.H., Fastook, J.L. and Lingle, C.S. 1981. The last great ice sheets: a global view, in G.H. Denton and T.J. Hughes (eds.), *The Last Great Ice Sheets*, 263–317. New York, Wiley.

Indrelid, S. 1973. Mesolitiske tilpasning-former i høyfjellet. *Stavanger Museum Årbok* 1972: 5–27.

1975. Problems relating to the early Mesolithic settlement of Southern Norway. *Norwegian Archaeological Review* 8: 7–18.

1978. Mesolithic economy and settlement patterns in Norway, in P.A. Mellars (ed.), *The Early Postglacial Settlement of Northern Europe*, 147–76. London, Duckworth.

Ingold, T. 1980. *Hunters, Pastoralists and Ranchers.* Cambridge University Press.

1981. The hunter and his spear: notes on the cultural mediation of social and ecological systems, in J.A. Sheridan and G.N. Bailey (eds.), *Economic Archaeology*, 119–30. Oxford, British Archaeological Reports International Series 96.

Inman, D.L. and Nordstrom, C.E. 1971. On the tectonic and geomorphological classification of coasts. *Journal of Geology* 79: 1–21.

Isaac, G.Ll. 1978. The food-sharing behavior of protohuman hominids. *Scientific American* 238: 90–108.

Isaac, G.Ll. and McCown, E.R. (eds.) 1976. *Human Origins.* Menlo Park, California, W.A. Benjamin.

Janssens, P., González Echegaray, J. and Azpeitia, P. 1958. *Memoria de las Excavaciones de la Cueva del Juyo (1955–1956).* Santander, Patronato de las Cuevas Prehistóricas.

Jarman, M.R. 1969. The prehistory of upper pleistocene and recent cattle, part I: East Mediterranean, with reference to north-west Europe. *Proceedings of the Prehistoric Society* 35: 236–66.

1972a. European deer economies and the advent of the Neolithic, in E.S. Higgs (ed.), *Papers in Economic Prehistory*, 125–47. Cambridge University Press.

1972b. A territorial model for archaeology: a behavioural and geographical approach, in D.L. Clarke (ed.), *Models in Archaeology*, 705–34. London, Methuen.

1976. Early animal husbandry, in Sir Joseph Hutchinson, J.G.D. Clark, E.M. Jope and R. Riley (eds.), 'The Early History of Agriculture'. *Philosophical Transactions of the Royal Society, London B* 275: 85–97.

Jarman, M.R. and Wilkinson, P.F. 1972. Criteria of animal domestication, in E.S. Higgs (ed.), *Papers in Economic Prehistory*, 83–96. Cambridge University Press.

Jarman, M.R., Bailey, G.N. and Jarman, H.N. (eds.) 1982. *Early European Agriculture.* Cambridge University Press.

Jessen, A. 1920. Stenalderhavets udbredelse i det nordlige Jylland. *Danmarks Geologiske Undersøgelse Series 2* 35: 1–112.

Jochim, M.A. 1976. *Hunter-Gatherer Subsistence and Settlement.* New York, Academic Press.

1979. Breaking down the system: recent ecological approaches in archaeology, in M.B. Schiffer (ed.), *Advances in Archaeological Method and Theory, vol. 2*, 77–119. New York, Academic Press.

Johansen, A.B. 1969. *Høyfjellsfunn ved Lærdalsvassdrag I.* Bergen, Universitetsforlaget.

1978. *Høyfjellsfunn ved Lærdalsvassdraget II.* Bergen, Universitetsforlaget.

Jones, R. 1980. Different strokes for different folks: sites, scale and strategy, in I. Johnson (ed.), *Holier than Thou*, 152–7. Canberra University, Department of Prehistory, Research School of Pacific Studies.

Jordá Cerdá, F. 1955. *El Solutrense en España y sus Problemas.* Oviedo, Diputación Provincial de Asturias.

1963a. Revisión de la cronología del Asturiense. *Actas del V° Congreso Nacional de Arqueología.* Universidad de Zaragoza, Seminario del Arqueología.

1963b. El paleolítico superior Cantábrico y sus industrias. *Saitabi* 13: 3–22.

1975. El paleolítico hispano. *Las Ciencias* 40: 23–30.

1977. *Historia de Asturias: Prehistoria.* Oviedo, Ediciones Ayalga, S.A.

Kaiser, K. 1960. Klimazeugen des periglazialen Dauerfrostbodens in Mittel- und Westeuropa. *Eiszeitalter und Gegenwart* 11: 121–41.

Keeley, L.H. 1979. *Experimental Determination of Stone Tool Uses.* University of Chicago.

Keene, A.S. 1979. Economic optimization models and the study of hunter-gatherer subsistence settlement systems, in C. Renfrew and K.L. Cooke (eds.), *Transformations: Mathematical Approaches to Culture Change*, 369–404. New York, Academic Press.

King, T.F. 1978. Don't that beat the band? Nonegalitarian political organization in prehistoric central California, in C.L. Redman, M.J. Berman, E.V. Curtin, W.Y. Langhorne Jr., N.M. Versaggi and J.C. Wanser (eds.), *Social Archeology: Beyond Subsistence and Dating*, 225–48. New York, Academic Press.

Klein, R.G. 1969. *Man and Culture in the Late Pleistocene.* San Francisco, Chandler.

1978. Stone age predation on large African bovids. *Journal of Archaeological Science* 5: 195–217.

1979. Stone age exploitation of animals in southern Africa. *American Scientist* 67: 151–60.

1980a. Review of *European Prehistory* by Sarunas Milisauskas. *American Antiquity* 45: 209–10.

1980b. Environmental and ecological implications of large mammals from Upper Pleistocene and Holocene sites in southern Africa. *Annals of the South African Museum* 81.

In press (a). Ungulate mortality and sedimentary facies in the late Tertiary Varswater Formation, Langebaanweg, south-western Cape Province, South Africa. *Annals of the South African Museum.*

In press (b). Stone age predation on small African bovids. *South African Archaeological Bulletin.*

n.d. El Juyo 1978 faunal report.

Klein, R.G., Wolf, C., Freeman, L.G. and Allwarden, A. 1981. The use of dental crown heights for constructing age profiles of red deer and similar species in archaeological samples. *Journal of Archaeological Science* 8: 1–31.

Klingel, H. 1965. Notes on the biology of the plains zebra *Equus quagga boehmi* Matschie. *East African Wildlife Journal* 3: 86–8.

1969. The social organisation and population ecology of the plains zebra (*Equus quagga*). *Zoologica Africana* 4: 249–63.

von Koenigswald, W., Müller-Beck, H-J. and Pressmar, E. 1974. *Die Archäologie und Paläontologie der Weinberghöhlen bei Mauern (Bayern).* Tübingen, Archaeologica Venatoria, 3.

Kopp, K.O. 1965. Límite de la nieve perpetua y clima de la época glaciar Würmiense en la Sierra de Aralar (Guipúzcoa-Navarra). *Munibe* 17: 3–20.

Kozlowski, J.K. 1961. Bemerkungen uber den Stand der Paläolith-forschung in Polen. *Archaeologica Austriaca* 30: 118–43.

Kroeber, A.L. and Barrett, S.A. 1960. Fishing among the Indians of Northwestern California. *Anthropological Records of the University of California* 21.

Kuhn, T.S. 1970. *The Structure of Scientific Revolutions*, 2nd edn. University of Chicago Press.

Kurtén, B. 1953. On the variation and population dynamics of fossil and recent mammal populations. *Acta Zoologica Fennica* 76: 1–122.

1964. Population structure in paleoecology, in J. Imbrie and N. Newell (eds.), *Approaches to Paleoecology*. New York, Wiley.

Lantier, R. 1974. *La Vie Préhistorique* ('Que Sais-Je?' No. 535). 7$^e$ Edition. Paris, P.U.F.

Lartet, E. 1861. Nouvelles recherches sur la coexistence de l'homme et des grands mammifères fossiles réputés caractéristiques de la dernière période géologique. *Annales des Sciences Naturelles* (Zoologie), 4$^e$ série 15: 177–253.

Laughlin, N.S. 1969. Foreword, in R.K. Nelson, *Hunters of the Northern Ice*, xiii–xvi. University of Chicago Press.

Laville, H. 1973. *Climatologie et Chronologie du Paléolithique en Périgord: Etude Sédimentologique de Dépôts en Grottes et sous Abris*. Thèse, Docteur des Sciences, Université de Bordeaux.

1975. Climatologie et chronologie du Paléolithique en Périgord: étude sédimentologique de dépôts en grottes et sous abris. *Etudes Quaternaires* 4. Marseille, Université de Provence.

1976. La Grotte du Pech-de-l'Azé. Livret-Guide de l'Excursion A4, Sud-Ouest (Aquitaine et Charente). Direction J-P. Rigaud et B. Vandermeersch, *IX$^e$ Congrès de l'Union Internationale des Sciences Préhistoriques et Protohistoriques*, 57–67. Nice.

Laville, H., Rigaud, J-P. and Sackett, J. 1980. *Rockshelters of the Perigord*. New York, Academic Press.

Lawrence, R. 1969. Aboriginal habitat and economy. *Australian National University Occasional Paper* 6.

Leach, E.R. 1981. Biology and social science: wedding or rape? *Nature* 291: 267–8. (Review of *Genes, Mind, and Culture: the Co-evolutionary Process*, by C.J. Lumsden and E.O. Wilson, Cambridge, Mass., Harvard University Press.

Leakey, R. and Lewin, R. 1977. *Origins*. London, Macdonald and Jane's.

Lee, R.B. 1968. What hunters do for a living, or, how to make out on scarce resources, in R.B. Lee and I. DeVore (eds.), *Man the Hunter*, 38–48. Chicago, Aldine.

1969. !Kung Bushman subsistence: an input-output analysis, in A.P. Vayda (ed.), *Environment and Cultural Behavior*, 47–79. New York, Natural History Press.

1972a. Work effort, group structure and land use in contemporary hunter-gatherers, in P.J. Ucko, R. Tringham and G.W. Dimbleby (eds.), *Man, Settlement and Urbanism*, 177–86. London, Duckworth.

1972b. Population growth and the beginnings of sedentary life among the !Kung Bushmen, in B. Spooner (ed.), *Population Growth: Anthropological Implications*, 329–42. Cambridge, Mass., M.I.T. Press.

1972c. The !Kung Bushmen of Botswana, in M.G. Bicchieri (ed.), *Hunters and Gatherers Today*, 326–68. New York, Holt, Rinehart and Winston.

1979. *The !Kung San*. Cambridge University Press.

Lee, R.B. and DeVore, I. (eds.) 1968a. *Man the Hunter*. Chicago, Aldine.

1968b. Problems in the study of hunter-gatherers, in R.B. Lee and I. DeVore (eds.), *Man the Hunter*, 3–12. Chicago, Aldine.

Lees, S. 1973. Sociopolitical aspects of canal irrigation in the Valley of Oaxaca. *Museum of Anthropology, University of Michigan Memoir* 6.

Legge, A.J. 1972. Cave climates, in E.S. Higgs (ed.), *Papers in Economic Prehistory*, 97–103. Cambridge University Press.

Lenoir, M. 1970. *Recherches Sédimentologiques concernant Quelques Gisements Magdaléniens de Guyenne Occidentale*. Thèse 3$^e$ cycle, Université de Bordeaux.

Leroi-Gourhan, A. 1965. *Treasures of Prehistoric Art*. New York, Abrams.

Leroi-Gourhan, Arl. 1959. Résultats de l'analyse pollinique de la grotte d'Isturitz. *Bulletin de la Société Préhistorique Française* 56: 619–24.

1967. Pollens et datation de la grotte de la Vache (Ariège). *Bulletin de la Société Préhistorique de l'Ariège* 22: 115–27.

1971a. Análisis polínico de Cueva Morín, in J. González Echegaray and L.G. Freeman (eds.), *Cueva Morín: Excavaciones 1966–1968*, 359–65. Santander, Patronato de las Cuevas Prehistóricas.

1971b. La fin du Tardiglaciaire et les industries préhistoriques (Pyrénées-Cantabres). *Munibe* 23: 249–54.

1980. Les interstades du Würm supérieur, in J. Chaline (ed.), *Problèmes de Stratigraphie Quaternaire en France et dans les Pays Limitrophes*, 192–4. Dijon, Association Française pour l'Etude du Quaternaire.

n.d. Análisis polínico, in G.A. Clark and L.G. Straus (eds.), *Excavaciones en la Cueva de la Riera (1976–1979): un Estudio Inicial*. Trabajos de Prehistoria.

Leroi-Gourhan, Arl. and Leroi-Gourhan A. 1964. Chronologie des grottes d'Arcy-sur-Cure (Yonne). *Gallia Préhistoire* 7: 1–64.

Lévêque, F. and Vandermeersch, B. 1980. Les découvertes de restes humains dans un horizon castelperronien de Saint-Césaire. *Bulletin de la Société Préhistorique Française* 77: 35.

Levine, M.A. 1979. Archaeo-zoological Analysis of Some Upper Pleistocene Horse Bone Assemblages in Western Europe. Unpublished Ph.D. dissertation, University of Cambridge.

Lewis, J.R. and Bowman, R.S. 1975. Local habitat-induced variations in the population dynamics of *Patella vulgata* L. *Journal of Experimental Marine Biology and Ecology* 17: 165–203.

Lewthwaite, J. 1981. Plains tails from the hills: transhumance in Mediterranean archaeology, in J.A. Sheridan and G.N. Bailey (eds.), *Economic Archaeology*, 57–66. Oxford, British Archaeological Reports International Series 96.

Lowe, V.P.W. 1967. Teeth as indicators of age with special reference to red deer (*Cervus elaphus*) of known age from Rhum. *Journal of Zoology* 152: 137–53.

de Lumley, H. 1971). *Le Paléolithique Inférieur et Moyen du Midi Méditerranéen dans son Cadre Géologique. II: Bas Languedoc-Rousillon-Catalogue*. Gallia Préhistoire 5$^e$ Supplement. Paris, C.N.R.S.

de Lumley, H. (ed.) 1976. *La Préhistoire Française*. Paris, C.N.R.S.

Lumsden, C.J. and Wilson, E.O. (1981) *Genes, Mind and Culture: the Coevolutionary process*, Cambridge, Mass., Harvard University Press.

Lustig-Arecco, V. 1975. *Technology: Strategies for Survival*. New York, Holt, Rinehart and Winston.

MacArthur, R.H. and Pianka, E. 1966. On optimal use of a patchy environment. *American Naturalist* 100: 603–9.

McBurney, C.B.M. 1973. From the beginnings of man to *c.* 33 000 B.C., In S. Piggott, G.E. Daniel and C.B.M. McBurney (eds.), *France before the Romans*, 9–29. Park Ridge, New Jersey, Noyes Press.

Macleod, D.A. and Vita-Finzi, C. 1982. Environment and provenance in the development of recent alluvial deposits in Epirus, north-west Greece. *Earth Surface Processes and Landforms* 7: 29–43.

MacNeish, R.S. 1964. Ancient Mesoamerican Civilization. *Science* 143: 531–7.

Madariaga, B. 1971. La fauna marina de la Cueva Morín, in J. González Echegaray and L.G. Freeman (eds.), *Cueva Morín: Excavaciones 1966–1968*, 401–15. Santander, Patronato de las Cuevas Prehistóricas.

1972. *Hermilio Alcalde del Rio: una Escuela de Prehistoria en Santander*. Santander, Patronato de las Cuevas Prehistóricas.

1980a. Estudio de las comunidades de moluscos de la cueva de El Pendo, in J. González Echegaray (ed.), *El Yacimiento de la Cueva de El Pendo*, 241–5. Bibliotheca Praehistórica Hispana 17.

1980b. La fauna marina de las cuevas de El Aguila, La Camara Superior y El Llongar. *Boletín del Instituto de Estudios Asturianos* 101: 703–9.

Madsen, A.P., Müller, S., Neergaard, C., Petersen, C.G.J., Rostrup, E., Steenstrup, K.J.V. and Winge, H. 1900. *Affaldsdynger fra Stenalderen i Danmark*. Copenhagen, C.A. Reitzel.

Mania, D. and Toepfer, V. 1973. *Königsaue*. Berlin, Veröffentlichungen des Landesmuseums für Vorgeschichte in Halle.

Mariezkurreña, K. 1979. Dataciones de radiocarbono existentes para la prehistoria vasca. *Munibe* 31: 237–55.

Marks, A.E. and Friedel, D.A. 1977. Prehistoric settlement patterns in the Avdat/Aqev, in A.E. Marks (ed.), *Prehistory and Paleoenvironments in the Central Negev, Israel: II. The Avdat/ Aqev Area Part 2 and the Har Harif*, 131–58. Dallas, Southern Methodist University.

Marks, S.A. 1976. *Large Mammals and a Brave People*. Seattle, University of Washington Press.

Marshack, A. 1976. Some implications of the paleolithic symbolic evidence for the origin of language. In S.R. Harnad, H.D. Steklis and J. Lancaster (eds.), *Origins and Evolution of Language and Speech*. Annals of the New York Academy of Science 280: 289–311.

Marstrander, S. 1956. Hovedlinjer i Trondelags forhistorie. *Viking* 20: 1–69.

Martínez Alvarez, J.A. 1965. *Rasgos Geológicos de la Zona Oriental de Asturias*. Oviedo, Instituto de Estudios Asturianos.

1975. Síntesis estratigráfica de Asturias. *Boletín del Instituto de Estudios Asturianos, Supl. Ciencias* 20: 135–58.

Mary, G., Medus, J. and Delibrias, G. 1975. Le Quaternaire de la côte Asturienne (Espagne). *Bulletin de l'Association Française pour l'Etude de Quaternaire* 42: 13–23.

Masters, P.M. and Flemming, N.C. (eds.) 1983. *Quaternary Coastlines and Marine Archaeology*. London, Academic Press.

Mathiassen, T. 1942. Bopladsen Dyrholm og dens betydning for den jyske Ertebøllekulturens kronologi, in T. Mathiassen, M. Degerbøl and J. Troels-Smith (eds.), Dyrholmen: en stenalderboplads på Djursland. *Det Kongelige Dansk Videnskabernes Selskab Arkæologisk-Kunsthistorisk Skrifter* 1: 3–75.

Mayor, M. and Diaz, T. 1977. *La Flora Asturiana*. Gijón, Ediciones Ayalga, S.A.

Mech, L.D. 1970. *The Wolf: the Ecology and Behavior of an Endangered Species*. New York, Natural History Press.

Megaw, J.V.S. (ed.) 1977. *Hunters, Gatherers and First Farmers beyond Europe*. Leicester University Press.

Meillassoux, C. 1973. On the mode of production of the hunting band, in P. Alexandre (ed.), *French Perspectives in African Studies*, 187–203. Oxford University Press.

Mellars, P.A. 1973. The character of the middle–upper palaeolithic transition in southwest France, in C. Renfrew (ed.), *The Explanation of Culture Change*, 255–76. London, Duckworth.

1974. The palaeolithic and mesolithic, in C. Renfrew (ed.), *British Prehistory*, 41–99. Park Ridge, New Jersey, Noyes Press.

1975. Ungulate populations, economic patterns and the mesolithic landscape, in J.G. Evans, S. Limbrey and H. Cleere (eds.), *The Effect of Man on the Landscape: the Highland Zone*, 49–56. London, Council for British Archaeology.

1978. Excavation and economic analysis of mesolithic shell middens on the island of Oronsay (Inner Hebrides), in P.A. Mellars (ed.), *The Early Postglacial Settlement of Northern Europe*, 371–96. London, Duckworth.

Méroc, L. 1953. La conquête des Pyrénées par l'homme et le rôle de la frontière pyrénéenne au cours de temps préhistoriques.

*1ᵉʳ Congrès International de Spéléologie, IV, 4*, 33–51. Paris.

Mertz, E.L. 1924. Oversigt over de sen- og postglaciale niveauforandringer i Danmark. *Danmarks Geologiske Undersøgelse Series 2* 41: 1–50.

Mikkelson, E. 1975. Mesolithic in Southeastern Norway. *Norwegian Archaeological Review* 8: 19–35.

Miquel, H. 1931. Découverte de haches de type acheuléen et moustérien dans une haute vallée de l'Ariège. *Bulletin de la Société d'Histoire Naturelle de Toulouse* 61: 381–3.

Mitchell, B. 1967. Growth layers in dental cement for determining the age of red deer (*Cervus elaphus* L.). *Journal of Animal Ecology* 36: 279–93.

Mitchell, B., Staines, B.W. and Welch, D. 1977. *Ecology of Red Deer*. Cambridge, Institute of Terrestrial Ecology, Natural Environment Research Council.

Moe, D., Indrelid, S. and Kjos-Hanssen, O. 1978. A study of environment and early man in the southern Norwegian highlands. *Norwegian Archaeological Review* 11: 73–84.

Møhl, U. 1970a. Oversigt over dyreknoglerne fra Ølby Lyng, en østsjællandsk kystboplads med Ertebøllekultur. *Aarbøger for Nordisk Oldkyndighed og Historie* 1970: 43–77.

1970b. Fangstdyrene ved de danske strande. *Kuml* 1970: 297–329.

1978. Aggersund-bopladsen zoologisk belyst: svanejagt som årsag til bosættelse? *Kuml* 1978: 57–76.

Mohr, E. 1971. *The Asiatic Wild Horse*. London, Allen.

Mörner, N-A. and Dreimanis, A. 1973. The Erie interstade. *Geological Society of America Memoir* 136: 107–34.

Morris, D. 1965. *The Mammals: a Guide to Living Species*. Zoological Society of London. London, Hodder and Stoughton.

Morris, P. 1972. A review of mammalian age determination methods. *Mammal Review* 2: 69–104.

Moser, F. 1976. Les remplissages des grottes et abris sous basalte en Haute-Loire, in H. de Lumley (ed.), *La Préhistoire Française*, I: 271–4. Paris, C.N.R.S.

Moure Romanillo, J.A. 1975. *Excavaciones en la Cueva de 'Tito Bustillo' (Asturias): Campañas de 1972 y 1974*. Oviedo, Instituto de Estudios Asturianos.

Moure Romanillo, J.A. and Cano Herrera, M. 1976. *Excavaciones en la Cueva de 'Tito Bustillo' (Asturias): Trabajos de 1975*. Oviedo, Instituto de Estudios Asturianos.

1978. Magdalenian habitation structure at Tito Bustillo Cave (Asturias, Spain). *Current Anthropology* 19: 392–4.

Mourer-Chauviré, C. 1962. *Les Gisements Fossilifères Quaternaires de Chatillon-Saint-Jean (Drôme)*. Thèse, 3ᵉ cycle, Université de Lyon.

1975. Conclusions générales sur les faunes de l'Aven I des Abîmes de la Fage (Corrèze). *Nouvelles Archives du Muséum d'Histoire Naturelle de Lyon* 13: 123–9.

1976. Les gisements de Chatillon-Saint-Jean. Livret-Guide de l'Excursion A8, Bassin du Rhone, Paléolithique et Néolithique. Direction J. Combier and J-P. Thevenot, 166–9. *IXᵉ Congrès de l'Union Internationale des Sciences Préhistoriques et Protohistoriques*, Nice.

Mourer-Chauviré, C. and Philippe, M. 1972. Géométrie du gisement paléontologique de la Fage. *Nouvelles Archives du Muséum d'Histoire Naturelle de Lyon* 10: 11–20.

Müller-Beck, H-J. 1957. *Das Obere Altpaläolithikum in Suddeutschland*, 1. Bonn, Habelt.

1961. Comments on Movius. *Current Anthropology* 2: 439–44.

Mulvaney, D.J. 1976. 'The chain of connection': the material evidence, in N. Peterson (ed.), *Tribes and Boundaries in Australia*, 72–94. Canberra, Australian Institute of Aboriginal Studies.

Musil, R. 1970. Domestication of the dog already in the Magdalenian? *Anthropologie* 8: 87–8.

Naber, F., Berenguer, D. and Zalles-Flossbach, C. 1976. L'art parietal paléolithique en Europe Romane. *Bonner Hefte zur Vorgeschichte* 14–16.

de Nahlik, A.J. 1959. *Wild Deer.* London, Faber.

Nelson, E.W. 1899. The Eskimo about Bering Strait. *Smithsonian Institution, Bureau of American Ethnology 18th Annual Report.*

Nelson, R.K. 1969. *Hunters of the Northern Ice.* University of Chicago Press.

Netboy, A. 1968. *The Atlantic Salmon: A Vanishing Species?* Boston, Houghton Mifflin.

Nie, N.H., Hull, C.H., Jenkins, J.G., Steinbrenner, K. and Bent, D.H. 1975. *Statistical Package for the Social Sciences.* New York, McGraw-Hill.

Nielsen, E.S. 1938. De danske farvandes hydrografi i Litorinatiden. *Meddelelser fra Dansk Geologisk Forening* 9: 337–50.

Noval, A. 1976. *La Fauna Salvaje Asturiana.* Gijón, Ediciones Ayalga, S.A.

Nummedal, A. 1929. Stone Age finds in Finnmark. *Institutt for Sammenlignende Kulturforskning Series B* 13. Oslo.

Oberg, K. 1973. The social economy of the Tlingit Indians. *Monograph of the American Ethnological Society* 55.

Obermaier, H. 1925. 2nd edn. El hombre fósil. *Comisión de Investigaciones Paleontológicas y Prehistóricas* 9. Madrid.

Odell, G.H. and Odell-Vereecken, F. 1980. Verifying the reliability of lithic use-wear assessments by 'blind tests': the low-power approach. *Journal of Field Archaeology* 7: 87–120.

Odner, K. 1966. Komsakulturen i Nesseby og Sφr Varanger. *Tromsφ Museum Skrifter* 12.

Odum, E. 1971. *Fundamentals of Ecology.* Philadelphia, Saunders.

Odum, H. and Copeland, B. 1974. Functional classification of the coastal systems of the United States, in E. McMahan, H. Odum and B. Copeland (eds.), *Coastal Ecological Systems in the United States,* 5–24. Washington, Conservation Foundation.

Osborn, A.J. 1977. Strandloopers, mermaids and other fairy tales: ecological determinants of marine resource utilization – the Peruvian case. In L.R. Binford (ed.), *For Theory Building in Archaeology,* 157–205. New York, Academic Press.

Oswalt, W.H. 1973. *Habitat and Technology.* New York, Holt, Rinehart and Winston.

1976. *An Anthropological Analysis of Food-Getting Technology.* New York, Wiley.

Otte, M. 1976. L'Aurignacien en Belgique, in J.K. Kozlowski (ed.), *Actes due IX$^e$ Congrès de l'Union Internationale des Sciences Préhistoriques et Protohistoriques, Colloque IX, Prétirage,* 144–63. Nice.

1977. Deux coquilles probablement d'origine anglaise, découvertes a Spy, Belgique, in J.B. Campbell (ed.), *The Upper Palaeolithic of Britain,* I, 211–12. Oxford University Press.

Paine, R. 1971. Animals as capital: comparisons among northern nomadic herders and hunters. *Anthropological Quarterly* 44: 157–72.

Pales, L. 1976. *Les Gravures de la March, II: Les Humains.* Paris, Ophrys.

Paludan-Müller, C. 1978. High Atlantic food gathering in northwestern Zealand, ecological conditions and spatial representation, in K. Kristiansen and C. Paludan-Müller (eds.), *New Directions in Scandinavian Archaeology,* 120–57. Copenhagen, National Museum of Denmark.

Paquereau, M. 1976. La vegetation au pleistocène supérieur et au début de l'holocene dans le Sud-Ouest, in H. de Lumley (ed.), *La Préhistoire Francaise,* 525–30. Paris, C.N.R.S.

Parkington, J.E. 1976. Coastal settlement between the mouths of the Berg and Olifants Rivers, Cape Province. *South African Archaeological Bulletin* 31: 127–40.

1980. Time and place: some observations on spatial and temporal patterning in the later Stone Age sequence in southern Africa. *South African Archaeological Bulletin* 35: 73–83.

Parmalee, P.W. and Klippel, W.E. 1974. Freshwater mussels as a prehistoric food resource. *American Antiquity* 39: 421–34.

Passemard, E. 1920. L'Abri Olha (Basses-Pyr.). *Association Française pour l'Avancement des Sciences, Strasbourg,* 553–60.

1922. La Caverne d'Isturitz (Basses Pyr.). *Revue Archéologique* 15: 1–45.

1935/6. Le Moustérien à l'Abri Olha en Pays Basque. *Revue Lorraine d'Anthropologie* 1935/6: 3–46.

1944. La Caverne d'Isturitz en Pays Basque. *Préhistoire* 9: 7–95.

Payne, R.H., Child, A.R. and Forrest, A. 1971. Geographical variation in the Atlantic Salmon. *Nature* 231: 250–2.

Payne, S. 1972a. Partial recovery and sample bias: the result of some sieving experiments, in E.S. Higgs (ed.), *Papers in Economic Prehistory,* 47–64. Cambridge University Press.

1972b. On the interpretation of bone samples from archaeological sites, in E.S. Higgs (ed.), *Papers in Economic Prehistory,* 65–82. Cambridge University Press.

1973. Kill-off patterns in sheep and goats: the mandibles from Aşvan Kale. *Anatolian Studies* 23: 281–303.

Perez, M. 1977. Presentación de algunos materiales procedentes de la Cueva Oscura de Ania (Las Regueras, Asturias). *Actas del XIV$^o$ Congreso Arqueológico Nacional,* 179–96. Universidad de Zaragoza.

Pericot García, L. 1942. *La Cueva del Parpalló.* Madrid, C.S.I.C.

1968. La vida económica de España durante el Paleolítico Superior, in M. Tarradell (ed.), *Estudios de Economía Antigua de la Peninsula Ibérica,* 19–31. Barcelona, Editorial Vicens-Vives.

Perkins, D. 1964. Prehistoric fauna from Shanidar, Iraq. *Science* 144: 1565–6.

1969. Fauna of Çatal Hüyük: evidence for early cattle domestication in Anatolia. *Science* 164: 177–9.

Perlman, S.M. 1976. Optimum Diet Models and Prehistoric Hunter-Gatherers: a Test on Martha's Vineyard. Unpublished Ph.D. dissertation, University of Massachusetts, Amherst.

1980. An optimum diet model, coastal variability, and hunter-gatherer behavior, in M.B. Schiffer (ed.), *Advances in Archaeological Method and Theory* III, 257–310. New York, Academic Press.

Peterson, G.M., Webb, T., Kutzbach, J.E., van der Hammen, T., Wijmstra, T.A. and Street, F.A. 1979. The continental record of environmental conditions at 18 000 yr B.P.: an initial evaluation. *Quaternary Research* 12: 47–82.

Peterson, N. (ed.) 1976a. *Tribes and Boundaries in Australia.* Canberra, Australian Institute of Aboriginal Studies.

1976b. The natural and cultural areas of Aboriginal Australia, in N. Peterson (ed.), *Tribes and Boundaries in Australia,* 50–71. Canberra, Australian Institute of Aboriginal Studies.

Peyrony, D. 1949. *Le Périgord Préhistorique: Essai de Géographie Humaine.* Périgueux, Société Historique et Archéologique du Périgord.

Philippe, M. 1970. Trois années de fouilles paléontologiques à Jaurens. *Compte-Rendu d'Activités Annuelles de l'Association Régionale pour le Développement des Recherches de Paléontologie et de Préhistoire et des Amis du Muséum,* 90–2.

1971. Fouilles paléontologiques de Jaurens et de Baudran (19): 1971. *Compte-Rendu d'Activités Annuelles de l'Association Regionale pour le Développement des Recherches de Paléontologie et de Préhistoire et des Amis du Muséum,* 74–81.

Piette, E. 1889. *Les Subdivisions de l'Epoque Magdalénienne et de l'Epoque Néolithique.* Angers, Imprimerie Burdin.

1891. 2nd edn. Notions nouvelles sur l'Age du Renne. Annexe A, in A. Bertrand (ed.), *Nos Origines: La Gaule avant les Gaulois,* 262–86. Paris, E. Leroux.

1895. Hiatus et lacune: vestiges de la période de transition dans la grotte du Mas d'Azil. *Bulletin de la Société d'Anthropologie de Paris, 4e série* 6: 235–67.

Piningre, J-F. and Vuillemey, M. 1976. Les civilisations du paléolithique moyen en Franche-Comte, in H. de Lumley (ed.), *La Préhistoire Française*, I: 1120–30. Paris, C.N.R.S.

Pitts, M. 1979. Hides and antlers: a new look at the gatherer-hunter site at Star Carr, North Yorkshire, England. *World Archaeology* 11: 32–42.

Plog, S. 1980. *Stylistic Variation in Prehistoric Ceramics*. Cambridge University Press.

Poplin, F. 1976. *Les Grands Vertébrés de Gönnersdorf, Fouilles 1968 (Gönnersdorf) 2*. Wiesbaden, Franz Steiner.

Prat, F. 1968. *Recherches sur les Equidés Pleistocènes en France*. Thèse de Doctorat, Faculté des Sciences de Bordeaux.

Quimby, D.C. and Gaab, J.E. 1957. Mandibular dentition as an age indicator in Rocky Mountain Elk. *Journal of Wildlife Management* 21: 435–51.

Rappaport, R.A. 1969. Ritual regulation of environmental relations among a New Guinea people, in A.P. Vayda (ed.), *Environment and Cultural Behavior*. New York, Natural History Press.

Reed, C.A. (ed.) 1977. *Origins of Agriculture*. The Hague, Mouton.

Reidhead, V.A. 1979. Linear programming models in archaeology. *Annual Review of Anthropology* 8: 543–78.

1980. The economics of subsistence change: a test of an optimization model, in T.K. Earle and A.L. Christenson (eds.), *Modeling Change in Prehistoric Subsistence Economies*, 141–86. New York, Academic Press.

Renfrew, C. 1975. Trade as action at a distance: questions of interaction and communication, In J.A. Sabloff and C.C. Lamberg-Karlovsky (eds.), *Ancient Civilization and Trade*, 3–59. Albuquerque, University of New Mexico Press.

Rick, J.W. 1980. *Prehistoric Hunters of the High Andes*. New York, Academic Press.

Rigaud, J-P. 1978. The significance of variability among lithic artifacts: a specific case from southwestern France. *Journal of Anthropological Research* 34: 299–310.

1979. A propos des industries magdaléniennes du Flageolet, in D. de Sonneville-Bordes (ed.), *La Fin des Temps Glaciaires en Europe*, I: 467–9. Paris, C.N.R.S.

Rindos, D. 1980. Symbiosis, instability, and the origins and spread of agriculture: a new model. *Current Anthropology* 21: 751–72.

Roper, D.C. 1979. The method and theory of site catchment analysis: a review, in M.B. Schiffer (ed.), *Advances in Archaeological Method and Theory*, II, 119–40. New York, Academic Press.

Rosenfeld, A. 1977. Profile figures: schematisation of the human figure in the Magdalenian culture of Europe, in P.J. Ucko (ed.), *Form in Indigenous Art*, 92–109. Canberra, Australian Institute of Aboriginal Studies.

Rosselló, V.M. 1971. Notas sobre la geomorfología litoral del sur de Valencia (España). *Quaternaria* 15: 121–44.

1972. Los ríos Júcar y Turia en la genesis de la Albufera de Valencia. *Saitabi* 22: 129–417.

Roule, L. and Regnault, F. 1895. Un maxillaire inférieur humain trouvé dans une grotte des Pyrénées. *Comptes rendus de l'Académie des Sciences, Paris* 121: 141–3.

Rowlett, R.M. and Schneider, M.J. 1974. The material expression of neanderthal child care, in M. Richardson (ed.), *The Human Mirror*, 41–58. Baton Rouge, Louisiana State University Press.

Rowley-Conwy, P.A. 1980. Continuity and Change in the Prehistoric Economies of Denmark 3700 bc–2300 bc. Unpublished Ph.D. dissertation, University of Cambridge.

1981. Mesolithic Danish bacon: permanent and temporary sites in the Danish mesolithic, in J.A. Sheridan and G.N. Bailey (eds.), *Economic Archaeology*, 51–6. Oxford, British Archaeological Reports International Series 96.

Rozoy, J-G. 1978. *Les Derniers Chasseurs*. Bulletin de la Société Archéologique Champenoise, Special No. June 1978. Reims, Imprimerie de Compiègne.

Rubenstein, D.I. 1978. Islands and their effects on the social organization of feral horses. Contribution to the 1978 ABS Symposium, *Social Behaviour of Islands*. Unpublished manuscript.

Sacchi, D. 1976. Cauna de Belvis, Aude. Livret-Guide de l'Excursion C2, Provence et Languedoc Méditerranéen, Sites Paléolithiques et Néolithiques, 306–12. Direction H. de Lumley. *IX<sup>e</sup> Congrès de l'Union Internationale des Sciences Préhistoriques et Proto-historiques*. Nice.

Sacchi, D. and Abelanet, J. 1980. Quelques données archéologiques sur le peuplement Paléolithique Supérieur du Conflent. *Actes du LI<sup>e</sup> Congrès de la Fédération Historique du Languedoc Méditerranéen et du Roussillon*, 11–29.

Sackett, J.R. 1973. Style, function and artifact variability in palaeolithic assemblages, in C. Renfrew (ed.), *The Explanation of Culture Change*, 317–25. London, Duckworth.

1977. The meaning of style in archaeology: a general model. *American Antiquity* 42: 369–80.

1982. Approaches to style in lithic archaeology, *Journal of Anthropological Archaeology* 1: 59–112.

Sahlins, M.D. 1974. *Stone age Economics*. London, Tavistock.

de Saint-Périer, R. 1920. Les migrations des tribus magdaléniennes Pyrénées. *Revue Anthropologique* 30: 136–41.

1924. Les fouilles de 1923 dans la grotte des Rideaux à Lespugue (Hte. Gar.). *L'Anthropologie* 34: 1–15.

1928. Engins de pêche paléolithiques. *L'Anthropologie* 38: 17–22.

1930. *La Grotte d'Isturitz. I: Le Magdalénien de la Salle de St.-Martin. Institut de Paléontologie Humaine* 7. Paris, Masson.

1936. *La Grotte d'Isturitz. II: Le Magdalénien de la Grande Salle. Institut de Paléontologie Humaine* 17. Paris, Masson.

de Saint-Périer, R. and de Saint-Périer, R.S. 1952. *La Grotte d'Isturitz. III: Les Solutréens, les Aurignaciens et les Moustériens. Institut de Paléontologie Humaine* 25: Paris, Masson.

Schalk, R.F. 1977. The structure of an anadromous fish resource, in L.R. Binford (ed.), *For Theory Building in Archaeology*, 207–50. New York, Academic Press.

Scheitlin, T. and Glark, G.A. 1978. Three-dimensional surface representations of lithic categories at Liencres. *Newsletter of Computer Archaeology* 13: 1–13.

Schiffer, M.B. 1976. *Behavioral Archaeology*. New York, Academic Press.

Schild, R. 1976. The final Palaeolithic settlements of the European Plain. *Scientific American* 234: 88–99.

Schoener, T.W. 1971. Theory of feeding strategies. *Annual Review of Ecology and Systematics* 2: 369–404.

Schrire, C. 1980. An inquiry into the evolutionary status and apparent identity of San hunter-gatherers. *Human Ecology* 8: 9–32.

Schwabedissen, H. 1970. Zur verbreitung der Faustkeile in Mitteleuropa, in H. Schwabedissen (ed.), *Frühe Menscheit und Umwelt* 61–98. Köln, Fundamenta series A, II.

Serjeant, R.B. 1976. *South Arabian Hunt*. London, Luzac.

Service, E.R. 1966. *The Hunters*, New Jersey, Prentice-Hall.

1971. *Profiles in Ethnology*. New York, Harper and Row.

Shackelton, J.C. and van Andel, T.H. 1980. Prehistoric shell assemblages from Francthi Cave and evolution of the adjacent coastal zone. *Nature* 288: 357–9.

Shackleton, N.J. 1969. The last interglacial in the marine and terrestrial records. *Proceedings of the Royal Society of London B* 174: 135–54.

1977. The oxygen isotope stratigraphic record of the Late Pleistocene. *Philosophical Transactions of the Royal Society of London B* 280: 169–82.

Shackleton, N.J., Imbrie, J. and Hall, M.A. In prep. Oxygen and carbon isotope record of core V19–30: implications for the formation of deep water in the Late Pleistocene North Atlantic.

Sharpe, L. 1952. Steel axes for stone age Australians, in E.H. Spicer (ed.), *Human Problems in Technological Change*, 69–90. New York, Russel Sage.

Sheridan, J.A. and Bailey, G.N. (eds.) 1981. *Economic Archaeology*. Oxford, British Archaeological Reports International Series 96.

Siegel, S. 1956. *Nonparametric Statistics for the Behavioural Sciences*. New York, McGraw-Hill.

Sieveking, A. 1976. Settlement patterns of the later Magdalenian in the central Pyrenees, in G. de G. Sieveking, I.H. Longworth and K.E. Wilson (eds.), *Problems in Economic and Social Archaeology*, 583–603. London, Duckworth.

  1979. *The Cave Artists*. London, Thames and Hudson.

Silberbauer, G.B. 1972. The G/Wi Bushmen, in M.G. Bicchieri (ed.), *Hunters and Gatherers Today*, 271–326. New York, Holt, Rinehart and Winston.

Skaarup, J. 1973. *Hesselø-Sølager: Jagdstationen der Südskandinavischen Trichterbecherkultur*. Copenhagen, Akademisk Forlag (Arkæologiske Studier 1).

Smiley, F.E., Sinopoli, C.M., Jackson, H., Wills, W.H. and Gregg, S.A. (eds.) 1980. The archaeological correlates of hunter-gatherer societies: studies from the ethnographic record. *Michigan Discussions in Anthropology*, 5.

Smith, B. 1979. Measuring the selective utilization of animal species by prehistoric human populations. *American Antiquity* 44: 155–60.

Smith, C.A. (ed.) 1976. *Regional Analysis: Economic Systems*. New York, Academic Press.

Smith, E.S. 1979. Human adaptation and energetic efficiency. *Human Ecology* 7: 53–74.

Smith, J.G.E. 1978. Economic uncertainty in an 'original affluent society': caribou and caribou eater Chipewyan adaptive strategies. *Arctic Anthropology* 15: 68–88.

Sømme, A. 1961. *A Geography of Norden*. Oslo, J.W. Cappelans.

de Sonneville-Bordes, D. 1960. *Le Paléolithique Supérieur en Périgord*. Bordeaux, Delmas.

  1963. Upper Paleolithic cultures of western Europe. *Science* 143: 347–55.

  1966. L'évolution du Paléolithique Supérieur en Europe occidentale et sa signification. *Bulletin de la Société Préhistorique Française* 63: 3–34.

  1973. The Upper Palaeolithic, in S. Piggott, G.E. Daniel and C.B.M. McBurney (eds.), *France before the Romans*, 30–60. Park Ridge, New Jersey, Noyes Press.

de Sonneville-Bordes, D. and Perrot, J. 1953. Essai d'adaptation des méthodes statistiques au Paléolithique Supérieur: premiers résultats. *Bulletin de la Société Préhistorique Française* 50: 323–33.

Sordinas, A. 1969. Investigations of the prehistory of Corfu during 1964–1966. *Balkan Studies* 10: 393–424.

Spencer, R.F. 1959. *The North Alaskan Eskimo*. New York, Dover Publications.

Spiess, A. 1976. Determining season of death of archaeological fauna by analysis of teeth. *Arctic* 29: 53–5.

  1979. *Reindeer and Caribou Hunters: an Archaeological Study*. New York, Academic Press.

Spinage, C.A. 1971. Geratodontology and horn growth of the impala (*Aepyceros melampus*). *Journal of Zoology* (London) 164: 209–25.

  1972. Age estimation of zebra. *East African Wildlife Journal* 10: 273–7.

  1973. A review of the age determination of mammals by means of teeth, with especial reference to Africa. *East African Wildlife Journal* 11: 165–87.

Spooner, B. (ed.) 1972. *Population Growth: Anthropological Implications*. Cambridge, Mass., M.I.T. Press.

Sterud, E. 1973. A paradigmatic view of prehistory, in C. Renfrew (ed.), *The Explanation of Culture Change*, 3–18. London, Duckworth.

Sterud, E., Straus, L.G. and Abramovitz, K. 1980. Recent developments in Old World archaeology. *American Antiquity* 35: 759–86.

Steward, J.H. 1969. Postscript to bands: on taxonomy, processes and causes, in D. Damas (ed.), *Contributions to Anthropology: Band Societies*, 288–95. Ottawa, National Museums of Canada, Bulletin 228, Anthropological Series 84.

Straus, L.G. 1974a. Notas preliminares sobre el Solutrense de Asturias. *Boletín del Instituto de Estudios Asturianos* 82: 483–504.

  1974b. Le Solutréen du Pays Basque espagnol: une ésquisse de données. *Munibe* 26: 173–81.

  1975a. A Study of the Solutrean in Vasco-Cantabrian Spain. Unpublished Ph.D. dissertation, University of Chicago.

  1975b. Solutrense o Magdaleniense inferior: significado de las 'diferencias'. *Boletín del Instituto de Estudios Asturianos* 86: 781–90.

  1975c. El Solutrense de las cuevas de Castillo y Hornos de la Peña (Santander). *Trabajos de Prehistoria* 32: 9–19.

  1976a. A new interpretation of the Cantabrian Solutrean. *Current Anthropology* 17: 342–3.

  1976b. Le Solutréen d'Isturitz et du Pays Basque: outillage lithique, in M. Escalon de Fonton (ed.), *Actes due XX$^e$ Congrès Préhistorique de France*, 595–604. Provence, C.N.R.S.

  1976c. Análisis arqueológico de la fauna paleolítica del Norte de la Península Ibérica. *Munibe* 28: 277–85.

  1977a. Of deerslayers and mountain men: paleolithic faunal exploitation in Cantabrian Spain, in L.R. Binford (ed.), *For Theory Building in Archaeology*, 41–76. New York, Academic Press.

  1977b. The Upper Palaeolithic cave site of Altamira (Santander, Spain). *Quaternaria* 19: 135–48.

  1977c. El Solutrense Cantábrico, in *XL Aniversario del Centro de Estudios Montañenses*, III: 309–19. Santander, Institución Cultural de Cantabria.

  1977d. Pointes solutréennes et l'hypothèse de territorialisme. *Bulletin de la Société Préhistorique Française* 74: 206–12.

  1977e. Thoughts on Solutrean concave base point distribution. *Lithic Technology* 6: 32–5.

  1977f. Posible atribución al Solutrense del yacimiento de la Pasiega (Puente Viesgo, Santander). *Ampurias* 36: 217–23.

  1978a. Observaciones preliminares sobre la variabilidad de las puntas solutrenses. *Trabajos de Prehistoria* 35: 397–402.

  1978b. Variabilité dans les industries solutréennes de l'Espagne cantabrique. *Bulletin de la Société Préhistorique Française* 75: 276–80.

  1978c. Of Neanderthal hillbillies, origin myths and stone tools: notes on Upper Palaeolithic assemblage variability. *Lithic Technology* 7: 36–9.

  1979a. Caves: a palaeoanthropological resource. *World Archaeology* 10: 331–9.

  1979b. Mesolithic adaptations along the northern coast of Spain. *Quaternaria* 21: 305–27.

  1979c. Cantabria and Vascongadas, 21 000–17 000 b.p.: toward a Solutrean settlement pattern. *Munibe* 31: 195–202.

  1979d. Notas teóricas sobre el Solutrense de Asturias. *Boletín del Instituto de Estudios Asturianos* 96/97: 473–84.

  1980a. Comment: the identification of prehistoric hunter-gatherer aggregation sites: the case of Altamira. *Current Anthropology* 21: 624–5.

  1980b. The role of raw materials in lithic assemblage variability. *Lithic Technology* 9: 68–72.

  1981a. On the habitat and diet of *Cervus elaphus*. *Munibe* 33: 175–82.

1981b. On marine hunter-gatherers: a view from Cantabrian Spain. *Munibe* 33: 171–3.

n.d. Comparison of La Riera assemblages with contemporary Cantabrian ones. Unpublished manuscript.

Straus, L.G. and Glark, G.A. 1978a. La Riera paleoecological project: preliminary report, 1977 excavations. *Current Anthropology* 19: 455–6.

1978b. Prehistoric investigations in Cantabrian Spain. *Journal of Field Archaeology* 5: 289–317.

1979. La Riera paleoecological project: preliminary report, 1978 excavations. *Current Anthropology* 20: 235–6.

Straus, L.G. Clark, G.A. and González, M. 1978. Cronología de las industrias del Würm Tardio y del Holoceno Temprano en Cantabria: contribuciones del Proyecto Paleoecológico La Riera, in M. Almagro Gorbea (ed.), *C-14 y la Prehistoria de la Peninsula Ibérica*, 37–43. Madrid, Fundación Juan March.

Straus, L.G. Bernaldo, F., Cabrera, V. and Clark, G.A. 1977. New radiocarbon dates for the Spanish Solutrean. *Antiquity* 51: 243.

Straus, L.G., Cabrera, V., Bernaldo, F. and Clark, G.A. 1978. Solutrean chronology and lithic variability in Vasco Cantabrian Spain. *Zephyrus* 28–9: 109–12.

Straus, L.G., Clark, G.A., Altuna, J. and Ortea, J.A. 1980. Ice-age subsistence in northern Spain. *Scientific American* 242: 142–52.

Straus, L.G., Altuna, J., Clark, G.A., González, M., Laville, H., Leroi-Gourhan, Arl, Menéndez, M. and Ortea, J.A. 1981. *Current Anthropology* 22: 655–74.

Struever, S. and Houart, G.L. 1972. An analysis of the Hopewell interaction sphere. In E.N. Wilmsen (ed.) *Social Exchange and Interaction.* Anthropological Papers, Museum of Anthropology, University of Michigan 46: 47–79. Ann Arbor.

Stringer, C.B. 1974. Population relationships of Later Pleistocene hominids: a multivariate study of available crania. *Journal of Archaeological Science* 1: 317–42.

Stuckenrath, R. 1978. Dataciones de carbono 14, in J. González Echegaray and L.G. Freeman (eds.), *Vida y Muerte en Cueva Morin*, 215. Santander, Institución Cultural de Cantabria.

Sturdy, D.A. 1972. Reindeer Economies in Late Ice Age Europe. Unpublished Ph.D. dissertation, University of Cambridge.

1975. Some reindeer economies in prehistoric Europe, in E.S. Higgs (ed.), *Palaeoeconomy*, 55–95. Cambridge University Press.

Suttles, W. 1968. Coping with abundance: subsistence on the Northwest Coast, in R.B. Lee and I. DeVore (eds.), *Man the Hunter*, 56–68. Chicago, Aldine.

Swadling, P. 1976. Changes induced by human exploitation in prehistoric shellfish populations. *Mankind* 10: 156–62.

Swanson, E. (ed.) 1975. *Lithic Technology: Making and Using Stone Tools.* The Hague, Mouton.

Tauber, H. 1973. Copenhagen radiocarbon dates X. *Radiocarbon* 15: 86–112.

de Terán, M. 1947. Vaqueros y cabañas en los Montes de Pas. *Estudios geográficos* 28: 493–536.

Thomas, D.H. (1973). An empirical test for Steward's model of Great Basin settlement patterns, *American Antiquity* 38: 155–76.

Thomas, R.A., Griffith, D., Wise, C. and Artusy, R. Jr. 1975. Environmental adaptation on Delaware's coastal plain. *Archaeology of Eastern North America* 3: 35–90.

Thomson, D.F. 1962. The Bindibu expedition. *Geographical Journal* 128: 1–14, 143–57, 262–78.

von Thünen, J.H. 1875. *Der Isolierte Staat in Beziehung auf Landwirtschaft und Nationalökonomie*, 3rd edn. Hamburg.

Tilley, C.Y. 1981. Economy and society: what relationship? In J.A. Sheridan and G.N. Bailey (eds.), *Economic Archaeology*, 131-48. Oxford, British Archaeological Reports International Series 96.

Tindale, N.B. 1953. Tribal and intertribal marriage among the Australian Aborigines. *Human Biology* 25: 169–90.

1974. *Aboriginal Tribes of Australia.* Berkeley, University of California.

Trigger, B.G. 1970. Aims in prehistoric archaeology. *Antiquity* 44: 26–37.

Tyler, S.J. 1969. The Behaviour and Social Organisation of the New Forest Ponies. Unpublished Ph.D. dissertation, University of Cambridge.

Ucko, P.J. and Rosenfeld, A. 1967. *Palaeolithic Cave Art.* London, Weidenfeld and Nicolson.

Utrilla, P. 1974. Reflexiones en torno a la industria lítica del Magdaleniense inicial cantábrico. *Munibe* 26: 183–92.

1976. *Las Industrias del Magdaleniense Inferior y Medio en la Costa Cantábrica.* Universidad de Zaragoza, Departamento de Historia Antigua.

Van den Brink, F.H. 1967. *A Field Guide to the Mammals of Britain and Europe.* London, Collins.

Vega del Sella, R., Duque de Estrada, Conde de la, 1914. La cueva del Penicial (Asturias). *Comisión de Investigaciones Paleontológicas y Prehistóricas* 4. Madrid.

1916. El Paleolítico de Cueto de la Mina. *Comisión de Investigaciones Paleontológicas y Prehistóricas* 13. Madrid.

1921. El Paleolítico de Cueva Morín (Santander) y notas para la climatología cuaternaria. *Comisión de Investigaciones Paleontológicas y Prehistóricas* 29. Madrid.

1923. El Asturiense, nueva industria pre-neolítica. *Comisión de Investigaciones Paleontológicas y Prehistóricas* 32. Madrid.

1930. Las cuevas de La Riera y Balmori. *Comisión de Investigaciones Paleontológicas y Prehistóricas* 38. Madrid.

Vézian, J. 1971. La grotte du Portel, commune de Loubens (Ariège). *Bulletin de la Société d'Etudes et de Recherches Préhistoriques*, 21. Les Eyzies.

Vézian, J. and Vézian, J. 1966. Les gisements de la grotte de St.-Jean-de-Verges (Ariège). *Gallia Préhistoire* 9: 93–130.

Vidal Lopez, M. 1947. La fauna malacológica de la cueva del Parpalló. *Trabajo Vario del Servicio de Investigación Prehistórica* 6: 57–61,

Vita-Finzi, C. 1978. *Archaeological Sites in their Setting.* London, Thames and Hudson.

Vita-Finzi, C. and Higgs, E.S. 1970. Prehistoric economy in the Mount Carmel area of Palestine: site catchment analysis. *Proceedings of the Prehistoric Society* 36: 1–37.

Voorhies, M.R. 1969. Taphonomy and population dynamics of an early Pliocene vertebrate fauna, Knox County, Nebraska. *University of Wyoming Special Contributions to Geology Special Paper* 1: 1–69.

Vuillemey, M. 1976. La Baume de Gigny, Livret-Guide de l'Excursion A7, Champagne, Lorraine, Alsace. Franche-Comte. Direction J.P. Millotte, A. Thevenin and B. Chertier, 150–7. *IX$^e$ Congrès de l'Union Internationale des Sciences Préhistoriques et Proto-historiques*, Nice.

Wagner, E. 1981. Eine Löwenkopfplastik aus Elfenbein von der Vogelherdhöhle. *Fundberichte aus Baden-Württemberg* 6: 29–58.

Wagner, P.L. 1960. *Human Use of the Earth.* Glencoe, Free Press.

Ward, J.H. Jr. 1963. Hierarchical grouping to optimize an objective function. *Journal of the American Statistical Association* 58: 236–44.

Watanabe, H. 1968. Subsistence and ecology of the northern food gatherers with special reference to the Ainu, in R.B. Lee and I. DeVore (eds.), *Man the Hunter*, 69–77. Chicago, Aldine.

1972. The Ainu ecosystem: environment and group structure. *The American Ethnological Society Monograph* 54.

Waterbolk, H.T. 1968. Food production in prehistoric Europe. *Science* 162, 1093–102.

West, R.G. 1968. *Pleistocene Geology and Biology.* New York, Wiley.

White, T. 1953. Aboriginal utilization of food animals. *American Antiquity* 18: 396–9.

Whittaker, R.H. 1975. *Communities and Ecosystems.* New York, Macmillan.

Wiessner, P. (1977) Hxaro: a Regional System of Reciprocity for Reducing Risk among the !Kung San, unpublished Ph.D. dissertation, University of Michigan, University Microfilms, Ann Arbor.

Wilmsen, E.N. 1973. Interaction, spacing behavior, and the organization of hunting bands. *Journal of Anthropological Research* 29: 1–31.

Williams, B.J. (1974) *A Model of Band Society*, Society for American Archaeology, Memoir 29.

Wilson, E.O. (1975) *Sociobiology: the New Synthesis*, Belknap, Cambridge, Mass.

Winterhalder, B.P. 1977. Foraging Strategy Adaptations of the Boreal Forest Cree: an Evaluation of Theory and Models from Evolutionary Ecology. Unpublished Ph.D. dissertation, Cornell University.

1980. Environmental analysis in human evolution and adaptation research. *Human Ecology* 8: 135–70.

Winterhalder, B.P. and Smith, E.A. (eds.) 1981. *Hunter-Gatherer Foraging Strategies.* University of Chicago Press.

Wishart, D. 1975. *Clustan 1C User Manual.* University College London.

Wobst, H.M. 1974a. Boundary conditions for paleolithic social systems: a simulation approach. *American Antiquity* 39: 147–78.

1974b. The archaeology of Band Society – some unanswered questions, in B.J. Williams, *A Model of Band Society*, v–xviii. Society of American Archaeology Memoir 29.

1976. Locational relationships in Paleolithic society. *Journal of Human Evolution* 5: 49–58.

1977. Stylistic behavior and information exchange in C.E. Cleland (ed.), Papers for the Director: research essays in honor of James B. Griffin. *Anthropological Papers, Museum of Anthropology, University of Michigan* 61: 317–42.

1978. The archaeo-ethnology of hunter-gatherers or the tyranny of the ethnographic record in archaeology. *American Antiquity* 43: 303–9.

Woillard, G.M. 1978. Grand Pile peat bog: a continuous pollen record for the last 140 000 years. *Quaternary Research* 9: 1–21.

1979. The last Interglacial–Glacial cycle at Grand Pile in northeastern France. *Bulletin de la Société Belge de Géologie* 88: 51–69.

Woodburn, J. 1968. An introduction to Hadza ecology, in R.B. Lee and I. DeVore, (eds.), *Man the Hunter*, 49–55. Chicago, Aldine.

1972. Ecology, nomadic movement and the composition of the local group among hunters and gatherers: an East African example and its implications, in P.J. Ucko, R. Tringham and G.W. Dimbleby (eds.), *Man, Settlement and Urbanism*, 193–206. London, Duckworth.

1980. Hunters and gatherers today and reconstruction of the past, in E. Gellner (ed.), *Soviet and Western Anthropology*, 95–107. London, Duckworth.

Wright, G. 1978. Social differentiation in the early Natufian, in C.L. Redman, M.J. Berman, E.V. Curtin, W.T. Langhorne Jr., N.M. Versaggi and J.C. Wanser (eds.), *Social Archaeology: Beyond Subsistence and Dating*, 210–11. New York, Academic Press.

Wynn, T. 1979. The intelligence of later Acheulean hominids. *Man* 14: 371–91.

Yellen, J.E. 1977a. *Archaeological Approaches to the Present.* New York, Academic Press.

1977b. Cultural patterning in faunal remains: evidence from the !Kung Bushmen, in D. Ingersoll, J.E. Yellen and W. MacDonald (eds.), *Experimental Archaeology*, 271–331. New York, Columbia University Press.

Yellen, J.E. and Harpending, H. 1972. Hunter-gatherer populations and archaeological inference. *World Archaeology* 4: 244–53.

Yengoyan, A.A. 1972. Ritual and exchange in Aboriginal Australia: an adaptive interpretation of male initiation rites, in E.N. Wilmsen (ed.), *Social Exchange and Interaction.* Anthropological Papers, Museum of Anthropology, University of Michigan 46: 5–9.

Yesner, D.R. 1980. Maritime hunter-gatherers: ecology and prehistory. *Current Anthropology* 21: 727–35.

Yonge, C.M. 1949. *The Sea Shore.* London, Collins.

INDEX

Printed in the United Kingdom by
Lightning Source UK Ltd., Milton Keynes
137634UK00001B/43-44/P